Contents

CONTENTS

REFORMATION DIVIDED

Catholics, Protestants and the Conversion of England

Eamon Duffy

B L O O M S B U R Y
LONDON · OXFORD · NEW YORK · NEW DELHI · SYDNEY

Bloomsbury Continuum
An imprint of Bloomsbury Publishing Plc

50 Bedford Square
London
WC1B 3DP
UK

1385 Broadway
New York
NY 10018
USA

www.bloomsbury.com

Bloomsbury, Continuum and the Diana logo are trademarks of Bloomsbury Publishing Plc

First published 2017

British Library Cataloguing-in-Publication Data
A catalogue record for this book is available from the British Library.

Library of Congress Cataloguing-in-Publication data has been applied for.

ISBN: HB: 978-1-4729-3436-9
         EPDF: 978-1-4729-3434-5
         EPUB: 978-1-4729-3437-6

2 4 6 8 10 9 7 5 3 1

Typeset by Integra Software Services Pvt. Ltd.
Printed and bound in Great Britain by CPI Group (UK) Ltd, Croydon CR0 4YY

To find out more about our authors and books visit www.bloomsbury.com.
Here you will find extracts, author interviews, details of forthcoming events
and the option to sign up for our newsletters.

Introduction

Divided Reformations

In 1517 an obscure German theologian from an undistinguished new university initiated a debate about popular religious practice which was destined to open up 'the greatest geological faultline in European civilisation'.[1] Martin Luther's angry critique of the sordid late medieval traffic in religious blessings known as 'indulgences' would rapidly escalate into a more fundamental challenge to the theological structures which had underpinned the evolution of Western society since the fall of the Roman empire. There ensued more than a century of fratricidal ideological conflict, in which many thousands would die, and the religious, social and political map of the European continent would be redrawn.

This stupendous upheaval has usually been known as 'the Reformation', an unsatisfactory designation concealing a battery of value judgements. Though the new religious identities which emerged from these conflicts shared a common repudiation of the papacy and of the allegedly materialistic religious system which the papacy headed, they were profoundly, often murderously, divided among themselves on almost everything else. 'Reformation', more-over, with its implication that a 'good' form of Christianity replaced a 'bad' one, begs the question of the credibility, health and religious worth of the beliefs and practices 'reformed' communities rejected. Till comparatively recently, these 'Reformation' movements were viewed as the product of a single energy, unwitting agents or heralds of modernity, and so, self-evidently superior to the medieval Catholicism they replaced. It was a superiority thought to have been demonstrated, among other ways, by the rapidity with which the old religion collapsed before them.

Hence older anglophone histories of the reformation commonly started with a brief résumé of the late medieval background, designed to demonstrate the dysfunctional character of late medieval Christianity, with the bulk of the narrative focused on the spread of Protestantism in the 50 years or so after 1517. The textbook which dominated the study of the English reformation in schools and universities for two generations from 1965 suggested that the reformation was all over, bar the shouting, by 1559.[2] And though it was recognised that the Catholic Church had itself engaged in an internal process of reform in the course of the sixteenth century, this reform, with various qualifications, was understood primarily as a response to the Protestant challenge, and hence more often than not designated the 'counter-reformation'.[3]

Few of these assumptions have worn well. We are far more aware now of the richness, resilience and social embedding of the late medieval religion so often caricatured or ignored in the older narratives. We are correspondingly more alert to the protracted and difficult labour involved in what Patrick Collinson called the 'birthpangs' of reformation, Catholic or Protestant.[4] The comparatively recent realisations that 'reformation' was not a confessional monopoly, but a fundamental aspect of the transformations of Catholic as well as Protestant communities in the sixteenth and following centuries, and that such transformations involve complexity and difference, and take a long time, are reflected in two of the best recent textbooks on early modern religion. Diarmaid MacCulloch's wide-ranging 2003 study, *Reformation: Europe's House Divided*, extended its time frame down to 1700, gave extensive coverage to Catholic as well as Protestant reform movements, emphasised the divisions and diversity of 'Protestantisms' in the plural, and devoted a third of its space to the long-term experience 'of Europe's Reformations and Counter-Reformations'.[5] The American historian Carlos Eire's even more massive 2016 survey similarly adopted a two-century span, gave more or less equal coverage to Catholic and Protestant reform, and embodied its insistence on the pluralism of the religious past in its title, *Reformations: The Early Modern World*.[6] MacCulloch's religious formation was Protestant (he is the child of an Anglican vicarage),

Eire is a Catholic originally from Cuba, making the convergence of their historiographical choices all the more telling.

The history of these reformations continues to fascinate – and to matter – because it is universally recognised that many of the dominant features of modernity originated in the religious upheavals of the sixteenth and seventeenth centuries. That legacy itself, of course, is highly contested. Everyone recognises that the split between Catholics and Protestants (easily parodied as the warm south versus the cold north, wine drinkers versus beer drinkers, and so on) created ideological, cultural and political divisions which constitute 'the shaping fact of European identity', and hence of Europe's impact on the rest of the world.[7] Opinions diverge radically, however, as to whether that influence was essentially benign or otherwise. A long tradition of anglophone historiography took it as axiomatic that the reformation (singular) was the midwife of the modern world, and therefore, in the words of *1066 and All That*, a Good Thing.[8]

By contrast, Brad Gregory's recent study of the long-term legacy of the reformation era suggested that the Protestant assault on the intellectual and moral underpinning of Catholic Christianity fatally if unintentionally undermined the coherence of the Western intellectual and moral tradition. Gregory, a distinguished American Catholic historian, is the author of the best study of the persecution of religious minorities in early modern Europe, and an authority on the radical early Protestant sectarians usually lumped together under the blanket term Anabaptists.[9] But in his polemical book *The Unintended Reformation*, he insists that the genesis of many of the intellectual ills of secular modernity must be laid fairly and squarely at the door of the Protestant reformation. Gregory accepts that late medieval Christianity was 'an institutionalised worldview . . . deeply marked by a gulf between its ideals and its realities'.[10] Nevertheless he believes that the market of values and the control of religion by the modern state in the name of religious liberty has brought about the progressive privatisation and exclusion of religion from the public sphere – problems, he argues, which stem either directly or indirectly from the activities of the sixteenth-century reformers.

Catholic polemics against the errors of the reformers have a long pedigree, of course, and in modern times it is easy to think of precedents for Gregory's approach, some of them very distinguished – Jacques

Maritain's *Trois Réformateurs* springs to mind.[11] And, of course, the links between the reformation and modernity have been asserted by many analysts with no Catholic axe to grind, most notably in Max Weber's *Protestant Ethic and the Spirit of Capitalism*, and in the more domestic British form given the argument by the Anglican Christian socialist R. H. Tawney.[12] In fact Gregory gives short shrift to the Weber thesis that the rise of capitalism was facilitated and advanced by a Protestant work ethic, and is emphatic that the reformers had no intention either of 'disenchanting the universe' or of legitimating acquisitiveness, both of which are Weberian themes. Nevertheless, he argues that in the long term the Protestant repudiation of a sacramental understanding of the material world opened the door to precisely such a disenchantment, by facilitating the removal of the question of God from scientific discourse about the natural world. The reformation's sharp distinction between the realms of matter and spirit and its hostility to scholasticism, he believes, ended more than a thousand years of Christianity as a framework for shared intellectual life in the Latin West.

Gregory's argument sharpens when he turns to the responsibility of the reformation for other aspects of secularism: the hyperpluralism of modern Western society, rooted in the absence of any rational basis for agreement about 'life questions' of value and truth, and hence of any rational way of arriving at a social platform based on shared beliefs. Here Gregory's trajectory as a historian of radical Protestantism is crucial to his argument. Protestantism is often thought of as a single force, comparable to the Catholic Church. But this, he insists, is an illusion, created by the accident of the social and political conservativism of magisterial reformers like Calvin and Luther, and the emergence of Protestant states which embraced one or other of those two Protestant syntheses and enforced a more or less traditional kind of political and moral order. In fact, however, underneath this apparent coherence, which was purely pragmatic, the fundamental reformation principle of *sola scriptura*, and the absolute rejection of tradition as a source of religious truth, proved a radical solvent which made impossible any agreement about truth elicited by communal effort within the context of a shared hermeneutic tradition.[13] Indeed the only thing about which the reformers agreed, he contends, was their repudiation of Catholicism. Those radical disagreements would ultimately lead to the emergence of societies like ours, which can maintain their unity only by banishing what Gregory calls the 'life questions' from the public forum. Religious toleration as a solution to the internal disunities of the early modern state in fact proved a powerful incubator of radical individualism, and ultimately of moral chaos. The murderous religious controversies of the early modern era persuaded many in the long term that, since religious disagreements could not be resolved, they should not matter, and did not matter.

And in this marginalising of religious truth as impossibly elusive, Gregory sees one of the roots of the acquisitive society. All the major reformers as well as their radical Protestant opponents denounced excessive wealth in traditional Christian terms, and the roots of both capitalism and consumerism were already evident in medieval and renaissance societies. Nevertheless, the abolition of the vowed religious life of monks and nuns removed a powerful if often compromised institutional witness to Christian ambivalence about material prosperity, while pulling in the opposite direction, the intractableness of post-reformation religious disagreements contributed to the emergence of societies which found their rationale in purely materialistic and acquisitive values – the protection of property and the contractual guarantee of the rights of the individual. In the pioneering early modern secular states, in particular the Dutch Republic, Gregory argues, men and women decided to stop killing each other over what seemed increasingly irresolvable religious differences, and went shopping instead. In the long run, religion became a private matter, and this privatisation became one of the building blocks of Enlightenment social theory. 'It does me no injury', declared Thomas Jefferson, 'for my neighbour to say there are twenty gods or no god. It neither picks my pocket nor breaks my leg.'[14]

Readers of Gregory's bracing but highly controversial book could be in no doubt about the abiding topicality of reformation history, though his razor-sharp distinction between the legacy of early modern Catholicism on the one hand (flawed but essentially benign) and that of its Protestant opponents on the other (well-intentioned but ultimately disastrous) is unlikely to command universal assent. The most original modern anglophone historian of the transition from medieval to modern Christianity was also, as it happens, by origin and education a Roman Catholic, but John Bossy's verdict on the rival confessions which emerged from the reformation conflicts might reasonably be summarised as 'a plague on both your houses'. Bossy's Jesuit education exerted a marked influence on his work long after he had ceased to practise his inherited faith. His best work grew out of a lifelong preoccupation with the context, meaning and social function of the sacraments. He was profoundly influenced by both the work of the French *Annales* school,[15] and by the 'Sociologie Religieuse' practised by Gabriel le Bras and his associates,[16] as also to a lesser extent by a youthful Marxist phase, later fiercely repudiated.

Bossy was bored by conventional political history, with its focus on elites (he once proposed as an examination question in an early modern European history paper, 'Did Charles V matter?') and, for a historian of his time, he was unusually well read in anthropology and sociology. His youthful Catholicism had given him an interest in and insight into the importance and social significance of ritual. His first major (and only full-length) book was a pioneering study of the English Roman Catholic community from the reformation to the restoration of the Catholic hierarchy in 1850. In it, he abandoned a narrative framework to focus on the processes of community formation in rites of passage, in the 'separation of meats and days' involved in the rituals of the Catholic household and in the social shifts from a community dominated and preserved by gentry patronage to the plebeian Catholicism of mid-Victorian England. Bossy's book was at once recognised as a major contribution not only to the history of English Catholicism, but of religious minorities in general. It was instrumental in liberating the study of the history of English Catholicism from a tribal focus on the 'sufferings of our Catholic forefathers', and its integration into the wider social and religious history of the island.[17]

Bossy's subtle and imaginative book advanced a consciously provocative thesis. Post-reformation English Catholicism, he argued, was not best understood as a survival of 'the old religion'. Far from being a dwindling remnant of a once universally Catholic population, it must be viewed as a new beginning, 'a small community gradually getting larger'. Membership of the Elizabethan and early Stuart Catholic community had to be assessed on the basis of overtly separatist behaviour of some sort. The gradual awakening of this new community to the fact of separation was accompanied by the transformation of the college at Douai founded by William Allen in the late 1560s from an academic haven for clerical dons awaiting the return of England to sanity and Catholic communion, into a training house for 'missionaries', dedicated to the perpetuation and expansion of a religious minority. In this awakening, from 'churchly nostalgia' to the practical reality of 'mission', activist Jesuit mission-aries played a key role, and Jesuits like Robert Persons were as close as Bossy's book got to heroes. By contrast, too many of the leaders of the secular clergy had, he thought, frittered their energies in pursuit of an antiquarian hierarchical ideal, based on the illusion that they were still the medieval *Ecclesia Anglicana*. This mirage was only set aside in the reign of James II, with the erection of four apostolic vicariates, a pragmatic form of Church government which aban-doned claims to continuity with the medieval English Church and recognised the 'missionary' status of England.

That bold scenario was rapidly challenged, and many of its details have not worn well. Bossy's insistence that Elizabethan Catholicism was essentially a new construct was unduly influenced by the work of A. G. Dickens on Yorkshire recusancy, from whom also he took a low estimation of the achievements of the Marian Church. As a bevy of critics led by Christopher Haigh insisted, Bossy radically underestimated the enduring importance of Marian Catholicism and the surviving Marian clergy in the shaping and consolidation of Elizabethan Catholic resistance.[18] Bossy's insistence on overt acts of 'recusancy' as constitutive of membership of the Catholic community, a perception carried over from an older Catholic his-toriography, was subjected to a diffident but devastating critique in Alexandra Walsham's MA dissertation on Church papistry. Walsham demolished one of Bossy's central contentions by demonstrating the long-term importance to the Catholic community of so-called 'schismatics', non-separating Catholics who on occasion attended services in their local Anglican parish, while retaining their allegiance to and connections within Catholicism.[19] And puzzlingly for a histo-rian whose best work engaged fruitfully with the history of early modern European Catholicism, Bossy failed to connect some of the preoccupations of the English secular clergy that he characterised as 'insular' and archaising, with major strands within the European counter-reformation.[20]

Nevertheless, Bossy was to build major elements of his argument, suitably refined and transformed, into a broader and more persuasive analysis of the entire reformation era, though, in this new form, Jesuits and other clerical activists were to feature much less flatteringly. Bossy's masterpiece was *Christianity in the West 1400–1700*, published in 1985,[21] an exploratory essay in book form which gathered together ideas broached over the previous ten years in a series of brilliant, idea-packed and highly influential articles.[22] The central contention of *Christianity in the West* was that medieval Christianity had been fundamentally concerned with the creation and maintenance of peace in a violent world. 'Christianity' then had denoted neither an ideology nor an institution, but a community of believers whose religious ideal – constantly aspired to if seldom attained – was peace and mutual love. The sacraments and sacramentals of the medieval Church were concerned to defuse hostility and to create extended networks of fraternity, spiritual 'kith and kin', enacting the 'social miracle' by reconciling enemies and consolidating the community in charity.

In the course of the sixteenth and seventeenth centuries, Bossy maintained, all this had changed. In the Renaissance era, reliance on symbol and image gave way to the privileging of the audible or visible word. While peace remained a fundamental Christian aspiration, ritual and sacrament gave way to persuasion and instruction as the means to achieve it. A newly professional breed of intellectuals and activists – the 'new clerks' – arose, who understood Christianity not as a community sustained by ritual acts, but a teaching enforced by institutional structures. The framework of moral teaching shifted from focus on the seven deadly sins, understood as wrong because anti-social, sin as malignancy against other people, to a preoccupation with obedience to the Ten Commandments, whose transgression was understood in the first place as an affront to God. Credal orthodoxy replaced *Communitas* as a supreme virtue, Christianity became a system of beliefs and moral behaviours, charity ceased to mean primarily the community-building state of love towards God and neighbour, instead signifying primarily an external act of benevolence to the poor and needy. By 1700 'the Christian world was full of religions, objectives and moral entities characterized by system, principles and hard edges'. Above that multiplicity loomed 'a shadowy abstraction, *the* Christian religion', and somewhere above that was 'religion with a capital R, planted in its new domain by people who did not usually believe in it'.[23]

Bossy's bravura essay, crudely summarised here, bristled with ideas and aphorisms, but also with breathtaking generalisations resting on slender empirical evidence. The book excited and infuriated reviewers in more or less equal measure, often simultaneously, not least because the total technical apparatus supporting its sweeping *tour d'horizon* consisted of just 17 footnotes and a handful of almost comically selective bibliographies. Bossy was also accused of romanticism, projecting back into the late Middle Ages a sentimentalised version of post-Vatican II Catholicism.[24] And certainly he was attempting to describe what he saw as a decline from a user-friendly popular religion into something harder, more abstract and more managerial. Protestantism was clearly a major factor in the changes he charted, and he titled a crucial chapter on the progress towards abstraction, 'The Institution of Christian Religion', in a reference to Calvin's most famous writing. But he was strikingly even-handed in attributing what he saw as decline equally to forces within as well as beyond institutional Catholicism: Carlo Borromeo featured as prominently as Calvin as one of the new clerks, and there was little to choose, on this account, between Jesuit priest and puritan minister.

The process Bossy traced in *Christianity in the West*, including the perception that 'the two Reformations – Luther's and Rome's – constituted ... two complementary aspects of one and the same process' had, of course, been noted by other historians, if rarely with such beguiling imaginative force. Conceived in narrower political terms, the imposition of orthodox belief and practice, Catholic or Protestant, was part of 'confessionalisation', the evolution and management of religious identities in militantly Catholic or Protestant states. Viewed as part of the evolution of docile civil societies, it could be viewed as the state's imposition of 'social discipline'. Bossy was resistant to such analyses, which he suspected of reductivism. Always alert to nuance, and for all his distaste for the direction which reforming Catholics and Protestants had taken Christianity in early modern Europe, he would probably have baulked, for example, at the starkness of Robin Briggs's assertion that the counter-reformation 'can be characterized, with only slight exaggeration, as one of the greatest repressive enterprises in European history'.[25] In the same way, despite his admiration for the author and his methods, he demurred from Jean Delumeau's characterisation of the early modern transformation of Western Christianity as a process of 'christianisation': medieval Christians, he thought, understood perfectly well what salvation was, and who was their saviour.[26]

For all its idiosyncrasies and blatant limitations, Bossy's brilliantly intuitive work has proved enormously fruitful. His influence has been pervasive even in fields into which he himself rarely ventured, as here, for example, in Blair Worden's insightfully Bossyesque observations on the nature of Puritanism:

> The challenge which Puritanism posed was not to hierarchy but to community. Dividing the world between saints and sinners, mixing only with the former and barring the latter from the Sacraments, the Puritans undermined the clergy's position as a parish conciliation service. It is true they wanted parochial unity – but unity on their terms. Theirs was a different conception of the minister's role from that envisaged for George Herbert's Country Parson, 'reconciling neighbours that are at variance', and charitably indulging, in the hope of correcting, the spiritual failings of weaker brethren.[27]

The essays which make up this book all, in one way or another, engage with aspects of the transitions in early modern English and Irish Christianity which Bossy mapped. This is a book about the reformation – or, rather, the attempted reformations – of Christian England, and about the divisions among and between those who sought to reform and convert it. The book falls into three distinct sections. The first broaches the theme of religious division and disputation, by considering the career of Thomas More, one of the first and certainly the most notable opponent of England's early Protestant reformers. More's English polemical writings, collected and republished by William Rastell in Queen Mary's reign, became an armoury of arguments drawn on again and again by Marian, Elizabethan and early Stuart controversialists. More appears in

Christianity in the West as a defender of a communitarian under-standing of tradition, an expositor of the 'social miracle', opposed to the dominance of mere text, whose sophistication neither Protestant opponents like Tyndale nor Catholic admirers like Reginald Pole then or subsequently understood or emulated.[28] When Bossy wrote, More's idealised humanitarian reputation, established by Chambers' beautiful biography[29] and the play and movie Robert Bolt based on it,[30] was already being harshly questioned by historians like Geoffrey Elton.[31] More recently, Hilary Mantel's brilliant but hostile fictions have ensconced a far more negative image of More in the public imagination. These three chapters therefore attempt to explore and explain More's vehement opposition to heresy and heretics, and thereby to open the discussion of reformation as a field of contes-tation, between Catholics and Protestants, but also within the opposing communions, which forms the subject of many of the chapters that follow.

The second section of the book offers a series of studies of Catholicism in England from the mid-sixteenth to the early eight-eenth century. That long time frame is now an established feature of thinking about the counter-reformation, which even in the Catholic heartlands of southern Europe was a long time in the making. In Europe's northern fringes where varieties of Protestantism were established, it was an even more drawn-out labour.[32] Chapters 4 to 6 examine the work of three key figures in the emergence and radicalisation of the post-reformation Catholic community in confrontation with Protestantism. Reginald Pole's legatine mission to re-Catholicise England in the mid-1550s failed, essentially because of his premature death and, crucially, that of his sovereign, Mary I. Bossy was inclined to be dismissive of the Marian Church and hence of Pole's achievements.[33] But Pole's theological legacy remained a potent influence on the development of Elizabethan Catholicism, and the discussion of Pole's preaching in Chapter 4 supplements the case I have made elsewhere for a more positive assessment of the Marian Catholicising project, and Pole's part in it.[34] Chapter 5 provides an overview of the career and objectives of the single most important leader of Elizabethan Catholicism, and Pole's successor as 'the Cardinal of England', William Allen. Allen's pastoral vision was central to the progress from church to mission on which Bossy had laid so much emphasis, but his conspiratorial political entanglements and commitment to re-Catholicisation by force of arms did nothing to moderate the Elizabethan regime's hostility to Catholics.

Chapter 6 considers the work of Allen's most important theological collaborator, Gregory Martin, whose career and writings throw into sharp relief the importance of the wider counter-reformation context of the English mission. In the conflicted history of seventeenth- and eighteenth-century English Catholicism, loyalty to the idea of Catholic unity round the Pope was a constant, but Rome itself was often viewed as a problem (an issue explored in Chapter 10). For Gregory Martin, however, the Rome of curial and papal management was less significant than the Rome of the mind and imagination, a Rome of saints and martyrs, *Roma Sancta*: this chapter offers a case study of some of the religious sentiments that energised the northern counter-reformation. Chapter 7 explores the devotional ethos of Elizabethan and early Stuart Catholicism by examining the history of its most important devotional book, the *Manual of Devout Prayer*. In the process, it traces both the dependence and independence of the English Catholic community on European resources. Chapter 8 continues this examination of recusant piety and pastoral organisation in their European contexts, arguing that elements which Bossy saw as symptoms of an insular and archaic mindset in fact featured prominently in the pastoral vision of the Italian and French Catholic pioneers of reform and conversion like Borromeo, Bérulle and Vincent de Paul. Chapter 9 offers a detailed account of the bitter early eighteenth-century disputes over Jansenism which seemed to threaten the integrity of the English Catholic community, once again illustrating the extent to which the history of the English mission was inextricably bound up with developments in counter-reformation Europe. The section concludes with a survey of Catholic polemical use of the history of the English reformation to contest the national Protestant narrative, from the writings of Cardinal Pole down to the subtler apologetic of Lingard in the age of Catholic Emancipation.

The book's final section turns from an examination of Catholic attempts at the reform and conversion of England, to consider the work of puritan 'new clerks' to convert the nation to a living and ardent Protestantism. The focus here is on the mid-seventeenth century, and especially on the ideals and activities of Richard Baxter and his circle. Baxter's vast collection of 'cases of conscience', *The Christian Directory*, a clerical guide to the dilemmas of the Christian life designed for the formation of earnest Protestants, featured prominently in both Weber's discussion of the evolution of the Protestant ethic and in R. H. Tawney's reworking of that theme in *Religion and the Rise of Capitalism*. In *Christianity in the West*, Bossy followed Weber and Tawney in taking Baxter's book as the epitome of the transformation of Christianity, both Catholic and Protestant, from a living community to a theorised 'religion', from collective to individual Christians, which was the subject of his book.[35] In these chapters I attempt to flesh out, I hope somewhat more sympathetically, the pastoral vision which underlay puritan understanding of what the Christian community could and should be. In the process, I examine the issue of the success and failure of Protestant attempts to reform the nation. The book concludes with a study of George Fox, a Protestant activist whose ecstatic and mystical vision of reform led him to reject and seek to overthrow the institutional vision of 'new clerks' like Baxter and his ilk. For Bossy, Fox and the radical milieu out of which Fox emerged formed 'only a footnote to the history of the transformations of Christendom'.[36] I hope that Fox's presence at the conclusion of this book as something more than a footnote may be a suitable reminder that the call to inner transformation and conversion has always been in uneasy and sometimes violent tension with the more institutional and ecclesial conceptions of what it is to be Christian, which form the substance of my book.

As should be evident by now, the work of John Bossy has been for me, as for so many other historians of early modern religion, a constant source of surprise, stimulus, inspiration, exasperation and disagreement. Only a few of the chapters of this book engage directly with his ideas, as often as not to qualify or dissent. But almost none of them would have been written without his example, and on occasion, direct encouragement. With some unease, I once sent him an early draft of an article criticising one of the central planks of his argument in *The English Catholic Community*.[37] I received in return a long and cordial letter in his inimitably looped and hasty handwriting, beginning 'I think you are *probably* right' and going on to suggest five or six ways in which the critique of his position could be strengthened and refined. It was entirely characteristic of him. He was a great historian, and a generous friend: this book is dedicated to his memory.

Notes

1 The description is Patrick Collinson's, *London Review of Books*, 26 (2004), pp. 22–3.

2 A. G. Dickens, *The English Reformation* (London, 1965).

3 Examples embodying these assumptions are A. G. Dickens, *Reformation and Society in Sixteenth Century Europe* (London, 1966), and H. J. Hillerbrand, *The Reformation in its Own Words* (London 1964); for the designation of Catholic reform, John O'Malley, *Trent and All That: Renaming Catholicism in the Early Modern Era* (Harvard, 2002).

4 Patrick Collinson, *The Birthpangs of Protestant England: Religious and Cultural Change in the Sixteenth and Seventeenth Centuries* (London 1988).

5 Diarmaid MacCulloch, *Reformation, Europe's House Divided 1490–1700* (London, 2003). Citations from the Penguin paperback edition of 2004.

6 Carlos Eire, *Reformations: The Early Modern World 1450–1650* (New Haven and London, 2016).

7 MacCulloch, *Reformation*, p. xxii.

8 For some reflections on that tradition see chapters 1 and 2 of my *Saints, Sacrilege and Sedition* (London, 2012).

9 Brad S. Gregory, *Salvation at Stake: Christian Martyrdom in Early Modern Europe* (Harvard, 1999).

10 Brad S. Gregory, *The Unintended Reformation: How a Religious Revolution Secularised Society* (Cambridge, Mass. and London, 2012); *Assessment of the Medieval Church*, pp. 129–45.

11 Jacques Maritain, *Trois Réformateurs* (Paris, 1925). Maritain's three culprits are Luther, Descartes and Rousseau.

12 Peter R. Baehr and Gordon C. Wells, *The Protestant Ethic and the 'Spirit' of Capitalism and Other Writings* (Harmondsworth, 2002); on Weber, H. Lehmann and G. Roth (eds), *Weber's Protestant Ethic: Origins, Evidence, Contexts* (Cambridge, 1993); Gordon Marshall, *In Search of the Spirit of Capitalism: An Essay on Max Weber's Protestant Ethic* (London, 1982); for Tawney, R. H. Tawney, *Religion and the Rise of Capitalism* (London, 1926) and many subsequent editions; Gary Armstrong and Tim Gray, *The Authentic Tawney: A New Interpretation of the Thought of R. H. Tawney* (Exeter, 2011).

13 Gregory, *Unintended Reformation*, p. 95 and Chapter 2 *passim*.

14 Ibid., p. 165.

15 André Burguière, *The Annales School: An Intellectual History* (Ithaca, NY, 2009), Peter Burke, *The French Historical Revolution: The Annales School 1929–89* (London, 1990); Stuart Clark (ed.), *The Annales School: Critical Assessments* (4 vols, London, 1999).

16 Gabriel le Bras, *Introduction à l'histoire de la pratique religieuse*, vol. 1 (Paris, 1942); vol. 2 (Paris, 1945); idem., *Études de Sociologie religieuse*, vol. I: Sociologie de la pratique religieuse dans les campagnes françaises et bibliographie (Paris, 1955); vol. 2: De la morphologie à la sociologie (Paris, 1956); idem., 'Sociologie religieuse et sciences des religions', *Archives de Sociologie des Religions*, no. 1 (1956), pp. 3–20; idem., *L'Église et le village* (Paris, 1976); F. Boulard, *Problèmes missionnaires de la France rurale*, 2 vols (Paris, 1945); idem., *Premiers itinéraires en sociologie religieuse* (Paris, 1954) (preface by Gabriel le Bras); F. Boulard and J. Remy, *Pratique religieuse et régions culturelles* (Paris, 1968).

17 John Bossy, *The English Catholic Community 1570–1850* (London, 1975).

18 Christopher Haigh, 'The fall of a church or the rise of a sect?', *Historical Journal*, 2 (1978), pp. 181–6; 'The continuity of Catholicism in the English Reformation', *Past and Present*, no. 93 (1981), pp. 37–69; 'From monopoly to minority: Catholicism in early modern England', *Transactions of the Royal Historical Society*, 31 (1981), pp. 129–47; Patrick McGrath, 'Elizabethan Catholicism: A Reconsideration', *Journal of Ecclesiastical History*, 35, (1984), pp. 414–28; P. McGrath and J. Rowe,

'The Marian Priests under Elizabeth I', *Recusant History*, 17 (1984), pp. 103–20; C. Haigh, 'Revisionism, the Reformation and the History of English Catholicism', *Journal of Ecclesiastical History*, 36 (1985), pp. 394–405; 'Reply' by McGrath, ibid., pp. 405–6: Andrew R. Muldoon, 'Recusants, Church-Papists, and "Comfortable" Missionaries: Assessing the Post-Reformation English Catholic Community', *Catholic Historical Review*, 86 (2000), pp. 242–57.

19   Alexandra Walsham, *Church Papists: Catholicism, Conformity and Confessional Polemic in Early Modern England* (Woodbridge, 1993).

20   Chapter 9 below.

21   John Bossy, *Christianity in the West 1400–1700* (Oxford, 1985).

22   Most importantly, 'The Counter-Reformation and the People of Catholic Europe', *Past and Present*, 47 (1970), pp. 51–70; 'Blood and Baptism: Kinship, Community and Christianity in Western Europe from the Fourteenth to the Seventeenth Centuries' in D. Baker (ed.), *Sanctity and Secularity: The Church and the World*, Studies in Church History, 10 (1973), pp. 129–43; 'The Social History of Confession in the Age of the Reformation', *Transactions of the Royal Historical Society*, 5th Series, vol. 25 (1975), pp. 21–38; 'Holiness and Society', *Past and Present*, 75 (1977), pp. 119–37; 'Essai de sociographie de la messe 1200–1700', *Annales*, 36 (1981), pp. 44–70; 'Some elementary forms of Durkheim', *Past and Present*, 95 (1982), pp. 3–18; 'The Mass as a Social Institution 1200–1700', *Past and Present*, 100 (1983), pp. 29–61.

23   Bossy, *Christianity in the West*, p. 170.

24   Review of *Christianity in the West* by Bob Scribner, *English Historical Review*, 101 (1986), pp. 683–6.

25   Robin Briggs, *Communities of Belief: Cultural and Social Tensions in Early Modern France* (New York, 1989), p. 230.

26   See Bossy's unpaginated preface to the English translation of J. Delumeau's *Le Catholicisme entre Luther et Voltaire, Catholicism Between Luther and Voltaire* (London, 1977).

27   Blair Worden, review article on the reformation in *London Review of Books*, 5 (1983), pp. 15–16.

28   Bossy, *Christianity in the West*, pp. 99–100.

29   R. W. Chambers, *Thomas More* (London, 1935).

30   Robert Bolt, *A Man for All Seasons* (London, 1960).

31   Chapters 1 and 2 below.

32   For a recent collection emphasising the diversity and extended time frame of the counter-reformation, Alexandra Bamji, Geert H. Janssen and Mary Laven (eds), *The Ashgate Research Companion to the Counter-Reformation* (Aldershot, 2013), pp. 1–14 and *passim*.

33   Bossy, *English Catholic Community*, p. 12.

34   Eamon Duffy, *Fires of Faith: Catholic England under Mary Tudor* (New Haven and London, 2009).

35   Bossy, *Christianity in the West*, pp. 149–51.

36   Ibid., p. 113.

37   A revised and expanded version of the article in question forms Chapter 8 of this book.

PART ONE

Thomas More and Heresy

I

Thomas More and the Strange Death of Erasmian England

In this first part of the book I want to consider Thomas More's role during the late 1520s and early 1530s in the collapse of what one may call the Erasmian moment in early Tudor culture and politics. England in those years saw the flowering, and then the destruction, of a devout and self-consciously orthodox Catholic humanism, propagated by More's circle of friends and intent on the reform of Christendom from within.[1] It was a circle which looked beyond merely English concerns, and which European humanists like the Dutchman Erasmus of Rotterdam and the Spaniard Luis de Vives were significant participants and indeed beneficiaries.[2]

In the last years of the fifteenth century Erasmus had painfully accumulated the skills and resources which would underpin his life's work. A spell of study at the University of Paris had convinced him of the bankruptcy of the scholastic method which dominated university theology, locked as he considered it to be into sterile theorising and narrow dogmatism.[3] As his acquaintance with the classical world grew he came increasingly to see the centrality of Greek for an understanding of early Christianity, and set himself to master the language and literature of classical and early Christian Greece. Erasmus seized eagerly on the still developing technology of the printing press, and over the next 30 years he was to publish a stream of classical and early Christian authors in ground-breaking editions.[4]

A key stimulus to his immersion in Greek was his first visit to England in 1499, under the patronage of the young Henry Blount, Lord Mountjoy, whom he had tutored in Paris. During this visit

Erasmus formed lifelong friendships with More and with John Colet, Dean of St Paul's.[5] Colet, the wealthy founder of St Paul's School, was an authority on the Greek New Testament, whose Oxford lectures on St Paul, based on the Greek text and saturated in the neo-platonic learning of Renaissance Italy, profoundly influenced Erasmus.[6] Contact with More, Colet and their circle during this and subsequent visits to England turned Erasmus decisively towards the study of early Christianity, and planted the seed of his great edition of the Greek New Testament, eventually published with a facing Latin translation in 1516. This *Novum Instrumentum*, as it was called, was to prove one of the world's most revolutionary texts, revealing the absence of biblical basis for dominant orthodoxies on the sacrament of confession and related practices like indulgences. Erasmus' *New Testament* would form the basis for the far more drastic reform activities of early Protestant leaders like Luther and Zwingli.

In 1500 Erasmus had issued the first edition of one of his most influential works, the *Adagia*, a small collection of mainly Latin proverbs and sayings, culled from his classical reading, round which he structured a series of commentaries and essays exploring various aspects of classical learning. Erasmus expanded the *Adagia* in each of its many successive editions, till by his death in 1536 it contained more than 4,000 Greek and Latin 'proverbs'.[7] Some of the component essays, most famously that on 'The Silenus of Alcibiades', were in effect free-standing treatises, expounding Erasmus' intensely ethical and anti-dogmatic religion. In this '*Philosophia Christi*', devotion to and moral imitation of the Jesus of the gospels took precedence over complex theology or external pious practices like fasting, pilgrimage or the monastic life. In 1503 he enshrined these emphases in a devotional handbook for lay people, the *Enchyridion Milites Christiani* (Manual for the Christian Soldier), which, after a slow initial reception, was to become a world bestseller. It ran through more than 70 editions in the course of the sixteenth century, and exerted a profound influence on both sides of the reformation divide.[8]

In 1505 Erasmus and More collaborated on a translation into Latin of a set of dialogues by the scurrilous and bawdy pagan Greek satirist Lucian of Samosata, which they published the following year.[9] Both men relished Lucian's risqué humour for its own sake. But they also argued that Lucian's ridicule of the follies and superstitions of the pagan world had urgent contemporary relevance, and applied just as well to superstitious Christians who, in More's words, swallowed 'feigned ... stories about a saint or horrendous tales of hell', rather than testing them by 'divinely inspired scripture' and the authentic teaching of Christ.

This collaboration, minor in itself, was to prove momentous. Both More and Erasmus would continue to deploy literary strategies derived from Lucian in some of their major works. More's *Utopia* (seen through the Parisian press by Erasmus in 1516), and Erasmus's *The Praise of Folly*, were both exercises in Lucianic wit, composed with a deadly serious reforming purpose. So too were the satiric dialogues, or *Colloquies*, of the 1520s, in which Erasmus would continue to lash the abuses and absurdities of the contemporary Church.

According to Erasmus *The Praise of Folly* was begun to while away the hours on horseback as he returned from a prolonged visit to Italy. It was completed during a week's stay in Thomas More's house in Bucklesbury Street, in the City of London, where Erasmus was recuperating from a kidney infection, and the book was intended as a public testimony to the two men's friendship. The Latin title of the work, '*Enconium Moriae*', means literally 'praise of folly', but was also a joking play on More's name (More frequently used the same pun to present himself, ironically, as foolish or dim-witted). The book even tells an anecdote about 'someone of (Folly's) name', a joker who presented his young wife with glass beads which he claimed were priceless jewels. The story is clearly about More himself, who relished practical jokes of this kind.[10]

Erasmus had gone to Italy to pursue his Greek studies, and was befriended by many cardinals and prelates. But he also saw at first hand the secular ambition of the Renaissance papacy and its court at its most blatant. He was in Bologna in November 1507 when Pope Julius II rode in at the head of his own army to take possession of the city. So both Erasmus' immersion in the Greek classics, and his disgust at the worldliness of the Church, dominate *The Praise of Folly*. The book is a Lucianic satire, a declamation in which Folly herself speaks, clothed in cap and bells and flaunting her foolish femininity (Erasmus, like More, was prone to misogyny). Folly rules everywhere, in the schoolroom, the church, the council chamber, the universities, the courts of law.

In the early and more generalised part of the book Folly is a comedian, portrayed as amused and indulgent towards human foibles. But in dealing with his own times, Erasmus' fictional mask slips, the humour fades, the satire sharpens and darkens, and we increasingly hear Erasmus' own voice, lashing in all earnestness the abuses of his own times, above all abuses in the Church. Go to church and see snoring congregations ignore the wisest and soberest preaching, but leap to rapt attention when some silly superstitious legend is recounted. Theologians lose themselves in mad complexities, obscuring the radical simplicity of the gospel with useless learning. The Apostles consecrated the Eucharist devoutly, but knew nothing of the doctrine of transubstantiation, they knew and revered the Virgin Mary personally, but 'which of them proved how she had been kept immaculate from Adam's sin, with the logic our theologians display'? Those so-called 'experts', who pride themselves on their theological subtleties, have never taken the time to read even once through the gospels or the epistles of St Paul, where they would find a simpler and more radical message.[11]

Some of Folly's most savage religious criticism was levelled at monks and monasteries, as Erasmus gave free rein to his disgust and regret at his own earlier vocation. Monks were sunk in 'filth and ignorance', universally despised, priding themselves for thinking that the 'highest form of piety is to be so uneducated that they can't even read'. They substitute 'petty ceremonies' and burdensome rules for the deeper demands of the gospel. Popes, cardinals, and bishops too abuse the gospel in their pursuit of wealth and power, although their predecessors the Apostles were all poor men. With Julius II's warrior papacy in mind, Erasmus insists that, had they a grain of the salt of the gospel in them, popes and prelates would exchange their wealth, pomp and pleasures for 'vigils, fasts, tears, prayers, sermons, study, sighs and a thousand ... hardships', instead of which, 'they leave everything, to devote themselves to war'.[12]

The final part of Erasmus' book struck a new and more intensely religious note, as Erasmus expounded the paradoxes of human and divine folly. Drawing on a tradition of Christianised Platonic mysticism encountered in the writings of the Greek Fathers, especially Origen, Erasmus portrayed the folly of the gospel as a kind of entry into divine madness, which takes the faithful soul beyond human reason into realms of the spirit no human wisdom can encompass. The deepest Christianity is of the heart, and beyond all rationalising. The gospel was revealed first to the simple and humble, to women and children, and the founders of the faith were lovers of simplicity, bitter enemies of learning. The happiness which Christians seek 'is nothing other than a kind of madness and folly', a spiritual repudiation of worldly values which makes no sense to the ungodly. Plato taught that the madness of lovers was the highest kind of happiness, and true religion is likewise a kind of crazy passion. The soul lost in God is truly 'beside itself', and those who taste mystic union with God can speak of it only incoherently: 'they lament their return to reason, for all they ever want is to be mad forever with this kind of madness'.[13]

The religious vision of *The Praise of Folly* was soon to be overtaken by events. Erasmus' satire against the abuses of institutional Christianity would be eagerly taken up by reformers like Luther, whose momentous attack on Indulgences in 1517 echoed many Erasmian themes. But Luther and his followers pushed the call to reform far beyond anything Erasmus had envisaged or could accept. His insistence on the primacy of the original text of the Bible became in their hands an insistence on the authority of *sola scriptura*, scripture alone, which challenged the doctrinal authority of the community of the Church. Erasmus was a passionate believer in order, and saw the unity of the Church as a sacrament of the unity God willed for the human race. A lover of peace, indeed a convinced pacifist, he watched in horror as religious disagreements became the cause of bloody warfare, and tore Christendom apart. Like the Protestant reformers he despised contemporary monasticism, and he sympathised with many of their positive emphases. But he saw in the Protestant rejection of Catholic teaching, and their desecration of sacred objects and buildings, a new and destructive kind of dogmatism, worse than those he had lampooned in the medieval Church.

Erasmus was not, however, deflected from his life's mission. Doggedly he went on editing the texts of early Christianity as a remedy for the ills of the modern Church. As religious divisions polarised and men increasingly took sides, Erasmus went on criticising abuse impartially wherever he saw it. In the mid-1520s he made clear his basic Catholic loyalties by attacking Luther's teaching on justification by faith alone, and on predestination.[14] In those same years, however, he published a series of satiric *Colloquies*, dialogues in the manner of Lucian, devastatingly lampooning Catholic abuses in institutions like fasting or pilgrimage.[15]

As we shall see, by the early 1530s, More by contrast may have had some regrets about his own early critical utterances about religion. But however evil the times, Erasmus had no such regrets. His Latin motto was *Cedo nulli*, 'I yield to no one', and he chose to die as he had lived, a Catholic priest. But in an age of violent dogmatism, retraction and second thoughts, he refused to be deflected from the path he had chosen as a young and eagerly reforming scholar. Unsurprisingly, both sides came to see him as a traitor. Protestants denounced his cowardice in not following his convictions into the reformed camp. Catholics blamed him for having 'laid the egg that Luther hatched'. The theologians of the Sorbonne got their revenge for his relentless polemic against scholasticism by condemning *The Praise of Folly* in 1527 and again in 1533: a series of sixteenth-century popes – Paul IV, Sixtus V, Clement VIII – followed suit. The book was also banned by the governments of some of the most powerful Catholic states – Milan and Venice, Portugal and Spain. After the Council of Trent, all Erasmus' writings were placed on the *Index of Forbidden Books*. *The Praise of Folly*, which had been translated into the major European languages and had run through 36 Latin editions before Erasmus' death in 1536, survived thereafter mainly in Protestant editions, in England, Switzerland and the Netherlands.[16]

More had achieved his own European celebrity as the author of *Utopia*, a short fictional dialogue in Latin, in two parts, published in December 1516.[17] The intriguing title 'Utopia' was a punning Greek word, which can mean both 'nowhere' and 'good place'. Travel and discovery were in the air: Amerigo Vespucci's voyages to the New World had been publicised a decade before, and More's fantasy purported to be an eyewitness account of an island somewhere in the South Atlantic, by one of Vespucci's companions, Raphael Hythloday. The little book immediately became an international bestseller, and it made More a literary superstar.

Utopia was a dream commonwealth ruled by elected officials, its population rationally distributed among 54 cities with identical street plans. No one was poor because goods were held in common and wealth despised. Gold and silver were made into pisspots, jewels given to children as toys, and there was no money. In Utopia there were no aristocrats and no idlers. Everyone dressed simply, everyone learned a trade and worked for a living. The citizens dined together at communal tables, the sick and elderly were cared for in spacious hospitals, capital punishment was a rarity reserved for the gravest crimes, war avoided as a calamity of last resort and hunting for sport despised as cruel. The religion of the Utopians was a rational pagan-ism. Religious disagreement was tolerated, though all accepted that the world was governed by a benevolent God who rewarded virtue and punished vice; those who denied this were viewed as criminals whose opinions threatened moral anarchy. Priests in Utopia were universally respected, because there were very few of them, and all were chosen for their wisdom and virtue.

Like *The Praise of Folly*, *Utopia* was of course a satire on the real Europe and, more specifically, the real England, in which government was harsh, priests and rulers often corrupt and the gulf between rich and poor wider every day. But not everything in *Utopia* represented More's ideal alternative. The regimented life of the island is some-times horribly reminiscent of an anthill, and Utopians sanctioned assisted suicide for the terminally ill, which More, a devout Catholic, certainly rejected. His book is a thought experiment, whose ideas are voiced wittily by the characters, making it hard for us to know where playfulness stops and serious advocacy begins.[18]

Between 1516 and 1519 most of More's literary activity was dedi-cated to the defence of Erasmus' edition of the New Testament against a phalanx of English and European critics. His open letters to the humanistically trained Louvain theologian Martin Dorp, to the University of Oxford, to the future Archbishop of York Edward Lee and to an anonymous monk of the Charterhouse, aligned More unequivocally with the movement for the reform of the Catholic Church by a return 'ad fontes', to the ancient sources, above all to Scripture and the Fathers, for which Erasmus was the chief spokesman.[19] These humanist tracts are notable for their Erasmian contempt for the aridities of university scholastic theology, and their ardent defence of Erasmus' biblical and patristic work, which, More claimed, does 'more fruitful work for the Church in one month' than all his opponents have done in many years.[20] From 1521, however,

More switched his literary activity to the fight against heresy as one of the leaders of Henry VIII's campaign against Luther.[21] He was one of the advisers and perhaps ghost writers of Henry's *Assertio Septem Sacramentorum*. In 1523, with the King's encouragement, More published pseudonymously a virulently abusive Latin '*Responsio ad Lutherum*', an extended rhetorical exercise in the form of a diatribe, which pressed humanistic learning into polemical use, drawing on classical models from Lucian, Horace and Juvenal to ridicule, insult and excoriate Luther and his errors.[22]

But More himself came to place a higher value on the remarkable stream of English works which seemed to gush from his pen in the five years leading up to his arrest and imprisonment in the Tower. Ironically, these works are nowadays read, if at all, mainly as evidence that More was losing his grip. They form a remarkable series – *A Dialogue Concerning Heresies*, and *The Supplication of Souls*, in June and September 1529 respectively; then the *Confutation of Tyndale's Answer* (Part 1, the Preface and Books I–III published in January 1532, and Part 2, Books IV–VIII, more than a year later, after his resignation as Chancellor). That same year, 1533, saw the last four in this astonishing polemical outpouring, in rapid succession the *Apology of Sir Thomas More*, the *Debellation of Salem and Byzance*, the *Answer to a Poisoned Book* and the *Letter Against Frith*.[23] Though these books were directed against a variety of authors, More's main target, implicit even in writings ostensibly directed against others, was the Bible translator and controversialist William Tyndale.[24] There was an irony in this: More's scathing dismissal of university theology in the *Letter to a Monk*, with the observation that 'young girls once understood what today's proud professors cannot' has some affinity with Tyndale's vow that by his Bible translation '*I wyl cause a boy that driveth the plough to know more of the Scripture, than [the pope]*'.[25] But More viewed Tyndale as the most important conduit for Lutheran ideas into England, and he saw in Tyndale's version of the New Testament the fountainhead from which lesser minds drew lethal draughts of error with which to poison the souls of unsuspecting English men and women. It is not too much to say that More *hated* heresy, and the actions issuing from that hatred have posed a problem which has dogged modern discussion of More's career, from Chambers' valiant attempt to exculpate it as in fact a fear of sedition, to more recent excoriations by Hilary Mantel. It already posed a problem for his earliest editors and biographers, which they dealt with by suppressing it.

At 3 p.m. on 16 May 1532 in the garden of York Place near Westminster Hall, Thomas More delivered the Great Seal of England in its white leather bag into the hands of Henry VIII, and thereby resigned as Lord Chancellor: his public career was at an end.[26] The immediate trigger for More's resignation was the Submission of the Clergy to the Royal Supremacy just the day before. More's abandonment of office represented his recognition that he had lost the political battle he had been fighting since 1529 to hold the King to the defence of the Church, her clergy and her doctrines, for which Pope Leo X had granted Henry the title 'Defender of the Faith' ten years before.

More had been England's most determined and highest profile public champion of orthodoxy since the publication of his *A Dialogue Concerning Heresies* in 1529.[27] The *Dialogue*, the outcome of a commission by More's bishop, Cuthbert Tunstall, was merely the first and best of the remarkable stream of books – more than a million words in all – which More produced over the next four years in defence of the Catholic faith – and of himself. It would continue with the *Supplication of Souls*, the *Confutation of Tyndale's Answer*, the *Letter Against Frith*, the *Apology of Sir Thomas More*, the *Deballation of Salem and Byzance* and the *Answer to a Poisoned Book*.

This immense literary and intellectual investment by More, a mountain of words heaped up in hours snatched from his political and public commitments, has, I suspect, often been dismissed largely unread. Certainly, in terms of literary appraisal we have advanced very little if at all beyond the assessment offered by C. S. Lewis more than half a century ago.[28] Lewis thought well of the art of *A Dialogue Concerning Heresies*, and a generation later Brendan Bradshaw, from a different perspective, made a persuasive case for the *Dialogue's* coherence and polemical force.[29] More recently, it has attracted sympathetic attention from a number of literary scholars and historians, notably Tom Betteridge.[30] But even in these days of industrial scale academic production on More and his milieu, there is surprisingly little detailed attention to the rest of the vast bulk of More's polemical writing. Even the editors of the Yale editions of the *Confutation of Tyndale's Answer* and the *Debellation of Salem and Byzance* did not venture to recommend them as a good read, and the widespread assumption that they are in fact unreadable has inhibited serious engagement with them.

Attention has turned, instead, to More's *actions* against heresy. Richard Marius, deploring More's writings against heresy, 'pages now seldom read and often embarrassing to those who love More', saw More's polemical works as 'emblems of his helplessness before events. He wrote because he could do nothing else.'[31] This sounds as if it ought to be a rather illuminating remark, but in fact it's not quite right. At least while he was writing the *Dialogue*, the *Supplication* and the first half of the *Confutation*, More was anything but helpless. Even as he generated this torrent of words, More was busily engaged as the Crown's chief law officer in devastatingly practical action against error. He was pushing his legal powers as Chancellor to the limit in a crack-down on the possession and circulation of heretical books, initiating a series of proclamations, nocturnal raids and confiscations. Somewhat less spectacularly but much more controversially, both then and since, he was arresting the heretics themselves. As a layman and secular law official, of course, More never himself presided as judge in a heresy trial, but he was instrumental in stirring bishops to action, and he himself was responsible for the arrest, imprisonment and interrogation of several doctrinal deviants who were subsequently condemned by their ordinaries and executed. These included James Bainham, John Tewkesbury and Richard Bayfield.[32]

Thus More's involvement in the campaign against heresy took on a new and unErasmian intensity with his elevation to the Lord Chancellorship in late October 1529. As Chancellor, More felt a special responsibility, since heresy undermined ancient law, custom and morality and threatened 'the final subversion and desolation of this noble realm'.[33] The proclamation of 1530 which More probably drafted underlined the King's detestation of the 'malicious and wicked sects of heretics and Lollards' who by perverting scripture and inducing error, 'soweth sedition among Christian people, and ... do disturb the peace and tranquillity of Christian realms, as late happened in some parts of Germany, where by the procurement and sedition of Martin Luther and other heretics were slain an infinite number of Christian people'. The proclamation called on civil officials, from the Chancellor himself down to the justices of the peace, to 'give their whole power and diligence to put away and to make utterly to cease and destroy all manner of heresies and errors'.[34] And so the pace of the London campaign against the underground book trade intensified. Several suspects were imprisoned and examined by More in his own house at Chelsea, and evidence collected by him was instrumental in securing the condemnation of three of the six heretics burned while he was Chancellor.[35]

Inevitably, the rumour mill got to work: allegations of torture circulated. More categorically and in detail denied all such allegations in the *Apology*,[36] but with John Foxe's help they persisted, reiterated in our time in Hilary Mantel's hostile portrayal of 'our friend in Chelsea', which looks like becoming the authorised portrait of More. For a generation this hostile take on More on heresy has been underpinned by elaborate psycho-sexual speculation about More himself. In a famous character sketch of More in a letter of 1519 to Ulrich von Hutten, Erasmus remarked that More had seriously considered a vocation to the priesthood or monastic life.[37] Discovering in himself, however, a strong attraction to women, he had opted instead for marriage, holding that it was better to be a good husband than a bad priest. On this flimsy base, modern interpreters of More have erected – the phrase is emphatically the *mot juste* – a theory that More's dealings with heresy were dogged by his own unresolved sexual problems, and that his writings about heresy are therefore obsessive, hysterical and increasingly uncontrolled. Sir Geoffrey Elton set the pattern with a series of debunking essays spread over 30 years, in which he argued that More had spent four 'idiot years'[38] trying to be a monk of the Charterhouse, and, having opted instead for marriage, spent the rest of his life struggling with a sense of failure. Elton's More was a repressed 'sex maniac', unable to shake off the conviction 'that he had failed to live up to what he regarded as God's ultimate demand on man', namely, celibacy. This, for Elton, was the explanation not only of what he considered More's morbid self-flagellation and hair shirt, but also of the tone of More's writings against the reformation, 'endless, nearly always tedious, passionate, devoid of humour and markedly obsessive', a display of 'helpless fury' rooted in More's own misanthropic pessimism, and above all in his unresolved and morbid sexuality.[39]

This psycho-sexual fantasy of the guilt-ridden failed monk was elaborated by the literary historian Alistair Fox in 1982 as the interpretative key to all More's English writings up to his arrest and imprisonment in the Tower. For Fox, More's controversial writings conceal an inner experience 'which . . . threatened to destroy his sense of providence and . . . eventually brought him close to despair'. In them we find 'a pattern of progressive deterioration: dialogue gives way to debellation, self-control yields to loss of proportion and perspective, candour is replaced by dishonesty'. More's 'snarling invective' and 'polemical ferocity' display 'an almost demoniac emotional violence towards his opponents', a 'vileness of sentiment', which he thinks went far beyond sixteenth-century convention, a sustained act of morbid compensation, to assuage his own guilt at not being a monk.[40]

There is a great deal of anachronism in such concerns. The ferocious language of More's polemical works, for example, both in Latin and in English, needs re-insertion into the rhetorical conventions of humanist writing.[41] But historians, literary critics, novelists and dramatists alike have professed revulsion from the bulk, vehemence and apparent lack of literary control in those writings, and have related their distaste to the apparent self-betrayal of More's actions. And the involvement of one of Europe's greatest humanist writers in a sometimes lethal campaign of repression, censorship and book-burning, and in the arrest and interrogation of suspects, has led historians to see More in the late 1520s and early 1530s as driven by a murderous panic about heresy rooted less in objective reality than in his own psychosexual pathology.

This is a familiar line of argument, according to which More, in the early 1530s, was 'a cruelly divided man', experiencing, in Alistair Fox's words, 'changes in his personality that threatened to destroy much of what was most attractive and admirable in him'.[42] This alleged deterioration explains, such writers suggest, the evident gulf in sensibility between the persecuting Chancellor with his hysterical and undisciplined anti-heretical outpourings, and the creator of *Utopia*, who only 15 years earlier had created that luminous fiction celebrating a rational commonwealth in which all religions were tolerated, where it was recognised that no one could be coerced into belief, and where even the most deviant opinions might be freely debated in private, provided those who held them did not air them in public or disturb the common people. In a judicious and fair-minded assessment of More's anti-heretical writings and actions in 2000, John Guy recognised that More undertook his polemical and repressive activities initially at least at the behest of others – Bishop Tunstall and, with supreme irony, Henry VIII. But he too finds in More's dealing with heresy a fundamental contradiction: More's language about heresy is, according to Guy, 'too severe', and 'the schizophrenia created by More's dual role as author of *Utopia* and inquisitor in heresy cases will never be dispelled'.[43]

I don't myself subscribe to this theory of schizophrenia between the humanist More and the persecuting and polemical Chancellor, and in Chapters Two and Three I will argue in detail for the formidable coherence and effectiveness of the key anti-heretical writings, including even the immense and repetitious *Confutation of Tyndale's Answer*.[44] More was indeed more urgent in action and more vehement in debate in the early 1530s. This, however, was not because he was having a nervous breakdown or being untrue to himself, but because the state of the world demanded vigorous action and urgency. By 1529 More was not the only rational man in Europe who believed that the Protestant reformation threatened the intellectual and moral coherence of Christendom as he (and for that matter Erasmus) understood it. And the intellectual foundations for the urgency of the 1530s are already there in his early humanist writings. *Utopia* is a portrait of a world before revelation, where rational debate about religious truth is essential, precisely because it is doomed to perpetual inconclusiveness. Dogmatism about religious truth is of course inappropriate in a world with no objective means of discovering where the truth might lie. But even the Utopians did not tolerate just anything: King Utopus, you may recall, allowed liberty of conscience in matters of religion, but 'By way of exception, he conscientiously and strictly gave injunction that no one should fall so far below the dignity of human nature as to believe that souls likewise perish with the body or that the world is the mere sport of chance and not governed by any divine providence'.[45]

Specifically, the Utopians insisted that 'After this life, accordingly, vices are ordained to be punished and virtue rewarded'. This reward of virtue was fundamental to rational society, so that 'if anyone thinks otherwise, they do not regard him even as a member of mankind, seeing that he has lowered the lofty nature of his soul to the level of a beast's body – so far are they from classing him among their citizens whose laws and customs he would treat as worthless if it were not for fear'.[46]

In other words, More's Utopian pagans believed that rational virtue was what marked mankind off from the rest of the animals, and no society could survive without an underlying belief in a divine providence. This belief manifested itself in the exercise of moral freedom shaped by a conviction that God would reward virtue and punish vice. And More, in common with most contemporary defenders of Catholicism, came to believe that Luther's denial of the place of good works and merit as conditions of salvation had precipitated precisely such a descent into bestial irrationality and social chaos. By their fruits ye shall know them. More's polemical vehemence was rooted in an appalled perception of the state of contemporary Europe in the grip of a heresy which he feared would 'frame this realme after the fassyon of Swycherlande or Saxony and some other partes of Germany where theyr secte hath alredy fordone the fayth / pulled downe the chyrches / polluted the temples / put out and spoyled all good relygyous folke / ioyned freres and nonnes togyther in lechery / despyted all sayntes / blasphemed oure blessyd lady / caste downe Crystes crosse / throwne out the blessyd sacrament / refused all good lawes / abhorred all good governaunce / rebelled agaynste all rulers fall to fyght amonge them selfe / and so many thousands slayne / that the lande lyeth in many places in maner deserte and desolate'.[47]

The key to this gloomy assessment of the consequences of Protestant teaching has more often than not been looked for in More's own degenerating psychological state. His vehemence and growing pessimism have been taken as a sign of psychic disturbance, rooted in self-loathing because of his choice of marriage over celibacy, a diagnosis based, to put it mildly, on the flimsiest of evidence. And there is no need for Freudian speculation to account for More's loathing of heresy, since almost everything in More on the subject can be paralleled in the writings of European contacts like Eck and Cochlaeus, who were equally apocalyptic. Both the general line of argument and the rhetorical pitch of passages like the one just quoted are typical of orthodox anti-Lutheran polemic. Five years before More wrote that passage, the German Catholic pamphleteer Simon Blich had declaimed in much the same tones in his *Shame and Desolation of the Nation and its People*:

> A runaway monk has turned everything upside down ... Pious virgin nuns have become whores, devout monks wicked carnal and unchaste men, and good Christians evil heretical dogs ... the people's deep devotion has been destroyed; instead of good works are base carnality; for freedom of the spirit, the freedom of the flesh; for love of God, hatred of neighbour; for moderation, eating, drinking and feasting ...

and so on.[48]

The Peasants' War in 1525 seemed to clinch decisively these alleged links between Protestantism and social chaos, and More's writing directly reflects this. But heresy brought more than disobedience and war: Luther's teaching on predestination seemed to More, as to other defenders of orthodoxy from Erasmus to Blich, an attack on the very roots of rational virtue. Luther, More believed, undermined the ethical framework of the Christian life as the Church had taught and practised it for a millennium and a half, and in effect denied the goodness of God himself by making him an arbitrary tyrant:

> finally that most abhomynable is of all / of all theyr owne ungra-cyouse dedes lay the faute in god / taking away the lybertye of mannes wyll / ascrybyng all our dedes to destiny ... whereby they take away all dylygence and good endevour to vertue / all wythstandyng and stryvyng agaynst vyce / all care of hevyn / all fere of hell / all cause of prayer / all desyre of devocyon / all exhortacyon to good / all dehortacyon from evyll / all prayse of welldoying / all rebuke of syn / all the lawes of the worlde / all reason among men / set all wretchednesse a broche / no man at lybertye / and yet every man do what he wyll / calling it not his wyll but his desteny / layng theyr syn to goddes ordenaunce / and theyr punysshment to goddes crueltye / and fynally turning the nature of man in to worse than a beste / and the goodness of god in to worse than the devyll ...[49]

Here was the sufficient cause of all More's urgency, for he was convinced that a descent into chaos like that afflicting Germany awaited England, too, unless the spreading poison of heresy was halted: 'all this good frute wold a few myschevous persons / some for desire of a large lybertye to an unbrydeled lewdness / and some of an hye devylesshe pryde cloked under pretexte of good zele and symplenes / undoubtedly bring in to thys realme / yf the prynce and prelates and the good faythfull people dyd not in the begynnyng mete with theyr malyce'.[50]

It would be possible, of course, to see in More's highly charged language a morbid overreaction. Protestantism had borne other fruits than warfare and iconoclasm, though you might never think so when reading More. But it bears reiterating that the links More made between heresy, rebellion and social breakdown were entirely conventional – Cochlaeus attributed the peasants' war to Luther just as he attributed the Hussite Wars to Wyclif. To dismiss More's fears as idiosyncratically alarmist or disproportionate is reminiscent of the way in which Churchill's opponents represented his anti-appeasement speeches in the 1930s as hysterical posturing. Time proved Churchill right, however, as, arguably, it vindicated More also, for within three years of More's execution Henry would indeed have 'put out and spoyled all good relygyous folke'. Within ten years, Henry's son would have 'ioyned freres and nonnes togyther in lechery / despyted all sayntes / blasphemed oure blessyd lady / caste downe Crystes crosse / [and] throwne out the blessyd sacrament'. More's apocalyptic vision had become sober reality, not hysteria, but history.

It needs to be emphasised that in itself More's turn to polemic had nothing in it that could be considered intrinsically unErasmian: the refutation of heresy had been a minor but definite element in More's humanist writings in support of Erasmus, many of the humanist clergy favoured by the Cardinal and the court were active in the campaign against the reformation after 1521, and after a good deal of shilly-shallying even Erasmus had entered the lists against Luther's teaching on Justification and free will in 1526.

There's no denying, of course, that More took a savagely negative view of the Reformation. For More, all heresy was inspired by demonic pride: it was a refusal to obey God, which took the form of the rejection of the manifest faith of the Church, 'the comen well-known bylefe of the comen known catholyke chyrche of all chrysten people / such fayth as by your selfe, and your fathers, and your grandfathers, you have knowen to be byleved',[51] 'preferrynge theyr owne fonde gloses against the old connynge and blessyd fathers interpretacyons'.[52] The heretic always rejected legitimate spiritual authority, 'boldely and stubbornly defending that syth they had connynge to preche they were by god bounden to preche. And that no man nor no lawe was made or coulde be made that had any authoryte to forbade them'.[53] This spiritual sedition, More thought, invariably issued in social breakdown, and heresy was always a solvent which fatally loosened the bonds of civil society. More returned time and again to this theme to justify his pursuit of heresy. 'Prynces and people have been constrained to punysshe heresyes by terryble deth', he wrote in 1529, because bitter experience has shown that 'outrages and myscheves' invariably 'follow upon suche sectes and heresyes'.[54] Heresy was primarily a crime against God, and for that reason alone intrinsically worthy of punishment. Yet for mercy's sake Christian people might have left the heretics to their errors, were it not for the fact that heresy was always seditious and destructive – 'while they forbore violence / there was little vyolence done to theym'.[55]

We may recall here that obnoxious opinions were only permitted in Utopia provided they were not preached to the common people. In the real world, however, error, puffed up with pride, was always proselytising. As More wrote in his *Apology* in 1533, 'heretykes wyll be doing'.[56] So it had been in Africa under the Donatists, in Greece under the Arians, in Bohemia under the Hussites. England had found this in the reign of Richard II, when the heretics were at first 'by many men wynked at, and almost by all folk forslouthed'. Free to 'spred theyr heresies about fro shyre to shyre and fro dyocise to dyocise', at last 'the heretykes were growen unto such number, corage and boldness' that they conspired 'not only the abolycyon of the fayth, and spoylyng of the spyrytualtye, but also the destruccyon of the kyng … with a playne subversyon and overturning of the state of hys hole realme'. This Oldcastle's rebellion made clear, and this was the inevitable course of all heresy, which was always intrinsically seditious.[57] And so it was in More's own times: if only the authorities in Germany and Switzerland had enforced their heresy laws at the outset of Luther's revolt, 'the matter hadde not there gone out at length to suche an ungracyouse endynge'.[58] Even the heretics themselves had come to realise the need to suppress error and in Germany, contrary to their own initial self-protective teaching on the sinfulness of the use of force in matters of faith, the Protestants sects were now locked in internecine war, and 'tone dreve tother to ruyne. For never shall that cuntre long abyde without debate and ruffle / where scysmes and factyouse hereses are suffered a whyle to grow'.[59]

Even at the height of his early defence of Erasmus against his critics More had been convinced that heretics were often impervious to argument, 'more intimidated by one little bundle of faggots than daunted by great bundles of syllogisms'.[60] More's later dedication to the fight against heresy in the 1520s and 1530s was informed by an urgent sense that Catholic England had become dangerously complacent. The heretics were few, but they were fervent, 'so besyly walkynge that in every ale house, in every taverne, in every barne, and almost every bote, as few they be a man shall alwaye fynde some'. Compared to the apathy of the orthodox, their zeal was 'as gret a difference, as bytwene frost and fyre'. The lazy tolerance by which heretics were indulgently 'suffred boldly to talk unchecked' gave error a foothold which would be ruthlessly exploited by the heretics. This was potentially a fatal negligence, for 'yf they thought theym selfe able to mete and matche the catholykes / they wolde not I wene lye styll in reste thre dayes'. Christ had promised that the gates of hell would never prevail against the Church, but that did not mean that individual local churches might not be overwhelmed by error. 'For as the see shal never surround and overwhelme all the lande ... yet hath it eaten many places in, and swallowed hole countries uppe'.[61]

This was the double rationale which More offered for his pursuit of heresy from the mid-1520s onwards. He was defending the common faith against the pride of those who would give the simple people poison in place of bread, and he was defending the commonwealth against those whose divisiveness would inevitably bring chaos and ruin. As Chancellor of the Duchy of Lancaster he was a key member of the commission for the suppression of heretical books established by Wolsey: in that capacity in 1526 More headed a series of spectacular raids on the Steelyards, the German mercantile colony which was one of the main channels for the importation of Lutheran books into London. And when, at the request of Cuthbert Tunstall, he began his English writings against heresy in 1529, he deliberately paraded his status as a Crown official. The title pages of *A Dialogue Concerning Heresies* and the *Supplication of Souls* proclaimed the author 'one of the privy counsayll of our soverayne lorde the kyng and Chancellour of hys duchy of Lancaster'. The second edition of the *Dialogue* and the first part of the *Confutation* announced More's elevation as Lord Chancellor. That official role as defender of the truths which bound Christian society together is insisted on in the *Confutation*. The King himself had shown his devotion to Catholic truth in the *Assertio Septem Sacramentorum*, and in the enforcement of a legal ban on 'those pernycyouse poysened books'. And so, 'seyng the kynges gracyouse purpose in thys poynt: I reken that beynge hys unworthy chancellour, it apperteyneth ... unto my parte and dewty, to folow the ensample of hys noble grace'. It was therefore his duty to persuade those in error to turn from their heresies or 'yf it happily be incurable, then to the clene cuttynge out the parte for infeccyon of the remnaunt: am I by myne office in vertue of myne othe, and every officer of iustyce thorow the realme for his rate, right especially bounden ...'[62]

By the time he wrote that passage in the spring of 1532, More was painfully aware that the King's earlier proactive opposition to heresy had been radically compromised by Henry's need to rally support from whatever quarter for the Divorce question. Within weeks of the publication of Part One of the *Confutation*, the King had asserted his supremacy over the Church, and More had resigned the Chancellorship. In 1533 he would defend both his own integrity and the fundamental principle of the legal pursuit and capital punishment of stubborn heretics in the second part of the *Confutation*, in his *Apology*, and in the *Debellation of Salem and Byzance*. This last was an attack on an anti-clerical tract by the lawyer Christopher St Germain, though More knew perfectly well that the author was articulating the regime's growing hostility to Church and clergy. In these books, therefore, More was fighting an increasingly fraught rearguard action to persuade the political elite of the continuing and urgent need to combat heresy. Without openly blaming the King he had to demonstrate how the escalating and officially fostered anti-clericalism played into the hands of the 'new broached brethren' and their poisonous doctrines. This involved the author of *Utopia* arguing against what he viewed as a specious and sentimental humanitarianism, which portrayed the use of force against religious deviance as inhumane or unnecessary. But more specifically, it also involved defending his own record as a pursuivant, interrogator and polemicist. More needed to rebut allegations of personal vindictiveness and the use of torture in his official pursuit of heretics, and of abusiveness in his controversial writing. That is the context for his well-known disclaimer of personal animus in the *Apology,* 'As touchynge heretykes, I hate that vyce of theirs and not theyr persones / and very fayne wolde I that the tone were destroyed, and tother saved.'[63]

To repeat, then, in these works More was thrown onto the defensive about his anti-heretical activities, forced to justify both the principle of persecution, and his own record as a persecutor. It is all the more remarkable, therefore, that More should continue in these late writings to present himself as a hammer of heretics, not merely defending or mitigating his proceedings, but actually emphasising his dedication to the fight against deviant doctrines and deviant doctors. This aspect of More's vernacular writings has not I think been adequately recognised. From *Utopia* onwards, all of More's best public writings involve the creation of one or more dramatic personae. It's often been noted that his three best books, *Utopia, A Dialogue Concerning Heresies* and the *Dialogue of Comfort* all take the form precisely of dialogues, in the first two of which a fictionalised More himself plays a leading – or should one say a misleading – role. But in all his anti-heretical English works, More uses these personifications to force the reader's attention to More's own actual agency in the struggle against Protestant error. Notoriously, this concern manifested itself in savage asides which make clear More's own loathing of heresy and of heretics, 'the devils stinking martyrs, well worthy to be burned'. More soberly, as we have seen, More was concerned to present his own activities as an expression of royal policy, a response to the lead given by the King as Defender of the Faith. He was also concerned to play the experience card, to document his claim that all heretics were driven by malice and the desire to deceive, from his extensive personal acquaintance with the culprits, and to set out the evidence of their duplicity. But in reporting these encounters, from *A Dialogue Concerning Heresies* onwards, More constantly presented a literary image of himself as an eager and determined hunter and interrogator of heretics. The English anti-heretical writings are larded with circumstantial vignettes of himself in action in that capacity. Notoriously, the *Dialogue* has detailed accounts of More's own involvement in the Hunne case and the investigation of Bilney's alleged recantation. The *Confutation* and *Apology* have many similar episodes – More's examination of James Bayfield, the interrogation of George Constantine and the book-busts carried out on the basis of Constantine's confessions, More's trick questioning of the book smuggler James Webb in the second part of the *Confutation*, and so on.

The opening of the story of the arrest and interrogation of Webbe is characteristic:

> Thys Webbe when I was Chancelloure to the kynges hyghnesse, was by dyvers heretykes detected unto me, that he had solde and used continually to sell many of those heretykes bookes forboden by the kynges gracyouse proclamacyon to be broght into the realme / and ferther I was by good and honest men enformed, that in Brystowe where he then dwelled, there were many of those pestilent bokes some throwen in the street and lefte at mennys dores by nyght, that where they durste not offer theyr poison to sell, they wolde of theyr cheryte poison men for nought . . . I gave out a commyssyon to certayne good wurshypfull folke at Bristowe to attach Richard Webbe . . .[64]

In such episodes More admittedly represents himself as always fair-minded and, where the accused was penitent, inclined to mercy, but also always as a shrewd and determined pursuivant. The extended anecdote about Webbe from which I've just quoted the opening, turns on More's possession of secret information from informers about Webbe's activities and associates in the illicit book trade , and hence his detection of Webbe in a series of barefaced lies. More's concern was to demonstrate from a specific case that heretics are invariably liars, but *en route* his own zeal as a hammer of heretics emerges into sharp focus. This was clearly deliberate, for the same point is emphasised in the epitaph More composed for himself in the aftermath of his resignation in 1532, and which he had carved in Chelsea parish church. The epitaph was designed to put on permanent record that More had resigned voluntarily from the Chancellorship ostensibly for health reasons at a time of his choosing, and that he retained the King's goodwill, but it included the notorious phrase that in the office of Chancellor he had been 'furibus autem homicides haereticisque molestus', 'to theves, murderers and heretikes grievous'.[65]

More certainly wanted to draw attention to his anti-heretical activities, despite their increasingly dangerous association with opposition to royal policy. He sent copies of the epitaph to friends, including Erasmus, who, notably, copied it on, adding a loyal defence of More's pursuit of heresy, which, however, included the false claim that no one had been executed for heresy during More's Chancellorship. For all his protestations of support, Erasmus may have been unhappy about More's activities in this area. If so, however, More brushed aside his friend's discomfort in a follow-up letter in the summer of 1533.

'If you think it expedient,' he wrote,

> don't hesitate to publish my letter. As to my declaration that I was grievous to heretics, 'hoc ambitiose feci', I meant every word. I absolutely detest that breed of men, and there are none I oppose more implacably, unless they come to their senses. For the more I have to do with them, the more I dread the calamities they will unleash on the world.[66]

More's epitaph has been insufficiently related to its proper context, and was evidently intended as an oblique comment on the increasingly vehement anti-heretical writings of the 1530s, with their deliberate focus on his heresy-hunting activities as counsellor and Chancellor. We have here more than an embarrassment for the *amici Thomae Mori*; we have a considered piece of self-representation by More, in which he features dauntingly as the hammer of heretics not only by his writing, but specifically as pursuivant, interrogator and accuser. In the epitaph, More relates his 'grievousness' to heretics precisely to his role as law officer, and places his handling of heretics on a par with his handling of murders and thieves: and the same equation is made throughout the *Confutation*, *Apology* and the *Debellation*.

Strikingly, this was a dimension of More's self-representation from which even his immediate circle of family and admirers sought to avert their eyes. His arrest, imprisonment and execution in any case switched attention from More the pursuer to More the victim. It would be More the martyr rather than More the hammer of heretics whom his admirers would transmit to the future. This reluctance of the More circle to engage with a theme which looms so large in More's English writings, and which he himself chose to underline in stone as well as in print, emerged intriguingly in the literary representations of More composed under Mary Tudor, and which did so much to determine More's recusant reputation more generally.

There is no space here to explore the management of More's memory in Mary Tudor's reign, except to underline the key role played in the process by Cardinal Pole himself.[67] Many of the episcopal leaders of the Marian Church had conformed under Henry VIII, and had defended both the royal supremacy and Henry's actions as King. For obvious reasons Stephen Gardiner and Edmund Bonner, both of whom had denounced More as a traitor, were not anxious to exalt his memory. But Pole himself had given a central place to More and Fisher as martyrs in his 1536 treatise on the Unity of the Church, an all-out attack on Henry. For Pole, More and Fisher were unique messengers from God, witnesses to the centrality of the papacy, their deaths letters from God written in blood and more weighty even than scripture. Pole and his family helped preserve More's writings in the aftermath of his execution, and Pole remained closely in touch with members of More's circle, including his nephew and publisher William Rastell, and More's close friend, the Lucca/London merchant Antonio Bonvisi, in whose house in Louvain members of the More circle, including William Roper and Nicholas Harpsfield, More's biographers, and William Rastell, his editor, all took refuge during the reign of Edward VI.

It is from this circle of Pole's contacts among More's relatives and friends that there emerged with Pole's encouragement in 1556 and 1557 a concerted campaign to use More's reputation in defence of the Marian campaign against heresy, and to present More the martyr as an antidote to the popular cult of Protestant martyrs.

The central documents here are the great folio edition of More's English *Workes* published by William Rastell at the end of April 1557, and Nicholas Harpsfield's splendid biography of More, ostensibly commissioned by More's son-in-law William Roper, and clearly intended to accompany Rastell's edition of the English *Workes*. The editing of the works and the writing of Harpsfield's life have usually been interpreted as private initiatives by More's family and friends. But both Rastell and Roper were close associates of the Cardinal, and were almost certainly working with his encouragement and help. Both men served as MPs for Canterbury; Roper lived there, and the Cardinal had Rastell appointed legal councillor for the city. Significantly, both men were activists in the Marian legal campaign against heresy: Roper was not only a member of the Canterbury heresy commission established by Philip and Mary in July 1556: he was involved in the examination and trial of the Kentish Protestant leader John Bland, and was also active outside Kent in the London dioceses, in the processes against Bartlett Green and John Philpott, and in the Protestant hotspot of Colchester. William Rastell was one of the legal officials nominated to the national heresy commission established with extensive powers across the country in February 1557 to step up the campaign against Protestant activity.[68]

This is the context both of the 1557 folio of More's English *Workes*, and of Harpsfield's *The Life and Death of Sir Thomas Moore*.[69] The English *Workes* appeared with a dedicatory epistle from Rastell to Queen Mary, signalling the volume's official status, and articulating the central preoccupation of the regime with heresy in the spring of 1557. The preface denounced the 'obstinate and stubborn malice, and also . . . proud and arrogant presumption' of unrepentant Protestants, while emphasising the utility of More's works for 'confuting of all perverse opinions, false doctrines and devilishe heresies'.[70]

Rastell's great folio contained all More's vernacular controversial writings, and culminated with his devotional treatises, prayers and letters from the Tower, the letters in particular providing a profoundly moving picture of a noble Catholic martyr following a very differ-ent road to martyrdom from what the regime saw as the arrogant and presumptuous self-immolation which motivated the victims of the burnings. For good measure Rastell added More's Chelsea epitaph, both in the original Latin and in an English translation.

Here, implicitly at any rate, were all the materials needed for a full picture of More's attitudes towards heresy and his actions against heretics.

And that pattern of martyrdom was handled explicitly in Nicholas Harpsfield's companion volume to the folio *Workes,* his *Life and Death of Sir Thomas Moore,* presented to More's son-in-law William Roper as a New Year's gift in January 1557. Harpsfield had been a refugee with the More family in Bonvisi's house in Louvain, and wrote the biography at Roper's request, drawing on Roper's own reminiscences as his main source. Now Harpsfield was Pole's right-hand man, Archdeacon of Canterbury and the principal agent of the reimposition of Catholicism in Canterbury and London. While writing the life of More in 1556, he had also conducted searching visitations in London and Canterbury, had been heavily involved in the legal work of the Court of Arches, and had composed what was probably intended as the regime's official Latin account of the last days and execution of Cranmer, for circulation in Europe. It is inconceivable that this hectically busy official and propagandist would have devoted so much time to writing More's biography in that frenetic year without Pole's knowledge and support, indeed at the Cardinal's request.

Harpsfield's book is designed to demonstrate the contention of Pole's treatise *De Unitate Ecclesiae,* that More's 'speciall peerless prerogative' was that he was above everything 'our blessed proptomartyr of all the laytie for the preservation of the unitie of Christ's Church'.[71] More's arrest, trial and last days were very fully treated, and, following More's own understanding of the nature of martyrdom, Harpsfield emphasises both More's determined attempts to avoid death and his patient resignation and confidence in God when it became inescapable. And he devoted an equal amount of space to More's controversial career, insisting on the permanent value of More's writings against heresy, and along the way informing the reader of the imminent publication of Rastell's edition.[72]

Revealingly, however, Harpsfield confined his account of More's opposition to heresy to his *literary* output: though he treated other aspects of More's work as a lawyer, judge and public servant, he said not a word about More's involvement in the actual pursuit and prosecution of heretics. This was certainly deliberate. Harpsfield includes a brief account of the series of raids on and the subsequent prosecution of the German merchants of the London Steelyards for importing Lutheran books in the mid-1520s. As he must have known, these raids had been masterminded from start to finish by More: in Harpsfield's account, however, More's *bête noire*, Cardinal Wolsey, is the one responsible, and nothing is said of More's involvement.[73]

Even more strikingly, though Harpsfield drew heavily on the English *Workes*, and devoted 20 pages to discussion of More's *Confutation, Apology* and the *Debellation*, the books in which More had devoted most space to justifying his pursuit and treatment of heretics, Harpsfield, himself a busy pursuivant of heretics, focused entirely on what these books have to say about More's literary activities: he explores and refutes Protestant accusations about More's rough writing against them.[74] On the accusations of torture and illegality, however, which later recusant writers would refute by repeating Erasmus' mistaken claim that no one had been executed for heresy while More was Chancellor, Harpsfield remained totally silent. Even more strikingly, he discussed More's epitaph in precisely the same way that he discussed the *Apology* and the *Debellation*, defending it from a charge of vaingloriousness, pointedly avoiding direct citation of the notorious phrase about being grievous to heretics, but tacitly glossing it as if it alluded only to his writings: 'in the endighting of this his Epitaphe,' Harpsfield wrote, More, 'had not so much regarde unto himselfe, or his owne estimation, as to God's cause and religion, which he had by open bookes against the Protestantes defended'. It would be impossible to guess from Harpsfield's life that More had used his office to pursue the heretics themselves, rather than merely writing to confute their works. At this high point in the Marian pursuit of heresy, one of the most active and effective pursuivants of heretics simply chose to eliminate that entire dimension of More's career. Though Harpsfield insisted that Sir Thomas 'was the most notable and valiant captain against these pestilent and poisoned heretics', according to Harpsfield it was exclusively by 'his noble books' that More had 'conquered' them.[75]

We are left with the question: did More renounce his youthful Erasmianism? Recusant writers like Harpsfield, anxious to present More as the patron of Tridentine orthodoxy, either suppressed details of More's friendship with Erasmus, or even suggested that he had rebuked Erasmus for his continued satire of corruption in the Church. No evidence of any such rebuke has survived, but Harpsfield's Marian generation was not the first to note the apparent contradictions between the younger Erasmian More and the controversialist and heresy hunter. According to William Tyndale, More's criticisms of Tyndale's New Testament applied equally to the biblical work of Erasmus, so 'how happeth it that M. More hathe not contended in lyke wise against hys derelynge Erasmus all this long whyle?' Perhaps he spared Erasmus, Tyndale suggested, for the sake of the fame More had reaped because Erasmus' *The Praise of Folly* had been written in More's house. But that very book was a monument to the gulf between the persecuting More and his earlier principle, and 'if [it] were in englische / then shulde every man se / how that he then was ferre other wise minded then he now writeth'.[76]

More's response to the accusation was twofold. In the first place, he insisted, intention was everything: he had not contended with 'Erasmus my derlynge' because Erasmus had none of the 'shrewde intent and purpose' that More found in Tyndale. Erasmus jested at abuses, Tyndale struck at fundamentals. In an explicit affirmation of the continuing value of Erasmian satire and humanist literary forms, More insisted that the satire in *The Praise of Folly* was much less pointed than that in More's own *Dialogue Concerning Heresies* published the previous year, and he pointed to the plausible presentation of the Protestant case against the Church 'which I have yet suffered to stand styll in my dialogue'. Nevertheless, times were changing, More went on, and new challenges demanded different responses. The humanist satirical project was entirely legitimate, but the propagation of 'pestilent heresyes' had 'so envenomed the hartes of lewdly disposed persons' 'that men can not almost now speke of such thynges in so mych as a play, but that such evyll herers wax a grete dele the worse'. Men now could be harmed by their own perverse misreading even of 'the very scrypture of God', and for that reason the King had forbidden the reading of the Bible in English, till men and times improved. And so, if anyone were now to translate *The Praise of Folly*, or More's own humanist writings into English, 'I wolde not onlely my derlynges bokes but myne own also, helpe to burne them with myne own handes, rather then folkers sholde (though thorow theyre owne faute) take any herme of them'.[77]

Does this carefully nuanced 1531 utterance constitute More's final abandonment of the humanist project, the death of Erasmian England? It's worth bearing in mind that More's concern is not the suppression of *The Praise of Folly* or any other humanist works, but concern about their availability in English in the changed and charged circumstances of the 1530s. His preoccupation is with the circulation of satire intended for a Latinate literate audience among the populace at large. More's love of Erasmus, and Erasmus' admiration of More, seem to have persisted to the end of their lives,[78] though the last of Erasmus' own colloquies satirising Catholic religious abuse was written and published in 1529, and Erasmus reissued the 50 already written, including such mordant satires as his 'Pilgrimage for Religion's Sake', in 1533. But these were Latin not vernacular texts, and it was specifically vernacular satire that More thought dangerous. And in that same year, 1533, Erasmus himself wrote to the King of Scotland urging that Tyndale's New Testament be suppressed there. The contrast between More the warrior against heresy and Erasmus the constant humanist, though real, is less stark than has often been alleged. It seems that by the early 1530s, in the face of the Protestant challenge, even for Erasmus himself the Erasmian moment may have passed.

Notes

1   James Kelsey McConicka, *English Humanists and Reformation Politics under Henry VIII and Edward VI* (Oxford, 1965); Constance M. Furey, *Erasmus, Contarini, and the Religious Republic of Letters* (Cambridge, 2008). A number of historians, most notably Professor George Bernard, have gone beyond McConicka in seeing the King himself as a committed 'Erasmian', and Bernard has even described Henry as a 'pupil' of Erasmus 'who was for a while his tutor', but Henry's 'Erasmianism' has been convincingly refuted by Richard Rex; G. W. Bernard, *The King's Reformation: Henry VIII and the Remaking of the English Church* (New Haven and London, 2005); G. W. Bernard, 'Reflecting on the King's Reformation' in T. Betteridge and S. Lipscomb (eds), *Henry VIII and the Court: Art, Politics and Performance* (Farnham, 2013), pp. 9–26; Richard Rex, 'The Religion of Henry VIII,' *Historical Journal*, 57 (2014), pp. 1–32.

2   E. E. Reynolds, *Thomas More and Erasmus* (Fordham, 1965); Dominic Baker-Smith, 'Erasmus and More, a friendship revisited', *Recusant History*, 30 (2010), pp. 7–25.

3   Eugene F. Rice, 'Erasmus and the Religious tradition, 1495–1499', *Journal of the History of Ideas*, 11 (1950), pp. 387–411; James D. Tracy, *Erasmus: The Growth of a Mind*, Travaux d'Humanisme et Renaissance, vol. 126 (Geneva, 1972).

4   For a stimulating if controversial reading of Erasmus' use of print as a means of self-construction and promotion, Lisa Jardine, *Erasmus, Man of Letters: The Construction of Charisma in Print* (Princeton, NJ, 1993).

5   Peter Iver Kaufman, 'John Colet and Erasmus' "Enchiridion"', *Church History*, 46 (1977), pp. 296–312.

6   J. B. Gleason, *John Colet* (Berkeley, Calif., 1989).

7   Good introduction and selection in Margaret Mann Phillips (ed.), *Erasmus on his Times: A Shortened Version of the Adages* (Cambridge, 1980).

8   Translation of the *Enchyridion* in John P. Dolan, *The Essential Erasmus* (New American Library, 1964).

9   Craig R. Thompson (ed.), *Translations of Lucian*, in *Complete Works of St Thomas More*, vol. 3 (New Haven and London, 1974).

10   Erasmus, *In Praise of Folly* (trans. Betty Radice) (London Folio Society, 2014), p. 63.

11   Ibid., pp. 76–83.

12   Ibid., pp. 94–7.

13   Ibid., p. 117.

14   Clarence H. Miller (ed.), *Erasmus and Luther: The Battle Over Free Will* (Indianapolis, 2012).

15   Representative selection in Craig R. Thompson, *Ten Colloquies of Erasmus* (Liberal Arts Press, 1957).

16   E. Rummel, 'Erasmus and the Louvain Theologians', *Nederlands Archief Voor Kerkgeschiedenis / Dutch Review of Church History*, vol. 70 (1990), pp. 2–12, and her two-volume *Erasmus and His Catholic Critics* (Nieuwkoop, The Netherlands, 1989).

17   Edited with a translation by Edward Surtz and J. H. Hexter, in *Complete Works*, vol. 4 (New Haven and London, 1965): there is also a good translation and useful introduction edited by George M. Logan and Robert M. Adams, *More, Utopia* (Cambridge, 1989).

18   Guidance on the vast literature on More's *Utopia* in Logan and Adams, *More, Utopia*, pp. xxxiv–vii.

19   The four defences of Erasmus are edited and translated by Daniel Kinney in vol. 15 of the Yale *The Complete Works of St. Thomas More* (New Haven and London, 1986).

20   *Complete Works*, vol. 15, pp. 141, 225, 297.

21   Richard Rex, 'The English Campaign against Luther in the 1520s', *Transactions of the Royal Historical Society*, 5th Series, vol. 39 (1989) pp. 85–106.

22   Edited as *Responsio ad Lutherum* by John M. Headley in More, *Complete Works*, vol. 5 (New Haven and London, 1969) with a translation by Sister Scholastica Mandeville.

23   *A Dialogue Concerning Heresies*, in *Complete Works*, vol. 6, eds Thomas M. C. Lawlor, Germain Marc'hadour and Richard C. Marius (New Haven and London, 1981); the *Supplication of Souls* and the *Letter Against Frith* are both in vol. 7, eds Frank Manley, Germain Marc'hadour and Clarence H. Miller (New Haven and London, 1990); *The Confutation of Tyndale's Answer* in vol. 8, eds Louis A. Schuster, Richard C. Marius, James P. Lusardi and Richard J. Schoeck (New Haven and London. 1973); the *Apology of Sir Thomas More* in vol. 9, ed. J. B. Trapp (New Haven and London, 1979); *The Debellation of Salem and Byzance* in vol. 10, eds John Gut, Ralph Keen, Clarence H. Miller and Ruth McGugan (New Haven and London, 1987); the *Answer to a Poisoned Book*, eds Stephen Merriam Foley and Clarence H. Miller (New Haven and London, 1985).

24   For whom see William A. Clebsch, *England's Earliest Protestants* (New Haven and London, 1964); David Daniell, *William Tyndale: A Biography* (New Haven and London, 1994).

25   More, *Letter to a Monk*, in *Complete Works*, vol. 15, p, 225; John Foxe, *Actes and Monuments online* (1563 edn), p. 570.

26   J. A. Guy, *The Public Career of Sir Thomas More* (Brighton, 1980), p. 201.

27   Ibid., pp. 141–74, and his *Thomas More* (London, 2000), pp. 106–25.

28   Lewis's assessment of More's writings is conveniently presented in R. S. Sylvester and G. P. Marc'hadour (eds), *Essential Articles for the Study of Thomas More* (Hamden, Connecticut, 1977), pp. 388–401.

29   Brendan Bradshaw, 'The Controversial Sir Thomas More', *The Journal of Ecclesiastical History*, vol. 36 (1985), pp. 535–69.

30   Thomas Betteridge, *Writing Faith and Telling Tales: Literature, Politics, and Religion in the Work of Thomas More* (University of Notre Dame Press, 2013).

31 Richard Marius, *Thomas More* (London 1993), p. 331.

32 Guy, *Thomas More*, pp. 106–25, and, more hostilely, Marius, *More*, pp. 386–406.

33 P. L. Hughes and J. F. Larkin (eds), *Tudor Royal Proclamations* (New Haven and London, 1964), vol. 1, p. 194 (=*TRP*).

34 *TRP*, vol. 1, pp. 181–6: the proclamation condemns books first published in 1530, making the date suggested by the editors (March 1529) impossible.

35 Summary of More's activities against heresy in Guy, *Public Career*, pp. 97–174; idem., *Thomas More* (London, 2000), pp. 106–25; for a sane and judicious overview of More's anti-heretical activities and attitudes, Richard Rex, 'Thomas More and the heretics: Statesman or Fanatic?' in George Logan (ed.), *The Cambridge Companion to Thomas More* (Cambridge, 2010) pp. 93–115.

36 More, *Apology*, pp. 116–20.

37 Erasmus' letter to Hutton is in P. S. Allen, H. M. Allen et al. (eds), *Opus Epistolarum Des. Erasmi Roterdami* (Oxford, 1992) (reissue); vol. IV, no. 999, p. 17.

38 G. H. Elton, *Studies in Tudor and Stuart Politics and Government,* 4 vols (Cambridge, 2003), vol. IV, pp. 148–9.

39 More's most influential modern biographer, Richard Marius, similarly saw in More a man 'cruelly divided' by his decision to marry on the one hand and his longing for the cloister on the other. These unresolved sexual and psychological problems gave a 'terrible intensity' to his anti-heretical writings, and in Marius' view account for the 'grim pleasure' he took in the burning of heretics – Richard Marius, *Thomas More*, pp. 35, 37, 42, 320–21, 331, 350, 391, 396, 403. For a refreshing recent counter-argument, Rex, 'Thomas More and the Heretics'.

40 Alistair Fox, *Thomas More: History and Providence* (Oxford, 1982), pp. 111, 119–20, 123, 125, 143, 145.

41 Constance M. Furey, 'Invective and Discernment in Martin Luther, D. Erasmus, and Thomas More', *Harvard Theological Review*, vol. 98, no. 4 (Oct. 2005), pp. 469–88.

42 Marius, *More*, p. 391: Fox, *More: History and Providence*, p. 205.

43 Guy, *Thomas More*, p. 122.

44 Chapters 2 and 3 below.

45 Edward Surtz and J. H. Hexter (eds), *Utopia*, in *Complete Works,* vol. 4 (New Haven and London, 1965), p. 221.

46 *Utopia*, loc cit.

47 *Dialogue Concerning Heresies* in *Complete Works*, vol. 6, part 1, pp. 427–8.

48 David Bagchi, *Luther's Earliest Opponents* (Minneapolis, 1991), p. 179.

49 *Complete Works*, vol. 6, part 1, p. 428.

50 *Complete Works*, vol. 6, part 1, loc. cit.

51 *The Apology of Sir Thomas More*, in *Complete Works*, vol. 9, p. 169.

52 *Complete Works*, vol. 6, part 1, p. 123.

53 Ibid., p. 124.

54 Ibid., p. 406.

55 Ibid., p. 407.

56 *Apology* in *Complete Works,* vol. 9, p. 123.

57 *Complete Works*, vol. 9, pp. 161–2.

58 Ibid., p. 139.

59 *Confutation of Tyndale's Answer*, in *Complete Works*, vol. 8, part 1, p. 29.

60 Letter to Dorp, *Complete Works*, vol. 15, p. 71.

61 *Apology* in *Complete Works*, vol. 9, pp. 159–60.

62 *Complete Works*, vol. 8, part 1, p. 28.

63 Ibid., vol. 9, p. 167.

64 Ibid., vol. 8, part 1, p. 813.

65 *The Workes of Sir Thomas More Knyght, sometime Lord Chancellour of England, written by him in the Englysh tonge* (London, 1557), pp. 1420–21.

66 P. S and H. M. Allen, *Erasmi Epistolae*, 12 vols (Oxford, 1906–58), vol. 10. p. 2831, my translation; another version in Elizabeth Rogers, *St Thomas More, Selected Letters*, pp. 178–83.

67   The classic discussion is J. K. McConica, 'The Recusant Reputation of Thomas More', in R. S. Sylvester and G. P. Marc'hadour (eds), *Essential Articles for the Study of Thomas More* (Hamden, 1977), pp. 138–49, which needs supplementing with my *Fires of Faith*, pp. 179–86.

68   *ODNB*, memoirs of Rastell by J. H. Baker, of Roper by Hugh Trevor Roper, of Bonvisi by C. T. Martin, and of Harpsfield by Thomas Freeman. See also Thomas F. Mayer and Courtney B. Walters, *The Correspondence of Reginald Pole*, vol. 4, *Biographical Companion, the British Isles*, pp. 251–2 (Harpsfield) and pp. 459–60 (Roper).

69   Elsie Vaughan Hitchcock (ed.), *The Life and death of Sr Thomas Moore, knight, sometimes Lord high Chancellor of England, written in the tyme of Queene Marie by Nicholas Harpsfield, L.D.* (Oxford and London, Early English Texts Society, 1932).

70   *Workes*, sigs c ii, recto and verso.

71   Hitchcock, *Life and death*, pp. 209–13.

72   Ibid., p. 100, 'we trust shortlye to have all his englishe works ... wherein Master Sargeant Rastell doth nowe diligently travell'.

73   Ibid., pp. 86–7.

74   Ibid., pp. 112–32.

75   Ibid., pp. 60–61.

76   William Tyndale, *An Answere unto Sir Thomas More's Dialoge*, edited by Anne M. O'Donnell and Jared Wicks (Washington, DC, 2000), p. 14.

77   *Complete Works*, vol. 8, part 1, pp. 178–9.

78   I follow here the sensitive appraisal of the friendship in Dominic Baker-Smith's 'Erasmus and More', above, note 2.

2

The Dialogue Concerning Heresies

•

A Dialogue Concerning Heresies, first published in June 1529, was the first of six interconnected vernacular treatises against the reformation, culminating in 1533 in the *Answer to a Poisoned Book*. This controversial broadside, totalling an astonishing one million words, was the most sustained literary effort of More's life, and was produced in just five years, for three of which More held the highest secular office in the land as Lord Chancellor of England, and was busy as a zealous heresy-hunter and censor of books.[1]

As I've already indicated in Chapter 1, these books have had few admirers. Charles Lamb thought them informed by a wit and malice 'hyper-satanic', Richard Marius saw in them a dispiriting parade of 'ferocity and dreary dullness', Alistair Fox detected in them 'a pattern of progressive deterioration' as 'dialogue gives way to debellation, self-control leads to loss of proportion and perspective, candour is replaced by dishonesty, and charity is displaced by violence'.[2] In particular, the sustained polemic in these works against heretics in general and the Protestant preachers burned in the early 1530s under the English heresy laws in particular, has alienated even commentators otherwise well-disposed to More. In the most extensive and sympathetic recent discussion of the *Dialogue*, Professor James Simpson nevertheless deplored the 'heartless mockery' and 'frankly vicious self-confidence' on display in these works as a group.[3]

In this general chorus of condemnation or dismissal, the *Dialogue* has admittedly fared somewhat better than the rest. Couched, like Book I of *Utopia* and the very different prison treatise, *A Dialogue of Comfort*, in More's favourite and most successful literary form, *A Dialogue Concerning Heresies* was written with evident zest, and published as the upward curve of More's career reached its zenith, with his appointment as Lord Chancellor in succession to Wolsey. C. S. Lewis put it in an altogether different class from the rest of the polemical works, written when 'the iron [had] not entered into More's soul': Lewis praised it as 'a great Platonic dialogue: perhaps the best specimen of that form ever produced in English'.[4] While considering that its length (150,000 words) 'threatens to destroy' the dialogue form, Professor Brian Cummings nevertheless sees in it 'a writer of genius writing at the extremity of his understanding of the meaning, significance and status of writing'.[5]

It needs to be insisted on that More intended the *Dialogue* as a real conversation between clashing accounts of Christianity. His fictional interlocutor, the 'Messenger', spokesman for the reformation, is elaborately deferential to the 'More' character, and ultimately declares himself convinced. He has accordingly been dismissed as 'only a foil', 'a straw man' offering no real resistance to the fictional More's persuasions.[6] But the Messenger is a far more complex character than such a verdict suggests. As his anonymous patron and friend declares in the 'letter of credence' at the beginning of the book, the Messenger has 'a very mery wytte' and is 'of nature nothynge tonge tyed'.[7] More not only gives him space to develop a 'plausible impersonation of the best arguments of [his] opponents',[8] but wraps these polemical points in muscular, racy and often telling language. The Messenger is given most of the best jokes and one-liners in the book. He is indeed presented as a callow young intellectual, breezily and crassly dismissive of a learning he does not possess, and which, like Thomas Bilney, he considers inimical to faith – 'Logycke he reckoned but bablynge / Musyke to serve for syngers / Arythmetrycke mete for marchauntes / . . . and as for Phylosophy / the most vanyte of all . . . For man he sayd hathe noo light / but of holy scrypture'.[9]

But there was plenty of warrant for these opinions in the writings of real Protestants, and in fact More distilled much of the Messenger's talk from the writings of Tyndale, and from the trial records of Bilney and his associates, to which he had privileged access.[10] The Messenger is certainly a stereotype, 'a wanton', the cocky youngster enamoured of the latest intellectual fad, delighted to shock his elders.[11] John Skelton deployed much the same stereotype against the Messenger's real-life Cambridge counterparts in his

1528 'Replication' against 'certain young scholars abjured of late': 'these demi-divines, and stoical students, and friskajolly younker-kins ... basked and bathed in their wild burbling and boiling blood, fervently reboiled with the infatuate flames of their reckless youth and witless wantonness'.[12]

More, however takes the Messenger and his opinions very much more seriously than Skelton took Thomas Bilney. The Messenger, though sometimes presented as thoughtless, is never witless. Indeed, More confessed himself 'halfe in a doute' about the wisdom and propriety of allowing his character to expound heresy 'so homely / and in maner somtyme unreverently spoken agaynst goddes holy halowes', and of giving him the 'tales and mery wordes whiche he mengled with his matter'.[13] There is a real issue here. Given More's ardent conviction of the intellectual and moral squalor of the teachings of Luther and his followers, we will need to consider later in this essay just why he opted to give the Devil so many of the *Dialogue's* best tunes.

The *Dialogue*, then, is the 'record' of a fictional conversation, in which the young Messenger is urged to throw caution to the winds and speak his mind fully to a patient and sympathetic 'More' – 'Doubt on quod I between us twayne and spare not'.[14] James Simpson has recently suggested, therefore, that 'trust surrounds and undergirds the text ... at almost every point'.[15] In fact it would be truer to say that the entire text is premised on suspicion rather than trust. More commits the *Dialogue* to paper in case the Messenger's account of their conversation, by malice or mischance, should mislead or distort. The More character indeed protests that he 'nothynge suspecte(s)' the Messenger, but over and over again the unfolding of the conversation between them makes it clear that this is exactly what he does do. The suspicion that the Messenger's account or recollection of their talk might not be reliable is implicit in the elaborate fiction on which the *Dialogue* is premised. An anonymous friend sends the impressionable young Messenger, his own 'speciall secret frend', to More, to have his mind set at rest about the seductive claims of the new religion. More spends several days in conversation with the Messenger, with a three-week interruption, during which the young man visits his old friends in Cambridge, returning to More's house full of outrage fuelled by university gossip about the burning of

Tyndale's New Testament, and the alleged clerical maltreatment of Thomas Bilney, abjured of heresy in 1528. The young man is charged to recount the substance of their conversations to the friend, but just in case he does not, and lest garbled versions should be put about by heretics, More composes his own verbatim report.

In this scenario, the Messenger is a sort of male *ingénue*, vulnerable to evangelical persuasions but in intention at least a docile Catholic seeking correction. In putting heretical arguments to More, there-fore, he is purportedly acting as a mere mouthpiece for other men's views, anxious to be shown what the snags are. But More repeat-edly complicates and indeed subverts this innocent version of things. The Messenger constantly reveals that he is no neutral reporter: he is relentlessly and rabidly anti-clerical, determined to believe the worst of every priest, 'loke the holy horeson never so saintly'.[16] His vehemence and eloquence in expounding the Lutheran case against Catholic belief and practice constantly betray that he is in fact committed to many of the views he claims merely to report. As More tells the anonymous friend, the Messenger 'set the matter so well and lustily forwarde / he put me somewhat in doubte whether he were (as younge scolers be sometyme prone to newe fantasyes) fallen in to Luthers secte'.[17] Thus, despite occasional protesta-tions of trust in his interlocutor's orthodoxy, all through Book I More slyly nudges the reader into questioning that orthodoxy. The Messenger is in constant danger of verbal slippage from a posture of well-intentioned neutrality, to an evident but unacknowledged commitment to 'Luthers secte'. So at one point the fictional More offers to prove to the Messenger the reality of miracles at the shrines of the saints 'whiche thynge ... ye seme to impugne'. Hastily the Messenger interjects 'Nay syr ... / I pray you take me not as thoughe that *I* dyd impugne it / but as I shewed you before / I rehersed you what I have herde *some other* say'. Undeflected, More begins his exposition 'And first, where ye say ...' Once more the Messenger nervously interrupts – 'Nay, Qoud he, where they say', to which More sardonically replies 'Well, quod I, so be it, where they say. For here ever my tongue tryppeth'.[18]

The *Dialogue* is, first and foremost, an occasional piece, addressed to very specific circumstances and to a very large extent shaped by them. More's vernacular polemics were the result of a direct commission from his friend and collaborator in the struggle against heresy, Cuthbert Tunstall, Bishop of London. In March 1528 Tunstall wrote to More, commissioning him to write some popular works in English which would help ordinary men and women, 'simplicibus et idiotis hominibus', to see through the 'cunning malice' of the heretics currently flooding the land with Lutheran propaganda. To help More target his writing most effectively, Tunstall sent him a bundle of confiscated books and tracts, including a marked copy of Tyndale's New Testament with the errors 'redy noted', and licensed him to read them.[19]

This invitation was one move in an ongoing campaign against heresy being waged by every available means in the diocese of London, and in which More himself was already deeply involved.[20] Thomas Bilney and his Cambridge disciple Thomas Arthur had abjured their preaching against images and relics in December 1527, after lengthy examinations by a panel of bishops and theologians which had included Wolsey, Fisher and Tunstall. Within a fortnight of Tunstall's commission, More would be an eyewitness at Tunstall's lengthy interrogation of Dr Thomas Farman, Cambridge-trained rector of All Hallows Honey Lane, whose preaching was a magnet for evangelicals, and whose rectory was a centre of the contraband book trade.[21] More would incorporate much detail from this campaign into the Dialogue, and the examinations of Bilney and Farman would provide major set pieces in the second half of the book.[22] The Dialogue is of course a polemic against the reformation as a whole, in which More touches on most of the substantive issues in contention between Catholics and their opponents, from justification by faith and predestination to papal authority and the value of images and relics. But it is formally structured round the issues and personalities involved in this London campaign against heresy.

At the beginning of Book I, therefore, More allows the Messenger to set out a list of complaints and queries arising out of the current push against heretics and their books, and then formulates his agenda for the Dialogue accordingly. More declares that he will begin where the Messenger began, with the abjuration of Bilney, and consider whether the complaints were justified that he had been 'borne wrong in hand' by his accusers and judges. From there he would move on to the condemnation and burning of Tyndale's translation of the New Testament. Thirdly, he would consider the nature and consequences of Luther's message, whom the Messenger claimed could not be all bad, 'for never was there heretyque that sayd all false'. Finally he would consider the legitimacy of the use of force in defence of Catholic orthodoxy.[23]

The Messenger is of course More's creation, and the agenda he sets out is the agenda More chose for his book. It is at first sight a puzzling one. Recent discussions of the *Dialogue* have focused on More's rejection there of the reformation doctrine of *sola scriptura*. Accordingly, the *Dialogue* has been seen as essentially a defence of the spoken as against the written word, and an extended discussion of how the Scriptures ought to be read. So for Brian Cummings, More's book is 'a radical attack on the grapheme in favour of the phoneme'; for James Simpson it is a dialogue mainly about 'the licit function and limitations of sacred texts'.[24] These issues do indeed loom large in the *Dialogue*, but I do not think that they are in fact its primary concern. A very large proportion of the *Dialogue* is focused, rather, on the defence of the cult of the saints, and, in general, of the practices and underlying assumptions of late medieval popular Catholicism. These practices were of course a major target of Protestant polemic, as they had been and remained a target for Erasmus' satire, but in the hierarchy of Protestant concerns they feature less prominently than the foundational doctrines of justification by faith or *sola scriptura*. Why then did More choose to lead his attack on the new religion with a defence of pilgrimage and images?

Certainly there was warrant for this focus in the much publicised recent proceedings against the Cambridge preacher Thomas Bilney. The articles alleged against Bilney during his London examination included attacks on the intercession of the saints, the veneration of images and the practice of pilgrimage, and these issues were to dominate the East Anglian preaching tour which led to Bilney's execution as a relapsed heretic in 1531.[25] But it was neither obvious nor inevitable that More should fasten on these aspects of the Bilney affair as the core of his defence of Catholicism, nor that he should devote almost half the *Dialogue* to them, deferring detailed discussion of Bilney's trial and the Messenger's other grievances for 250 pages.

Nevertheless, the *Dialogue* starts with Bilney, because the Cambridge reformer's attack on images and pilgrimage allowed More to build the first half of his book round his own central conviction, the reality of Christ's guiding presence in the common life of the visible Church. This choice of opening theme of course had implications for the debate about whether Christians look for guidance primarily to scripture or to unwritten tradition. For More the Church cannot err in fundamentals, because of Christ's promise 'I am with you all the dayes tyll the end of the worlde'. For his interlocutor that promise was fulfilled in the gift of the scriptures to the Church. Christ is present, the Messenger declares, 'bycause his holy scrypture shall never fayle / as longe as the worlde endureth'. More dismisses this as a confusion between mere text and the living word of God. Christ had promised that he and the Holy Ghost would abide with the Church, but 'wherto all this yf he ment no more but to leve the bokes behynde them and go theyr way?'.[26] Texts may perish, and many scriptural texts have in fact perished. Those that survive may become corrupted in transmission by the ravages of time, or by some fault in the translator, or the writer, and, with a nod at the new technology, 'or nowe a dayes in the printer'.[27] But the substance of God's word, his living truth embodied in the teaching and practice of the Christian community through the ages, can never perish, and is not dependent on the survival or stability of any text.

Yet it is important to grasp that for More this was not in essence a debate about the primacy of the spoken as against the written word. Though he cites a proposition as an example of the Church's unwritten tradition – the belief that Mary had remained perpetually a virgin – he does not think of God's truth as consisting primarily of spoken propositions, any more than of written ones. By the 'lawe of Crystys faith' he meant 'not onely the wordes written in the bokys of his evangelystes', but, much more, 'the substance of our fayth itselfe / which oure lorde sayde he wolde wryte in mennes hartes'. This he did by 'the secret operacyon of god and his holy spyryte' in the work of grace – the regeneration of the baptised and the sanctification of believers – as well as by the fact that he revealed the heavenly mysteries 'fyrste without wrytynge ... by his blessyd mouth / thorowe the eres of his apostles and dyscyples in to theyr holy hartes'. But More insists that in this transmission of the life and truth of God, the heart is just as important as the ear or mouth. Like the written word, even the *spoken* word was secondary. Indeed,

God's truth was given to St Peter 'the prynce of the apostles', without any words at all: 'as it semeth it was inwardely infused in to saynt
Peter his harte / by the secrete inspyracyon of God / without eyther
wrytynge or any outwarde worde'.[28] The word of God was indeed
first spread 'by the mouthes of his holy messengers', but it was the
heart, not the ear or the eye, which received it. 'And so was it convenient for the lawe of lyfe / rather to be wrytten in the lyvely mindes
of men / than in the dede skynnes of bestes'.[29]

All this did indeed have far-reaching consequences for the reading of scripture. More devotes a good deal of the later part of Book
I to refuting the notion that the written scriptures and the faith
of the Church can ever be truly at variance. The Bible can only
be properly understood in the light of the Church's credo and its
divinely inspired exegetical tradition, as embodied in the writings of
'the olde holy fathers'. The hermeneutic of suspicion, that systematic 'dyffydens and mistrust' which More thought characterised the
exegesis of Lutherans like Tyndale, caused them to set Bible and
Church over against each other, and so to question the reality of
Christ's living presence in his community in all ages. 'Of all wreches
worst shall he walke / that forsynge lyttell of the fayth of Crystes
chyrche / cometh to the scrypture of god to loke and try therin
whyther the chyrche byleve aryght or not.'[30]

But this opposition is not More's principle concern. For him the
living truth of Catholicism was not primarily a matter of the spoken
word, any more than the written word, whether those words be Bible,
creeds, conciliar decrees, or doctrinal statements, though naturally he
acknowledged that Catholic tradition necessarily involved all these
forms of expression. His principle concern in the *Dialogue* is, rather,
to defend the presence of Christ in the life of the Church as embodied in its devotional and sacramental practice, the 'rytys & sacraments
and the articles of our fayth', transmitted 'from hande to hande from
Cryst & his apostles unto our dayes',[31] specifically in all the concrete
forms of the cult of the saints. For that reason, the discussion of the
right place and understanding of scripture comes as the conclusion
of a far more extended discussion of the legitimacy of the symbolic
forms in which devotion to the saints is expressed – pilgrimage, the
veneration of relics and images, and the miracles worked by their
intercession. These forms of devotion were as ancient as Catholic

Christianity itself: 'For I trowe that pylgrymages and miracles done at them be very olde thynges and not thynges newly begon nowe a dayes', but attested in 'the godly bookes' of the 'olde holy doctour(s) of Crystes chyrche'. If, therefore, the devotion to the saints was indeed an appalling error, as Bilney maintained, 'dysplesaunt to God / and by hym reputed as a mynyshment and a withdrawynge of the honoured dewe to hym selfe . . . and taken as Idolatry', this would mean that the Church had for fourteen hundred years been out of the truth, remote from the mind and heart of Christ. Christ's promises to abide with his Church and keep in her 'the right fayth' would have failed.[32]

The whole of Book I of the *Dialogue*, therefore, is a defence of and appeal not so much to a body of teaching, written or unwritten, as to the immemorial devotional practice of the Church, understood as a concrete manifestation of the life of God within her. For More, participation in that living tradition was the test of true understanding of the Gospel, and took precedence over all forms of argumentation. At the very outset of his exposition he declared that the best way for a simple layman like himself (!!) to discover the truth is 'in all thyngys (to) lene and cleue to the comen fayth and byleue of crystys chyrche'.[33] All sorts of evidence might be mustered to prove the legitimacy of pilgrimage, not least the many miracles which God had worked through the saints: but for More 'the thynge that I holde stronger than any miracles . . . is as I sayd afore the fayth of Crystes chyrche / by the common consent wherof these matters be decyded and well knowen'.[34]

The main purpose of Book II of the *Dialogue* is the exploration of the meaning and implication of this 'common consent' for the nature of the Church itself. At the outset of the book, the Messenger concedes that perhaps Christ has indeed promised to remain personally present with the Church, and to ensure that she cannot err in faith. But since, as the reformers believe, scripture condemns the cult of the saints as idolatrous, might it not be that the true Church is not 'the people that ye take it for', but instead a hidden and persecuted remnant of true believers (like Tyndale or Bilney)?[35]

Characteristically, More's reply to this was to insist that the true Church cannot be hidden, and is known precisely in the visibility of its common life. Even in times of persecution, the early Church had

come together 'to the prechynge and prayer', and had expressed its
identity in a shared public life of grace, in 'fastyngys / vygylys kepte /
the sondayes hallowed / the masse sayd / holy service songe / and
theyr people howselyd'. What was true then must be true now:
'such thyngys must there be therin / yf it be any Congregacyon of
Cryste'.[36] This common cult was the expression of a common faith
and a shared life of grace. The early Church 'were all of one mynde
and of one harte', for the indwelling of the Holy Spirit 'maketh
all of one mynde in the house of God'. The Messenger countered
this by pointing to the visibility of an alternative Church rejecting
superstition, to be seen among Luther's followers in Saxony, and the
Hussites in Bohemia. More, however, seizes on this as corrobora-
tion of his point, because these heretics manifestly have no unity of
heart or mind. 'For in Saxony first and amonge all the Lutheranes
there be as many heddes as many wyttes. And all as wyse as wylde
geese . . . the maysters them selfe chaunge theyr myndes and theyr
oppynyons every day.' And Bohemia was the same: 'One fayth in the
towne / another in the felde. One in prage [Prague] / a nother in
the next.'[37] There is therefore no hidden remnant with special access
to an allegedly pure gospel truth: Christ's church 'is knowen and not
hyd . . . and he wolde have his fayth dyvulgyd and spredde abrode
openly / not always whispered in hukermoker'. The Church must
always be 'the comen knowen multydtude of crysten men good and
bad togeyther'.[38]

It is notable that in the *Dialogue* this appeal to the common life
of the Church as the ultimate criterion of Christian authenticity
never becomes merely or mainly an appeal to hierarchy, or to the
teaching authority of the clergy. Though he insisted that Peter was
Christ's Vicar and head of the Church, 'and alway synce the succes-
sours of hym continually', More never once appeals to the teaching
of a pope or council to clinch his argument. Though the authority
of 'the olde holy fathers' is repeatedly invoked in defence of current
practice, it is always as a witness to the shared faith of the Church
as a body. 'I take not one doctour or twayne but of the consent and
comen agreement of the olde holy fathers', expressing the 'comen
consent of the chyrche'.[39] Even when More's argument might seem
to be leading him inexorably towards an appeal to clerical authority,
he steers instead towards this insistence on the shared belief of the

whole Church. So at one point he asks the Messenger to suppose that, as at the time of the Arian controversy, some fundamental truth such as the divinity of Christ were to be called in doubt, which the balance of biblical texts seemed unable to resolve. If God were then to reveal that there was a wise man who understood the true interpretation of such texts, would we not be bound to seek him out and accept his judgement, rather than remain in doubt? The Messenger agrees that we would have to believe such an infallible guide, at which point More invokes neither the Pope nor the bishops, but asks 'What yf it were a certayne knowen company of men and women togyder?' Here the deliberate inclusion of women in the 'known company' makes explicit the non-hierarchical nature of this appeal to the 'common corps of Christendom' as the ultimate authority.[40]

That same non-clerical emphasis surfaces again in the course of More's defence of pilgrimage. The Messenger characteristically suggests that pilgrimage thrives mainly because the clergy 'norysshe this superstycyon . . . to the parell of the peoples soules / for . . . lucre and temporall advauntage'. More dismisses this, partly on the factual grounds that shrine offerings form only a small part of the income of the clergy. But he goes on to insist that this devotion had been 'planted by goddess owne hand in the hertes of the whole chyrche', *not* among the clergy only, 'but the hole congregacyon of all crysten people'. As a result, 'yf the spyrytualyte were of the mynde to leue it / yet wolde not the temporalyte suffer it'.[41] For More, the most fundamental mark of the Church was this holy unanimity, as much a lay as a clerical possession. Correspondingly, the mark of heresy was the pride and love of singularity which set heretics 'in spekyng and prechyng of such commune thynges / as all crysten men knowe' to 'shewe them selfe . . . merueylous' and set out 'paradoxis and straunge opynyons / against the commen fayth of Crystes hole chyrche'.[42]

So far, I have alluded only in passing to More's use of humour as a controversial weapon. Humour, however, and particularly that of the 'mery tales' which punctuate the text, is integral to More's purpose in these first two books of the *Dialogue*. The insistence on the devotional and doctrinal unanimity of 'the comen corps of Christendom' which undergirds these books might have become an argument for inertia and the total irreformability of Christian belief and practice. If what the Church did and taught was the expression of the mind of Christ, must it not be considered perfect? For the humanist author of *Utopia* and the dedicatee of Erasmus' great satire on the absurdities of contemporary Christendom, *Encomium Moriae*, such an argument would indeed have represented a retreat to reaction. And some influential interpreters of the *Dialogue* have read it in just this way, as when Richard Marius characterised the *Dialogue* as a 'rigid affirmation of unshakeable certainty'.[43]

The *Dialogue*, however, is far from rigid, and More's defence of traditional religion, however benign, is by no means uncritical. Convinced of the essential wholesomeness of Catholic religious practice, he can simultaneously poke fun at its excesses and abuses, while making the case for the value of the basic institutions. More's handling of Protestant criticisms of traditional religion in the *Dialogue* is therefore self-consciously pragmatic and moderating, puncturing rhetorical posturing, challenging sweeping generalisations. When the Messenger attacks pilgrimage on the grounds that it 'smells of idolatry' to seek God this place or that, as if we would be 'better herde with our lorde in Kent than in Cambrydge, at the north dore of Poules then at the south dore', More replies that the same logic would lead to the abolition of all churches, 'For God is as mighty in the stable as the temple'. He is also insistent that by portraying the laity as the helpless dupes of the clergy, the reformers traduce them. 'The flocke of cryst is not so folysshe as those heretyques bere them in hande.' If even a dog can tell 'a very cony from a cony carued and paynted', then 'crysten peple that have reason in theyr heddys / and therto the light of fayth in theyr soulys' are in no danger of thinking that images of the Virgin 'were our lady her selfe'.[44]

In this defence of religion as it is actually practised, the 'mery tales' allow More to highlight religious foibles and abuses while maintaining that abuse does not outlaw right use. More gives most of these scandalous stories against orthodox piety to the Messenger, and most of the fun in the Messenger's stories has a sour edge to it, in line with More's belief in the self-righteous censoriousness of the reformers. But the humour is nevertheless genuine, not least in the most notorious (and funniest) story in the book, the Messenger's long, rude and ribald account of the shrine of St Walery in Picardy. There, he claims, pilgrims resorted for the healing of genital diseases and impotence. The *ex voto* offerings hung round the shrine were 'none other thynge but mennes gere and womens gere made in wax'; male pilgrims offer candles measured to the length of their penises and an alarmed wife refuses to allow one such candle to be burned, in case her husband's member should dwindle sympathetically.[45]

Richard Marius rightly pointed to the similarity between these 'mery tales' and the humour in Erasmus' *Colloquies*, the satirical dialogues in which, into the mid-1520s, Erasmus lampooned aspects of popular Catholic practice which he judged to be remote from Gospel teaching. *Naufragium* (The Shipwreck), published in 1523, and *A Pilgrimage for Religion's sake*, of 1526, ridicule many of the very practices complained of by the Messenger, and in much the same terms. So the panic-stricken travellers in '*Naufragium*' make extravagant vows to curry favour with the saints, chant hymns to the Virgin to still the waves, or deploy 'queer little prayers like charms to ward off danger': the somewhat supercilious narrator, who of course knows better, by contrast resorts 'straight to the Father himself, reciting the Pater Noster'.[46]

More was undoubtedly prepared to tolerate a good deal that Erasmus deplored as 'superstition'. So, the fictional More listens to the Messenger's hair-raising catalogue of abuses – 'ryot / revelynge and rybawdry' in pilgrimages, the confusion of simple souls between the images of the Virgin and the Virgin herself, the wives of London praying to St Wilgefortis or 'Uncumber', to uncumber them of their husbands, the universal resort to particular saints for special purposes – St Scythe (Zita of Lucca) to find keys, St Roke against plague, St Loye (St Eligeus) to heal horses – not to mention glaring abuses like the procession with an image of St Martin in Germany, where the people poured the contents of their pisspots on the statue if the weather has been bad.

More agrees that dousing St Martin with urine may be stretching the legitimate bounds of piety, and concedes that the French authorities should perhaps look into the goings-on at St Walery's shrine. But he dismisses most of the Messenger's other complaints as hyercriticism. 'Somewhat is it in dede that ye say / and yet not all thynge to be blamed that ye seme to blame'[47] because 'a fewe dotynge dames make not the people'.[48] Even simple women well understand the difference between a favourite statue and the spiritual reality it represents. More saw 'nothing moche amysse' in the practices the Messenger condemned: it is 'no wytchecrafte' to pray for relief from the toothache to St Appolonia, 'consyderynge that she had her tethe pulled out for Crystys sake', or to pray to St Loye, who had been a smith, 'for the helpe of a poore mannes horse'. These were natural Christian intuitions in time of need, a legitimate extension of faith in God's providence in all our necessities, fully in the spirit of the petition of the Lord's Prayer, 'Give us this day our daily bread'.[49]

More treads a delicate line here, guying the ludicrous and scandalous side of popular religious practice jokingly in his own fictional persona or more abrasively through that of the Messenger, freely conceding the existence of occasional deceptions and abuse, but defending the essential soundness of the institutions themselves and the intelligence and religious instincts of the laity who used them. A great deal has been made of the contrast between More's intentions in the *Dialogue*, and those of the Erasmus of the *Colloquies*. Richard Marius declared that 'Erasmus ends by attacking popular piety and More by defending it', and suggested that, though Erasmus was not mentioned explicitly by name, 'much in the Dialogue sounds like a refutation of views expressed in the Familiar Colloquies'.[50] The implication here is that in the *Dialogue* More repudiated his earlier concern for the reform of Christendom, abandoned his erstwhile Erasmianism, and exerted himself instead to defend precisely those aspects of religion which Erasmus most deplored. It was a claim made in More's own time. As we saw in Chapter 1, and as I will explore in more detail in Chapter 3, Tyndale, in his reply to the *Dialogue*, claimed that he, not More, was following in the footsteps of Erasmus, and speculated that More had held back from attacking his 'derlynge' Erasmus only because the great humanist had written *The Praise of Folly* in More's house. But from that same book, 'if it were in englishe / then shulde every man se / how that [More] then was ferre other wise minded than he nowe writeth'.[51]

It is true that Erasmus' *Colloquies* and More's merry tales poke fun at the same targets, but do so for rather different ends. To left-leaning correspondents, Erasmus could confess that the cult of the saints had indeed 'run to idolatry'. He was careful to insist that 'practices good in themselves should [not] be condemned because they are abused', but he thought the Church had itself to blame for the

Protestant rebellion. Catholics, he insisted, 'instead of repenting of their sins, pile superstition on superstition'.[52] He told the Dominican polemicist Johann Fabri that the best way to refute Luther was to reform the abuses which had provoked Luther's protest.[53] That was why, when the rest of Europe was polarising religiously in the 1520s, he went on doggedly producing his satirical dialogues, to orthodox Catholic outrage, determined not to be deflected from the course of reform from within which he had marked out for himself before Luther had ever been heard of. More, by contrast, thought that Protestant denunciations of abuses were a mask for outright rejection of essential Catholic practices themselves. This no reform would ever quieten, since what they looked for was not to purify but 'to mynyshe and quenche mennes devocyons'.[54] Both men were aware that, despite all they shared in common, therefore, their religious instincts did not exactly coincide. Erasmus regretted More's polemical writings, but he defended his activities against heresy as Lord Chancellor, and he understood the respect for traditionalist piety which motivated More. As he told Fabri in 1532, just after More's resignation as Chancellor, More 'hates those seditious teachings which are currently tearing the world apart. He makes no pretence about this, nor does he wish to hide it, being so wholehearted in his religious practice that if he has an inclination in either direction, he seems to be closer to superstition rather than to impiety.'[55]

For his part, More never criticised, much less repudiated, Erasmus or his writings, but, unlike the less grounded Erasmus, he did think that changing circumstances made a profound difference to how those writings were likely to be perceived. In 1531 he denied Tyndale's claims to kinship with Erasmus, who 'detesteth and abhorreth the errours and heresyes that Tyndale plainly teacheth'. Erasmus' satire was licit because it was without 'malycyouse intent' towards the saints, their relics and images. *The Praise of Folly* 'doeth but in dede but ieste upon the abuses of suche thynges', like a jester in a play, '& yet not so far neyther by a grate deale, as the messenger doth in my dyaloge'. But 'erroneous bokes . . . settynge forth Luthers pestilent heresyes' by Tyndale and others had so poisoned public discourse about religion 'that men can not almost now speke of such thynges in so much as a play, but that such evyll herers wax

64

a grete dele the worse'.[56] In this fraught context, More lamented, where men could take harm from the 'very scrypture of god', it might even be necessary 'to burne ... with myne owne handes' not only 'my derlynges bokes but myne owne also ... rather than folke sholde (though throw theyr own faute) take any harme of them'.[57]

More made that gloomy assessment when, riding on the back of the King's divorce, anti-clericalism and heresy were gaining ground in England, 'turning all hony in to posyn'. It was a prescient judgement: the humanist movement would indeed be hijacked by the proponents of far more drastic reform, Erasmus himself would be annexed posthumously as a Protestant *avant la lettre*. Even as early as 1528 Tunstall was turning up heresy suspects in his diocese who attributed their fall from orthodoxy to reading Erasmus. Thus Thomas Topley, Augustinian friar of Stoke-by-Clare, began his recantation, 'All Christen men beware of consentyng to Erasmus fables, [i.e. the *Colloquies*] for by consentyng to them, they haue caused me to shrinke in my fayth'.[58] Given his closeness to Tunstall, and their shared love of Erasmus, More must certainly have known about Topley's examination and recantation, throughout which Erasmus features very negatively. That makes all the more striking, therefore, his unequivocal public defence of Erasmus' innocence and orthodoxy in 1531, as well as his lavish deployment of Erasmus' satirical technique in the merry tales of the *Dialogue* in 1529. These are emphatically not the actions or attitudes of a man in denial about his humanist past.

In Books III and IV of the *Dialogue*, More changes gear and mounts a detailed defence of Tunstall's (and Wolsey's) campaign against heresy, and of the role of the clergy in general in combating heresy. This he develops into a general consideration of the solvent effects of heretics and heresies on Church and society, ending with a rationale and defence of the use of force in suppressing error. *En route*, the discussion involves him in a consideration of the legitimacy of the vernacular Bible in general, and of Tyndale's version in particular. After the relatively leisurely pace and comic interludes of Books I and II, this second half of the *Dialogue* is more closely focused on specific events, and its later pages are fiercer and more urgent in their analysis of what More sees as the radical destructiveness of Lutheran teaching, and the measures needed to fight it.

Influential modern readers of the *Dialogue* have recoiled from these chapters especially. Richard Marius, convinced that the *Dialogue* in general represented an abandonment of More's earlier humanism, was baffled by More's apparent advocacy of a vernacular Bible in Book III, which he thought wholly 'at odds with his general and oft-expressed thoughts on the Bible'. Marius speculated that More might have included this material against his better judgement, to curry favour with Henry VIII.[59] James Simpson focuses instead on More's justification of the burning of heretics. In these chapters, Simpson argues, More contradicted the humane views he had espoused in *Utopia* about the futility of the use of force in religion. The 'weak' argumentation More deploys in favour of persecution stems in Simpson's view from his unwitting surrender to the 'exclusivist, distrustful and utterly self-convinced' understanding of Christian truth maintained by his evangelical opponents.[60] At the risk of appearing perverse, however, I want to maintain that in these final two books it is More's remarkable consistency in defence of Christian humanism which is strikingly on display. The apparent discrepancies between the earlier More and the author of these parts of the *Dialogue* which some commentators have discerned arise from a failure to grasp the nature and force of More's urgent analysis of the special dangers threatening Catholic Christendom in the 1520s.

As Book III opens, the Messenger has returned to Chelsea after a visit to Cambridge where all the talk has been of the abjuration of Thomas Bilney for heresy, and where 'some of them semed to take very sore to hart / the hard handelyng of the man' by his clerical judges. As More knew, Bilney had a reputation for personal holiness and theological zeal: anger against the clerical establishment was being fuelled by rumours that Bilney had been framed for heresies he never held by implacable heresy-hunters. More, who had been present at Bilney's examination, knew better. He had heard the testimony of 20 witnesses about Bilney's preaching, and he had seen incriminating letters in Bilney's own hand which had not been brought in evidence against him. He knew that Bilney had previously been summoned before Wolsey himself on suspicion of heresy, but that the Cardinal 'for hys tender favour borne to the unyversyte' had chosen not to proceed against him. Bishop Tunstall had

66

also delayed sentence against Bilney even when his heterodoxy had become clear, and Bilney was eventually offered a form of abjuration so laxly ambiguous that More's professional instincts as a lawyer were outraged.[61]

More's severe account of these proceedings was not in fact unfair to Bilney. The most thorough modern examination of his trial concluded that Bilney throughout displayed 'a degree of contrivance and calculation difficult to reconcile with his pose as an injured innocent', and that this 'shrewd young man' was 'more a schemer than a saint'.[62] But whatever the facts, in addition to exonerating Bilney's judges, More was concerned to present the man himself, whom he never names since he had abjured and was at liberty, as a paradigmatic case of lapse into heresy. More's Bilney is the victim of religious neurosis, pride and *amour-propre*, whose reluctance to confess his errors, simply and sincerely, boded ill for the future. (In the light of Bilney's relapse two years later, More here showed himself remarkably percipient.)

More's portrayal of Bilney's religious trajectory has considerable psychological plausibility, and was crucial for the overall scheme of the last two books of the *Dialogue*, through which some of its key themes would be elaborated. Afflicted with neurotic scruples which drove him to obsessively literal religious observance, Bilney, according to More, had eventually recoiled into antinomianism. 'Wyth the werynesse of that superstycyouse fere and servile drede / he felle as farre to the contrary'. So, under pretext of Christian love and liberty, he 'waxed so drunke of the new muste of lewd lyghtnes of mynd and vayn gladnesse of harte / whyche he toke for spyrytuall consolacyon. That what so ever hym selfe lysted to take for good / that thought he forthwith approved by God'. Thus deluded, he 'framed hym selfe a fayth / framed hym selfe a conscience / framed hym selfe a devocion'.[63]

Bilney provided More with an exemplum of a talented man's progress into heresy, in reaction to a diseased and disproportionate piety. There was, More tells the Messenger with characteristic humanist emphasis, 'a mene [that] may serve' between fanaticism and carelessness.[64] But the arch-heretic of the *Dialogue* is not Bilney, but William Tyndale. Outrage at the solemn burning of Tyndale's translation of the New Testament was another of the complaints the

Messenger had encountered in Cambridge, and in chapter eight of Book III More turns to justify this apparently obscurantist act. Such a defence was certainly a test of his own fidelity to the humanist project. A decade earlier he had thrown his weight behind Erasmus' controversial new Greek and Latin edition of the New Testament, in the *Letter to Dorp* and related writings.[65] Some of the most controversial renderings in Tyndale's English version had their origins in Erasmus' rejection of the vocabulary of Jerome's vulgate for his new Latin translation, and the substitution of words free of the theological freight of the medieval schools. More himself had defended one such controversial substitution ('sermo' for 'logos' in the prologue of St John's Gospel), in the *Letter to Dorp*.[66] In defending the banning and destruction of Tyndale's translation, therefore, More's own integrity and consistency were on the line.

More tackles this delicate task by confining his discussion to just three words. The marked copy of the New Testament supplied by Tunstall had noted 'wrong and falsly translated above a thousande textys by tale', More tells the Messenger, but he will demonstrate Tyndale's malicious error by focusing on the terms *priest, church* and *charity*. Tyndale systematically substitutes for these the words 'senyor', 'congregacyoun' and 'love'. More's objections to Tyndale's renderings are both linguistic and theological. By rejecting the traditional terms Tyndale deliberately drives a wedge between the text and the Church's understanding of the text, developed over fourteen hundred years of divinely guided reflection, prayer and preaching. In the three examples he has chosen, More insists, a tendentious Lutheran agenda masquerades as scholarly objectivity. Luther and Tyndale deny the sacramental priesthood and so translate the Greek word *presbyteros* to exclude the notion of priesthood altogether. Yet Tyndale's preferred translation, 'senior', according to More has no claim to greater fidelity to the Greek. In implying *age* it is overliteral – St Paul's protégé, the presbyter Timothy, was a young man – and its semantic resonances in English were both inadequate and misleading: 'In our englysshe tonge this worde senyor sygnyfyth no thing at all / but is a frenche worde used in englysshe more than half in mockage / whan one wyll call another my lord in scorne.'[67]

In the same way, More argues, the tendentious use of 'congregation' instead of 'church' is rooted in Tyndale's repudiation of the visible Church in favour of 'an unknown congregacyon of some folke here two and there thre no man wote where'. Tyndale deliberately empties the New Testament concept of the Church of its resonance as a *holy* assembly, for the term 'congregation' makes no distinction between 'a company of crysten men or a company of turkes'. And the systematic choice of the word 'love' in place of charity is intended to underpin Luther's doctrine of justification by faith alone. More accepts that there is a linguistic rationale for that particular translation. Though he thinks that 'charity' better conveys 'the name of that holy virtuous affecyon', yet 'If he called charyte sometyme by the bare name of love / I wolde not stycke therat'. Tyndale's real agenda, however, is revealed in the fact that he 'studiously flee(s)' the traditional term, and so 'laboureth of purpose to mynysh the reverent mynde that men bere to charyte'.[68] His repudiation of Tyndale's work, therefore, is not a rejection of the possibility or desirability of translation, but of the tendentious nature of the translation which Tyndale has produced to a Lutheran agenda.

And so More's justification of the suppression of Tyndale's translation is balanced by robust and forceful argument for the legitimacy and desirability of English Bible translation.[69] There were those among the clergy, he conceded, who thought it best to withhold the Bible because if it were to be in every man's hand 'there wold grete parell aryse and that sedycyous people sholde do more harme therwith / than good and honest folke sholde take fruyte therby'. But that argument, he declared, weighed nothing with him. The fact that 'sedycyous' readers might twist meaning to their own purposes could not make it right to deny the majority of well-intentioned Christians the nourishment of the Scriptures. The Messenger's eager agreement that lay people can easily understand the Bible is slapped down by More, who insists on the inability of lay people to grasp the 'high secrete mysteryes of God / and harde texts of hys holy scrypture': scripture often exceeds 'the capactye and perceiving of men'. And so disputing God's mysteries in 'pot parlementes', when 'the wyne were in and the wytte out' can breed only 'folyshe wordes and blasphemye': interpretation is a task for the Church's theologians and approved preachers. But that was no reason for withholding an English Bible from the people. English was a language well fitted to translation, the sacred writers had written in the vernacular in the first place and 'I wolde not for my mynde withhold the profyte that one good devout unlerned ley man myght take by the redyng / not for the harme that an hundred heretykes wolde falle in by theyr owne wylfull abusyon'.[70]

More somewhat took the shine off this heartfelt apologia for lay Bible-reading by suggesting that a reverent and devotional use of scripture might be ensured if individual books of the Bible were to be printed in separate fascicles, to be doled out by each bishop 'to suche as he perceyveth honeste sad and virtuous'.[71] It is hard to believe that, in an age of commercial printing houses, More seriously imagined such a paternalistic scheme was remotely workable. But however that may be, his support for an orthodox Bible translation was in any case to be rapidly overtaken by events. In May 1530 Henry VIII, anxious to offset his increasingly menacing behaviour towards the clergy by proving his credentials as Defender of the Faith, summoned the leading bishops and theologians from the two universities to discuss measures against the heresies threatening the realm. The assembly condemned a long list of evil opinions from Tyndale's writings, and advised the King that, given the spread of 'pestilente bookes and . . . evill opynyons', the production of an English New Testament at this stage would be likely to bring 'confusion and destruction' rather than the edification of souls.[72]

More was the only layman present at the Whitehall consultation: he signed its *acta*; he must certainly have had a hand in its detailed condemnation of Tyndale's writings; he probably drafted and vigorously enforced the proclamation banning those writings which was issued in June 1530. In 1531, he would include a brief defence of the halting of the official translation of the New Testament in his *Confutation of Tyndale's Answer*.[73] All the more remarkable, then, that, despite all this, in the 1530 reissue of the *Dialogue* More retained his long and vehement argument for the legitimacy of lay Bible-reading whatever the dangers, even though it directly contradicted the official rationale for the Whitehall ban. This cannot have been an oversight, for this second edition was significantly revised and expanded. It therefore seems likely that the prohibition of an official English New Testament originated with the clerical members of the consultation, or with some of Henry's lay counsellors. If More did eventually retreat from his Erasmian commitment to the benefits of lay Bible-reading, that retreat was the reluctant product of the changed and increasingly fraught circumstances of his last two years as Chancellor, when anti–clericalism was being given its head by Thomas Cromwell, and heresy was establishing a foothold even at court. But there is no such retreat in the *Dialogue*.

The last book of the *Dialogue* is in many ways its craggiest. In it, More argues two positions. Luther's teaching, however speciously attractive, was the worst of heresies, lethal to Christian society, because his exaltation of faith alone as the key to salvation made virtue irrelevant and thereby dissolved all order and moral cohesion. From this it followed that Christian rulers had a duty to protect their people from this demonic teaching, and in doing so the use of force, including the death penalty, was both legitimate and necessary. More was unusual among Luther's Roman Catholic opponents in the 1520s in laying great stress on the Wittenbergers' teaching on justification. But like other Catholic writers, including King Henry, he interpreted Luther's teaching on justification by faith as leading directly to antinomianism, 'plunging [men] headlong into that licentious way of life which you strive to introduce under the pretext of evangelic liberty'.[74]

For More this aspect of Luther's doctrine had a special horror, for he recognised that Luther's teaching of justification was underpinned by his teaching on predestination, and by his outright repudiation of the notion of human free will. This was the issue on which Erasmus and Luther had decisively quarrelled just three years earlier, and it went to the heart of More's own Christian humanism. For him salvation was the crowning and purification by grace of man's natural inclination towards virtue. As we saw in Chapter 1, even before conversion the Utopians believed that, in the afterlife, vice is punished and virtue rewarded. This was the *only* religious opinion the Utopians would not permit to be disputed, and 'hym that is of a contrary opinion they counte not in the number of men', since such a man put humanity on a level with the beasts, placed himself beyond the reach of morality, and could have no respect for anything but force.[75] More shared all the Utopians' horror at what he took to be Luther's repudiation of the foundations of human morality and, specifically, Christian virtue. That, and not some personal sexual obsession, was the significance for More of Luther's marriage.

A friar in bed with a nun was bad enough, but also the routine stuff of the *Decameron* and a thousand medieval satires. But a friar in bed with a nun claiming that this was a Christian marriage, that solemn religious vows had no power to bind, and that holy chastity was an offence against the Gospel, was of a different order of heinousness, an explicit repudiation of the Christian moral order.[76] More regarded the religious iconoclasm and violent acts of desecration which accompanied the early reformation, and the secular upheavals of the Peasants' Revolt, as the inevitable outcomes of the antinomianism of Luther's Gospel, a conviction strengthened by the atrocities perpetrated during the Sack of Rome. And by the same token, for More the doctrine of predestination was an attempt by the reformers to absolve themselves of any moral responsibility for their evil actions: 'he that beleveth thus / what careth he what he dothe . . . ?[77]

It is these convictions which underlie More's passionate insistence that the reformation had to be halted at all costs before it took hold in England. Otherwise, the fate which had befallen Germany would befall England. That belief underlies one of the most eloquent passages in the *Dialogue*, the extraordinary single sentence in which More passionately evoked Luther's doctrine as the ruin of Christian coherence as he and Erasmus had imagined it. In Germany:

> theyr secte hath all redy fordone the faythe / pulled downe the chyrches / polluted the temples / put out and spoyled all good relygyous folke / joined freres and nonnes togyther in lechery . . . caste downe Crystes crosse / throwne out the blessyd sacrament / refused all good lawes / abhorred all good governaunce / rebelled agaynste all rulers . . . and fynally that most abhomynable is of all / of all theyr owne ungracious dedes lay the faute in god / taking away the lybertye of mannes wyll / ascrybyng all our dedes to desteny . . . whereby they take away all dylygence and good endeavour to vertue / all withstanding and stryvyng against vyce / all care of hevyn / all fere of hell / all cause of prayer / all desyre of devocyon . . . all the lawes of the worlde / all reason among men / set all wretchedness abroche / no man at lyberty / and yet every man do what he wyll / calling yt not his wyll but his destiny / layng theyr syn to goddess ordenaunce / and theyre

punysshment to goddess crueltye / and fynally turning the nature of man in to worse than a beste / and the goodness of god in to worse than the devyll.[78]

And it is that vision of the chaos and destruction, which inevitably flow from Luther's Gospel, which lies at the root of More's apologia for the use of force against heresy and its propagators, with which the *Dialogue* concludes. James Simpson, deploring what he took to be the feebleness of More's arguments here, suggested that More had weakened an already weak case by dragging in just-war theory.[79] But this is to miss the specificity of More's argument. Heresy, More believed, was always a force for destruction, oppression, rebellion. It was this inherent violence, he argued, which had moved St Augustine to call for the forcible repression of heretics. In England a century ago, Oldcastle's rebellion had demonstrated that heresy ran always true to type.[80] But the rhetorical weight of More's argument turns on a comparison between the duty of Christian rulers to resist militant Islam in the form of the Turkish threat to Eastern Europe and their corresponding duty to use force against internal heresy.[81]

More here was invoking a very real danger, and one which preoccupied him and his humanist friends. Suleiman the Magnificent had taken both Belgrade and Rhodes, 'the outworks of Christendom', and in 1526 his armies occupied Budapest. A stream of humanist publications lamented the divisions of Christian Europe, and Erasmus himself called for unity against the common enemy. Suleiman's attempts to buy the neutrality of the protestant Schmalkaldic League, and Luther's teaching that the Turk was the scourge of God for the sins of Europe and therefore not to be resisted, seemed to More proof of a demonic conspiracy against 'the comen corps of Christendom'. More would deepen and spiritualise this comparison in the greatest of his Tower works, *A Dialogue of Comfort*.[82] In *The Dialogue Concerning Heresy*, however, the comparison, though no less deeply felt, is strictly practical. Christendom was in deadly peril from without and within. The same imperative which required the princes to defend Christian civilisation from Turkish conquest mandated and demanded the forcible elimination of the equally destructive threat of heresy.

More's argument here has about it something of the manifesto. In the London campaign against heresy, no evangelical had so far been burned, and More at this stage did not believe that any heretic possessed the courage or conviction to persist in the face of death. 'I never yet founde or herde of any one in all my lyfe', he tells the Messenger, 'but he wolde forswere your fayth to saue his lyfe'.[83] For their part, Tunstall and his colleagues had bent over backwards to avoid sending anyone to the flames, if only because, as the Messenger declares early on in the *Dialogue*, 'of the asshes of one heretyque spryngeth up many'.[84]

More makes much of that reluctance in defending the clergy against charges of cruelty. But he clearly foresaw the possibility that Protestant resistance might force Church and state to resort to the ultimate sanction, and at the conclusion of the *Dialogue* he mounts a vehement defence of such a step. Notoriously, as Chancellor he would translate theory into grim fact. No modern reader of the *Dialogue* is likely to find that defence compelling. In its own time and place, however, it carried great weight, and most of More's contemporaries would have felt its force. Twenty-first-century hand-wringing about the horridness of persecution seem a poor gauge of the contemporary effectiveness of More's urgent advocacy.

The *Dialogue* is More's most effective polemical work. Its apparent conversational sprawl masks a carefully controlled argument setting the teaching of Luther, Tyndale and their English followers over against the holy and immemorial unanimity of 'the comen corps of Christendom'. More defends the religious value of traditional religious practice while laughing at its absurdities, and comes forward as the champion of the religion of ordinary Christian men and women. But he also advocates the renewal of lay piety by devout encounter with an English Bible. He deploys an unrivalled mastery of the detail of the Henrician campaign against heresy to defend the bishops and clergy, while resisting a clericalist ecclesiology. He offers a powerful if one-sided analysis of the evils of Lutheran teaching, informed by a humanist vision which he had laboured alongside Erasmus to develop and to defend, and which he never repudiated. And at the end of his book he defended the use of the death penalty against unrepentant heretics, summoning up a sombre and terrifying vision of the devastating consequences for the fabric of Christian belief and practice if the new religion were to gain its head in England. What he would have considered the worst elements of that dire vision – the destruction of the religious life, the rejection of the cult of the saints, the dismantling of the Catholic sacramental system – would all be realised within a generation, testimony to the prescience of the polemical masterpiece in which he had predicted exactly such an outcome.

Notes

1   Survey by Louis A. Schuster in More, *Complete Works*, vol. 8, part 3, pp. 1137–1268.

2   *Complete Works*, vol. 8, part 3, p. 1208; Richard Marius, *Thomas More* (London, 1993), p. 138; Alistair Fox, *Thomas More: History and Providence* (Oxford, 1982), p. 111. The outstanding exception to this negative consensus is Brendan Bradshaw's seminal defence of the controversial writings, to which the argument of this chapter is much indebted: 'The Controversial Thomas More', *Journal of Ecclesiastical History*, 36 (1985), pp. 535–69.

3   James Simpson, *Burning to Read* (Harvard, 2007), p. 265.

4   In R. Sylvester and G. Marc'hadour (eds), *Essential Articles for the Study of Thomas More* (Hamden, Conn., 1977), pp. 392–3.

5   Brian Cummings, 'Reformed Literature and Literature Reformed' in David Wallace (ed.), *The Cambridge History of Medieval English Literature* (Cambridge, 1999), pp. 834–5.

6   Marius, *Thomas More*, p. 346; David Daniell, *William Tyndale: A Biography* (New Haven and London, 1994), pp. 263–4. A not dissimilar conclusion, more judiciously expressed, is reached by Roger Deakins in 'The Tudor Prose Dialogue: Genre and Anti-Genre', *Studies in English Literature*, vol. 20 (Winter 1980), pp. 5–23 at p. 14.

7   *Complete Works*, vol. 6, part 1, p. 25.

8   Cummings, 'Reformed Literature', p. 834.

9   *Complete Works*, vol. 6, part 1, p. 33: one of the articles alleged against Bilney in 1527 was that he had denied 'moral Philosophy and natural, to preuaile any thing for the better vnderstanding of the scriptures, & for the exposition and defence of the truth': *John Foxe's Actes and Monuments online* (1583 edn), p. 1000; H. C. Porter, *Reformation and Reaction in Tudor Cambridge* (Cambridge, 1958), p. 61.

10 For parallels in Tyndale's *Obedience of a Christian Man* to the Messenger's jaundiced views of the value of philosophy, for example, Thomas Russell (ed.), *The Works of the English reformers William Tyndale and John Frith*, vol. 1 (London, 1831), pp. 190–94.

11 *Complete Works*, vol. 6, part 1, p. 287.

12 Philip Henderson (ed.), *The Complete Poems of John Skelton,* 3rd edn (London, 1959), p. 415.

13 *Complete Works*, vol. 6, part 1, p. 23.

14 Ibid., p. 109.

15 Simpson, *Burning to Read*, p. 240.

16 *Complete Works*, vol. 6, part 1, p. 83.

17 Ibid., p. 34.

18 Ibid., p. 63: I have added punctuation and emphasis to clarify More's irony. And see More's sarcastic implication that the Messenger shares the slippery insincerity of heretics on trial, *Complete Works*, vol. 6, part 1, p. 84.

19 E. F. Rogers (ed.), *The Correspondence of Sir Thomas More* (Princeton University Press, 1957), pp. 386–8; *Complete Works*, vol. 8, part 3, p. 1139, n 4.

20 Indispensable context for More's dealings with heresy is provided in J. A. Guy, *The Public Career of Sir Thomas More* (Brighton, 1980), pp. 97–174.

21 For the campaign against heresy in London in 1528, Susan Brigden, *London and the Reformation* (Oxford, 1989), pp 110–18. The commonly accepted form of Farman's name, 'Robert Forman', is incorrect, as entries relating to him in Queens' College archives and his own signature in his copy of Erasmus' Jerome in St John's College Library make clear. My thanks to my colleague Professor Richard Rex for this correction.

22 *Complete Works*, vol. 6, part 1, pp. 255–80, 378–84.

23 Ibid., pp. 28–36.

24 Cummings, 'Reformed literature', p. 835; Simpson, *Burning to Read*, p. 243.

25 The articles are set out in *John Foxe, Actes and Monumentes online* (1583 edn), pp. 999–1000, and for the content of his East Anglian sermons, ibid., pp. 1010–11.

26 *Complete Works*, vol. 6, part 1, p. 114.

27 Ibid., p. 127.

28 Ibid., p. 143.

29 Ibid., pp 143–4. The reference to 'dead skins' is of course an allusion to velum pages.

30 Ibid., pp. 152–3.

31 Ibid., p. 152.

32 Ibid., p. 112.

33 Ibid., p. 37.

34 Ibid., p. 62.

35 Ibid., pp. 189–90.

36 Ibid., p. 190.

37 Ibid., pp. 191–2.

38 Ibid., p. 205.

39 Ibid., p. 169.

40 Ibid., p. 161.

41 Ibid., pp 53-4.

42 Ibid., p. 123.

43 Marius, *Thomas More*, p. 345.

44 *Complete Works*, vol. 6, part 1, p. 56.

45 Ibid., pp. 227–9.

46 Erasmus, *Ten Colloquies*, trans. and ed. Craig R. Thompson (Indianapolis, 1957), pp. 6–8. I have emended Thompson's translation, which takes 'Erant, qui peculiares quasdam *preculas* habebant, non dissimilis magicis, adversus pericula' to mean 'some had certain queer *beads*, like charms, to ward off danger', a perfectly possible rendering, though in the context I take the word to mean short prayers. Latin text from *Desiderii Erasmi Roterdami, Colloquia Familiaria et Enconium Moriae* (Leipzig, 1829), vol. 1, p. 197.

47 *Complete Works*, vol. 6, part 1, p. 232.

48 Ibid., p. 237.

49 Ibid., pp. 232–3.

50 Marius, *Thomas More*, pp. 339, 342.

51 Anne M. O'Donnell and Jared Wicks (eds), *An Answere Vnto Sir Thomas Mores Dialogue* (Washington, 2000), p. 14.

52 Erasmus to Johann Botzheim, 13 August 1529, in Richard De Molen (ed.) *Erasmus* (London, 1973), pp. 170–71.

53 J. A. Froude, *Life and Letters of Erasmus* (London, 1895), pp. 342–3.

54 *Complete Works*, vol. 6, part 1, p. 47.

55 Quoted in Dominic Baker-Smith, 'Erasmus and More: a friendship revisited', *Recusant History*, 30 (2010,) p. 13.

56 *Complete Works*, vol. 8, part 1, pp. 176–9.

57 Ibid., p. 179.

58 Foxe, *Actes and Monuments online* (1583 edn), pp. 1046–7; James McConica, *English Humanists and Reformation Politics* (Oxford, 1965), pp. 106–49, esp. 145–7.

59 Marius, *Thomas More*, pp. 348–9.

60   Simpson, *Burning to Read*, pp. 261–71.

61   *Complete Works*, vol. 6, part 1, pp. 268–71.

62   Greg Walker, 'Saint or Schemer? The 1527 Heresy Trial of Thomas Bilney Reconsidered', *Journal of Ecclesiastical History*, vol. 40 (1989), pp. 219–38.

63   *Complete Works*, vol. 6, part 1, pp. 257–8.

64   Ibid., p. 258.

65   Above, chapter 1, p. 25.

66   For which see *Complete Works*, vol. 15, pp. lxxii–xcii.

67   Ibid., vol. 6, part 1, p. 286.

68   Ibid., pp. 286–8.

69   It is prefaced by a lengthy rebuttal of the Messenger's accusation that the English clergy have always been the enemies of an English Bible, in which More argues that the fifteenth-century legislation forbidding unauthorised translations had been intended to outlaw only heretical versions. He claimed that it had always been possible for bishops to allow 'suche as he know for good and catholyke folke' to read the bible, and many had done so. There was special pleading here, and More was undoubtedly making a small amount of evidence go a long way, but his basic claim is in fact borne out by recent study of the circulation and censorship of the so-called 'Wyclifite' Bible: *Complete Works*, vol. 6, part 1, pp. 317–30; Mary Dove, *The First English Bible* (Cambridge, 2007), pp. 37–67.

70   *Complete Works*, vol. 6, part 1, pp. 333–40.

71   Ibid., p. 341.

72   D. Wilkins, *Concilia Magnae Brittaniae et Hiberniae* (London, 1737), vol. 3, pp. 727–37.

73   *Complete Works*, vol. 8, part 1, pp. 178–9.

74   David V. N. Bagchi, *Luther's Earliest Opponents, Catholic Controversialists 1518–1525* (Minneapolis, 1989), pp. 159, 129 – quoting Henry VIII's *Assertio Septem Sacramentorum*.

75   *Complete Works*, vol. 4, pp. 221–3: on this subject, see Brendan Bradshaw, 'More on Utopia', *Historical Journal*, 24 (1981), pp. 1–27, esp. 9–14.

76   Ibid., vol. 6, part 1, p. 434.

77   *Complete Works*, vol. 6, part 1, p. 403.

78   Ibid., pp. 427–8.

79   Simpson, *Burning to Read*, p. 263.

80   *Complete Works*, vol. 6, part 1, p. 409.

81   Ibid., pp. 411–8.

82   Ibid., vol. 12, pp cxxii–cxxxv.

83   Ibid., vol. 6, part 1, p. 201.

84   Ibid., p. 31.

3

The Confutation of Tyndale's Answer

Unsurprisingly, More's pursuit of heresy and heretics was already calling his reputation as a humanist into question in his own lifetime, and after his death was a problem for those who believed him to be a saint. As we saw in chapter 1, allegations of maltreatment and torture of suspects began to circulate in the early 1530s, and though More categorically denied them,[1] they persisted, and have been reiterated in our time by popular historians from Jasper Ridley to Brian Moynahan. Most recently they formed the basis of Hilary Mantel's brilliantly hostile portrayal of More, in her Booker-Prize-winning historical novel, *Wolf Hall*, and the sour portrait was if anything heightened in Mike Poulton's stage adaptation, and in Anton Lesser's acidulated More in the television version. It all seems a long way from the wise and genial saint of Catholic hagiography, or the martyr for liberal individualism celebrated in Robert Bolt's superbly misleading *A Man for All Seasons*.

Admirers of More, not least his first major twentieth-century biographer, R. W. Chambers, have variously tried to minimise, explain or ameliorate More's implacable pursuit of heresy and heretics.[2] For the last 30 years or so, however, such exculpation has been out of fashion. Instead, it has become customary to emphasise the alleged harshness and imbalance of More's attitudes to heresy and heretics, and the morbid vehemence of his language against them in his polemical writings. This hostile take on More on heresy has been underpinned by elaborate psycho-sexual speculation about More himself.

On this account, the man for all seasons was a repressed 'sex-maniac', 'preoccupied with the problems of sexuality', and in his anti-heretical writings returned to the alleged sexual misdemeanours of Luther and the other reformers with 'obsessional frequency'.[3] This, for Sir Geoffrey Elton, was the explanation not only of what he considered More's morbid self-flagellation and hair shirt, but also of the tone of his writings against Tyndale. The *Confutation* in particular was for Elton one 'interminable high-pitched scream of rage and disgust which at times borders on hysteria', a display of 'helpless fury' rooted in More's unresolved and morbid sexuality.[4]

As we saw in Chapter 1, Elton's picture received further influential endorsement in 1982 from Alistair Fox's highly charged reading of More's entire literary output. Fox deployed this psycho-sexual account of More, the guilt-ridden, failed monk, as the interpretative key to all the writings up to his arrest and imprisonment in the Tower, and, above all, as the explanation for what Fox took to be the *literary* failure of More's vernacular writings against heresy. For Fox, the combination of a deep Augustinian pessimism about human moral endeavour and a disordered sexuality underlie and explain More's negative reaction to the reformation. His controversial writings thus conceal an inner experience 'which . . . threatened to destroy his sense of providence and . . . eventually brought him close to despair'. In them we find 'a pattern of progressive deterioration: dialogue gives way to debellation, self-control yields to loss of proportion and perspective, candour is replaced by dishonesty'. More's 'snarling invective' and 'polemical ferocity' display 'an almost demoniac emotional violence towards his opponents', a 'vileness of sentiment', which went far beyond sixteenth-century convention. This 'descent into subjective involvement' and the evident accelerating 'deterioration of his self-composure' was rooted in an 'interior psychological conflict arising from a continuing preoccupation with problems of sexuality'. More's astonishing stream of books against the reformation was therefore a sustained act of morbid compensation, the attempt to assuage his own guilt at not being a monk: 'by continuing to write one book after another he was seeking to prove a central private conviction: that human imperfection was no cause for despair.'[5]

Three related charges, of moral, mental and of literary failure, are embodied in this now very widespread perception of More's writing and legal action against heresy and heretics. It is widely held both that More's dealings with heretics reveal him, in Brian Moynahan's words, as a 'strange, tortured and cruel man'[6] and that, in writing against heretics, More lost all literary restraint and judgement, and became verbose, repetitive, boring and incoherent. The picture of More as a relentless sadist is, of course, itself a literary construction, invented by John Foxe in the 1560s, drawing on evangelical testimony which More explicitly and categorically repudiated.[7] But the fiction has persisted, given new and brilliant currency in Hilary Mantel's *Wolf Hall*, where More is portrayed as a master torturer, deploying rack, scourge and the vile machine known as 'Skeffington's Daughter' in 'the twin arts of stretching and compressing the servants of God'.[8]

As will be evident, most scholarly writing on this subject since Elton has depended on a highly suspect cod psychology, and the mistaken notion that ascetical practices accepted as routine by medieval Christians, like the hair shirt More wore under his robes of office, constitute evidence of a morbid sexuality. But these negative perceptions also rest to a large extent on the simple and undeniable fact that More unblinkingly endorsed the use of the death penalty against unrepentant or relapsed heretics, and as chief law officer of the Crown acted on this conviction. There is a complex and perhaps ultimately unresolvable issue here about what we are to make of the acceptance by otherwise admirable people in the past of moral axioms and actions which we now find repellent.

But these are all issues for another occasion. My specific concern here is with the widespread perception that More's vernacular writings against heresy fail, individually and cumulatively, as *literary* constructs, and that the *Confutation of Tyndale's Answer* in particular is a shapeless, repetitious and boring work whose immense bulk and inflamed rhetoric reflects the collapse of More's control over his material, and hence his failure as artist, persuader and polemicist. In this general chorus of condemnation, the *Dialogue Concerning Heresies* has fared rather better than the books that followed it. The young Lutheran spark who is More's interlocutor in the book is of course ultimately convinced of the Catholic truth, but along the way he is given many of the *Dialogue's* wittiest lines and all the best jokes.[9]

By contrast, the *Dialogue's* far lengthier sequel, the *Confutation of Tyndale's Answer*, has found few sympathetic readers, and no advocates for its literary merits. Treated as a shapeless mountain of abuse at odds with More's earlier humanism, it has been quarried for nuggets of lurid rhetoric. Notoriously, these include More's deliberately shocking dismissal of Tyndale's disciple Thomas Hitton, burned at Maidstone in February 1530, as 'the devil's stinking martyr', and what Elton called More's 'relentless harping' on Luther's marriage and the marriages of other leading reformers, as men 'runne oute of relygyon and fallen to fleshe and caryn and lyve in lechery with a none under the name of wedloke, and all the chyfe heddys of them, late monkys and freres, and now apostates and lyvynge with harlots under the name of wyves'.[10] This allegedly 'tedious and hysterical' invective has been variously treated as symptomatic of More's secret envy of the reformers' sex lives, of a 'frankly vicious self-confidence' and heartlessness, and of a 'fanatical, frenzied loathing' of the victims of the Henrician heresy hunt.[11]

The *Confutation*, especially Part 1, published in the spring of 1532, is indeed a ferocious book, which deploys all More's formidable resources of invective and an unrelenting battery of argument against Tyndale and his fellow reformers. But it is neither hysterical, shapeless, nor evidence of failing emotional or artistic control. It is indeed a very different kind of book from the *Dialogue*, but the difference is not a matter of loss of grip, but of considered literary choice. In More's judgement the religious situation in England had worsened dramatically since the publication of the *Dialogue*. The need to alert the literate public to the true nature and threat of heresy and the heretical books now flooding into the country, and to expose the speciousness of their arguments, had become ever more urgent. More therefore dropped the leisurely fictional framework of the *Dialogue* as inadequate to this changed situation. There is indeed still a dialogue in progress in the *Confutation*, but now More brought all his legal skills to bear on protestant teaching, not as in the *Dialogue* through the ironical fiction of a discussion with a wavering Cambridge scholar, but in a detailed forensic deconstruction of Tyndale's own words, quoted at length and scrutinised minutely for every negative nuance and insinuation. In the process More deployed a literary form new in English, though already in use in Latin polemic against Luther by Fisher, Latomus and others,[12] in which long passages from an opponent are given verbatim, and then answered sentence by sentence, clause by clause. More was well aware of the dangers implicit in such a form – excessive length, redundancy and repetition, boredom, not to mention the fact that it unavoidably gave added circulation to forbidden heretical opinions. He addressed those formal issues and explained his strategy in risking them explicitly in the *Confutation* itself, and then in more detail in 1533, in the *Apology of Sir Thomas More*. Once that strategy is understood, the *Confutation* takes on an altogether more formidable appearance. And as we shall see, the form More devised for the *Confutation* was far from being considered self-defeating by his contemporaries. It was in fact to exercise a direct and decisive influence on confessional debate in the reign of Elizabeth and beyond.

To understand what More was up to in the *Confutation* and its sequels, we first need to register the context in which it was published. The two previous years, an anxious time of famine and epidemic disease, had also seen a steady escalation both in the spread of heresy and in the campaign to halt that spread. In May 1530 Henry had established an Ecclesiastical Commission of court clergy and theologians from both universities to consider the problem of heresy. Presided over by Warham and Tunstall, the Commission had only one lay member, More himself. Despite the inclusion of closet reformers like Edward Crome and Hugh Latimer, the Commission produced an immense list of condemned propositions, culled mainly from Tyndale's writings. It also issued a homily to be read from the pulpit by all preachers, denouncing heretical books and explaining why at this juncture the King had decreed that it was neither necessary nor desirable to have the New Testament in English translation.[13]

Despite the increased vigilance of the authorities, however, the trade in forbidden books continued unabated. Three thousand copies of Tyndale's venomous anti-Divorce tract, the *Practice of Prelates*, were in circulation by the summer of 1530. Henry himself was determined to halt this flood of contraband literature. The return of the new and fiery Bishop of London, John Stokesly, from diplomatic service overseas the same month was reflected in an immediate intensification of the campaign against heresy in London, as More and Stokesly joined forces to increase the pressure on the city's evangelicals.[14] More was active in a number of arrests and trials that year. His interrogation of George Constantine proved particularly devastating to the evangelical cause, for Constantine turned King's evidence, and his circumstantial revelations about book smuggling and distribution networks led to a series of arrests and confiscations. In August 1531 the Cambridge preacher Thomas Bilney was burned as a relapsed heretic in Norwich, and December 1531 saw the executions of Richard Bayfield and John Tewkesbury, both of whom had been arrested and interrogated by More at Chelsea.[15]

But this royally endorsed campaign against heresy was complicated by Henry's growing impatience over the Divorce question, and by the consequent escalating campaign of intimidation against the clergy, designed to bully the Church into line over the King's Great Matter. The exigencies of the Divorce even led Henry to authorise friendly overtures to hitherto hunted Protestant activists, who might be useful in mustering international support behind the King's cause. Tyndale himself, whom Henry loathed, was approached by royal agents in the early months of 1531, and the runaway friar, abjured heretic and wanted book-smuggler Robert Barnes, who had taken refuge in Wittenberg, was recruited to bring Luther on side. By November 1531 Barnes was back in London under royal safe conduct, appearing openly in lay dress and consorting with known dissidents. On 13 January 1532 the third session of the Reformation Parliament opened, and it became clear at once that lay grievance against clerical jurisdiction generally, and the *ex officio* powers used in heresy proceedings in particular, were to be a major focus of Commons attack. These rumblings, orchestrated by Cromwell, were to culminate in March with the presentation of the *Commons Supplication against the Ordinaries.* Despite ritual protestations of horror at the spread of 'new, fantastical and erroneous opinions', the *Supplication* struck at the very roots of the episcopal campaign against heresy, portraying the suspects as innocent victims of the bishops and their agents.[16]

It was against this background that the first part of the *Confutation of Tyndale's Answer* appeared. More has been widely perceived as a desperate man at this stage, aware that power was slipping from him as his known disaffection over the Divorce brought a showdown with Henry ever closer, and conscious that he and the bishops were losing the battle with the heretics. His modern editors endorsed this perception by heading their account of the year 1531 'More's Gethsemane'.[17] But there is too much hindsight here. More was well aware of the danger he stood in, but in January 1532 there was still everything to play for. For all his flirting with Tyndale and Barnes, Henry remained a determined opponent of sacramental heresy. The Protestant sympathies of many of Cromwell's protégés were as dangerous to them as More's opposition to the Divorce was to him. The *Confutation* is therefore not the long despairing cry of a doomed loser, but a considered and powerful play in a battle which More had grounds to think might yet be won.

The first point to be made about the 1532 *Confutation of Tyndale's Answer* is that, though it would ultimately form just under half of the completed work, in fact it stands alone and works well as a self-contained book. It is slightly shorter than the *Dialogue Concerning Heresies*, and like the *Dialogue,* it is carefully structured into four discrete parts. A 40-page 'Preface to the crysten reader' sets out More's reasons for writing the book, emphasising the seditious and destructive character of heresy and the urgency of the fight against it, stressing Henry VIII's leadership in the campaign which More and the bishops had been waging for the last three years, and deploying More's unrivalled knowledge of evangelical personnel and networks in England to discredit the claims of the reformers to superior Christian insight or holiness. The rest of the 1532 publication tackles successively three distinct aspects of Tyndale's teaching. Book I picks up from the preoccupations of the *Dialogue Concerning Heresies* and examines Tyndale's polemic against the Church's sacraments, ceremonies and pious observances, including the institution of vowed celibacy. Book II expands More's reflections in the *Dialogue* on the legitimacy of biblical translation, by returning to the problems of Tyndale's translation of the New Testament, and the third and final book, by far the longest, opens up a new set of issues by examining the related questions of whether the Church existed before the Gospel or the Gospel before the Church, and the authority of God's word, written and unwritten.

Tyndale had begun his *Answer* to More's *Dialogue* with an extended preface which his modern editors describe as a 'foundational essay', setting out all the main planks of his teaching.[18] Throughout the *Confutation*, More focused his fire on this essay, exploiting the clarity and focus of Tyndale's Preface to give a uniting theme to successive sections of his own reply. There is no space here to examine each of the component parts of the 1532 *Confutation*, so I want to focus instead on just three of the issues which have most often been taken to demonstrate the failure of the *Confutation* as a literary construct – More's invective against the executed evangelicals Thomas Hitton, John Tewkesbury and Richard Bayfield, his repeated denunciations of the marriages of the reformers, and the repetitive nature of the literary form he devised for the *Confutation*. In fact, most writing about the *Confutation* has ignored the work's formal structure, on the assumption that it has none, only hysterical incoherence. Yet shape and purpose are very much in evidence, and, despite the harshness of tone, there is no hysteria. More, I want to argue, is perfectly in control of his material, which he marshals into a vehement but carefully crafted piece of advocacy.

For all its monumentality, the 1532 *Confutation* was an occasional piece, directed to very specific circumstances. The mounting and managed anti-clericalism, which was soon to culminate in the *Commons Supplication against the Ordinaries*, presented the London campaign against heresy as the arbitrary clerical oppression of innocent victims. More was concerned to vindicate that campaign by demonstrating the poisonous nature of heresy itself, the forbearance of the bishops and their officials in dealing with it and the duplicity and guilt of the heretics. His own encounters with heretics over the previous seven years, and the ambiguities, evasions and downright deceit which they had understandably deployed to escape detection, had given him a low opinion of their honesty and integrity. 'But and yf they were ones founde out and examined / we se them alwaye first redy to lye and forswere them selfe yf that wyll serve', he had declared in the *Dialogue*. 'And whan that wyll not helpe but theyr falshed and periury proved in theyr faces / than redy be they to abiure and forsake it / as longe as that may save theyr lyves.'[19]

More made that claim before the executions had begun: the burning of six Protestant martyrs since then seemed to give him the lie. In his *Answer* to More's *Dialogue*, therefore, Tyndale claimed that those burned were glorious martyrs for the gospel truth, and he named especially the priest Thomas Hitton, executed at Maidstone in February 1530.[20] That is why More devotes the bulk of the Preface of the *Confutation* to showing that heresy could never make saints, and that these victims in particular had been dupes of the devil and were themselves incorrigible deceivers. The nuggets of abuse which have so scandalised modern commentators are part of that sustained argument, in which More drew on his own detailed knowledge of individual cases to establish a wider point.

England had for several years been in the grip of famine and epidemic disease. More's opening sentence links the failure of the crops directly to God's hatred of heresy: 'Our lorde sende us nowe some yeres as plenteouse of good corne, as we have hadde some yeres of late plenteous of evyll bokes.' God punishes sin with the scourge of disease and death, especially 'that odyouse and hatefull synne of the soule, that spyleth the frute from all manner of virtues, I meane unbelyefe, false fayth and infydelyte, and to tell you all at ones in playne englyshe heresye'.[21] England, therefore, stands under God's judgement so long as she tolerates heresy. Books full of 'pestylent poisoned heresyes' had 'in other realms all redy kylled by scysmes and warre many thousande bodyes . . . and many mo thousand soules'. Now a few 'malycyouse myschevouse persones', in defiance of the King's proclamations, were flooding England with such books, 'to corrupte and infecte all good and vertuouse people'.[22] Naming some of these propagators of error – Tyndale himself, John Frith, George Joye, George Constantine, Robert Barnes – More put the best face he could on official connivance at the open presence in London of Barnes, 'at thys daye comen to the realme by saufe conducte'. This was by the 'blessyd diposycyon' of the King, who hated heresy, yet who indulged heretics like Barnes 'to thende that yf there might yet any sparke of grace be founden in hym, yt myghte be kepte, kyndeled and encreaced, rather than the man be caste away'. But More recalled ominously that the King had been ill-requited for the similar indulgence granted to Richard Bayfield and George Constantine, who had both returned to Tyndale's heresies, 'lyke a dogge returnynge to his vomyte'.[23]

All this is the prelude to More's central concern in the Preface, his repudiation of the claim that executed heretics like Bayfield and Hitton were Christian martyrs. For Tyndale, More insisted, such deaths were a cause of obscene and unholy triumph: 'the grete feste and glory of Tyndales develysh prowde dyspytouse harte, to delyte and reioyce in the effusyon of such people's blode as hys poisoned bokes have miserably bewyched, and from trew crysten folke, turned into false wycked wreches'.[24]

More's accusation, that Tyndale had no pity for the spilled blood of these victims, may baffle and even repel. More, as we shall see, insisted that most of those burned had gone straight to the eternal fires of hell, and that they were therefore the devil's martyrs. This insistence has struck even well-disposed modern readers as 'heartless mockery' of their deaths.[25] But we need to grasp the precise terms of More's argument here. For him, as for St Augustine and the whole of mainstream medieval Christian theology, heresy was not a matter of legitimate personal opinion, but always a culpable choice, and the damnation of a heretic was never a cause for pity. The stubborn or relapsed heretic was emphatically not the victim of some unfortunate mistake. The heretic had been shown the saving truth, and God always gave souls the grace to embrace that truth. Through pride and perversity, therefore, they had rejected God's grace, and, in the process, turned away from God. To die in that state of refusal was to be damned, and the damned were, in a perfectly literal sense, hateful. They had deliberately turned their back forever on love, and were therefore themselves impossible to love. As fellow mortals we may lament their tragedy, we may pity the waste, we may grieve at the ruin of one of God's creatures, but we can never forget that they have of their own free will renounced truth, light, love, and placed themselves forever beyond the reach of charity, outside the common life of the redeemed.

More believed that the damned have *chosen* their own destruction, for human will is free. Each had had 'myche favour shewed hym, & myche labour charytablye taken for the saving of hym'. The legal process against heresy and the clergy who administered it were both just and merciful. But in the end for their obstinacy each victim had been delivered to the secular arm and 'burned uppe in hys false fayth and heresyes, whereof he lerned the great parte of Tyndales holy bokes', and the spirit of lies 'hath taken his wreched soule with hym from the shorte fyre to the fyre everlastyng'.[26]

But they had been propelled towards that ruin by the influence of others, and More points again and again to Tyndale as the murderer of these men's souls. Hitton, Bayfield and Tewkesbury were indeed damned, since they had died 'of hard herte and malycyouse mynde incurable'.[27] But in hell their damnation would deepen and increase the misery of the one who had perverted them. More dwells on these double deaths, of body and soul, not to gloat, or because he rejoiced in suffering, but to bring out the full scale and horror of Tyndale's responsibility for the ruin of these immortal souls. Tewkesbury, he insisted, would never have fallen from grace 'yf Tyndales ungracious bokes had never come in hys handes'. Because of Tyndale, 'the pore wreche lyeth now in hell and cryeth out on hym / and Tyndale yf he do not amende in tyme, he is lyke to fynd hym when they come togyther an hote fyrebronde burnynge at hys bakke, that all the water in the worlde wyll not be able to quenche'.[28] That horrifying vision would not be out of place in Dante's Inferno, but, like Dante's poem, it springs not from the writer's psychic disorders, but from More's imaginative assimilation of beliefs which were part of the mainstream eschatology of medieval Christendom.

To offset these appalling images of souls doomed to a shared damnation by their own pride and stubbornness and the malign influence of Tyndale's teaching, More offers a contrasting portrait of a heretic saved at the very last by the grace of repentance. As we saw in Chapter 2, More had discussed the first trial and abjuration of Thomas Bilney at length in the *Dialogue*, though, since Bilney *had* abjured his errors, More refrained from naming him there. In the *Dialogue*, More had nevertheless been unimpressed by Bilney's protestations of good intent, and he had predicted his eventual relapse. So it is all the more striking that in the *Confutation* More returns to Bilney for a portrait of a repentant heretic. Bilney had once been every bit as proud and deceitful as Hitton, Bayfield and Tewkesbury, like them had lied and dissembled to escape detection, had abjured like them, and then, like them, had relapsed through pride and had sought to pervert others from the truth.

Yet, according to More, by God's grace at the very last, Bilney had renounced his errors and had died repentant, an orthodox Catholic lamenting especially his sacramental errors and the contempt for 'Crystes catholyke knowen chyrche' which was the root of all heresy. During his examination, Bilney had 'waxed styffe and stoburne in hys opynyons'. But by the grace and goodness of God, 'he was finally so fully converted unto Cryste and hys trewe catholyke fayth that not onely at the fyre, as well in wordes as wrytynge, but also many dayes before / he had revoked, abhorred and detested such heresyes as he before had holden'.[29] The legal penalty for a relapsed heretic could not be set aside, and Bilney had been duly burned. But the man himself had been saved: God 'hath forthwith from the fyre taken hys blessed soule to heven'. Bilney, though no martyr, *was* a saint. Though every unrepentant heretic was doomed to eternal torment, God would accept the repentant Bilney's suffering in the fire as his purgatory, 'and settynge the merytes of hys owne paynefull passion theunto, hath forthwith from the fyre taken hys blessed soule to heven, where he now prayeth incessauntly for the repentaunce and amendement of all suche as have ben by hys meanes whyle he lyved, into any suche errours induced or confyrmed'.[30]

The reliability of More's claim that Bilney died a devout and penitent Catholic has been much debated. As a consequence, the literary purpose of his portrait of Bilney, as a deliberate foil to those of the 'devils stinking martyrs', has been largely ignored. Whatever the facts about Bilney's end, More's skilful handling of the episode is designed to balance and contrast with his portraits of the unrepentant heretics Hitton, Bayfield and Tewkesbury, acquiescent victims of Tyndale's false teaching. We are dealing here not with random abuse and relish in burnings, but with a careful if daunting polemical construction.

I have been arguing that a psychological interpretation of More's invective against heresy has blinded readers to the literary and argumentative function of that invective, which is to be found mainly in the opening section of the *Confutation*. The same is true of his much more widespread attacks on the marriage of the reformers. The frequency and vehemence of More's language about the 'bestely bychery' of monks and nuns in bed together has been taken as a reflection of his own sexual preoccupations. In fact, any reader of More's account in the *Dialogue* of the shrine of St Walery in Picardy, famed for its cures of sexual ailments and impotence, hung about with *ex voto* replicas of 'men's gear and women's gear in wax', and ablaze with candles measured to the dimensions of the male pilgrims' genitalia, will realise that More had a robustly Rabelaisian sense of humour about sex. And in the *Confutation* he displays no interest whatever in the details of what these former monks and nuns are actually *doing* to each other in bed. For him, the simple fact that they have not only abandoned vowed chastity, but have sanctimoniously disguised that abandonment of their solemn vows with a pretence of positive Christian virtue and a repudiation of a millennium of teaching about celibacy was the outrage. More importantly, it pulled the rug from under any Protestant claims to truth or holiness. More returns to the marriages of the reformers again and again because he saw in them a devastating common-sense disproof of their claims to the moral high ground. He knew, too, that his conservative Tudor audience was likely to share his take on the credibility of a preaching friar who bedded down every night with a nun. For a millennium and a half monks and nuns had taken solemn vows to God to live in chastity, and the whole Christian people had recognised clerical unchastity as an abomination. Medieval literature from the pulpit invective of the Gregorian reformers to the dirty jokes of the *Decameron* was full of contempt for the squalors of unchaste monks and nuns. But however laughable, it was also shocking, and so, More pointed out, people 'have always iested that Antecryste sholde be borne between a frere and a none'.

Even as More wrote, the Protestant presses of Germany were pouring out propaganda prints satirising the sexual misbehaviour of Catholic priests and religious. Within three years of his writing, Cromwell's monastic visitors would use just such alleged misbehaviour to close down religious houses. More, therefore, was playing a very strong card by reiterating that the leading reformers, monks and friars who had renounced chastity and taken women into their beds, had turned a sick medieval joke into sober modern reality. In defiance of 'the hole consent of crystendome so many hundred yeres ... foure or five fond freres runne out of relygon and lyvynge in lechery, take upon themselfe to preche and saye to the people of theym selfe, we be the spyrytuales, we serche the botome of God's secrets ... and all that have been called holy doctors and interpretours before our dayes, were eyther false or folyes and ... brought all crysten nacyons oute of the right fayth / tyll now that god of hys high goodnes sent us and our wyves to preche fayth, and teche heresy, and show lechery to torne the worlde to grace'. More's references to the reformers and their wives always carries this polemical point, because he was confident that even the most unlettered layman or woman who reflected on this single fact about the reformers would thereby see through them, 'syth ye se Tyndale now teche and allowe theyr lechery and avowe it solempnely for good and laufull matrimony: I nothing fere your iudgement in this matter'.[31] In confronting the *Confutation*'s constant jibes against the reformers' marriages, we are dealing not with the obsessive scratching of a sexual itch, but the strategic reiteration of what its author felt to be an unanswerable populist argument.

I turn finally to the literary form in which the *Confutation* is cast. I've suggested that Part 1 of the *Confutation* can be treated as an integral work in its own right, and its Preface and successive books focus effectively on distinct aspects of Tyndale's teaching and the wider Protestant challenge. But the technique of learned literary debate which More was adapting here for a vernacular readership, citing extended extracts from Tyndale and then refuting them at length, inevitably makes for repetitiveness. He was accused of both tedium and redundancy by his evangelical opponents, as he has been by critics ever since. It has also been suggested that the form is doubly self-defeating, because the refutation gives wider circulation to the works being refuted.

More was well aware of all these criticisms, and offered a robust defence in the *Apology*. He quoted Tyndale at such length, he wrote, so that no one should accuse him of distortion – 'lothe would I be to miss reherse any mannys reason against whome I wryte, or to reherse hym slenderly'.[32] More claimed that Tyndale's book could be reconstructed simply by omitting his own refutation, a claim conceded by the far from friendly Victorian editors of the Parker Society edition of Tyndale's works. In this More certainly differed from Tyndale, who, he claimed, distorted by selective or tendentious quotation and 'rehersyth myne in every place faintly and falsely to / and leveth out the pyth and strength'.

As for its length, that was unavoidable. The most ignorant heretic could spread a heresy in a single page of eye-catching aphorisms: to unpick the errors in that single page might take the wisest man in the world 40 times as long. For all the charge of tedium, nonetheless, More insisted that he knew of good men who had read his book three times over as a comprehensive source of orthodox arguments, making 'tables thereof for their own remembraunce'.[33]

As that suggests, More insisted that his book was not *meant* to be read consecutively or as a whole. The *Confutation* was a compendium, a manual of controversies, which could be randomly browsed, or searched for specific issues. 'I sometyme take the payne to reherse some one thynge in diverse fashions in mo places than one, bycause I wolde that the reder sholde in every place where he fortuneth to fall in redynge, have at hys hande without remyttynge ellys where or labour of ferther sekynge for it, as myche as shall seme requysite for that mater that he there hathe in hande.' Readers were prone to 'wexe wery to rede over a long boke': he had designed this book so that 'they shal not need to rede over any chapyter but one, and that yt shall not force greatly whych one thorow all the boke'.[34] So whether some 'yndyfferent' reader picked up the *Confutation* at random, or 'the beste evangelyste of all this evangelycall bretherhed' searched to see what More had to say about 'some chosen piece in whyche hym selfe had went that hys evangelycall father Tydale had sayed wonderfull well', he would find a complete refutation.[35]

Nor did More fear that his book gave fresh currency to forbidden ideas. He knew better than anyone the reach of the trade in evangelical books, and in the Preface to the *Confutation* argued that heretics even gave their books away free, 'so greate a pestilent pleasure have some develysh people caught, with the labour, travayle, coste, charge, parell, harme and hurte of them selfe, to seke the destruccyone of other'.[36] So heretical books were already everywhere, to say nothing of the 'bold erroneous talkynge that is now allmoste in every lewde laddys mouth'.[37]

More had declared in the *Confutation* that he would far prefer it if nobody read either his book or the evangelical writings which had elicited it. 'The very tryacle [antidote] were well loste, so that all venome and poison were utterly loste therwyth.' But where there was heresy, there must be refutation, and the defenders of orthodoxy must not sleep while Judas went about his work. 'Evyl and ungracyouse folke shall ever fynde the meanys that suche bookes shall never in some corners lakke, wherby good people may be deceived and corrupted: yt ys more thenne necessary that men have agayne suche bookes as may well arme them, to resyste and confute theym.'[38] But it is clear that in adapting a learned Latin argumentative form to provide that necessary vernacular antidote to heresy, More was conscious of creating a different kind of work, combative, baggy, encyclopaedic, cyclical, a form which should be judged by the targeting and effectiveness of its individual parts, rather than its correspondence to some modern notions of what makes a good read.

Judged in this way, the *Confutation* stands up far better to scrutiny than has been allowed. Entire books can stand alone, especially Book VIII, a sustained polemic against Robert Barnes which returns brilliantly to the comic mode of the *Dialogue*, in a series of extended conversations in which Barnes is bested in debate by women, most devastatingly his landlady, 'the good wife of the botell of Botolph's wharf'.[39] But the rest of the *Confutation*, read in short bursts as More envisaged it would be, is full of good things, as in the passages where More deploys common usage or his humanist training in Greek to challenge Tyndale's translation of contested terms,[40] or as in the following passage, in which he picks on one of Tyndale's stylistic habits to score a debating point:

Tyndale is a great marker / there is nothynge with hym now but marke, marke, marke. It is pytye the man were not made a marker of chases in some tenys playe. For in good fayth he sholde be therin mych better occupyed than he is in this / when he sytteth and marketh all other mennis fautes and leveth hys owne unmarked / which every other man marketh well inough.[41]

One test of the value of any literary innovation is whether or not the form is adopted by other serious writers. And the vernacular debating form More had introduced into English was indeed to have a decisive influence on the shape of the religious debates of the Elizabethan era. In Queen Mary's reign, the *Confutation* was included in William Rastell's magnificent folio edition of More's English works, a collection designed to provide the Marian Church with a major polemical resource.[42] Eight years later, in 1565, the former Marian activist Thomas Harding, now a Louvain exile, adopted both the title and the distinctive literary form of the *Confutation* for his own *Confutation* of John Jewel's *Apologie for the Church of England*. Harding justified his adoption of the form in much the same terms as More – 'That I might seme to deale uprightly', he wrote, 'I would leave out nothing.'[43] Perhaps more surprisingly, Jewel responded in kind, once again using More's form to structure his own even vaster

Defence of the Apology.[44] Archbishop Parker thought well enough of Jewel's book to order copies placed in every parish church in England, despite the misgivings of those like Bishop Parkhurst of Norwich, who thought that the form of the book gave hostages to fortune – Catholics too poor to buy Harding's books 'shall finde the same already provided for them'.[45] But the polemical advantages of More's novel form were evidently deemed to outweigh any such drawbacks.

And in one way at least, Jewel outdid More. In Renaissance writing, *copia*, abundance or copiousness, was considered a species of merit, not a defect. Jewel's immense treatise weighed in at more than twice the length of More's *Confutation*. Yet though many have doubtless found Jewel's book tedious, no one so far as I am aware has seen in the Elizabethan Protestant bishop's adoption of More's literary innovation a symptom of mounting hysteria, moral collapse, or evidence of a mind at the end of its tether.

Notes

1   More, *Apology*, pp. 116–20.
2   R. W. Chambers, *Thomas More* (Bedford Historical Series edn, London, 1938,) pp. 274–82.
3   Elton, *Studies*, vol. III pp. 352–5.
4   Richard Marius, *Thomas More* (London 1993), pp. 35, 37, 42, 320–21, 331, 350, 391, 396, 403.
5   Alistair Fox, *Thomas More: History and Providence* (Oxford, 1982), pp. 111, 119–20, 123, 125, 143, 145.
6   Brian Moynahan, *William Tyndale: If God Spare My Life* (London, 2003), p. 349.
7   For a representative example, Foxe's anecdote of 'the cruel answer of Sir Thomas More . . . not here to be passed ouer, who at that time being Chauncelor of Englande, when as those which shuld burn Bilny came vnto him, requiring a letter of his hand, wherby they might be discharged after his death, he answered vnto them, sayinge: goo to good fellowes, burn him first, and then come after and aske a bil of my hand.' Foxe, *Actes and Monuments online* (1563 edn), p. 535; and see the account of the pursuit of James Bainham, ibid., pp. 548 ff.
8   Hilary Mantel, *Wolf Hall* (London, 2009), pp. 298–9.
9   For a recent positive discussion of the *Dialogue* which sees it as the signal for a new and sterner phase in the anti-heresy campaign, Craig D'Alton, 'Charity or Fire? The argument of Thomas More's 1529 Dyaloge', *Sixteenth Century Journal*, xxxiii (2002), pp. 51–70.
10 More, *Confutation,* in *Complete Works*, vol. 8, part 1, pp. 17, 41–2.
11 Elton, *Studies*, vol. III, pp. 347, 349, 352, 446; Fox, *History and Providence*, p. 23; James Simpson, *Burning to Read: English Fundamentalism and its Reformation Opponents* (Cambridge, Mass., 2007), p. 263; David Daniel, *William Tyndale: A Biography* (New Haven and London, 1994), p. 185.
12 A point I owe to my colleague Richard Rex.
13 Proceedings of the Commission in Daniel Wilkins, *Concilia Magnae Brittaniae et Hiberniae* (London, 1737), vol. 3, pp. 727–37. These measures were reiterated in a proclamation of 22 June 1530, which More almost certainly drafted, so it has been assumed that he endorsed and perhaps even initiated

this ban on an English Bible. In fact the ban probably originated with the more conservative clerical members of the Commission, and as I argued in chapter 2, More probably disagreed with it. He had argued at length for a Catholic translation of the New Testament in the *Dialogue*. Despite the official moratorium on such a translation till the populace 'do utterly abandon and forsake all perverse, erroneous and seditious opinions', More retained his arguments for an official Bible translation in the revised edition of the *Dialogue* published in 1531. As Chancellor he was obliged to defend the ban in justifying royal measures against heresy in the *Confutation*, but he reiterated his personal support for an English New Testament in the *Apology* a year later.

14 For a (slightly overheated) account of the 1530–31 campaign and More's part in it, Susan Brigden, *London and the Reformation* (Oxford, 1989), pp. 179–98.

15 Guy, *Public Career*, pp. 165–74.

16 Stanford E. Lehmberg, *The Reformation Parliament 1529–1536* (Cambridge, 1970), pp. 138–9.

17 So, for example, Brigden, *London and the Reformation*, p. 181, 'This Chancellor's campaign against heresy was desperate because he knew that time was short'. For 'More's Gethsemane', *Confutation, Complete Works*, vol. 8, part 2, p. 1229.

18 Anne M. O'Donnell and Jared Wickes (eds), *An Answere Unto Sir Thomas More's Dialoge* (vol. 3 of *The Independent Works of William Tyndale*), Washington, DC, 2000, p. xxxv.

19 *Dialogue, Complete Works*, vol. 6, part 1, pp. 201, 422.

20 Tyndale, *Answere*, p. 112; for the six victims, ibid., pp. 424–6.

21 *Confutation, Complete Works*, vol. 8, part 1, p. 3.

22 *Complete Works*, vol. 8, part 1, pp. 11–12.

23 Ibid., p. 17.

24 Ibid., pp. 16-7, 34.

25 Simpson, *Burning to Read*, p. 265.

26 *Complete Works*, vol. 8, part 1, p. 16.

27 Ibid., p. 18.

28 Ibid., p. 22.

29 Ibid., p. 23.

30 Ibid., pp. 23–5.

31 Ibid., pp. 131, 141.

32 Apology, in *Complete Works*, vol. 9, p. 6.

33 *Complete Works*, vol. 9, p. 8.

34 Ibid., vol. 9, p. 10.

35 Ibid.

36 *Confutation*, in *Complete Works*, vol. 8, part 1, p. 12.

37 *Apology, Complete Works*, vol. 9, p. 11.

38 *Confutation, Complete Works*, vol. 8, part 1, pp. 36–9.

39 Ibid., part 2, pp. 883–905.

40 Ibid., part 1, pp. 169–73.

41 Ibid., part 1, p. 139.

42 *The Workes of Sir Thomas More Knyght* (London, 1557) (STC 18076); the *Confutation* occupies pp. 614–832.

43 Thomas Harding, *A confutation of a booke intituled An apologie of the Church of England* (Antwerp, 1565); Alexandra Walsham, 'The Spider and the Bee: the perils of printing for refutation in Tudor England' in John King (ed.), *Tudor Books and Readers* (Cambridge, 2010), pp. 163–90, quotation at p. 169. Surprisingly, Professor Walsham makes no allusion to More's responsibility for or use of the form.

44 John Jewel, *A defence of the Apologie of the Churche of Englande conteininge an answeare to a certaine booke lately set foorthe by M. Hardinge, and entituled, A confutation of &c* (London, 1567).

45 Walsham, 'Spider and the Bee', pp. 172, 174.

PART TWO

Counter-Reformation England

4

Cardinal Pole Preaching

Thomas More's reputation as a martyr, and the immense literary and polemical reservoir of his writings against Protestantism which were the subject of Chapters 1–3, were both to be central to the self-understanding of Elizabethan Catholicism. But both More's reputation, and his literary and polemical legacy, had fallen into eclipse in the wake of his execution for treason in 1535. Even after the restoration of Catholicism in 1553, his memory, with that of Fisher, remained an embarrassment to many of the leaders of the Marian regime, who had condemned and opposed the two martyrs' loyalty to the papacy, and some of whom had connived at their executions.

The man responsible above all others for the recovery of the reputations of More and Fisher, and their symbolic role at the heart of a newly resurgent Catholicism, was Reginald Pole, friend and ardent admirer of More and Fisher, and humanistically educated cousin of Henry VIII. Elevated to the Cardinalate by Pope Paul III and appointed Legate and Governor of Viterbo, Pole had become the centre of the reforming circle of Italian Catholics (which included Michelangelo), known as the 'Spirituali'. He had presided at the opening of the Council of Trent, and had come within a single vote of the papacy in the Conclave of 1547. In the mid-1530s, while still only in minor orders, he had been mooted as a possible husband for his cousin the Princess Mary, in the event of a conservative coup against Henry VIII. On Mary's accession to the throne, he was recalled to England as Papal Legate, and had replaced Thomas Cranmer as Archbishop of Canterbury.

Pole's centrality to the Marian counter-reformation, and his consequent responsibility for many of the distinctive themes and emphases of the Elizabethan Catholicism which was in many ways the heir of the Marian Church, have long been overlooked, but have now begun to be appreciated. In this chapter I examine Pole's attitude to preaching and Bible-reading, reforming themes that were at the heart of Pole's own ardently papalist but also distinctively Augustinian theology, and which go to the heart of his vision of a reformed Catholicism.

★ ★ ★

In the spring of 1558 the Spanish Ambassador in London, Count Feria, put on record a series of judgements about Reginald Pole which have coloured perceptions of the Cardinal and of the effectiveness of the Marian restoration of Catholicism ever since. To Feria it seemed that Pole was sleepwalking through his task of re-Catholicising England. He was a 'dead man', whose fatal listlessness could be stirred to ardour only by news from the Italy he manifestly pined for. Radically deficient in the zeal necessary for the reconversion of England, he was the wrong man in the wrong place at the wrong time. 'The Cardinal', Feria wrote, 'is a good man, but very lukewarm: and I do not believe the lukewarm go to Paradise, even if they are called moderates.'[1]

Some of these remarks were addressed to King Philip II of Spain, but the occasion of this latter oft-quoted judgement was a letter to the Jesuit activist Pedro Ribadeneira, briefly based in London, in which Feria attempted to explain (and exculpate) his own failure to persuade Pole and Queen Mary to establish the Society in England. Such apparently inexplicable resistance to a Jesuit presence, Feria thought, must spring from the Cardinal's lack of zeal or insight, and could only be the mark of a secret son of the Church of Laodicea, condemned in the Book of Revelation as being 'neither hot nor cold', a symbol of the spiritually half-hearted, whom the apocalyptic Christ had threatened to 'spew out of [his] mouth'.[2]

Given Pole's friendship with Ignatius and his financial support for new Jesuit enterprises in Italy, it does not seem very likely that he would indefinitely have declined Jesuit help in England. But had he done so he would have been by no means the only counter-reformation bishop with reservations about the unqualified value of the Jesuit order. In the mid-1550s the Society was pastorally still something of an unknown quantity, whose independence of episcopal control and extra-parochial base of operations ran counter to some of the most fundamental emphases of the reform party at Trent. Even two generations later, and in territory in which, as in Marian England, the Church was fighting to reclaim hearts and minds after a period of Protestant dominance, so successful a counter-reformation activist as Archbishop Matthew Hovius of Mechelen would fight tooth and nail to prevent an able seminarian from joining the Jesuit order.[3]

More recent studies of Pole's relationship with the Society have helped clarify the complex of reasons which may have informed his caution.[4] Nevertheless, Pole's rejection of the Jesuits (if that is what it amounted to) has been regularly linked to his supposed lukewarmness, and consistently read by historians as one aspect of a general disinclination on his part towards the more adventurous expressions of the counter-reformation spirit, indicating a fatal lack of imagination which would have doomed the Marian restoration even if death had not brought it to an abrupt end. The seminal work here was that of Rex Pogson, whose pioneering study of Pole's legatine mission exhaustively documented both the difficulties confronting Pole and the careful solidity of his administrative and financial reconstruction. However, Pogson also stressed what he took to be Pole's lack of imagination. The Cardinal, Pogson thought, 'possessed valuable gifts for leadership of a Church in peaceful times', but 'nothing more': he recoiled from the extraordinary measures which the reign of Mary demanded.

Above all, Pogson insisted, the Cardinal distrusted preaching: 'right to the end of the mission he took the line that preaching was useless for the time being, for people were corrupted by the schism and so listened with avarice in their hearts and were untouched by God's Word'. In this, Pole could not entirely be excused simply as a man of his times: others saw what had to be done, even if he did not, and so he 'differed crucially' from advisers as various as Queen Mary, King Philip and Pope Julius III, on the 'urgency to be attached to the organisation of vigorous widespread preaching'. For Pole, preaching would become valuable only when the people had been 'compelled to realise the truth by a terror of the law'. In June 1558, just a few months before his death, Pogson claimed, Pole wrote to his Dominican friend and former collaborator Bartolomeo Carranza, recently appointed Archbishop of Toledo and Primate of Spain, a letter in which he spelled out these fundamental reservations about the value of preaching, declaring, 'I think it is better to check the preaching of the Word rather than to proclaim it, unless the discipline of the Church has been fully restored.'[5]

For the rest of the twentieth century, Pogson's line was closely followed by most of those who wrote about Pole, even historians who have consciously striven to do justice to the Cardinal and his methods. For the late David Loades, Pole and his colleagues 'were not slack or inept, but they were committed to a long-term policy which ignored certain important features of the immediate situation', above all 'the desperate need for spiritual leadership of a high calibre'. Pole, Loades thought, drew back from the Jesuits who might have provided such leadership because he 'simply did not want men with the fire of the counter-reformation in their bellies'. He belonged to an 'older generation' (though Pole was in fact nine years younger than St Ignatius) which 'saw the future in terms of the past', he valued right behaviour above right belief, and feared sermons as 'liable to be controversial'. The Cardinal was thus 'unenthusiastic about preaching', 'seldom preached himself', and when he did 'his main theme was exhortation to gratitude and obedience'.[6]

Christopher Haigh, who makes a vigorous case for the effectiveness of Pole's efforts, nevertheless agreed that 'Pole regarded energetic evangelism as unnecessary and inappropriate', and cited the letter to Carranza in support of this judgement.[7] For Diarmaid MacCulloch, Pole and his collaborators 'showed themselves weak in understanding the need to communicate a dynamic message, having embarked on the negative work of dismantling Protestantism and tidying up after it'. Pole distrusted 'preaching campaigns' which he associated 'with brilliant former associates like Peter Martyr or Bernard Ochino, who had betrayed the Church by turning Protestant'.[8] For the Jesuit historian Thomas McCoog, also, Pole's bitter experience as leader of the Italian *Spirituali*, and the damaging apostasy of evangelists like Martyr and Ochino, led him to renounce his earlier enthusiasm for preaching as an indispensable instrument of reform, and this disillusion was the root cause of his rejection of the Jesuits, who were above all else preachers. Predictably, McCoog backed up his argument about Pole's distrust of preaching by recycling Pogson's 'quotation' from Pole's letter to Carranza.[9]

In fact, all these judgements rest on a disastrous misreading of what Pole himself actually said. Rex Pogson was an admirable historian, but his Latin evidently left something to be desired. He misunderstood Pole's letter to Carranza, which offers a far more specific, nuanced and subtle estimation of the value of preaching – and of controversial writing – than Pole has been given credit for. Pogson's mistranslation was unquestioningly reproduced by almost everyone writing about Pole since 1975, and decisively shaped all but the most recent estimates of the Cardinal's outlook and intentions.[10] A more accurate reading of the letter to Carranza is thus the place to begin a reconsideration not only of Pole's attitude to preaching, but of his openness to the newer energies of the counter-reformation more generally.

Pole's letter to Carranza, written on 20 June 1558,[11] is a highly defensive document. Detractors had evidently told Carranza that Pole, almost permanently at court and preoccupied with affairs of state, was neglecting both his diocese of Canterbury and also the 13 London parishes which fell under his peculiar jurisdiction. Carranza duly passed these accusations on to Pole, and his motives in doing so may not have been entirely spiritual. Philip II and his advisers had cause to be worried about Pole's acknowledged influence over the Queen as inimical to Spanish interests, and Carranza may have had his royal master's concern in mind in urging Pole to leave the court and attend to his episcopal responsibilities. At any rate, his criticisms touched Pole on a raw nerve, for episcopal responsibility was a high priority with him. The momentous sixth session of the Council of Trent had produced a trenchant decree on the necessity of episcopal and canonical residence, and this Tridentine insistence had been forcefully reiterated in the third decree of Pole's own Legatine Synod.[12] In this matter the Marian Church practised what it preached: the Marian bench of bishops was dominated not by lawyers and diplomats, but by theologians and pastors, whose ministries were strikingly characterised by punctilious attention to the religious concerns of their own dioceses.[13]

Stung by these insinuations of neglect, therefore, Pole vigorously defended his record. He was indeed often absent from his diocese and at court (the letter was written from Richmond), but the times demanded this, for his advice was needed not only on religious affairs but on matters of state. Pole nevertheless was content to be judged by his record: let those who thought he was not doing his job properly consider the woeful state of the country and of the Church in the very recent past, down to the previous year, and compare it with the present, when the 'face of religion' [*facies Religionis*] was at last beginning to recover its pristine form. [*quo iam pristinam formam recipere incipit*]. Above all, he was bound to assist Queen Mary. He had often petitioned her to be allowed to go back to look after his diocese, but she and her counsellors considered his presence vital for the good of Church and state, and he could not refuse Mary, as she held the helm of state in stormy waters. She was the nursing mother to whom God had committed the care of the Church in England, the woman to whom, indeed, the English Church owed everything [*cui tanquam matri, et secundum Deum conservatrici obedientiae Ecclesiae in hoc Regno, omnia ipsa debet Ecclesia . . .*] Thus he could be of most use not only to the country but even the Church, by being present at court. For the foreseeable future much of his time would be absorbed by the task of sorting out the Church's finances after the depredations of earlier reigns, now happily reversed by the piety of the King and Queen.

But the pastoral effectiveness of the clergy and the restoration of proper Church discipline depended on the outcome of those efforts to restore the Church's possessions, and hence provision for her ministers. In the light of the many demands on his time, he was, he said, only too well aware of his own inadequate performance as a pastor, which he daily lamented. He knew that Carranza's informants took a cynical view of these protestations, however, since they argued that even if his responsibilities for the English Church as a whole took him away from Canterbury, he could at least look after his London parishes better than in fact he did, since he was near them while at court. And indeed he knew the urgency of London's need, which he was eager to help even more than Canterbury.

It was at this point in the letter that Pogson imagined that Pole had told Carranza that it was better to 'check' preaching than to advance it, 'unless the discipline of the Church has been fully restored', and that the people should be 'compelled to realise the truth by a terror

of the law'.[14] The second claim seemed strange in a man who notoriously shrank from strong-arm techniques. The first was even more
improbable: Pole was deeply imbued with Pauline theology, and
would have been horrified by the mere thought of 'checking' or
hindering the word of God. And in fact he said nothing of the sort.
What he actually wrote to Carranza was very different. Many people
thought that what London needed most was the medicine of more
and more preaching. But, in truth, Pole told Carranza,

> From ample daily experience I learn how corrupt and diseased is
> the state of that body, [the city of London], [and] I find that wher-
> ever the word most abounds, men least profit from it, when it is
> misused: we see this to be nowhere more so than in London. Of
> course I don't on that account deny the necessity of preaching the
> word, but I do say that the word can be more of a hindrance than
> a help, unless it is proceeded or at the same time accompanied by
> the establishment of church discipline, because carnal men turn
> [preaching] into an empty ear-tickling entertainment, rather than
> a health-giving discipline and food for the soul.[15]
>
> [*Ego vero qui quotidie magis experientia disco, qui sit infecti atque
> infirmi hujus corporis status, hoc reperio, ubi major est verbi copia, ibi
> minus homines proficere, ea abutentes; quod nusquam magis videmus
> accidere, quam Londini; nec tamen nego necessarium esse verbi praedica-
> tionem, sed nisi vel ante sit, vel simul constituta Ecclesiastica disciplina,
> dico potius obesse verbum, quam prodesse, quia hoc carnales homines ad
> inanem aurium delectationem, non ad salutarem animi disciplinam, et
> alimentum transferunt*].

He then quoted Ezekiel 33.31–2 – 'they sit before thee as my people,
and they hear thy words, but they will not do them: for with their
mouth they show much love, but their heart goeth after their covetousness. And lo, thou art unto them as one that hath a pleasant voice.'
And so it is in London – despite the preaching of the word, people
neglect the celebration of divine worship, except when compelled
by the fear of the law, and the Church's discipline is almost wholly
ignored. So in Pole's opinion at this particular point in time it is in
the people's interests that more effort be put into sorting out discipline than into preaching. But we need to give full weight to his use

of the word '*simul*' – preaching and discipline must go together and at the same time, and Pole adds that in fact discipline itself can't be established rightly unless there is preaching. [*Quare si in iis constituendis atque confirmandis, quae ad disciplinam pertinent, maior opera, quam in praedicando verbo ponatur, id certe huic populo utilius esse ad tempus video, quanquam hoc sine verbo recte fieri non potest*].

But in any case, he insisted, there is no question of the people of London lacking preaching. The 'good bishop of London' has made this a priority, and there is preaching in many places in the city, and in particular every Sunday at St Paul's Cross, to which great assemblies of people come. Pole himself has provided for frequent preaching in the parishes under his direct care, appointing pious and learned men to do this work, and his Chancellor, Henry Cole, is also tireless in parochial reform and reconstruction. So contrary to these accusations, Pole was fulfilling his duty as a pastor, even if he had to do it by proxy. Indeed he claimed that he felt easier in his mind about London than about the other parts of the Church under his care, because, as he had shown Carranza, London had plenty of preaching [*verbi copia*]. But if it was still thought that the shepherd's own voice was essential, then Pole's sheep were not deprived of that, either: he himself preaches often, both in his Metropolitan Church, and in many other parts of his diocese, he has preached twice in London itself, and with God's help he intends to go on preaching.

Moreover, he has tackled the problem of warning, instructing and correcting his people not simply by the *spoken* word, but by the use of the press. In this task he has good collaborators, men who have advised him that orthodox and wholesome printed works in English were an urgent need, because, they tell him, heretic writings had played a bigger part in corrupting the people even than the spoken word. That was why, as Carranza well knew, the bishops at the Legatine Synod had insisted on the need for doctrinal and devotional instruction, above all on truths which had been contradicted by the heretics, and that was why they had called for the preparation of a set of English homilies by pious and learned men. Among these he singles out the Bishop of Lincoln, Thomas Watson,[16] and, rather more surprisingly, the Queen's secretary, John Boxall:[17] some of their writings, Pole declared, were already in print, and some were in the press. Carranza's own excellent catechism was at this very moment being translated out of Spanish for use in England. [*tuo . . . docto et pio Catechismo . . . qui nunc in nostram linguam vertitur*].[18]

There were now, therefore, so many suitable writings of this kind that Pole himself might well be excused from adding to them. In fact, however, he had been persuaded to publish some of the things he had written on controverted questions, and he would do so after they had been vetted by friends and advisers, including Carranza himself. Pole offered all this as proof that he was far from neglecting the pastoral duties in which, as Primates of their respective Churches, he and Carranza were joined in a single responsibility. But Carranza was fortunate to minister in a Spain in which, blessedly and almost uniquely, no one had been led astray by corrupt teachers, and Satan had not been able to find a chink through which he could insinuate the poison of heresy. Pole added drily that he hoped that in offering welcome advice and admonition in the future, Carranza would draw on his own pastoral experience rather than on book learning. The implication was that Toledo did not offer the sort of difficulties that Pole had to contend with in England, where the going was tougher and the pastoral challenges far greater.[19]

This is a remarkable utterance, as near as Pole ever got to a comprehensive rationale and defence of the whole teaching programme of the Marian restoration, and in effect a retrospective, composed a matter of months before that restoration came to an abrupt end with his own and Mary's deaths. Its importance in assessing the relationship between Pole and Carranza has been recognised by Spanish historians, but in England it has been either ignored or disastrously misunderstood.[20] Of all those who have used it, only Pole's recent biographer, Thomas Mayer, has grasped that, far from providing evidence of Pole's distrust of preaching, the letter constitutes evidence that 'preaching was important to him, and he put effort into it'.[21] And no one at all has recognised or explored the letter's importance as an account of Pole's overall pastoral strategy.

The letter to Carranza is a very rich source for Pole's understanding of the Marian enterprise, not least for what it reveals about his own reverence for Mary as 'established by God as the maintainer of obedience to the Church in this realm' [*secundum Deum conservatrici obedientiae Ecclesiae in hoc regno*], a strikingly full-blooded expression from so zealous an opponent of the royal supremacy as

Pole.[22] Equally emphatically, Pole here asserts a coherent preaching and teaching strategy by the Marian Church, appealing both to the actual provision of such teaching, and to the programmatic legislation of the Legatine Synod, whose emphases on episcopal residence and visitation, instruction, preaching and publishing is carefully echoed and at several points quoted directly in his letter.[23]

Moreover, Pole claims that this strategy had been effectively implemented and was working, as he contrasts the woeful state of English religion in the recent past with the present time in which 'it is just beginning to recover its pure form'. That sense that some sort of corner had been turned by the summer of 1558, however, was certainly not born of complacency. Pole's letter is throughout informed by a sense of the daunting scale of the tasks and dangers confronting the regime, and of the extent to which the reformation had 'deformed' the religious sense of the people. Pole is often accused of seriously underestimating the extent and strength of the Protestant penetration of English lay religious culture, of imagining that 'the breach with Rome had been the work of a tiny faction' and of lacking 'an informed overall judgement of the schism's impact'.[24] There is no sign in the letter of any such lack of awareness, though he was admittedly playing up his own difficulties as a form of self-defence. For our purposes, however, perhaps the most striking features of the letter are the careful balance of what Pole has to say in it about preaching, and the specific reference of what he does say, not to preaching in general, but to preaching in the city of London, which he thinks and says is a special and desperate case.

It should not surprise us that Pole defended so vigorously his record on preaching. In the early 1540s he devoted a good deal of time and labour to composing a long treatise on the art of preaching, *De Modo Conciandi*, consulting his friend and mentor Cardinal Contarini as well as expert preachers like Nicholas Bobadilla: sadly, the resulting manuscript 'a large volume, but imperfect' (i.e. unfinished), has not survived.[25] Preaching and teaching dominate three of the first four decrees of his Legatine Synod, signalling the high priority he placed on them from the outset of his mission. The first decree indeed invented a ground-breaking propagandist technique, normally associated with the Protestant regimes which succeeded Mary. The decree provided for an annual procession

and thanksgiving Mass on St Andrew's Day, the anniversary of the reconciliation of England with the papacy, in the course of which 'a sermon shall be preached to the people in which the reason for this solemnity shall be explained'. The Synod directed that where there was no qualified preacher, an official homily on the subject should be read out by the parish priest, and John Harpsfield duly produced such a model sermon for St Paul's in 1556, which was published for wider use on the instructions of Bishop Bonner.[26] Historians have recently recognised the importance and effectiveness of *Protestant* anniversary celebrations, and the role which 'bonfires and bells' with their accompanying sermons commemorating events like Queen Elizabeth's accession or James' deliverance from the Gunpowder Plot, played in consolidating Protestantism within popular culture.[27] It has not, I think, been noted that the invention of this innovatory technique is Pole's, and its introduction certainly does not suggest a timid reluctance to use preaching for propagandist purposes.

The Synod's second decree introduced tight control of the press to eliminate heretical books, prohibited heretical preaching, emphasised the need for orthodox teaching above all on the principal reformation targets of papal primacy and the seven sacraments, and, since Trent had not yet produced a compact formulation on the sacraments as a whole, the Synod provided clergy with a brief but comprehensive summary of Catholic sacramental teaching, derived from the Council of Florence. That sacramental teaching was given symbolic endorsement in new provisions for the public reservation of the Blessed Sacrament in a tabernacle on the high altar of every church. The third decree was devoted to enforcing clerical residence, but decree four explained that the point of all this was to ensure the proper discharge of their pastoral duties by the clergy, from the bishop down, and that 'the pastoral office ... chiefly consists in the preaching of the divine word'. This was above all the bishop's task: he must preach often in person, and he must ensure that all parish priests 'feed the people committed to them with the wholesome food of preaching', at least on Sundays and other feast days. They must also catechise, taking special care to admonish and if necessary threaten lay people who had been seduced into heresy, and they must be specially vigilant against anyone 'unauthorised by the apostolic see, or by the catholic bishop of his diocese', who dares 'usurp the office of a preacher'. Finally, the decree ordered the preparation of English homilies for use 'by such curates as are not capable of preaching'.[28]

All this, it must be emphasised, was Pole's own agenda, not some alien programme thrust upon him by others more committed to preaching than he was himself, and all these concerns are revisited in the letter to Carranza. That letter makes it clear that Pole did not distrust preaching as such; he distrusted heretical preaching by self-appointed evangelists who operated without proper authority. He thought preaching to be the principal duty of all pastors, but he insisted that it should be orthodox and programmatic, focused on fundamentals of the Christian life like the nature and use of the sacraments and the unity of the Church. He thought it the special responsibility of the bishops to preach themselves, to choose parish clergy able to preach, to determine and to police the content of parochial preaching and to provide model sermons for the inept or uneducated clergy to read. Far from discouraging preaching, he was active in securing all that. As we shall see, however, he was also convinced that there were special problems in London, corrupted by years of Protestant polemics, preached and printed, in which sermons had become sources of dissension rather than of consolidation in the Christian life. Preaching in such an environment was prone to become separated from the sacramental life of the Church, the practice of charity and penitential asceticism. In such a culture of contestation the proper reception of the word of God, a matter of humble openness rather than fractious judgement, was a rarity, and audiences were liable to become opinionated and hardened against the life of grace. So he thought the restoration of a Catholic pattern of sacramental practice, including regular use of the sacrament of penance, a vital and compelling context for preaching. But he did not on that score think preaching should be outlawed or discouraged, for he recognised that sermons and catechizing were needed to explain and underpin the restoration of sacramental discipline. He commended the record of Bonner and his own record in the provision of pastoral preaching in London parishes, as well as the set-piece official (and controversial) weekly sermons at St Paul's Cross.

But in any case, claims about Pole's supposed lack of commitment to preaching were made in the face of voluminous surviving evidence of Pole's own sermons, which even his most recent (on the whole sympathetic) biographer has ignored.[29] Pole himself told Carranza that he preached 'frequently' [*saepius*]. This is a pardonable exaggeration. Archbishops of Canterbury were great officers of state as well as busy ecclesiastical administrators: few medieval or early modern archbishops have been 'frequent' preachers, and Pole's archbishopric was more fraught than most. Nevertheless, the late Thomas Mayer, Pole's most learned biographer, pointed out that in terms of frequency, Pole's record as a preacher compares favourably with that of his successor at Canterbury, Matthew Parker.[30] We badly need an edition of Pole's English sermons, of which five survive more or less complete, together with a number of other extended fragments.[31] Pole's style has been disparaged,[32] but in fact these vernacular sermons display a keen sensitivity to audience and occasion, and a literary skill displayed not so much in fine language (he was almost certainly happier writing in Latin or Italian) as in a remarkable ability to develop key ideas by an almost musical technique of variations on recurring texts and topics, sustained through the length of a sermon.

The surviving sermons include two preached on St Andrew's Day 1556 and 1557, as part of the observances prescribed by the Legatine Synod for the annual commemoration of the schism and reconciliation with Rome. In 1556 Pole preached the first of these in his own diocese, presumably in Canterbury Cathedral, taking as his text the apposite psalm '*Laetatus Sum*' (Psalm 121), which evidently formed part of the celebratory liturgy of the day. The sermon was a thoroughly biblical exercise, in the first half of which Pole offered a meditation on the Church as the embodiment of the heavenly Jerusalem on earth, the one centre of unity out of which there could be no grace: in the words of the psalmist, 'I was glad when they said unto me: we will go into the house of the Lord. Our feet shall stand in thy gates, O Jerusalem. Jerusalem is built as a city that is at unity in itself'. He then went on to reflect on the account of the calling of St Andrew in St John's Gospel,[33] in which Andrew and his companion ask Jesus where he lives, and Jesus replies, 'Come and see'. After spending a day in the home of Jesus, Andrew goes to tell his brother Simon Peter, 'We have found the Messiah'. The first question the Apostles had asked Jesus was 'Master, where do you dwell?', and that remained the great question confronting all who would be saved. The answer, Pole emphasised, was that Christ dwelt in his Church, and was only to be found there. Those who seek Christ must, like the Apostles, 'come and see', by returning to the unity of the Church.[34] The 1556 sermon concluded with an extended reflection on the nature of the faith which allows us to see Jesus, namely the '*fides patrum*', the faith of our fathers, humbly received from our spiritual fathers, the appointed pastors and teachers of the Church. This faith had descended from Abraham through the Apostles, above all through Peter and his successors, and in England had been transmitted by a metaphorical Jacob's 'ladder', the succession of Catholic archbishops in communion with Peter, from the time of St Augustine to Pole himself, a succession in which Cranmer had been the only broken rung. But Pole notably refrained from any extended scolding of his audience for their part in abandoning that faith and falling into schism – 'I doo not utterly accuse you, nor I can not say yt was your desyres, for you dyd yt beynge thereunto constrayned'.[35]

The 1556 St Andrew's Day sermon displays Pole's characteristic handling of the Bible, and his other surviving English sermons are equally distinctive. His first public sermon in England had been preached earlier that year, on the feast of the Annunciation (25 March), just four days after Cranmer's execution, when Pole had received the Pallium marking his formal assumption of Archiepiscopal authority as Cranmer's successor at Canterbury. The ceremony took place in the church of St Mary le Bow (St Mary Arches), a Canterbury 'peculiar', in the city and diocese of London but officially under the Archbishop's direct jurisdiction. Pole had originally delegated the task of preaching that day to one 'which hath . . . more use and practice', but a petition from the priest and people of the parish had persuaded him to preach himself. As in the Canterbury St Andrew's Day sermon, Pole used two texts for his sermon, the opening greeting of an archbishop to the people 'Peace be with you', (Christ's words to the Apostles in the upper room after the resurrection), and then the Gospel of the day, the Lucan account of the Annunciation.[36]

I have discussed the St Mary Arches sermon elsewhere, and will only summarise that discussion here.[37] Perhaps because it was his first utterance as Archbishop, perhaps because he was conscious of addressing a London audience, where the reformation had penetrated more deeply than in Canterbury, it is a sterner utterance than the earlier St Andrew's Day homily, commending the congregation for their desire to hear the word of God, but deploring the restless pride of the many who 'for no necessitie theye fynde but rather for curiositie to see whatt bread their newe pastours bring with them, some also to tempt their Curates, making them selfes iudges of their sayings, redye to reprove them when thei maye take any occasion thereof by any cavilation, which be all greate abuses, and such as God never faileth to punnyshe'.[38] To receive real spiritual food, however, they must receive the word of God without vain questioning, in the spirit of peace which the Archbishop's greeting represented, and as Mary had received the angel's message not taking 'godes meaning' lightly but letting it 'penetrate your hart, and move your hart, altering the same with the effect of feare at the furst hearyng'. There had never been an age more preoccupied with preaching the word of God, 'nor more diligent studie putt to com to the understanding therof', never more 'professors' of the word of God. Yet there had never been more heresies and 'never more licentious disorder in the lyffes of Christen men then is at this tyme'. The legitimate 'desyer of knowledge of those things that be written in scripture' was commendable in itself, as was the desire to hear sermons, and it was the duty of pastors like Pole to nourish and encourage such longing. But right reading and hearing had to be undertaken in the spirit of humility and obedience. It could not be permitted to everyone 'to feade hym selfe as hym lyste and his owne wytt leadeth hym', for that 'is the most perilouse state that the wyll and wytt of men can putt ytt self unto'.[39]

These themes were picked up and developed in the series of sermons intended for publication which Pole composed to meet the desire of the people of his diocese and 'universallie in the people throughout the realme' for instruction 'in the trew doctrine' of the word of God. As the Pope's Legate and their chief pastor, Pole's preaching, like his liturgical greeting 'Pax Vobiscum', was intended to bring peace to those who had been 'moche travailed wyth diversities of opinions and doctrines touching the faith, wherewith all quietnes of conscience hath bene taken from you ... by yll preachers and teachers, and inordinat reading of scriptures'.[40] The sermons explore characteristic counter-reformation themes; the evils of schism and heresy, the need for unity around the Pope, the Church as the one ark of salvation and the need for the docile reception of the faith of our fathers. But these themes were given Pole's very distinctive expression. Aware of the hold that the vernacular Bible had established even among many otherwise conservative laity in Edward's reign, he was intensely conscious of the danger of appearing to seek to suppress the word of God. But he dwelt at length on the chaos and division which indiscriminate preaching and Bible-reading had brought.

> And now shew me all yow that have had experience of these yeares past, when you were out of the obedience of the Churche, was there ever a tyme that Scripture was more studied in, was there anye tyme that the precheng and teaching thereof was more divulgate ... [when] also the Latten service used ever before in the Churche [was] cast out, and all to be sett fourthe in Englusshe, to the extent that nothing should sownde in the peoples eares, but onely scripture transform'd and taught in that maner.

And yet

> what fruite cam off all this, yow that have seene the one, have seene the other, for was God ever lesse honoured, was proper wyll [self-will] ever more followed, of those that were moste authours of this order to communicat Scripture wyth all kind of men, and generallie the rest ...[41]

In some of these sermons Pole's Augustinian theology of grace is clearly on display, and may well have troubled the conservative English theological censors to whom he submitted his draft text. The third of these homilies in particular addressed the obligation to do good works. Much of the sermon is conventional enough, emphasising the duty of every Christian, from the monarch in council to the husbandman at the plough, to take up the cross and follow Jesus by labouring in their own vocations. But Pole stressed 'the ryall spirit and sacerdotal wythall' of all Christians in pursuing their vocation, 'as well the plough man that dyggeth and delveth the ground ... as onye kyng of a realme or Busshop beside'. He related those priestly and royal dignities to the 'holiness and justice' spoken of by Zachary in the Benedictus canticle from Luke's Gospel, a holiness and justice which belonged to Christ, and which derived from the one 'good work' of God, the Cross, of which all our good works were merely the fruit. Unfortunately, only the anonymous and theologically cautious censor's comments on Pole's second sermon have survived,[42] so we have no way of knowing whether he detected the faint whiff of Lutheranism which hung about such phrasing, and which Pole's arch-enemy Pope Paul Caraffa would certainly have pounced upon, had the sermons ever appeared in print.[43]

The manuscript of Pole's last public sermon is lost, but the sermon survives, largely complete, thanks to its printing from John Foxe's papers by the Protestant historian John Strype in the early eighteenth century. Delivered as it was on the eve of Pole's last year as Archbishop and Legate, it offers a particularly rich insight into Pole's priorities. This was the sermon he preached at Whitehall on St Andrew's Day 1557, the third anniversary of the nation's reconciliation with Rome.[44] In this major set-piece utterance before the Queen, the court, the legal profession and the Mayor and Aldermen of London, Pole confronted head-on the problem of London, the nature of the city's apostasy, its continuing role as a centre of dissent and his own vision of the best means of restoring it. Preached just over six months before his letter to Carranza, the St Andrew's Day sermon deals in greater detail with issues touched on in that letter. Between them, the two documents offer a striking corrective to much of the conventional wisdom about the limitations of Pole's pastoral vision.[45]

Pole's St Andrew's Day sermon was the culmination of a day of extraordinary Catholic triumphalism. That morning (a Tuesday) the procession, Mass and 'godly sermon' stipulated in the first synodal decree had been duly held at St Paul's, with a priest from every parish in London participating. Later that day, the Queen and the Cardinal rode from St James's to Whitehall, for a display of Catholic chivalry at which Sir Thomas Tresham was installed as Prior of the newly revived Order of St John, and four Knights of Rhodes were made. The ceremony was attended by all the bishops, and by the Judges and Sergeants of the law, and it took place in the context of a solemn Mass and procession at Westminster Abbey at which Abbot Feckenham presided in his mitre. After dinner the court and the legal profession moved to the Chapel Royal, where they were joined by the Lord Mayor and all the aldermen of London, who had presumably attended the Mass and Sermon at St Paul's that morning. There, in the presence of the legal profession, the city governors and of 'many Lordes and knyghtes, and lades and gentyllmen', Pole preached.[46] He is often accused of being out of touch with the English scene, insufficiently aware of the extent of the impact of the reformation, his antennae for English affairs and English sensibilities dulled by years of residence in Italy. His sermon that day, however, suggests quite another picture. It forcefully targets some of the different constituencies who made up his audience, and it intervenes tellingly in the affairs of the city, in particular the fraught issue of the city hospitals and their confessional significance. Pole tackles head-on some of the thorniest problems confronting the regime in London, above all the city's continuing sympathy for Protestantism, or at any rate for the victims of the Marian regime's campaign of repression.

In the course of his sermon Pole observed that St Andrew had seen Jesus walking by the Sea of Galilee, an incident from the Gospel prescribed for St Andrew's Day, Matthew 3.18–22.[47] The sequence (hymn between the readings at Mass) for the day, however, specifically identified Andrew as a preacher of repentance, and, perhaps following this clue, Pole took as his text a passage in Matthew 3, in which John the Baptist urges the people of Judaea to 'bring forth fruits meet for repentance', and warns that trees that fail to bear such fruit will be cut down and cast into the fire.

In a city which had witnessed many recent burnings, it was a pointed and uncomfortable choice of text. The opening of the sermon is missing, but in it Pole had evidently identified as one of the chief sins of reformation England the dissolution of the monasteries and the theft of monastic property, 'whereby . . . was overtoorned the welthe of the realme, and of the prynce also himselfe'. Pole hastened to reassure his audience, of lords, gentlemen and city fathers, that they were not required as the fruit of their repentance to rebuild the monasteries, 'which I knowe you be not able to do'. Rather, 'yf you were able, and had such a gay mynde to restore the ruynes of the chyrches', they should help their parish churches, which 'have byn sufferede to fawle downe of themselves maynye, and yn lyke maner spoyled as the monasteryes were'. With his eye on the judges and the city magistrates, he presented such restoration as an act of common prudence, for respect and care for the churches was part of the maintenance of civic society, 'the whyche you maye yn no wyse fayle to doo, excepte you wyll have your people wax brutyshe and wylde, and your commonwealthe wythout foundacyon'.[48]

Though Pole thus absolved his audience from the obligation to restore monastic property, he did not leave the matter there. As the letter to Carranza was to make clear, he was much preoccupied with the Church's finances, and he reminded his hearers that they held monastic property by the concession of the Church, their indulgent mother, and not by right. The recent appetite for Church property which had impoverished and weakened religion was, he thought, an infantile disorder, and those affected by it were like a greedy child gobbling an overlarge apple given by his mother, which she 'perceyvinge him to feade too much of, and knowynge yt sholde doo him hurte ... would have him give her a lytyll pece therof'. They should attend to the requests of their loving mother Church, famished as she was for sustenance, when they had far more than was good for them, or else, like an angry father intervening in a mother–child stand-off, Christ would come and take the apple away altogether, and cast it 'out of the wyndowe'. The Church herself would not constrain her children in this matter, but Pole hoped that in a little while, 'you by [Christ's] grace waxinge a lytyll stronger, youre appetite shal be retourned to his natural course. As I have harde that some have begonne veray well al readye . . .'[49]

Pole now turned to the fraught issue of charity and poor relief. He was preaching at a time of desperate social hardship and recurrent dearth and disease. The city had responded to this mid-century crisis by founding or recasting the city's five hospitals, St Bartholomew's, St Thomas's, Bethlem, Christ's Hospital and Bridewell, as centres for poor relief and social discipline. These measures had been supported across the religious spectrum of reformation London. Thomas White, founder of Trinity College, Oxford, and an ardent Catholic, was involved, as was that archetypical establishment conformist the former Lord Mayor and MP Sir Martin Bowes, reviled by John Stow for his prominent role in the dismantling and sale of pre-reformation monuments, and a pillar of the Edwardine Chantry Commission for

London, yet whose personal religious views were conservative, and who 'of his benevolence and good wille, paid for the gilding and painting of the rood, Mary and John' in his parish church in 1557.[50] But the pace in Edward's reign had been set by reformation activists like the printer and chronicler Richard Grafton, while Bishop Ridley and other Protestant clergy had urged the use of former Church property for poor relief and especially the establishment of hospitals which would be 'truly religious houses'. Christ's Hospital had been established as a reception centre for foundling children in the premises of the former Greyfriars. The Franciscans, led by William Peto, were to make determined but unsuccessful efforts to recover their house, if necessary at the cost of dissolving the hospital, early in Mary's reign. The imposition of moral discipline on the erring poor confined in Bridewell, moreover, cut across the jurisdiction of Bonner's restored Church courts. So to many people the future of the Edwardine social initiatives in London looked uncertain, and the city hospitals were in danger of becoming confessional footballs, in a quarrel in which Protestants occupied the high moral ground with an apparent monopoly on charity. As a character in a dialogue on the hospital question by Grafton's servant John Howes asked, 'Could not the Pope's clergy and Bridewell be friends?'[51]

Pole now intervened directly in this highly charged debate, to demonstrate that Protestants had no monopoly on concern for the poor. Indeed, the citizens must make use of their ill-gotten Church wealth to 'enlarge your hande more to the helpe of the poore'. Christ would judge men not by empty professions, but by what they did for the needy. Almsgiving went along with prayer and penance as 'special means to injoie the goodnes of God'. But in this, England compared wretchedly with Catholic Italy, 'where is more almes gyven to monasteryes and poore folkes in one monthe, than yn this realme in a hole yeare'. There were fewer than ten hospitals and religious houses to relieve the poor in London. As Pole could personally testify, there were, by contrast, hundreds in Milan, Bologna and Rome. The reason for this was plain: in Catholicism, unlike Protestantism, charity as well as faith was required for salvation. In a characteristically careful formulation, avoiding any crude notion of justification by works, Pole insisted that 'the doctryne of the chyrche ys the doctryne of the mercye and almes of God. Whyche mercye is receyved more wyth comforte: but of them that use mercye, and gyve almes to other, that ys the veraye waye to enjoye all the grace and benefyts of God graunted to the chyrche.' They, who had specially offended in stealing from the Church, must above all bring forth this fruit of repentance, charity to the poor.[52]

Having thus neatly stolen the reformers' clothes on the question of poor relief, Pole pressed home his argument. Robbing the poor was just part of the sin of the reformation in stripping the Church of her property. They had also stripped their priests, and, in the process, the Christ whom the clergy represented. In this the English 'have gone further than any schismaticall natyon hath done, that ever I redde of', 'dyshonouringe [God's] prystes, wythdrawinge from them that shoulde be theyr lyvinge, by the appoyntment of God'. Contempt of priests was excused by complaints of the unedifying lives of the clergy, but they should be honoured for what they taught, whatever their lives, and the people should pray for good clergy, especially that they might be spared the priests they deserved, men who instead of opposing sin and error 'wyll conforme themselves to your desyres'. The clergy were their spiritual fathers, and the mercy of God would be withheld from any who rejected their authority. That was why the special mark of a heretic was hatred of priests, 'that are onlye the stay and lett, that theyr pernycyouse attempts take none effect'.[53]

The mention of the curse of a docile clergy who would not challenge the errors and vices of their people introduces a section of the sermon in which Pole considered the fruits of schism, and the way in which the rejection of papal authority had led inexorably to the undermining of morality and godly order, as well as the utter rejection of the sacraments. Heresy was a calamity in society, for 'there ys no kynd of men so pernycyouse to the commonwelthe ... no theves, no murtherers, no advouterers, nor no kynd of treason to be compared to theyrs', since true religion was the foundation of the commonwealth, and heresy overthrew that foundation.[54] Pole was speaking to judges and city worthies, and could take it for granted that most of them were likely enough to be opposed to religious radicalism. Equally clearly, he was aware that most of those sitting before him had acquiesced in and in many cases directly benefited from the reformation, and that even the many alienated by the drastic Protestantism of Edward's reign might be more ambivalent about the demerits of the Henrician schism. And so he pressed on them the necessity of communion with Rome, and the inexorable momentum of the reformation towards extremes once that communion had been broken. To the worst excesses of the reform, when the priesthood, the laws of the Church and the sacrament 'were cast awaye, and troden underfoote', he told them, 'you cam not sodenlye', for at first 'you toke nothynge from the chyrche, but the preemynence and prerogative of the supreme hed, whiche you toke from the highest pryste, and gave yt to the Kynge: all the sacraments standynge and remaynynge wyth streight lawes, that they sholde not be violated, but reverentlye kept'. But all in vain: though the sacraments were maintained under Henry despite his 'straunge tytle', yet the realm received no grace from them, being in schism. They had been like a withered branch, cut off from the vine, or like the Philistines when they stole the ark of the covenant from the Israelites, receiving only cursing and disease from the presence of God among them. And the English had sinned more deeply than the Philistines. In the ark of the covenant had been the rod of Aaron, symbolising priestly authority, and the miraculous manna, symbolising the Mass. These the Philistines had left unharmed, but under Edward England had rejected both.[55]

Pole here was deploying standard arguments, familiar from many of the official publications of the Marian restoration.[56] He now mounted a critique of the Henrician schism and its consequences linked directly to the publication of the folio edition of the English *Workes* of Thomas More earlier that year.[57] More and Fisher had long been iconic figures for Pole: their executions had precipitated him into open opposition to Henry and his reformation, and they loom large in his first major publication, the treatise *Pro Ecclesiasticae Unitatis defensione*, addressed to Henry VIII in 1536.[58] In the sermon, the theme first explored by Pole in *De Unitate*, that More and Fisher were miraculous witnesses and sacrificial victims raised up for the salvation of England as it stood poised on the edge of schism, is elaborated and focused: they are invoked specifically as witness not merely to England, but to London in particular. England, Pole declared, had been greatly blessed from her first reception of the Gospel, and in

Catholic times had brought forth 'nobyl fruytes to the honore of him that planted you', till at last, by their own fault, their branch had been cut off and would have withered entirely, if the schism had not been ended. 'What countrye hathe ever had the lyke grace?'[59] And London had special cause for gratitude, not merely in being the first part of the realm to be reconciled, but for 'having more dyligent labour bestowede upon you, to make you a grounde to bryng furthe all fruyte of sanctitie and justice, wyth more frequent rayne of preachynge and teachinge than all the realme besyde'. Instead of bearing good fruit, however, it seemed that London had produced nothing but thorns. In a gruesome and daring joke, Pole allowed that this might be an optical illusion. It is true that 'a greater multytude of thes brambles and bryars were cast in the fyre hear among you, than yn any place besyde', but they might have grown elsewhere, since London was the epicentre of the Marian campaign against heresy. So, many of those burned there for heresy were not native Londoners, which 'maye gyve occasyon that you have the worse name wythoute your deserte'.[60]

Be that as it might, God had raised up for Londoners marvellous witnesses, whose miraculous example should have preserved them 'when the realme was fawlinge from the unytie of the churche'. Of these witnesses the greatest was Thomas More, 'a cytesyn of yours', assaulted on all sides on this very question of the unity of Christendom, and like other lay people bound by bonds of family affections and obligation, concern for which might have plucked him from the unity of the Church. Pole illustrated his account of More with a vivid anecdote he had received from the rich Lucca/London merchant Antonio Bonvisi, one of More's oldest and closest friends, godfather to his son John and purchaser of his house in Bishopsgate. Bonvisi had been a key member of the More circle and of Catholic resistance to the reformation after More's death, and had been banished from England as a consequence. He had sheltered Pole's future archdeacon and More's biographer, Nicholas Harpsfield, together with members of the More family, in his house in Louvain, and before Pole's arrival in England Bonvisi had acted for him as a go-between with Mary.[61] A translation of an ardently affectionate letter to Bonvisi from More formed the penultimate item in the 1557 folio edition of More's English *Workes*,[62] and Pole clearly expected his audience to recognise him, introducing him as a familiar city figure 'whom I thinke you all knowe'.[63] He tells how when Bonvisi at the outset of the Henrician reformation had asked More's opinion about papal primacy, More had answered at first that he thought it a matter of secondary importance, 'rather inventyd of men for a polytical ordre, and for the more quyetnes of the ecclesiasticall bodye, than by the verye ordynance of Cryste'. Regretting this hasty judgement, however, he told Bonvisi that he would study more and deliver a considered opinion. In due course he returned to the subject, declaring, 'Alas! Mr Bonvyse, whither was I fawlinge, when I made you that answer of the prymacye of the chyrche? I assure you, that opinione alone was ynough to make me fawle from the rest, for that holdyth up all'.[64]

Alongside More, an example to the laity of constancy to the Pope and hence to the unity of the Church, Pole set as an example to the clergy John Fisher, whom Henry VIII himself had recognised as the most learned clerk in Christendome. The pairing was of course another Marian convention, given its most spectacular expression at the execution of Cranmer by Pole's chancellor, Henry Cole, who declared that as the death of Northumberland would atone for More's death, so those of the heretical bishops Ferrar, Cranmer, Ridley and Latimer would atone for Fisher's.[65] Pole now put a personal mark on this conventional pairing, recalling how, on his first return from study in Italy, Henry had quizzed him about the learned men he had met, boasting that there was none to compare with Fisher: yet when his conscience was challenged by Fisher, he had him beheaded. This beheading was symbolic, Pole declared, a sign of the cutting off of the realm from the true head of the Church, the Pope. London had received further witnesses in the deaths of the martyred priests and religious 'oute of those religiouse howses that were most reformed' – from the London Charterhouse, from Syon, from the Observant Franciscans. 'And why was all this, but for your staye? And but for your example?' And here Pole picked up the ruling metaphor of the sermon again: despite such examples, they had fallen, and tasted the bitterness of the fruit 'receyved by the swervynge from the unytie of the churche. Whiche at the fyrste semed verey sweete, as dyd the apple to our fyrst mother, eaten agaynst the commandement.'[66]

All that had happened when royal authority was pressing men into schism. Yet even now, when the authority of the King and Queen was on the side of Catholicism, and 'the favour of heaven and earth agree together', still the city harboured Protestants. So Pole turned to examine London's continuing infidelity. As his letter to Carranza would make clear, he was under no illusions about the resistance of many in the city to the restoration of Catholicism. Early in his legation he had been jeered as he passed through Cheapside with the Queen, blessing the people, and he was well aware of the continuing support for arrested heretics in the city.[67] Who then was to blame, 'whome shall I fyrst accuse?'

Pole's first attempt at an answer to his own question was the suggestion that the reformation was a youth movement.[68] He considered first as 'one great cause' the attractions Protestantism exercised over the London apprentices and other 'yowthe brought up yn a contrarye trade', ignorant of the true faith and prejudiced against it by the polemic of the Protestants, 'and herein I have great compassyon of the youthe'. But the real blame, he thought, lay with those who had charge of the young, and who tolerated such youthful rebellion, and failed 'to bringe the youthe to followe the same [religion], that your fathers afore have followed'. Disorder and error would never cease 'untyll the fathers and masters cease to suffer any alteracyon yn his sonne or servant touching religion'. And there is now nothing to prevent every man in the city enforcing true religion in his own house, 'And so I truste they do'. Yet Pole knew, he told them, that whenever heretics were carried through the city to execution, each one was comforted and encouraged to die 'in his perverse opinions', and they were much cherished in prison. The city's alibi was that it was the young who were responsible for all this, and that more time was needed to reform them. Pole was unimpressed: three years had passed since the reconciliation, 'this beinge a thinge not to be suffered one houre'.[69]

But for Pole the key to London's sympathy for the heretics lay in the debate about real and pretended martyrdom. More's English writings were the main quarry for the Marian Church's arguments against the martyr status of condemned heretics, the 'pseudo-martyr' debate. As we have seen, Pole's sermon was certainly shaped by the recent publication of those works, and there are striking parallels between his presentation of More and Fisher and that of his arch-deacon, Nicholas Harpsfield's life of More, written in the same year to accompany the English *Workes*.[70] It was entirely natural therefore that Pole should raise the 'pseudo-martyr' issue.[71] But given the numbers of Protestants burned for heresy in the city, he could hardly have avoided it, and there had been a much publicised burning of three city heretics at Smithfield, only a fortnight before. One of those burned then, Richard Gibson, was a very prominent Londoner, whose grandfather had been Lord Mayor, and whose father was bailiff of Southwark.[72] Even so conservative a London commentator as Henry Machyn displayed an unusual interest in the circumstances of Gibson's burning, almost certainly because of his distinguished city connections, and sympathy for such a sufferer was bound to be widespread.[73] Pole therefore tackled this issue head-on. He told the listening aldermen that the cause of Protestantism in London was being nourished by the citizens' mistaken admiration for the cour-age and constancy of the heretics in death, courage which seemed to confirm the truth of their teaching, especially in the eyes of those who knew no better. 'Thys, men say, ys a greate stoppe, and a great blocke yn theyr way that have none other lernyng than theyrs, to let them to come to the ancyent doctryne, as I thynke yt be indeed.' But this was a terrible error: what heretics displayed was not holy courage in defence of the truth, but a 'develysche pertynacye'. Stubbornness in death for one's own opinion was not martyrdom. True martyrs like More and Fisher had died for the ancient faith, inherited from their fathers, not for some concocted gospel, pieced together from books and citations of the ancient fathers 'that were not harde of in our fathers dayes'. A faithful man is known, 'not by the faythe he hath found of himselfe, or taken of the fathers so fur off, not allegyng his next father, but by the fayth of his next father, contynuyng the same untyll he come to his fyrst father'. Nor was his cause vindicated by an apparent lack of fear at his death, for rash courage might be a sign of error rather than truth. Christ at his death, the paradigm of all martyrdom, had not displayed the arro-gant defiance which characterised the heretics burned in London, but had showed more 'heavynes and doloure at his dying houre' than the thieves with whom he was crucified. It was the wicked thief on Calvary who showed no fear, 'and so doe these heretykes at their deathe lyke the blasphemer, whatsoever theyr wordes be yn honour of Chryste'.[74]

Pole drew all this together in the final section of his sermon, in which he considered how the true Christian may see and follow Christ, as Andrew did in Galilee, to which his answer is, by humble openness to the grace of God in the Church, and by participation in the sacraments and in the life of charity. That day had been a day of ceremonial, and accordingly he focused in this final section on ceremonies, as a concrete expression of the state of mind needed for salvation. The good Christian follows the commandments of Christ, and of Christ's spouse, the Church. For a great while the Church's commandments have been despised, especially her ceremonies, which are always the first target of the heretics. But 'of the observation of ceremonyes, begynneth the verye educatyon of the chylderne of God': it is the 'pedagogium in Christum' of which Paul speaks. Heretics despise such things, and their dismissal of them seemed plausible: 'yt semed nothing here amongst you to take awaye holy water, holy breade, candells, ashes, and palme'. But from little things great consequences flow, and 'what yt came to, you sawe, and all felt yt' – the breakdown of all order, the triumph of heresy and the loss of the sacraments. Obedience in the small things commanded by the Church is the sign of submission to the will of God. 'What lesse thinge woulde there be commanded, than to forbeare the eating of an apple', but Eve's apple had been a poisoned fruit which killed the whole of humanity.

Pole made it crystal clear that he was talking here about inner dispositions, not external ceremony. Without the Spirit of God, neither ceremonies 'whiche the heretykes doe rejecte, nor yet the Scripture whereunto they so cleve' are of any use. It is not that ceremonies bring salvation, but that contempt of ceremonies brings damnation. The 'thinge that gyveth us the veraye light, ys none of them both; but they are most apt to receive light, that are the more obedyent'. So obedience in ceremonies is the mark of the 'parvuli', the little ones to whom (unlike the assertive youth of reformation London) belongs the kingdom.

Many think there is 'no better nor spedyer waye ... for to come to the knowledge of God and his lawe, then by reading of books, wherein they be sore deceyved', though 'so yt be done in its place, and with right order and circumstance, [reading] helpeth muche'. But the light of God is not got by reading: where have the prophets enjoined on anyone the reading of scripture? It is the works of mercy, joined with fasting, prayer and true repentance, expressed in the sacrament of penance, 'that makyth all in this waye to come to light'. At Judgement Day it will be by the measure of our acts of mercy that we will be weighed. What a terror to this realm this should be, he warned them, where there is so little charity, so little mercy, so little repentance, where they not only do no mercy but 'have taken away the fruyte of the almes that was gyven by other'. Never had a country been shown such mercy, restored from schism, but in no other country has there been such excess, 'bothe on your bodies and yn your houses' and yet 'the churches remaynynge bare, robbyd and spoyled'.[75]

If they wanted quietness of mind, therefore, and sought the high-way to paradise, they must 'utterly leave your own wyll'. They must abandon the vain and presumptuous itch for 'more knowledge than God hath lymyted unto us' which is the mark of the reformation, the sin which misled Eve and brought poisoned fruit into the world. And they must forsake the carnal pleasure of the body, resting instead in the joy of the heavenly manna, the body of Christ in the Mass, the food which quietens all our cravings of body and spirit. Then they will have fulfilled the prophetic injunction to keep a true holy day, and can return to their houses rejoicing.[76]

In some ways Pole's St Andrew's Day sermon is conventional enough. Most of his theological and polemical arguments can be paralleled from his own writings or in those of other apologists for the Marian Church. What is striking about it, however, is Pole's tough and specific analysis of the problems confronting the Church in London, his stark confrontation of lay resistance to the burn-ings, his understanding of the role of youth culture in that resistance and the subtlety, clarity and force of the Catholic account of salva-tion he opposes to the Protestant gospel. There is nothing vague or generalised about this preaching, and there is considerable rhetorical resourcefulness in the way in which he rings the changes on the unifying theme of good and bad 'fruits'. Pole displayed here, too, an acute sense of his audience and their interests: this is emphatically a London sermon. Church property, poor relief in the city, turbulent apprentices and the campaign against heresy were all topical in 1557:

and Pole confronted them all. In this he was strikingly and unexpect-
edly in tune with another very different London polemicist. Pole is
not normally thought of as a populist writer or preacher, but most
of these issues had been addressed by the artisan polemicist Myles
Hogarde a year before, in his savagely effective *The Displayinge of
the Protestantes*, and there are striking similarities between Hogarde's
and Pole's handling, especially on the pseudo-martyr issue.[77] In one
respect at least, however, Pole went beyond Hogarde. Pole understood perfectly well that Papal Supremacy was a difficult doctrine
to sell after a generation of schism, and he mobilised the history of
More, Fisher and the other London martyrs skilfully to highlight
and support it. Hogarde, too, had recalled the witness of the English
martyrs of Henry's reign, but in his brief recital More was not
singled out for special attention. The much more prominent place
given to More in Pole's sermon, and the deployment of theological
arguments first aired in More's polemical writings against heresy, and
of the extended anecdote credited to Bonvisi, both given new topicality by More's recently published English *Workes*, indicates Pole's
own long-standing personal regard for More, but also, in its link to
the publication of the English *Workes*, a cohesion and direction in
the developing Marian restoration that has yet to be fully explored.[78]

Finally, Pole's stern discussion of the continuing hold of
Protestantism in London, and his subtle and balanced dissection of
the problematic place of knowledge and reading in faith, and of the
corresponding need for the disposition of a humble learner, underlay his qualified endorsement of the value of preaching in the city, an
exaggerated and negative estimate of which has exercised and misled
readers (or, rather, *non*-readers) of the letter to Carranza. Debate will
no doubt continue about the merits or otherwise of Pole's strategy
for the restoration of Catholicism in Marian England. But the St
Andrew's Day sermon and the letter to Carranza between them
surely establish that he was guilty neither of inattention to preaching,
nor of lack of realism about the challenges confronting the Marian
Church. And, as we shall see in subsequent chapters, Pole's distinctive
theological emphases, above all his insistence on the witness of More
and Fisher and the centrality of loyalty to the papacy as the guaran-
tor of the unity of the Church, would help determine the shape of
Elizabethan Catholicism.

Notes

1 Royall Tyler (ed.), *Calendar of Letters, Despatches and State papers relating to the negotiations between England and Spain*, vol. xiii (London, HMSO 1954), pp, 366, 370.
2 Revelation 3.15–16.
3 Craig Harline and Eddy Put, *A Bishop's Tale: Matthew Hovius among his flock in Seventeenth Century Flanders* (New Haven and London, 2000), pp. 178–94.
4 Thomas M. McCoog, 'Ignatius Loyola and Reginald Pole: a Reconsideration', *Journal of Ecclesiastical History*, 17 (1996), pp. 257–73; Thomas Mayer, 'A test of wills: Pole, Loyola and the Jesuits in England' in T. M. McCoog (ed.), *The Reckoned Expense: Edmund Campion and the early English Jesuits* (Woodbridge, 1996), pp. 21–8; John Edwards, *Archbishop Pole* (Farnham, 2014), pp. 196–201; Edwards' biography, while in many ways indebted to Thomas Mayer's work on Pole, is now the best introduction to Pole's career. For Pole's English legation, see also Eamon Duffy, *Fires of Faith: Catholic England under Mary Tudor* (New Haven and London, 2009), pp. 29–56.
5 Rex H. Pogson, 'Reginald Pole and the Priorities of Government in Mary Tudor's Church', *Historical Journal*, vol. 18 (1975), pp. 3–20, quotations at pp. 19, 18, 13, 16, in that order.
6 David Loades, *The Reign of Mary Tudor* (2nd edn, London, 1991), pp. 272, 276, 293.
7 Christopher Haigh, *English Reformations* (Oxford, 1993), p. 224.
8 Diarmaid MacCulloch, *The Later Reformation in England, 1547–1603* (2nd edn, London, 2001), p. 20.
9 McCoog, 'Loyola and Pole', pp. 269–70.
10 An exception was the late Thomas F. Mayer's, *Reginald Pole, Prince and Prophet* (Cambridge, 2000).
11 *Epistolarum Reginaldi Poli* (ed. Angelo Maria Quirini, Brescia, 1744–57), vol. v, pp. 69–76.
12 N. P. Tanner (ed.), *Decrees of the Ecumenical Councils* (London and Washington, DC, 1990), vol. 2, pp. 681–3; Gerald Bray (ed.), *The Anglican Canons 1529–1947* (Church of England Record Society, vol. 6, 1998), pp. 94–101 (Bray's edition is now the most convenient text of the decrees of Pole's Legatine Synod, providing a parallel Latin/English text).
13 See David Loades, 'The Marian Episcopate' in E. Duffy and D. M. Loades (eds), *The Church of Mary Tudor* (Aldershot, 2006), pp. 33–56.
14 Pogson misread 'obesse' as a transitive verb, with 'verbum' as its object, rather than as intransitive, in an accusative and infinitive construction in which 'verbum' is in fact the subject: Thus the sentence 'sed nisi vel ante sit, vel simul constituta Ecclesiastica disciplina, dico potius obesse verbum, quam prodesse,' means literally 'I say that the word may hinder more than help, unless it is proceeded or accompanied by the establishment of church discipline'. Pogson, however, translated this as 'I think that it is better to check the preaching of the Word than to proclaim it, unless the discipline of the Church has been fully restored', wrecking the careful balance of what Pole has to say about the timing of the restoration of discipline. Pogson also misunderstood Pole's complaint that Londoners are unresponsive to preaching and only go to church when they are made to do so, 'nisi terrore legum impellerenter, nec sacris ac divinis officiis interessent', as a general *prescription* for reconversion – that they *should* be 'compelled to realise the truth by a terror of the law'. Once again, Pole's thought has been coarsened and distorted by a misreading of what he actually wrote.
15 *Epistolarum Reginaldi Poli*, v, pp. 72–3. I am indebted to the superior Latinity of my colleague Professor Richard Rex for help with Pole's sometimes elusive Latin prose.
16 Pole was evidently referring to Watson's collection of sermons on the sacraments, one of the most effective publications of the Marian restoration: *Holsome and Catholyke doctryne concerning the seven Sacramentes of Chrystes Church, expedient to be knoen to all men, set forth in maner of short e Sermons to bee made to the people* . . . (London, 1558).
17 Pole is quite explicit about the writer in question's role as royal secretary, so Boxall is certainly the person referred to in the printed text of Pole's letter as 'Brexallus', though so far as I am aware Boxall published no homilitic material under his own name.
18 For Carranza's Catechism, see John Edwards, 'Spanish Religious influence in Marian England' in Duffy and Loades, *Church of Mary Tudor*, pp. 201–24.

19   *Epistolarum Reginaldi Pole*, v, pp. 74–5.

20   It was published *in extenso* in J. Ignacio Tellechea Idigoras, *Fray Bartolome Carranza y el Cardenal Pole: Un navarro en la retauracion catolica de Inglaterra (1554–1558)* (Pamplona, 1977), pp. 191–6.

21   Mayer, *Prince and Prophet*, p. 250.

22   *Epistolarum Reginaldi Poli*, v, p. 71.

23   For example, Bray, *Anglican Canons*, p. 104, Synodal decree 4, on the preparation of Homilies by 'piis et doctiis viris', and the same formula in *Epistolarum*, v, p. 74.

24   Rex Pogson, 'The Legacy of the Schism' in J. Loach and R. Tittler (eds), *The Mid-Tudor Polity c 1540–1560* (London, 1980), p. 122.

25   Thomas Mayer, *A Reluctant Author: Cardinal Pole and his Manuscripts, Transaction of the American Philosophical Society*, vol. 89, part 4 (1999), pp. 74–5.

26   Bray, *Canons*, pp. 75–7; John Harpsfield, *A Notable and learned Sermon made upon Saint Andrewes daye last past 1556 in the cathedral churche of St Paule in London . . . set forth by the bishop of London* (London, 1556).

27   David Cressy, *Bonfires and Bells: National Memory and the Protestant Calendar in Elizabethan and Stuart England* (London, 1989).

28   Bray, *Anglican Canons*, pp. 101–5.

29   John Edward's brief treatment of Pole's preaching acknowledges the existence of Pole's manuscript sermons, but discusses only the single example printed by John Strype more than three centuries ago, *Archbishop Pole*, pp. 215–19.

30   Mayer, *Prince and Prophet*, p. 250.

31   They are catalogued by Mayer, *Reluctant Author,* pp. 68–74.

32   J. W. Blench, *Preaching in England in the late Fifteenth and Sixteenth Centuries*, (Oxford, 1964), pp. 164–5.

33   Gospel of St John, ch. 1, verses 35–42.

34   Vatican Lat. 5968, fols 277–303, with some possible additional material fols 227r–47 v, 248r–56v.

35   Vatican Lat. 5968, fol. 247r.

36   Ibid., fols 379r–399r.

37   Duffy, *Fires of Faith*, pp. 52–6.

38   Vatican Lat. Fol. 380r.

39   Duffy, *Fires of Faith*, pp. 53–4.

40   Vatican Lat. 5968, fol. 420r: brief summary of the subsequent sermons in Duffy, *Fires of Faith*, pp. 54–6.

41   Vatican Lat. 5968, fol. 437r.

42   Vatican Lat. 5968, fols 444 r & v.

43   Vatican Lat. 5968, fols 446r–82v, easily the most theologically distinctive of these homilies.

44   The manuscript, once among the Foxe manuscripts, appears to be lost, and the sermon survives only in a long but still incomplete edition by John Strype, *Ecclesiastical Memorials Relating Chiefly to Religion and its Reformation under the Reigns of King Henry VIII, King Edward VI and Queen Mary* (Oxford, 1816), vol. III, part 2, pp. 482–510; Mayer, *Reluctant Author*, pp. 70, 72. Mayer's discussion of the likely occasion of this sermon, however, is confused – Strype does not pronounce the sermon 'lost', as Mayer claims, merely noting that some parts are 'wanting' (Strype, *Memorials*, vol. III, part 2, pp. 21, 482) and Henry Machyn does not link Pole's sermon to Sir Thomas Tresham's installation as Prior of the order of St John's, though both took place at Whitehall on the same day, and Pole was present for the installation ceremony; this took place in the course of a Mass and procession at Westminster Abbey in the morning at which Abbot Feckenham presided, Pole's sermon was preached in the Chapel Royal in the afternoon – cf. John Gough Nichols, *The Diary of Henry Machyn* (Camden Society, 1848), p. 159. There can be no doubt that Strype's text was the sermon preached by Pole in the afternoon of 30 November 1557; the deliberate and rather artificial reference to St Andrew is inexplicable otherwise (Strype, *Memorials*, vol. III, part 2, p. 501) and together with Pole's remark that 'three years and mo' had passed since the reconciliation (p. 498) pinpoints the date: this is a St Andrew's Day sermon, it cannot have been preached earlier than 30 November 1557, and Pole was dead by 30 November 1558. There is not the slightest reason to think, as Mayer

suggests, that the Cardinal might have preached twice on the same day, and, given the length of the surviving sermon, the suggestion is unlikely in the extreme. As will emerge from the discussion below, moreover, the target audience of the sermon fits Machyn's account of those present.

45 It has been surprisingly neglected: it was summarised at length by Philip Hughes, who recognised that it was 'the nearest thing we possess to a public review of the quality of the Marian restoration', and it has been quarried by many writers about the Marian restoration and about Pole, but Hughes' insight was not developed by him and has been pursued by nobody else: cf. Philip Hughes, *The Reformation in England*, vol. 2 (London, 1953), pp. 246–53. For another recent (and rather different) discussion of the Carranza letter and St Andrew's Day sermon, Dermot Fenlon, 'Pole, Carranza and the Pulpit' in John Edwards and Ronald Truman (eds), *Reforming Catholicism in the England of Mary Tudor: The Achievement of Friar Bartholome Carranza* (Aldershot, 2005) pp. 81–98.

46 John Gough Nichols (ed.) *The Diary of Henry Machyn* (Camden Society, 1848), p. 159.

47 F. E. Warren (ed.), *The Sarum Missal in English* (London, 1913), part 2, pp. 246–9: Strype, op. cit., p. 501.

48 Strype, loc. cit., p. 482.

49 Ibid., p. 483.

50 Claire S. Schen, *Charity and Lay Piety in Reformation London 1500–1620* (Aldershot, 2002), pp. 31, 80. My thanks to Professor Peter Marshall for this reference, and for helpful discussion of Bowes' religious position.

51 Paul Slack, 'Social policy and the Constraints of Government 1547–1558' in Jennifer Loach and Robert Tittler (eds), *The Mid-Tudor Polity c 1540–1560* (London, 1980), esp. pp. 108–13; Susan Brigden, *London and the Reformation* (Oxford, 1989), pp. 620–23.

52 Strype, loc. cit., p. 484.

53 Ibid., p. 486.

54 Ibid., p. 487.

55 Ibid., pp. 488–9.

56 For a similar account of the disastrous consequences of the breach with Rome, for example, see Henry Pendleton's homily on the authority of the Church in *Homilies sette forth by the right reverend father in God, Edmunde Byshop of London* (London, 1555), RSTC 3285.7, fols 41v–42r.

57 *The Workes of Sir Thomas More Knyght, sometyme Lorde Chancellour of England, wrytten by him in the Englysh tonge*, edited by William Rastell (London, 1557).

58 Discussed in Mayer, *Prince and Prophet*, pp. 13–61: occasionally problematic English translation by J. G. Dwyer, *Pole's Defense of the Unity of the Church* (Westminster, Md., 1965); there is also an excellent annotated French translation by Noelle-Marie Egretier, *Reginald Pole, Défense de l'Unité de l'Eglise* (Paris, 1967).

59 Strype, loc. cit., p 489.

60 Ibid., p. 490.

61 Archivio Segreto Vaticano Bolognetti 94, fols 29r–v, 63v–70r, 73v–77r; references from the late Thomas Meyer via Dr Thomas Freeman, to whom many thanks.

62 *Workes of Sir Thomas Moore*, pp. 1455–7.

63 Strype, loc. cit., p. 491.

64 Ibid., p. 493.

65 Nicholas Harpsfield, *Bishop Cranmer's Recantacyons* (London, 1877–84), pp 96–7; my thanks to Tom Freeman for reminding me of this reference.

66 Strype, loc. cit., p. 494.

67 John Gough Nichols (ed.), *Narratives of the Days of Reformation* (Camden Society, 1859), pp. 209–10 (Autobiography of Thomas Mountayne).

68 On which topic see Susan Brigden, 'Youth and the English Reformation', *Past and Present*, no. 95 (May 1982), pp 37–67.

69 Strype, loc. cit., p. 498.

70 E. Vaughan Hitchcock (ed.), *The Life and Death of Sir Thomas Moore . . . written in the tyme of Queene Marie by Nicholas Harpsfield* (Early English Text Society, 1932), pp. 209–13.

71 Anne Dillon, *The Construction of Martyrdom in the English Catholic Community 1535–1603* (Cambridge, 2002), pp. 18–71; Brad Gregory, *Salvation at Stake: Christian Martyrdom in Early Modern Europe* (Cambridge, Mass., 1999), pp. 315–41.

72 *Diary of Henry Machyn*, pp. 157–8.

73 Machyn's account makes it clear that the execution of Gibson was postponed for a day as the result of an intervention by Abbot Feckenham, perhaps to buy time to persuade Gibson to recant; it is likely that the regime was anxious about the fallout from the execution of a member of a leading city family. I am indebted to Dr Tom Freeman for comment on this point.

74 Strype, *loc. cit.*, pp. 499–501.

75 Ibid., pp. 506–8.

76 Ibid., pp 508–9.

77 Myles Hogarde, *The displaying of the Protestantes*, 2dn edn (London,) 1556, fols 44–51 (campaign against heresy and pseudo-martyrs), 93v–95v (turbulent apprentices and the protestant young), 110–112v (monasteries, church property and charity to the poor): for Hogarde's importance, Duffy, *Fires of Faith*, pp. 174–7.

78 It is often claimed that the publication of More's English *Workes* was exclusively a More/Roper family venture entirely independent of direct involvement by Pole: I do not think this view can be sustained in view of Pole's handling of More here: cf. Duffy, *Fires of Faith*, pp. 179–87.

5

Founding Father: William, Cardinal Allen

Any attempt to understand the nature and trajectory of the English Catholic community in the Elizabethan age has to come to terms with the figure of William Allen. A product of Edwardian Oxford and a participant there in the project to restore the nation to Catholicism under the first Tudor Queen regnant, Allen went on to mastermind the reconstruction of the secular priesthood for a mission to Elizabeth's England. He devoted the rest of his life to radicalising what he saw as a broad but dangerously unfocused Catholic survivalism into something more militant and ideologically committed. He has been dismissed as a 'mild, scholarly rather dull man':[1] if so, he was transformed by the urgency of his circumstances into something and someone else, the inspiration, patron and energiser of men of more remarkable talents, like Gregory Martin and Edmund Campion. He is also a figure of some moral ambiguity, the apostle of a more ardent Catholicism who was also a political plotter, whose entanglements in the corridors of power, and advocacy of the overthrow of the Protestant monarch, would help cement into place English Protestant equation of popery with tyranny and treachery.

In May 1582 the papal nuncio in Paris wrote to Cardinal Galli, Pope Gregory XIII's Secretary of State, to update him on yet another scheme to reconvert England and Scotland to the Catholic faith. The plan had been concocted by the Spanish Ambassador in London, Don Bernardina de Mendoza, in consultation with Esme Stuart Duke of Lennox, the French Duke de Guise, and the Jesuits William Creighton and Robert Persons. It involved landing an invasion force of 8,000

Spanish and Italian soldiers in Scotland. Expanded to 20,000 by an expected rush of devout local recruits, the army would march south into England, overthrow Elizabeth, liberate Mary Queen of Scots, and set her on the throne of both kingdoms. This half-baked scheme, which was welcomed by the Pope as a glorious new crusade, needed a religious figurehead who could command the loyalty of all English Catholics and serve as a rallying point for soldiers, gentry and the devout Catholic faithful. Everyone agreed that there was only one possible choice. The President of the English College at Rheims, William Allen, should be appointed to the key religious and secular post in the north of England, the bishopric of Durham. Allen, the nuncio claimed, was a man whose authority and reputation 'stand so high with the whole nation that his mere presence ... will have a greater effect with the English than several thousand soldiers ... all the banished gentlemen bear him such reverence that at a word of his they would do anything'.[2]

Five years earlier Mary Queen of Scots herself had written to Allen, expressing her conviction that 'the good opinion every one of them hath of yow' was the best hope of bringing 'reunion and reconcilement' of the faction-ridden English Catholics, and she expressed her confidence in him by giving him *carte blanche* to use her name in his activities.[3] In August 1587 Sixtus V recognised Allen's role in the preservation of English Catholicism by appointing him 'Cardinal of England', and he took formal direction of Roman affairs relating to England from then until his death in October 1594.

The man courted and honoured in this way by princes, popes, politicians and plotters was a schoolmaster and pamphleteer who in another age might well have enjoyed an uneventful career in a minor academic post, or ended his days in a cathedral prebend or a North Country rectory. Instead he found himself manoeuvred by circumstance and his own strong convictions to the centre of the European stage. In the pantheon of English Catholic heroes he features as a saintly and eirenic patriarch, the founder of Douay College, and, later, of the English College in Rome, the originator not only of the Seminaries, but of the whole notion of the Elizabethan mission, and hence the man who, more than anyone else, was one of the 'new clerks' who spearheaded the attempt to turn the English Catholic community from ignoble and demoralised external conformity in their parish churches, to principled religious resistance.

Allen wrote some of the best prose of the Elizabethan age, defending the integrity of his persecuted community, and he was the moving spirit behind the Rheims-Douay version of the Bible. In the internal affairs of the Catholic community he was a man of peace, whom Catholics of all parties and persuasions respected and obeyed, and who, so long as he lived, was able to hold together even the rival bodies of Jesuits and secular clergy. Above all, from 1574 Allen sent a stream of young priests from his colleges to England, in many cases to prison, torture and execution. The Elizabethan regime insisted that these men died for treason. Allen eloquently maintained that they died purely for their religion. Two generations of saints, martyrs and confessors looked to him as their spiritual inspiration, their protector, their father.

This picture of Allen is perfectly accurate, as far as it goes, but it leaves a great deal out, for Allen was also a political figure of some ambivalence. From 1572 at the latest he was actively involved in a series of plots for the deposition of Queen Elizabeth, and the forcible reconversion of England. In 1581 and in 1584 he published two skilled and moving defences of the Catholic mission, insisting on its non-political nature. 'No man can charge us', he insisted, 'of any attempt against the realm or the prince's person', and he absolutely repudiated any 'mislike' of Elizabeth and her ministers 'whose persons, wisdoms, moderation and prudence in Government, and manifold graces, we do honour with al our hart in al things: excepting matters incident to Religion'.[4] But for Allen that phrase 'matters incident to Religion' was a very wide rubric, and, to put it mildly, he was being economical with the truth in affirming his loyalty and respect to Elizabeth and her ministers. For, by any standard recognised in Elizabethan England, Allen was a traitor. Even as he wrote his protestations of innocence he was up to his neck in political schemes for the deposition of Elizabeth. Sixtus V created him Cardinal of England, bad-temperedly and with some reluctance, under immense pressure from Philip II of Spain and his Ambassador in Rome, Count Olivares, and Allen's appointment was universally and correctly understood as an integral part of the 'Enterprise of England', an unmistakable signal of the imminence of the Armada. Inevitably, he was intended to be Cardinal Legate and Archbishop of Canterbury when Spanish forces invaded England and reimposed

Catholicism. It was Allen who was chosen to summon Englishmen to rally to the Spanish flag in 1588 in a pamphlet attack on Elizabeth so savage and so scurrilous that generations of Catholic historians preferred to believe that someone else, probably a Jesuit, had written it. For all his transparent private integrity and the undoubted warmth and generosity of his temperament, Allen is a complex figure whose career illustrates the dilemmas, and the deviousness, forced upon good men in an age of religious violence.

Allen was born in 1532 into a gentry family at Rossall in the Fylde of Lancashire, one of the most conservative parts of England. Even at the end of the sixteenth century large tracts of the county would be barely touched by the forces of reformation. Allen never set foot in England after his second departure for the Netherlands in 1565, and Lancashire as he remembered it in the early 1560s became his vision of grassroots England. This England of the mind – and heart – was populated by robust northern gentry and farmers who did not believe a word of the new religion whose services they were forced to attend, in contrast to the effete south with its merchants, shopkeepers and courtiers whom, he knew, were much infected with heresy.[5] As late as 1584 he still cherished the illusion that the majority of the population were Catholic at heart, and that Protestantism was sustained only by 'the partiality of a few powerable persons'.[6]

Oxford had an even profounder effect on him. His early adult years were spent first as an arts student during the stormy years of the Edwardian reformation, and then as a fellow of Oriel and Principal of St Mary's Hall,[7] in the triumphant period of Catholic restoration under Queen Mary. Lancashire and Oxford marked him for life. All his essential convictions were in place by the time he was 30, and he never abandoned or altered the perspective on English affairs and the nature of the English reformation which he gained from his conservative home background and from the easy and almost total reversal of Protestantism in which he had participated in the Marian university.

Allen went up to Oxford in 1547, took his BA in 1550 and was immediately elected fellow of his college, Oriel. To a greater extent even than Cambridge, Oxford had proved highly resistant to Protestantism, and Allen's student opinions were formed in an intensely and militantly orthodox environment. The Edwardian regime tried to bulldoze the university into the new religion by a combination of sackings and promotions. From 1548 religious controversy in Oxford was fuelled by the presence there of the Italian reformer Peter Martyr as Regius Professor of Theology. Allen's tutor, Dr Morgan Phillips (nicknamed 'the sophister' for his debating skills) played a prominent role on the Catholic side in a great set-piece debate against Martyr at the end of May 1549, and Allen must have been vividly conscious of the perfervid and rancid atmosphere of religious controversy which characterised the university at this time.[8]

Despite Martyr's efforts and mounting government pressure, however, Oxford remained a largely Catholic university, and the accession of Queen Mary in 1553 triggered a heady period of Catholic restoration, into which Allen was quickly drawn. Two new Catholic colleges, Trinity and St John's, were founded, the latter with special provision for the teaching of canon law. Catholic scholars ousted under the Edwardian regime were restored, notably Richard Smyth, who took up once again the Regius Chair from which he had been ejected in favour of Peter Martyr – Smyth would preach at the burning of Latimer and Ridley in Oxford in 1555. But the Oxford counter-reformation was also fed from Europe: in particular the Queen's marriage brought to the university a series of distinguished Spanish theologians. Cardinal Pole, as Chancellor of the university, appointed the Dominican Fray Bartolomé Carranza, future Archbishop of Toledo and Primate of Spain, to conduct a formal visitation on his behalf to purge the university of heresy and disorder. Carranza's theological pedigree should warn us against easy assumptions that this Spanish influence was in any straightforward sense 'reactionary', for he was an Erasmian, and by the standards of the time a theological liberal. Despite his ultimately exalted office he was spectacularly to fall victim to the Spanish Inquisition in his own country, and spent the last 17 years of his life in gaol. A brilliant Valladolid theologian, Juan de Villa Garcia, succeeded Smyth as Regius Professor in 1556, and was instrumental in the re-establishment of a Dominican house in Oxford in the following year. Another Dominican, Peter Soto, reintroduced the formal teaching of scholastic theology: he was credited with restoring Oxford theology single-handedly to its pre-reformation state of shining orthodoxy. Allen would never share the suspicion many, even of his Catholic fellow countrymen, felt towards Spain and all things Spanish: he never budged from the perception of the Spaniards as champions of Catholic truth which he formed in these Oxford years.[9]

In 1556 he succeeded his tutor Morgan Phillips as Principal of St Mary's Hall, a post which involved some basic undergraduate teaching for the arts course but was essentially that of tutor to a couple of dozen unruly undergraduates. There, and as Proctor for two successive years, he was actively involved in the Marian purge of the university, and the religious revival which was to produce a remarkable generation of Catholic students. Among them were Gregory Martin, subsequently Allen's colleague and friend and the translator of the Rheims-Douay Bible, and Thomas Stapleton, one of the most voluminous, learned and bitter-tongued of counter-reformation theologians. Seven products of Marian Oxford would go on to become Jesuits; nearly 30 would become seminary priests.[10]

These men of Marian Oxford were a new breed, less tolerant or at any rate less easy-going than their predecessors. Edward's reign had thrown a starker light on the choices between Rome and reformation, and issues which had been fudged or genuinely obscure in Henry's reign were now visible for what they were. Men now understood better the need to take sides, and take sides they did. Thomas Harding, who had himself been an ardent disciple of Peter Martyr and a proselytising Protestant in Edward's reign, had not a good word for his former fellow Protestants – they were 'theeves', 'Ministers of Antichrist', 'loose Apostates', 'apes', driven by profane malice, rancour and spite. Thomas Stapleton would one day publish an entire lecture devoted to a discussion of whether heretics were chiefly motivated by wickedness or low cunning.[11] Allen fully shared these attitudes. He was almost certainly a witness of Cranmer's Oxford trial and burning, but if so he felt no pity for the old man's agonised indecision and successive recantations, describing him later as that 'notorious perjured and oft relapsed apostate, recanting, swearing, and forswearing at every turn'.[12] He wholeheartedly endorsed the Marian counter-reformation, including the persecution of Protestants. Why, he asked 'should any man complain or think strange for executing the laws which are as ancient, as general and as godly against heretics as they are for the punishment of traitors, murderers, or thieves?' Those who shed their blood for heresy 'can be no martyrs but damnable murderers of themselves'.[13] For the men of his generation, there could be no halting between opinions. Right was right, wrong was wrong, and the Catholics had a monopoly on right: as Allen memorably put it, 'To be shorte, Truth is the Churchis dearlinge, heresy must have her maintenaunce abrode'.[14]

Catholicism at Allen's Oxford, then, was upbeat, pugnacious, articulate. It was also highly successful. By the end of Mary's reign the Protestant coup which had taken place in Edward's reign had been totally reversed. John Jewel told Bullinger that in the university 'there are scarcely two individuals who think with us . . . That despicable friar Soto, and another Spanish monk . . . have so torn up by the roots all that Peter Martyr so prosperously planted, that they have reduced the vineyard of the Lord into a wilderness.'[15] But the extent of that triumph was to become evident only when it had in turn been overthrown. Mary's reign was too short, and the millions of words of controversy in refutation of the new religion and its advocates which gushed from Allen and his colleagues, Harding, Stapleton, Sanders, Smith, in exile in the 1560s were in a sense the late-gathered first fruits of Marian Oxford and its counter-reformation.

The accession of Queen Elizabeth put an end to Allen's Oxford career. Between 1559 and 1561 all but one of the Catholic heads of colleges were ejected, and Allen left his post as Principal of St Mary's Hall. He lingered a while in the university, which remained largely Catholic in opinion despite the government purge, but in 1561 he joined the drift of displaced Marian academics to the Catholic Low Countries.[16] During the brief Protestantising of Oxford under Edward, many Oxford men had gone to the University of Louvain to continue theological work in a Catholic environment, and Louvain once more drew the new wave of Oxford exiles. Like others, Allen seems to have led a hand-to-mouth existence there, continuing the theological studies he had begun at Oxford and supplementing his income with private tutoring. In 1562 a severe bout of illness brought him home to Lancashire to convalesce, and it was here that his view of the Elizabethan reformation took its final form.

It is now generally accepted that the Elizabethan Church took more than a decade to make serious inroads on the Catholic convictions and instincts of the population at large. What Patrick Collinson called the 'birth-pangs of Protestant England' were protracted and painful, and most of the adult population in 1559 viewed the new religious regime with something very far short of enthusiasm.[17] Yet by and large the parish clergy conformed to the new order, serving Elizabeth as they had once served Mary, and most parishioners, whatever their reservations, followed the clergy's lead and continued to attend services in their parish church. Social conformity, as much as the new twelve-penny fine for absence, brought the people to sit under the new teaching.[18]

Allen was horrified to discover these compromises among his Lancashire neighbours, where he found that not only did the majority of the Catholic laypeople attend Prayer Book services, many even communicating, but also that many priests 'said mass secretly and celebrated the heretical offices and supper in public, thus becoming partakers often on the same day (O horrible impiety) of the chalice of the Lord and the chalice of devils'. He launched a vigorous campaign to persuade them to 'abstain altogether from the communion, churches, sermons, books and all spiritual communication with heretics'. We perhaps catch an echo of the overconfidence of this cocksure young man from Oxford in his later account of how he went from one gentry household to another and 'proved by popular but invincible arguments that the truth was to be found nowhere else save with us Catholics'.[19]

Allen remained in England for three years, though his polemical activities made Lancashire too hot to hold him. He spent some time in the Oxford area, where he was able to note at first hand the persistence of Catholicism within the university, and then in the household of the officially Protestant but fellow travelling Duke of Norfolk. In 1565, the year in which he was finally deprived of his Oriel fellowship for non-residence, he left England for the last time, settling this time in Malines where he was ordained to the priesthood, and where he found a teaching post in the Benedictine college there.[20]

Throughout these years Allen was also establishing himself as a writer. The polemical programme he developed in Lancashire and afterwards was distilled into a 'Scroll of Articles' which he himself never published, but which circulated in manuscript and which was adopted as the basis for controversial treatises by several other writers.[21] Shortly after settling in Malines he published a treatise

defending Catholic belief in Purgatory. This had been largely written three years before as a contribution to the controversy stirred up
by John Jewel's *Apology* for the Church of England.[22] It's a vigorous
book, which shows the ferocity of Allen's rejection of Protestantism –
'this wasting heresy ... nothing else but a canker of true devotion,
an enemy to spirituall exercise, a security and quiet rest in sinne', a
'gathered body of no faithe', taught by 'cursed Calvin ... that miserable forsaken man'.[23] It also demonstrates his way with words, and
his eye for the telling phrase – as in his summary of the disastrous
moral effects of the doctrine of justification by faith – 'Feasting
hathe wonne the field of fasting: and chambering allmost bannished
chastitye', or his contemptuous dismissal of Protestant apologists as
obscure denizens of the night – 'owle light or moonshyne I trowe, or
mirke midnight were more fit for theyre darke workes and doctrine,
our way is over much trodden for theves'.[24]

But the *Defense and Declaration* is far more than a polemical
put-down. It contains some of the richest English theological writing
of the sixteenth century, and the tendency to disparage Allen as 'in
no sense distinguished' compared to the other Louvainists altogether
fails to take account of the quality of his writing.[25] He was indeed
singled out by C. S. Lewis as the author of prose on a par with that
of Richard Hooker,[26] and the *Defense and Declaration* in particular
reveals his writing at its most powerful. Consider the theological and
rhetorical splendour of this passage on the Church, which reveals,
incidentally, something of his own passionate dedication:

This socyety is called in oure crede, *communio sanctorum*, the
communion of Sanctes, that is to say a blessed brotherhood under
Christe the heade, by love and religion so wroght and wrapped
to gether, that what any membre off this fast body hath, the other
lacketh it not: what one wanteth, the other suppliethe: when
one smartethe, all feeleth in a maner the lyke sorowe: when one
ioyethe, thother reioysethe wythall. This happy socyety, is not
inpared by any distance of place, by diversity off goddes giftes, by
inequalyty off estates, nor by exchaunge of liefe: so farre as the
unity of goddes spirit reacheth, so farr this fellowship extendethe,
this city is as large, as the benefite of Christes deathe takethe place.
Yea within all the compasse of his kingdom, this fellowship is

fownde. The soules and sanctes in heaven, the faithful people in earth, the chosen children that suffer chastisement in Purgatory, are, by the perfect bond of this unity, as one abundeth, redy to serve the other, as one lacketh, to crave of the other ... Christe oure heade, in whose bloude this city and socyety standeth, wil have no woorke nor way of salvation, that is not common to the whole body in generall, and perculierly proffitable, to supply the neede of every parte thereof.[27]

But Allen's mind was already turning to other more practical measures for the defence of Catholicism. The Elizabethan purge of the universities had created a Catholic diaspora in France and the Low Countries every bit as remarkable as that of the more celebrated Protestant exiles of Mary's reign. More than a hundred senior members left the University of Oxford for religious reasons in the first decade of Elizabeth's reign, at least 33 from New College alone. They naturally gravitated to university towns like Louvain and, later, Douai. In 1563 Nicholas Sanders, Thomas Stapleton and John Martial, all former fellows of New College, were sharing accommodation in Louvain, and two short-lived houses of study were eventually formed there, nicknamed Oxford and Cambridge. John Fowler, a former New College man, set up a printing house in Louvain which published more than 30 devotional and controversial works in English. Douai University, which received its charter in 1559 as the stream of refugees from the Elizabethan Settlement was just beginning, availed itself of the sudden flood of academic talent and became something of an English institution, its first Chancellor being Richard Smyth, and a number of its professors being recruited from among the exiles.[28]

These exiles produced a remarkable body of controversial and devotional literature, but the potential for moral and educational disaster among them was enormous. Many had no visible means of support, many were young and in need of academic guidance and moral discipline. It appears that by the mid-1560s alms from the Catholic gentry and aristocracy in England, as well as subventions from Spain, were already being sent to support these poor scholars, but the whole process was hit and miss, and was causing trouble among the exiles.[29] It was to meet just such problems that the halls and colleges had emerged in the medieval universities, and Allen felt intensely the lack of an institution, offering 'regiment, discipline, and education most agreable to our Countrimens natures, and for prevention of al disorders that youth and companies of scholers (namely in banishment) are subject unto'.[30] Out of this concern Douay College emerged, and in its wake the rest of the English seminaries abroad.

The story of the founding of the English College at Douai, Allen's greatest achievement, is well-known, but Allen's precise intentions have not been perfectly understood.[31] By the 1580s Douay was being seen, and saw itself, as the first Tridentine seminary, and as a forcing ground for missionary stormtroopers in the fight against Elizabethan Protestantism. It has been widely conceded, I think too readily, that in 1568 Allen had no such thoughts in his head. In the autumn of 1567 he made a pilgrimage to Rome, in company with his former tutor, Morgan Phillips, and a Belgian friend, John Vendeville, Regius Professor of Canon Law at the new University of Douai, and future Bishop of Tournai. Vendeville was an intensely pious counter-reformation activist, who wanted papal approval for a missionary enterprise to the Muslim world, but he evidently did not have the right Roman connections and so was refused an audience with Pius V. On their return journey Allen persuaded him to divert his interest, influence and financial backing to establishing a college for English students of theology in the Low Countries. To begin with, the objectives were modest: to provide a single institution in which the scattered scholarly exiles might study 'more profitably than apart', to secure a continuity of clerical and theological training, so that there would be theologically competent Catholic clergy on hand for the good times ('were they neere, were they far of') when England returned to Catholic communion, and, finally, to provide an orthodox alternative to Oxford and Cambridge, thereby snatching young souls 'from the jaws of death'. But Vendeville would hardly have adopted the new college as a substitute project for his Barbary mission, unless he had felt that Douai itself would have some missionary dimension, and in 1568 he told the Spanish authorities in the Netherlands that the students were to be specially trained in religious controversy and, after a two-year preparation, sent back to England to promote the Catholic cause 'even at the peril of their lives'.[32]

Much has been made of the apparent difference of vision between Vendeville and Allen, with Allen seen as an unimaginative conservative, intending nothing much more dynamic than St Mary's Hall or Oriel in exile. He himself later claimed that at this stage, while he thought they should be ready to seize any opportunity to promote the faith in England, little could be done 'while the heretics were master there'. John Bossy, in a brilliant discussion of Allen's intentions, suggested that he was still trapped in the static theological vision of the Marian Church, unable to think of the Church working as anything other than an establishment backed by the Crown, and so unable to conceive of mission as such, and that he only slowly came round to Vendeville's more activist conception. Indeed, Bossy sees this as a watershed between Marian and Elizabethan Catholicism, with the newer missionary spirit represented by Elizabethans like Gregory Martin and Edmund Campion, men with more in common with their puritan opposite numbers in England than with the older Louvain exiles, and who, almost as much as their Protestant sparring partners, had 'no ties with the Marian Establishment, and [who] treated it with some contempt'.[33]

This is certainly to drive too sharp a wedge between Marian and Elizabethan Catholicism. The Marian regime in the universities was anything but moribund or static, least of all in the universities.[34] Gregory Martin himself was its product, and nearly 40 others would become seminary or Jesuit priests. It is true that Allen's later description of his thinking about this time plays down his own missionary awareness, and so lends support to a conservative reading of the foundation of Douai, but that description comes in a letter where he is complimenting Vendeville by attributing all the foresight to him. We should not in any case lay too much stress on the absence of the vocabulary of mission in Allen's utterances. As late as June 1575 he described the college as 'this college for English theologians, this refuge of exiles, this seat and home of Catholics, this place of true worship for those who have left the Samaria of the Schismatics and who have the faces of those going to Jerusalem'.[35] That last phrase, with its deliberate allusion to Jesus' journey to Jerusalem and his passion in Luke's Gospel, hints at confrontation, but the rhetoric as a whole doesn't suggest much missionary awareness, and it comes in a letter in which Allen talks of Douai simply as a place of Catholic education which will save souls who would otherwise have been led astray at Oxford or Cambridge. Yet by the time the letter was written he had already begun to send priests back to England, and, as we shall see, by now was most certainly thinking of the active reconversion of England by every means available, from bibles to bullets.

And in fact from a very early stage Allen and his fellow exiles were aware of a missionary dimension to any such enterprise in theological education, though they had difficulty in formulating it explicitly. In 1568 an anonymous memorandum written in Allen's circle, if not by Allen himself, asked either that the English Hospice in Rome should become a seminary both for established scholars and young hopefuls, who might be theologically trained for the overthrow of heresy, or else that its revenues should be diverted to support the work just being begun at Douai, which would provide 'ideally qualified workers' when England should once again 'emerge' from heresy. The word 'emerge' suggests that the memorialist had no very clear view of how the 'emerging' might happen, but theology, controversy and mission – or at any rate the overthrow of heresy – were firmly if vaguely linked by this stage.[36] That link rapidly resolved itself into a recognised need for missionaries in England. By 1572 some of the English Louvainists, describing themselves as 'the College of Preachers', were asking for papal support for the formal establishment of an English College there, whose primary purpose would be to provide preachers and catechists for the scattered English exile communities in Europe, but which would also undertake to send missionaries to England.[37]

In these years of confusion and improvisation, then, it looks as if even some of the older activists among the exile community were feeling their way towards the conception of the mission to England: we are not dealing here with a distinctively 'Elizabethan' invention into which Marian veterans, even relatively young veterans like Allen, were dragged, blinking and mumbling. And in fact we know that even before his trip to Rome with Vendeville, Allen was well aware of the damaging consequences of any merely passive 'waiting game'. In the preface to his treatise on the priesthood, written during Lent 1567, he lamented the 'great desolation of christian comfort and all spiritual functions' which the Elizabethan Settlement had brought to the parishes, and the dangers of leaving the people to the ministrations of schismatic and heretical parish clergy. He saw quite clearly that time mattered, and that the acceptance of the ministry of these clergy would ultimately attach the Catholic population to the new Church. He wrote:

> For how can it be otherwise. Baptisme is ministered by here-tikes, they helpe forth such as passe hence, they keepe visitation of the sicke ... and to be short, they minister the mysteries of holy communion: so that, in time, though the libertie of Christes religion be restored againe, the youth shal take such likinge in heretikes practices, to whom by love and custom, they are so fast knit, that it will be hard to reduce them home to truth againe.[38]

Given such a perspective, the emergence of something approaching the Elizabethan mission seems inevitable: it is a short step from this sort of awareness to the activist frame of mind reflected in the saying recorded by the preacher at his funeral – 'Better times don't come by waiting: they have to be made'.[39]

The College began in a hired house near the theological schools in Douai at Michaelmas 1568, and received papal approval the same year. Allen was joined by a handful of former Oxford academics and a couple of Belgian theology students, for Vendeville envis-aged a role for the house in training stormtroopers for the northern European counter-reformation in general, though the Belgians soon tired of the austere conditions in the house and took themselves off. Despite contributions from local religious houses, its funding was from the start precarious, though Allen's appointment to the Regius Chair of Theology in 1570 put the house's finances on a slightly better footing. Nevertheless, the College quickly began to attract other exiles, including celebrities like Thomas Stapleton, who took up residence as 'tabler', or paying guest, in 1569.[40] In 1570 Morgan Philips died and left his entire estate to the College: on the strength of the legacy eight new theology students were taken in, including Gregory Martin and Edmund Campion. The growing numbers and the mixed character of the community called for miracles of tact on Allen's part: he encountered widespread incomprehension and outright hostility. Some of the former Marian dignitaries among the exiles suspected him of self-aggrandisement, or of designs on the alms and pensions for which they jostled: the grant of the Pope's pension in 1575 rankled particularly.

To counter such suspicions and to tempt established scholars to join in the project Allen treated the senior recruits with almost exaggerated deference, and kept the regime of the house flexible. 'A little government ther is and order', he wrote in 1579,

> but no bondage nor straitenes in the world: ther is nether othe, nor statute, nor other bridle nor chaticement but reason and every man's conscience in honest superiority and subalternation eche one towardes other. Confession, communion, exhortation hath kept us this ix yeare I thanke God in great peace amongest ourselves, in good estimation abrode, with sufficient lyvelihod from God, and in good course of service towardes the Church and our contry.[41]

Although it has now been demonstrated that the actual numbers of priests sent from Douai and the later colleges to England has been overestimated,[42] the growth of the College between 1570 and 1580 is an astonishing story. Recruitment was very varied. Some of the students were gentlemen's sons, in search of a Catholic education unobtainable in England, and who came often in defiance of conformist families fearful of government attention. There was a continuing haemorrhage from the English universities, especially Oxford, which Allen encouraged and exploited, and which brought to Douai not only Martin and Campion, but the proto-martyr of the seminaries, Cuthbert Mayne, a graduate of St John's College and, like a good many of the early recruits, a priest of the new Church. Some of these men were already convinced Catholics, some were seekers 'doubtful whether of the two religions were true'. Allen claimed that many were schismatics or heretics, disgusted with the collapse of moral and academic standards in reformation Oxbridge, some even mainly in search of educational bursaries, an attraction which became greater after 1575, when the Pope settled a monthly pension of one hundred crowns on the college. He rejoiced in the despoiling of the Protestant universities and set himself 'to draw into this College the best wittes out of England', a pardonable boast given the calibre of men like Martin and Campion.[43] He deliberately exploited the evangelistic potential of these young men, setting them to write to friends, family and former teachers and colleagues to urge them to become Catholics, even to 'make for once a trial of our mode of life and teaching'. The most spectacular example of this technique was the letter Campion wrote from Douai to his friend and patron Bishop Cheney of Gloucester, urging the old man to follow his secret convictions, renounce heresy and 'make trial of our banishment', but we have a similar, somewhat later, letter by Gregory Martin, presumably once again instigated by Allen.[44]

The College proved a magnet for other English exiles in the Low Countries, and had a resident local English satellite community which included a number of gentry families. It also had a stream of visitors, ranging from the casually curious about an increasingly notorious institution, to relatives or friends of the students. All were welcomed, and pressed to take instruction in the faith. Poor visitors were given a month's free board and lodging, a course of religious instruction and the offer of reconciliation and the sacraments. By May 1576 there were 80 students in the College, by September the same year 120. The growing numbers created constant problems of accommodation and finance, and the foundation of the Venerabile in Rome was among other things an attempt to deal with the overflow. Nevertheless, Allen resisted pressure to set fixed limits on the intake, since so many of those who came were refugees who had no other resource, or waverers who might lapse back into Protestantism if turned away. At the end of the decade he reckoned that there were on average a hundred students in the College in any one year, and that they were ordaining 20 men to the priesthood annually. The first four priests left the College for England in 1574, and by 1580 about a hundred in all had been sent on the mission.[45]

The regime devised by Allen for his men is very striking, and differed in several important ways both from university theology courses and from the normal seminary syllabus of the late sixteenth century.[46] Late medieval training manuals for priests emphasised practical skills — seemly performance of the liturgy, sacraments and sacramentals, basic expertise in hearing confessions and a grounding in the essential elements of catechesis. To these Allen added an overwhelming emphasis on expertise in the Bible, a good grounding in dogmatic theology through the study of St Thomas, and constant practice in preaching and in disputation. The centrality of St Thomas perhaps reflected the influence of Soto and his fellow Dominicans in Marian Oxford, though it was also shared with the programme of studies outlined for Jesuit colleges by St Ignatius, and the scheme of studies at Douai had a number of elements in common with those pursued in the Society of Jesus and formulated from the later 1580s in successive revisions of the *Ratio Studiorum*.[47]

But it was the needs of the English mission which gave the distinctive character to Allen's regime. He was intensely aware of the crucial importance of the English Bible to the success of the English reformation, and was determined to eliminate the advantage this gave Protestants. The publication of Gregory Martin's translation of the New Testament in 1582 was part of this project, but even before its appearance Allen saw to it that his men had the Bible at their fingertips. Between three and five chapters of the Old or New Testaments were read aloud at each of the two main daily meals, followed while still at table by an exposition of part of what had been read, during which students were expected to have their bibles open before them and pen and ink to hand. In three years the students heard the Old Testament read through in this way 12 times, the New Testament 16 times. Each was expected to do private preparatory work on the passages read communally, there was a daily lecture on the New Testament, Hebrew and Greek classes and regular disputations on the points of scripture controverted between Catholics and Protestants. There were two lectures each day on St Thomas and a weekly disputation on points from the week's lectures. The men also studied Church history, especially English Church history, the canons and decrees of Trent and the catechisms of Trent and of Peter Canisius, and they received practical instruction in the techniques of catechesis. There was a strong emphasis on the reconciliation of penitents in confession, and so on moral theology and cases of conscience, using the standard textbook of the day by the Navarese theologian Martin de Azpilcueta, supplemented by cases of conscience specially devised with the English mission in mind.[48]

To this new-style theological training he added a new spirituality, focused on daily Mass and regular weekly communion, twice weekly fasting for the conversion of England, regular meditation on the mysteries of the Rosary. A fundamental element in this new, more intense piety was the use of confession as a means of spiritual growth 'not in a perfunctory way as we used to do when for custom's sake we confessed once a year'. That dismissal of the medieval Sarum past is significant: Allen believed that the reformation was a judgement on the sins and superficiality of the people, and so a deeper more self-conscious penitence was a necessary condition of the restoration of Catholicism. For this purpose he especially valued and promoted among the students and staff the Jesuit Spiritual Exercises 'in order to the perfect examination of our consciences', and the choice of 'a holier state of life', another link between his regime and the spirit of the Society.[49]

In the early days of the seminary Allen's recruits were a miscellaneous lot, from seasoned and sometimes very senior academics to raw lads from country grammar schools. He was realistic about what could be achieved with much of the material he had to hand: Mercury, he told a critic of the seminary, 'cannot be made of every logg'.[50] He was in the business of producing 'plaine poor priests', for whom 'zeal for God's house, charity and thirst for souls' were more important than academic achievement.

Nevertheless, he knew quite well that his regime was producing a different kind of priest, more professional, better instructed, altogether more formidable 'than the common sort of curates had in old tyme'. He thought his men compared well with those emerging from any seminary in Europe, and even in some respects with the Jesuits, for whom he had an unqualified reverence and admiration. He believed in the special value of a graduate clergy, and academic distinction was highly prized at Douai: Masters of Arts and Doctors at Douai were appointed humbler students as servitors to wait on them at table, and sat in due order of precedence at high table. As long as funds were available for it, members of the College were encouraged to take theological degrees in the University of Douai, and Cuthbert Mayne kept the exercise for his baccalaureate in theology just days before returning to England and martyrdom in 1575. There is no doubt that this emphasis on theological excellence derived directly from Allen himself, and was part of the legacy of Marian Oxford to the Elizabethan mission. By contrast, graduates going from Douai to Rome noticed and frequently resented the lack of deference the

Jesuit regime there paid to scholastic distinction.[51] He regretted the way in which missionary demands and funding priorities inexorably forced the theological concerns of the College to the margins, and to the end of his life nursed a project for a College where English priests might pursue advanced theological studies.[52] In all this he also had his eye on Elizabethan Oxford and Cambridge, and the need to excel them, above all in their boasted excellence in biblical knowledge. There were more and better theological courses, including training in scripture, he claimed, 'in our two colleges, then are in [the Protestants] two Universities conteining neere hand 30 goodly Colleges'.[53]

By the same token he was impatiently dismissive of nostalgic comparisons made by his fellow Catholics – 'that golden world is past, yf ever any such were'.[54] He resented the criticism, made by conservatives like the veteran English Carthusian Maurice Chancey, of the youth, inexperience and unpriestly deportment of the seminarians going in 'disguised gear' of ruffs and feathers on the mission.

For above all Allen was intensely aware of the dangers his men incurred. It has been calculated that of the 471 seminary priests known to have been active in England in Elizabeth's reign, at least 294 (62 per cent), were imprisoned at some time or another. A hundred and fifteen fell into government hands within a year of arrival, 35 while still in the ports at which they landed, 116 were executed, 17 died in gaol, 91 were banished, of whom 24 subsequently returned at great risk. Allen worried about the power of life and death he exercised over these men. When in 1585 20 of them were expelled from England and duly reported to Allen for duty, he did not feel he had the right to send them back on the mission: in his last years in Rome as a cardinal he would contrast the comfort and safety of his own life with the danger and suffering of his priests.[55] Most men, he told Chauncey,

> mark there [their] misses, and few consider in what feares and daungers they be in and what unspeakable paines they take to serve good menus tornes to there least perill. I could recken unto youe the miseryes they suffer in night journeyes, in the worst wedder that can be picked; perill of theves, of water, of watches, of false brethrene; there close abode in chambers as in pryson or dongeoon withowt fyre and candell leest they gyve token to the

enemy where they bee; there often and sudden raisinge from there
bedds att mydnight to avoyde the diligent searches of haeretikes; all
which and divers other discontentments, disgraces and reproches
they willinglye suffer, which is great penannce for their fethers,
and all to wynne the soweles of there dearest countreyemen.[56]

Yet these sufferings were fundamental to the spirituality Allen
encouraged among the seminarians, and to the message he wished
through them to impress upon the Catholics in England. Their sufferings, he told his priests, were stronger intercession for their country
'than any prayers lightly in the world' – 'Bloude so yielded maketh
the forciblest meane to procure mercie that can be'. The likelihood
of martyrdom was actually one of the inducements Allen offered
to persuade Campion to go to England, and in the wake of his and
his companions' executions Allen told the Rector of the Venerabile
that 'ten thousand sermons would not have published our apostolic
faith and religion so winningly as the fragrance of these victims,
most sweet both to God and men'. He was distributing fragments
of Campion's 'holy ribbe' as relics by May 1582.[57] Some of his most
moving writing occurs in the exhortation to constancy in martyrdom with which the *Apologie* for the two colleges ends:

> Our daies can not be many, because we be men: neither can it be
> either godly or worldly wisdom, for a remnant of three or foure
> yeres, and perchance not so many moneths, to hazard the losse
> of all eternity. They can not be good in these evil times ... And
> were they never so many or good, to him that refuseth his faith
> and Maister, they shal never be joyful, but deadly and dole-
> ful. Corporally die once we must every one, and but once, and
> thereupon immediatly judgement, where the Confessor shal be
> acknowledged, and the Denyer denyed againe.
>
> No Martyrdom of what length or torment so ever, can be more
> grevous, then a long sicknes and a languishing death: and he that
> departeth upon the pillow, hath as little ease as he that dieth upon
> the gallowes, blocke, or bouchers knife. And our Maisters death,
> both for paines and ignominie, passed both sortes, and all other
> kinds either of Martyrs or malefactors. Let no tribulation then,
> no perill, no prison, no persecution, no life, no death separate us

from the charity of God, and the society of our sweete Saviours passions, by and for whose love we shal have the victory in all these conflictes.[58]

The whole seminary was in a sense heroic, confrontational, its objective the separation of the Catholic community from an acquiescent conformity which, he understood perfectly well, would ultimately absorb and undo it. And so his men were nursed not only in readiness for martyrdom, but in a robust hatred of Protestantism:

> By frequent familiar conversations we make our students thoroughly acquainted with the chief impieties, blasphemies, absurdities, cheats and trickeries of the English heretics, as well as with their ridiculous writings, sayings and doings. The result is that they not only hold the heretics in perfect detestation, but they also marvel and feel sorrow of heart that there should be any found so wicked, simple and reckless of their salvation as to believe such teachers, or so cowardly and worldy-minded as to go along with such abandoned men in their schism or sect, instead of openly avowing to their face the faith of the catholic church and their own.[59]

That was the point – to bring the laity to see the necessity of recusancy, of making a clean break with the parish churches, thereby ensuring the survival of an uncompromised Catholicism. Less than ten years after the establishment of Douai, Allen could rejoice that 'innumberable nowe confesse there faithe and abhorreth all communion and participation with the sectaryes in there servyce and sacraments, that before, beinge catholykes in there hart, for worldly feare durst not so doo'.[60] Insistence on this point was a major theme in the writings of Allen, and his circle, and in the casuistic formation of the seminary priests themselves,[61] but it was uphill work, and, for all his own conviction, Allen understood the pressures Catholics in England were under. His last briefing with each of his priests on their departure for the mission concerned 'how and where to condiscende withowt synne to certain feablenesse growne in manns lyfe and manners these ill tymes, not alwayes to be rigorous, never over scrupulous, so that the churche discipline be not evidently infringed, nor no acte of schisme or synne plainly committed'.[62] This should not be interpreted as willingness to legitimate church-papistry or occasional conformity, but he did his best to meet the realities of the English situation. When the draconian law imposing a £20 fine on recusants for persistent non-attendance was passed in 1581 Allen responded to lay panic by seeking some relaxation of the Vatican line on this matter, lobbying the nuncio in Paris and consulting the leading Jesuit casuist. He was clearly relieved at the refusal of the authorities to soften their line, however, and told the Jesuit rector of the Venerabile that 'no other decision was possible'.[63] Yet if connivance was forbidden, compassion was not. As persecution mounted in the early 1590s he instructed his priests to hold the line on the sinfulness of outward conformity, yet to deal gently with those who fell into it through fear – 'be not hard nor roughe nor rigorous ... in receavinge againe and absolving them ... which mercie you must use, thoughe they fall more than once, and though perhaps you have some probable feare that they will of like infirmity fall againe ... *tutior est via misericordiae quam justitiae rigoris*'.[64]

The question of confrontation and constancy in the faith brings us at last to Allen's politics, for all his politics were tuned to the reconversion of England. The first thing to be said is that Allen believed that he knew how to convert England: between 1553 and 1558 he had seen it done and had taken part in the process. He never doubted that what was needed for the success of this great work of God was, in essence, the repetition of the Marian restoration, and in 1588, when the Armada was about to sail, he sent for the complete Vatican files on the Legatine mission of Cardinal Pole.[65] His blueprint for the reconversion included the removal of Queen Elizabeth, and the implementation of a sternly Catholic regime. He did not believe in the toleration of error, and he did not believe that Catholics and Protestants could live in peace together. In this last, it has to be said, he had history, observation and cold common sense on his side. North-western Europe in the 1560s and 1570s seemed to be falling apart at the seams for the sake of religion. France was descending into religious civil war, and his arrival in the Low Countries coincided with the outbreak of the Calvinist revolt which would separate the northern provinces from Spanish rule and the Catholic faith. From the moment of his settlement in the Low

Countries, Allen's personal wellbeing, the existence of his College and the future of his projects for the reconversion of England were inextricably involved with the political dominance of Spain. Spain's weakness was his College's peril, as he discovered when in 1578 the English College was forced by the ebb and flow of the Revolt to abandon Douai and take up temporary residence at Rheims.[66]

In the early 1560s the loyalty of Catholics was hardly an issue: the possibility of the death, the Catholic marriage or the conversion of the Queen had not yet been ruled out and the main preoccupation of the exiles was the polemical campaign against the new religion, and the simple business of survival. But the arrival of Mary Queen of Scots in England in 1568, the Rising of the Northern Earls in 1569 and the excommunication of the Queen the following year changed all that. The Elizabethan regime was bound to treat Catholicism as a political threat, and Catholics were bound to take stock of the courses of action open to them. By now it was clear to everyone that the Elizabethan Settlement was not just going to go away. Something would have to be done, and the key to what might be done was the Bull of Excommunication.

Regnans in Excelsis solemnly declared the Queen an apostate from the Catholic faith, a heretic and a tyrant, and it absolved English Catholics of their allegiance to her. But it was issued quite irresponsibly, without any serious attempt to secure political help from Spain or anywhere else to enforce it. It therefore made the conditions of English Catholics much worse, exposing them to charges of treason without any compensating hope of liberation. It also created serious problems of conscience for them: it was clear that they *need* not now obey the Queen, but would they themselves incur excommunication if, out of fear, prudence, or natural loyalty they *did* obey her? In 1580 a ruling was secured from Gregory XIII which absolved Catholics from obedience to the Bull until its enforcement became practicable, and in the meantime it was tacitly allowed to drop. There were theologians, in any case, who questioned the extent of the Pope's authority in matters of civil allegiance, and therefore the legitimacy of the Bull.[67]

But Allen was not among them. An ardent papalist, who saw in the Pope the surest defence of the Church and the 'rocke of refuge in doubtful daies and doctrines', he was to place the excommunication and deposition of Elizabeth, and the theoretical and practical right of the Pope to perform such an act, at the centre of his political thinking.[68] In 1572 he was one of the signatories of a petition from a group of exiles at Louvain to Pope Gregory XIII, asking him to take some action to implement the Bull against the 'pretended Queen', and to extirpate Protestantism in England, from which the infection of heresy was spreading like cancer to the surrounding nations. In 1584, in a pamphlet defending the loyalty of English Catholics, he would devote three chapters to an extended defence of the deposing power of the Pope.[69]

Yet it was one thing to accept *Regnans in Excelsis*, another thing to act on it, and here the only realistic hope was to involve the King of Spain. Allen was in any case in constant touch with Spain and Spanish officials in northern Europe by virtue of his growing position of leadership among the exiles: the management of pensions, the procurement of ecclesiastical and civil preferment for his growing circle of supplicants and clients, above all the protection of his College, demanded it. But he went beyond this, and throughout the 1570s and early 1580s Allen was a key figure in a succession of plans for a Spanish invasion of England. Early in 1576 he took part in a consultation in Rome on English affairs: the foundation of the Venerabile was one consequence of this visit.[70] But that was a by-product of what was in fact a council of war, whose main outcome was a plan for invasion of England by a papal force led by Don John of Austria, to set Mary on the throne. Allen prepared a lengthy document of advice for this invasion, the first of many, in which, among other things, he suggested that the expenses should be met from the confiscated property of Protestant ecclesiastics.[71] For any such plan the support of Philip II was essential, but Spanish problems in the Netherlands meant that in the event nothing was done, and Allen was increasingly aware that simple reliance on Spain would be a mistake. However zealous for religion he might be, Philip was a politician first – as Allen's friend Nicholas Sander told him, 'wee shall have no stedy comfort but from God, in the Pope not the King of Spain. Therefore I beseech you, take hold of the Pope.'[72]

Allen's own involvement in political schemes was not continuous: his part in the invasion plans of 1576 was almost certainly directly provoked by an attempt of Elizabeth's ministers to secure an agreement with Spain for the expulsion of the exiles, in particular the College, from the Low Countries. But the wave of persecution which followed the arrival of Campion and Persons in 1580 pushed him in this direction again. His letters in the wake of the martyrdom of Campion are a curious mixture of grief, anger and exaltation, but there is no mistaking the growth of his hostility to Elizabeth, 'our Herodias', who bathed her hands in the 'brightest and best blood' of Catholics.[73] In 1583 he was actually named as Papal Legate and Bishop of Durham in the event of the success of the proposed invasion by the Duc de Guise with which this chapter began, but the discovery of the Throckmorton plot prevented its implementation.[74] 'If [the invasion of England] be not carried out this year', he told Cardinal Galli in April 1584, 'I give up all hope in man and the rest of my life will be bitter to me.'[75]

His political involvements in the fight against international Protestantism deepened, and he was drawn into the negotiations which led to the formation of the Catholic Holy League in France in 1584 and 1585: to the end of his life he remained hostile and suspicious towards Henri IV of France, whom he regarded even after his 'conversion' as a crypto-Protestant.[76] In these years Allen exerted all his influence to commit the King of Spain and the Pope to the 'Enterprise of England', and his postbag was stuffed with the explosive matter of high espionage: when he fell seriously ill in the summer of 1585 he panicked and burned everything, including his cipher books.[77]

The election of a new Pope, Sixtus V, in 1585 brought the still convalescent Allen hurrying to Rome, partly to secure continued papal support for the College, but largely for political reasons. If the enterprise of England was to become a reality, the Pope had to be persuaded of its importance. Allen worked hard to scotch rumours of the easing of persecution in England, in case these should cool enthusiasm for the invasion, and in September 1585 he drafted an elaborate memorial for the Pope, describing the religious geography of England, pressing on him the widespread support in the north and west of the country for Catholicism, the unwarlike character of the urban supporters of Protestantism and the 'common and promiscuous multitude', the ease with which an invasion might be carried through.[78]

The Franciscan Pope Sixtus V was a volatile and formidable figure who was deeply committed to the re-Catholicising of Europe, but he distrusted the dominance of Spain and resented the interference of Philip in ecclesiastical affairs. If he was to be brought to back – and to help finance – the enterprise of England, every ounce of pressure and persuasion would be needed. The Spanish Ambassador in Rome, Count Olivares, recognised the role Allen could play in this and detained him in Rome. There is no doubt that he now became, to all intents and purposes, a Spanish servant, receiving detailed briefings from the maladroit Olivares on the management of the Pope.[79] Allen's own centrality to the enterprise, in any case, was obvious, and became critical after the execution of Mary Queen of Scots: as the unquestioned religious leader of the English Catholics, he was now the only conceivable figurehead for a crusade. But if he was to serve that role he would need to be more than Dr Allen; he had to be made a cardinal. Sixtus V bowed to immense Spanish pressure, orchestrated in part by Robert Persons, Allen's closest political collaborator, and he created Allen cardinal in August 1587. Elaborate plans for his role in the invasion were drawn up, in part at least based on Pole's Legatine mission: interestingly, Allen intended to hold the office of Lord Chancellor as well as that of Archbishop of Canterbury.[80] There is no doubt in all this that the Pope saw Allen as a Spanish stooge, and when in October 1588, at Philip II's command, Allen sought permission to go to the Netherlands to be in readiness when the call to England came, Sixtus V threw a series of spectacular tantrums, abusing Allen, according to Olivares, 'like a negro'.[81]

It is against these developments that we have to assess Allen's role not only in politics in general, but in the martyrdom of his priests. In the face of the Elizabethan regime's insistence that the priests died for treason, Allen vehemently maintained their total innocence. In 1581 and again in 1584 he published pamphlets claiming that none of the priests had any political involvement, and in these works and in his account of the martyrdoms of Campion and his companions he insisted that it was the government, not the Catholics, who were making an issue of the Bull of Excommunication, which Catholics had allowed to fall into harmless oblivion. He insisted that no discussion of the Bull was allowed at Douai, and this was certainly true.[82]

Yet he himself repeatedly defended the validity of the Bull in the published writings which his priests helped circulate in England, and he actively sought the armed implementation of the Bull and the deposition of Elizabeth in 1572, 1576, 1583, 1586 and 1588. In 1586, moreover, he told the Pope that the 'daily exhortations, teaching, writing and administration of the sacraments ... of our priests' had made the Catholics in England 'much more ready' for an invasion, and that no good Catholic now 'thinks he ought to obey the queen as a matter of conscience, although he may do so through fear, which fear will be removed when they see the force from without'. The priests, he added 'will direct the consciences and actions of the Catholics ... when the time comes'. This perception of the role of the clergy was generally shared by the Catholic authorities: when the invasion by de Guise was being planned three years earlier, the nuncio in Paris told the Cardinal Secretary of State that the leading Catholics would be informed 'per via de sacredoti' – through their priests.[83]

Yet Allen was not lying: he rigorously kept from all but a handful of his friends and his pupils any knowledge of his own political activities, and certainly approved of the *breve* of Gregory XIII formally allowing the excommunication to be held in abeyance indefinitely, which Campion and Persons took with them to England in 1580.[84] He himself observed a scrupulous distinction in his writings between the work of priests – which was to preach the Gospel and to endure martyrdom for it when the time came – and the role of princes and fighting men; 'the spiritual [sword] by the hand of the priest, the [material sword] by the hand of the soldier'.[85]

The 'readiness' his priests contributed to, therefore, was indirect, a strengthening of loyalty to the papacy, and a willingness to choose God rather than man when put to the test, as the Henrician and Edwardian Catholics had so signally failed to do. The English reformation was for him a sacrilegious invasion of the spiritual sphere by the secular power. It followed that any recovery of Catholic understanding and commitment, however apolitical and spiritual its ministers, its methods and its aims, must inevitably lead to a confrontation with the Protestant state. The more clearly the people saw in the light of the Gospel, the more resolutely they would reject the claims of the royal supremacy over their consciences. A straight line runs from Allen's efforts in the early 1560s to persuade his Lancashire neighbours out of their token conformity, to his promotion of the enterprise of England in the 1580s, and the spiritual mission of the seminary priests lies squarely along that line.

But in any case the whole notion that a Catholic might be rebellious seemed to him a nonsense. It was the Protestants who were rebels, 'opinionative and restless brains to raise rebellion at their pleasure under pretense of religion', following 'their own deciptful wils and uncertain opinions, without rule or reason', stirring up civil war in France, rebellion against the lawful sovereign in the Netherlands and in Scotland, fastening on the weakness of the body politic – 'they make their market most', he claimed, 'in the minority of princes or of their infirmity'. Catholics, by contrast, as men of 'order and obedience', took no such liberties, but 'commit the direction of matters so important to the Church and to the chief governors of their souls'. The deposing power was a God-appointed safeguard, stretching back to Old Testament priests and prophets like Samuel, and entrusted to the Pope for the preservation of the prince and people in due obedience to the law of Christ. Catholics therefore proceed by reason and conscience, Protestants by 'fury and frenzy'.[86] It was the Elizabethan government, then, with its murder of priests and war against Catholic truth which sinned, in forcing Catholic men and women to choose between civil and religious obedience, between God and the prince.

These views were never concealed by Allen – he proclaimed them in the works he published in the early 1580s: but their consequences were finally spelled out in the two open calls to resistance which he produced in 1587 and 1588. In 1587 an English commander with the Earl of Leicester's expedition to help the rebels in Holland, Sir William Stanley, surrendered the town of Deventer to the Spanish forces. Allen published a defence of his action, claiming that English involvement in a war against Philip was sinful and unjust, Stanley's action that of an informed conscience, and that any Catholic should do the same. He further declared that 'al actes of iustice within the realme, done by the Quenes authoritie, ever since she was, by publike sentence of the Church, and Sea Apostoloke, declared an Haertike ... and deposed from al regal dignitie ... al is voide, by the lawe of God and man ...' He called for the formation of companies of English soldiers on the continent to be trained 'in Catholike and old godly militare discipline', just as the seminaries were training priests, to undo the evil of the reformation: 'it is as lawful, godly and glorious for you to fight, as for us Priestes to suffer, and to die'. To labour in either of these ways for the defence of the faith 'is alwaies in the sight of God, a most precious death, and martyrdom'.[87] In the following year Allen finally burned his boats with his *Admonition to the Nobility and People of England*, calling on them to join the Spaniards and overthrow Elizabeth, whom he denounced as a sacrilegious heretic, an incestuously begotten bastard, guilty not only of oppressing the people but of ruining the commonwealth by a whole range of ills, from the promotion of base-born upstarts to the enjoyment of nameless acts of sexual debauchery with her young courtiers.[88]

There is no doubt that his political involvements contributed to the sufferings of his priests, for the Elizabethan government knew much about his activities, and guessed a good deal more. Yet his priests shared with Allen a sense of the spiritual issues at stake, and the dilemmas on which they were impaled were not of his or their making. For him and for them there could be no peace with a state which claimed an absolute authority over consciences: his perception of that claim, and his solution to the dilemma it posed, was not so very different from that of Bonhoeffer in our own times.

Yet if in the conditions of his own time he can hardly be blamed for seeking to overthrow Elizabeth, so that the Gospel might be free, Allen cannot entirely be absolved of responsibility for the disasters of Catholicism in the 1580s and 1590s. He can be blamed, I think, for his lack of realism about the likelihood of the success of any such attempts. We are less prone now than we once were to dismiss the optimism of Elizabethan Catholics about the persistence of widespread sympathy for the old religion among the people at large: there was nothing inevitable or easy about the triumph of the reformation. But, perhaps in part at least to counter a growing scepticism at the Spanish court about support for the enterprise, Allen persisted in the conviction that even into the mid-1580s two-thirds of the people were Catholics in their hearts, and so discontented with Elizabeth's rule,[89] the 'pure zelous heretikes' very few and 'effeminate, delicate and least expert in the wars'. He persuaded himself that the indifferent remainder 'will never adore the setting sun, nor follow the declining fortune of so filthie, wicked and illiberal a Creature' as Elizabeth.[90]

Dazzled by the extraordinary impact of his priests, he never grasped, or allowed himself to acknowledge, the extent of anti-Spanish feeling in England, or the unlikelihood of the population of late Elizabethan England flocking to the Pope's banner. And he consistently underestimated his enemy, declaring in 1581 that no intelligent person could be a sincere Protestant. Even the promoters of reformation must certainly be mere *politiques*, 'who, because they be wise, can not be Protestants 23 yeres, that is to say, any long time together'.[91]

It is easy with hindsight to be superior about this. Successive popes and the most experienced king in Christendom took the same optimistic view as Allen of the prospects of success, and Philip committed the sea-borne might of the world's greatest power to it. And Allen was driven by longing for restoration and return, the restoration of the true faith and the lost greatness of a Catholic England, above all the longing of one who had eaten the bitter bread of exile for almost half his life. In 1581 he had publicly lamented that he and his like, 'for our sinnes . . . be constrained to spend either al or most of our serviceable yeres out of our natural countrie', and the longing for his 'lost fatherland' tolls persistently through his writings. In 1580, as Campion set out for England, he told him that he and his like 'will procure for me and mine the power of returning'.[92]

An autumnal air hangs over Allen's last years as Cardinal. He had an immensely high understanding of his office as an instrument of the papacy he so much revered. Though he was the poorest of the cardinals, he was an active and effective member of the curia, involved in the affairs of Germany, the revision of the Vulgate and the Congregation of the Index.[93] He enjoyed friendship with and was treated as an equal by the greatest men of his age – Bellarmine in his last years, as Borromeo earlier. He was a man of affairs, keeping open house to English visitors, Catholic or Protestant, in his relatively modest home beside the English College, the hub of a network of information, clientage and organisation.

More than ever, he was the central figure in the concerns of the English Catholics, and his eirenical temperament and passionate concern for unity were exerted to the full in holding together a community increasingly riven by the bitterness of defeat, in particular the ominous gap opening between the secular clergy and his revered Jesuits.[94]

Half-hearted attempts were made by the King of Spain to appoint him Archbishop of Malines, so as to be nearer England, but nothing came of them. And he himself was a disappointed man, aware that now there was little chance of a dramatic restoration of Catholicism, and forced to consider seriously the notion, which he had not very convincingly canvassed in the early 1580s, of securing some minimal toleration for Catholics in a Protestant England. In a world in which almost nobody believed in toleration, it was a project as hopeless as invasion, but we catch a remarkable glimpse of his changed perceptions in the spring and autumn of 1593, through the eyes of an English government go-between, John Arden. Arden, the brother of Allen's Jesuit confessor and closest English friend in Rome, was encouraged by the Cardinal to broker a protracted negotiation for the granting of freedom of conscience to Catholics and a marriage between 'one of Elizabeth's blood' to a Spaniard, to secure the succession. In return, Allen would call off the Pope, the King of Spain and the Catholic League, and all the Catholics would 'do that duty is due to the Queen, religion excepted, and would take arms in defence of her person and realm against the King of Spain or whosoever'. A striking feature of the whole negotiation was Allen's willingness to shrug off his Spanish involvements. When Arden asked him why he was so keen to unite an English heir with a Spaniard, Allen replied that 'he would never wish it if they might have liberty of conscience', and he excused his and other exiles' writings against Elizabeth with 'alas, it was to get favour of the King of Spain who maintained them'. A key to his deepest feelings appeared from an impassioned outburst, when he snatched up a bible and swore 'as I am a priest' that to secure the free practice of Catholicism he would rather 'leave here and all . . . and be content to live in prison all the days of my life' in England.[95]

By the time of Allen's death on 16 October 1594 the first heroic phase of the Elizabethan mission was drawing to its close. English colleges on the continent were multiplying, and the succession of martyrs would continue – Robert Southwell would go to Tyburn within six months of Allen's death. But the creative verve and the excitement and imaginative power of the mission in the 1580s would never quite be equalled, just as the opportunities which had faced it then were slipping away with the years. The first seminary priests and their Jesuit colleagues, themselves sent to England at Allen's urging, represented one of the most original and most effective experiments of an exceptionally creative and turbulent period of Christian history, and it was Allen's vision they incarnated. No English Protestant attempt to rethink ministry, or to equip men for ministry, was half so radical, or quarter so professional. No one else in that age conceived so exalted nor so demanding a role for the secular priesthood, and no one else apart from the great religious founders produced a body of men who rose to that ideal so eagerly, and at such cost. The times had demanded invention, decisive action, and he had risen to the challenge. 'The quarell is God's', he told one of his critics, 'and but for Hys holy glory and honor I myght sleepe att ease, and let the worlde wagge and other men worke.'[96]

Allen's political entanglements ultimately yielded nothing but grief. But his creation of generations of clerical stormtroopers for counter-reformation, and the energy, humanity and management of men by which he inspired and preserved them, showed pastoral resource and vision on a par with that of Carlo Borromeo in his own generation, or Vincent de Paul in the next. He understood perfectly well what he had achieved, and six months before his death wrote of 'the semynarie of Doway, which is as deere to me as my owne life, and which hath next to God beene the beginning and ground of all the good and salvation which is wrought in England'.[97] Because of him, English Catholicism was given an institutional lifeline to the larger world of Christendom, and a surer, clearer sense of its own identity: because of him, it survived.

Notes

1   The phrase is A. L. Rouse's, quoted by John Bossy, *The English Catholic Community 1570–1850* (London, 1975), p. 13.

2   T. F. Knox (ed.), *The Letters and Memorials of William Cardinal Allen* (London, 1882) [hereafter *Memorials*], pp. xli, 407: T. F. Knox (ed.), *The First and Second Diaries of the English College, Douay* (London, 1878), [hereafter, *D.D.*], pp. 337–8; L. F. Von Pastor, *The History of the Popes* (St Louis, 1930), [hereafter *Pastor*], vol. 19, pp. 429–433.

3   *Memorials*, pp. 29–30.

4   Robert M. Kingdon (ed.), *A True, Sincere, and Modest Defense of English Catholics*, 1584. (Ithaca, NY, 1965), p. 127 [hereafter, *Modest Defense*]: *An Apologie and True Declaration of the Institution and endeavours of the two English Colleges . . .* (Henault [*vere* Rheims] 1581), p. 12 verso, [hereafter, *Apologie and Declaration*].

5   *Memorials*, pp. 5, 181, 213; on Tudor Lancashire and its religious conservatism, see Christopher Haigh, *Reformation and Resistance in Tudor Lancashire* (Cambridge, 1975); for Allen's view of the state

of England in the mid-1580s see Garrett Mattingly, 'William Allen and Catholic Propaganda in England', *Travaux d'Humanisme et Renaissance*, 28 (1957), pp. 325–39.

6   *Memorials* p. 213; *Modest Defense*, p. 56.

7   For the role of the halls in Tudor Oxford, James McConica, *The History of the University of Oxford*, vol. 3 (Oxford, 1986), pp. 51–5; Alan B. Coban, *The Medieval English Universities: Oxford and Cambridge to c. 1500* (London, 1988), pp. 145–60. They were in effect colleges within the colleges, many of them having been annexed lo larger institutions, as St Mary's had been acquired by Oriel, though they continued to offer teaching both for the basic arts course and for further studies in theology and laws.

8   On the course of the reformation at Oxford, and martyr's part in it, Jennifer Loach, 'Reformation Controversies' in McConica, *The History of the University of Oxford*, vol. 3, pp. 363–74; an unsuccessful attempt was made in 1550 to impose a Protestant head on Allen's own college, Oriel.

9   J. Ignacio Tellechea Idigoras, *Fray Bartolomé Carranza y el Cardenal Pole* (Pamplona, 1977), and the same author's *Inglaterra, Flandres y Espana 1557–1559* (Vitoria, 1975). As professor of theology at Dillengen until 1553 Soto had been a key figure in the German counter-reformation; Villa Garcia had been instrumental in securing several of Cranmer's recantations. For the Spanish influence in Marian England more generally, see the essays gathered in John Edwards and Ronald Truman (eds), *Reforming Catholicism in the England of Mary Tudor: The Achievement of Fray Bartolome Carranza* (Aldershot, 2005).

10   Loach, op. cit., p. 378.

11   John E. Booty, *John Jewel as Apologist of the Church of England* (London, 1963), p. 63: M. R. O'Connell, *Thomas Stapleton and the Counter Reformation* (New Haven, 1964); Michael Richards, 'Thomas Stapleton', *Journal of Ecclesiastical History*, 18 (1967), pp. 187–99.

12   *Modest Defense*, p. 104.

13   Ibid., pp. 95, 115.

14   *A Defence and Declaration of the Catholike Churchies Doctrine Touching Purgatory* (Antwerp, 1565), [hereafter, *Purgatory*], p. 286.

15   H. N. Birt, *The Elizabethan Religious Settlement* (London, 1907), p. 257.

16   *D.D.*, pp. xxii–xxiii: on the Elizabethan Settlement and its enforcement in Oxford, Penry Williams, 'Elizabethan Oxford: State. Church and University', in McConica, op. cit., pp. 397–440.

17   Patrick Collinson, *The Birthpangs of Protestant England: Religious and Cultural Change in the Sixteenth and Seventeenth Centuries* (London, 1988), especially p. ix: the case is set out in my *The Stripping of the Altars: Traditional Religion in England 1400–1580* (London and New Haven, 1992), pp. 565–93, and in Christopher Haigh, *English Reformations* (Oxford, 1993), pp. 235–50.

18   A sub-committee at the Council of Trent in 1562 considered, and refused, a request that English Catholics should be permitted to attend Book of Common Prayer services, in order to avoid persecution. Alexandra Walsham, *Church Papists: Catholicism, Conformity and Confessional Polemic in Early Modern England* (Royal Historical Society Monograph, 1993), pp. 22–3; for the Trent adjudication, Ginevra Crosignani, Thomas J. McCoog and Michael Questier (eds), *Recusancy and Comformity in Early Modern England* (Rome, 2010), pp. 1–25, 30–71.

19   *D.D.*, pp. xxiii–xxiv, *Memorials*, pp. 56–7.

20   *D.D.*, pp. xxv–xxvi; Martin Haile, *An Elizabethan Cardinal: William Allen* (London, 1914), pp. 57, 67.

21   A. C. Southern, *Elizabethan Recusant Prose 1559–1582* (London, 1950), pp. 517–23; one such publication was *A Notable Discourse, plainelye and truely discussing, who are the right Ministers of the Catholike Church* (Douai, 1575).

22   For the Jewel controversy, Southern, *Recusant Prose*, pp. 59–118 (Allen's contributions discussed in detail pp. 103–9); Booty, *Jewel*, pp. 58–82; Peter Milward, *Religious Controversies of the Elizabethan Age* (London, 1978), pp. 1–16.

23   *Purgatory*, pp. 37 verso, 282–3.

24   *Purgatory*, p. 12 verso; Southern, *Recusant Prose*, p. 109.

25 John Bossy, *The English Catholic Community 1570–1850* (London, 1975), p. 13. For a critique of this general view, and an assertion of Allen's 'keen intelligence' see Mattingly, 'William Allen and Catholic Propaganda', pp. 335–6.

26 C. S. Lewis, *English Literature in the Sixteenth Century* (Oxford, 1954), pp. 438–41.

27 *Purgatory*, pp. 132–3.

28 Loach, in McConica, op. cit., p. 386; Peter Guilday, *The English Catholic Refugees on the Continent 1558–1795* (London, 1914), pp. 1–27, 63–65: Southern, *Recusant Prose*, pp. 14–30; Bossy, *English Catholic Community*, pp. 12–14; J. Andreas Löwe, 'Richard Smyth and the foundation of the University of Douai', *Nederlands archief voor kerkgeschiedenis/Dutch Review of Church History*, 79 (1999), pp. 142–69.

29 J. H. Pollen, ed., *Memoir of Robert Parsons, S.J.*, Catholic Record Society, *Miscellanea*, 2 (1906), p. 62.

30 *Apologie and Declaration*, p. 19.

31 By far the most stimulating and valuable account is that in Bossy, *Catholic Community*, pp. 14–18, to which I am greatly indebted though, as will be seen, I dissent from some of his central contentions. A cruder and somewhat facile statement of a similar view to Bossy's will be found in J. C. H. Aveling, *The Handle and the Axe* (London, 1976), pp. 53–6.

32 *D.D.*, p. xxviii; *Memorials*, p. 22.

33 Bossy, *English Catholic Community*, p. 15.

34 For the Marian regime's handling of the universities, see Cerianne Law's 2014 Cambridge PhD thesis, *Religious change in the University of Cambridge, c. 1547–84*.

35 P. Renold (ed.), *Letters of William Allen and Richard Barrett 1572–1598* (Catholic Record Society, 1967), pp. 4–5 [hereafter, *Letters*]. The allusion is to Luke 9.52–3, Vulgate version.

36 P. Ryan (ed.), 'Correspondence of Cardinal Allen' in Catholic Record Society, *Miscellanea*, 7 (1911), pp. 47–63, quotation p. 63 [hereafter, 'Correspondence'].

37 J. H. Pollen, *The English Catholics in the Reign of Queen Elizabeth* (London, 1920), p. 247.

38 *A Treatise Made in Defence of the lauful power and authoritie of Priesthood to remitte sinnes* (Louvain, 1567), preface (unpaginated). He is actually quoting from St Basil, but makes the application to England and 'our new ministers' explicit.

39 *Memorials*, p. 367.

40 He and Allen took their Doctorates in Divinity together in 1571.

41 *D.D.*, pp. xxvii–xxxi; *Letters*, pp. 8–11.

42 Patrick McGrath and Joy Rowe, 'Anstruther Analysed: the Elizabethan Seminary Priests', *Recusant History*, 18 (1986), pp. 1–13.

43 *Apologie*, p. 22 verso; 'Correspondence', pp. 66–7.

44 Printed in Richard Simpson, *Edmund Campion* (London, 1896), pp. 509–13; for Martin's letter, Gregory Martin, *A treatyse of Christian peregrination, written by M. Gregory Martin Licentiate and late reader of divinitie in the Englishe Colledge at Remes* ([Paris] 1583), 'The copy of a letter written to M. Doctour Whyte Warden of the new Colledge in Oxforde' (the final item in the book, unpaginated, dated 15 October 1575).

45 *D.D.*, p. xxxviii; *Memorials*, pp. 61–2.

46 For a good account of which see T. Deutscher, 'Seminaries and the Education of Novarese Parish Priests, 1593–1627', *Journal of Ecclesiastical History*, 32 (1981), pp. 303–19.

47 On the Jesuits, the *Ratio Studiorum* and St Thomas, see James Broderick, *The Life and Work of Blessed Robert Francis Cardinal Bellarmine* (London, 1928), vol. 1, pp. 374–84. An annotated translation of the 1599 Ratio is available online at http://www.bc.edu/sites/libraries/ratio/ratio1599.pdf

48 Allen's own account of the syllabus is in *Memorials*, pp. 62–7, translated *D.D.*, pp. xxxviii–xliii: it is helpfully expanded by Gregory Martin in *Roma Sancta* (ed. G. B. Parks) (Rome, 1969), pp. 114–9; the cases of conscience devised for the College are edited by P. J. Holmes, *Elizabethan Casuistry* (Catholic Record Society, 1981).

49 *D.D.*, pp. xxxix.

50 *Memorials*, pp. 32–3.

51 *D.D.*, p. xxxi–xxxii; Godfrey Anstruther, *The Seminary Priests*, vol. I (Ware and Durham, 1968), p. 224.

52 *Memorials*, p. 17.

53 *Apologie*, pp. 67–8.

54 *Memorials*, p. 33.

55 *Letters*, pp. 131–4; *Memorials*, p. 344.

56 *Memorials*, p. 36.

57 *Apologie*, pp. 109 verso – 110; for Allen's own account of his advice on martyrdom to Campion, *A Briefe Historie of the Glorious Martyrdom of XII Reverend Priests* (n.p., 1582), sig. d. iii. Verso; for the comment to Fr Aggazari, Rector of the Venerabile, see the preface to J. H. Pollen's edition of the *Briefe Historie*, p. ix; *Memorials*, p. 135.

58 *Apologie*, pp. 117 verso – 118.

59 *D.D.*, p. xliii: *Memorials*, p. 67.

60 *Memorials*, p. 35.

61 Alexandra Walsham, *Church Papists: Catholicism, Conformity and Confessional Polemic in Early Modern England* (Woodbridge, 1993), pp. 22–49.

62 *Memorials*, p. 34; see Walsham, *Church Papists*, pp. 62–3, though I think that Professor Walsham interprets Allen's text more permissively than Allen intended.

63 *Letters*, pp. 30–33.

64 *Memorials*, p. 354.

65 *Letters*, pp. 194–5.

66 *D.D.*, pp. li–lvi.

67 On the Bull in general, and Catholic opinion about it, A. O. Meyer, *England and the Catholic Church under Queen Elizabeth* (London, 1916), pp. 37 ff., 52–55, 76–90, 138–41; T. H. Clancy, *Papist Pamphleteers* (Chicago, 1964), pp. 46–9.

68 *Apologie*, p. 17.

69 *Letters*, pp. 276–84; *Modest Defense*, pp. 146–214.

70 Anthony Kenny, 'From Hospice to College 1559–1579', *The Venerabile*, 21 (1962) (Sexcentenary Issue), pp. 228–9.

71 *Letters*, pp. 284–92; Pollen, *The English Catholics in the Reign of Queen Elizabeth* (London, 1920), pp. 197–200.

72 *Memorials*, p. 38.

73 *Memorials*, 131; *Letters*, p. 75.

74 *Memorials*, pp. 217–18; Philip Hughes, *The Reformation in England*, vol. III (London, 1954), pp. 297–300.

75 *Memorials*, p. 233; Mattingly, 'William Allen', p. 333.

76 Mattingly, 'William Allen', p. 332.

77 The most extended treatment of Allen's political involvement at this time is Knox's introduction to *Memorials*, pp. li–lxxi.

78 *Letters*, pp. 156–66: the memorial for the Pope was identified and edited by Garrett Mattingly, loc. cit. The reference to the 'promiscuous multitude' comes from *Memorials*, p. lxvii.

79 For one of which see *Memorials*, pp. c–ci.

80 *Memorials*, pp. cvi–cviii.

81 Ibid., p. cxi

82 See especially *Modest Defense*, pp. 124–6; *A Briefe Historie of the Glorious Martyrdom of XII Reverend Priests*, Preface to the Reader, sig. c ii.

83 The evidence is assembled by Mattingly, loc. cit., pp. 336–7.

84 See, for example, 'Correspondence', p. 45, recommending Thomas Stapleton as a potentially valuable member of the invasion fleet of 1576 'but he knows nothing at all about the enterprise'.

85 *Modest Defense*, p. 196.

86 Ibid., p. 141; Clancy, *Papist Pamphleteers*, p. 51.

87 *The Copie of a Letter Written by M. Doctor Allen: concerning the yeelding up, of the Citte of Daventrie, unto his Catholike Maiestie, by Sir William Stanley* (Antwerp, 1587), pp. 17, 29.

88 *An Admonition of the Nobility and People of England . . . made for the execution of his Holines Sentence, by the highe and mightie Kinge Catholike of Spain. By the Cardinal of Englande* (1588).

89   *Modest Defense*, p. 224.
90   *Admonition to the Nobilitie*, sig. D5.
91   *Apologie*, p. 4 verso.
92   Ibid., p. 7; Simpson, *Campion*, p. 134.
93   *Pastor*, vol. 21, p. 250; vol. 22, p. 391; vol. 23, p. 311.
94   See, for example, his letter to John Mush in March 1594, *Memorials*, pp. 357–8.
95   R. B. Wernham (ed.), *Lists and Analyses of State Papers Foreign Series Elizabeth I* (London, HMSO, vol. 1, 1964), no. 627, vol. 4 (1984), nos 638–43, vol. 5 (1989), no. 627; and see the remarkable letter to Richard Hopkins, 14 August 1593, *Memorials*, pp. 348–51, about just such a 'reasonable toleration' – ''I thank God I am not estranged from the place of my birth most sweet, nor so affected to foreigners that I prefer not the weal of that people above all mortal things.'
96   *Memorials*, p. 37.
97   Ibid., p. 358.

6

The Mind of Gregory Martin

Elizabethan Catholicism was till fairly recently thought of as in some way incidental to the history of Elizabethan culture. Its religious and political history had for generations been written as an exercise in confessional *pietas*, its men of action remembered primarily as tribal heroes, its major authors, from Robert Persons to Robert Southwell, marginalised or excluded altogether from the canon of significant Elizabethan writing.[1] This marginalisation is in the process of correction, as the history of early modern Catholicism has moved out of its denominational embedding. The claims of these writers to serious consideration have increasingly been recognised, with the appearance of critical editions and biographies,[2] and projects like the 'Who were the Nuns' database. A list of significant recent work would have to include the names of Peter Lake, Michael Questier, Alex Walsham, Alison Shell, Victor Houliston, Paul Arblaster, Christopher Highley, Ann Dillon, Gerard Kilroy and Katy Gibbon. But we have still much to do to map the stature and cultural significance of two remarkable generations of Catholic Elizabethans, and the complex and varied impact of the early modern English Catholic exile community in Italy, Spain, France and the Low Countries on the politics and religious development not only of England, but of the territories in which they took refuge, and on the wider counter-reformation.

William Allen's claim that his new college in Douai would 'draw ... the best wittes out of England' to the service of the Catholic Church was an exaggeration, but, given the talents of many in his circle, a pardonable one. The Elizabethan Catholic exiles included a galaxy of men of European stature – Nicholas Sander, Thomas Stapleton, Thomas Harding, Edmund Campion, Richard Verstegen and Robert Persons were by any measure men of genius whose lives or writings resonated across the continent, and remind us that Eliza's beleaguered isle is not known at all if only known in isolation from counter-reformation Europe.

And of that still comparatively unexplored Elizabethan Catholic diaspora,[3] Gregory Martin is one of the most unjustly half-forgotten. Martin, as a scholar of St John's, Oxford, a late product of Marian England's brief counter-reformation, was one of the handful of English Catholic activists who shaped a vigorously aggressive 'recusant' response to the Elizabethan religious settlement.[4] The Queen's reign still had more than 20 years to run in 1582 when Martin died from tuberculosis, still in his early forties. But in the decade leading up to his death Martin had been one of William Allen's most energetic collaborators in giving the Douay College curriculum a distinctive emphasis on biblical apologetic, in transforming the English pilgrim hostel in Rome into something resembling a Tridentine seminary, in publishing pioneering and formidably effective polemics against both Church papistry and Protestant Bible translations,[5] while in a mere and scarcely credible 18 months he had produced the 'crowning glory' of English recusant prose,[6] the Bible translation which would serve English-speaking Catholics for the next four centuries.[7]

Unsurprisingly, John Bossy ranked Martin alongside Allen and Robert Persons as the most distinguished of the 'new men' who brought a vigorous and hard-edged 'reforming idealism' to the Elizabethan Catholic community.[8] Yet unlike the comparatively better known members of that trio, Martin has never quite had his due. Modern literary critics have echoed Elizabethan Protestant polemicists in panning his greatest achievement, the Rheims-Douay Bible, as 'wooden, literal and unidiomatic', and Martin himself rates just three mentions in the most recent scholarly discussion of the significance of the Douay-Rheims version.[9] Martin's 1578 *Treatise of Schisme* was the first published Catholic polemic against the practice of occasional conformity, Church papistry, in which he laid out most of the arguments subsequently deployed against Catholic attendance at Protestant services. Yet Robert Persons' hastily composed and incomplete *Reasons why Catholiques refuse to go to church*, published two years later, has received more scrutiny both from Martin's Protestant contemporaries and from subsequent historians of recusancy. Martin's treatise is now most often remembered for the fact that its printer, William Carter, was executed for treason, ostensibly on account of Martin's unfortunate citation of the biblical Judith, slayer of the tyrant Holofernes, as a model for Catholic gentlewomen, an allusion which the regime chose to interpret as an incitement to Catholic court ladies to cut Queen Elizabeth's throat.[10] And, as we shall see, *Roma Sancta*, Martin's ardent celebration of the religious energies of counter-reformation Rome, and Martin's greatest achievement apart from his Bible translation, was doomed by a convergence of circumstances, not least his own untimely death, to lie unpublished and unknown for four centuries. More than any other Elizabethan Catholic vernacular prose work,[11] *Roma Sancta* explicitly sought to promote militant recusancy in England by relating the English struggle *both* to the heroic age of early Christian martyrdom *and* to the extraordinary contemporary Catholic revival under Pope Gregory XIII. Had Martin's masterpiece been published in the years immediately following his death, Elizabethan recusancy might have looked different both to Martin's own contemporaries and to subsequent historians, less particular and insular, more explicitly and obviously an aspect of the response of a globalising Catholicism to the challenges of reformation.

Gregory Martin was the only surviving son of a minor gentry family from Guestling in Sussex. Little is known of his family, but a posthumously published and markedly affectionate letter to his married sisters, written sometime in the 1570s, suggests that while Martin's widowed mother was probably a Catholic, the rest of his family were conforming members of the Elizabethan Church. In 1557 he won a foundation scholarship at Sir Thomas White's new foundation of St John in Oxford, where he was an exact contemporary of Edmund Campion, with whom he proceeded both BA and MA, and who would remain his closest friend. Both men held fellowships in St John's from 1564, Martin's in Greek, Campion's in rhetoric. Early Elizabethan St John's was a notorious nest of papists: more than 30 of the early members of the college left Oxford for ordination at Douai or Rheims, and almost a third of Martin's and Campion's cohort of 20 founding members of the college eventually became Catholic priests. Martin's academic specialisation in biblical Hebrew and Greek must also have brought him into close contact with Thomas Neale, Regius Professor of Hebrew from 1559, but a staunch Catholic who avoided harassment from the university authorities by living just outside the university bounds in the recusant household of Edward Reynolds at Cassington, and with George Etheridge, Regius Professor of Greek, deprived in 1559 for refusing the Oath of Supremacy and who thereafter 'constantly adhered to the R. Catholic religion': Etheridge nevertheless remained in Oxford tutoring private pupils in Greek throughout the 1560s and 1570s.[12]

Even in so Catholic an enclave, Martin and Campion were probably not able to avoid attendance at Prayer Book worship altogether, and Campion at any rate must have received communion in the reformed rite at least once, at his ordination to the diaconate sometime before July 1568. But by the later 1560s pressure for more general conformity was mounting within the university. Correspondingly, from the safety of Catholic Europe, English Catholic leaders in exile like Thomas Harding, Nicholas Sander and Laurence Vaux were advocating sterner restrictions on the absolution of laypeople who attended Prayer Book services to avoid persecution: the opinion of a committee of theologians at Trent in 1562 against such occasional conformity was being circulated in manuscript in England, and was read by Martin among others.[13] In December 1568 Martin resigned his fellowship at St John's and left Oxford to take up a position as tutor to the children of Thomas Howard, fourth Duke of Norfolk, among them the future martyr St Philip Howard. Here for a time Martin was able to live 'after his conscience', but after Norfolk's arrest at the start of October 1570 the household was placed under hostile oversight and its members pressured to take Anglican communion. Martin resigned his post and went into hiding, and soon took ship for Allen's new College at Douai, *en route* writing to urge Campion to join him in exile, which, after some hesitation and a stay in Ireland, Campion eventually did in June 1571. Together once more in Douai, both men immersed themselves in theological reading, and together they completed the exercises for the BD degree in January 1573.[14] Almost immediately, however, Campion set out on foot on the pilgrimage to Rome which would take him into the Jesuit order and to work for the counter-reformation in Rudolf II's Prague.[15] Martin stayed in Douai to continue his theological studies, in January 1575 completing the exercises for the Licentiate, a necessary qualification for university teachers of theology.

But he did not proceed at once to teaching. In February 1575 Martin left Douai for a secluded country life in the household of a pious patron in the province of Hainault, perhaps as chaplain or family tutor ('*rusculum habitans cum meo Danusio*'). But the needs of the English mission and the burgeoning success of the College remained at the forefront of Martin's mind. That autumn he wrote an urgent persuasive to Thomas White, crypto-Catholic warden of New College, Oxford, urging him to renounce his preferments, acknowledge his true beliefs and join the exiles in the Low Countries.[16] A long letter to Campion at the end of the year bemoaned his own lack of literary productivity, and is packed with news from Douai – details of the curriculum there, of prestigious converts, of the flocks of students attracted to the College by rumours of Pope Gregory's recent grant of an annual subvention, and even an account of a Eucharistic miracle in one of the city's churches, seized on in Allen's sermons as confuting heretical doubts about the real presence. In April 1576 Martin returned to Douai and immediately began offering lectures in Hebrew, specifically designed to equip English priests to confound the 'arrogant ignorance of our heretics' ('*hereticorum nostrorum imperitissimam superbiam*').[17]

He was not, however, permitted to settle. On 9 November that same year, Allen despatched him and Thomas Stapleton to Rome with a party of students to help establish an English seminary there under the patronage of Reginald Pole's friend and colleague Cardinal Morone, in the former pilgrim hospice in Via Monserrato.[18] Martin was to remain in Rome for a year and a half, overseeing the establishment of a new regime of study there, an eager participant in the religious ferment which was the legacy of the recently concluded 1575 Jubilee, but also an uneasy witness of the rising tensions between the students and the distinguished but maladroit last Custos of the pilgrim hostel and first Rector of the new College, Morys Clennock. The troubles were in part the product of ancient racial animosities, and suspicions that the Welsh rector was guilty of nepotism and favouritism to his countrymen. But beneath these atavistic rivalries, two contrasting visions of the new College and its purpose were also in contention. For Clennock and the other veterans, members of a generation 'that remembered High Mass in Westminster Abbey, and (had become) accustomed to rapid changes of religion', the Elizabethan Settlement could seem a temporary setback. Accordingly, they viewed the refounded Hospice as a house of studies for exiles, pending the swing of the pendulum and the inevitable reconciliation of England with the papacy. To judge by the statutes authorised by Morone in 1577, this essentially conservative understanding of the refoundation was also shared by the Cardinal Protector, and perhaps by the Pope. But for Allen and his students, as for Martin himself, the new College, like the establishment at Douai, was being created to train men for the dangerous mission to re-evangelise England, as the Jesuits and others were evangelising the Indies.[19] The war between these different perceptions would come to a head in open student rebellion in 1579, a year and a half after Martin's return to the Low Countries, and led to the placing of the College under Jesuit government. Martin, who shared Allen's admiration for the Society, would certainly have approved, but the troubles were still containable during his time in Rome, and he never alludes to them.

We have little direct information about how Martin spent his time in Rome, but it's clear that in addition to establishing a pattern of studies closely modelled on the regime at Douai, he made full use of the religious opportunities offered by the great hub of counter-reformation. *Roma Sancta*, the celebration of Rome he was to write two years after his return to Rheims, is packed with recollections and glimpses of his involvements there. Like every pilgrim to Rome Martin prayed in the seven basilicas, venerated the major relics and attended solemn papal liturgies, an eagerly appreciative and self-conscious 'tramontane', utterly glamorised by the abounding religious energies released by the Jubilee and displaying none of Montaigne's cynical conviction that Rome's religiosity showed more of pomp than of piety.[20]

Martin said Mass in St Peter's, where he was struck by the efficiency and lavishness of the sacristy provision for visiting clergy;[21] he visited churches of special interest to English Catholics, like the chapel of *Domine Quo Vadis*, restored by Cardinal Pole, or the monastery of San Gregorio in Caelio, where, as he reported, one could pray in 'the verie closet where that holie man prayed'.[22]

He attended public recitations of the Rosary and joined in the Lenten stational liturgies, marvelling at the vast crowds of pious citizens, that 'goe and come continually so thicke like bees about their hive'.[23] He climbed the *Scala Sancta* at the Lateran on his knees, recalling that on Good Friday especially 'thou must watch for a place, so many there are continually upon them, four in a ranke upon every stayre'. He visited the catacombs, he took part in Corpus Christi processions and *Quarant'Ore* veneration of the Blessed Sacrament,[24] he attended open-air sermons by Jesuits and Oratorians, and was struck by the fervour of Italian preaching.[25] A seminary teacher himself, he noted the Pope's generosity to the many seminaries and colleges in Rome, commented characteristically on the unfamiliar pronunciation in use in the liturgies at the Greek College, and he travelled to Grottaferrata to observe the Byzantine liturgy of the Basiliean monks there.[26] Access to all this was facilitated by the friendship and patronage of Thomas Goldwell, Marian Bishop of St Asaph and now at the centre of Roman religious life as assistant bishop to the Cardinal Vicar of Rome. Goldwell had special responsibility for the instruction and baptism of converted Jews, and Martin was an eyewitness of the notorious compulsory sermons in the Ghetto, and took a keen interest in particular in the activities of 'M. Andreas the Christian Rabine and great preacher to the Jews'.[27]

Martin's 18-month immersion in Gregory XIII's Rome ended in July 1578, when Allen recalled him to Rheims, where the College had relocated after their expulsion from Douai. Robert Persons suspected that Allen had been alarmed that Martin might be recruited into the Society of Jesus if he remained in Rome.[28] However that may be, once back in the Netherlands Martin plunged into intense activity. He arrived in Rheims on 23 July: by the end of August he was lecturing on biblical Hebrew and Greek.[29] He was also writing: by the first week in November he had completed *A Treatise of Schisme*, directed at Catholics in England who were attending Anglican services to avoid harassment, arguing strongly the sinfulness of even such external compliance. Martin was here reflecting a hardening of attitudes by Allen and his circle. Students at Rheims in the late 1570s were being trained in cases of conscience which recognised that in certain circumstances it might be legitimate for the Catholic servants of Protestant masters, and for Catholic noblemen at court, to attend Anglican worship, a view endorsed by theologians and canonists at Rome.[30] But Allen and others were increasingly conscious of the dangers of assimilation, and they sought to stiffen Catholic resistance. Martin's pamphlet, printed clandestinely in England and carrying an imprimatur from Allen declaring the work 'published at this time out of necessity for schismatics', was the first public indication of this new hard line. Martin's tract set out incidents and arguments from Scripture, from the writings of the Fathers and from the history of the Church which were routinely used to justify occasional conformity, and offered refutations of them all. The *Treatise* became a standard point of reference in late Elizabethan disputes over Church papistry, and provided an arsenal of arguments for hard-line opposition to occasional conformity.[31] But Martin's treatment of these issues bears the mark of his own recent immersion in papal Roman. Countering the often cited precedent for occasional conformity of Namaan the Syrian, the convert pagan permitted by the prophet Elisha to accompany his master the Canaanite king when he went to worship in the temple of Rimmon, Martin introduced a distinctively papal slant to the story, not taken up by subsequent Catholic writers. Namaan's action, he suggested, was licit (if at all) only because it had the express permission of Eliseus (Elisha), whereas 'he that is Eliseus nowe, [i.e. the Pope] doth give you no such leave, but doth commaund the contrary'.[32]

Formidable as *A Treatise of Schisme* was, however, it must have been written at high speed, and, even before it had been sent to the printers, Martin was launched on a far more momentous task, the translation of the whole Bible. In September 1578 Allen wrote to John Vendeville, co-founder of the College, outlining the course of studies at Douai and emphasising the centrality of biblical study, since priests working in England needed to 'have at their fingers' ends all those passages ... impiously misused by the heretics in opposition to the church's faith'. For the same reason, the students also needed familiarity with the Bible in English, 'a thing on which the heretics plume themselves exceedingly, and by which they do great injury to the simple folk'. An English Catholic version of the Bible was therefore urgently needed, and, provided the Pope approved, Allen told Vendeville, the College would undertake it, 'for we already have men most fitted for the work'.[33]

Just one month later to the day, Martin, unquestionably the man most fitted for the work, was launched on that mammoth project, working from the Latin Vulgate, as was inevitable for any counter-reformation translation, given the Council of Trent's privileging of that version above all others for doctrinal purposes,[34] but with constant reference to the Hebrew and Greek. He turned out copy at the breakneck speed of two chapters a day. [*ipse vertendo quotidie duo capita absolvit*] These chapters were then checked and where necessary the renderings emended by Allen himself and by Richard Bristow, who between them also supplied most of the doctrinal and polemical notes to the published version.[35] In addition to consulting the Hebrew and Greek texts alongside the Vulgate, Martin paid close attention to previous Tudor Protestant Bible versions, and his scorn for heretical mistranslation did not prevent him from borrowing liberally from Tyndale and his successors. But Martin's main reason for trawling through the English Protestant translations was to cull examples of heretical depravity in mistaking or deliberately perverting the original meaning to support their own doctrines. The outcome of this hostile scrutiny was a substantial tract of more than three hundred pages, published more or less simultaneously with the New Testament, in 1582, as *A discoverie of the manifold corruptions of the holy scriptures by the heretikes of our daie*. It was a relentlessly hostile case for the prosecution, designed to show that all heretics systematically 'deny some whole bookes and parts of books . . . call other some into question . . . expound the rest at their pleasure . . . picke quarels to the very original and Canonical text, [and] fester and infect the whole body of the Bible with cankred translations . . .'[36]

From its first appearance, Martin's Bible was attacked – for its use of the Vulgate as its base text, for its wooden literalism, for its allegedly clunky rhythms and for its excessive use of Latinisms. Such criticisms were of course confessionally motivated, and Martin's versions of the Gospels and the narrative sections of his Old Testament can in fact stand comparison with other Tudor Bibles. Many of his distinctive turns of phrase were vivid and idiomatic improvements on the renderings that had preceded them: '*The footstool of thy feet*' (Mt. 12.44; '*Why what evil hath he done*' (Mt. 27.23); '*throng and press*' (Lk. 8.45); '*his rainment white and glistering*' (Lk. 9.29); '*set at nought*' (Lk.

23.11); *'strive for mastery'* (1 Cor. 9.25); *'to live is Christ and to die is gain'* (Phil. 1.21); *'questioned among themselves'* (Mk 1.27); *'blaze abroad the matter'* (Mk 1.45); *'mourn and weep'* (Lk. 6.25); *'it came to pass'* (Lk. 17.11); *'distress of nations'* (Lk. 21.25).

Nevertheless, many of the objections to Martin's work had substance, not least his use of the Latin Vulgate rather than the Greek New Testament as his base text. And his close adherence to the language of the Vulgate, often involving transliteration rather than translation, produced many oddities. Martin's version of the Psalms, and his rendering of the New Testament epistles especially, yield many notoriously clumsy or impenetrable examples: 'Purge the old leaven, that you may be a new paste, as you are azymes. For our Pasche, Christ, is immolated' (1 Cor. 5.7.); 'For our wrestling is not against flesh and blood, but . . . against the rectors of the world of this darkenes, against the spirituals of wickedness in the celestials' (Eph. 6.12); 'Beneficence and communication do not forget: for with such hosts God is promerited' (Heb. 13.16). In Philippians 1 Christ 'inanites' rather than 'empties' himself, in Hebrews 'brotherly love' is rendered 'charity of the fraternity'. Martin was conscious of the problematic character of many of these Latinisms, but insisted they were the price that had to be paid for faithfulness to the (Vulgate) original: 'We presume not in hard places to mollifie the speaches or phrases, but religiouslie keepe them word for word, and point for point, for feare of missing or restraining the sense of the holy Ghost to our phantasie.'[37] And many of his Latinisms were in fact successful, subsequently being adopted by the translators of the King James Bible, and, as he was convinced they would, passing from there into the language – in the Epistle to the Romans alone these include *separated, consent, impenitent, propitiation, remission, concupiscence, revealed, emulation, conformed, instant, contribution.*[38]

Martin's was unquestionably the most consistently literal Tudor Bible translation, and his policy of translating the same Hebrew or Greek word by the same English equivalent, while not without its own problems, gave him a decided polemical edge on his Protestant opponents. In his tract against Protestant corruptions of scripture, he made telling use of Protestant inconsistency in translating the Greek word *'paradosis'*, 'tradition', for example: Martin scored a palpable hit with his charge that the inconsistency of the Protestant versions sprang in this instance from reluctance to acknowledge that scripture here supported Catholic teaching on the positive value of tradition.

> Wheresoeuer the Holy Scripture speaketh against certaine traditions of the Iewes, partly friuolous, partly repugnant to the Law of God, there al the English translations folow the Greeke exactly, neuer omitting this word, *tradition*. Contrariewise wheresoeuer the holy Scripture speaketh in the commendation of Traditions, to wit, such traditions as the Apostles deliuered to the Churche, there al their said translations agree, not to folow the Greeke, which is still the self same word, but for, *traditions,* they translate, *ordinances,* or *instructions.* Why so and to what purpose? we appeale to the worme of their conscience, which continually accuseth them of an heretical meaning, whether, by vrging the word, *traditions,* wheresoeuer they are discommended, and by suppressing the word, wheresoeuer they are commended, their purpose and intent be not, to signifie to the Reader, that al traditions are naught, & none good, al reprouable, none allowable.[39]

Together, Martin's *Discoverie of the Manifold Corruptions* and his New Testament translation, both of which appeared in 1582, posed the Elizabethan religious establishment with one of its most alarming challenges. The stream of Protestant replies, by such heavyweights as John Reynolds, William Whitaker, Thomas Cartwright, Thomas Bilson, Edward Bulkeley and the egregious William Fulke, who reprinted the entire Rheims New Testament in order to refute it, would flow on to the end of the reign.[40] And it is worth noting that the publication of Martin's New Testament in 1582 was a landmark event for the counter-reformation as a whole: Catholic Bible versions were a rarity in late sixteenth-century Europe, liable to bring their translators under suspicion of heretical leanings. By contrast, the Rheims New Testament, its margins dense with controversial and expository notes upholding the Catholic cause, had been produced with Rome's approval and would be a major source for the notes included in Jakob Wuzek's 1593 Polish Catholic Bible.[41]

Martin had completed the gargantuan task of translation by July 1580,[42] and might have been expected to lay down his pen for a while. In fact he moved restlessly on. While still at work on the translation he had despatched a long letter of remonstrance to a 'maried priest, his frend', not named in the published version, but who had evidently been chaplain to Ralph Baynes, 'your olde Maister and Lorde, the last true bishopp of Lichefilde'. Now, with his translation complete, he turned once more to literary polemic against one of the champions of Elizabeth's Church.[43]

The immediate occasion for the writing of Martin's greatest original work, *Roma Sancta,* was an attack on Rome and the papacy by one of the most persistent Elizabethan anti-Catholic theological gladiators, William Fulke, Master of Pembroke College, Cambridge, who was to publish two large attacks on Martin's biblical work, and who was to be the ablest of Campion's opponents in the Tower disputations in October 1582.[44] In February 1580 Fulke published A *Retentive to stay good Christians in true faith and religion,* an attack on a pamphlet by Martin's Rheims colleague Richard Bristow, 'Motives unto the Catholic Faith', itself a reworking of William Allen's celebrated 'scroll of articles'.[45] In the *Retentive* Fulke reiterated the charge that the Pope was antichrist, and claimed that every traveller in Italy, 'whether he be protestant, Papist, or Newter' was aware that at Rome 'where be most Atheists of any region almost in the world', 'vnder the Popes nose, . . . is greatest ignorance . . . [and] open blasphemies are as common, yea oftentimes in the Popes mouth, as the praises of God are among true christians'.[46] So there was, he claimed, 'more . . . of vertue and lesse of vice in England at this time, then is or hath beene at any time with in those fiue hundred yeeres in Rome . . .'[47]

This was a red rag to Martin, who had lost none of the devotional ardour his year and a half's residence in Gregory XIII's Rome had inspired in him. Fulke prefaced the *Retentive* with a tendentious 'reasonable request and protestation to the learned papists', to 'leaue of all vayne discourses, and needelesse questions', and deal with controverted issues solely 'in the strict forme of Logicall argumentes'.[48] What Martin produced, however, was not logical confutation, but an ardent devotional rhapsody, designed to persuade by empathic evocation. The book's value as a unique window into a crucial moment in the late sixteenth-century counter-reformation has gained increasing recognition; according to John Hedley, 'for its comprehensive treatment of the religious life in Rome, the confessional commitment and emotional impact . . . [*Roma Sancta*] constitutes one of the most important statements of the counter reformation church'.[49]

But *Roma Sancta* is not only a unique source of information, and a programmatic expression of counter-reformation self-perception. It is also a literary construct utterly unlike any other product of the bitter disputes between Catholics and Protestants in early modern England, or, for that matter, any other contemporary account of the Rome of Gregory XIII. The book is intensely personal: not even Martin's posthumously published letter to his much loved but conformist sisters, urging them to embrace Catholicism, displays anything like the same degree of emotional urgency, and that letter is far less revealing about the springs of Martin's own passionate Catholicism. Yet like everything else he wrote, *Roma Sancta* was an occasional work, almost certainly written at Allen's behest, and directly addressed to the immediate needs of controversy with English Protestantism. But to understand the sources of its distinctive focus and power, we need to consider changing perceptions of Rome in the second half of the sixteenth century.

It's a historical commonplace that many of the reformation debates turned on the right to possession of the past – crudely, was Apostolic Christianity Catholic or Protestant, and hence *whose* were the Fathers? Sixteenth-century Catholics and Protestants both invoked and evoked the past to legitimate present belief and practice. In the decades after 1550 a series of formidable polemical projects, of which the Magdeburg *Centuries*, Foxe's *Actes and Monumentes* and Baronio's *Annales Ecclesiastici* are just the best known, laid claim to the present possession of saving truth, by drawing out alleged continuities with the Christian past. As the Protestant centuriator Matthew Flacius insisted, *historia est fundamentum doctrinae*, or, as the Catholic Thomas Stapleton wrote in the preface to his 1565 translation of Bede's Ecclesiastical History, . . . 'touching . . . what the faith first planted among us englishmen was, how and when we received it, because it is a matter historicall, in an Historie ye shall read it'.[50]

Both Catholics and Protestants, then, claimed ownership of the Christian past. But for Catholics that claim took a distinctive form. Rejecting the innovations in belief, institution and custom which they believed characterised the churches of the reformation, they repudiated counter-accusations of corruption and decline by asserting unbroken continuity between the Tridentine and the early Church. The Church was visibly, even materially *semper eadem*, always the same, and hence always itself. Protestantism might seek to recover the primitive past, but Catholics claimed to *remember* it, a living memory, embedded and encoded in the teaching, institutions, practices and material culture of contemporary Catholicism.

In that newly assertive polemical claim to *remembrance* of authentic Christian truth, the city of Rome and its bishop had a central place. Against Protestant claims that papal Rome had fallen away from primitive purity to become the synagogue of Satan, the seat of antichrist, and the great harlot of Revelation, Catholics asserted an unbroken continuity of belief and practice between the Church of the martyrs and the Church of Post-Tridentine Rome, a continuity increasingly testified to by the archeological record. The very soil of the papal city was, in the words of Pope Pius V, '*inzuppata col sangue dei martiri*' 'steeped in the blood of the martyrs' like a sop of bread in soup.[51] Pagan Rome had persecuted the saints, but papal Rome had become their shrine, and the principal conduit and guardian of the faith for which they had died. That claim was foundational for the reform and reconstruction of Catholicism in the wake of Trent. As Pope Paul IV insisted in his 1558 Bull, *Ineffabilis divinae providentiae*, extending the solemn observance of the feast of the Chair of St Peter at Rome to the universal Church, the city had been consecrated by the blood of the Apostles 'so that where the head of superstition had been, there should be the head of holiness, and where the princes of the pagans had lived, there the princes of the churches should die, and so that she who was once the mother of error should become the mother of truth'.[52]

The pre-Christian antiquities of Rome, its ancient buildings and the institutions they represented had, of course, always been fundamental to European cultural memory, a symbol of ancient continuities and, for the humanists of an earlier generation, a resource for social, political and artistic renewal. The tragic ruin of classical Rome, and the contrast between the 'immortal glory' of the ancient city and the parasitic squalor of the 'bastard Rome' which now perched ignominiously among the ruins, had long been a conventional theme for humanist lamentation and regret, most famously perhaps in the sonnets of Joachim du Bellay, with their evocations of a city of ancient greatness 'fallen to heaps of stones', nowadays teeming with shameless whores and ruled by sleazy ecclesiastics whose main occupation was financial and political intrigue.

> Si je monte au Palais, je n'y trouve qu'orgueil,
> Que vice déguisé, qu'une cérémonie,
> Qu'un bruit de tambourins, qu'une étrange harmonile,
> Et de rouges habits un superbe appareil:
> . . . .
> Si je vais plus avant, quelque part où j'arrive,
> Je trouve de Vénus la grand bande lascive
> Dressant de tous côtés mille appas amoureux.
> Si je passe plus outre, et de la Rome neuve
> Entre en la vieille Rome, adonques je ne treuve
> Que de vieux monuments un grand monceau pierreux.[53]

Much the same sentiments would surface 30 years on in the early 1580s in the Italian journal of Michel de Montaigne.[54] The pathos of the 'ruins of Rome' was a theme reiterated throughout the century, for example by the English traveller William Thomas,

> the wonderfull maiestee of buildynges that the onely rootes therof doe yet represent, the huge temples, the infinite great palaices, the vnmeasurable pil|lers, . . . and a noumbre of other lyke thynges, not to be founde againe thoroughout an whole worlde: imaginyng withall, what maiestee the citee myghte be of, whan all these thynges flourished, Than didde it greeue me to see the onelie iewell, myr|rour, maistres, and beautie of this worlde, that neuer had hir lyke, nor (as I thynke) neuer shall, lie so desolate and disfigured, that there is no lamentable case to be harde, or lothesome thyng to be seen, that maie be compared to a small parte of it.[55]

Classical Rome, of course, retained its fascination even for pious Catholic visitors. From 1557 onwards the most widely used and influential guidebook to Rome, *Le Cose Meravigliose dell'alma citta di Roma*, incorporated Antonio Palladio's illustrated pamphlet on the remains of classical Rome, *l'Antichita di Roma*, alongside his more conventionally pious *Descrizione de le chiese, stationi & reliquiie . . . che sonno in la Citta di Roma*, which listed the sacred sites of papal Rome and provided itineraries for visiting the churches and gaining their indulgences.[56] Even so single-minded a pilgrim as the Jesuit Robert Persons, in Rome for the Jubilee of 1575, could admit that he had carried 'little devotion' out of the city, because he 'had attended more to see profane monuments of Caesar, Cicero and other such like then to places of devotion'.[57]

But at least from the Jubilee of 1550 onwards a different emphasis on Rome's past was gaining favour, shaping a rhetoric which rejected, denounced or ignored the city's pagan past, and denied or minimised its modern vices, instead locating Rome's abiding imaginative power in a revival of devotion rooted in its Christian antiquities. Fostered by Filippo Neri's prayer vigils in the catacombs and his famous devotional visits to the Seven Churches,[58] this newer emphasis was nourished especially by the work of the antiquarian and epigrapher Onofrio Panvinio. Panvinio's major works included a map and topographical guide to classical Rome, and histories of the Roman Triumph and the Roman Republic, so he was no enemy to the study of classical antiquity. But his account of the catacombs in his treatise on early Christian funerary practice, the *De Ritu Sepeliendi Mortuos apud veteres Christianos*, published in Cologne in 1568, and based primarily on literary and liturgical sources, was an important stimulus for the revival of religious interest in *Roma Sotteranea*, fully ten years before the momentous rediscovery of a hitherto unknown Christian cemetery in the Via Salaria fired counter-reformation fascination with the archaeology of the catacombs.[59] Onofrio's historical and devotional treatise on the seven basilicas and their relics, the *De Praecipuis Urbis Romae Sanctioribusque Basilicis*, published the same year, and which was to run through at least 14 editions in ten years, provided both a stimulus and a quarry for the flood of publications on Christian Rome related to or flowing from the Jubilee of 1575, by writers like Pompeio Ugonio, Marco Serrano and others.[60] Panvinio's *De Praecipuis* provided a brief history of the foundation of each of the ancient basilicas, citing the key patristic and medieval sources, listing the major inscriptions and relics and providing brief and austerely

liturgical forms of prayer to be recited before the major altars. The
De Ritu Sepeliendi used similar epigraphic, liturgical and historical
sources to describe the devotional and ritual practices surrounding
burial in the early Church. Both books provided a crucial prelude
to the monumental labours of Cesare Baronio, who began work on
his great compilation on early Christianity, the *Annales Ecclesiastici,*
in the immediate wake of the Jubilee, while *De Ritu Sepeliendi* was
one of the main inspirations for Antonio Bosio's pioneering archaeological work in the catacombs.[61] The accidental discovery of an
unknown complex of catacombs in Via Salaria in 1578 excitedly
described by Baronio *'quod nullo magis proprio vocabulo dixerimus prae
eius amplitudine, multisque atque diversis viis, quam subterraneam civitatem'*,[62] 'a subterranean city' unleashed centuries of imaginative
fantasy about the early years of Roman Christianity which both
Neri's Oratorians and Mercurian and Aquaviva's Jesuits consciously
fostered. During the Jubilee of 1575 the Jesuit General petitioned
Gregory XIII for permission to search for martyr relics in the catacombs. Baronio's major revision of the Roman Martyrology, with
its historical and archaeological notes, was a seminal influence, as
was his triumphant reinstallation in the late 1590s of the relics of
the titular saints in his Cardinalatial titular church of San Nereo e
Achilleo, a much imitated exercise in Christian antiquarianism.[63]
The cult of early Christian martyrdom would find more gruesome expressions in the 1590s, in Nicolo Circignani's horrifying
martyrological fresco cycles at San Stefano in Monte Caelio, and at
the Venerabile, both of these Jesuit or Jesuit-inspired commissions,
and in the Oratorian Antonio Gallonio's *Trattato degli instrumenti di
martirio e delle varie maniere di martoriare usate da' gentilicontro christiani*
(1591–4), with engravings by Antonio Tempesta after drawings by
Giovanni Guerra which left nothing whatever to the imagination.[64]

This revived emphasis on the spiritual glories of early Christian
Rome as inspiration for the present would blossom fully at the
end of the century, but, perhaps as a result of Cardinal Pole's ardent
papalism,[65] it was affecting English Catholic sensibilities already by
the early 1560s. Reporting rhapsodically about his discovery of the
relics and Christian antiquities of Italy in general and of Rome in
particular, Nicholas Sander assured his friend and Oxford contemporary John Rastell

These are the glorious trophies Rastell, to see which holy martyrs and confessors came themselves to Rome, and invited others to take the same road ... I am not surprised if Rome fills my pages, since with the fame of her name she has filled the whole world ... For not only is doctrine incorrupt there, but the traces (vestigia), nay, the express images of the discipline, which flourished in the primitive church, are to be seen at Rome.[66]

By the '*vestigia*' of primitive Christianity Sander had in mind something more contemporary than Rome's ancient churches or the relics of its saints. Well aware of humanist and Protestant satire on the vices of modern Rome, and despite the brothels and the licence, luxury and ambition which du Bellay had so sardonically observed, for Sander papal Rome remained still the holy city it had been from Christianity's earliest days. As he told Rastell,

Though I do not deny that there are vices at Rome ... still I think I shall be speaking the truth when I say that it is the one place above all others, in which the holiest life is led ... In the Lent that I was there, not a day passed without my seeing sixty, and often a hundred men receive the Body of the Lord in one and the same church. The learned confessors in many churches do not leave the confessional all the early morning. Indulgences are offered to those about to communicate ... There are a great many magnificent hospitals for the poor ... I have specially mentioned all this because I know the Devil is harder at work than ever traducing the Supreme See ...[67]

What Christian Rome had been in the Church's infancy, it was still. The early Christian past presented a mirror in which could be discerned a reflection of the face of modern Catholicism. Remembrance of things past was therefore vital for continued fidelity to the gospel. As Thomas Stapleton insisted in the preface to his translation of Bede,

... if we looke to Italy, to Fraunce, to Spaine, to the catholike territories of Grece, of Germany, of Suicerland, to the kingdomes of Poole, of Portugall, and of other maine landes in other places off the worlde dispersed, where the precious iewell of this faith is knowen and enioyed, we shall finde that all those countres haue and do therefore yet continew in the same, bicause they varie not from the first faith receiued . . . For why? They haue well remem-bred the admonitions of S. Paule to the Corin|thians . . . when he wrote vnto them and saied, *Vigilate & state in fide.* Watch and stande in the faith . . . Al Christened Catho|like countrees haue wel remembred these lessons of the Apo|stle. And as many as haue remembred and folowed them, haue remained and do yet remaine in the faith of Christ, haue long enioyned and do yet enioye this rare and inestimable iewell . . .

And so he offered his translation of Bede precisely as an act of remembrance, 'that we may remembre *vnde exiderimus*, from whence we haue fallen', and 'to put thee in mind, (Christen Reader) of this precious iewell of our faith in Christ'.[68]

But Stapleton's use of the word 'remember' as the act of 'putting in mind', in his preface to Bede, was far from neutral, for at that precise moment the word and concept of remembrance was sharply dividing Catholic and Protestant. In September 1560 Elizabeth had issued a '*proclamation against breakinge or defacing of monumentes of antiq-uitie, beyng set up in churches or other publique places for memory and not for supersticion*', in which she attempted to halt radical Protestant iconoclasm by forbidding the destruction of any monuments 'that haue ben in times past erected and set vp, for the only memory of them to their posteritie in common Churches, and not for any reli-gious Honour'.[69] That distinction between simple memorialisation and memory as something altogether more dynamic and interac-tive, intrinsically involving the paying of 'religious honour', featured prominently in William Allen's first controversial publication, a defence of purgatory and prayers for the dead, published in the same year and from the same printing house as Stapleton's preface to Bede. In it Allen insisted that remembrance of the dead was part of the 'holy consent of good woorkes, and mutuall agreement of prayer, to the continuall supplying of eche others lackes' which constituted the communion of saints. As St Augustine had said, 'The soules off the faythfull deceased, be not seuered from the Churche . . . elles there shulde be no memory kepte for theime at the altare, in the communion of the body of Christe.' The reformation's reduction of remembrance of the dead to mere recollection, therefore, was in effect a repudiation of belief in the community of saints, under the delusion that 'the Lord hathe taken the deade owte of our company'. But 'all this forgetfullnesse, coommethe by the wicked suggestion of these late deuelishe opinions, which maynteyne that the prayers of the lyuing, or theire workes, doo not extende to the deade in Christe'. Christian remembrance was therefore emphatically not the mere recollection of bygone people and events, inexorably separated from us by the passing of time, but an act of communion. In the Christian dispensation, the remembered dead were our contemporaries, and the act of remembrance made us present to each other in a mutually beneficial exchange of charity, 'the common utilitie'.[70]

What applied to the Christian dead in purgatory, applied doubly to the holy dead in heaven. The tombs and relics of the saints were their 'glorious memories', and there could be no question of such *memoria* being 'for the only memory of them ... and not for religious honour'. As Gregory Martin was to write in his posthumously published treatise on pilgrimage, there had always been 'gowing, running, kneeling [and] burying at the Apostles memories'. 'All the best Christians in the primitive Church' loved such sacred sites, and went 'farre and neere unto them, to touch, to kisse, to licke them, to weepe in the place, to conceive such a livelye imagination of thinges done there by Christ or his sayntes ... that it was a payne to remove from thence, a death to dwelle farre off'.[71]

It was out of this milieu of awed fascination with the material holiness of Rome that Martin's masterpiece was drawn. *Roma Sancta* falls into two distinct parts or books. The first juxtaposes lavish citations from early Christian writers with vivid recollection and description of his own experiences in Rome, in order to evoke 'the devotion of the citie of Rome' as a living continuum from past to present. The second part lists and describes the wide range of charitable foundations, confraternities, hospitals, orphanages and religious communities, which that devotion inspired in contemporary Rome. The division was programmatic, designed to confute Protestant insistence on salvation by faith alone by demonstrating the superiority of the true faith through the evidence of its abundant good works: 'we gladly leave unto them theyr only faith or rather no faith'. For Martin as for Sander, Rome's extraordinary flood of charitable action and organisations flowed seamlessly from its practice of the ardent piety which was the product of right faith. Rome's religious life proved the 'unspeakable gifte and wonderfull providence' of God, who had preserved 'these two, Fayth and good works, jointly together in his Church, and specially in the Head Citie and Apostolike See, which is a Rocke for the one, and a candell on a candelsticke for the other'.[72] Rome itself was the best possible evidence of the truth of the Catholic faith, its distinctive religious observances, like its stational liturgies, attested since antiquity:

> And so we are descended from S. Paule to S. Jerom, from him to S. Gregorie, and from him to three hundred yeares after, and at this verie day we see it with our eies increased rather then diminished, and this is authoritie and antiquitie sufficient to stoppe al our adversaries mouthes, and to confirme and enflame al good Catholikes to the practice of the like devotion . . .[73]

'It were a thing much to be wished' therefore, that all good Christians 'once at leest within xxv years, did see with their own eies this blessed Citie.' But because of England's descent into heresy, Martin wrote to share his ardour for the holy city with his 'deere contriemen', that 'dwell far of'.[74]

In evoking the ancient and modern pieties of Rome, Martin was covering territory familiar enough in the scholarly writings of Panvinio, and Serrano, in guidebooks like the *Cose Meravigliose*, and in the flood of publications elicited by the 1575 Jubilee. More than half the first part of *Roma Sancta* deals with the seven ancient basilicas, the liturgy of the stational churches, and the relics venerated in the holy places in Rome. In describing them, Martin quarried Panvinio's and Serrano's work, just as in the second part of his book, on Rome's charity, he draws a long chapter on the charitable and devotional activities of the city during the Jubilee year from the Dominican Angelo Pientini's *Pie Narrationi dell Opere piu memorabile fatte in Roma l'anno del Giubileo*.[75] But the highly personalised tone of Martin's work makes it quite unlike any of his sources. This distinctiveness is evident in part in idiosyncratic choice of subjects, for example his marked interest in the pronunciation of liturgical

Greek by the members of the Greek College in Rome, a reflection of his own Oxford writing on the pronunciation of Greek.[76]
Martin's fascinating but disturbing discussions of the treatment of
Rome's Jews and the preaching of convert Rabbis, reflect both his
own interest in Rabbinic and Hebrew studies and his friendship
with Thomas Goldwell, Marian Bishop of St Asaph. As a refugee
bishop forced by persecution to settle in Rome, Goldwell himself
represented for Martin a living testimony of the continuity between
early Christian and counter-reformation Rome, for, as he wrote,
'thou shalt never see Rome without some Athanasius and Paulus, I
mean some Catholike bishops driven from their Sees'.[77] Goldwell
was also now vice-gerent to the Cardinal Vicar of Rome, and so the
bishop responsible for the instruction and baptism of convert Jews,
which probably helps account for Gregory's extended discussions
of such matters.[78] But Martin's avid personal interest in all aspects
of the religious ferment of Gregory XIII's Rome makes his book a
unique eyewitness source for a host of topics, from early Jesuit and
Oratorian preaching to the activities of the Roman Confraternities,
and many other matters ignored by other contemporary writers.

But it is above all Martin's mode of address which makes *Roma
Sancta* unique. He addresses his readers as one excitedly remembering the past – Rome's remote past, constantly referenced in
extensive quotations from St Jerome, St Augustine, St Leo the Great,
St Ambrose, St Gregory the Great, Prudentius and Procopius, but also
his own recent time in the city, now recalled for their benefit, and for
the confounding of heresy. Even Martin's many extended citations
from patristic sources are marshalled as if they were recent memories.
'Consideryng in what tyme we do live ... upon whom the ends of
the worlde is come', he wrote, it seemed impossible that the ardour of
the early Christians, 'in whose partes the bloud of Christ was warme
as yet' could be matched. Yet in Rome he had seen that ardour with
his own eyes, 'I mean it is the self same now that the auncient fathers
have heretofore described it ...'[79] So Martin offers not mere history,
but first-hand testimony, enthralled reportage: only an extensive
quotation from the book's opening can convey the effect:

Being at Rome, gentle Reader, almost two yeeres in this time
of Gregorie the thirteenth, & seeing there wonderful varietie of

blessed monuments, of devout persons, of godlie and charitable exercises from day to day never ceasing: the churches, the Martyrs, the glorious ashes of undoubted Sainctes, the places where they prayed, preached, fasted, were imprisoned, dyed: when I saw moreover the good examples of all degrees, the preaching, teaching, Confessing, Communicating, visiting of holy places which they call Stations, kneling, knocking, sighing, weeping, creeping, al other maner of fervent, comelie and unfeigned devotion: when I saw the almes ... the mercifull & bountiful provision for al kind of poor and nedie persons; ... And (that which is a great cause of all the rest) when I saw the majestie of the See Apostolike, his holiness among his Cardinals, as Michael among the Angels, Aaron or Moyses among the other preistes, Peter among the rest of the Apostles, their solemnitie in Chappel, Wisedom in Consistorie, audience at home in their chambers, courtesie in al places mixt with great Discretion and singular gravitie: ... I was in maner rapt besides my self with admiration therof, & sayd within me ... It is a verie true report which I have heard and read of this noble Citie, I did scarse thinke it credible til my self came & saw it with mine eyes & found that the half part was not told me.[80]

The first part of Martin's book was largely concerned with evocations of ancient Christian Rome and its remains, what he calls 'the antiquities of godliness'. But this was a past recalled not through arduous historical research, though Martin is copious in patristic quotation, but by constant insistence on the deep continuities which defined Holy Rome. He quotes the admonition of Proverbs 23: 'O my sonne ... despise not thy mother when she is old': Rome, our spiritual mother,

> ... in very deede is old many wayes, old fayth, old charitie, old devotion, old Churches, old Relikes, old Sainctes. In al these so old verie neere as in Christianitie it self which Peter and Paule taught them. And this is one principal pleasure among the rest which they take that come to this Citie, and that thou (gentle Reader) mayst take of this booke, to se how Rome after so many yeres & so great alterations in a great part of the world besides, is notwithstanding always like it self.[81]

Martin had no interest in the past for its own sake: 'worldlie and prophane antiquitie' was best left 'to them that for curiositie, or gayne, or whatsoever other vanitie, take great paines to abuse their travel and tyme in paltrie'.[82] When he had first arrived in Rome, Campion had written to him from Prague, urging him to make the most of his time in the holy city, but warning

> Do you see the corpse of the Imperial city? What in this life can be glorious, if so much wealth and beauty can come to nothing? But who and what have stood firm in these miserable shifts of time? The relics of the saints and the throne of the Fisherman![83]

Martin might well have adopted that as the epigraph for his work: instead, he prefaced the book with a sonnet, the sestet of which reflected just so on the ruins of pagan Rome:

> Where are thy Temples and triumphant bowes
> Wt marble shafte that shott them selves to heaven
> Thy bathes thie signes thie Theaters thy showes
> Nay where is Rome yt rydd on Mountayns seven
> One Rome there was in all the world of yore
> But now o fatall anagram Noe more.[84]

The Christian pilgrim should rejoice 'to se the ruines therof, and how they are neglected, al Christian monuments coming in their places; to se the victorie of Christ over the Divel, of peter [sic] over Nero, of the See Apostolike over the earthly Empyre, of Rome the spouse of Christ over Rome the whoore of Babylon'. By contrast, 'if thou wilt rather know the antiquities of godliness, thou shalt fynd here infinite treasures . . .'[85]

In Rome, the history books put on flesh, the past became present:

> Read me in Eusebius the triumphant monuments of the two chief Apostles . . . so we find them at this day . . . Read in S. Jerom that . . . Peter lying buried in the Vatican was solemnly honoured with the concourse of the whole Citie; that him self being a yong man & student there, went upon Sundayes & holy dayes with his other felowes to the Churches, and under the ground among

Saintes bodies, where little holes only gave in a darksome light: that prophane monuments fel to the ground, and Christian Churches were erected in their places: al is even so until this verie day.[86]

Rome's profane monuments were tokens of a deserved oblivion, and it was 'Ethnish follie', the product of 'the faithless haeresie of our unhappie time' to accept the identification of pagan ruins like the Capitol or the Circus Maximus, so long 'neglected and defaced', while questioning the authenticity of sacred relics and shrines 'so diligentlie preserved, religiously frequented and by suche authoritie of Christian authors commended unto us'. Such 'holy monuments' were not like the pagan city, the ruins of a dead past, but living parts of Catholic consciousness. The relics of the saints, even 'some one word of theirs coming to our minde, striketh up the hart, and reneweth our memorie, efftsones frail and forgetfull': grace and devotion were 'engendered in the mind by the visiting of relickes'.[87]

But Martin does not confine himself to portraying the Christian city as a memory-palace to evoke devotion. The literary form of his book as personal testimony again and again evokes the process of remembering itself. In describing the devotional observances of contemporary Rome, he constantly represents himself in the very act of recollection. So in two separate passages he presents himself as struggling to recall the precise number of steps on the Scala Sancta at the Lateran 'the self same that oure Saviour went up into Pilates house, having (*as I remember*) xxviiitie steppes'.[88] He records the large numbers of devout communicants at the city's Masses, 'which I have seen to my great comfort, and edification'. Describing the outdoor preaching of the Oratorians he recalled, 'Often have I bene in the garden where I could scarce come within hearing of the preacher for the prease'. Evoking the elaborate piety of the Roman churches allocated to Catholic nations, 'I remember many times, and as if I were present, so doe I see and take comforte, and I hartely honour S James Churche of the Spanyardes; S. Jhons of the Florentines; and the Neoplitanes of the Holy Ghost ...': recalling the piety of the religious orders, 'I can never forget the Companie of Charita in S Jeroms Churche the Domincan of Minerva, the Franciscans of Aracoeli ... What order, what majestie, what uniformitie, what lightes, what musicke, what odoriferous savour more than the best frankincense.'[89] Even when the concept of memory is not explicitly invoked, Martin's constant slippage into autobiographical mode never lets his reader forget that these descriptions are first-hand testimony, experience recalled so that it can be shared, as in his vivid account of the solemn displaying of relics in the city's churches.

> it is a wonder to see, how long before they take their places, how thicke they stand, in how little ease for the most part, and yet how willingly, and reverently, and earnestly harkening, and quietly hearing the name of everie Relike, and if they chaunce not to heare this or that, they are so carefull to ask their neighbour, and as sone as ever the sound of the name cometh from the Criers mouth, they are so ravished with devotion and sodenly touched with sweete compunction, that I was ashamed of my own hardnesse and coldnesse, when I heard their harty shout at every Relike, and this general voice, O *Signor misericordia*, and their sighinges and groninges, and joyful departure.[90]

The second and less original part of *Roma Sancta*, 'principally concerninge the charitie of Rome', presents an idealised picture of the pious benevolence of counter-reformation Rome. This starts with Pope Gregory XIII's own charities, in particular his seminary foundations for Catholic communities under persecution in Europe and elsewhere, especially the recent foundation of the English College in Rome. Martin took the opportunity to set out in detail the training regime and syllabus at Rome and Douai, which of course he himself helped establish and operate.[91] From seminaries he moved on to orphanages, refuges for 'mal-maritate', asylums for the insane, credit institutions like the *montes pietatis*, hospitals 'for the sicke and sore', and the charitable activities of Rome's many confraternities.[92] Description again and again gives way to apologetic and instruction. A short account of the Rosary Confraternity leads into a set of instructions on the manner of reciting the Rosary, and an explanation of the Mysteries.[93] A discussion of houses for 'convertites' or reformed prostitutes mutates into an extended discussion of the problem of prostitution in a Christian society, the efforts of recent popes to reform the sexual mores of Rome and the theological reasoning for and against the toleration of brothels.[94] A discussion of outdoor relief for Rome's beggars incorporates a long paraphrase from a sermon on charity by Gregory Nazianzen, 'which I thought good to put downe at large ... that my countrie men also might hereby be moved to have pitie on the poore, and not be hard or severe towards them'.[95] An account of Rome's nunneries and monastic communities for men provides the opportunity for extended apologetic discourses on the religious life, drawing liberally on patristic sources, designed 'to informe the yonger sorte of our countrie men that are not yet so happie as to have them and to live among them, what maner of men they are, and how ancient and Apostolick and venerable their profession is'.[96]

Martin's most extended discussion of the religious life is devoted entirely to the Society of Jesus, an ardent 20-page eulogy of Jesuit learning, spiritual formation, linguistic talents, missionary heroism in Europe, the Americas and Asia, and singling out for special praise Campion's work in Prague.[97] The descriptive parts of Martin's book concluded with extended accounts of the holy lives and episcopal generosity of 'two notable cardinals', offered as exemplary counter-reformation prelates, Gabriele Paleotti of Bologna, singled out for his generosity to English clergy travelling between Rome, Rheims and England, and Carlo Borromeo of Milan.[98]

Martin had completed *Roma Sancta* by the end of April 1581, when he signed the dedicatory letter to William Allen, and the one surviving manuscript is a fair copy prepared for the printer. But his masterly account of 'these wonderful fruites of the Catholike Romane faith'[99] remained unpublished till 1969, although a collection of other unpublished writings, including a short treatise on pilgrimage, drawing on some of the same materials as *Roma Sancta* and probably written about the same time, was printed in Paris by Richard Verstegen in 1583.[100] The conjecture of the editor of the 1969 edition that *Roma Sancta* had remained unpublished because Douay College could not afford to print it, has been accepted by most of those who have used or discussed Martin's work.[101] I know of no discussion of Martin's book which takes note of the extraordinarily charged moment at which *Roma Sancta* was written, but that moment profoundly influenced its character and may help explain why Allen chose to leave Martin's book unpublished.

Martin began writing *Roma Sancta* immediately on the completion of his bible translation in July 1580, and the bulk of the book
was composed between then and April 1581, for Martin makes a
number of unmistakable reference to events which he cannot have
known about before the summer or autumn of that year, and incorporates several letters written from northern Italy in late September
and early October 1580.[102] Martin's immediate target, as we have
seen, was Fulke's *Retentive*, which had been entered in the Stationers'
Register as early as February 1580, though Martin's translation work
meant he was not free till the summer to answer Fulke. The final
phase of work on the Rheims Bible coincided with the arrival in
Rheims of two of Martin's closest friends, bound for England on a
momentous mission. On 24 April the 80-year-old Bishop Goldwell,
one of Martin's closest Roman contacts, who, as we have seen, features
prominently in the pages of *Roma Sancta*, arrived in the College, a
very reluctant participant in the mission to England of Campion
and Persons. Three days later the two Jesuits themselves arrived, and
remained in the College till early June, when, without Goldwell,
they set off for England. And within a month, Martin had begun
writing *Roma Sancta*. The sequence can hardly be coincidental.

There is no way of knowing whether Martin was aware of
Campion's mission before his old friend turned up in Rheims.
However that might be, the mission is woven prominently into
Martin's long chapter on the Jesuits, with a glowing eulogy of
Campion 'sometime my deere companion, and now my father and
maister in al virtue and learning'. Even in her 'better days', Martin
declared, presumably with Mary's reign in mind, England had had
no Jesuits. How marvellous then 'now first to have them in the
middes of persecution'. Like his predecessor Pope Eleutherius at
England's first conversion, Pope Gregory had sent 'two religious
fathers' to 'make it Christian'.[103] Englishmen should esteem themselves happy 'to have such men as are willing to shed their bloud for
you and yours unto salvation', and they should receive them joyfully,
as one would receive a prophet.[104] Campion's mission shaped other
aspects of the book less directly as well. Martin's extended eulogies
of Cardinals Paleotti of Bologna and Borromeo of Milan for their
generosity to English clerics must owe something to the fact that
Goldwell, Campion and Persons had benefited from the hospitality

of each of them only weeks before, in the course of the journey which had brought them to the College in Rheims.[105]

Martin presented the manuscript of *Roma Sancta* to William Allen at Rheims on 9 April 1581. This intensely personal work was almost certainly the only one of Martin's literary enterprises since his return to Rheims which had not been initiated by Allen. So Martin left to his superior the decision 'whether, when, what and in what order, it may or may not be published, onely to the honour of God, the profite of our Countriemen, and disadvantaging of the Adversaries'.[106] Campion by then had been in England nine months, and in January 1581 Elizabeth's government had declared sheltering a Jesuit to be a capital offence. On 17 June Campion was apprehended at Lyford Grange in Berkshire. His arrest, trial and execution triggered an outburst of national anti-Catholic and anti-Jesuit paranoia, fanned by news of the abortive Spanish invasion of Ireland in which Martin's Oxford acquaintance Nicholas Sander played so disastrous a part. This was no time for the publication of eulogies of the Jesuits in general, and of the most notorious Catholic priest in England in particular. In the wake of Campion's execution on 1 December 1581 a flood of denunciatory pamphlets and broadsheets seemed to demand direct and detailed confutation, like that provided in Allen's *A Briefe Historie of the Glorious Martyrdom of XII Reverend Priests*, rather than the oblique and empathic strategy which underlay *Roma Sancta*.[107] Martin's book could not in any case have been published without a complete rewriting of the chapter on Campion and the Jesuits, and by now Martin was dying of tuberculosis, his remaining energies fully engaged in seeing his New Testament translation through the press. By April 1582, with that task finished, he was in the hands of physicians in Paris, and six months later he was dead. He was not yet 42.

It is pointless to speculate how effective an apologetic tool Martin's remarkable book might have proved had it been published in the fraught years following its completion. The right moment might have been in the summer of 1582, when Anthony Munday's vividly hostile autobiographical account of three months spent as a seminarian in the English College in Rome in 1579 appeared under the title *The English Romayne lyfe*.[108] Munday's opportunistic polemic, with its sneering accounts of carnival, pilgrimage, relics and a visit to the catacombs, is in many ways the mirror image of Martin's, and there are some startling and often piquant overlaps of material.[109] Read alongside each other, the eloquence and imaginative power of Martin's work becomes even more obvious. But in the summer of 1582 Martin died, and neither Allen nor any of his associates had leisure for such sophisticated appositions. The moment for *Roma Sancta*'s eloquent evocation of the antiquities of godliness had passed, and would not come again for 400 years.

Notes

1   Alison Shell, *Catholicism, Controversy and the English Literary Imagination, 1558–1660* (Cambridge, 1999), pp. 1–20 and *passim*; Victor Houliston, *Catholic Resistance in Elizabethan England: Robert Persons's Jesuit Polemic 1580–1610* (Aldershot, 2007), pp. 1–2.

2   For example, Victor Houliston (ed.), *Robert Persons, The Christian Directory* (1582) (Leiden, 1992), Gerard Kilroy, *Edmund Campion: A Scholarly Life* (Farnham, 2015).

3   This is not, of course, intended to disparage valuable older works like Albert J. Loomie's, *The Spanish Elizabethans* (New York, 1963).

4   Useful though incomplete outline of Martin's career in *ODNB* by T. McCoog.

5   *A treatise of schisme. Shewing, that al Catholikes ought in any wise to abstaine altogether from heretical conventicles, to witt, their prayers, sermons, &c* Douai (false imprint) [London] 1578, STC 17508; *A discoverie of the manifold corruptions of the holy scriptures by the heretikes of our daies* (Rheims, 1582), STC 17503.

6   The phrase is A. C. Southern's, *Elizabethan Recusant Prose* (London, 1950), p. 231.

7   *The New Testament of Jesus Christ, translated faithfully into English, out of the authenticall Latin . . . with arguments of books and chapters, annotations and other necessary helps . . . in the English College of Rhemes* (Rheims, 1582), STC 2884. The Old Testament was not printed till 1609, *The Holie Bible Faithfully translated into English out of the Authenticall Latin . . . By the English College of Doway* (Douai, 1609, 1610), STC 2207.

8   John Bossy, *The English Catholic Community 1570–1850* (London, 1975), p. 15.

9   The most sustained Elizabethan attack on Martin's translation was by William Fulke, *The Text of the New Testament of Jesus Christ, translated out of the vulgar Latine by the Papists of the traitorous Seminarie at Rhemes . . . with A Confutation . . .* (London, 1589), STC 11456; other responses listed in Peter Milward, *Religious Controversies of the Elizabethan Age* (London, 1978), pp. 46–50; for two represent-ative modern discussions, David Norton, *The King James Bible: A Short History from Tyndale to Today* (Cambridge, 2011), pp. 28–32, and David Daniell, *The Bible in English* (New Haven and London, 2003), pp. 358–68; fullest recent treatment, Alexandra Walsham, 'Unclasping the Book? The Douai Rheims Bible' in *Catholic Reformation in Protestant Britain* (Farnham, 2014), pp. 285–314, Martin treated, pp. 291, 301, 304.

10   Robert Persons, *A brief discours containing certain reasons why Catholiques refuse to goe to church* ('Doway' [false imprint, vere London, the Greenstreet Press] 1580), STC 19394; for William Carter and his fate, T. A. Birrell, 'William Carter (c. 1549–84): Recusant Printer, Publisher, Binder, Stationer, Scribe – and Martyr', *Recusant History*, 28 (2006), pp. 22–42. Martin's fatally ambiguous allusion to Judith, *Treatise of Schisme* sigs Dii–Dii (v), is confusingly expressed, but the nub seems to be that Judith overcame Holofernes even before she decapitated him by telling him plainly that 'being in his house, yet she must serve her Lorde and God stil', and refusing to eat of the unclean meats set before her: similar abstention from attendance at church by Catholic gentlewomen tempted to compliance would destroy the metaphorical Holofernes, 'the master heretike, and amase al his retinew, and never defile their religion by communicating with them in any small point'.

11 The illustrated martyrological works by Richard Verstegen are in a different category.

12 For a vivid account of the Catholic ethos of Oxford in general and St John's in particular in the 1560s, Gerard Kilroy, *Edmund Campion: A Scholarly Life* (Farnham, 2015), pp. 29–60.

13 For the text of the Trent adjudication, and examples of the subsequent hardening of opinion within the leadership of the English Catholic community, Ginevra Crosignani, Thomas J. McCoog and Michael Questier (eds), *Recusancy and Conformity in Early Modern England* (Rome, 2010), pp. 1–25, 30–71. For Martin's knowledge of the Tridentine adjudication, *Treatise of Schisme*, sig c vi (verso).

14 Kilroy, *Campion*, pp. 83, 86.

15 Ibid., p. 88.

16 Gregory Martin, *A treatyse of Christian peregrination, written by M. Gregory Martin Licentiate and late reader of divinitie in the Englishe Colledge at Remes* ([Paris] 1583) (STC 17507), 'The copy of a letter written to M. Doctour Whyte Warden of the new Colledge in Oxforde' (the final item in the book, unpaginated, dated 15 October 1575).

17 T. F. Knox (ed.), *The First and Second Diaries of the English College, Douay* (London, 1878), pp. 103, 104, 308–14.

18 Knox, *Douai Diaries*, p. 113.

19 For what follows on the early days of the Venerable English College I follow Anthony Kenny, 'From Hospice to College' in *The English Hospice in Rome* (Rome, 2012), pp. 218–73, quotation at p. 244; see also Jason A. Nice, 'Being British in Rome: the Welsh in the English College 1578–84', *Catholic Historical Review*, 92 (2006), pp. 1–24. Alex Walsham has emphasised similarities in missionary outlook and understanding between seminary priests in England and missionaries to the New World in Alexandra Walsham, 'Wholesome milk and strong meat; Peter Canisius's catechisms and the conversion of Protestant Britain', *British Catholic History*, 32 (2015), pp. 293–314.

20 Contrast Montaigne's tart observation of the irreverence of the papal entourage during mass in *Complete Works*, ed. Donald M. Frame (New York, London, Toronto, 2003), p. 1144, with the reverential tone of *Roma Sancta*, pp. 240–46.

21 *Roma Sancta*, pp. 60–62.

22 Ibid., pp. 33, 43.

23 Ibid., pp. 48, 216–18.

24 Ibid., pp. 64, 86–8.

25 Ibid., pp. 70–74.

26 Ibid., pp. 119–25, 152.

27 Ibid., pp. 75–83, 129–30.

28 Richard Simpson, *Edmund Campion: A Biography* (London, 1896), pp. 129–30.

29 Knox, *Douai Diaries*, pp. 142, 144,

30 Peter Holmes (ed.) *Elizabethan Casuistry* (Catholic Record Society, 1981), pp. 3, 50, 51; Crosignani, McCoog and Questier, *Recusancy and Conformity*, pp. 90–110.

31 For example, Crosignani, McCoog and Questier, *Recusancy and Conformity*, pp. 167–72, 199–200, 226–30, 369.

32 *Treatise of Schisme*, sig ⋆⋆iij (verso).

33 Knox, *Douai Diaries*, pp xl–xli: Latin original printed in T. F. Knox (ed.), *Letters and Memorials of Cardinal Allen* (London, 1872), pp. 64–5.

34 Excellent discussion of the counter-reformation rationale in Walsham, 'Unclasping the book', n. 6 above.

35 Knox, *Douai Diaries*, p. 145.

36 *A discoverie*, sig aiij.

37 Martin's preface to the Rheims New Testament (slightly abbreviated) is conveniently printed in Alfred W. Pollard, *Records of the English Bible* (Oxford, 1911), pp. 301–13, quotation at p. 308.

38 The most thorough discussion of all these issues is James B. Carleton, *The Part of Rheims in the Making of the English Bible* (Oxford, 1902); see also Brooke Foss Westcott, *A General View of the History of the English Bible*, revised by William Aldis Wright (London, 1905), pp. 105–8, 256–65.

39 *A discoverie*, sig bv ff.

40 The replies are listed in Milward, *Religious Controversies of the Elizabethan Age*, pp. 46–50, nos 166–79.

41 David A. Frick, 'Anglo-Polonica: the Rheims New Testament of 1582 and the making of the Polish Catholic Bible', *Polish Review*, 36 (1991), pp. 47–67.

42 E. H. Burton and T. L. Williams (eds), *The Douay College Diaries, Third, Fourth and Fifth, 1598–1654, with the Rheims Report, 1579–80*, vol. 2 (Catholic Record Society Record Series, XI, 1911), p. 565.

43 The (unpaginated) letter was posthumously published in *A treatyse of Christian peregrination* (n. 13 above).

44 Kilroy, *Edmund Campion*, pp. 283–94.

45 For which see Southern, *Elizabethan Recusant Prose*, pp. 144–8, 519–23; Milward, *Religious Controversies of the Elizabethan Age*, pp. 39–46, nos 146–65.

46 Fulke, *Retentive*, p. 89.

47 Ibid., p. 170.

48 Ibid., p. iiij.

49 *Annali d'Italianistica*, vol. 8 (1990), p. 462.

50 Thomas Stapleton, T*he History of the Church of Englande. Compiled by Venerable Bede, Englishman* (Antwerp, 1565), p. 41.

51 I am indebted for Pius V's vivid phrase to Simon Ditchfield's presidential address to the Ecclesiastical History Society Summer Conference, 2014.

52 'Petrus, et cum eo Gloriosus Coapostolus Paulus vas electionis Romanam Ecclesiam plantarent, et suo sanguine consecrarent, ut ubi caput superstitionis erat, illic caput existeret sanctitatis, et ubi Gentilium Principes habitant, Ecclesiarent Principes morarentur, et quae prius erat magistra erroris, fieret magistra veritatis . . .'
Bullarum, privilegiorum ac diplomatum romanorum pontificum amplissima collectio, cui accessere pontificum omnium vitae . . . Opera et studio Caroli Cocquelines (Rome, 1745), vol. 4, part 1, p. 342 (6 January 1558).

53 Joachim du Bellay, 'Regrets', sonnet 80, in David R. Slavin, *The Regrets, A Bilingual Edition* (Evanston, Ill. 2004), pp. 174–5.

54 For Montaigne's views on the 'immortal glory' of the ancient city, and the parasitic squalor of modern 'bastard Rome', trans. and ed. Donald M. Frame, *Michel de Montaigne, The Complete Works* (New York and London, 2003), p. 1151.

55 William Thomas, *The Historie of Italie* (London, 1549), p. 22.

56 Innumerable editions: I have used *Le Cose Meravigliose Dell'Alma Citta Di Roma: Dove Si Tratta Delle Chiese, Stationi, & Reliquie de' corpi Santi*, ed. Girolamo Franzini (Rome, 1592), available online at http://reader.digitale-sammlungen.de/de/fs1/object/display/bsb11095239_00024.html.
For the evolution of *Le Cose*, Andrea Palladio, *The Churches of Rome*, trans. and ed. Eunice D. Howe (Binghampton, NY, 1991); Barbara Wisch, 'The Matrix: Le sette chiese di Roma of 1575 and the Image of Pilgrimage', *Memoirs of the American Academy in Rome*, 57 (2012), pp. 277–8.

57 Kilroy, *Edmund Campion*, p. 141.

58 Vincenzo Fiocchi Nicolai, 'San Filippo Neri, le catacomb di San Sebastiano e le origini dell'archeologia Cristiana' in *San Filippo Neri nella realta Roma del XVIe secolo* (Rome, 2000), pp. 105–30.

59 Jean Luis Ferrary, *Onofrio Panvinio et les Antiquites Romaines* (Rome, 1996); V. F. Nicolai, 'Storia e topografia della catacomb anonima di Via Anopo' in *Die Katacombe Anonima di Via Anopo, Reportorium der Malerein (*Citta del Vaticano, 1991), pp. 2–23; Simon Ditchfield, 'Baronio storico nel suo tempo' in Giuseppe Antonio Guazzelli et al. (eds), *Cesare Baronio tra santita e scrittura storica* (Rome, 2012), pp. 3–21, esp. p. 8.

60 Marco Serrano, *De Septem Urbis Ecclesiis, una cum earum Reliquiis, Stationibus & Indulgentiis* (Rome, 1575), obtainable online at https://play.google.com/books/reader?printsec=frontcover&output=reader&id=h8JTAAAAcAAJ&pg=GBS.PP4; Pompeo Ugonio, *Historia delle Stationi di Roma che si celebrano la Quadragesima* (Rome, 1588), available online at https://play.google.com/books/reader?printsec=frontcover&output=reader&id=tgRXpge1avAC&pg=GBS.PP4:

61 For Bosio, Simon Ditchfield, 'Text before trowel: Antonio Bosio's Roma Sotteranea revisited' in R. N. Swanson (ed.), *The Church Retrospective: Studies in Church History*, 33 (Woodbridge, 1997), pp. 343–60.

62 The quotation is from Baronio's *Annales Ecclesiastic*, vol. 2 (Rome, Ex Typographia Congregationis Oratorii, apud S. Mariam in Vallicella, 1594), p. 81: '[...] Mirabile dictu: vidimus, saepiusque lustravimus Priscillae coemeterium, haud pridem inventum atque refossum via Salaria tertio ab Urbe lapide: quod nullo magis proprio vocabulo dixerimus prae eius amplitudine, multisque atque diversis eiusdem vijs, quam subterraneam civitatem: quippe quod ipsius ingressu primaria via ceteris amplior pateat, quae hinc inde vias diversas habeat, easdemque frequentes, quae rursum in diversos viculos dividantur, et angiportus; rursus, ut in civitatibus, statis locis velut fora quaedam, ampliora sint spatia ad conventus sacros agendos, eademque sanctorum imaginibus exornata; nec desint, licet nunc obstructa, ad lumen recipiendum desuper excisa foramina'; see Ditchfield, 'Baronio Storico', p. 8.

63 R. Krautheimer, 'A Christian Triumph in 1597' in Douglas Fryer et al. (eds), *Essays in the History of Art presented to Rudolf Wittkower,* vol. 2 (London, 1967), pp. 174–8; Alexander Herz, 'Cardinal Cesare Baronio's Restauration of SS Nereo ed Achilleo & S Cesarea de Appia', *The Art Bulletin*, 70 (1988), pp. 590–620; Kelley Magill, 'Reviving Martyrdom: Interpretations of the Catacombs in Cesare Baronio's patronage' in John B. Decker and M. Kirkland Ives (eds), *Death, Torture and the Broken Body in European Art 1300–1650* (London, 2014), pp. 86 ff.

64 David Nelting, 'Nicolo Circignanis Fresken In Santo Stefano Rotondo und Anotonio Gallonios 'Tratatto de gli Instrumenti di Martirio'; Zwei Beispiele manieristischer Praxis unter den Bedingungen der Gegenreformation', *Romanische Forschungen*, vol. 113 (2001), pp. 70–81; K. Noreen, 'Ecclesiae Militantis Triumphi: Jesuit Iconography and the Counter-Reformation', *Sixteenth Century Journal*, 29 (1998), pp. 689–715 see also Carol M. Richardson, 'Durante Alberti, the Martyrs' Picture and the Venerable English College, Rome', *Papers of the British School at Rome*, 73 (2005), pp. 223–63.

65 Eamon Duffy, 'Rome and Catholicity in mid-Tudor England', *Saints, Sacrilege and Sedition: Religion and Conflict in the Tudor Reformations* (London, 2012), pp. 195–210.

66 'Some Letters and Papers of Nicholas Sander', ed. J. B. Wainewright in Catholic Record Society, *Miscellanea XIII*, 26 (1926), pp. 3–5.

67 CRS, *Miscellanea XIII*, p. 5.

68 Stapleton, *History of the Church of Englande*, pp. 39–40.

69 *A proclamation against breakinge or defacing of monumentes of antiquitie, beyng set up in churches or other publique places for memory and not for supersticion,* Imprinted at London in Powles Churcheyarde: By Rycharde Iugge and Iohn Cawood, Printers to the Quenes Maiestie, [1560], STC (2nd edn)/7913, reproduced in P. L. Hughes and J. F. Larkin (eds), *Tudor Royal Proclamations* (New Haven, 1964–9), vol. 2, p. 146. For discussion of the proclamation, Ralph Houlbrooke, *Death, Religion and the Family in England* (Oxford, 1998), p. 348: Margaret Aston, *England's Iconoclasts*, I, *Laws against images* (Oxford, 1988), pp. 266-7, 269, 314–15.

70 William Allen, *A defense and declaration of the Catholike Churchies [sic] doctrine, touching purgatory, and prayers for the soules departed* (1565), STC 371, p. 134.

71 *A treatyse of Christian peregrination*, pp. 16, 19, 30, 36. He claimed in the cited passage to be quoting St Augustine.

72 *Roma Sancta*, p. 262.

73 Ibid. p. 51.

74 Ibid. p. 8.

75 *Roma Sancta*, chapter 32, pp. 229–40; Angelo Pientini, *Le pie narration dell'opere piu memorabilia fatte in Roma l'Anno del Giubileo 1575* (Viterbo, 1577), available online at https://play.google.com/books/reader?id=-ucqbiuH3IIC&printsec=frontcover&output=reader&hl=en&pg=GBS.PR4.

76 Martin's early treatise on Greek pronunciation was published as *Gregorius Martinus ad Adolphum Mekerchum pro veteri & vera Graecarum literarum pronunciatione* (Oxford, 1712); for the Greek College and pronunciation, *Roma Sancta*, pp. 122–5.

77 *Roma Sancta*, p. 10.

78   On Goldwell, see the biography by Thomas Mayer in *ODNB; Roma Sancta*, pp. 75–83, 129–30.

79   *Roma Sancta*, pp. 8–9.

80   Ibid. p. 7.

81   Ibid. p. 9.

82   Ibid. p. 10.

83   Edmund Campion, *Decem Rationes . . . et Opuscula selecta* (Antwerp, 1631), p. 389. Translated (slightly differently) in Richard Simpson, *Edmund Campion*, p. 125.

84   *Roma Sancta*, p. 4.

85   Ibid., p. 10.

86   Ibid., p. 9.

87   Ibid. pp. 25, 27, 45.

88   Ibid., pp. 35, 93.

89   Ibid., pp. 64, 72, 74, 81, 99, 98.

90   Ibid., p. 53.

91   Ibid., pp. 107–25.

92   Ibid., pp. 131–3, 182–95.

93   Ibid., pp. 214–19.

94   Ibid., pp. 143–51. On the background behind Gregory's concern, Tessa Storey, *Carnal Commerce in Counter-Reformation Rome* (Cambridge, 2008).

95   *Roma Sancta*, pp. 189–93.

96   Ibid., pp. 134–43, 151–8.

97   Ibid., pp. 160–79.

98   Ibid., pp. 246–56.

99   Ibid., p. 239.

100 A. F. Allison and D. M. Rogers, *The Contemporary Printed Literature of the English Counter-Reformation between 1558 and 1640*, vol. II, *Works in English* (Aldershot, 1994), no. 523.

101 For example, by Thomas McCoog in his biographical article on Martin in *ODNB*.

102 *Roma Sancta*, pp. 59 (discovery of an ancient icon of the Virgin in St Peter's, 26 April 1580), pp. 256–9 (letter of Owen Lewis from Milan, 29 September 1580), pp. 263–4 (letter of William Sheprey from Bologna, 5 October 1580).

103 On the Eleutherius legend and its polemical use in the reformation, Felicity Heal, 'What can King Lucius do for you? The Reformation and the Early British Church', *English Historical Review*, 120 (2005), pp. 593–614.

104 *Roma Sancta*, pp. 173–4.

105 Ibid., pp. 246–60, 263–4, Kilroy, *Campion*, pp. 150–51. Paleotti had in fact written to David Lewis in Rome a year earlier to express his admiration for the heroism of English missionary clergy, and pressingly offering hospitality to English students or priests travelling to and from Rome: but Campion's stay in Bologna must certainly have been fresh in Martin's mind. Knox, *Douai Diaries*, p. 150, *Roma Sancta*, p. 251.

106 *Roma Sancta*, p. 3.

107 For the publications surrounding Campion's mission, trial and execution, Kilroy, *Campion*, pp. 349 ff.; Milward, *Religious Controversies of the Elizabethan Age*, nos 222–35.

108 Modern critical edition edited by Philip J. Ayres, *Anthony Munday: The English Roman Life* (Oxford, 1980). The original was entered in the Stationers' register 21 June 1582; Anthony Kenny, 'Anthony Munday in Rome', *Recusant History*, 6 (1962), pp. 158–62; Donna Hamilton, *Anthony Munday and the Catholics 1560–1633* (Aldershot, 2005); Christopher Highley, *Catholics Writing the Nation in Early Modern Britain and Ireland* (Oxford, 2008), pp. 91–8.

109 Compare Martin's description of the veneration of relics in Rome, with Munday's account of the same devotion.

      'The maner of goinge is, with grave and sober gate, beades in their hand, the minde occupied in good meditations and inward prayer or soft moving of the lippes (for al inordinate and vehement gesture owtwardly is not so wel liked, but a moderate and comely maner of devotion, more in the hart then to the shewe,) in the Church, the first reverence upon the knees is to the blessed

Sacrament, if it be there; then at the high aultar before the principal Relikes, where there stand al the day one or two in surplices, to take the beades of them that wil (and who wil not?) and with them to touche al the Relikes . . . Which being done everie Station day throughout the year, imagine what precious beades they are, which byside the popes benediction . . . and the indulgences annexed, have also touched so many Relikes, as are thus shewed in Rome in a yeare and therefore manie to this purpose being little bundles tied together, to send afterward to their frendes. This done, they visite other special monuments in that Church . . . and so returne home in like maner as they came, giving almes by the way . . . to so manie and so miserable persons which in every Station hedge the way on both sides, that I never saw the like.'

Roma Sancta, p. 49.

'In all these churches there be divers relics which make them haunted of a marvellous multitude of people: whereby the lazy lurden friars that keep the churches get more riches than so many honest men should do. For either at their coming into the church, or else at the altar where the relics be, there standeth a basin, and the people cast money therein with very great liberalitie. And there standeth a friar with a forked stick in his hand, and thereupon he taketh everybody's beads that lays them on the altar, and then he wipes them along a great proportioned thing of crystal and gold, wherein are a number of rotten bones which they make the people credit to be the bones of saints; so wiping them along the outside of this tabernacle, the beads steal a terrible deal of holiness out of those bones, and God knows, the people think they do God good service in it: O monstrous blindness!'

The English Roman Life, pp. 45–6.

7

Praying the Counter-Reformation

On 15 February 1586–7 the head of a staunchly Catholic Oxfordshire family, William Lenthall of Lachford, Great Haseley, made his will. Related on the distaff side to the Tempests of Holmside, Co. Durham, and through them to an extended cousinage of northern Catholic families, Lenthall himself had married Jane Brome of Ixhill Lodge at Boarstall, a notorious Mass centre in the 1580s. William and Jane's daughter Elinor married into another Great Haseley recusant family, the Horsemans, while a younger son, also William, married Francis Southwell of Horsham St Faith in Norfolk, sister of the Jesuit martyr and poet. The family's recusancy would end with the next generation, though, because William's grandson, yet another William, was to put the family on the map by apostatising and entering the history books as Speaker of the Cromwellian House of Commons, and subsequently one of Oliver's peers. But in 1587 that calamity was not yet to be imagined, and William senior's testament is an emphatically Catholic document.

But although emphatically Catholic, it was not unambiguously so. In it, among many benefactions to the poor, Lenthall provided for four frieze (coarse woollen) coats to be given annually at Hallontide (All Saints Day) to four of the poorest men in the parish, on condition that they assemble at his grave in the parish church, 'yearly for ever upon Sondayes and ffestivall Dayes', to recite the *De Profundis* psalm kneeling upon their knees 'ymediatly when service is done, in token or profession of my faith', concluding with a prayer for the repose of his soul. In a piquant and very characteristic Tudor mix of piety and pragmatism, this colourful annual observance was to be funded from the income of local confiscated chantry lands, which William had acquired by purchase from the Crown.

Such a benefaction in 1587 is striking enough. I've dwelt on it, however, because of the curiously equivocal texts Lenthall prescribed for the use of his four bedesmen. The shortened version of the *De Profundis* which he stipulated and spelled out in the will corresponds to no Tudor translation, and appears to be his own paraphrase from the Latin. To it, he added the 'I know that my redeemer liveth' passage from the book of Job which features in the Catholic office of the Dead, but which Lenthall quoted word for word as it occurs in the Book of Common Prayer (hereafter BCP) funeral service. And the bedesmen were to conclude with the following collect, recited in unison.

Almightye god with whome doe live the spiritts of them whiche doe departe hence in the Lorde and in whome the sowles of them that be elected after they be delivered from the burden of the fleshe be in ioye and felicitye, wee give the harty thancks for that it hathe pleased the to deliver this our brother William Lenthall owte of the miseries of this sinnefull worlde beseeching the that it maye please the of thy gracious goodnes shortly to accompte him in the number of thy Electe And to hasten thy Kingdome that we with this our brother and all others departed in the true faithe of the holye Catholique Churche maye have our perfecte Consum'ac'on and blisse bothe of bodye and sowle in thy eternall and everlasting glorye Amen.[1]

That prayer is a carefully bowdlerised version of the penultimate collect of the 1559 Elizabethan Book of Common Prayer burial service, a fiercely reformed prayer dwelling on predestination.[2] In Lenthall's will, however, it has been subtly Catholicised by replacing the phrase 'shortly to accomplish the number of thine elect', with 'shortly to account him in the number of thy Electe', a transformation that throws open the door to the doctrine of purgatory. And the shift in the direction of Rome is clinched by the replacement of the Prayer Book's 'all other departed in the true fayth of thy holy name' with 'all others departed in the true faithe *of the holye Catholique Churche*'.[3]

It would be possible to view Lenthall's post-mortem provisions simply as a cunning piece of subterfuge, designed to smuggle Catholic eschatology into the parish church by subtle modification of the Prayer Book wording. Lenthall's careful insistence that the prayers he was requesting were 'taken oute of the holye scripture' makes it clear he was indeed anxious to allay likely Protestant suspicions. But while that is doubtless true enough, it seems to me that something more complicated is going on here. For Lenthall was clearly familiar with the words of the Prayer Book burial service, and willing to incorporate them into his carefully planned and expensively funded intercessory arrangements. To some degree or other, these Protestant prayers had become part of the vernacular religious culture of a staunchly Catholic country gentleman, and they are a testimony to the attraction which the vernacular exercised even over convinced early-modern Catholics. For all the Lenthall family's recusancy, and the unmistakably papistical intentions of Lenthall's will, we glimpse here something of the double-edged character of Church papistry, and the threat it might pose to the identity and cohesion of the Catholic community in late Elizabethan England.

The clerical leaders of the Elizabethan Catholic community were, of course, aware of this phenomenon and sought to challenge it. The publication of the Rheims-Douai New Testament in 1582 was one part of that response.[4] But the Douai Bible was a polemical not a devotional tool and its physical layout, bristling with the argumentative apparatus of marginalia and endnotes, repeatedly drags the reader into sharply phrased religious controversy. If the pull of the vernacular at prayer was to be neutralised and counteracted, more than debate and invective was needed. Early modern Catholicism needed its own distinctive vernacular idiom of prayer. What follows is an attempt to explore what I take to have been the most crucial aspect of the evolution of such an idiom.

Long before Elizabeth's accession, successive Tudor regimes had recognised the crucial role of private prayer in the shaping of a common religious consciousness. From the 1490s onwards English prayers were increasingly present in the most popular of all printed devotional books, the Primer, or Little Office of Our Lady.[5] The first fully bilingual Primers appeared in the mid-1530s, after the break with Rome and sponsored by the Henrician regime. At first many of these were printed in France, but the import of Primers printed abroad was effectively outlawed in 1538, and in 1545 Henry's government issued its own official reformed and expurgated Primer, and banned all others.[6] Edward's government went one step further, producing a 'Primer' which was really a supplemented form of morning and evening prayer from the Book of Common Prayer, bulked out with emphatically Protestant and rather wordy devotions: the book contained no Latin and had little continuity with the traditional books.[7]

Mary's restored Catholic regime permitted the free import of traditional Sarum Primers, many of them entrepreneurial ventures from commercial presses in France or the Low Countries. But the Marian regime followed the lead of Henry and Edward in recognising the need to regulate the potent attraction of English prayers, and was well aware that the vernacular devotional idiom which had emerged during 20 years of the schism could not simply be wished away. So Cardinal Pole authorised and the regime promoted an official bilingual Primer, in which the Latin of the traditional offices which made up the bulk of the book appeared in small type in the margins, alongside the much larger English text, borrowed from the bilingual Primers of the 1530s.[8] English was therefore the dominant language of this official Catholic Primer, and the copious additional prayers and pious exercises which supplemented the Offices were printed in English only: many of them indeed were drawn from reformed sources, especially Henry's *King's Primer* of 1545.[9] Despite the scrupulous Catholic orthodoxy of the book, the sombre and penitential character of the supplementary prayers in Pole's book maintained clear rhetorical continuity with the immediate Protestant past. Astonishingly, the prayers retained from the era of schism included even a Protestantised version of the *Salve Regina*, addressed not to Mary but to Christ – 'Hail Holy King, Father of Mercy'![10] Despite the wide circulation of the Marian Primer – a remarkable 14 editions in just three years – the Marian regime did not last long enough to establish a distinctive Catholic vernacular idiom, though perhaps the sacramental preaching of Thomas Watson, the translations of the Tower writings, meditations and prayers by Thomas More included in the 1557 *English Works*, and Cuthbert Tunstall's *Certaine godly and devout prayers*, issued in 1558, suggest the direction in which things might have moved.[11]

But there, as far as Catholics were concerned, the evolution of a vernacular devotional idiom froze for an entire generation. The end of the Marian restoration threw Catholic academics, writers and printers alike into disarray, and triggered an exodus from all three groups to the continent. By the time the elite personnel of the Marian counter-reformation still at liberty had regrouped in France and the Low Countries in the early 1560s, and the Catholic literary and polemical riposte to the Elizabethan Settlement had got underway, polemic and apologetic seemed the most urgent needs, and the production of vernacular devotional works was high on nobody's agenda. Of the 66 surviving Catholic titles printed in English between 1559 and 1574, there was not a single Prayer Book or devotional text.[12] The substantial fardel of 'unlawful' Catholic publications confiscated from John Stowe's house in February 1569 consisted entirely of catechetical, homelitic or controversial texts, and included no ascetical or devotional writings.[13]

By contrast, when the lodgings of the sisters Elizabeth and Bridget Brome were raided in August 1586, among the 'superstitious bookes and reliques' discovered there was a shelf-ful of recent works of piety in English – an otherwise unrecorded edition of the *Manual of Godly Prayers* with the *Jesus Psalter*, printed that same year, first edition 1583; Stephen Brinkley's translation of the Jesuit Gaspar Loarte's *Exercise of a Christian Life*, with prayers for confession and communion attached, first edition 1579, expanded edition 1584; Vaux's *Catechism*, with an appendix on the 'laudable ceremonies' of the liturgy, 1584; Person's *Christian Directory*, 1582; a treatise on penance which was probably John Fowler's *Briefe Form of Confession*, translated from Spanish and dedicated to Jane Dormer, Duchess of Feria, with an appendix of prayers by Sir Thomas More, published in 1576; and Richard Hopkin's translation of Luis de Granada's *Memorial of a Christian Life*, dedicated to the gentlemen of the Inns of Court and fresh from the press in 1586.[14] Even so modest a library of newly minted Catholic piety could not have been assembled in England before the 1580s. The trickle of Catholic devotional publications in English which began in the mid-1570s had swelled to something approaching a flood by the time the pursuivants broke into the Brome ladies' lodgings ten years on, and that very notable shift in the priorities of writers and publishers, which has been surprisingly little noticed or commented upon, requires some explanation.

It will be obvious at once that this resumption of Roman Catholic devotional publication coincides very neatly with the arrival in England of the first seminary priests. Reflecting in 1581 on the remarkable impact of the first priests, William Allen claimed that 'the enterance to this spiritual attempt and traffike was wel opened *before*, [my emphasis] by bookes written from these partes',[15] but he had in mind not devotional preparation, but the flood of polemic for which he and his collaborators were responsible. Allen's first priests found themselves ministering with no devotional or pastoral vernacular resources other than Laurence Vaux's not entirely satisfactory catechism, and whatever ragged remnant of vernacular catechetical, devotional and ascetical literature happened to survive from the reign of Mary. Certainly this must have included hundreds and perhaps thousands of Primers or Books of Hours, both bilingual and Latin. But Latin Books of Hours were of limited pastoral utility, though even an imperfectly comprehended Latin book might function as a defiant badge of identity, as it did for John Hardy of Brompton in 1577, who attended his parish church but 'doth there in the time of divine service reade so loude upon his latin popish primer (that he understandeth not) that he troubleth both the minister and the people'[16]. The official Marian Primers, by contrast, which had been produced relatively cheaply in their tens of thousands, were a different matter: many remained in circulation and some certainly went on being used, in the absence of more up-to-date provision.

But after 1571 the use of even these books became increasingly problematic, at least for some of the clergy. In 1571 Pope Pius V issued a revised Primer, as part of the general revision of the liturgy undertaken in the wake of the Council of Trent. The new book was designed not only to purge lay piety of anything hospitable to heresy (so, for example, prayers by Erasmus disappear[17]), but to prune away all the apocryphal legends, miraculous promises and spurious indulgences which 'by the greed of printers' had been marketing devices in the unauthorised Primers, and which 'ad varias superstitiones facile rudes ipsos inducere possunt'. The Marian Primers were of course themselves the product of a careful counter-reformation revision. They carried no indulgences, real or spurious, and were free of all apocryphal and superstitious material, but their many borrowings from Protestant sources, and even their inclusion of now suspect humanist material by Erasmus and others, would certainly not pass muster in the increasingly polarised religious climate of the 1570s and 1580s. Allen himself was clear that the Sarum Primer, whether in its original Latin or in translation, did not in fact come under the prohibitions of Pius V's Primer Bull of 1571, and so was still licit in England. But the continuing lay use of such Primers was clearly becoming a matter of concern to some missioners, for it was anxiously debated in casuistry classes at Douai in the late 1570s.[18]

This situation would not be rectified till 1599, when the multi-talented and furiously energetic 'Jesuited' layman Richard Verstegan produced a parallel Latin and English edition of the Tridentine Primer for English readers.[19] It is tempting to look for specifically English circumstances to explain the elapse of 28 years, an entire generation, between the first promulgation of the Tridentine Primer, whose recitation, as Pius's Bull emphasised, seemed so well suited to the capacities of the *pusillis et rudibus christifidelibus*, the 'feeble and uncultivated laity', and the production of a version which a largely monoglot as well as rude and uncultivated English laity could actually understand. But that would probably be a mistake, because the appearance of vernacular versions of the Tridentine Primer was slow to happen everywhere. Though the Council of Trent did not rule on the legitimacy of vernacular prayers and Bible translations in general, since the mid-century there had been widespread nervousness in Catholic Europe about the promiscuous circulation of vernacular scripture in the post-Tridentine Church, and those years saw a rowing back from the early sixteenth-century proliferation of Catholic vernacular biblical and devotional texts. Even in late sixteenth-century France, where the Council's decrees were not received, the same reservations about the virtues of the vernacular were widespread. Leading French clergy in the 1560s and 1570s insisted on the necessity of retaining Latin; the impeccably orthodox Parisian theologian René Benoist, future Bishop of Troyes, was expelled by the Sorbonne in 1572 for his biblical translations; and Michel de Montaigne famously deplored the fact that the sacred book was now 'tossed up and down and plaid withal, in a shop or a hall or a kitchin', and thought it desirable to keep both Bible and Mass still in Latin.[20] These attitudes were softening by the 1580s, but the first edition of the post-Tridentine Primer for

French readers, by the Jesuit Pierre Coton, did not appear till the early seventeenth century, and though his edition included many additional vernacular prayers, the offices themselves remained conservatively in Latin.[21]

The history of the Tridentine Primer in English has been usefully studied by J. M. Blom, and the 1599 edition was the basis for one of John Bossy's most characteristic, controversial and bravura performances, the marvellous 1990 Royal Historical Society lecture simply entitled 'Prayers'.[22] But I am going to put that book to one side, and focus instead on the origins of the other great pillar of recusant vernacular piety, the *Manual of Prayers*. The *Manual*'s history began two decades earlier than Verstegan's translation of the Primer, and it would far outreach the Primer in the affections of generations of English Catholics. A simple statistic illustrates this. By the outbreak of the English civil war, the Primer had run through 15 editions, no fewer than five of them concentrated in the reign of Charles I. By the same date, the *Manual* had gone through 28 editions, and they were far more evenly spread, with a new edition appearing on average every two or three years.[23] That momentum was maintained down to the end of the eighteenth century, even after the advent of Challoner's *Garden of the Soul*, which ultimately displaced it, with the *Manual* notching up 83 editions to the Primer's 42, on top of which the *Manual* itself gave rise to a series of multi-editioned spin-offs and imitations, from William Clifford's now largely forgotten *The Little Manual of the Poor Man's daily Devotion*,[24] first published in 1669, down to Challoner's *Garden of the Soul*, first published in 1740 and still in print.[25]

The *Manual* was the outcome of the new sense of pastoral urgency which emerged in about 1575. After almost 20 years of neglect, Catholic missioners and lay activists seem suddenly to have awakened to the long-standing need to provide the materials for Catholic prayers in English. The way was led by the Louvain-based publisher, John Fowler, who had reissued More's *Dialogue of Comfort* in 1573. In 1575 Fowler printed three separate editions of an early Tudor devotional classic, also from the More circle, Richard Whytford's *Jesus Psalter*, first published in 1529 but subsequently included in some of the printed Primers of the early 1530s. To one of these editions Fowler attached a translation of another even more constant item in medieval and early Tudor Books of Hours, the so-called 'Psalter of St Jerome', a catena of supplicatory verses from the psalms. To another he added instead a charming set of woodcuts with minimal text, on the life and Passion of Christ, the 'Godly Contemplations for the Unlearned'.[26] In the following year he issued his translation of the *Brief form of confession*, dedicated to Jane Dormer, and with an appendix of prayers by Sir Thomas More.[27]

In England itself, this renewed interest in devotional material comes suddenly into focus in the activities of one of the most significant of Elizabethan Catholic activists, the layman, printer, binder, stationer and scribe William Carter, who was hanged, drawn and quartered for treason in 1584, and beatified by John Paul II in 1987. Carter was a London draper's son, born sometime before 1549. He was apprenticed in 1563 to the Catholic printer John Cawhood, who had been printer to the Crown under Mary I, responsible for producing crucial counter-reformation texts like Bonner's *Necessary Doctrine* and *Homilies*.[28] From 1573 Carter established another link between the Marian and Elizabethan counter-reformations by becoming secretary and amanuensis to Nicholas Harpsfield, then still a prisoner in the Fleet, and he was in due course to inherit Harpsfield's papers, including the manuscript of his life of More. After Harpsfield's death in 1575 Carter joined forces with George Gilbert and Stephen Brinkley to establish a secret Catholic press in London: on Person's arrival in England, he was involved in the establishment of the clandestine Greenstreet Press at East Ham. Carter was also responsible for the transcription of Campion's disputations. Several times arrested and imprisoned, and severely racked in 1583, Carter was eventually executed for treason for printing Gregory Martin's *Treatise of Schisme* (1578), convicted on the basis of an unlucky passage in which Martin had urged Catholic gentlewomen to religious constancy in the face of temptation, by comparing them to the biblical Judith, a passage which the regime chose to interpret as direct incitement of Elizabeth's Catholic ladies-in-waiting to murder the Queen, as Judith had murdered Holofernes.

Between 1575 and 1582 Carter was responsible for printing and publishing at least 16 Catholic books. These included the *Treatise of Schisme* itself, Peter Canisius's short catechism and Alfield's account of Campion's martyrdom. Strikingly, the other 13 books were all purely devotional texts, and, as you might expect from a man with Carter's personal history, they represent a fascinating blend of old and new devotional fashions. Four of Carter's books were translations from the contemporary Spanish Jesuit, Gaspar Loarte, including both Loarte's influential treatise on meditating the Rosary, and Stephen Brinkley's translation of Loarte's *Exercise of a Christian Life*, one of the books which was found in the Brome sisters' lodgings. In 1576 Carter also published a small treatise on meditating the passion by Peter Canisius, and a 'Short and Absolute order of confession' designed as a practical guide, and clearly extracted from some much larger ascetical treatise. All the rest of the devotional output of his press were venerable devotional classics, most of them with a previous life in early Tudor England. Also in 1576, Carter printed a short set of Rosary meditations by John Mitchell, an English Carthusian based in the charterhouse at Bruges: this had a substantial appendix containing the *Fifteen Oes* of St Bridget together with other affective prayers, which had first appeared three generations earlier under the Lady Margaret's patronage. A translation of Henry Suso's Office of Jesus with specially fine renderings of the *Jesu dulcis memoriae* hymn was in effect a revival of an early Tudor devotion, since in a different translation Suso's text had been a favourite in the bilingual Primers of the 1530s. Carter also reissued Richard Whytford's fine translation of Kempis's *Imitation of Christ*, with a false title page attributing the edition to the reign of Queen Mary. In 1578 he printed John Fisher's *Spiritual Consolation*, a rather gloomy letter of direction written to Fisher's sister Elizabeth, and his Good Friday Sermon, in each case of course derived from Harpsfield's manuscripts, thereby ensuring the survival of both texts, which were probably translated from Carter's edition for the Latin *Opera Omnia* of 1597. In the same year he revived Wynkyn de Worde's much printed translation of a medieval text by Peter of Blois, *The Mirror of Consolation*, and in 1579 he printed the so-called *Jesus Psalter*, an elaborate and repetitious devotion to the name of Jesus which was also probably Whytford's work, and which the Louvain-based publisher John Fowler had printed twice the previous year.[29]

Carter's press was therefore responsible for a very high proportion of the total devotional output aimed at English Catholics in the late 1570s. He and his collaborators were clearly trying to fill what they saw as a yawning gap in basic spiritual reading and practical devotional instruction. But the scattering of such material through a series of individual publications, hard to get hold of and expensive when one did, was a severe drawback. Several of Carter's books contained small collections of prayers, including devotional classics like the *Fifteen Oes*.[30] But, as yet, there was no single publication which brought together in a systematic way a repertoire of prayers for all eventualities, and which provided basic guidance not merely for devotional meditation, but for essential Catholic observances like going to confession or preparing to receive communion, the kind of material which had been a regular feature of English and bilingual Primers up to and including the official Primers of Mary's reign.

An attempt to bring this scattered material between a single pair of covers, in which Carter was probably involved, was made sometime after October 1580, at the Greenstreet Press in East Ham. From that press there issued *A Manual or Meditation, with a Memoriall of Instructions, also a Summary of Catholike Religion*.[31] As its clumsy title suggests, this was an *omnium gatherum*, made up of nine separate components. These began with Canisius's *Meditations on the Passion*, which Carter had printed separately in 1576, then a set of prayers and reflections for prayer from morning to evening based on a Latin source, about which more later, a 'Briefe summarie of Christian religion', derived from a now lost controversial broadsheet by Allen's chief lieutenant Richard Bristowe, and then a short catechism in the form of a dialogue between doctor and novice, covering the same topics. This was followed by a tidied-up and expanded version of the *Short and Absolute form of confession* which Carter had issued separately in 1577, together with prayers to be recited before and after confession and communion, including some prayers by Thomas More borrowed from the *Brief form of confession* which John Fowler had published in 1576. The collection concluded with Whytford's *Jesus Psalter*, together with the Golden Litany, another early Tudor Christocentric devotion, and a long prayer of thanksgiving addressed to the Holy Trinity, which may have been a fresh composition.

In the face of what its editor described as 'the scarcitie of devoute bookes treating of pietie and direction of godly life'[32] the *Manual or Meditation* was evidently considered useful enough to run to three editions by the mid-1590s. But it was fundamentally a rag-bag, an eclectic amalgam of materials with no very obvious structure and with major gaps in its provision – it offered, for example, no prayers for the sick or dying, a serious omission in a country where the majority of the laity were likely to die without the benefit of Catholic clerical ministrations.

But it was not, of course, only in mission territory that the need for such a devotional *vade mecum* was felt. In the wake of Trent, the great devotional outpouring of the late Middle Ages had come to seem to many fastidious theological minds far too promiscuous by half. The Pian reform of the liturgy, in which the Tridentine Primer was just one item, was an attempt to purge the liturgical and devotional life of Catholics of error, superstition and excess.[33] Much of the energy of the leaders of the late sixteenth-century counter-reformation was poured into the production of catechetical and devotional material which would offer wholesome and orthodox spiritual milk for the laity, and keep them from the poison of Protestant religious writing.

In the Low Countries, the most important single contribution to that effort came from a Brabantine grammarian and schoolmaster, Simon Vereept, who published under the Latinised form of his name, Verepaeus. Vereept is now a largely forgotten figure, but his pedagogical and grammatical writings remained in use in schools and colleges all over northern Europe well into the eighteenth century, and were still being printed in the 1860s. And in terms of the number of its sixteenth- and early seventeenth-century editions and translations, and its direct religious influence, Vereept's 1565 devotional compilation, the *Enchyridion Precationum Piarum*, once ranked alongside the writings of his now far more famous friend Peter Canisius. And it was Vereept's *Enchyridion* which was to provide the core round which would form the most important of all recusant devotional texts, the *Manual of Prayers*.

Simon Vereept was born in Dommelen in North Brabant in 1522, and proceeded MA at Leuven in 1545. In the 1560s and 1570s he combined a distinguished career as a Latin teacher and educational theorist with the spiritual direction of the nuns of the convent of Mont Thabor on the outskirts of Malines, a spiritual distinction he blazoned on the title pages of his books: he ended his career as rector and professor of Latin at the Chapter school at Bois le Duc, and Canon of the Cathedral there till his death in 1598. Vereept was a humanist in the mould of Erasmus and Juan de Vives (whose letters he edited). Like them he combined professional immersion in the Greek and especially Latin classics with a deep commitment to Christian renewal. Unlike them, however, he lived out that commitment in the midst of the traumatic religious upheavals which shattered the unity of the Low Countries in the 1560s and 1570s, and he was himself a victim of those upheavals. In 1566 he was driven from his post at Mont Thabor, and fled Malines, in the wake of the Calvinist 'iconoclastic fury'. The convent itself was sacked, restored and then reduced to ashes again in 1572: these '*miserabili et deploranda afflictioni*', and especially the '*calamitoso incendio*' of the convent, loomed large in Vereept's consciousness.[34]

Vereept produced two compilations of prayers, the first and more important, the *Enchyridion Precationum Piarum*, in 1565,[35] the second, derived from it but differently arranged, the *Precationes Liturgicae in dies septem digestae*, in 1574. Both became immensely popular, and the *Enchyridion* in particular ran through dozens of editions before the end of the century, was translated into both French and German and was excerpted and abbreviated.[36] It is not hard to see why. The *Enchyridion* was a self-consciously Tridentine book, designed to provide devout Catholics with collections of eloquent and orthodox prayers, free from superstition or excess, drawn exclusively from approved Catholic writers, ancient and modern. The dedicatory letter addressed to Gerard de Groesbeck, prince Bishop of Liège, which Vereept added to a reissue of the *Enchyridion* the year after the iconoclastic fury of 1566, presents the book as a spiritual weapon for a Church beset by militant enemies, designed to displace from the hands of simple readers the flood of 'pernicious' and 'pestilential' Protestant Prayer Books, lavishly illustrated and ornately phrased to mislead the unwary, and to provide a sound and attractive Catholic alternative.[37]

A prominent feature of the preliminary matter in the *Enchyridion* was a long list of the sources, extending to several pages, from which Vereept had collected the prayers – Greek and Latin liturgies, the early Church Fathers and especially St Augustine, medieval theologians and devotional classics from Anselm to Thomas à Kempis, and approved modern Catholic writers from Johannes Faber, Luis de Vives and John Fisher, to Luis de Blois, Stanislaus Hosius, Peter Soto and Peter Canisius. Vereept arranged the prayers in the *Enchyridion* thematically into 15 chapters: these included prayers for morning and evening, prayers at Mass, prayers for protection against various calamities including heresy, prayers of penitence and of intercession for various states of life, prayers of thanksgiving, prayers to the persons of the Trinity, prayers of the passion, prayers to the saints, prayers for the dying and the dead, prayers on the glories of heaven. Vereept provided a suggested weekly framework for reading the various chapters, and in the *Precationes Liturgicae* went one better by rearranging a selection of his material into devotions formally allocated to the days of the week. Each prayer in both collections was carefully attributed to its author, including those prayers contributed by Vereept himself. These attributions were important. For all its devotional emphasis, Vereept's *Enchyridion* is manifestly a product of the age of the Magdeburg centuries and Cesare Baronio, in which an exclusive claim to the inheritance of the Fathers and the primitive ages of the Church was a key weapon in the struggle between rival confessions.

We know that the *Enchyridion* had reached English Catholic circles by the mid-1570s. In 1575, as Fowler and Carter were issuing their devotional *libelli*, Thomas Tallis and William Byrd published their great musical collection, the *Cantiones Sacrae*. Despite its dedication to Queen Elizabeth, and its elaborate structuring round the number 17, to mark the Queen's accession on 17 November 1558, just 17 years before, the *Cantiones*, with its settings of texts from the Catholic liturgy of Lent, of the dead, and of Corpus Christi, positively reeks of popery, which may partly account for its commercial failure.[38] One of the finest items in the book is Byrd's setting of a non-liturgical text, an invocation to the Trinity beginning *Tribue Domine*. This has been recognised by the musicologists as an extract from chapter 33 of a medieval Pseudo-Augustinian text, the *Meditationes*. What has not been recognised is that Byrd almost certainly took the text not from a full text of the *Meditationes*, but from Vereept's *Enchyridion*, where the paragraphs Byrd set form the second item in the chapter of prayers to the Trinity.[39] Five years on, Vereept's work was also drawn on by the compiler of the *Manual or Meditation*, whose section of prayers for morning, evening and times of the day were taken from the *Enchyridion*.

But Carter's *Manual or Meditation* turned out to be a trial run for a far superior compilation, the *Manual of Prayers* itself, the first surviving edition of which appeared from the press established at Rouen by Robert Persons in 1583. The *Manual*'s compiler and editor was not Persons, however, but the layman George Flinton, the 'molto pio e zeloso' English merchant recruited by Persons to print for the English mission.[40] In an address from 'the Collectour and translator' to the Catholike and Christian reader, Flinton commented on the recent surge in devotional publications, 'which in the judgement of many are presently more necessary than farther to treate of any controversy'. This little manual, he declared, 'hath bene collected in greate haste', and without naming Vereept he acknowledged his debt to the prayers 'collected and translated out of dyvers famous and holy authors as well auntient as of the time present' which 'to the great increase of devotion' had been published 'in many countries and in dyvers tonges, before this my collection and translation'.[41]

Flinton's *Manual* was indeed heavily dependent on the *Enchyridion*, but was by no means a straightforward translation. For a start, Flinton's manual was much shorter than Vereept's book. He reduced the *Enchyridion*'s 15 chapters to 13 by omitting the section of Eucharistic prayers for priests, scarcely relevant in a book aimed primarily at the laity, and omitted also the final chapter of prayers 'on the heavenly Jerusalem'. Within the sections he retained, Flinton dropped or shortened many individual items. Nevertheless, more than 70 per cent of the material in the *Manual* was lifted from the *Enchyridion*, and, with minor modifications to take account of the omitted material, Flinton even reproduced Vereept's diagrammatic reading scheme for working through all the chapters of prayers twice a month.[42] Like the *Enchyridion*, the *Manual* provided a comprehensive range of prayers for morning and night, prayers to be said at Mass, prayers of intercession for the Church, for friends, for enemies, for benefits spiritual and temporal, prayers of thanksgiving, prayers to the persons of the Trinity, prayers to the saints, and prayers for the dying and the dead. It would have been perfectly possible for Flinton to compile a satisfactory Prayer Book using nothing but Vereept's material, and at first glance it might seem that that is what he did. But a closer look reveals that Flinton was exercising considerable editorial discretion, and, in particular, that he was at pains to inject into the book a large quantity of distinctively English material, drawn mainly from publications originating in the circle of Thomas More, including prayers by More himself, by Fisher, by Cuthbert Tunstall and by Richard Whitford.

This is most obvious in the inclusion at the end of the manual, under a separate title page, of the *Jesus Psalter* and the *Golden Litany*, 80 pages' worth of ardent early Tudor devotional invocation, to the end of which Flinton tacked on Thomas More's *Godly and Devoute Prayers*, the Tower prayers, which include the famous marginalia from his Primer beginning, 'Give me thy grace Good Lord', and which had been included in Fowler's 1576 *Brief form of confession* dedicated to Jane Dormer.[43] Flinton put another four prayers by More into the chapter of prayers on the Blessed Sacrament, again taken from those printed in Fowler's book.[44] His longest text by More, however, was the only Latin prayer included, 'for the use of those that are desirous to rede latine prayers'. This was More's long catena from the Psalms, *Imploratio Divini Auxilii contra tentationum*, first published in Cologne in the 1520s, but which had been reissued under a false imprint from a secret press in London in 1572, along with Fisher's rather similar *Psalmi seu Precationes*, an obvious enough pairing.[45]

There were other signs of Flinton's self-conscious use of more sober native English material, and perhaps of a deliberate desire to connect the Elizabethan mission with the key figures in early Tudor Catholicism. He rejected most of Vereept's prayers to the Virgin, and instead substituted a prayer by Cuthbert Tunstall, 'All hayle un-defiled Virgin Mary . . . elected and chosen', taken from Cawood's 1558 edition of Tunstall's *Certaine Godly and Devoute Prayers*. Another of Tunstall's prayers, to the Crucifix, replaced some of Vereept's prayers on the Passion.[46] Flinton included a shortened version of the popular medieval prayer to Mary, *O Intemerata*, with a heading ascribing it to 'S. *Edmundus Arch. Cantuariensis*', and a prayer to Mary and the saints, taken from the Sarum Primer.[47] In the same way, he replaced most of Vereept's prayers to the Trinity with a long address to the Three Persons taken from the material at the end of William Carter's edition of Loarte's *Exercise of a Christian Life*. Vereept had included some short extracts from John Fisher's Latin *Psalmi seu Precationes*, the collection of exclamatory prayers which Fisher had composed out of verses culled from Scripture, first published at Cologne in 1525. Flinton translated some of Vereept's selections, but added three more, Fisher's lengthy thirteenth, fourteenth and fifteenth 'psalms'. Astonishingly, rather than translate them himself, Flinton took his versions of these prayers by Fisher from a Protestant source, the translation of the *Psalmi seu Precationes* by Queen Katherine Parr, first published, without any mention of Fisher, by Thomas Berthelet, Henry VIII's official printer, in 1544.[48]

The same independence and resort to early Tudor sources is evident in Flinton's handling even of Thomas à Kempis's *Imitation of Christ*. The *Imitatio* was one of the counter-reformation's most admired texts, Ignatius Loyola's favourite reading, and Vereept unsurprisingly included many extracts from Kempis in the *Enchyridion*, mostly in the form of short prayers from the sacramental material in Book 4.[49] Flinton jettisoned most of these, instead opting for longer extracts from Book 3, in the translation by Richard Whytford which Carter had reissued in 1576.[50]

Flinton's *Manual* of 1583, deeply indebted to Vereept and the European counter-reformation, yet deliberately and consciously drawing on native early Tudor material, decisively established the framework of the vernacular prayer of English Catholics for two centuries. His book had a number of obvious omissions, but the most significant of them were deliberate. In impeccable Tridentine fashion, Flinton emphasised in the preliminaries to the *Manual* that a collection of private devotions like his should never supplant or challenge the official prayer of the Church, and so the laity should be assiduous in the use of the Rosary, the Little Office of the Virgin, the *Dirige* for the dead, the penitential psalms and the Litany of the saints: in effect, he was insisting on the need for his readers to own a Primer as well as his *Manual*, though there would be no way of supplying that desideratum for monoglot English readers for the best part of another generation.

As a self-denying ordinance, Flinton's *Manual* included no litanies, not even the Litany of the Saints, which Vereept had included, and it offered few psalms and fewer hymns. But his book was recognised immediately as offering an invaluable and flexible framework into which these and many other items could be inserted. Over the next 40 years additional material would accrete in the editions which poured steadily from presses both in Europe and clandestinely in England.[51] In successive editions, Flinton's work was supplemented and reshaped, while remaining recognisably the same book. The *Manual* acquired sections containing a calendar, a synopsis of the Catholic faith (modelled closely on the corresponding material in

Vereept's *Enchyridion*), the regulations on fasting and other seasonal observances for Catholics in England, the method of serving the priest at Mass, and detailed instructions for going to confession and preparing to receive communion.

Flinton had jettisoned the rather preachy meditations on the passion by Peter Canisius which had opened Carter's *Manual or Meditation*, and replaced them with a shorter and less hectoring set of 15 sweetly devotional prayers on the wounds and sufferings of the Passion, punctuated by a repeated prayer beginning 'O myld and Innocent Lambe of God, thus hartely didst thou love me, these things thou didest for me'. This Jesus-centred devotion at the start of the book, like the *Jesus Psalter* and *Golden Litany* at its end, anchored the *Manual* firmly in the affective piety of the late Middle Ages.[52] The prayer evidently touched a chord in the hearts of Flinton's readers, and became an invariable feature of future editions. The second edition of 1589 dropped More's Latin *Imploratio*, redistributed the bulk of the prayers under the days of the week and provided a set of litanies for Thursday (of the Blessed Sacrament) – Friday (of the Holy Name of Jesus) – and Saturday (of the Virgin). Subsequent editions followed this pattern, and litanies would multiply till there was one provided for every day: the free use of prayers in Litany form would remain one of the most distinctive features of English Catholic piety well into the nineteenth century, and in the eighteenth century formed a staple of public para-liturgical services in Catholic chapels and households.[53]

These early litanies could be very striking formularies: the Thursday litany of the Sacrament invoked Christ as

Chief memorial of divine love, medicine of immortality, bread of the Almighty Word made flesh, unbloody sacrifice, most sweet banquet wherein the ministering angels attend, sacrament of piety, bond of charity, offerer and oblation, spiritual sweetness tasted in his proper fountain, refection of holy souls, voyage food of those who die in the Lord, pledge of future glory.[54]

The suffrages attached to the Wednesday litany of the Blessed Saints dwelt vividly on the beleaguered condition of English Catholics themselves:

That thou wouldst mercifully convert the heart of his majestie, to take compassion of our miseries.

That thou wouldst comfort and fortifie al such as suffer imprisonment, losse of goodes, or other affliction for the catholick faith.

That neither by frailties, enticements, or any torments, thou permit any of us to fall from thee.

That thou wouldest mercifully hasten the conversion of England, Scotland and Ireland, from the infection of heresie and infidelitie.

That thou wouldest reduce from errour and heresie our parents, Friends and Benefactors, whom thou hast so dearly bought with thy precious blood.

That thou wouldest illuminate the harts of al schismatikes, which live out of the Church, to see the grievous danger of their estate.

That thou wouldest mercifully looke downe from heaven upon the bloud of so many Martyrs, as have given their lives to convert us unto thee.[55]

By 1620, the fully evolved *Manual* had essentially done away with the need for any other book, since editions now routinely incorporated the most valuable parts of the Primer – the Litany and penitential psalms, Lauds, Vespers and Compline for Sunday and the days of the week, and in many cases the hymns, antiphons and proper collects for all the major feasts. As the editor of the 1620 edition pointed out, '. . . it hath bin thought good to adde . . . the holy Song of our Blessed Lady, and others, with the psalms of King David used throughout the Primer, which are divided and digested (for the more easie exercise of such devoute people, who know not the use of the said Primer) into the dayes prayers of the weeke', an aside about ignorance of the Primer which perhaps suggests something about the relatively humble social status of the expected readership of the edition.[56] At any rate, a Catholic with a copy of the *Manual* in his or her closet, and a Rosary at her belt or in his pocket, needed no other devotional aid.

I have space here only for the briefest of reflections on what the history of the *Manual* might tell us about the nature of the English counter-reformation. Whether one leans towards Bossy or towards

Haigh in the now rather tired debate about continuity (Haigh) or new beginnings (Bossy) in the history of Elizabethan recusancy,[57] it is obvious that the arrival of the seminary priests and the start of the Jesuit mission coincided with a new sense of pastoral urgency, and a new resourcefulness and energy in compiling, printing and disseminating a devotional literature to service that new pastoral drive. It is obvious, too, that Robert Persons and his associates, archetypical 'new clerks', to borrow a phrase from John Bossy again, had a major hand in initiating and shaping that response. The *Manual* was itself a new kind of Prayer Book, deeply indebted to the scholarly, carefully orthodox and ecclesiatically correct piety of the international counter-reformation and represented by men like Vereept, proponents of a reformist piety militant on two fronts, battling Protestantism without and ignorance and superstition within the post-Tridentine Church.

But it is equally obvious that in compiling their new Prayer Books, Flinton and those who came after him had no sense or intention of breaking with the past. William Carter was Person's collaborator at Greenstreet House: but he had first been amanuensis to Nicholas Harpsfield and was the conduit by which crucial texts of Henrician and Marian Catholicism were preserved and disseminated. In selecting material for their publications, these first devotional compilers were as likely to draw on the affective devotion of the fourteenth or fifteenth century as on the more sententious and controlling orthodoxies of the age of Trent. The bulk of the prayers included in the *Manual* were medieval or even older, and most of the distinctively English material added to the *Manual* had been generated or translated no later than the 1520s or 1530s. So users of the *Manual* were encouraged to think of themselves as stepping into a stream that ran back into a time when there had been no Protestants, and they were aware of standing fast in the faith of their fathers. Interestingly, and perhaps puzzlingly, successive redactors of the *Manual* quickly dispensed with one of the most obvious markers of these continuities, for after 1596 most editions of the *Manual* dispensed with Vereept's and Flinton's attributions of individual prayers to Chrysostom or Augustine, Bede or the ancient liturgies, though the title pages continued to advertise that the prayers were drawn from 'many famous and godly' men, both ancient and modern. With or without those specific attributions, however, the *Manual* was the product of a Catholicism which felt no need for a hermeneutic of rupture in understanding its own medieval and early Tudor past.

Notes

1   I am indebted to Mr Tony Hadland, Chairman of the Oxfordshire Local History Association, who drew my attention to Lenthall's will and provided a transcript. See his 'An Oxfordshire Recusant's Pick and Mix Will' in *Catholic Ancestor, Journal of the Catholic Family History Society*, 14 (April 2013), pp. 199–205. Details of the Lenthall and Brome families and their recusancy in the 1970 Bristol DPhil thesis by D. Alan Davidson, 'Roman Catholicism in Oxfordshire from the late Elizabethan Period to the Civil War', pp. 138 ff.

2   The most convenient edition of the 1559 Prayerbook is now Brain Cummings (ed.), *The Book of Common Prayer* (Oxford: 2011), pp. 99–181; the prayer under discussion is at p. 174.

3   PCC Prob 11/ 71.

4   Alexandra Walsham, 'Dumb Preachers: Catholicism and the Culture of Print' and the same author's 'Unclasping the Book: the Douai Rheims Bible', both reprinted in Walsham, *Catholic Reformation in Protestant Britain* (Farnham, 2014), pp. 235–314.

5   Eamon Duffy, *Marking the Hours: English People and their Prayers 1240–1570* (New Haven and London, 2006), pp. 121–46.

6   *The primer, set foorth by the kynges maiestie and his clergie, to be taught, lerned and read: and none other to be used throughout all his dominions* (London, Richard Grafton, 1545), STC 16034.

7   *The Primer and Catechism, set forth by the King's highness, and his clergy; to be taught, learned and read of all his loving subjects, all other set apart . . .* (London, Richard Grafton, 1551), STC 16053.

8   *An uniforme and catholyke prymer in Latin and Englishe . . . to be only used of al the kyng and queens maiesties loving subiectes* (London, J. Waylande, 1555), STC 16060.

9   *The Primer set forth by the King's majesty, and his clergy; to be taught, larned and read, and none other to be used throughout all his dominions*, Richard Grafton (London, 1545). For this book's contents, Edgard Hoskins (ed.), *Horae beatae mariae Virginis, or, Sarum and York primers with kindred books . . .* (London, 1901), pp. 237–44.

10   These developments are discussed more fully in Eamon Duffy, *The Stripping of the Altars* (New Haven and London, 1992), pp. 444–7, 537–43.

11   For Tunstall's prayers, *Certaine godly and devout prayers made in latin and translated by T Paynell* (London, 1558), STC 24318.

12   But the dedicatory epistle of Stephen Brinkley's translation of Gaspar Loarte (below, n. 11) is dated 1572.

13   Janet Wilson, 'A Catalogue of the "Unlawful" Books found in John Stow's study', *Recusant History*, 20 (1990), pp. 1–30.

14   A. C. Southern, *Elizabethan Recusant Prose* (London, 1950), pp. 40–41. For the works mentioned, see A. F. Allison and D. M. Rogers, *The Contemporary Printed Literature of the English Counter-Reformation between 1558 and 1640*, vol. II, *Works in English* (Aldershot, 1994) (= *ARCRE*), nos 193 and 200 (Manual and Jesus Psalter), 63 (Brinkley's Loarte), 751 (Vaux), 616–17 (Persons), 311 (Fowler), 439 (Hopkins' Granada).

15   *An Apologie and true declaration of the institution and endeavours of the two English Colleges, the one in Rome, the other now resident in Rhemes* (1581), *ARCRE* no. 6, p. 26.

16   Brief comments on these issues in E. Duffy, *Marking the Hours* (New Haven and London, 2006), pp. 175–7.

17   Another aspect of the 'strange death of Erasmian England' discussed in chapter 1.

18   Full text of Pius V's Bull in *Bullarum Diplomaticum et Privilegiorum Sanctorum Romanum Pontificem* (Rome, 1857–72), vol. VII, pp. 897–901, (Latin) summary in Edgar Hoskins, *Horae Beatae Mariae*

Virginis, or, Sarum and York Primers (London, 1901), pp. 349–50. For Allen's opinion and the Douai debates, P. J. Holmes, *Elizabethan Casuistry* (Catholic Record Society, 1981), p. 24.

19   *The Primer, or office of the blessed virgin Marie, in Latin and English: according to the reformed Latin* (Antwerp, 1599), SRC 16094; for Verstegan, Paul Arblaster, *Antwerp and the World: Richard Verstegan and the International Culture of Catholic Reformation* (Leuven, 2004).

20   'Of Prayer and Orisons' in Michel de Montaigne, *Essays*, vol. 1 (London, 1910), p. 361 (John Florio's translation).

21   Émile Pasquier, *Un curé de Paris pendant les guerres de Religion. René Benoist, le Pape des Halles (1521–1608)* (Paris, Angers, 1913); Bruno Petey Girard, 'Latin ou Langue vulgaire. La Prière Catholique en France à la fin du xvi siècle' in Jean-François Cottier (ed.), *La Prière en Latin de l'Antiquité au xvie siècle* (Turnhout, 2006), pp. 379–89; Virginia Reinburg, *French Books of Hours: Making an Archive of Prayer c 1400–1600* (Cambridge, 2012), pp. 96–100.

22   John Bossy, 'Prayers', *Transactions of the Royal Historical Society*, 6th Series, 1 (1991), pp. 137–50.

23   Figures from the lists in J. M. Blom, *The Post-Tridentine English Primer* (Catholic Record Society, 1982), pp. 168–88.

24   For the surviving editions of Clifford's book, Thomas H. Clancy, *English Catholic Books 1641–1700* (Aldershot, 1996), nos 230–33.

25   Richard Challoner, *The Garden of the Soul: or, a Manual of Spiritual Exercises and Instructions for Christians who living in the world aspire to devotion* (London, 1740); the standard bibliography of eighteenth-century English Catholic books lists 31 editions of *The Garden of the Soul* between 1740 and 1800, compared with the *Manual*'s 26 editions between 1705 and 1793 – F. Blom, J. Blom, F. Korsten and G. Scott (eds), *English Catholic Books 1701–1800* (Aldershot, 1996), nos 544–74, nos 1780–1805.

26   *ARCRE*, nos 193–5.

27   Above, n. 6.

28   STC nos 3281.5–3285.10.

29   For a discussion of Carter's output, T. A. Birrell, 'William Carter (c. 1549–1584) Recusant printer' in *Recusant History*, 28 (2006–7), pp. 22–42.

30   For which see *Stripping of the Altars*, pp. 249–54.

31   *ARCRE*, no. 664.3, STC 17278.4.

32   Phrases from the preface to the 1596 edition 'The Collectour to the devout Catholike and Christian Reader', *ARCRE*, 664.7, STC 17278.6.

33   On the reform of the liturgy after Trent, Simon Ditchfield, *Liturgy, Sanctity, and History in Tridentine Italy: Pietro Maria Campi and the Preservation of the Particular* (Cambridge, 1995).

34   For his career, M. A. Nauwelaerts, 'La Correspondence de Simon Verepaeus' in *Humanistica Lovaniensia, Journal of Neo-Latin Studies*, 23 (1974), pp. 271–340. The Latin phrases are from the 1574 dedicatory epistle to the *Precationes Liturgicae in septem dies*, addressed to Cardinal Granvelle.

35   For the sake of accessibility I have worked from the 1577 edition, which is available online at http://books.google.co.uk/books/about/Precationum_Piarum_Enchiridion.html?id= d4RUAAAAcAAJ&redir_esc=y

36   Marcel A. Nauwelaerts, 'Bijdrage tot de bibliographie van Simon Verepaeus', *De Gulden Passer*, 25 (1947), pp. 52–90, esp. 61–6, supplemented and corrected in Gilbert Tournoy, 'Bouwstenen voor een nieuwe verepaeusbibliografie', *De Gulden Passer*, 74 (1996), pp. 439–450, esp. 442–4. For a discussion of the early Dutch (Flemish) versions, see the article by Nauwelaerts in *Het Boek*, 30 (1951), pp. 357–63. I am grateful to Professor Win Francois of Leuven, to whose comradely help I am indebted for these references, and for providing copies of material from Leuven.

37   'ut perniciosi illi precationum libelii (quos videbam quotanni fere prodire novos magnis laudum encomiis, styli ac dictionis ornatu, plerosque etiam elegantis picturae levociniis, magnifice quidem commendates) simplicium lectorem manibes, paulatim hac ratione ac excuterentur, atque in eorum locum Catholici pii ac salutares succederunt'.

38   The most recent recording of the complete motets of the *Cantiones Sacrae* is the two-CD edition by Alamire, directed by David Skinner, Obsidian Records 706 (2011).

39 For a recent discussion of the motet, though without reference to Vereept, Kerry Robin McCarthy, 'Byrd, Augustine and *Tribue, Domine*', *Early Music*, 32 (2004), pp. 569–75. The best edition of *Cantiones Sacrae*, with a comprehensive bibliography, is part of the British Academy's Early English Church Music series, *Thomas Tallis and William Byrd, Cantiones Sacrae 1575*, transcribed and edited by John Milson (London, 2014).

40 Victor Houliston (ed.), *The Christian Directory (1582): The First Booke of the Christian Exercise, appertaining to Resolution*, by Robert Persons (Leiden, 1998), pp. xxi–xiii; Southern, *Elizabethan Recusant Prose*, pp. 359–62, mistakenly attributes these works to the press of George l'Oyselet, cf. *Short Title Catalogue*, vol. 3, p. 132. col. 2, 'Fr Persons' Press'.

41 *Manual 1583* (*ARCRE*, 200, STC 17263, printed in facsimile by Scolar Press, English Recusant Literature series no. 372). 'The Collectour and translatour of this present Manual, to the Catholick and Christian Reader'). The history of the *Manual* was first discussed by Joseph Gillow, 'Origin and History of the Manual', *Ushaw Magazine* (1910), pp. 276–312: Blom, *Post-Tridentine Primers*, pp. 112–36.

42 Vereept's Schema in the address 'Ad piam lectorem' at the end of the *Enchyridion*: Flinton's schema in *Manual 1583* in the preliminary 'Argument of the Chapters', both unpaginated.

43 *Manual 1583* fol. 181–5.

44 *Manual 1583* fols 190, 194.

45 Alison and Rogers, *The Contemporary Printed Literature of the English Counter-Reformation between 1558 and 1640*, vol. 1, *Works in Languages other than English* (Aldershot, 1989) (= *ARCR0*), nos 423–7.

46 STC 24318: *Manual 1583* fol. 122.

47 *Manual 1583* p. 123.

48 STC 3001.7; for the history of Queen Katherine's version, Janel Mueller (ed.), *Katherine Parr, Complete Works and Correspondence* (Chicago and London, 2011), pp. 197–213. The psalms included by Flinton are in *Manual 1583*, fols 97–106, Mueller, pp. 338–56. Flinton included another extract from Fisher's Psalm 15 in his own version, fol. 108v.

49 For translations of the *Imitatio*, Maximilian von Habsburg, *Catholic and Protestant Translations of the Imitatio Christi, 1425–1650* (Ashgate, 2011).

50 *Manual 1583* fols 42v ff. (cf. Whitford's *The Following of Christ* (1575) *ARCRE*, no. 803), fol. 67 ff.); *Manual 1583* fol 51 ff. (cf. Whitford fol. 64); *Manual 1583* fol. 53 ff. (Whitford fol. 76v ff.); *Manual 1583* fol. 57 ff. (cf. Whitford 87v–88); for a duplicated version of this prayer, *Manual* 76v–77.

51 Twenty-nine editions by 1639: STC 17263–17278, plus a Protestant bowdlerised version, 17278.1.

52 *Manual 1583* fols 5–14. I have not yet identified the source of these 15 meditations.

53 Useful discussion of the changing contents of the Manual in Blom, *Post Tridentine Primer*, pp. 116–25.

54 *ARCRE*, no. 212 (1613) [STC 17273], pp. 334–5.

55 Ibid., pp. 312–13.

56 Blom, *Post Tridentine Primer*, p. 121.

57 John Bossy, *The English Catholic Community, 1570–1850* (London, 1975); Christopher Haigh, 'The fall of a church or the rise of a sect?', *Historical Journal*, 2 (1978), pp. 181–6; 'The continuity of Catholicism in the English Reformation', *Past and Present*, no. 93 (1981), pp. 37–69; 'From monopoly to minority: Catholicism in early modern England', *Transactions of the Royal Historical* Society, 31 (1981), pp. 129–47; Patrick McGrath, 'Elizabethan Catholicism: A Reconsideration', *Journal of Ecclesiastical History*, 35 (1984), pp. 414–28; P. McGrath and J. Rowe, 'The Marian Priests under Elizabeth I', *Recusant History*, 17 (1984), pp. 103–20; C. Haigh, 'Revisionism, the Reformation and the History of English Catholicism', *Journal of Ecclesiastical History*, 36 (1985), pp. 394–405; 'Reply' by McGrath, ibid., pp. 405–6; Andrew R. Muldoon, 'Recusants, Church-Papists, and "Comfortable" Missionaries: Assessing the Post-Reformation English Catholic Community', *Catholic Historical Review*, 86 (2000), pp. 242–57; M. C. Questier, 'What Happened to English Catholicism after the Reformation?' *History*, 85 (2000), pp. 28–47.

8

The English Secular Clergy and the Counter-Reformation

The century from the calling of the Council of Trent to the conclusion of the Treaty of Aix-la-Chapelle stands out as one of the most creative in the pastoral history of Christian Europe. The great number of new apostolic orders, the devotional flowering in France which tamed and domesticated the mysticism of Spain for everyman, the renovation of the parish and the priestly life aspired to by Carlo Borromeo, Pierre Bérulle and Vincent de Paul, are all aspects of a transformation which is the spiritual face of the baroque.[1] The practice of confession stands somewhere near the centre of this transformation. From an annual social rite concerned essentially with the restoration of peace and the guaranteeing of restitution, it became a monthly or even weekly private rite of reconciliation of the penitent with God.[2] It became, too, the focus for the direction of souls which was now seen, supremely in the work of François de Sales, as a central part of the work of the priest. The Salesian tradition was to dominate the flood of devotional manuals published in every European language in the seventeenth century, and in it the practice of confession was developed beyond the juridical and canonical framework of Trent, and turned into a subtle and highly personal instrument of spiritual direction.[3]

The revival of confession was intimately linked with the renewal of the ideal of the secular priest. The Tridentine emphasis on confession was part and parcel of a tightening of the parochial structure in which the centrality of the parish priest, and above him of the bishop, was the key factor.[4] Accordingly, the seventeenth-century French emphasis on the spiritual director was harnessed to a rehabilitation of the secular clergy. Pious laypeople desired holy men to be their ghostly fathers. The lack of prestige of the secular clergy, and the assumption that only the religious orders produced men devout enough to guide others, came increasingly under attack from those, like Cardinal Bérulle or Monsieur Vincent, who sought to exalt the parochial clergy. Spiritual direction and the holiness which validated it must not be separated from hierarchical authority, an impeccably Tridentine sentiment which often took on the air of a polemic against the regulars. As Bérulle wrote:

> God preserved authority, sanctity and doctrine, uniting these triple perfections in the sacerdotal order . . . Alas . . . the malignity of the world in which we live has cast us down from this dignity. It has passed into strange hands [the religious orders] and we may justly adopt the words of Lamentation, *Hereditas nostra versa est ad alienos*; but however much they [the religious orders] are naturalized in grace and in the unity of the Body of Jesus they are yet strangers in the ministry, and God, in his original plan, did not choose them for that.[5]

The revival of the secular clergy was accompanied by a renewed sense of urgency, the discovery of *France, pays de mission*, and the launching of an offensive against a popular religiosity perceived in terms of pagan survivalism and ignorance, the impact of which was still reverberating into our own times.[6] Hierarchy and holiness, counsel and confession, the gargantuan task of converting a continent never wholly purged of paganism, or newly enmeshed in the desolation of Protestantism, these are grand themes in the history of counter-reformation Europe.

How do these themes appear in seventeenth-century England? *Pays de mission* certainly, its secular clergy 'missionary priests', the products, for the most part, of one of the earliest Tridentine seminaries. They were, moreover, preoccupied throughout the period with problems of hierarchy and order. One of the tragedies of the English counter-reformation was the bitter division of its agents, most notoriously in the hostility between the secular clergy and the Jesuits. England was effectively without a bishop for the 50 years before 1685 because of the failure of Richard Smith, Bishop of Chalcedon and 'ordinary of England', to establish his authority over the regular clergy and their lay clients on this very matter of confession and the right to absolve. He retreated to France, to be comforted by his patron Richelieu and by the disciples of his friend and mentor, Bérulle, not least the Jansenist heresiarch (if such he was) Saint-Cyran.[7] Behind him he left a clergy without any organisation that Rome was prepared to recognise, a situation not rectified till James II introduced a Catholic episcopal structure into England, the only successful venture of his reign.[8]

It would not, then, be surprising to find the Tridentine, Borromean and Bérullian ideals of the priesthood penetrating the English secular clergy in the early seventeenth century. Yet, in the view of the most distinguished and most influential modern historian of English Catholicism, these ideals penetrated hardly at all. According to Professor John Bossy, the English secular clergy were trapped 'in a sterile wilderness of unreality' by the conviction that they were *not* a missionary group seeking to *create* a Catholic community, but the continuing *Ecclesia Anglicana* of the Middle Ages. Refusing to face reality, they sought, in Bossy's view, to recreate a hierarchical structure in which the religious orders, above all the Jesuits, would be subordinated to the secular clergy and their bishop, a structure 'ludicrously unadaptable to English conditions'. This obsession with the 'mirage' of a 'ghost church' prevented the seculars settling down to the business of a mission. Professor Bossy traces this 'mirage' through a long development dating from the Elizabethan period – from the Wisbech Stirs and the Appellant disputes under the pro-Jesuit archpriest Blackwell – through the attempts by William Bishop and Richard Smith to extend episcopal control over the religious orders and the Catholic laity.

To exercise episcopal control *sede vacante*, Bishop erected, and Smith confirmed, the 'Chapter' of the secular clergy, a body which was to be tacitly accepted though never formally recognised by Rome as the *de facto* canonical authority for the English secular mission between Smith's death in 1655 and the coming of the first vicars apostolic in 1685. And it was, above all, by the men of the Chapter that the illusion of being a Church rather than a mission was fostered, their energy being frittered away on the obsessive pursuit of an episcopal hierarchy. This quest was accompanied by a conviction that the proper place for a monk was the cloister, certainly not in pastoral activity. For the secular clergy, according to Bossy, the 'beauty and significance of the church lay in its just (hierarchical) proportion, and not in anything the clergy might be doing'. With far greater realism and practicality, the Jesuits, and then the other regulars, notably the Benedictines, accepted the fact that England was no longer a Church, but a mission, adapted themselves to a flexible variety of ministries and resisted the secular clergy's attempts to impose upon them the straitjacket of hierarchical structures and all the unwieldy machinery of the canon law. The activities of the Chapter under its secretary, John Sergeant, in the mid-century were in this account the last struggles on behalf of an increasingly unreal ideal. By the time that John Leyburne, the first of James's vicars apostolic, was appointed in 1685, the secular clergy were ready to abandon the mirage of a Church, to accept the realities of the mission and to settle down to make a success of it, as the regulars had long since done. And so Bossy discerns 'a general sense of effort' among the clergy in the last quarter of the century and an accompanying growth in missionary effectiveness.[9]

As for the great renaissance of pastoral care associated with the work of Borromeo, Bérulle, Francis de Sales and Vincent de Paul, this, too, save for its hierarchical trappings, 'passed them by'. Though Bossy concedes that there *were* links with Borromeo and Bérulle,[10] he concludes that 'when all the evidence is assembled, it may appear that these new continental models provided for the English secular clergy only a few trimmings to a notion of the Church which depended for its substance on an appeal to the inviolable tradition of the past, and was accordingly insular as well as extremely conservative'. Even Smith's preoccupation with the licensing of confessors in the 1620s was primarily a concern with confession as a jurisdictional rather than a pastoral problem. 'Pastoral needs and realities, though they did not ignore them, seem still to have taken second place among the objects of their concern.'[11]

This interpretation has much to commend it. It is comprehensive, simple and in the best sense imaginative. I believe it, however, to be defective at a number of crucial points and to oversimplify an intractably complex situation. That antiquarian and insular attitudes motivated some of the clergy is doubtless true. But, in an age in which insistence on hierarchical order and the primacy of the secular clergy over the religious was one of the dominant themes of clerical reformers throughout Western Europe, to suggest that English insistence on these things was insular and backward-looking seems to me perverse. English clergy were trained in Italy and Spain, in France and the Low Countries. Many of their most distinguished members made careers in the churches of Italy, France and Flanders, while retaining influence over their clerical compatriots.[12] Even the most apparently negative and backward-looking attitudes of the secular clergy, their obsessive hierarchicalism and their deep distrust of and hostility to the Society of Jesus, can be amply paralleled elsewhere in counter-reformation Europe, and in contexts which demonstrate the interaction of English and European attitudes. This parallelism and interaction is nowhere more obvious than in Holland. An examination of the shared attitudes of Dutch and English secular clergy will do much to undermine the notion of English insularity.

Parallels between the Dutch and the English scenes are sufficiently obvious. In each case the official hierarchy was wiped out by political changes in the later sixteenth century. The appointments of Sasbout Vosmeer as vicar apostolic of Holland in 1592 and of George Blackwell as archpriest of England in 1598 marked the first stage in the ecclesiastical reconstruction of the two countries as mission territory. Vosmeer was consecrated Archbishop of Philippi in 1602: England had to wait a further 21 years before William Bishop was elevated to the see of Chalcedon. The secular clergy of both countries were involved throughout the century which followed in a bitter struggle with the religious orders, and especially with the Jesuits. In Holland the vicars apostolic negotiated demarcation agreements in 1610, 1624 and 1652, but were no more successful than Bishop or Smith in enforcing their rule on the regulars. In both countries Jesuits moved from place to place, heard confessions, granted indulgences and minor dispensations without episcopal approval. In each case this produced bitter hostility against what Neercassel called 'our rivals', and what an English secular priest called 'our opposites'.[13]

The seculars of both nations recognised their common cause and fostered it. Philip Rovenius, greatest of the Dutch vicars apostolic, wrote to sympathise with and support Smith in his struggles with the religious in 1628. The English Chapter negotiators for a bishop in the 1650s sought the help of Rovenius's successor, Jacques de La Torre. In the 1690s the English vicars appealed to Dutch precedents for their attempts to restrain Benedictine and Jesuit indiscipline. In 1710 and again in 1728 the Utrecht Chapter's apologist, Van Erckel, published extracts from Sergeant's *Account of the English Chapter* to underpin the claims of the Utrecht Chapter, while the consecrations of Bishops Stonor and Petre by single bishops were among the precedents cited for the consecration of the Archbishop of Utrecht by the Bishop of Babylon. John Leyburne, Philip Howard and a significant number of English secular priests corresponded with Jan van Neercassel, Quesnel and even the Utrecht Chapter itself. In 1714 the Utrecht group applied to Bishop Giffard to ordain priests for them and, although unwilling to compromise himself by doing so, he seems to have made no secret of his sympathy for them. Though both sides recognised limits to their community of interest – the English Chapter, for example, rejected for England bishops appointed, like the Dutch, 'ad beneplacitum Sanctae Sedis' – their sense of common purpose is unmistakable.[14]

The values common to both Dutch and English seculars included a sombre and rigorist attitude towards many aspects of the Christian life, and severity in ecclesiastical discipline, especially in the sacrament of penance.[15] In Holland this culminated in full-blown Jansenist schism, but it is important once again to put such rigorism in its proper counter-reformation perspective. In an important article, Pierre Chaunu argued that, on what he called the 'frontiers of Catholicism', that is to say, in areas with strong Protestant majorities or close Protestant neighbours, 'Jansenism' might signify not the negative and often political factionalism so often associated with French Jansenism, but a 'compensatory Augustinianism', a rigorous reformist Catholicism stripped to essentials to meet the Protestant challenge, based on an Augustinian theology of grace.[16]

In practice this Augustinian Catholicism drew its strength from the Borromean and Bérullian rigorist strands of the counter-reformation. The link hardly needs documentation for Holland. Rovenius planned with Jansenius himself the introduction of Bérulle's French Oratory into the Low Countries. Neercassel was trained by the Oratorians. Peter Codde was himself an Oratorian, and when Neercassel's *Amor Poenitens* was attacked at Rome it was defended by Cardinal Grimaldi as 'entirely agreeable to the . . . sentiments and to the practice of S. Charles [Borromeo]'.[17]

The Borromean tradition was characterised by two principal emphases: the reform of the Church by the enforcement of episcopal discipline which involved the relegation of the religious orders to a strictly ancillary role in support of the diocesan clergy; and the reform of the lives of individuals by a strictly penitential discipline which included practices coming to be looked upon as characteristic of Jansenism, such as the postponement of absolution until the penitent had shown clear signs of a sincere purpose of amendment.[18] Such severity naturally ran counter to many of the more exuberant and popular expressions of seventeenth-century devotion, which often seemed to offer 'cheap grace'. Since these devotions were often patronised by the regulars, they served to increase the suspicions of the rigorist party of regular (and especially Jesuit) 'lax morals'. It is these considerations that underlay a series of fierce but apparently trivial disputes in England over such matters as Lenten observance and the English secular clergy's use of 'deferred absolution'.[19]

In England the lack of a settled organisation brought a distinctly competitive element into the secular clergy's quite genuine rigorist disapproval of the methods of the regulars. There were no formal means of allotting priests to missions, or even of discovering which and how many priests were in the country. Hence, though most Catholics lived in the north-west, most priests were to be found in the south-east, a fact which Neercassel used in 1670 to back his own case for tighter episcopal control in Holland.[20] A further consequence of this lack of discipline was the fact that the gentry chose their own chaplains. And it is here that the element of competition occurred, for the religious orders sought to make their ministry attractive to the laity by offering their clients special religious privileges. This was one of the secular clergy's grievances during the mission of Gregorio Panzani to the court of Charles I. It remained a live issue throughout the century. In the 1690s the vicars apostolic challenged the claim of the Benedictines to be able to grant certain marriage dispensations for which the vicars themselves had to apply to Rome.[21]

Indulgenced devotions were another sore point and provide a vivid illustration of the significance of this whole area. Gerard Saltmarsh, chaplain to the dowager Duchess of Norfolk and one of the most influential of secular priests, had been nominated in 1707 to the vacant Western Vicariate. At the last minute, however, after his bulls of consecration had already been drawn up, his candidature was quashed because of his active sympathy for the supporters of Peter Codde, the deposed Jansenist vicar apostolic in Holland.

In 1712 Saltmarsh applied to Rome for permission to establish a confraternity under the title *De Bona Vita*. Though the practices of this confraternity were to include recitation of the Rosary and the Litany of Loretto, its principal emphases were on daily meditation on the four last things, examination of conscience, monthly confession and communion, daily spiritual reading and regular attendance at special sermons or instructions 'towards promoting the duty of a good life'. Saltmarsh's motive was a simple one, to prevent the flock wandering 'from their natural pastors' into the care of the religious orders. He admitted that his zeal for confraternities 'is not so very great because I observe these pious Institutions are subject to great abuse', often leading the ignorant to substitute 'the observance of some Rote practices' for 'the more substantial duties of Christianity'. Nevertheless, he felt that 'unless something of this sort be obtained for the Secular Clergy they may pack up shop and be idle, or turn Regulars, for the Dominican draws by Rosary Indulgence, the Fryer by Cords, the Carmelite by Scapulars, and now, as the good Fathers of the Society have order'd matters, they carry all the rest away by *Bona Morte* privileges and Indulgences'.[22] Saltmarsh spoke feelingly; he had himself been supplanted as chaplain to the Duke of Norfolk by a Jesuit. His request for an indulgenced devotion was refused, but the episode neatly brings together the secular clergy's rigorism, their distrust of 'cheap grace' and popular religion, their concern for the primacy of an ordered diocesan ministry over the encroachments of what one secular clergy petition called '*i banditti gesuitici*', with the naked economic competition of missioners for 'places' in gentry households, a competition unregulated by any missionary structure, and one which gave urgency and point to the theoretical issues.[23]

Thus the secular clergy's insistence that 'the Clergy are the only persons, that by divine institution and the principal Design of their vocation are entrusted with the care of souls', and that 'the Regulars can only pretend their own private zeal and the approbation of their superiors for offering their assistance' takes its place with other elements within the tradition of Bérullian and Borromean thinking which is a major element in the counter-reformation of seventeenth-century Europe.[24] No less a protagonist in the Jansenist debate than Abbé Saint-Cyran himself testified to this. In 1632-3 he intervened as *Petrus Aurelius* to defend Richard Smith against the English Jesuits, Floyd and Knott, who had rejected his authority. Saint-Cyran's work contained a defence of the Bérullian doctrine of the priesthood and an emphatically Borromean assertion of the importance of episcopal hierarchy in the reform and ordering of the Church. The regulars, especially the Jesuits, resisted this episcopalism in the interests of their own freedom of action. Purveying devotion capable of abuse, they seemed on all counts enemies of the godliness and good order by which the seculars believed Catholic religion alone could be forwarded. The claim, made both by English and Dutch Jesuits, 'that all jurisdiction had perished, and that therefore they needed no further authorisation for their stations than that of their own superior', *may*, as Bossy claims, have been prompted by counter-reformation zeal and flexibility, but was believed by the secular clergy and their leaders to be simple opportunism. The Jesuits, Christopher Bagshaw insisted, were forever 'seeking uniuste and unfit superioritye, wch the Pope him selfe hath warned them of, & hath made them odiouse wth Bishopps, Pastors, Universityes & all ordinarie Ecclesiastical estate in many places of Christendome'.[25] Thirty years on, the Dutch vicar apostolic Philip Rovenius agreed. 'The regulars, according to their custom', he told Richard Smith in 1628, 'subvert all order: Nay, they do this eagerly, so that order being overturned they may themselves act as they please and make piety a traffic.'[26] Against this anarchy Rovenius and his successors in Holland attempted to construct an orderly and rigorist ecclesiastical system on the Borromean pattern, a pattern fully in the spirit of Trent, a pattern to which the English, too, aspired.

There is no need, of course, to argue that a hierarchical model *was* necessarily the most appropriate for England or Holland: the pastoral limitations of the episcopal rigorism which characterised the Borromean tradition in Holland have been criticised even by the most sympathetic Dutch historian of Neercassel's work.[27] Nevertheless, Dutch experience does not seem to me to support Bossy's claim that an episcopal structure was 'ludicrously unadaptable' to a mission to Protestants. The parallels between England and Holland, moreover, and the fact that Dutch episcopalism was firmly rooted, politically and spiritually, in the counter-reformation does suggest that the English clergy's preoccupation with these matters cannot be dismissed as merely 'insular' or 'antiquarian'. [28]

In the rest of this chapter I want to consider the *pastoral* dimensions of this preoccupation with episcopal order and the dignity of the clergy. I want to take up Bossy's invitation and, in his phrase, to 'assemble the evidence' for the pastoral concern of Smith and the clergy associated with him. I think it will emerge that 'these new continental models', far from providing mere 'trimmings' to a basically insular and static antiquarianism, were in fact profound and far-reaching elements in a fully counter-reformed concept of ministry, based on the direction of souls and a heightened spirituality. It will also emerge that these models were transforming the English secular clergy in the same ways, and at more or less the same time, as similar changes in France and elsewhere. [29]

We may begin with the rhetoric of these disputes, noting that, whether or not secular clergy preoccupations with hierarchy were indeed archaising and impractical, at any rate in defending their concerns they certainly invoked the language of pastoral and missionary effectiveness. So, when the last of the archpriests, William Harrison, and his eleven assistants wrote to Pope Paul V to complain of Jesuit designs on the English seminary at Douai, the case they made was that an independent secular clergy seminary free of control by regulars was essential to ensure a supply of missioners, committed by oath to return to England as 'pastors ... obliged *ex officio* to the care of souls in those places'. Such missionaries should be 'persons of learning and singular erudition, to promote virtue and establish religion, not only among the better sort but among the common people'. For this reason Allen had founded Douay College to qualify clergy who would be 'equal to their task, in attempting the conversion of England ... converting heretics, instructing the faithful and acquitting themselves of their duty in any other part of the sacerdotal function'. The Jesuits, however, persistently tried to draw seminarians into their own organisation and its objectives, and therefore away from commitment to parochial ministry. For that reason Carlo Borromeo, who had at first committed his seminary in Milan to Jesuit government, 'removed them, and gave the whole government up to the [secular] clergy'.[30]

That this was a consistent preoccupation of the secular clergy leadership is confirmed if we turn to the explicit pastoral concerns of Richard Smith himself. An examination of his treatise, *Of the best kind of Confessors*, published as late as 1651, seemed to Bossy to bear out his view that Smith was largely concerned with confession as a juridical and not as a pastoral phenomenon. The 'best kind of Confessors' of the title are not priests of superior sanctity or insight but those with the status of *parochi* as opposed to those who are mere *regulari vagantes*. In fact, however, the distinction is a dangerous one: Smith sets the whole of his discussion in the context of the Tridentine *Catechismus ad Parochi*, where jurisdictional and pastoral concerns are of course inseparable. Still, it may be conceded that apart from a reiterated concern that the poor should have priests obliged *ex officio* to minister to them, there is little detailed discussion of the priest as pastor and spiritual guide in Smith's work.[31]

To conclude from this that Smith was unconcerned, however, or only secondarily concerned, with pastoral issues would be a mistake. For Smith had already published a treatise devoted to the pastoral work of the clergy, issued first in 1630 and reissued in an expanded edition in 1647. This was that 'golden-treatise', *Monita Quaedam utilia pro Sacerdotibus Seminaristis... quando primum veniunt in Angliam*.[32] This highly compressed work – 36 tiny pages in the first edition – ranges over the whole scope of a missioner's life, from the cultivation of an intense personal piety based on mental prayer and the sacramental life, to the conduct of chaplains towards their gentry patrons. There is guidance on matters ranging from the best means of deciding cases of conscience to details of clerical dress and diet. Preaching and individual instruction is heavily emphasised, and, significantly, there is a strong emphasis on the overriding claims of the poor on the missioner. The rulings of Trent and the obligations of the mission oath feature prominently.[33]

Smith's *Monita* were highly compressed but they covered an astonishing amount of ground, and central to them was an insistence on the need for a selfless zeal for souls, rooted in a personal sanctity which is the essence of priesthood: Smith's language here was entirely in the Bérullian tradition.[34] The means to this sanctity were to include the exercise of mental prayer, 'quo usi sunt in Seminariis'. Mental prayer was to be taught to such of the clergy's penitents as were capable of engaging in it, and Smith recommends the use of St Francis de Sales' *Introduction to a Devout Life* as a text-book.[35] Smith's direct appeal to Salesian piety was a pointer to a development which had been taking place among the clergy since 1613, when the first English translation of the *Introduction* appeared.[36] This had run through five editions before being replaced by a more accurate version produced by the English secular clergy of Tournai College.[37] It was joined in 1630 by a fine translation of Francis's *Treatise of the Love of God*, by Miles Carre, one of the staff at Douay College. Carre followed this up in 1632 with translations of two works by Jean Pierre Camus, Bishop of Belley, Francis's principle disciple and publicist.[38]

It is easy to understand the attraction of the Salesian tradition for secular priests, with its insistence on the pursuit of a practical humane piety, and its emphasis on the vital role of the spiritual director. As Carre's translation of Camus' *Spirituall Combat* has it:

Now to whom doth it belong to communicate to others this knowledge of the God of knowledge, but to those who are called the Salt of the Earth, and the Light of the World, who together with the Holy Ghost ... received the knowledge of the voice, by the imposition of hands in their ministrie ... who are to be a Law, and a Rule of Life to their subjects, and to the soules of whom they are liable to give an accompt?[39]

More than this, the Salesian tradition provided pointed material for a polemic against the religious orders, since Francis, and Camus after him, insisted on the primary role of the secular clergy. It is, therefore, no surprise to find in 1633, shortly after the debacle of the brief *Britannica* which overthrew Smith's claims to control the rights of regulars to give absolution, the publication of an English translation of Camus' most controversial work *A Spirituall Director Disinteressed*.[40] This work is famous, or notorious, for its assertion of the superiority of parochial clergy as confessors over the religious orders, since 'Hierarchical order' was established by Jesus Christ himself, so that He loves it 'with a love of election ... before all the Cenobiticall Orders which are onely of humane and positive lawe and which the Holie Sea [sic] may as well abolish, as it hath approved them'.[41]

Behind Smith's recommendation of mental prayer to his priests, then, lies a growing identification of the English secular clergy with the French *dévot* tradition and its central concept of spiritual direction. This identification had been given institutional expression already, in the work of the new English seminary at Lisbon.

Lisbon College had been established in the 1620s to train secular priests. Its Portuguese founder and his English clerical associates were bitterly hostile to the Jesuits and resolute partisans of the secular aspiration for a settled hierarchy. Its first president, Joseph Haynes, was one of the original canons of the Chapter and had played a key role in securing a bishop for England.[42] In the same year as the publication of the *Monita* Smith appointed a new president of Lisbon. This was Thomas White, alias Blacklo, the eponymous head of 'Blacklo's Cabal', the group most fanatically committed to the establishment of an episcopal structure for the English mission, and the group identified by Bossy as principally responsible for the delayed attainment of pastoral realism by the English seculars.[43] Blacklo drew up the rules of the new college, which were unusual among English seminaries in giving the bishop total control over the college and its officers, even the president's appointment being revocable at will. This is hardly surprising in 1630, at the height of the jurisdictional conflicts in England, and from the first it was intended that Lisbon should be a fully Tridentine seminary in its dependence on the bishop. Timing, personnel and insistence on hierarchy, on Bossy's analysis, should have made Lisbon the centre for the insular and antiquarian pursuit of a 'ghost church'. In fact it became the principal centre for the propagation in England of counter-reformation ideals of a reformed priesthood. These ideals are apparent in the course of spiritual instructions drawn up by Blacklo for the Lisbon seminarians, that 'honourable Societie of ... Collegiats', called by 'God and their superiors to assist their Country in an active life, and to undertake the sublime function of Priesthood'. These 'Divine Considerations', in fact, form a short treatise on the whole of the Christian life, but White included among them a set of meditations on priesthood and the missionary vocation which illuminate the ideals of the secular clergy in the early 1630s.[44]

White's meditations on the priesthood draw on two principal sources, Smith's *Monita* and the pervasive rhetoric of the Bérullian and Vincentian exaltation of the secular clergy. His picture of the missionary life, with its danger and dedication in poverty, and its obligation of service and sanctity rooted not in special vows but in ordination itself, in the mission oath and in charity, in places simply paraphrases the *Monita*. His passages on the glories of the priestly office are rhapsodies in the most exalted manner of Bérulle:

> Consider, of how much dignity it is, and honour, to have received the administering of God himself, to bear him in your hands, to have him in your power, to give him to whom you will . . . see how the Priest hath received that which is not granted to the Angels, nor was ever lawfull for any but only to his blessed Mother . . .[45]

White left Lisbon in 1634, but the preoccupation of the college with the ideals of a reformed priesthood persisted. On his return to France in 1631, Smith was employed by the Archbishop of Paris to deputise for him at ordinations. In this way he was brought into contact with Vincent de Paul and frequently ordained the groups of secular priests prepared by Vincent in the famous ten-day retreats at St Lazare.[46] Smith was deeply moved by the renewal of the secular clergy being achieved at St Lazare. He repeatedly spoke of it to English associates 'with much fervour and high approbation', saying that 'the primitive tymes seemed to him to be renewed againe in those holy young men'.[47] His interest in the Vincentian reform of the clergy seems to have found a natural expression in his continuing influence over his new seminary.

Throughout the 1630s the Lisbon clergy wrestled with these issues. A central figure here was Henry Gilmet, who was procurator of the college from 1634 to 1636. In August of that year he returned to England to serve on the mission. In August 1641 he wrote from Norfolk to one of his former students who had asked him for an account of 'my course of life, which you would strive to imitate when you should come for England'. Gilmet's letter, written after consultation with another unidentified priest, 'whom I account as my master in the business', represents the fullest and clearest statement of the ideals of an active secular missioner in the first half of the century, and is a moving revelation of the spirit of the tradition taught at Lisbon. It begins with an account of 'what we conceive in general concerning the body of the secular clergie, of which wee are members: the which is this: that it doth not exclude any perfection of the most perfect religious orders, but rather include it, though not *in voto*, yet in practice of life and conversation'. In language echoing Bérulle and Camus, Gilmet lamented the ascendancy of the religious orders:

> all others who have flourished and doe now flourish are but as bowes and branches sprung from the body of our tree, which in very deed is the root and stock from whence all grafts and setts have been taken: and yet now wee find by experience they make lesser esteem of the old tree, than it deserves, thinking it fruitlesse in comparison of them.'

He went on to define the apostolic mission of the secular clergy, the spirit 'which was in our fore fathers':

> finding that the mission and coming of our Blessed Saviour into the world, was *evangelizare pauperibus*; wee began to think that in this consisted the finall end and perfection of an Apostolicall life ... that coming into this vineyard wee might labour amongst the poore.'

Gilmet listed four means or 'pillars' to this end: the practice of voluntary poverty to enable charitable giving and the sharing of a common purse among clergy; obedience 'to the disposition of the superiors of the Clergie, as if we had obedience *in voto*'; sharing of spiritual resources with other seculars, in the form of regular meetings for prayer, contemplation and study of the life of Christ 'that thus we may conserve and augment the fire once kindled, having comfort and helpe one of another'; and, finally, 'the perfect performance of our vow of chastitie and ... the exact performance of our office and function in all things whatsoever ... contained in the Lord Bishop of Calcedon his *Monita*, which booke we have always at hand, and doe endeavour to putt them in execution upon ever[y] occasion'. [48]

Gilmet's outline of the priestly life was clearly an *ideal*, with its heavy emphasis on the priest's duty to the poor, and was practised as yet by relatively few of the clergy. What is important about it, however, is the way in which it incorporates those elements of rivalry with the religious orders and insistence on hierarchy which Bossy sees as archaic and destructive of missionary effectiveness, in a setting which makes clear their relationship to the most positive and vigorous developments in contemporary reformed Catholicism. Nor was it an isolated example. Within a year of Gilmet's letter a new president was appointed to Lisbon with the express purpose of fostering a reformed ideal of priesthood. Edward Daniell was one of Blacklo's closest friends and disciples, one of the founding staff at Lisbon, confessor and professor of theology under Blacklo's presidency. Recalled to Lisbon after only a year on the mission, his presidency was one of continuous promotion of reform ideals. [49] He brought with him classical works on the priesthood, such as James Marchant's Borromean *Hortus Pastorum*, which was soon being eagerly read by the students.[50] Within months of his arrival he compiled a register or *Liber Missionis* for students departing for England, into which he copied Smith's *Monita* and Gilmet's letter, to be taught 'to all priests most particularly before they receive their faculties for their Mission'.[51] Daniell also drew up for the use of his seminarians a manual of meditations on the spiritual life, which was printed in 1649. As might be expected, this book contained a special section on priesthood, which drew on White's *Divine Considerations*, Smith's *Monita* and on the Bérullian tradition.[52]

In 1647 Smith's *Monita*, greatly enlarged, were reprinted, with a long letter to the secular clergy at large from the late dean of the Chapter, Anthony Champney, dated 1643. Champney was 74 years old in 1643 and a veteran of the Appellant Controversy, but his 'Legacy', as he called his letter, was entirely in the spirit of the new age. It is an eloquent sermon on the dignity and responsibility of the priestly life, and the obligations of sanctity and discipline which it laid on all missioners. He dwelt at length on the merits of Marchant's *Hortus Pastorum*, and at even greater length on Antonio de Molina's *Instructio Sacerdotum*, the textbook on the priestly life used by Vincent de Paul at the St Lazare retreats. De Molina's treatise was a work much patronised by Jesuits, and 'laxist' in its teaching on frequent communion.[53] The praise bestowed on it by Champney is all the more striking testimony of the prestige among the English seculars of the Priests of the Mission, to whose work he refers. He dwelt also on the activities of Daniell at Lisbon and the need for a clergy whose mission was nourished by mental prayer and a rigorous training.[54] The whole treatise was now unmistakably a reformist tract, explicitly Borromean in character.[55]

All this was directed at the clergy themselves, though clearly the instruction of priests in the Salesian piety recommended by Smith, and exemplified in Gilmet's letter and Daniell's *Meditations*, was bound to have a direct and profound effect on their penitents, as Smith had meant it to. From the mid-century onwards a stream of works of direction for laypeople emanated from Lisbon clergy which continued well into the next century. Daniell's *Meditations* was republished in 1663, by which time Blacklo's *Divine Considerations* had been edited for lay use by William Clifford. Clifford had been Blacklo's vice-president, but since 1640 had been teaching at Tournai College, the institute for higher studies which Smith and Richelieu had established for English priests. In 1655, the same year as that of his edition of Blacklo's *Considerations*, Clifford issued the first edition of his *Christian Rules Proposed to a Virtuous Soul*. This was a Salesian treatise, teaching simple methods of meditation, containing instructions for every aspect of the Christian life. Clifford acknowledged his debt to 'the winning and cheerfully attractive piety, which that skilful master of all spirituality and devotion Blessed Sales hath so happily infused into Christian hearts', and he recorded with gratitude his own friendship, 'one of God's greatest blessings', with 'that blessed Man, Monsieur Vincent de Paul, Institutor and first General of that holy Congregation of the Father of the Missions'.[56] Clifford was to follow this up in 1670 with an even more attractive work, *The Little Manual of the Poor Man's Daily Devotion*.[57] This was a comprehensive work of direction aimed, as its title suggests, at a readership lower down the social scale, but including still a dissertation on mental prayer and a set of sample meditations modelled on those in the first part of the *Introduction to a Devout Life*.[58]

These were examples of a growing genre traceable directly to Lisbon, and the college's influence spread in other ways. Daniell and Clifford were engaged in clerical education in other English colleges, at Douai and Tournai respectively. John Perott, president of Lisbon from 1662 to 1670, and dean of the Chapter from 1676, reissued the *Monita* in obedience to a resolution of the Chapter of 1674, and the most influential priest of the late seventeenth century,

John Gother, whose devotional works were to become the centre of the secular clergy's work and 'the best helps they have for carrying on their mission', was a Lisbon priest.[59]

But Lisbon had no monopoly of reform ideals. Thomas Carre, the translator of Francis and Camus, had no direct Lisbon connections, but his translations played a vital role in educating English clergy and laypeople. In 1666 he, too, published an account of the work of Vincent de Paul, the fullest which had yet appeared in English, in which he gave a detailed account of the St Lazare retreats and of Smith's response to them.[60] By the last quarter of the century other colleges were excelling Lisbon. A letter from Thomas Hall, a Lisbon priest studying at St Gregory's, Paris, to a friend in Lisbon reveals both the continuing interest in these matters at the college, and the spread of the ideals: '... if ever I saw devotion practised in my life', Hall wrote, 'I have seen it here. I have made a Reflection upon the Oratorians with you, but I must confess ingenuously that the Clergy here far surpass them.' His account of the regime at St Gregory's is what might be expected from what we have already seen – daily meditation, sessions with a spiritual director, spiritual reading and training in counselling, cases of conscience, and in catechising, sermons in 'a more than Oratorian Spirit'.[61] The growth of this 'more than Oratorian spirit' is marked, too, by the circulation among the secular clergy of works on the priesthood such as Bourgoing's *Lignum Vitae* or Marchant's *Hortus Pastorum*.[62] By the 1690s the tradition had reached full maturity with Gother, a completely successful Englishing of the counter-reformation ideals embodied in the French *dévot* tradition, a tradition which would be further refined and streamlined in the following century by Richard Challoner.[63]

I think it is clear, then, that Professor Bossy's picture of a secular clergy only cosmetically involved in the counter-reformation renewal of priestly ideals and trapped in a structure-bound antiquarianism, will not do. Many of the very individuals and groups of secular clergy singled out by him as principally responsible for this sterility can be shown to have been passionately and systematically engaged, from the 1630s at the latest, in the transmission of the spiritual insights of Francis de Sales, Pierre Bérulle and Vincent de Paul. It is true that this work reached its full flowering in the later seventeenth century, but that is equally true of the work of the French clerical reformers.

The great age of the foundation of groups like the Priests of the Mission and St Sulpice was the period from 1625 to 1650, but it took more than a generation for that work to begin to bite.[64] The foundation of Lisbon in the late 1620s is entirely of a piece with these French activities and, indeed, in that it was a fully-fledged seminary, was even ahead of its time. Thus, the undoubted increase in clerical effectiveness after the Restoration in England was not the product of a belated awakening from the last enchantments of an ecclesiological middle age, nor the mushroom growth of a new missionary seriousness. It was, rather, the maturing of a long-held and carefully fostered priestly spirituality, formulated in the white heat of counter-reform by Richard Smith and the men of 'Blacklo's Cabal'.

Notes

1   General survey in J. Delumeau, *Catholicism between Luther and Voltaire* (London, 1977), esp. pp. 175–202; François Lebrun (ed.), *Histoire des Catholiques en France* (Toulouse, 1980), pp. 111–19, 148–77; Louis Chatellier, *The Religion of the Poor: Rural Missions in Europe and the Formation of Modern Catholicism c 1500–c 1800* (Cambridge, 1997).

2   J. Bossy, 'The social history of confession' in *Transactions of the Royal Historical Society*, 5th Series, 25 (1975).

3   Despite its age and distinctive slant, the best account of the Salesian tradition as a whole remains Henri Bremond's monumental *Literary History of Religious Thought in France* (London, 1928–36), vol. 1 *passim* and vol. 2, pp. 394–429.

4   G. Alberigo, 'L'Ecclesiologia del concilio di Trento', *Rivista di storia della Chiesa in Italia*, 18 (1964), pp. 227–42.

5   Bremond, op. cit., iii, pp. 137–8; for *Bérullisme* and the priesthood, see the excellent summary in P. Cochois, *Bérulle et l'École Française* (Paris, 1963), pp. 124–33.

6   As revealed in the work of G. Le Bras and his associates, to which the most convenient introduction is F. Boulard, *An Introduction to Religious Sociology* (London, 1960).

7   Most useful narrative, P. Hughes, *Rome and the Counter-Reformation in England* (London, 1942), pp. 271–420; brief account in J. C. Aveling, *The Handle and the Axe* (London, 1976), pp. 68–121. On Smith and his French connections, A. F. Allison, 'Richard Smith, Richelieu and the French marriage', *Recusant History*, 7 (1964), pp. 148–211. For Saint-Cyran's intervention, see J. Orcibal in *Dictionnaire d'Histoire et de Géographie Ecclésiastiques*, vol. 14, cols 1216–41, especially the section 'La Défense du Bérullisme', cols 1221–3. See also the useful though partisan 'Argumentum' prefixed to *Petri Aurelii Theologi Opera* (Paris, 1646).

8   B. Hemphill, *The Early Vicars Apostolic* (London, 1954), pp. 1–26.

9   J. Bossy, *The English Catholic Community 1570–1850* (London, 1975), pp. 11–74.

10 Ibid., pp. 27–9.

11 Ibid., pp. 29, 53.

12 The most outstanding example is the Benedictine William Gifford who became Primate of France, but there were many others, including Richard Smith himself, Dr Henry Holden and Dr William Clifford.

13 Neercassel's remark, J. M. Neale, *A History of the so-called Jansenist Church of Holland* (London, 1858), p. 166; the English priest's remark (John Bennet) is in M. Tierney (ed.), *Dodd's Church*

History of England (London, 1843), vol. 5, appendix cclii. For Vosmeer's ministry, including his hostility to the Jesuits and other religious orders, Charles H. Parker, *Faith on the Margins: Catholics and Catholicism in the Dutch Golden Age* (Cambridge, Mass., 2008); for Neercassel's pastoral views and the hostility they provoked, G. Ackermans, 'Good Pastors in the Missio Holandica in the second half of the Seventeenth century', *Nederlands Archief Voor Kerkgeschiedenis/Dutch Review of Church History*, 83 (2003), pp. 260–70; on the Dutch mission generally, in addition to Parker, *Faith on the Margins*, see also the important review article by James Tracy, 'With and Without the Counter-Reformation: The Catholic Church in the Spanish Netherlands and the Dutch Republic, 1580–1650: A Review of the Literature since 1945', *Catholic Historical Review*, 71 (1985), pp. 547–75.

14   Matthew Spiertz, *L'Église catholique des Provinces-Unies et le Saint-Siècle* (Louvain, 1975), pp. 72–6; Neale, *Jansenist Church*, pp. 200–201; T. A. Birrell, 'English Catholics without a bishop', *Recusant History*, 4 (1958), pp. 142–78; for a comparison of England and Holland from a very different perspective, see J. Bossy, 'Catholicity and nationality in the northern Counter-Reformation' in S. Mews (ed.), *Religion and National Identity (Studies in Church History)*, vol. 18 (Oxford, 1982), pp. 285–96.

15   Delumeau, *Catholicism*, pp. 99–128, 161, 201; P. Burke, *Popular Culture in Early Modern Europe* (London, 1978), pp. 207–43; J. Bossy, 'The Counter-Reformation and the people of Catholic Europe', *Past and Present*, 47 (1970), pp. 51–70; Parker, *Faith on the Margins*, pp. 123 ff.; Robin Briggs, *Communities of Belief* (Oxford, 1989), pp. 277–339.

16   P. Chaunu, 'Jansenisme et frontière de catholicité', *Revue Historique*, 227 (1962), pp. 116 ff.

17   Neale, *Jansenist Church*, p. 187.

18   Exemplified, most famously, in A. Arnauld's *De Frequenti Communione Liber* (Paris, 1647), *Praefatio*, 62 ff.

19   Bossy, *English Catholic Community*, pp. 270–71; John M. Headley and John Tomaro (eds), *San Carlo Borromeo: Catholic Reform and Ecclesiastical Politics in the Second Half of the Sixteenth Century* (Washington, DC, London and Toronto, 1988).

20   Birrell, 'English Catholics', p. 163.

21   J. Berington, *Memoirs of Gregorio Panzani* (Birmingham, 1793), p. 250; Geoffrey Scott, *Gothic Rage Undone: English Monks in the Age of Enlightenment* (Bath, 1992), pp. 63–72.

22   For the context, below, chapter 10, Archives of the Archbishop of Westminster (hereafter AAW), *Ep. Var.*, IV, no. 66; *Ep. Var.* VI, no. 20.

23   AAW, 'A' series 36, fol. 181, draft petition to Rome, June 1698.

24   Phrases from AAW, Old Brotherhood papers, iii (i), no. 6.

25   Thomas Graves Law (ed.), *The Archpriest Controversy: Documents relating to the dissensions of the Roman Catholic Clergy 1597–1602* (Camden Society, 1896,) vol. 1, p. 209.

26   Hughes, *Rome and the Counter-Reformation*, pp. 360–62; n. 7, above. Saint-Cyran had also translated and edited Rovenius's *De Missionibus*, see J. Orcibal, *Saint Cyran et le Jansenisme* (Paris, n.d.), p. 15.

27   M. Spiertz, 'Pastoral problemen in de Noordnederlandse Katholieke Kerk van de zeventiende eeuw', *Historie als Vriend: opstellen voor Dr. P. S. M. Geurts OFM* (Utrecht, 1979), pp. 42–7.

28   Bossy, *English Catholic Community*, p. 29. The archbishopric of Utrecht, so central to the Dutch secular clergy's hierarchical claims, had been established by Philip II as part of a centralising and counter-reformed programme. The Dutch vicars apostolic remained ardent supporters of Spanish influence in the Netherlands, Spiertz, *L'Eglise Catholique*, passim.

29   Bossy, *English Catholic Community*, p. 29.

30   Memorial printed in M. A. Tierney (ed.), *Dodd's Church History of England*, vol. 5 (London, 1843), pp. ccxxii–cccxxix, quotes from pp. ccxxiv–ccxxv.

31   *A Treatise of the Best Kinde of Confessors By which Preists in England may see how they may be, and lay Catholicks see how they may chose the best kinde of Confessors. Composed by the most Reverend Father in God, Richard Bishop of Chalcedon, Pastor of the Catholicke in England* (n.p. 1651) passim.

32   *Monita quaedam utilia pro Sacerdotibus Seminaristis praesertim, Quando primum veniunt in Angliam* (Douai, 1630).

33   Ibid., sections 2 (Mission oath), 11 (Trent).

34 Ibid., sections 1–3.

35 Ibid., sections 4, 8.

36 *An Introduction to a Devoute Life . . . Translated into English by I.Y.* (n.p. 1613).

37 *A new edition of the Introduction to a Devout Life . . . set forth by the English Priests of Tournay College at Paris* (Paris, 1648).

38 *A Treatise of the Love of God. Written in French by B. Francis de Sales . . . Translated into English by Miles Car Preist of the English Colledge of Doway* (Douai, 1630); *A Draught of Eternitie. Written in French by John Peter Camus . . . Translated . . . by Miles Car . . .* (Douai, 1632); *A Spirituall Combat: A Tryall of a Faithfull Soule OR Consolation in Temptation. Written in French by I. P. Camus . . . and Translated in English by MCP of the Eng. Coll. of Doway* (Douai, 1632). For Carre, see J. Gillow, *Bibliographical Dictionary of the English Catholics* (London, 1885), vol. 5, pp. 313–17; G. Anstruther, *The Seminary Priests*, vol. 2 (Great Wakering, 1975), pp. 245–6.

39 *A Spirituall Combat*, pp. 4–5; for Camus' extraordinary series of treatises on the prerogatives of the secular clergy over against the religious orders, see the list in in F. Boulas, *Un Ami de François de Sales: Camus évêque de Belley* (Lyon, 1879), pp. 331–3.

40 *A Spiritual Director Disinteressed According to the Spirit of B. Francis of Sales . . . By the most Reverend Father in God John Peter Camus, Bishop of Bellay* (Rouen, 1633).

41 *Spiritual Director Disinteressed*, p. 639.

42 On the foundation of Lisbon, Simon Johnson, *The English College at Lisbon*, vol. 1 (Stratton on the Fosse, 2014), pp. 42–99: Tierney's *Dodd*, vol. 4, pp. 123–33; Michael Sharratt, 'Blacklow and Coutinho in 1633', *Ushaw Magazine*, 88 (1977), pp. 16–25, vol. 90 (1978), pp. 18–26. For Haynes, see Anstruther, *Seminary Priests*, vol. 2, p. 153.

43 For White's influence at Lisbon, and its waning, Johnson, *English College at Lisbon*, pp. 177–257; Gillow, *Dictionary*, vol. 5, pp. 578–81; Anstruther, *Seminary Priests*, vol. 2, pp. 349–54. Bossy, *English Catholic Community*, 62 ff.; Kenneth L. Campbell, *The Intellectual Struggle of the English Papists in the Seventeenth Century. The Catholic Dilemma* (Lewiston, New York. 1986); George H. Tavard, *The Seventeenth Century Tradition: A Study in Recusant Thought* (Leiden, 1978); Albert J. Loomie, 'Oliver Cromwell's Policy toward the English Catholics: The Appraisal by Diplomats, 1654–1658', *Catholic Historical Review*, 90 (2004), pp. 29–44; Beverley C. Southgate, 'Blackloism and Tradition: From Theological Certainty to Historiographical Doubt', *Journal of the History of Ideas*, 61 (2000), pp. 97–114; Beverley Southgate, 'Cauterising the Tumour of Pyrrhonism: Blackloism versus Skepticism', *Journal of the History of Ideas*, 53 (1992), pp. 631–45.

44 *A Manuall of Divine Considerations, Delivered and Concluded by the Reverend Thomas White. Translated out of the Original Latine Copie* (n.p. 1655), phrases quoted from the epistle 'To the Reader', which is by the editor, William Clifford.

45 Ibid., pp. 159–75, quotation at pp. 168–9.

46 On the exercises of St Lazare, and the Vincentian reforms in general, see P. Coste, *Monsieur Vincent* (Paris, 1934); *La Congrégation de la missio* (Paris, 1927); P. Broutin, *La Réforme pastorale en France au XVII siècle* (Paris, 1956).

47 Thomas Carre, *Pietas Parisiensis or a short Description of the Pietie and Charities commonly exercised in Paris . . .* (Paris, 1666), pp. 38–9.

48 For Gilmet, see Anstruther, *Seminary Priests*, vol. 2, p 295; Gilmet's letter is transcribed in the MS *Liber Missionis* of Lisbon College, now among the Lisbon Papers at Ushaw College, Durham. A modernised transcription was published by Dr Michael Sharratt, the custodian of the Lisbon Collection, in *Mount Carmel* (Spring 1977), pp. 44–52.

49 For Daniell, see Gillow, *Dictionary*, vol. 2, pp. 9–11; Anstruther, op. cit., vol. 2, pp. 244–5. See C. Haigh, 'From monopoly to minority; Catholicism in early modern England', *Transactions of the Royal Historical Society*, 5th Series, 31 (1981), pp. 129–47. For further examples of concern by secular clergy with the mission to the poor in the 1630s, see M. J. Havran, *The Catholics in Caroline England* (Stanford and Oxford, 1962), pp. 78–9, and refs there cited. Haigh, cynically, attributes this growth of interest in the poor to the fact that by the 1620s all available gentry chaplaincies had been filled, 'and some priests were forced to turn to the poor and adopt a more populist approach'. Haigh seems to me seriously to underestimate the number of priests in the Elizabethan and Jacobean

period who 'assisted' the poor, while the close links between the growth of concern for the poor in Europe and in England argued for here makes his interpretation seem unsatisfactory.

50   For Marchant, see *Dictionnaire du Théologie Catholique*.

51   Lisbon Archive, Ushaw College, *Liber Missionis*, unpaginated.

52   I have used the second edition, *Meditations collected and ordered for the use of the English Colledge of Lisbon, by the Superiors of the same Colledge* (Douai, 1663). The *appendix* of meditations on priest-hood is on pp. 436–54.

53   *Monita quaedam utilia pro sacerdotibus seminaristis . . . cui adiectum est Legatum Antonii Champnei Doctoris Sorbonici, Fratribus suis Cleri Anglicani Sacerdotibus, testamento relicturm . . . Editio nova* (London, 1695), pp. 107–42; Molina's work was translated into many languages. I have used the Latin edition, *Instructio Sacerdotum Ex SS Patribus el Ecclesiae Doctoribus Concinnata . . . Auctore RPF Antonio de Molina Monacho Carthusiani impressionem Latinitate donavit RPF Nicolaus Ianssenius* (Antwerp, 1618). The book was in seven treatises or 'tractates', of which the seventh, '*De Frequentatione SS Sacramenti*, was Arnauld's target. Tractate three, *De Sancio missae sacrificio*, appeared in an English translation, with additional devotions for the laity, by Smith's Jesuit opponent, Fr John Floyd, in 1623, *A treatise of the Holy Sacrifice of the Masse and Excellencies therof* (St Omer, 1623); tractate one, *De eminentinium Sacerdotum Dignitate* appeared in an English translation, from the Birchley Hall press, in 1642 as *The Catholike Younger Brother; OR A short Discourse, wherein the Author propoundeth unto Catholike Younger Brothers . . . to take upon them, the Sacred Order of Priesthood . . . Heerunto is adioyned . . . a Translation of a Treatise made by the Reverend Mons. Antonius de Molina . . . entitled De dignitate Sacerdotum* (n.p. 1642). For Champney, see Gillow, *Dictionary*, vol. 1, pp. 462–6; Anstruther, *Seminary Priests*, vol. 2, pp. 70–71.

54   *Monita . . . Editio nova*, pp. 134–6.

55   Ibid., p. 130.

56   William Clifford, *Christian rules proposed to the vertuous soul aspiring to holy perfection*, (n.p. 1655). I have used the third edition of 1665. Reference to St Vincent, pp. 260–4, St Francis, p. 265. For Clifford's career, see Gillow, *Dictionary*, vol. 1, pp. 514–16; Anstruther, *Seminary Priests*, vol. 2, pp. 62–3.

57   I have used the edition of 1705, *A Little Manual of the Poor Man's Daily Devotion; Collected out of several Pious and Approved Authors. By W. C.* (London, 1705).

58   Ibid., pp. 268–89. St François' meditations, *Introduction à la vie dévote*, in *Oeuvres De Saint François de Sales*, Edition Complete, vol. 3 (Annecy, 1893), pp. 15 ff.

59   For Gother, E. Duffy (ed.), *Challoner and His Church: A Catholic bishop in Georgian England* (London, 1981), pp. 1–3, and refs there cited, and chapter 9 below, n. 10.

60   *Pietas Parisiensis*. Most of the book is devoted to various aspects of Vincent's work; the St Lazare exercises are described, pp. 27–43.

61   Ushaw College, *Lisbon Papers*, Thomas Hall to Richard Moseley, 25 September 1684.

62   The presence of multiple copies of *Lignum Vitae*, *Hortus Pastorum* and Molina's *Instructio Sacerdotum* in the Oscott College Library, gathered largely from former mission libraries, testifies to this. A number of these works contain the signatures of seventeenth-century English clergy. A copy of *Lignum Vitae*, now in my possession, belonged formerly to Edward Kyn or Kinn, the Chapter's rural dean of Worcestershire from 1667. It is probably in this context that the abortive attempts in the 1690s to establish an 'Institute' of secular clergy, living a common life, should be seen. The planned institute embodied many of the ideals expressed in Gilmet's letter: see *Archives of the Archbishop of Birmingham* C 168: 'Mr Coles' reason why the Institute ought not to be laied down; nor suppressed by your Lordship's authority'. C 172: 'Reason why those who will not lay aside the Institute should not be admitted into the common fund'; AAW Old Brotherhood papers, iii (ii), no 140, John Sergeant to the Brethren of the New Institute.

63   For which see my essay 'Richard Challoner and the Salesian Tradition', *Clergy Review*, 66 (1981), pp. 449–55.

64   For example, in Italy, cf. Luigi Mezzadri, 'Le Missioni popolari della Congregazione della missione nello stato della Chiesa 1642–1700', *Rivista di Storia della Chiesa in Italia*, 33 (1979), pp. 12–44. For the implementation of the reforms in France from 1660, see Lebrun, *Histoire des Catholiques*, pp. 147–214.

9

A rubb-up for old soares: Jesuits, Jansenists and the English Secular Clergy

Chapters 7 and 8 explored some of the ways in which, in lay devotion and in clerical self-understanding, as in so much else, interaction with the European counter-reformation was fundamental to the survival of English Catholicism. John Bossy's suggestion that the Catholic community was best understood sociologically as in effect an English nonconformist denomination has proved enormously fruitful as an historical tool. But it risks obscuring a radical difference between English Roman Catholicism and other dissenting bodies. It is not simply that Roman Catholics vehemently insisted that they, and they alone, were representatives in England of the one true Church – many sects claim as much. But Roman Catholics were, as a social reality, a community on both sides of the sea. Links with Rome, and loyalty to the papacy, however grudging at times, constantly shaped, modified and even hindered their response to specifically English problems.

The leaders of the clergy were appointed at Rome, and many of the most existential problems they faced, from allegiance to government to the authority of their bishops over the religious orders, were determined at Rome, not always to English satisfaction. All English clergy were trained abroad, and many of them made careers in Europe. In the early seventeenth century one of them, William Gifford, even became Archbishop of Rheims and Primate of France.[1] Dozens of priests at any one time served in teaching, pastoral or administrative work in English institutions in Europe, or as officials of the local churches of France, the Netherlands, Spain or Italy. In addition to the secular clergy trained in the English seminaries at Douai, Lisbon, Valladolid and Rome, hundreds of members of the religious orders spent years, even entire lifetimes (in the case of the thousands of nuns professed in English institutions abroad between 1598 and 1800), in European monasteries and convents.[2] The sons and, to a lesser extent, the daughters of many of the gentry were educated in Europe, and the secular priest who declared in 1710 that Douai contained 'all the Catholic youth of this nation', was exaggerating, but pardonably so.[3] And for three generations after the banishment of the Catholic Stuart monarchy in 1688, the political loyalties of many Catholics centred on the Stuart court in exile, another magnet drawing them into the affairs of the counter-reformation Church. What Charles Parker has said about the wider counter-reformation links of the mission in Holland 'to a matrix of exiles in Northern Europe, to nuncios, prelates and superiors in Brussels, Louvain . . . and to the *Propaganda Fide* in Rome, all of which were at war with Protestantism', applies equally to its English counterpart.[4]

For many, perhaps most, Catholics, that involvement felt integral to their identity. When it was first suggested in the wake of the French Revolution that a college to train priests and educate lay boys might be set up in England, Thomas Eyre of Hassop erupted.

'I hate the very idea of it', he wrote.

> I can never approve of a scheme which would prevent a great number of our young people for ever acquiring a practical . . . and ocular information, conviction and demonstration of the universality, respectability & prevalence of their religion, over the several new-fangled, pied, patched & piebald sects & sectaries, which under the name of Protestants (a glove which fits every hand, from the claws of Lucifer to the rat, that eats a hole in your wainscote) are spreading desolation over, or more properly speaking tearing up Christianity root and branch.[5]

In this chapter I want to consider a particularly fraught episode in the long history of English involvement in the affairs of the European churches. From the 1630s, the Church of France and, increasingly, the Church in other parts of Europe, was troubled by conflict over the doctrine of grace which had been left ambiguously

unresolved by the definitions of Trent, and over the rigorist movement known as Jansenism. In fact, Jansenism was less a single
movement than a convergence of causes – a severely Augustinian
understanding of salvation which emphasised human helplessness
without divine grace, an emphasis on the centrality of scripture
for the Christian life, which seemed to some to lean unduly in
the direction of Protestantism, and a respect for the pastoral discipline and liturgical purity of the early Church in preference to
modern and more permissive devotional fashions, especially those
associated with the newer religious orders, above all the Jesuits.[6]
In the mid-seventeenth century this cluster of ideas, emphases
and pastoral practices became entangled with technical questions
of doctrinal orthodoxy, and threatened to shatter the unity of the
French Church. The debates unleashed ferocious hostilities between
'Jansenist' supporters and fellow travellers, and their opponents, led
by the Jesuits. Pascal's *Provincial Letters*, a savagely satirical attack on
the moral and religious integrity of the French Jesuits, was merely
the most famous contribution to the vast lake of bitter polemic
which flowed from these debates.[7] In what follows, I want to
consider the impact of disputes over Jansenism on English Catholics
in the immediate aftermath of the collapse of their hopes for toleration under James II. In the process, we get a glimpse into London's
plebeian Catholicism – of clubs and sodalities of Catholic tradesmen and artisans organised for charitable relief, of Catholic clergy
and doctors ministering in the garrets and cellars of the poor, and of
a busy and at times violent exchange of ideas in booksellers' shops,
taverns and even in the open streets, as the theological controversies
convulsing Catholic Europe found their sometimes strident echo in
the England of Queen Anne.[8]

The year 1688 was for England a religious as well as a political turning point, and nowhere more so than among the English
Roman Catholics. The post-Revolution Church was maintained
and led by the same clergy who had flourished under James II, but
in very different circumstances. The hectic triumphalism of the years
before 1688 gave way to a period of slow and cautious consolidation.
The change can be seen in the careers of two men, Bonaventure
Giffard and John Gother. Giffard had been provocatively consecrated Bishop of Madura in the Banqueting Hall at Whitehall in

1688. In the same year he had gone to Oxford, to preside over 12 Catholic dons at Magdalen College, intruded in the place of the evicted Protestant Fellows. There he had confirmed and sung the Mass, while Protestant undergraduates stormed and howled outside the chapel windows. The Revolution brought a 14-month prison sentence in Newgate, from which he emerged, a chastened man, to oversee the formation and consolidation of congregations and clergy funds and organisations in the Midland District and, after 1702, to take charge of the London District with its mission to the London poor and unchurched.[9] A similar shift from controversy to pastoral concern can be seen in John Gother. Gother, a Lisbon-trained missioner originally a London catechist, became in the reign of James II the chief Catholic controversialist, breaking lances with the most notable Anglican polemicists of that stormy reign. After the Revolution, however, he renounced controversy, and set himself to the production of a corpus of devotional and catechetical material which became the basis for a missionary and educational enterprise to the farming, trading and labouring classes with whom the future of Catholicism in England increasingly lay.[10]

In a community thus concerned with internal reconstruction the international issue of Jansenism might seem at first sight an irrelevance. In fact, however, there was much in the ethos of English Catholics to incline them to sympathy with the Jansenist, or at least the anti-Jesuit, party in the debates which raged within the European Church.

As we saw in chapter 8, throughout the seventeenth century the English secular clergy had increasingly viewed the religious orders, and particularly the Jesuits, as their natural enemies, intruders and hireling shepherds usurping the place of the lawful pastors of the flock. Rooted in the late Elizabethan internecine quarrels between Jesuits and their opponents among the prisoners cooped up together in Wisbech Castle, these quarrels would fester in the wake of Rome's imposition of a Jesuitically inclined 'archpriest', George Blackwell, to govern the secular clergy. 'All Catholics must hereafter depend upon Blackwell', snarled William Watson, one of the secular clergy leaders, in 1601, 'and he upon Garnet and Garnet upon Persons, and Persons upon the Devil.'[11] This mutual animus deepened and sharpened as Jesuit and Benedictine missionaries, and their lay patrons, resisted the attempts of Richard Smith, Bishop of Chalcedon, to assert his authority as vicar apostolic from 1625 onwards.[12] During his eight months in England, Smith's predecessor, William Bishop, the first vicar apostolic, had set up a Chapter of canons to help administer the secular mission: the Chapter would become a self-perpetuating body, and its members would become the custodians of the anti-regular tradition.[13]

By the 1640s and 1650s, the arch-exponents of such views were 'Blacklo's Cabal', the group of clergy and gentry associated with Thomas White, alias Blacklo. These men, many of whom were prominent in the Chapter, saw themselves as defenders of the 'rights of the clergy' and the traditional hierarchical government of the English Church. They were dedicated to the restoration of episcopal government in opposition to the 'Presbyterianism' and anarchy of the Jesuits, but were equally determined that any bishop appointed for England should be a bishop 'in ordinary', and not a mere vicar apostolic, at the beck and call of the papacy. During the Commonwealth period they had sought a political accommodation with Cromwell's regime, in order to secure a government-sanctioned hierarchy, and the deportation of all Jesuits, whom they portrayed as seditious and un-English.[14]

In furtherance of their aims 'Blacklo's Cabal' had developed and fostered a distinctive theological position, a 'secular tradition' of a loyal *English* Church, a Catholicism shorn of alien factors. This position was formulated most clearly by Henry Holden in his *Analysis of Divine Faith*, which jettisoned all but the essentials of Catholic belief, abandoning all 'monkish disputation' or 'Jesuitical wrangling'.[15] A basically similar if more nuanced approach was employed by John Gother, most notably in the 'simplified' Catholicism of *A Papist Misrepresented and Represented*, but also in the catechetical and apologetic works written after 1688.[16]

This 'minimalism' was evident at a devotional level, too, and resulted in attitudes which might loosely be termed 'Jansenistical'. Gother's coolness towards the Rosary, his suspicion of 'confraternities', scapulars, or other devotional aids, his unvarying emphasis on the saints as exemplars rather than intercessors, are all manifestations of this tendency.[17] More directly still, his extremely rigorous preparations for confession and communion, his suggestion that the faithful should receive the sacrament of penance more often than that of communion, and the restrictions with which he hedged around the reception of the Eucharist, are representative of a cast of mind which persisted among the secular clergy throughout the eighteenth century.[18]

All this fell far short of Jansenism, but it is no surprise to find that Arnauld's *De la fréquente Communion* was in circulation among English Roman Catholics, and in the 1690s at least one secular priest was denounced to Bishop Giffard as a 'sort of Jansenist-Heretick' for his over-severe confessional discipline. [19] Indeed, overt correspondence or sympathy with Jansenists was by no means unknown in later seventeenth-century England. John Leyburne, the first of James II's vicars apostolic, was a friend and correspondent of Arnauld, and wrote appreciatively of his *Fantome du Jansenisme*, while both Leyburne and Cardinal Howard were friendly with Jan van Neercassel, Bishop of Castoria and vicar apostolic in Holland.[20] Neercassel's treatise on confession, *Amor Poenitens*, was well calculated to appeal to the rigorist strain in English Catholic piety, and there was in any case much in the situation of the Dutch Catholics to arouse the sympathy of the English clergy.

In Holland as in England a series of vicars apostolic sought to make good their claims to 'ordinary' jurisdiction, independent of Rome, with an accompanying right to erect Chapters possessing legal authority during vacancies. In Holland as in England they were resisted by the Jesuits, who sought to undermine the episcopal claims of successive vicars apostolic, to evade their jurisdiction, to have the 'missionary' status of their territory recognised.[21] The Jansenist struggles, in fact, presented to English clergymen an opportunity of arousing sympathy for a cause older than Jansenism, and the Jansenists themselves were seen as fellow combatants in the struggle against the 'mystery of Jesuitisme', loose morals and hostility to hierarchy and order.[22] These affinities and sympathies did not pass unnoticed; accusations of Jansenism were levelled at Howard, Leyburne, and at Bonaventure Giffard.[23] In 1686 a secular clergy chapel, financed in part by John Gother, opened in Lime Street in the city of London. Within months the priests in charge, who included bishop Giffard's brother Andrew, were being denounced as Blacklosts and Jansenists, and were duly replaced by Jesuits.[24] The disasters of Revolution eclipsed such quarrels, but by the beginning of the new century they were ready to emerge once more.

As the eighteenth century opened, Jansenism was creating a good deal of excitement in those parts of Europe which impinged most closely on English Catholics. In France the uneasy slumber which had descended on the Jansenist debate was broken in 1701 by the publication of the *Cas de Conscience*, in which 40 doctors of the Sorbonne ruled that a penitent might be given the sacraments on the strength of a submission of 'respect and silence' to the papal rulings on the 'question of fact' in *Augustinus*, though without interior assent or belief.[25] The ultra-orthodox held that such a position called the infallibility of the Church into question, but enthusiasm for the *Cas* ran high at Douai, where one bookseller sold more than 600 copies in a matter of days, and the doctrine of the *Cas* was publicly defended within the university.[26]

In July 1702 the English College at Douai became involved. A '*concours*' or series of public debates was being staged as part of the selection process for the Royal Professor of Divinity, and these debates became the cockpit for pro- and anti-Jansenist forces. The vice-president and professor of divinity at the English College, Edward Hawarden, was a candidate for the chair. Hawarden was far from being an ultramontane; his attitude to the papacy was Gallican, he shared the standard attitude of the secular clergy to the Jesuits and their 'loose' casuistry, and his doctrine of grace was sternly Augustinian. His candidacy was being backed by the Bishop of Arras, Guy de Sève, a man of known Jansenist sympathies, and he was opposed by a group led by Adrian Delcourt, the university vice-chancellor and the leader of an emergent anti-Jansenist mafiosa.[27]

With Jesuit assistance Delcourt began to collect subscriptions attesting that Hawarden had taught the doctrine of the *Cas* during the debates. This was subsequently denied by English College sources, but there is no doubt that the English were in general sympathy with the moderation of the *Cas*, and Laurence Mayes, the second divinity professor at the English College, was heard to declare during the autumn of 1702 that 'were he to Answer from the Dictates of Dr. H he should scarce make any other than the Forty Doctors had done ... concerning *respectful silence*'.[28] Sympathy for the *Cas* did not, of course, imply Jansenist beliefs, and in any event, since the *Cas* was not formally condemned until the following spring, the refusal of the English divines at Douai to censure it was legitimate enough. Nevertheless, the circumstance was noted, and rumours of Hawarden's heterodoxy persisted.[29]

Douay was by now in the grip of an ecclesiastical and academic vendetta on the grand scale; rumours of *lettres de cachet* against suspected Jansenists began to circulate.[30] Matters were worsened by internal troubles at the English College itself. In October 1703 one of the college subdeacons, Augustine Newdigate Poyntz, was sent to cool his heels for a few months at the Arras diocesan seminary. The reasons for his exile are not altogether clear, but they included public and scurrilous allegations of Jansenism among the college staff. He was also cultivating the friendship of a number of Jesuits in the town.[31] Poyntz returned to Douay at the beginning of 1704, apparently a reformed character, but the college authorities remained suspicious of him and delayed his admission to the diaconate. He became the centre of a small group of malcontent students. In November he was sent back to England, having been told by Dr Paston, the college president, that 'the clergy ought to be all of a piece', evidently a reference to his Jesuit friendships. Back in London, Poyntz approached Dr Jones, Bishop Giffard's vicar general, with accusations of the college staff's '*secret morals*, disrespect to the decisions of the Court of Rome, and to the Persons of the Popes themselves', as well as their 'contempt of Regulars'.[32] Poyntz was treated with extreme courtesy and care by the senior English clergy. Bishop Giffard offered to finance the rest of his ordination training at any French seminary, and there was even a suggestion that Bishop Witham might ordain him in England. In the event, however, Poyntz adopted the expedient of almost all disgruntled eighteenth-century ordinands; he set out for the English College at Rome, which was in the hands of the Jesuits.[33]

The kid-glove treatment he had received from the vicars apostolic was evidence that the question of Jansenism was beginning to trouble them. Already the cold winds of suspicion had begun to play round one of the elder statesmen of English Catholicism, the preceptor to his majesty 'king James III' at the exiled court of St Germain, Dr John Betham. Betham was a Chapter man, a disciple of

Blacklo's, a friend of John Gother, a doctor of the Sorbonne. He was deeply suspicious of notions of papal infallibility, of indulgences, of excessive devotion to the saints or the use of devotional 'aids' such as scapulars. The austerity of his temperament drew him to the evident sanctity of Arnauld, and to the vigour and rigorousness of the devotional writings of the Jansenist Oratorian, Pasquier Quesnel. Betham was inclined to favour the doctrine of the *Cas de Conscience*, and he had no liking for the Jesuits and the lax morality he believed them to purvey. He concealed none of these views from the young King, and the queen mother, a client of the Society of Jesus, took alarm. Despite the sympathetic intervention of the Cardinal de Noailles, Betham was banished from the Stuart court in January 1705. His disgrace was purely temporary, and he was back at his post within a matter of months, but the incident was a foretaste of things to come.[34]

Other warnings might have been observed in England. In 1703 there had appeared in London a translation of Etienne de Champs' *Secret Policy of the Jansenists*.[35] The publication of this work in England is difficult to see in any other light than that of an act of aggression against the secular clergy, a renewal of the bitter disputes of the seventeenth century, using Jansenism as a convenient brickbat. The book claimed that the secular clergy were the chief means of spreading Jansenism, for the heretics knew that 'the Pastors being once corrupted' they would 'lead their sheep to the wolves that seek to devour them'. The jurisdictional claims of the secular clergy against the regulars, and especially the Jesuits, were no more than a device to cut the faithful off from sound teaching, under the pretence that 'the people are bound to be directed in their consciences by Secular Priests'. Jansenism itself was characterised in terms which suggested that the traditional emphases of the 'secular tradition' were heretical. It was Jansenism, asserted the author, to teach that indulgences 'are to be layd asside', or to insist on 'severe penances' and to condemn the 'softness' of the Jesuits on the pretext that 'their manners are corrupted, their direction hurtful to soules'. The book included a newly composed 'Memorial on the State and Progress of Jansenism in Holland' which attacked Monsignor Neercassel, the vicar apostolic, and the head of his Chapter, Jan Christian Van Erkel, and condemned a list of Jansenistical tenets and practices 'very unwarrantable and uncommon' with which many English clergy would certainly have sympathised: these included discouraging confessions to members of religious orders, delaying absolution on account of habitual venial sins, or when the penitent's contrition seems imperfect, speaking disrespectfully of 'indulgences, relics, pictures beads and suchlike, nay also of confraternities approv'd by the Holy See'.[36]

The moving spirit behind the reissue in England of this provocative work was probably Fr Thomas Fairfax SJ, who had been one of Bishop Giffard's Catholic fellows of Magdalen, and who was now living in London as procurator of the English province. Fairfax appears to have appointed himself doctrinal watchman of England's little Sion, and to him can be traced the first 'printing and publishing those books of controversy concerning Jansenism' which were soon to prove so divisive.[37] In the same year as the appearance of the *Secret Policy of the Jansenists*, Fairfax, alert to the potential attractions of the *Cas de Conscience* to the English clergy, produced an English translation with some related papers designed to highlight the heterodoxy of the *Cas* and its supporters.[38] Fairfax presented copies of this work to Bishop Giffard and other senior clergymen; not very surprisingly the gift was coolly received. Giffard, who had never head of the *Cas*, told him that 'there were none *here* concerned for or with that Party'.[39] Secular clergy resentment was increased by the fact that copies of the *Secret Policy* were being 'sent down into the country by dosens [*sic*]' and 'dispersed thourough most of the Catholique familys in England'.[40] To the unsympathetic eyes of secular clerics this seemed nothing more nor less than an exercise in spiritual sheep-stealing, an attempt to win away the penitents of the secular clergy on the pretext that their teaching and 'great Penances ... savour very much of an heretical intent'.[41]

Such jars and rubs created an atmosphere of tension which persisted through 1704 and 1705. The general unease was increased by the continuing presence of Poyntz at the English College in Rome, the darling of its Jesuit masters. On leaving Douai he had handed over his notes on Hawarden's lectures to his Jesuit friends at Douai, and, with his wild talk of heresy, he was feared as a dangerous man. These fears lingered into 1706; in the late summer of that year they were fulfilled beyond the bounds of nightmare. Thomas Roydon, one of the disgruntled Douai students formerly associated with that 'turbulent fellow', Poyntz, now came forward with a confession as appalling as it was circumstantial. According to Roydon, Poyntz had been encouraged by an English Jesuit named Piggott, and a Walloon Jesuit named Weidart, to collect evidence of Jansenism at Douai. He had drawn Roydon and another student into this enterprise, and in October 1704 these three had signed affidavits, in the presence of a burgess of Douai, two Jesuits and an apostolic notary, in which they recounted Laurence Mayes's indiscreet remarks about Hawarden and the *Cas*, as well as 'some Words once or twice spoken concerning Indulgences, Beads and Scapulars'. Roydon also alleged that Poyntz had received two letters from Fr Lewis Sabran SJ, commending his resistance to 'Tyranny and Rigorism', and urging him to build up a faction within the college.[42]

Some, at least, of these serious allegations were subsequently denied by Fr Sabran, but it seems likely that he had heard of Poyntz through his Jesuit contacts, and reassured him about any adverse effects on his ordination prospects which his resistance to 'Jansenism' might have.[43] Whatever the facts of the case, there were powerful *a priori* reasons why the alarmed college authorities should accept Roydon's claims at face value. Lewis Sabran was a figure to strike a chill to the heart of any secular clergyman. He was president of the episcopal seminary at Liège, an establishment which until 1699 had been in the hands of the secular clergy. In that year the prince bishop had conducted a purge of the house, which he suspected of Jansenism, and had installed Sabran, at the head of 200 troops from the local garrison, as president and professor of divinity.[44] Sabran was a dedicated opponent of Jansenism, and he was to make no bones about his conviction that Edward Hawarden had indeed propagated that detestable error at Douai.[45] Roydon's disclosures, therefore, raised fears that Sabran was hatching imperialist designs against Douai College, as he had at Liège. That he was doing so is in the highest degree unlikely, but the bishops in England despatched a volley of panicky letters to the college and to St Germain, expressing their fears that Dr Paston's 'family' was about to be 'purged and modelled upon another foot'.[46] Poyntz's continuing presence at Rome, at the ear of Propaganda, now seemed more menacing than ever – 'he is not kept there for nothing this year after priesthood'.[47]

The secular clergy girded themselves to do battle. At Douai, the president, Dr Edward Paston, was a slow-moving, rather ineffectual character, who hid himself behind a studiedly remote manner, 'too starch'd and reserv'd' for English tastes, too indecisive for swift action.[48] The chief manager of the coming campaign at the college, therefore, was to be the college procurator and professor of syntax, Edward Dicconson. This 35-year-old sardonic Lancashire man had a relish for intrigue and a 'secret correspondence'. He loathed the Jesuits, the 'Walkers' as he liked to call them, and he had already begun to collect materials for a history of English Catholicism which Paston dreaded would 'rubb-up and renew old soares' by reviving the quarrels 'which were formerly amongst the Clergie and the Religious'.[49] At Rome the secular clergy agent managing business for the vicars apostolic and the college was none other than Laurence Mayes, one of the accused 'Jansenist' divinity teachers, who had taken up his new post in Rome in August 1706.[50] These two, with John Betham at St Germain, set up an information and policy-making network which was to be crucial in the years ahead.

They had more to concern them than Sabran's apparent threat to Douai College. The Western Vicariate had been vacant since 1705, and the vicars apostolic were anxiously lobbying to prevent the appointment of another regular to the post, which had previously been held by a Benedictine.[51] The secular clergy candidate for the vicariate was Gerard Saltmarsh, chaplain to the dowager Duchess of Norfolk. In many ways he was an excellent choice, an able and experienced missioner, well-connected and recently returned from the Grand Tour with the Duke of Norfolk, during which he had spent a good deal of time fraternising with the cardinals of Propaganda.[52] By 29 January 1707 Laurence Mayes had been assured that the Bulls for Saltmarsh's consecration would be expedited within the next four days; within that short period disaster struck.[53] On 30 January Fr Sabran arrived in Rome, apparently on business connected with his order. At the same time Cardinal Fabroni received a letter from Mgr Bussi, papal internuncio at Cologne, accusing Saltmarsh of Jansenism.[54]

The origins of this thunderbolt lay in Holland. In 1702 Peter Codde, the Jansenist Archbishop of Sebaste, had been suspended from his functions as vicar apostolic of Holland. He refused to accept

Rome's decision, and was supported in his stand by his Chapter at Utrecht, led by Jan Christian van Erkel. By the spring of 1705 an ugly confrontation had developed between the papacy, represented by Bussi, and Bishop Codde and his supporters.[55] With matters in this condition Saltmarsh had passed through The Hague on his way homeward from the Grand Tour. While there he had struck up an acquaintance with van Erkel, for whom he conceived a considerable admiration as a man of spirit, defending the rights of the clergy. He also renewed his acquaintance with Mgr Bussi, whom he had known previously in Italy and Brussels. The internuncio noticed that 'Mr. Gerard was ever in company with the Jansenists, and the very stiffest of 'em'. His suspicions of Saltmarsh's orthodoxy were confirmed when, during a conversation about the situation in Holland, the Englishman 'with a great deal of heat and passion' began openly 'to defend the Jansenists, advancing that the H(oly) Sea [sic] persecuted good and holy men, to favour Regulars'.[56] Saltmarsh's version of this conversation differed slightly, but there is no doubt where his sympathies lay; he admitted defending the rebellious clergy as peaceable men, and advocating a 'submission of respect and silence' in the manner of the *Cas*.[57]

Bussi's report of these transactions scuppered any hope of Saltmarsh's appointment to an English vicariate, but the internuncio's accusations had not stopped there. 'Many of the English Missioners pass frequently into Holland', he reported, 'to conferr with the Jansenists, with whom the Bishops, Vicars Apostolical, keep a most strict corrispondence [sic] . . . Jansenism makes farther progress in England, than even in Holland or Flanders . . . something likewise had happen'd att Douay, which afforded matter of suspicion against the English Colleges there'.[58] The English clergy reacted with considerable bitterness to these allegations against their 'poor suffering church'. 'Alas', wrote Bishop Giffard, 'the great and continual afflictions we are oppressed with . . . leave us no time and less inclination to meddle in such controversies as exercise the wills of such as live at ease, and feel nothing of what is our portion *in foris pugna*'. He urged Mayes to vigilance 'to discover all sinister designs of our Enimys', but at all costs to avoid antagonising anyone.[59] The vicars themselves drew up a 'very firm letter' to Propaganda, protesting their and Saltmarsh's innocence.[60] Mayes set about collecting testimonials on Saltmarsh's behalf from Italian notables, but Bussi's revival of the Douai affair seemed to call in question the orthodoxy and character of the agent himself. 'God grant your name is not among the accused', wrote Paston to Mayes, and Betham was even more forceful. 'You must not be passive in this matter', he urged, 'for being once blasted in things of that nature, you would find it prejudicial to your selfe and imploiment.'[61] Mayes evidently purged himself by signing all the papal rulings on Jansenism, and the vicars' nightmare of having to plead their innocence through an agent himself under suspicion passed. Edward Hawarden from Douai hastened to clear himself in a similar way, but for the sake of the college he was asked to resign as divinity professor and to return to England. With extreme reluctance he did so. [62]

The clergy were now divided on the question of tactics. Some, like Dicconson, were for loud protests to Rome and public denunciations of their calumniators. The vicars, Paston, and Betham on the other hand, favoured a more cautious and discreet approach. On one point, however, all were agreed. Behind Bussi's unwarranted interference in English affairs must lie the dirty doings of the Society of Jesus. What did Bussi know of England or of Douai, and could anyone believe that it was a mere coincidence that Sabran had arrived in Rome at the same time as Bussi's letter? The difficulty lay in finding hard evidence of Jesuit malice. 'The Walkers do work all they can behind the Curtain I know', wrote Edward Dicconson, 'and that makes me the more industrious to get proofs of their practices.'[63] He was assisted in England by Bishop Giffard's brother Andrew, whose ejection from the Lime Street Chapel in 1686, on the pretext of Blackloist and Jansenist heresy, and the conversion of the building to a Jesuit residence, rankled still. 'Those gentlemen' were worse than any Protestants. As he recalled with bitterness:

About a year and a half after departure from Lime Street House, I was made Fellow of Magdalen College, where I stayed until we were turned out by the return of the Protestant Fellowes into their college again. I compared these two passages together, my being turned out of Lime Street House by the Jesuits, and out of Magdalen College by the Protestant Parsons, and I must needs do justice to the truth and to those of Magdalen College, that

I was dismissed that place with much more civility and much less reproach than what I found at my dismissal from Lime House ...[64]

Late in 1707 Giffard managed to get hold of an intercepted letter between Fr Sabran and Fr Philip Medcalfe, a Jesuit living in Northumberland. 'Come over with all expedition', wrote Sabran, 'for I have a great Employment and preferment for you, bring along with you all the information and *proofs* (if possible) you can against Cl(ergy) and All those who are against our Factory.'[65] Here, it seemed, was proof positive of Sabran's scheming. This 'preferment' could surely be nothing else than the presidency of Douai College, and Medcalfe's arrival in London seeking a passport for Flanders seemed to clinch the matter.[66] Sabran himself wrote to Andrew Giffard to deny any plot against Douai; his trip to Rome had been on strictly Jesuit business, and no Jesuit whatever bore any ill will towards the secular clergy: 'there may be young men of a warmer temper and less prudent Amongst my Relations, but I doe not find they turn that warmth towards any prejudices to those of your Family; I wish I (might) say the same of the most warm among yours'. The invitation to Medcalfe was to assist Sabran in his new post as visitor and vice-provincial of the English Jesuits; the 'proofs' against the clergy referred to heterodox books being circulated by missioners in the north of England, word of which had reached Sabran, as vice-provincial, from zealous Jesuits, fearful for the souls of the faithful in those parts.[67]

Skirmishings had, indeed, commenced between seculars and Jesuits in the north, but they were as nothing to the battle which had been joined in the London District. [68] Paradoxically, its central figure was neither a Jesuit nor a secular clergyman, but a Catholic physician, Dr Richard Short. Though a layman, Short was one of the pillars of the London mission. He had been one of Bishop Giffard's Catholic fellows of Magdalen, and after the Revolution spent two years at Douai College studying philosophy. After a medical training at Montpellier and Paris he settled in practice in London.[69] The London mission was very much one of 'cellars and garrets',[70] and Short became renowned for the generosity with which he gave his professional services to those who could afford no fee. He also maintained open house for clergy temporarily 'out of place'.[71]

This 'charitable Phisician' did not confine himself to tending the bodies of his patients and clerical friends; he was a deeply devout man, with a keen interest in theology, and his medication was often accompanied by pious exhortation. Unfortunately, Short was heavily involved with the Jansenists of Holland, and his devout conversation began to reflect this involvement. His interest in Holland had been aroused initially by the writings of Jan van Neercassel, especially the *Amor Poenitens*. He collected works on the struggles of the Church in Holland with the papacy and the Jesuits, and eventually entered into correspondence with van Erkel and the Utrecht Chapter.[72] For Short the clergy of Holland were all 'choice divines', confessors suffering for their refusal to abandon a 'fine church to an Inundation of loose morality and probabilism', or blindly to submit to 'the unlimited desires of the court of Rome'.[73]

Short began to send van Erkel translations of material relating to the English disputes of the sixteenth and seventeenth centuries between Jesuits and seculars, 'materials for workmen' in the struggle against the 'exorbitant power of Rome' and its auxiliaries, those 'Emperours by Sea and Land', the Jesuits.[74] His friendships among the London secular clergy gave him access to the archives of the Chapter, and he sent van Erkel material from there, too.[75] Short also imported defences of the Utrecht Chapter through a bookseller in the Strand, and circulated these among his clerical friends, or among influential catholic laymen like the Towneley brothers of York.[76] Through his Dutch associates Short eventually contacted Pasquier Quesnel himself, and they became fast friends, Short sending the refugee gifts of money and even offering him a haven in his London home. Between 1706 and 1709 Short supervised the translation into English of Quesnel's *Moral Reflections*, presiding over a team which included an elderly Catholic squire, two eminent members of the Chapter and a Benedictine monk.[77]

One of these collaborators was Dr Sylvester Jenks, former professor of philosophy at Douai, formerly court preacher to James II, and currently the Chapter's archdeacon of Surrey and Kent. His involvement in Short's project throws a good deal of light on the range of theological sympathies which were now being drawn into the conflicts over Jansenism. Jenks, an ardent Thomist, was one of the mission's best theologians, with a special concern for pastoral counsel in confession.[78] He was certainly no Jansenist, but his bestselling treatise *A contrite and humble heart* aligned him with the opponents of the view, often attributed to Jesuit moral theologians, that 'attrition' (repentance based on fear) rather than 'contrition' (repentance based on love) was a sufficient basis for sacramental absolution.[79] Jenks had become involved in June 1706 through gratitude for Short's medical treatment, which he believed had save his life, but he later claimed that his role in the project had been simply to revise and correct the notes on St Matthew's Gospel. He claimed to have been concerned then about the work's orthodoxy, and to have done what he could to improve it.

> As for the preface to it, I made bold to burn it, and took care to have the first sheet printed without it', though 'there are still faults left in the English notes upon S. Matthew, which are enough to deserve the Pope's censure.[80]

Short, however, had no such reservations, and was incapable of keeping his views to himself. 'We live', he wrote, 'in a world either indifferent to the Interests of Religion, or not caring to trouble itself in the behalf of Innocency oppress'd.'[81] This situation he determined to remedy. He held meetings at his house to disseminate information about the Dutch clergy's 'defence of the grace by which we are Christians'. Wherever he went, among the poor, among his patients, among friends, he talked endlessly of the love of God insulted by Jesuit casuists, pedlars of cheap grace, who told their penitents that they need not love God, but only fear him. He denounced the opponents of Quesnel, he castigated the extravagant claims of the papacy.[82]

Not unnaturally, the London Jesuits took notice. Nor did they confine their attentions to him. Short's friendships among the secular clergy were well known; Bishop Giffard himself was his confessor. Since these friends shared many of the doctor's attitudes to the papacy, to penance, and above all to the Jesuits, they too came under attack, and in particular John Vane, a former Anglican clergyman, who had been received into the Catholic Church in Newgate prison by Giffard in 1689.[83] Vane seems to have worked mostly among the traders and small businessmen who formed the backbone of the Catholic mission in the Holborn area. A group of these tradespeople was in the habit of meeting regularly 'in order to the relieving their poor starving neighbours'. Many of these men were patients of Short's, some were the penitents of Vane and other secular clergymen, and some penitents of the Jesuits. By the end of 1707 divisions had appeared among them, and the charitable aims of the meeting were being forgotten as bakers, lawyers' clerks, cobblers and bodice-makers argued vehemently about attrition and contrition, efficacious grace and irresistible grace, limited or unlimited atonement, the doctrinal irregularities of Pope Honorius, and the question of papal infallibility.[84] The tradespeople took sides, and sometimes changed them – a Dutch baker who had translated some pamphlets for Short was 'recovered' by Fr Charles Kennet, procurator of the Jesuits, and became an invaluable informer, revealing John Vane's conversational indiscretions to great effect.[85]

One of the most active anti-Jansenist accusers – 'a chief man employed to bring accusations against us', as Andrew Giffard reported – was a young convert, Richard Gomeldon, son of a London jeweller. Among the priests Gomeldon accused of heresy was Christopher Piggott, 'a most laborious priest who helps the poore people in and about Southwark, and seldom returns home from his labours until ten or eleven a clock at night'. Gomeldon also drew up a paper of 20 allegedly heretical propositions entitled 'Several of Dr Short's tenets' 'affirming that he had heard the Doctor speak them all'. According to his opponents, Gomeldon was 'a young debauchee' 'who had spent his patrimony', like the prodigal son, 'vivendo luxoriose cum meretrice' and now 'dares not shew his head for fear of arrests'. He was also, it seemed a religious enthusiast, 'a visionaire, who according to his own words often sees heaven open, but oftener converses with hell, for he saies the devil sits by his bedside many nights, and they talk and converse familiarly for several hours'. All the same, Gomeldon's accusations evidently stuck, and Short was obliged to make a solemn protestation of his innocence before the Benedictine abbot James Corker, friend of Oliver Plunkett and custodian of his relics, and, as a veteran of the restoration Catholic Church and a confessor of the faith, considered to be an honest broker. Short asked for communion from Corker 'and after communion upon the sacrament which he had received, took oath that not one of all the propositions was his'.[86]

The disputes were not confined to tradespeople, but spread to the gentry staying in London. Fr Francis Mannock SJ, chaplain to the Fitzherbert family, happened incautiously to speak 'against Jansenism', to find himself set upon by the entire family with talk of 'the imaginary heresy', and attacks on the overzealousness of the opposers of the 'new errores'. Mannock himself, a zealot with little sense of proportion, 'ran from house to house to desire ... that their children might come to him' in order that he might undo the evil teaching of the secular clergy.[87] There was an appalling series of public confrontations between one Fr Smith and John Vane, culminating in a scene in the street in Holborn.[88] The pastoral disruption and scandal was prodigious; penitents became bewildered, suspicious of their confessors, and one woman was said to have died without the sacraments rather than receive them from a secular priest.[89] Members of the tradesmen's charitable club began to withdraw. Lists of indictments against Short, Vane and their associates were drawn up, to be sent to the Jesuit provincial for transmission to Rome; half a dozen of these letters were intercepted by Fr Kennet's brother, who was a secular priest, and provided yet more evidence of the duplicity of the 'padri'.[90]

These disputes could not be ignored by the leaders on either side. Thomas Fairfax complained to Giffard of Short's activities, and both Bishop Giffard and Bishop Smith cautioned the physician against meddling in matters 'out of his sphere and understanding'. They refused, however, to consider him as in any sense representative of the secular clergy. 'The Dr. is but a particular layman, must answer for himself, without affecting others and making them answerable for his follies.'[91] Short was, indeed, cautioned by many of the secular clergy, including Edward Hawarden, now in England; he promised amendment, but his persistence in his controversial activities alienated many of his clerical friends, and Giffard asked him to find another confessor. Giffard also commanded the tradesmen in their meetings to 'content themselves to be obedient children of the church ... and to confine their discourse only to such things as might increase charity, peace and unity'.[92]

Charity, peace and unity were sadly wanting. Hawarden's departure from Douai had done nothing to settle the disruption there. Rumours spread that his return to England was the flight of a guilty man, that Rome had banished him, that he had narrowly escaped arrest.[93] Doggedly the college authorities mounted their counter-measures, declarations of orthodoxy, testimonials from theologians, parish priests, heads of colleges, superiors of religious houses, from the Bishop of Arras; petitions from the London clergy in favour of their alma mater; minute and exhaustive arguments to prove the disastrous consequences which would follow if the college were handed over to the Jesuits.[94] Betham and Dicconson began to collect materials relating to the Chinese Rites controversy, in which the Society of Jesus was at odds with the papacy; this material might prove 'of great use towards the putting to confusion our detractors . . . who seem to approve and support in their own brethren the same disobedience which they blame and persecute in others, and wrongfully cast upon us'.[95]

The seriousness with which the vicars apostolic viewed these conflicts is reflected in the fact that in 1709 they applied to the Holy Office for some formula by which they might settle once and for all their orthodoxy and submission to Rome. That Rome viewed the issue with equal concern is reflected in the fact that the vicars apostolic were asked to subscribe jointly to the *Formulaire* of Alexander VII, as explained by Clement XI four years earlier in the Bull *Vineam Domini*.[96] This was not as easy to do as might appear, for a joint submission of all three vicars presented special difficulties. Giffard, a slow-moving and cautious individual at the best of times, had learned by long experience never to trust incriminating documents to the mails; the prospect of sending a signed copy of a papal Bull round England was unthinkable.[97] Yet a meeting between all three vicars was difficult to arrange, particularly since Smith was engaged on the visitation of his vast district, and was unreachable by post. In the long delay which ensued, fresh accusations against the vicars and their clergy were sent to Rome, probably by Fr Kennet. Though Quesnel's *Moral Reflections* had been condemned in July 1708, a translation was being published and circulated by the secular clergy. The condemned *Cas de Conscience* was also in circulation, and the constitution *Vineam Domini* which condemned it had not been promulgated.[98]

Giffard's reaction to these charges was bitter. 'Good God!', he wrote to Laurence Mayes, 'how little doe these great men understand our circumstances. I wish one of them were in my place for a month or two.' He had known nothing of the condemnation of Quesnel till a few days before, when a messenger from the nuncio at Brussels had brought it to him. He had instantly commanded Dr Short to stop the presses on the offending translation, which was done, at considerable financial loss to Short. As for *Vineam Domini*, 'I never heard of it, till I received your letter, nor have I ever seen it, or know how to get it.' Nor could he be blamed for the circulation of the *Cas*, since it was a Jesuit, Fr Fairfax, who published it '*animo impugnandi*'.[99] This *apologia* evidently had little effect. By July 1709 Giffard had still not managed to contact Bishop Smith, and Rome reiterated its complaints and demands. Giffard was exasperated, and his reply was something of an ultimatum. Did the cardinals imagine that he could exercise control over the English press? Did they wish him to bring renewed persecution on his flock by drawing the State's attention to them? This he would not take upon himself, 'Wherefore that I may not be blam'd by our Masters there for not publishing their orders, nor by our friends here by bringing new troubles on them, I desire that what decree they will have me publish, they will signify their positive commands to me in writing.'[100]

Rome's reply to this was prompt. On 17 August 1709, Clement XI promulgated the brief *Dilecti Filii*, addressed to the Catholics of Great Britain and Ireland. The document cautioned the faithful against erroneous books, urged them to shun persons of suspected orthodoxy, especially those who under pretence of 'rigid morality' attacked the authority of the Holy See. The laity were cautioned to be especially careful whom they chose as confessor.[101] This was gall and wormwood to the secular clergy. Here were 'the very same accusations wich our unjust adversarys have bin endeavouring for many years to disperse amongst the people, and now they obtain a Bull from the Pope to confirm men in the same bad opinion of us'. The Pope was insinuating that 'there are priests amongst us infected with these evill errores'. Behind all this must be the Jesuits. 'Is it not pla(i)n from whence and from whom . . . these informations . . . come?'[102]

Disaster followed disaster. On 23 November the Cardinal Secretary of State, Cardinal Paolucci, despatched an extremely curt letter to Giffard and his two episcopal brethren, accusing Douai College of containing 'many professors and schollars' who 'did openly teach and learn the falce doctrine of Jansenius', and demanding that they be dismissed forthwith, on pain of stoppage of the papal pension to the college. Paolucci's list of culprits, based on information received from Poyntz via Bussi, was ludicrously garbled and out of date; all the individuals concerned had long since left Douai, and most of them had never taught theology, or even studied it at an advanced level.[103] Nevertheless, the letter galvanised the vicars into action. Giffard began to talk of resignation, but the long-delayed subscriptions to the *Formulaire* were suddenly achieved and hastily despatched to Rome. The vicars met in London for a summit conference with the heads of the religious orders. The meeting satisfied no one. The Jesuit superiors made generalised accusations against the clergy, but would name no names, and were unimpressed by Giffard's attempts to convince them that 'such general clamour serv'd only to raise divisions, disturb the minds of the Laity, cause scandals, and expose us all to the scorn and reproach of Protestants'.[104]

The clouds continued to gather. There were rumours of a blanket condemnation of Gother's writings. Although Short had died in December 1709, the debates among the London laity had survived him. In January 1710 Bishop Giffard was forced to depute his brother Andrew to set up a 'commission' or tribunal at the Portuguese Ambassador's residence to hear the many heresy charges which were circulating. 'The people', wrote Andrew Giffard, 'are divided into party and party, faction and faction, who have not less animosity to each other than high church and lowchurch.'[105] Sylvester Jenks, anxious about Short's Jansenist friendships and involvement in promoting suspect literature, and convinced that 'it was a great Pity so important a Matter as Jansenism would be so universally talk'd of, and so little understood', published a theological and historical *Review of the Book of Jansenius*. This was a damage-limitation exercise, designed to play down claims of a crisis or orthodoxy – 'Notwithstanding all the confident Reports of a Jansenian Invasion from Holland, we have hitherto been more afraid than hurt'– and to distance himself and the secular clergy from Jansenist error, while stoutly defending Douai and its Thomist teaching on grace from the insinuations of Fairfax and others that Douai priests were fellow travellers with heresy.

'As for all that I have said in Defence of Thomistry', he wrote,

tis only to do Justice to the Thomists, and to force the Jansenists out of a Lurking Hole, which does not belong to them. I long since suck'd this milk of Alma Mater, our Mother-Colledge at Doway; and have been all of a piece, from the beginning of my Studies, to the present Hour. Six years I spent in learning Thomistry, and as many more in teaching it; since which I have had above twenty Years to consider it; and am still of the same Mind. *Que didici, ac docui, doceo.* I humbly thank God I am a Catholic. And, in my daily Prayers, I humbly beg, that I may always be so happy as to have Grace, without understanding it; rather than once be so uncomfortably miserable as to understand it without having it.[106]

But such sophistications cut little ice. From France came rumours that the Pope had written to the (Stuart) King to enquire about the state of Douai College. At home, the Duke of Norfolk dismissed Gerard Saltmarsh as his chaplain, and replaced him with a Jesuit. Saltmarsh's dismissal may well have been part of the marriage agreement between the Duke of Norfolk and his future father-in-law, Sir Nicholas Sherburne, a devoted client of the Jesuits notorious for his hostility to the secular clergy. The new Jesuit chaplain to the Norfolks was Fr Thomas Hunter, formerly chaplain to Sir Nicholas. The Society, it was said, not content with stealing the clergy's college, were seeking now to take their chaplaincies as well, to snatch the very bread from their mouths – 'they might as well cut our throats'.[107]

In the general atmosphere of apocalypse men brooded on desperate measures. A group of the 'hotter' men among the secular clergy were determined 'never to suffer such unjust proceedings'; they drew up a petition to the House of Lords, suggesting that the Jesuits should be banished, since they were 'endeavouring to ingross to themselves the conduct and education of all the Catholick youth of this nation, that they might infuse them with pernicious principles, dangerous to the persons of princes and destructive of government'. This 'Blacloesque' document was never presented, but it was brandished. If the Jesuits did not amend, Andrew Giffard told Dicconson, 'you may expect to hear strange news from hence'.[108]

Matters were, if anything, more desperate still at Douai. For months the college staff had been cultivating the nuncio at Paris, Mgr Cusani, and he had promised to procure an official visitation of the college which would put an end to the calumnies of the last decade. In April 1710 the name of the chief visitor was announced. Incredibly, it was the college's principal local enemy, Adrian Delcourt. 'Thus has Mgr. Cusani managed things so well for the advantage of the children of the Holy See', snarled Dicconson, 'that of all the world, the person who showed himself the greatest enemy and accuser of our house and people in it, is constituted its judge.'[109]

At this point, however, Providence itself intervened. On 22 April 1710, the day after Delcourt's visitation commenced, the English army under the Duke of Marlborough invaded Douai, and the college was evacuated to Lille, under the friendly escort of a British redcoat. God, it seemed, was indeed an Englishman.[110] Delcourt's visitation was destined never to be resumed. Indeed, the nadir of secular clergy affairs had been reached, and passed. 'James III', after long sitting on the fence in the disputes, at last wrote to Rome in defence of the college. The staff of the English College had been cultivating the young 'James III' in order to gain his support. In December 1708 he had visited the college, where he had been delighted by 'the number of young men who followed him everywhere he went gazing at and admiring him'. Dicconson had told Mayes that 'you may imagine the obvious compliments were not wanting to let him know their ... eagerness to follow him proceeded from the principles of their education here'. The royal intervention, and the avalanche of petitions and protestations from England and Douai, had the desired effect, and Rome smiled once more.[111]

Though Sabran sent a lengthy letter to Propaganda in November 1710, complaining of the slanders being circulated against the English Jesuits in general and himself in particular, and enclosing a series of Fr Kennet's charges against Short and the clergy, it was of no avail.[112] In February 1711 the Cardinal Secretary of State wrote to the vicars apostolic to assure them of the Pope's great joy in their evident zeal and orthodoxy. Here at last, it seemed, was an end to the affair. The letter, wrote John Ingleton from St Germain, is 'look'd upon as a justification of the Cleargy on both sides of the sea, and I am apt to think the Examen of Doway college will be let fall, or favourably performed . . . the Fathers talk of nothing but peace and union'.[113]

The 'examen' was indeed favourable; the new visitors of Douai College were the Dean of Mechlin and the president of the seminary there, both of them sound Thomists, and full of goodwill towards the Englishmen. Their visitation was carried out in November 1711; it was searching, meticulous, but, in the event, favourable. They did find matter for concern in Hawarden's dictates on such topics as papal authority, indulgences and the value of the Rosary, as well as more technical points about the sense in which the Atonement might be considered limited. A civil exchange of letters between the visitors and Edward Hawarden, however, disposed of these difficulties, and, in short, 'they thought some expressions very blunt . . . but they thought there was not anything condemnable'. Rome declared itself 'edified' by the results of the visitation; the college and its pension were safe. [114]

And there, it seemed, the matter might rest. On 13 September 1713, however, Clement XI promulgated the Bull *Unigenitus*, condemning 101 propositions extracted from the writings of Quesnel.[115] On 15 October, Fr Charles Kennet SJ presented himself before Giffard, and asked him if he had heard of the Bull. Predictably, Giffard said he had not, so Kennet gleefully informed him of its contents. *Unigenitus* was the outcome of a prolonged fencing match between the papacy and Cardinal Noailles, in which the sympathies of the English clergy were entirely on the side of 'our Cardinal'. In addition, the writings of Quesnel were popular among English Catholics. Giffard, there-fore, listened to Kennet in glum silence, and although the English Jesuits printed *Unigenitus* with a translation, the bishop took no steps to promulgate it.[116] Even Dicconson considered this dilatoriness a tactical error and one which could not easily be justified; Kennet and his associates dwelt lovingly on it, and reported the matter to Mgr Santini, internuncio at Brussels.[117]

At this juncture appeared an anonymous pamphlet, *The History of the English College at Douai*. Purporting to be an account of the college by one of the Protestant chaplains of the English army which had so providentially invaded Douai in 1710, this was in fact a vigor-ous Catholic polemic, in the best 'Blackloist' tradition, against the Jesuits. Its potted version of the history of the college was a saga of the various alleged Jesuit attempts to gain control of it, from rascally

Fr Persons to rascally Fr Sabran. The pamphlet concluded with a warning to the clergy that 'their adversaries are restless and indefatigable. They only wait to see the two remaining Bishops expire, and then they certainly will be ready to play the old Game over again ...The useful Calumny of Jansenism stands their Enemies in good stead upon such like Occasions, and obstructs all.' The author suggested that the accusation of Jansenism was being systematically employed to prevent the appointment of any bishops for England, thus giving the Jesuits a free hand.[118]

This stirring of the hornets' nest was the last thing the vicars desired, and 'all the Chief of the Clergy' hastened to disown it. Dicconson considered it a 'contrivance of our enemies', and grimly noted that the English Jesuits were maliciously demanding that Bishop Giffard should suppress the work, 'which they know (not) to be in his power'. They intend, he concluded 'to have it believed our work'.[119] Indeed, there was little doubt that the pamphlet expressed the widespread worries of the clergy. Bishop Smith had died in 1711, and the long delay in filling his vicariate, and that of the West, had already been attributed by Bishop Witham to the accusations of Jansenism which were current at Rome. Witham's brother Robert, moreover, was told by one prominent Jesuit, Fr Thomas Lawson, that 'he never desired to see another Bishop come into these parts'. The very hierarchy itself seemed threatened.[120]

The spring of 1714 brought trouble of a different sort. Two apostate priests, Barker and Mottram, turned priest-catchers, and there was a rash of arrests among the London clergy. Warrants were out for Bishop Giffard himself, and his brother Andrew died of a fever caught by fleeing from his sickbed to escape arrest. In the midst of all this an aggressive letter arrived from Mgr Santini at Brussels, demanding that *Unigenitus* should be promulgated forthwith. In the circumstances Giffard could do little more than notify it to such of the clergy as had not gone underground.[121] By way of contrast, in August a messenger arrived from van Erkel and the schismatic Church of Utrecht, to ask Giffard to ordain priests for them. Giffard was sympathetic and friendly, and declared himself 'moved' by the plight of the Dutch clergy, but even had he been willing to help he could hardly have risked compromising himself further, and so declined. That the English vicars apostolic could be considered a possible source of ordinations for the schismatic Church is itself, however, significant.[122]

By the beginning of 1715 hostilities between the contending parties in England had, it seemed, ceased. The calm was deceptive, for the last and most swingeing attack in the whole dispute was about to be launched, and in a totally unexpected form. The *History of the English College* had evoked a Jesuit reply in 1714, Fr Thomas Hunter's *A Modest Defence of the Clergy and Religious*. Hunter was the priest who had 'usurped' Saltmarsh's place as chaplain to the Duke of Norfolk, and although his book professed to be conciliatory, an olive branch from his hand was not altogether convincing. In any case Hunter had not entirely managed to conceal his view that the ranks of the secular clergy probably did in fact conceal Jansenists, as they once had Blackloists.[123] In February 1715 appeared the first six of a series of 24 printed letters addressed to the provincial of the English Jesuits, under the title *The Secret Policy of the English Society of Jesus*. Modelled on Pascal's *Provincial Letters*, this work was intended as a reply to Hunter's *Modest Defence*, and took the form of a detailed review of the history of English Catholicism, in the course of which every event which could be turned against the Society was raked up and interpreted with the maximum hostility. Letters 19 to 21 dealt with the recent Jansenist troubles, and the overall conclusion of the book was that in Hunter's *Defence*, as in all their doings, the aim of the Society was 'to cut the Clergies Throats, after you had tript up their Heels by an accusation of *Jansenism*, for according to your Scheme ... their Ancestors were nurs'd up in *Schism* and *Faction*, and now these of our Days must end in *Jansenism* and *Heresy*. Oh! *The Modest Defence of the Clergy*'.[124]

These letters put all in uproar. The Jesuit provincial made repeated visits to Giffard as successive parts of the work appeared, demanding that he prevent the publication of any further letters, or else 'he would be obliged to defend the English Jesuits in a public answer which could not be done without exposing the Clergy to a great degree'.[125] There was, of course, nothing Giffard could do to stop the publication. No one knew the identity of the author, though it seemed clear that he was also responsible for the *History of Doway College*, and as in the case of the earlier pamphlet, the printer was a Protestant. Jesuit efforts, therefore, were concentrated on persuading the bishop to issue a condemnation of the book as calumny and falsehood. This Giffard would not do: the furthest he would go was a declaration that the letters were 'injurious and against charity'. To Jesuit eyes this was tantamount to a declaration of agreement with the book. 'B(ishop) Giffard gives no satisfaction', wrote one of Fr Sabran's correspondents, 'so declares himself head of the party.'[126]

The fact was that the book, for all its venom, did indeed enshrine the secular clergy view of the Jesuits, and nothing alleged by the author in the section on Jansenism had not already been alleged by Andrew Giffard or Edward Dicconson, in words almost as bitter. Few secular clergymen could find it in them to be hard on such a book. Even Robert Witham, the new president of Douai College, and a moderate man, found no harsher words for it than 'indiscreet and provoking'. By 1716 secular clergymen were lending their copies around to penitents; no condemnation of the book by any of the vicars ever appeared.[127]

Nor was any Jesuit reply published, though one at least was written.[128] The year 1715 brought more than these 'Provincial Letters'; it brought armed rebellion, and the gallows for Catholic Jacobites.[129] This was no time for defending Jesuits, and nobody did. The appointment of a moderate successor to Paston at Douai, acceptable to Jesuits and, indeed, chosen in part as a result of Jesuit lobbying, eased the internal tensions which had so rent the Catholic community, as did the nomination in the same year of a pro-Jesuit Franciscan friar to the Western Vicariate.[130] In any event, a new personality had appeared on the English Catholic scene and was monopolising the attention of its leaders. John Talbot Stonor, the ruthlessly ambitious nephew of the Earl of Shrewsbury, had come on the English mission in 1714. Within three months he was vicar general to Bishop Giffard; within a year he was actively plotting to have himself put over Giffard's head as 'coadjutor'; within two years he was vicar apostolic of the Midland district.

Stonor set the English Catholic community by the ears; for almost a decade his outrageous activities dominated the workings of the mission and its leaders, and Jansenism was forgotten.[131] Thus, though visitors from the Utrecht Church continued to pay visits to some of the London clergy, and maintained a sympathetic interest in Giffard and Vane until their deaths in 1733, though Vane and

Saltmarsh themselves kept up an occasional correspondence with the Dutch Jansenists on such topics of common interest as the sins of Jesuits and regulars, yet these were no more than civilities.[132] The publication from time to time of translations of works relating to the Bull *Unigenitus* perhaps indicates some continuing sympathy for the Jansenist cause among the English Catholics, but such sympathies, if they existed, sought no public expression, and although English clergymen retained a firmly independent attitude to Rome they found no occasion to make an issue of it. By 1729 Bishop Stonor could claim that *Unigenitus* was of no real relevance to the English mission: 'to require a general acceptation might put a new Stumbling Block in the way of the Protestants, would fill the heads of our Missionaries with the Disputes of other Countries very forraign to their present purpose, and might very likely, raise in some a spirit of opposition to the Pope's decrees of which they had nothing before'.[133]

Yet the Jansenist troubles did have profound and long-lasting effects on the lives of English Catholics. The English secular clergy in the seventeenth century had produced some notably adventurous thinkers, especially but not only in the circle round Thomas White. But David Milburn has noted the growing conservativism and introversion of the teaching at Douai College throughout the eighteenth century, and the increasing reluctance of the college to take a full part in the life of the university at large.[134] This shrinking of the horizon can be traced to the regime of Robert Witham; his 'Advice to a President of Douay College', drawn up for the guidance of his successors, is a clear indication of the way in which the fear of a recurrence of the dangerous disputes of Paston's presidency cramped the intellectual life of the college. The president, Witham wrote, 'must be watchfull least any of the masters of divinity or philosophy advance any new or singular opinions either as to morality or grace, which may the least favour the Jansenists or Quesnellists ... He must also be attentive least any one in the house by their discours favour these or any heretical and erroneous or new opinions.' Though the effects of this narrowing must not be exaggerated, they are plainly to be seen in men like Alban Butler and Richard Challoner, and contributed to a greater sense of English insularity.[135]

There was a yet more momentous consequence. The struggles of the first 15 years of the eighteenth century produced a new crystallisation of ancient hostilities between seculars and regulars, which remained unresolved well past the mid-century. Edward Dicconson, in particular, became a man dedicated to the task of bringing the religious orders to heel.[136] His most determined effort in this cause was to be made during his episcopate in the 1740s, but as chaplain to Peter Giffard of Chillington in the 1720s he made a contribution hardly less important. Here he came into contact with another Giffard chaplain, Hugh Tootell.[137] It was by then an open secret that Tootell, the nephew of one of the Lime Street veterans, was the author of both the *History of Doway College* and the *Secret Policy of the Jesuits.* Tootell was a dedicated Jesuit-hater, and an historian. Dicconson, therefore, put at his disposal the collection of historical records relating to the English Catholics which he had been building up even before the Jansenist troubles, and Tootell used these collections in his masterwork, the *Church History of England*, published under the name of Charles Dodd.[138] Dicconson's patronage was no accident: the spirit of the Jansenist troubles of the age of *Unigenitus* was being deliberately perpetuated, and would shape the attitude of secular priests and their clients for another century.

Gabriel Glickman, in an insightful reading of Dodd's *Church History*, has rightly emphasised Dodd's apologetic purpose, drawing together 'two fashionable but seemingly contrary, historical sensibilities: grounded upon antiquarian recoveries of the gothic past, but shaped by a cosmopolitan spirit of "reason" that drew upon continental reformist schools' in order 'to construct a new intellectual platform for his co-religionists within their national community'.[139] The point is well made, but risks obscuring the fact that the overwhelming majority of Dodd's readers were fellow Catholics: his major impact was not to be on the Protestant general reader, but as the principle literary channel through which the internecine rivalries of early modern Catholicism were communicated to the age of Emancipation. Glickman recognises the importance of Dodd's work for the Cisalpine attempts at the end of the century to present the Catholic community as patriotically enlightened, free of undue papal or Jesuit influence, and therefore worthy of political freedom. But Glickman suggests that a century after his death in 1743 'Dodd was a waning figure in the English Catholic imagination, his works offering little to feed the triumphalist, ultramontane hunger of the Victorian revival'.

This, however, seems rather wide of the mark. For, exactly a century after Dodd's death, one of the most learned secular priests in England, Mark Tierney, chaplain to the Duke of Norfolk and a gifted antiquarian, was busily engaged in reissuing a new and vastly expanded edition of Dodd's work.[140] He was assisted by no less a figure than the historian John Lingard, and the immense scholarly apparatus of additional documentation, which makes his edition still valuable, was drawn from the 50 volumes of manuscripts accumulated by the veteran Cisalpine warrior John Kirk, who had himself planned a continuation of Dodd's work. Tierney was persuaded to discontinue his edition in 1843, incomplete after five volumes, not because Dodd's work was felt to have nothing to offer the Catholics of Victorian England, but because it was feared that the new edition was all too likely to reignite animosities smouldering still not far below the surface. Tierney himself embodied many of the more rebarbative attitudes of the secular clergy participants in the Jansenist stirs. A resolute opponent of Wiseman and the new ultramontanism, he considered that the Catholic cause had been 'thrown back at least a century' by 'the appearance of so obnoxious a person as a cardinal, the pomp and style of an archbishop, and above all, the lordly tone of power and domination . . . by which... the new cardinal announced his elevation and proclaimed his authority'. It was sentiments like these that led ultramontanes like Mgr George Talbot to suspect in the 1860s that the English clergy still harboured too many men hankering after 'a National, Anglican, Jansenistic Church'.[141]

For, over and above his apologetic intentions, the dominant theme of Dodd's work, in so far as any book so sprawling can be said to have a theme, is that of the *Secret Policy of the Jesuits*. The aims and motives of Dodd's heroes and villains (and the *Church History* is rich in both) are already indicated in his two earlier books. English Catholic history, on Dodd's reading, was a struggle between the forces of decency, order, sense and Catholic Christianity, on the one hand, and the criminal lunacy of ultramontanes and Jesuits, on the other. This is the pattern burned into Dodd's historical consciousness by the troubles of 1705–15, and in the *Church History* he did much to transmit the same pattern to every historian of English Catholicism after him.

And it is, perhaps, here that the most enduring result of the Jansenist troubles is to be discerned. As Tierney's edition indicates, Dodd's *History* was to play a crucial role in the subsequent development of English Catholic historiography; it would hardly be too much to describe English Catholic historical writing until well into the present century as a dialogue between the disciples and the critics of Dodd.[142] The positions adopted by the two parties in that dialogue received their definitive formulation in Dodd's response to the supposed 'secret policy' of the clergy's enemies. The disputes considered in this chapter were quite clearly, at one level, no more than a storm in a very small ecclesiastical teacup, a storm conjured out of the air by the paranoid fear, suspicion and wilful misunderstanding which has been the disgrace, as well as a good part of the fascination of English Catholic history. In so far as those disputes produced 'Charles Dodd', however, it could be argued that much of the writing about that history is little more than commentary upon them.

Notes

1   Michael E. Williams, 'Gifford, William (1557/8–1629)', *ODNB*.

2   This extraordinarily important but till now comparatively neglected aspect of recusant Catholicism is at last receiving systematic study, thanks to the 'Who were the Nuns?' project and website organised at Queen Mary University, London, by Dr Caroline Bowden and Dr James Kelly http://wwtn.history.qmul.ac.uk/

3   Eamon Duffy, *Peter and Jack: Roman Catholics and Dissent in 18th Century England* (London, 1982), pp. 18–21.

4   Geoffrey Scott, *Gothic Rage Undone: English Monks in the Age of Enlightenment* (Bath, 1992), pp. 1–8: Gabriel Glickman, *The English Catholic Community 1688–1745: Politics, Culture and Ideology*, (Woodbridge, 2009); Charles H. Parker, *Faith on the Margins: Catholics and Catholicism in the Dutch Golden Age* (Cambridge, Mass., and London, 2008), p. 15.

5   Ushaw College, Durham, Ushaw Coll. Hist. MSS 224 'Mr Eyre of Hassop's Sentiments'.

6   Useful short overview in William Doyle, *Jansenism: Catholic Resistance to Authority from the Reformation to the French Revolution* (New York and London, 2001).

7   A. J. Krailsheimer (trans.), *The Provincial Letters* (Harmondsworth, 1967). Richard Parish, 'Pascal's *Lettres Provinciales*' in N. Hammond (ed.), *The Cambridge Companion to Pascal* (Cambridge, 2003), pp. 182–200; L. W. B. Brockliss, 'The *Lettres provincials* as a Jansenist calumny: Pascal and moral theology in mid-seventeenth-century France', *Seventeenth-Century French Studies*, 8 (1986), pp. 5-22; Robin Briggs, *Communities of Belief: Cultural and Social Tensions in Early Modern France* (Oxford, 1989), pp. 286–90.

8   On plebeian Catholicism in seventeenth-century London, Michael Gandy, 'Ordinary Catholics in Mid Seventeenth Century London', in Marie B. Rowlands (ed.), *Catholics of Parish and Town 1558–1778* (Catholic Record Society, 1999), pp. 153–78.

9   W. Maziere Brady, *Annals of the Catholic Hierarchy in England and Scotland* (Rome, 1877), pp. 149–51, 202. For Giffard's activities as vicar apostolic of the Midlands, see Marie Rowlands, unpublished Birmingham MA dissertation, 1965, 'Catholics in Staffordshire from the Revolution to the Relief Acts, 1689–1791' : J. Anthony Williams, 'Giffard, Bonaventure (1642–1734)', *ODNB*.

10 Gother is a seriously neglected figure: the best account is that in Fr Godfrey Anstruther's *The Seminary Priests* (Great Wakering, 1976), vol. 3, pp. 81–4. See also Sister Marion Norman, 'John Gother and the English Way of Spirituality', in *Recusant History*, 11 (1972), pp. 306–17; Stuart Handley, 'Goter, John (*d.* 1704)', *ODNB*, and my 'Poor Protestant Flies: conversions to Catholicism in early eighteenth-century England' in D. Baker (ed.) *Religious Motivation: Biographical and Sociological Problems for the Church Historian* (*Studies in Church History,* vol. 15, Oxford, 1978), pp. 289–304, especially pp. 293–6; A list of Gother's writings will be found in G. F. Pullen (ed.), *Recusant Books at St. Mary's, Oscott*, part II, *1641–1830* (New Oscott, 1966), pp. 77–80; Thomas Clancy, *English Catholic Books 1641–1700* (Aldershot, 1996), nos 431–73; F. Blom et al. (eds), *English Catholic Books 1701–1800* (Aldershot, 2000), nos 1217–334.

11 Philip Hughes, *Rome and the Counter-Reformation in England* (London, 1942), p. 298.

12 Ibid., pp. 329–430; David Lunn, *The English Benedictines 1540–1688* (London, 1980), pp. 151–4; A. F. Allison, 'Richard Smith, Richelieu and the French marriage', *Recusant History*, 7 (1963–4), pp. 148–211; A. F. Allison, 'Richard Smith's Gallican backers and Jesuit opponents', *Recusant History*, 18 (1986–7), pp. 329–401; 19 (1988–9), pp. 234–85; 20 (1990–91), pp. 164–205. ·

13 Hughes, *Rome and the Counter-Reformation*, p. 323.

14 M. V. Hay, *The Jesuits and the Popish Plot* (London, 1934), pp. 1–120; John Miller, *Popery and Politics in England 1660–1688* (Cambridge, 1973), pp. 42–8; T. A. Birrell, 'English Catholics without a Bishop 1655–1672' in *Recusant History*, 4 (1958), pp. 142–78; T. A. Birrell, introduction to the Gregg Press reprint of *Blacklo's Cabal Discover'd . . . by R. Pugh* (n. p. 1680); John Bossy, *The English Catholic Community 1570–1850* (London, 1975), pp. 60–69; R. I. Bradley, 'Blacklo and the Counter-Reformation: An Inquiry into the Strange Death of Catholic England' in *From Renaissance to Counter-Reformation*, ed. C. H. Carter (New York, 1965), pp. 348–70; Beverley C. Southgate, 'Blackloism and Tradition: From Theological Certainty to Historiographical Doubt', *Journal of the History of Ideas*, 61 (2000), pp. 97–114; Jeffrey R. Collins, 'Thomas Hobbes and the Blackloist Conspiracy of 1649', *Historical Journal*, 45 (2002), pp. 305–31; Albert J. Loomie, 'Oliver Cromwell's Policy toward the English Catholics: The Appraisal by Diplomats, 1654–1658', *Catholic Historical Review*, 90 (2004), pp. 29–44.

15 Henry Holden, *The Analysis of Divine Faith, or two treatises of the resolution of Christian Belief* (Paris, 1658), 'Epistle to the Reader'; Nigel Abercrombie, *The Origins of Jansenism* (Oxford, 1936), p 252.

16 John Gother, *A Papist mis-represented and represented, or, a two-fold character of Popery . . .* (London, 1685); *Mr. Gother's Spiritual Works* (London, 1718), vol. 7, pp. 427–38.

17 *Mr. Gother's Spiritual Works*, vol. 7, pp. 367–76, 386–8; vol. 4, sig A2–A3v and *passim*.

18 'Instructions for Confession, Communion and Confirmation', in *Mr. Gother's Spiritual Works*, vol. 8. *passim*, vol. 6, pp. 264–327; Bossy, *Catholic Community*, pp. 269–72; Alban Butler, *Meditations and Discourses on the Sublime Truths . . . of Christianity* (London, 1791), (posthumous publication), vol. 1, pp. 102–229, vol. 2, pp. 1–46, 120–30.

19 There were a number of copies of Arnauld's work at Oscott, from former mission libraries–information from the late G. F. Pullen, and cf. Pullen, op. cit., p. 17; Myles Davies, *The Recantation of Mr. Pollet* (London, 1705), pp. 10–11. For Davies, the priest in question, see my article 'Over the Wall, Converts from Popery in 18th century England', in *Downside Review*, 94 (1976), pp. 7–8, 16, 21.

20 Ruth Clarke, *Strangers and Sojourners at Port Royal* (Cambridge 1932), pp. 149–59, 164, 181–3 (hereafter Clarke, *Strangers*).

21 J. M. Neale, *A History of the so-called Jansenist Church of Holland* (Oxford, 1857), pp. 158–196 (hereafter cited as Neale, *Jansenist Church*); Ludwig von Pastor, *The History of the Popes* vol. 32 (London, 1940), pp. 487–92 (hereafter cited as *Pastor* with volume number). C. P. Voorvelt OFM, *De Amor Poenitens van Johannes van Neercassel (1626–1686)* (Kerckebosch, 1988); Gian. Ackermans, 'Good Pastors in the *Missio Hollandica* in the second Half of the Seventeenth Century', *Nederlands Archief Voor Kerkgeschiedenis/Dutch Review of Church History*, 83 (2003), pp. 260–70; and the essays in J. van Bavel and M. Schrama (eds), *Jansenius et le jansenisme dans les Pays-Bas.Melanges Lucien Ceyssens* (Louvain, 1982).

22 *Blacklo's Cabal*, pp. 13, 19, 102, 107; Birrell, art. cit., pp. 149–50.

23 Clarke, *Strangers*, pp. 158–9.

24 John Kirk, *Biographies of English Catholics in the Eighteenth Century* (London, 1909), pp. 98–9 (hereafter *Kirk*); G. Macdonald, 'The Lime Street Chapel (part I)' in *Dublin Review*, 180 (1927), pp. 257–265.

25 Abercrombie, op. cit., pp. 307–8.

26 *Pastor*, vol. 33, pp. 179–83.

27 *Kirk*, pp. 113–15; Fr Alphonsus Bonnar OFM, 'The English Franciscans and Jansenism' in *Clergy Review*, 2 (1931), pp. 122–32, esp. pp. 125–6; Ushaw College, Durham, Ushaw Collection of Manuscripts, i. fols 211–12 (hereafter UCM. I am indebted to the President of Ushaw College for permission to quote from these papers. References are normally to volume and item number. Folio numbers are given, as here, only when necessary to avoid confusion with item numbers).

28 UCM. i fols, 215–16, 224. In quoting from MSS I have silently expanded conventional abbreviations; spelling is otherwise unaltered.

29 UCM. i fols 227–8.

30 Philip Harris (ed.), *Douai College Documents* (Catholic Record Society, vol. 63, 'Diary of Edward Dicconson', pp. 86–7 (hereafter *Dicconson Diary*); Archives of the Archbishop of Westminster (hereafter AAW), *Epistolae Variorum* (hereafter Ep. Var.) i no. 47; Edward Dicconson to Laurence Mayes, 18 December 1706.

31 UCM. i fols. 217–18, 225; AAW. Ep. Var. i no. 37: Peter B. Tunstal to James Gordon 14 December 1705.

32 UCM. i fols. 218–25; Archives of the English Province of the Society of Jesus, Farm Street, London (hereafter *Arch. SJ*) A. iv. 21, MS of Fr Thomas Hunter's 'Answer to the four and twenty Letters, Intitled the secret Policy of the English Society of Jesus', fol. 49 (extract of a letter from Poyntz himself); (Fr Thomas Hunter SJ), *A Modest Defence of the Clergy and Religious* (n.p. 1714), p. 121.

33 *Arch. SJ*, A. iv. 21 fol. 50; Hunter, *Modest Defence*, p. 122.

34 Charles Dodd, *The Church History of England, from 1500 to 1688, chiefly with regard to Catholicks*, 'Brussels' (false imprint) 1737–42, vol. 3, p. 485; *Historical Manuscripts Commission, Stuart Papers at Windsor* (HMSO, 1904), vol. 1, pp. 188–93, vol. 2, p. 520; AAW. Paris Seminary volume, fols 231–45, 'A Ruff draught of the reasons given and the methods taken for removing from St. Germans John Betham preceptor to King James the 3rd'. This is Betham's own account of the proceedings against him, and contains a detailed and revealing account of Noialles's sympathetic interview with Betham. Among the charges mentioned by the cardinal was one that Betham had told the King (James Edward Stuart) that 'Mons. Arnold would be canonised'. This, Betham assured Noialles, was a mistake. He had not said Arnauld would be canonised, but that the last pope had intended to make him a cardinal, a thing, as Betham drily observed 'very different from Canonisation'. The account in Clarke, *Strangers*, based on the *Stuart Papers*, is incomplete, and mistakenly implies that Betham's banishment was permanent. For his return to St Germain, see AAW. Ep. Var. i no. 30: John Betham to James Gordon, 13 April 1705. For Jansenism and the Stuart court at this time more generally, Glickman, *English Catholic Community*, pp. 175–83.

35 (Etienne Agard de Champs), *The Secret Policy of the Jansenists and the present State of the Sorbon . . . To which is premis'd A brief Abstract of the Memorial concerning the State and Progress of Jansenism in Holland . . .* (n. p. 1703). This translation of the *Secret Policy* had first appeared in 1667.

36 Ibid., pp. 40–43, 68–70, 72, 75, 95, 98; for the context of accusations of Jansenism against the Dutch clergy, Parker, *Faith on the Margins*, pp. 24–46, 83–4.

37 *Kirk*, pp. 76–7; ODNB, xviii, p. 149; H. Foley, *Records of the English Province of the Society of Jesus* (London, 1877–1883) (hereafter *Foley*), vol. 5, pp. 821–3. For Fairfax see J. A. Williams, *Catholic Recusancy in Wiltshire 1660–1791* (Catholic Record Society Monograph, 1968), pp. 151–3.

38 *A Case of Conscience Propos'd to, and Decided by Forty Doctors of the Faculty of Paris, in Favour of Jansenism*, n. p. 1703; AAW. 'A' series, xxxviii, no. 55; Fr Thomas Fairfax to Sylvester Jenks (23? November) 1710.

39 AAW. 'A' xxxviii, 55.

40 Archives of the Old Brotherhood of the Secular Clergy (the Chapter), iii, no. 106: 'A Short and True (account) of the uncharitable persecution raised and carried on against the clergy'.

41 Myles Davies, *Recantation of Mr. Pollet*, p. 12.

42　UCM. i fols 219–225; AAW. Ep.Var. I no. 37: Peter B.Tunstall to James Gordon, 14 December 1705; AAW. 'A' xlviii, no. 15; Thomas Roydon to Laurence Mayes, 25 February 1708.

43　The evidence concerning Fr Sabran's relations with Poyntz at this period is difficult to assess. Roydon's evidence is plausible because self-incriminating, and he was emphatic that he had seen and read two letters from Sabran to Poyntz: AAW. 'A' xlviii, no. 15. Fr Sabran's denials of involvement were confined to denials of any plot against Douay College, with a view to a Jesuit takeover. When taxed with writing to Poyntz his words seem carefully chosen – see for example Geoffrey Holt SJ (ed.), *The Letter Hook of Lewis Sabran SJ*, vol. 62 (Catholic Record Society, 1971), pp. 240–41, where his denial of correspondence with Poyntz seems to be limited to correspondence on the subject of 'Dr. Paston's tyranny'. Sabran's later relations with Poyntz, using him as an informer against suspected Jansenist teaching and teachers at Douai, and procuring him an annuity in the aftermath of Charles Dodd's denunciations of Poyntz in 1713–15, suggest that they were indeed previously known to each other; *Sabran Letters*, 35, 41, 47–8, 181, 183–4. See also Hunter, *Modest Defence*, pp. 121, 129; *Arch. SJ.* A. iv, 21 cols, 48–9; UCM. i. fol. 249 'Fr. Sabran's Answer to some queries put to him by F. Eyre'.

44　Hubert Chadwick SJ, *St. Omers to Stonyhurst* (London, 1962), p. 249; Archives of the Old Brotherhood, iii, no. 106.

45　UCM. i. fols 281–2: Lewis Sabran to Andrew Giffard ('Jonathan Coles'), 22 June 1708.

46　AAW. Paris Seminary Volume, fol. 257: Bishop James Smith to John Betham, 10 September 1706; Ep.Var. i no. 41; John Betham to Laurence Mayes, 18 October 1706; *Dicconson Diary*, p. 87.

47　AAW. *Ep. Var.* i no. 40; Edward Dicconson to Laurence Mayes, 13 October 1706.

48　Dodd, *Church History*, vol. 3, p. 480; *Catholic Record Society*, vol. 28, 'The Seventh Douai Diary', containing 'Dr. Robert Witham's Advice to a President of Douay College', p. 308.

49　*Kirk*, pp. 63–4; AAW. Ep.Var. vi no. 3; Robert Witham to Laurence Mayes, 20 February 1716; I no. 29: Edward Paston to James Gordon, 23 March 1705.

50　*Kirk*, pp. 160–61.

51　The previous incumbent, Michael Ellis, a careerist Benedictine who had lived abroad since 1689, finally resigned his neglected vicariate in 1705, reluctantly accepting instead the small Italian see of Segni which, however, he did much to convert into a model Tridentine diocese: see the article by Geoffrey Scott in *ODNB*.

52　*Kirk*, p. 204.

53　*Dicconson Diary*, p. 107; *Kirk*, p. 204; UCM. i fols 233–4.

54　AAW. 'The Roman Agency books of Laurence Mayes' (hereafter 'Mayes Agency'), i fols 53–5; *Dicconson Diary*, p 107.

55　*Pastor*, vol. 32, pp. 651–8, vol. 33, pp. 314–31; Neale, *Jansenist Church*, pp. 209–24.

56　AAW. Ep.Var. i no. 110: Gerard Saltmarsh to Laurence Mayes, 4 November 1707; i no. 118: same to same, 22 December 1707; 'Mayes Agency', i fols. 53–5, 148–51.

57　AAW. Ep.Var. i no. 110: Saltmarsh to Mayes, 4 November 1707.

58　AAW. 'Mayes Agency', i fol. 55.

59　AAW. Ep.Var. i no. 64: Bishop Bonaventure Giffard to Laurence Mayes, 13 March.

60　AAW. 'Mayes Agency', i fols 61–3, 79–88.

61　AAW. 'Mayes Agency', i fols 55–60; Ep.Var. i no. 68: Edward Paston to Laurence Mayes, 22 March 1707; i no. 72: John Betham to Laurence Mayes, 11 April 1707.

62　AAW. Ep.Var. i no. 73: Edward Paston to Laurence Mayes, 16 April 1707; i no. 95; same to same, 6 October 1707; i no. 106: Fr. Tomson (*sic*) to Laurence Mayes, 30 October 1707; 'Mayes Agency', i fols 67–8.

63　AAW. Ep. Var. i no. 102: Bishop Giffard to Laurence Mayes, 24 October 1707; i no. log: Edward Dicconson to Laurence Mayes, 1 November 1707; ii no. 18: same to same, 10 April 1708.

64　*Kirk*, pp. 98–100.

65　UCM. i fols 284–5; AAW. Ep.Var. ii no. 23: Edward Dicconson to Laurence Mayes, 12 May 1708; *Foley*, vol. 7, p. 449.

66　*Kirk*, pp. 161–2; UCM. i fol. 279: Andrew Giffard to Edward Paston ('Jo. Coles' to 'Mr. Everard'), 7 July 1710.

67 UCM. i fols 281–3; Lewis Sabran to Andrew Giffard, 22 June 1708 (with notes by Giffard); Hunter, *Modest Defence*, pp. 128–9, 132–3.

68 For troubles in the north see Dodd, *Church History*, vol. 3, p. 519; AAW. Ep.Var. i no. 109: Edward Dicconson to Laurence Mayes, 1 November 1707; i no. 119; Edward Paston to Mayes, 23 December 1707; UCM. i fol. 309; Fr Francis Mannock SJ to Fr Charles Kennet SJ, 11 March 1709/10; AAW. Ep.Var. i no. 120; Bishop Smith to Mayes, 30 December 1707.

69 Dodd, *Church History*, vol. 3, p. 460; *Kirk*, p. 210.

70 Cf. Dodd, *Church History*, vol. 3, p. 360; *Kirk*, p. 100.

71 AAW. Ep.Var. i no. 114; Bishop Giffard to Laurence Mayes, 5 December 1707.

72 Clarke, *Strangers*, pp. 164–70.

73 UCM. i no. 96: Richard Short to Charles Towneley, n.d.; i no. 97: same to same, 24 September 1706(?); i no. 91: same to same, no date.

74 UCM. i no. 98: Richard Short to Charles Towneley, February (1706/7?).

75 Clarke, *Strangers*, p. 169.

76 AAW. xxxviii no. 54: 'Fr. Fairfax's remarks on the Review of Jansenius'; no. 55: Fr. Fairfax to Sylvester Jenks, 23 November 1710.

77 Clarke, *Strangers*, pp. 166–7; 'the persons concerned were "old squire Whetenhall"' (Henry Whetenhall of East Peckham, Kent), his nephew Francis Thwaites, a Douai priest, Sylvester Jenks and Dom Thomas Southcote, though Southcott seems to have subsequently denied involvement – cf. Geoffrey Scott, *Gothic Rage Undone* (Bath, 1992), p. 251, n. 457; *Kirk*, pp. 215, 235, 247; UCM. i no. 84: Sylvester Jenks, letters to Thomas Fairfax concerning Jansenism, 9–11; AAW. Ep. Var. ii no. 88: Edward Dicconson to Laurence Mayes, 21–24 July 1709.

78 He published a series of bestselling treatises on penitence and contrition: *The Blind Obedience of a Humble Penitent. The Best Cure for Scruples* (n.p. 1698) (three editions by 1699); *The Security of an Humble penitent Asserted in a Letter to a Friend* (n.p. 1700).

79 *A Contrite and Humble Heart* (Paris 1692) – three further editions by 1698.

80 Jenks's testimony printed in Joseph Gillow, *Biographical Dictionary of the English Catholics*, vol. 3, p. 621.

81 UCM. i no. 91: Richard Short to Charles Towneley, no date.

82 AAW. 'A' xxxviii no. 54; for some indications of Short's 'Jansenist' views, suggesting that they centred on the question of papal authority and the doctrine of Neercassel's *Amor Poenitens*, see Archives of the Old Brotherhood iii nos 17 (Short on papal authority), 21 (Short to Richard Gomelden on dogmatic facts, no date), 23 (untitled paper on the Five Propositions), 27 (Copy of Dr. Short's Answer to the Paper of accusations against him), 28 ('Dr. Short's tenets' – a hostile 'Syllabus' of Short's errors). This last item seems to contain the 'propositions' solemnly disowned by Short after receiving the Sacrament from abbot James Corker. They were not, as is wrongly suggested by Clarke, *Strangers*, p. 170, the 'Five Propositions'; cf. UCM. i no. 75 (fol. 308), evidently misread by Clarke.

83 For Vane, see Anstruther, *Seminary Priests*, vol. 2, pp. 237–8, and W. Croft and J. Gillow, *Historical Account of Lisbon College* (London, 1902), pp. 261–2.

84 AAW. Ep.Var. i no. 114: Bishop Gillard to Laurence Mayes, 5 December 1707; UCM. i nos. 68, 71: copies of a letter from Francis Mannock SJ to Charles Kennet SJ, written before 8 March 1708, with notes by Andrew Giffard; *Arch. SJ*, Fr. John Thorpe's 'Notes and Fragments' (hereafter 'Notes and Fragments'), fols 76, 78; Charles Kennet to Fr. Powil (?) December(?) 1707, May 1709, August 1709.

85 AAW. 'A' xxxviii no. 43: 'An account of wh(at) hapned (*sir*) between Mr. Smith S J. and Me November 1707' (by John Vane); no. 44: fair copy, idem., with some additional material.

86 Andrew Giffard to Edward Dicconson, 30 June 1710, printed in Gillow, *Biographical Dictionary*, vol. 3, pp. 66-7; the original is in UCM.

87 UCM. i no. 75 fols 309–11: copy of a letter from Francis Mannock to Charles Kennet 11 March 1709/10, with notes by Andrew Giffard; AAW. 'A' xxxviii no. 43. For Mannock see J. C. Aveling, *Catholic Recusancy in York 1558–1791* (Catholic Record Society Monograph, 1970), pp. 156–7; *Foley*, vol. 6, pp. 485–6; *Kirk*, pp. 157–8.

88 AAW.'A' xxxviii no. 45:'A Relation of the Abuses offered to me by Mr. S(mith) in Long Acre on Saturday night 24th of July 1703' (by John Vane). It is not clear whether the Fr. Smith concerned was John or Thomas Smith – *Foley*, vol. 7, pp. 718, 721.

89 See AAW.'A' xxxviii nos. 50, 51, documents compiled in 1710 by Andrew Giffard relating to these disruptions; Clarke, *Strangers*, p 163.

90 *Arch. SJ.*, 'Notes and Fragments', fol. 83: Charles Kennet to Richard Plowden, January 1714.

91 AAW.'A' xxxviii no. 54: Fairfax's 'Remarks on the Review of Jansenius'; Ep.Var. i no. 104: Bishop Smith to Laurence Mayes, 28 October 1707.

92 AAW. Paris Seminary Volume, fol. 318: Andrew Giffard to Edward Dicconson 9 May 1710; Ep.Var. i no. 114: Bishop Giffard to Laurence Mayes, 5 December 1707.

93 UCM. i. fols 234–5.

94 AAW.'A' xlviii nos 18–20;'Mayes Agency', i fols 108–37, 141–4, 152–64, 168–96; Ep.Var. ii no. 9: Edward Dicconson to Laurence Mayes, 25 February 1708; ii no. 12: Bishop George Witham to Laurence Mayes, 4 March 1708.

95 AAW. Ep.Var. ii no. 55: John Betham to Laurence Mayes, 10 December 1708; ii no. 73: Edward Dicconson to Laurence Mayes, 25 April 1709.

96 AAW.'Mayes Agency', i fols 229–35, 253–6; text of the Bull in *Magnum Bullarum Romanum . . . Editio Novissima,* vol. 8 (Luxembourg, 1727), pp. 33–5.

97 AAW. Ep. Var. iii no 34: Bishop Smith to Laurence Mayes, April 1710. Fears about circulating incriminating documents by post were not illusory: for some recusant letters stolen from the public mails by spies of Archbishop Tenison, see *Catholic Record Society*, vol. 56, pp. 130–64.

98 AAW. 'Mayes Agency' i fols 235–240. For the probable origin of these accusations *see Arch. SJ.* 'Notes and Fragments', fol. 79.

99 AAW. Ep.Var. ii no. 85: Bishop Giffard to Laurence Mayes, 16 May 1709.

100 Ibid., 7 July 1709.

101 Summary in A. Bellesheim, *A History of the Catholic Church in Scotland* (Edinburgh and London, 1890), vol. 4, pp. 200–201.

102 UCM. no. 68 fol. 267, notes on the brief by Andrew Giffard.

103 AAW. Ep. Var. iii no. 2: Bishop Giffard to Laurence Mayes, 18 January 1709/10; iii no. 42: John Ingleton to Laurence Mayes, 26 May 1710 (Ingleton had succeeded Betham, who died in 1709, as Preceptor to 'James III'); UCM. i fol. 305, notes by Andrew Giffard.

104 AAW. Ep. Var. iii no. 24: Bishop Giffard to Laurence Mayes, 8 March 1710; *Arch. SJ.* 'Notes and Fragments', fols 79–80.

105 AAW. Ep. Var. iii no. 17: Bishop Giffard to Mayes, 22 February 1710; 'A' xxxviii nos 50–51, 'Mr. Andrew Giffard's Commission'; UCM. i no. 81: Andrew Giffard to Edward Dicconson, 3 April 1710.

106 Sylvester Jenks, *A Short Review of the Book of Jansenius* (London, 1710), pp. 152–3.

107 AAW. Ep. Var. iii no. 25: Edward Paston to Laurence Mayes, 15 March 1710; iii no. 28: Sister Elizabeth Mevnell to Laurence Mayes, 30 March 1710; iii no. 54: Henry Howard to Mayes, 25 July 1710; iii no. 88: Andrew Giffard to Mayes, 31 December 1710; UCM. i no. 81: Andrew Giffard to Edward Dicconson, 3 April 1710.

108 UCM. i. no. 81: Andrew Giffard to Edward Dicconson, 3 April 1710; AAW. Ep. Var. iii no. 38: Edward Dicconson to Laurence Mayes, 14 May 1710; iii no. 42: J. Ingleton to Mayes, 26 May 1710. Such a scheme had been publicly proposed in 1705 in the anonymous pamphlet *A Short Way with the Papists*, which pleaded the loyalty of the secular clergy and their flocks, but denounced the 'Jesuit party' as disloyal and dangerous. I have not been able to find a single surviving copy of this pamphlet, which is possibly the work of John Sergeant, but a summary will be found in British Library Add. MS 29612,'Letter book of Sylvester Jenks', fols 36–8.

109 AAW. Ep.Var. iii no. 33: Edward Dicconson to Laurence Mayes, 22 April 1710.

110 AAW. Ep.Var. iii no. 36: Edward Dicconson to Laurence Mayes, 7 May 1710.

111 Dodd, *Church History*, vol. 3, p. 521; HMC *Stuart Papers*, vol. 2, p. 236: AAW. Ep. Var. ii no. 56: Dicconson to Laurence Mayes, 22 December 1708.

112 AAW.'Mayes Agency', i fols 330–344: Lewis Sabran to Cardinal Caprara (the cardinal protector of England), 5 November 1710. Sabran was also endeavouring to convince 'James III' that the secular

clergy were indeed guilty of Jansenism, but Sabran's letter to Caprara, which Mayes managed to copy, instead convinced the young King that Fr Sabran was activated by malice: Ep.Var. iii no. 74: J. Ingleton to Mayes, 10 October 1710; iii no. 85: Laurence Green to Mayes, 13 December 1710; iv no. 25: Edward Dicconson to Mayes, 23 May 1711; *Arch. SJ.* 'Notes and Fragments', fol. 79.

113 AAW. Ep.Var. iv no. 15: J. Ingleton to Laurence Mayes, 29 March 1711; iv no. 38: Andrew Giffard to Laurence Mayes, 29 July 1711; 'Mayes Agency', i fol. 383: Cardinal Paolucci to the Vicars Apostolic, 17 February 1711; ibid., 386–8; Cardinal Caprara on Paolucci's letter, 20 February 1711–throughout the entire proceedings Caprara showed himself a zealous and energetic friend to the secular clergy; UCM. i no. 123: Robert Witham to Mr Midford, 9 August 1712.

114 AAW. Ep.Var. iv no. 45: Peter B. Tunstall to Mayes, 25 September 1711. For details of the visitation, see Ep.Var. iv no. 53: Paston to Mayes, 5 November 1711; iv no. 54: Cuthbert Haydocke to Mayes, 9 November 1711; iv no. 56: Dicconson to Mayes, 22 November 1711; iv no. 60: same to same, 8 December 1711; iv no. 61: same to same, 20 December 1711; 'Mayes Agency', i fols 566–87, ii fols 35–40; 'A' xlviii no. 28: the Visitors to Hawarden, 12 February 1712. It is clear from this last letter that some of the 'blunt' parts of Hawarden's dictates drew directly on Gother; Paris Seminary Volume, fols 329–30; E. H. Burton *The Life and Times of Bishop Challoner* (London, 1909), vol. 1 pp. 30–33.

115 Text in *Bullarum*, vol. 8, pp. 118–22; J. F. Thomas, *La Querelle de l'Unigenitus* (Paris, 1950); Toon Quaghebeur, 'The Reception of Unigenitus in the Faculty of Theology at Louvain, 1713–1719.' *Catholic Historical Review*, vol. 93 (2007), pp. 265–99; J. M. Gres-Gayer, 'The Unigenitus of Clement XI: a fresh look at the issues', *Theological Studies*, vol. 49 (1988), pp. 259–82; Lucien Ceyssens (ed.), *Le sort de la bulle Unigenitus. Recueil d'études offert à Lucien Ceyssens à L'occasion de son 90e anniversaire* (Louvain, 1992).

116 AAW. Ep.Var. iv no. 46: Henry Howard ('Paston') to Mayes, 2 October 1711; iv no. 49: J. Ingleton to Mayes, 9 October 1711; *Arch. SJ.* 'Notes and Fragments, fols 92, 94; *Sabran Letters*, p. 13.

117 AAW. Ep.Var. v no. 81: Dicconson to Mayes, 27 December 1714; 'Mayes Agency', ii fols 183–88. For evidence of Kennet's responsibility for these accusations compare fol. 186 of this last reference with *Arch. SJ.* 'Notes and Fragments', fol. 99^v. See also Ep.Var. v no. 56: Henry Howard to Mayes, 12 June 1714.

118 (Hugh Tootell, alias 'Charles Dodd'), *The History of the English College at Doway. By R.C. Chaplain to an English Regiment* ... (London, 1713), pp. 33–6.

119 AAW. Ep.Var. v no. 34: Dicconson to Mayes, 2 November 1713; v no. 36: Dr. Thomas Witham to Mayes, 11 December 1713; v no. 37: Dicconson to Mayes, 29 December 1713; 'Mayes Agency', ii fols. 85–7.

120 AAW. 'A' xxxviii no. 78: Bishop George Witham to Mayes (1713); Ep.Var. v no. 46: Robert Witham to Mayes, 1 March 1714.

121 W. Maziere Brady, *Annals of the Catholic Hierarchy*, pp. 151–3; AAW. Ep.Var. v no. 56: Henry Howard to Mayes, 12 June 1714; v no. 60: Dicconson to Mayes, 29 July 1714; UCM. i no. 65 fols 261–2: Mgr Santini to Edward Paston, 18 May 1714.

122 Clarke, *Strangers*, pp. 175, 211; Neale, *Jansenist Church*, p. 235; cf. James Mitchell, 'The Ordination in Ireland of Jansenist Clergy from Utrecht, 1715–16: The Role of Fr Paul Kenny, ODC, of Co. Galway (Part One).' *Journal of the Galway Archaeological and Historical Society*, 42 (1989), pp. 2–29.

123 (Thomas Hunter), *A Modest Defence*, pp. 123–4, 130–31, 137–8. Much of the historical material for Hunter's pamphlet was supplied by Fr Sabran – *Sabran Letters*, pp. 21, 65, 100.

124 (Hugh Tootell, alias 'Charles Dodd'), *The Secret Policy of the English Society of Jesus. Discover'd in a Series of Attempts against the Clergy. In ... twenty four Letters Directed to their PROVINCIAL* (London, 1715), quotation from p. 330.

125 *Arch. SJ.* 'Notes and Fragments', fol. 84; *Sabran Letters*, pp. 246, 257; AAW. Ep.Var. v no. 88: Henry Howard to Mayes, 18 March 1715; v no. 39: Dicconson to Mayes, 28 March 1715.

126 *Arch. SJ.* Notes and Fragments', fol. 86; *Sabran Letters*, p. 259.

127 *Arch. SJ.* 'Notes and Fragments', fol. 88; AAW. Ep.Var. vi no. 4: Robert Witham to Mayes. 4 March 1716.

128 Hunter's 'Answer to the Four and Twenty Letters ...' *Arch. SJ.* A. iv. 21.

129　J. Baynes, *The Jacobite Rising of 1715* (London, 1970); Daniel Szechi *1715: The Great Jacobite Rebellion* (New Haven and London, 2006), though this is mainly concerned with Scotland.

130　For Jesuit lobbying for both appointments, see *Sabran Letters*, pp. 121, 130–31, 162, 180–84, 187, 194–5, 213. In February 1716 Fr Sabran hinted to the new president of Douai, Dr Robert Witham, the extent of his endeavours 'in favour of my being chosen'. Witham was not impressed – 'I am not well pleased with my obligations to such friends. I rather pitie our late misfortunes that could make us indebted to such tools': Ep.Var. vi no. 3: Witham to Mayes, 20 February 1716.

131　Dom Basil Hemphill, *The Early Vicars Apostolic of England* (London, 1954), 41–69: Eamon Duffy, 'Englishmen in Vaine: Roman Catholic Allegiance to George I', in S. Mews (ed.) *Religion and National Identity, (Studies in Church History*, vol. 18, Oxford, 1982), pp. 345–65; Gabriel Glickman, *The English Catholic Community 1688–1745: Politics, Culture and Ideology*, (Woodbridge, 2009), pp. 129–57.

132　Clarke, *Strangers*, pp. 175–80. The 'M. Herbert' discussed by Professor Clarke is in fact John Vane, who used the alias Herbert.

133　AAW. 'A' xxxviii no. 160: Bishop Stonor to (?), 21 July 1729. Stonor was probably reacting to the publication of the anti-Jansenist *The Bull Unigenitus clear'd from Innovation and Immorality* (London, 1729).

134　David Milburn, *A History of Ushaw College* (Durham, 1964), pp. 9–12.

135　*Catholic Record Society*, vol. 33, pp. 316–7. Examples of this frame of mind in Alban Butler may be found in my unpublished Cambridge PhD thesis (1973, 'Joseph Berington and the English Catholic Cisalpine Movement 1772–1803', pp. 76–7, 85–7.

136　*Kirk*, pp. 63–4: Gillow, *Biographical Dictionary of the English Catholics,* vol. 2, pp. 56–9; Thompson Cooper, 'Dicconson, Edward (1670–1752)', rev. J. A. Hilton, *ODNB*.

137　Anstruther, *Seminary Priests*, vol. 3, pp. 230–31.

138　*Kirk*, p. 63.

139　Gabriel Glickman, 'Gothic History and Catholic Enlightenment in the works of Charles Dodd (1672–1743)', *Historical Journal*, 54 (2011), pp. 347–69.

140　*Dodd's Church History of England from the Commencement of the Sixteenth Century to the Revolution of 1688, with notes, additions and a continuation by the Rev. M. A. Tierney* (5 volumes, London, 1839–43). The project broke off at the year 1625.

141　Richard Schiefen, 'Anglo-Gallicanism in Nineteenth-Century England', *Catholic Historical Review*, vol. 63 (1977), pp. 14–44, quotes at pp. 28, 37; Rosemary Mitchell, 'Kirk, John (1760–1851)', *ODNB*; Thompson Cooper, 'Tierney, Mark Aloysius (1795–1862)', rev. Richard J. Schiefen, *ODNB*; Joseph Gillow, *Bibliographical Dictionary of the English Catholics*, vol. 5 (London n.d.), pp. 545–7. For Lingard's assistance, Peter Phillips, *John Lingard, Priest and Historian* (Leominster, 2008), pp. 157, 345, 346, 358, 416, 420.

142　Chapter 10 below; and for a brief account of the subsequent history of the 'Dodd' tradition see Professor T. A. Birrell's introduction to the Gregg Press reprint of Joseph Berington's *The Memoirs of Gregorio Panzani* (Birmingham, 1793). For a virulent attack on this tradition, M. V. Hay, *The Jesuits and the Popish Plot* (London, 1934), *passim*. Something like a reworking of these disputes, from a pro-Jesuit standpoint, can be found in John Bossy's *The English Catholic Community 1570–1850* (London, 1975), pp. 9–74. For a fascinating example of the way in which the 'Dodd' pattern could be read back into the secular/Jesuit disputes of the seventeenth century, see the eighteenth-century MS annotations in the front fly-leaves of the Cambridge University Library copy of (Peter Talbot), *Blackloanae Haeresis Olim in Pelagio Et Manichaeis Damnatae . . . Auctore M. Lomino Theologo* (Ghent, 1675). Discussing the doctrinal disputes in which John Sergeant was involved with Archbishop Talbot and other Jesuits in the 1670s, the annotator, a secular priest who knew Paston and Andrew Giffard, writes, 'The violence with which this matter was carried on by the *Society* shows that they were in hopes to have made some great advantage thereof, to their body, by depressing the whole sett of the Engl(ish) Clergy on both sides the sea which here' (in the attack on Sergeant's 'Pelagianism') 'they endeavour to hook into the guilt of Heresy . . .'

10

From Sander to Lingard:
Recusant Readings of the Reformation

Asked to name the single book which shaped almost everything subsequently written about the English reformation, most of us would be likely to come up with John Foxe's *Actes and Monuments*.[1] Down to the late twentieth century even the most ostensibly secular historiography of the English reformation bore traces of Foxe's Protestant providentialism, if only in the form of a residual historical whiggery.[2] But it's easy to forget that in terms of European readers and editions, Foxe's account of the English reformation was challenged and in some cases eclipsed by the rival accounts of Catholic opponents like Nicholas Harpsfield, in his powerful polemical *Dialogi Sex,* published in 1566,[3] by the works of Robert Persons and, above all, by those of Nicholas Sander.[4] Persons' *De Persecutione Anglicana* ran through 11 editions in Latin, French, German and Italian in the first year after its first publication in 1581:[5] it was the text behind Richard Verstegan's martyr picture books,[6] and in the decades either side of the sixteenth and seventeenth century divide, helped shape European perceptions of what was going on in England. Sander's *De Origine ac Progressu Schismatis Anglicani,* completed down to 1584 by Edward Rishton and first published in 1585, was certainly the most influential account of the English reformation ever written.[7] Over the next 40 years it ran through eight Latin and five French and German editions, and it became the basis for a flood of derivative accounts of the English reformation, in Italian, Spanish, German and Latin, which ran in their turn to more than two dozen further editions: for most of continental Europe Sander's reformation *was* the standard version of the English reformation.[8]

For the most part, of course, the readership of these conflicting accounts of the reformation didn't overlap. Sander, Persons and Harpsfield wrote for a European Catholic audience, Foxe, after his first Latin edition, for an English Protestant one. But we can make too many assumptions about the universal triumph of Foxe's book in England. In the 1670s Gilbert Burnet complained of the failure of Protestant historians to rise to the challenge of recusant historical writing, and singled out for comment the strange Protestant silence about Sander's work, which he believed had led to the widespread acceptance of his account of events, and the fact that 'in this age that Author is in such credit, that now he is quoted with much assurance' especially but by no means exclusively by Catholic writers.[9]

For the recusant writers, the story of the reformation was that of the unnatural overthrow of all right order. Henry's lapse from the radiant and gifted Catholic prince of his youth into concubinage, bigamy and wife-murder kept pace with his wading ever deeper into heresy and into blood. God's rejection of this fundamental defiance of the divinely ordered course of things was manifest in the fact that Henry's objectives were thwarted when he was succeeded by a feeble child, whose weakness could be exploited by unscrupulous careerists like Somerset and Northumberland, and hypocritical heresiarchs like Cranmer. The succession of Henry's heretic bastard daughter Elizabeth completed the overthrow of the natural order by arrogating to a woman not merely temporal but spiritual supremacy. As Sander commented at the end of his contribution to the *De Origine*, 'Then came the hour of Satan, and the power of darkness took possession of the whole of England.'

Like so much else in Elizabethan Catholicism, this story in its essence was deeply indebted to the thought of Cardinal Reginald Pole, in particular Pole's extraordinary open letter to Henry VIII, the *De Unitate*, 'on the unity of the Church'.[10] There Pole had set out the portrait of Henry which would be absorbed and elaborated in subsequent Catholic historiography: the devout, talented young Catholic prince, whose accession to the throne had seemed to promise a golden age, 'For what did your distinguished virtues not promise ... piety ... justice, clemency, liberality and ... prudence.'[11] But lust for a shameless harlot and greed for the goods of the Church had degraded Henry himself into a tyrant worse than the Turk, spilling

288

the innocent blood of the holiest men in the kingdom, Thomas More and John Fisher, and bringing spiritual and material ruin on his people. Pole had elaborated the arguments of *De Unitate* in his programmatic address to Parliament in 1554, when he returned as Legate to reconcile the nation to the papacy. In that speech he traced the ruin of the kingdom by Henry's tyranny and lust, the hand of Providence in the preservation of Princess Mary, and the contrast between Henry and the martyrs Fisher and More whose blood had preserved the nation from even worse calamities.[12]

Pole's seminal interpretation of Henry's reign and its disastrous consequences for England had been rapidly absorbed into the official polemic of Marian Catholicism, and underlay the emergent cult of More and Fisher (carefully purged of incriminating association with Erasmus) with momentous consequences for subsequent Catholic perceptions of the Tudor age.[13] And in elaborating Pole's understanding of Henry's reign and legacy, Sander established a series of benchmarks for subsequent Catholic interpretation of the reformation,[14] perhaps most notably in his notorious, entertaining and immensely influential account of the Divorce, and of Anne Boleyn. The main features of that account were destined for endless repetition: the Divorce was first suggested by Wolsey, who, full of frustrated ambition at his failure to become Pope, struck at the marriage to Catherine as a way of detaching Henry from her nephew Charles V, whom he blamed for blocking his path to the papacy. Wolsey wanted Henry to remarry into the French royal family, but at this point the devil and Anne Boleyn intervened, and the reformation began.

Sander believed, or at any rate claimed, that Henry had seduced Anne's mother as well as her sister, and that Anne was in fact his own daughter, so that his marriage to her was a particularly horrible – and deliberate – act of incest as well as of bigamy. Anne herself was a rampant lecher, deflowered in her teens by her father's butler and his chaplain, and then at the French court earning the nickname 'the English mare' for her sexual exploits. In France she embraced Protestantism, whose doctrine of justification by faith meant she could be as immoral as she pleased. Having become the mistress – Sander says the 'mule' – of the French King, she returned to England to work on Henry. For Sander she was in fact a sort of witch, who enchanted the King, her seductive powers a triumph of artifice over nature. I cannot forbear quoting Sander's account of Anne's appearance.

> Anne Boleyn was rather tall of stature, with black hair, and an oval face of a sallow complexion, as if troubled with jaundice. She had a projecting tooth under the upper lip, and on her right hand six fingers. There was a large wen under her chin, and to hide its ugliness she wore a high dress covering her throat, in which she was followed by the ladies of the court, who also wore high dresses, having formerly been in the habit of leaving their necks and bosoms bare. She was handsome to look at, with a pretty mouth, amusing in her ways, playing well on the lute, a good dancer: she was the mirror of fashion to the court ... But as to the disposition of her mind, she was filled with pride, ambition, envy, and lust.[15]

So, following Pole, Sander established the fundamental reformation narrative for Catholics, you might say the Catholic myth, of a reformation solely triggered by a tyrannical king's lust for a scheming courtesan. And Sander elaborated the delicious though spurious claim of Pole's disciple, Nicholas Harpsfield, that Archbishop Cranmer had concealed his marriage from Henry VIII by carrying his German wife around with him in a padded wooden box. The story, sadly, is pure fiction, but it proved so irresistible that it recently found its way into an episode of Michael Hirst's ludicrously enjoyable TV series *The Tudors*.

This was crude stuff, about as subtle and nuanced as John Foxe's hostile portrait of Sir Thomas More in *Actes and Monuments*. It lies at the heart of Sander's account, though, providing the key to all that was rotten in the reformation. He quoted St Paul, 'He who is joined to a harlot is made one body with her' ... 'Now, all English protestants – Lutherans, Zuinglians, Calvinists, Puritans and Libertines – honour the incestuous marriage of Henry and Anne Boleyn as the well-spring of their Gospel, the mother of their church, and the source of their belief' – and he quoted in support of this claim Matthew Parker's 1573 eulogy of the 'truly blessed and providential wedlock' which had given birth to the Protestant Judith, Elizabeth.[16]

During the first half of the seventeenth century both Catholic and Protestant historians accumulated new atrocities without any fundamental change of emphasis. Protestant convictions about the anti-Christian and persecuting character of Catholicism were nourished by the treatment of French Huguenots, the Thirty Years War and the massacres of 1641 in Ireland, while Catholics added to their armoury the heroism of the Catholic martyrs of the 1580s and 90s, and a sharpening of the attacks launched by the first recusant generation against the Church of England. The emergence and elaboration in the reign of James I, for example, of the Nag's Head Fable, in which it was alleged that Parker and the other new Elizabethan bishops, thwarted of consecration in the apostolic succession by the refusal of Bishop Kitchin of Llandaff to oblige, were invalidly made bishops after a drunken dinner at the Nag's Head in London by having bibles placed on their heads by John Scory. Catholic concentration on this story is only explicable in terms of a new sensitivity within the Church of England about the nature of apostolic succession, a new interest in the maintenance of a line of ordination passed on through the Catholic episcopate of the pre-reformation period. The story had only the flimsiest of foundations, but it became increasingly circumstantial in the telling, and by 1614 Archbishop Abbot took it seriously enough to arrange for a committee of four senior Catholic priests to be rounded up from the London gaols and brought to examine the account of the actual consecration in Parker's register at Lambeth for themselves.[17]

In other respects, too, elements of the recusant rather than the Protestant account of the reformation established themselves. Foxe's demolition job on the integrity and character of More, given fresh currency in our own time by Hilary Mantel's *Wolf Hall*, was on the whole not accepted. The more reverential emphases enshrined in the lives by Roper, Harpsfield[18] and Stapleton[19] made their way into the public perception of More, and indeed of Fisher, and in the process influenced perceptions of the reign of Henry VIII, though it was not until 1655 that a very much bowdlerized version of the early anonymous life of Fisher appeared under the editorship of Thomas Bailey.[20]

But by the mid-seventeenth century in any case the Elizabethan agenda which had conditioned most of what was written on either side about the reformation of the sixteenth century had been radically modified by the revolutionary upheavals of the 1630s, 1640s and 1650s. The Restoration was to see a blossoming of English historical writing which would last well into the Hanoverian period, and which would transform perceptions of the reformation as a whole. Much of this work was on the Middle Ages, and marked a renewed interest in the patristic and medieval past – and the medieval legal structure – of the Churches of England and Ireland, a dimension of their history which Foxe had effectively edited out. It was heavily based in the antiquarian tradition, but also highly politicised by the divisions of the Restoration and Hanoverian Church, divisions which stemmed from the civil war and Interregnum – writers like Peter Heylyn and Jeremy Collier, for example, were attempting to rewrite the history of the Church of England in more ways than one. Heylyn was a Laudian, determined to secure a Restoration which preserved for the Church its property, and as much of its medieval jurisdiction and influence as could be secured.[21] Collier, writing a generation later, was a non-juror, and his treatment of the history of the medieval Church of England, the most extended narrative account so far published by a Protestant, was designed to demonstrate that the royal supremacy, as commonly understood in early modern England, was a novelty, and that the extension of royal power into spiritual matters was a usurpation – not a message English Protestants as a whole wanted to hear.[22] As we shall see, Catholics were to make capital out of both Heylyn and Collier's work.

The first flowering of English patristic and medieval scholarship was explored two generations ago by Greenslade, Douglas, Sykes and others and has been revisited more recently by Jean-Louis Quantin.[23] The accompanying blossoming of reformation studies, however, has received less attention, despite the fact that we continue to be its beneficiaries. A hundred years on, Foxe's apocalyptic take on the reformation was given a soberer suit of clothes in Gilbert Burnet's *History of the Reformation of the Church of England*, the first volume of which appeared in 1679, and third and final volume in 1715. Scottish by birth and whiggish by persuasion, Burnet wrote his book to fuel the vicious anti-Catholicism of the late 1670s. The first volume was published at the height of the murderous frenzy over the Popish

Plot, and was recognised at once as valuable ammunition in the fight against political Catholicism. The ostensible occasion of his *History* was the publication of a new French edition of Sander's *Origin and Growth*, so Burnet's first volume was intended as a vindication of the reformation under Henry VIII, which had been Sander's main target.[24] Burnet himself was in fact rather lukewarm about Henry, who like Foxe he saw as an inconstant figure tugged in different directions by factions and rival favourites. With more confidence he followed Foxe in his admiring portraits of Anne Boleyn, Thomas Cranmer and especially Thomas Cromwell, all of whom he presented as heroes of the early Protestant cause.

Burnet's whig political connections gave him access to import-ant deposits of public records, including the amazing library of Sir Robert Cotton, containing many important state papers from Tudor England. Burnet embedded many of these documents in his text, and added a large collection of original records, not always accurately transcribed, to back his narrative. Burnet's book had no literary graces, but its copious documentation and its robustly Protestant tone quickly established it as the standard account of the English reformation, a status it retained for more than a century. And the main lines of his account were consolidated by a stream of works by his like-minded friend and fellow whig, the Reverend John Strype. Strype, son of a Huguenot family from Brabant, was an ardent Protestant who shared Burnet's hatred of popery and the High Church. He was also a complacent Anglican, who thought the Church by law established the pinnacle of Christian perfection, and disapproved accordingly of all its critics, from the Elizabethan puritans to the dissenters of his own day.[25] Strype was a dedicated collector of manuscripts, and between the early 1690s and the late 1730s he produced a stream of books designed to illustrate the prog-ress of Tudor Protestantism – lives of Archbishops Cranmer, Parker, Grindal and Whitgift, of Bishop Aylmer, of Sir Thomas Smith, and Sir John Cheke, and a multi-volume series of *Ecclesiastical Memorials*, covering the reformation under Henry, Edward and Mary, and another series of *Annals of the Reformed Church of England*, devoted to the reign of Elizabeth.

Like Burnet, Strype presented himself as producing authen-tic history straight from the archives. And his greatest coup was to secure the loan and, eventually, by rather shady means, the ownership of Foxe's surviving papers, as well as the papers of Lord Burghley's secretary Sir Michael Hickes, and he, too, printed scores of documents as appendices to his biographies and annals. These appendices were treasure trove for other historians, and became a plausible alibi for those who wouldn't or couldn't undertake difficult research in the archives themselves. The most influential history of England of the eighteenth century, by David Hume, notoriously involved no archival search whatever. The footnotes to his coverage of the reformation reveal again and again his reliance for fact, incident and narrative shape on Foxe, Burnet and Strype. And a century on it still seemed to the Syndics of Oxford University Press worth reprinting Strype's complete works in an enormous and costly 25-volume edition, because of their sound Protestant tone and their value as a storehouse of inaccessible archival material. For all their fairly obvious deficiencies, these histories remain valuable even in the age of State Papers online, if only because of the huge quantities of more or less accurately transcribed source material they made readily available. Both Strype and Burnet were staunch Protestants and defenders of the established Church, and Burnet's book was something of a manifesto for the Latitudinarian party: his research work had the support and backing of Bishop Lloyd, and the future Bishops Stillingfleet and Tillotson, as well as of aristocratic lay defenders of the Protestant settlement like Robert Boyle and Daniel Finch.[26]

Manifesto or not, however, Burnet claimed a new level of scholarly honesty and accuracy for his book, emphasising the 'vouchers' which he printed in the form of detailed documentation, especially from the Cotton and Petyt manuscripts which had been his main sources. But he conceived his book not as an exercise in objective scholarship, but as a contribution to the fight against popery. Its appearance at the height of public agitation over the Popish Plot guaranteed intense public interest in Burnet's book, and earned him the formal thanks of both houses of parliament, with a request that he should publish volume two with all speed: when completing the third and final volume of the work in the almost equally fraught year of 1715 he underlined his overall objective, to paint the evils of Catholicism and the benefits of Protestantism in their true colours – 'How much soever we may let the fears of popery wear out of our thoughts, they are never asleep, but go on steadily, prosecuting their designs against us. Popery is popery still, acted by a cruel and persecuting spirit, and ... therefore we see what reason we have to be ever watching and on our guard against them.'[27]

The crisis of the Popish Plot and the reign of James II reactivated many of the controversies of the Elizabethan and Jacobean years: the presses groaned under the weight of pro- and anti-Catholic propaganda. Inevitably, the history of the reformation was pressed into service on both sides. The nature of monastic life and the motives for its dissolution, the character of Henry and Anne, Mary and Elizabeth, above all the nature of the Marian regime and the persecution of Protestants under Bloody Mary, were endlessly rehearsed. So too were the claims to the Church of England to continuity through the apostolic succession. The Nag's Head was taken for a trot again, though Catholics concentrated their fire on the defect of form which they maintained characterised the Edwardian Ordinal, and the defect of intention in the consecrators of the Edwardian and Elizabethan episcopate, which Catholics maintained this defect of form demonstrated.[28]

One of the contributors from the Catholic side to this debate was a remarkable convert, Thomas Ward, a Yorkshire Presbyterian layman who had served for a while as a private tutor and had been converted to Catholicism in his late teens or early twenties. He travelled in France and Scotland, and in the late 1670s served as a member of the papal guard in Rome. During the reign of James II he was a vigorous contributor to the pamphlet wars against the reformation, under the *nom de guerre* 'The Roman Catholic Soldier': Ward was answered by a range of Protestant apologists, including the future Archbishop Tenison, who was convinced that he was a Jesuit in disguise. His writings ranged over a series of reformation issues, including the tendentious character of Protestant Bible translation, for which he drew heavily on the writings of Gregory Martin, but he focused in particular on the defects in Protestant ordinations: he used the Nag's Head Fable, but concentrated on the firmer ground of the defect of form in the first Ordinal.[29]

Like every other Catholic controversialist, Ward fell silent in 1688, and in fact he went to live in France. While there, he composed his best-known – and best – work, a four-canto poem in the skipping octosyllabic couplets of Samuel Butler's *Hudibras*, entitled *England's Reformation*, posthumously published at Hamburg in 1710.

At one level, Ward's poem is a sometimes clever versification of the age-old repertoire of Catholic accusations against the reformation: it is scurrilous, hostile and unsubtle. The opening of Canto one is a fair sample:

> When old King Harry youthful grew
> As Eagles do, or Hawks in Mew
> And did, in spite of *Pope* and *Fate*
> Behead, Rip and Repudiate
> Those too-too long-liv'd Things, his Wives,
> with Axes, Bills and Midwives Knives;
> When he the Papal Power rejected
> And from the Church the Realm dissected,
> And in the Great St PETER'S stead
> Proclaimed himself the Church's Head.
> When he his ancient Queen forsook,
> And buxom *Anna Boleyn* took,
> Then in the *Noddle* of the Nation
> He bred the Maggot, *Reformation* . . .
> But Heralds grave, report this Odd-piece
> That from old Harry's monstrous *Cod-piece*
> It had its rise, as they do trace
> Its Pedigree – a blessed Race!
> Race like its Parent, whom we find
> A man to every vice inclined,
> Revengeful, cruel, bloody, proud,
> Unjust, unmerciful and leud . . .[30]

Like its model, *Hudibras*, Ward's poem had an apparatus of historical and theological notes drawn 'not only' as its publisher assured the public 'from Statutes, Injunctions, Articles, Canons, Liturgies Homilies etc., but likewise from the most approved historians, as Holinshed, Heylyn, Stow, Camden, Speed, Baker, Burnet, Clarendon etc'.[31] Burnet was particularly maddened by the way in which his judicious treatment of Henry VIII – a bad man, but raised up as an unstoppable instrument to clear the ground for a reformation which would otherwise have been smothered – was invoked in defence of Ward's crude hatchet job. Burnet recognised that in many ways Ward's book was Sander versified, 'impious abuse' 'apt enough to take with those who were disposed to divert themselves with a shew of wit and Humour, dressed up to make the reformation appear both odious and Ridiculous'. Sander's description of Anne Boleyn – unfashionably black hair, pointed oval face, buck tooth, sallow complexion, wart under her chin, six fingers on one hand, is the source for Wolsey's grotesque description of Anne, as reported by Ward:

   . . . Her Hair, black as the Plume of Crow
Encroaches on each Side of Brow;
She's colour'd like one in Green-sickness
When free from Paint an Inch in Thickness;
Large Balls of Cheeks, taper to Chin,
From Ear to Ear she's mouth'd, and in
Her upper Gum there sticks a Tooth
That wants Room for it in her Mouth.
Above her Breast, beneath her Chin,
There grows an ugly Sort of Wen,
   . . . Clad with soft Down, and here and there
It bristles out a Sort of Hair
That's seen in threes and fours to stand.
She has six Fingers on a Hand,
All this considered, can a King
Affect so hideous a Thing?[32]

In fact, Ward's account of the reformation did have some notably distinctive elements: he paid a good deal of attention to changes in the Prayer Book, and dwelt on the progress of Edwardian icono-clasm: he was interested in the practical consequences of Protestant liturgical and theological changes, as in his account of the differ-ence between the communion service in the first and second Prayer Books, which draws on Marian polemical publications:

This second Book, in other Rubricks,
Has also many pretty new tricks:

As turning Altar into Table,
And setting Minister to gabble
At the North-side, and on the South
Communicants with open Mouth
To take in Lumps of leavened Bread
On Trenchers in square Gobbets laid.
And none being stinted to their Parts
Drink hearty draughts of Wine in Quarts,
And what escapes their greedy Throttles
The drunken Parson puts in Bottles.
What bless'd Communion Bread remains
Falls to the Sexton for his Pains.
Where waiting for't the hungry Gull
Crams both his leathern Pockets full.[33]

There are other distinctive features, including a lengthy and quite shrewd section devoted to the shortcomings and idiocies of metric psalmody (in the course of which he draws on the satirical verse of Laudian writers like Richard Corbett). Canto three deals with Elizabeth's reign, including the Nag's Head Fable,[34] with a splendidly gruesome set piece for her death scene, in which Henry VIII returns to tell her that she, like him, is damned.[35] Canto four is devoted to an account of the renewed Jacobean debate about Anglican orders, and a savage attack on the Laudians for aping Rome while denying the substance of Catholic teaching. Ward's treatment of civil war and Restoration focuses almost exclusively on the transformation of the Prayer Book which they brought, and the proof this offered that the Prayer Book was perceived even by the Laudians as defective to start with: the poem concludes with a burlesque account of the Popish Plot and the Rye House Plot.

Ward's poem proved surprisingly popular: it had new editions in 1715, 1716, 1719, and 1747, and it clearly found a readership outside the Catholic community: Burnet noted its dependence on Sander, but thought the poem appealed to the fashionable libertine ethos, for which anything cheerfully anti-clerical or anti-religious was grist to the mill.[36] Its popularity indicated the resilience of some Elizabethan controversial ploys, and the abiding force of Sander's polemic: but in its use of material from Heylyn, and its focus on the dissatisfactions of the High Churchmen of the Laudian and Restoration period with the foundation documents of Elizabethan Anglicanism like the Prayer Book and articles, it also indicated the presence of a new factor in Catholic reformation historiography, an ability to harness internal Anglican debates in the service of Catholic apologetic.

This trend was materially advanced by the publication between 1708 and 1714 of Jeremy Collier's *Ecclesiastical History of Great Britain*, the second volume of which was devoted to the long English reformation. Burnet had complained that Heylyn's history of the reformation sometimes read as if it had been written by a closet papist, 'though I doubt not that he was a sincere protestant'. He felt less sure about Collier, as well he might. Collier's book was written to an agenda absolutely different from Burnet's, and designed to defend a high clericalist reading of the history of the English Church. Collier was a sacramentalist who took pains to demonstrate uncomfortable and forgotten truths such as Calvin's richly patristic and high Eucharistic teaching, and he emphasised wherever he could the Catholic dimension of the English reformation. He defended the monasteries as edifying places of retirement, prayer and rational poor relief, and he was also at pains to castigate the invasions of ecclesiastical jurisdiction by Crown and Parliament, and in tracing the history of the reformation saw as much to blame as to praise. The results could be startling, and, to early Hanoverian Protestant readers, at times deeply shocking. His assessment of the merits of Queen Elizabeth can stand as representative.

> If this Queen's Usage of the clergy was compared with what they met with in the reign of Henry VIII, tis to be feared it might be said, her little finger was thicker than her father's loins: and that he disciplined them with whips, but she chastised them with Scorpions. And as to the parallel between the princess and her Sister Queen Mary: may it not be affirmed, that the one made Martyrs in the Church, and the other beggars? . . . And therefore, reserving the honour of the reformation to Queen Elizabeth, the question will be, whether the Resuming of first fruits and tenths, putting many of the Vicarages in this deplorable condition, and settling a perpetuity of poverty upon the Church, was not much

more prejudicial than fire and faggot? . . . But this only by way of Query: and so much for Queen Elizabeth's reign.[37]

It is hard to avoid the suspicion that Collier has his tongue firmly in cheek here, but such sentiments from a Protestant writer horrified readers nourished in the certainty that the reformation's greatest blessing was the delivery of the nation from the fires of Smithfield, and that Queen Elizabeth was the nation's deliverer: his formidably learned and extremely readable book provided a new slant on the English reformation, considerably less wedded than Burnet's to a Foxeian historiography, and far more likely to appeal to Catholics. For the rest of the century, Collier would be treated by Catholic writers as a valuable ally and resource.

Collier's work underlies a good deal of the narrative sections of the most monumental Catholic contribution to reformation history of the eighteenth century, Charles Dodd's *Church History of England,* published in three folio volumes between 1737 and 1742, nominally at Brussels though in fact at Wolverhampton, near which, at Harvington Hall, Dodd was the Catholic missioner.[38] He himself was a Lancashire man and a secular priest, Douai- and Paris-trained, whose real name was Hugh Tootell.[39] Dodd's work was a semi-official project: he had the financial backing and moral support of the Duke of Norfolk, the Worcestershire landowner Sir Robert Throckmorton and the wealthy Yorkshire antiquary Cuthbert Tunstall, as well as of two of the vicars apostolic, Bishops Stonor and Hornyhold. It was not his first venture into historical writing: as we saw in chapter 9, in 1713, under the thin disguise of a Protestant chaplain in the English army in Flanders, he had published a history of the foundation of the English College at Douai, which was in fact a savage attack on the Society of Jesus.[40] The English Catholic community both in London and in France and Flanders was currently deeply involved in the Jansenist debate. Some of the leading secular clergy saw in the controversy a rerun of their own troubles over the past century: under the theological quarrel they saw a profound conflict of ecclesiologies, identifying the Janesenists in Holland in particular as the defenders of right order and hierarchy, and a rigorous and primitive doctrine of penance, against the subversive usurpation and presumption of mushroom religious orders like the Jesuits. The staff at Douai had therefore come under suspicion of heterodoxy, and Dodd's pamphlet was an intervention on their behalf. He followed it in 1715 with a series of scurrilous public letters to the Provincial of the English Jesuits, *The Secret Policy of the English Jesuits*, in imitation of Pascal's *Provincial Letters*, rehearsing a hundred years of grievance – the stirs between Jesuited priests and the secular clergy in Wisbech Castle in Elizabeth's reign, the quarrels over the archpriest Blackwell, the condemnation of the Oath of Allegiance, the Jesuit frustration (as Dodd saw it) of the secular clergy's attempts to secure a bishop for England, and the maltreatment of Richard Smith in the reign of Charles, down to the ousting of the secular clergy from control of the Lime Street Chapel in London in the reign of James II.[41]

Dodd's *Church History* is therefore a complex work, with more to it than a single agenda, and which added to the emphases derived from Sander's generation the internecine Catholic rivalries which had ripened and festered in the course of the seventeenth century. Its first volume treats the reformation down to the end of Mary's reign, volume two covers the reigns of Elizabeth and James, volume three takes the story down to the Revolution, but includes a coda on the Jansenist disturbances at Douai. While volume one is designed to correct Protestant accounts of the reformation, the later parts of the work, more than half the total, have a very different target, and are a continuation of the polemic against the Jesuits and in favour of a distinctive reading of the history of the seventeenth-century Catholic community as the struggle of a loyal English Church to assert its independence and maturity against Roman craft or sheer incomprehension, fomented by the self-interest of the Jesuits.

This is not, of course, how Dodd presents the work: his preface adopts the lofty high-minded tone of an Enlightenment writer:

So many things happen to bypass our opinions, and viciate our taste; that the strongest resolution of impartiality will prove insig-nificant unless we be carefully guarded against those temptations, whereby men are not only daily surprised, but as it were driven into errors and mistakes. *Ignorance, education, religion, passion* and *party disputes*, are in a kind of confederacy to seduce mankind. Under their influence we become both writers and readers; and place ourselves on the bench of judges ....[42]

Protestants might take offence that he portrayed the Catholic opponents of the reformation in a good light, as able and conscientious men, but Protestants had nothing to fear:

> My design not being to enter into the capital quarrel about religion, I presume all mankind are upon a level as to personal merit. And if I either extoll or depreciate particular persons, I am only accountable to justice and decency in my characters. Nature has very little regard either to religion or climate. She deals her favours with an impartial hand ... Neither church nor *state* can suffer in their just claims, by representing a Catholick handsome, learned, or patient under afflictions. Tis depriving God and nature of their due, not to acknowledge and bow to excellence, wheresoever they are found; and an instance of sottish partiality to confine them within the limits of our idle speculations.[43]

Dodd's handling of the key moments of reformation – the Divorce, the characters of Henry VIII, Anne Boleyn, Cranmer, Elizabeth – try to strike a sometimes painfully self-conscious balance, citing writers on both sides, refusing to make sweeping judgements, avoiding the shriller notes of earlier Catholic historiography. Foxe, Burnet and secular historians like Echard are all pressed into service. But Collier was an enormous help here, for from his non-juring perspective he made many of the strictures and insinuations a Catholic might want to emphasise: Dodd's long treatment of the Divorce, for example, is heavily dependent on the corresponding sections of Collier, and his implacably hostile account of Cranmer is clinched with quotations from Collier. Dodd, however, breaks with the Sander tradition, recently revived by Ward, in his handling of the ordinations of the first Elizabethan bishops. He devotes a great deal of space to the issue, presenting a lucid account of the Nag's Head Fable but also summarising the evidence against its truth, printing the relevant section of Parker's register, listing the controversialists on both sides, and in the end refusing to pass a judgement one way or the other, though he made no secret of his conviction that Parker and his colleagues, because of the deficiencies of the ordinal, were not in any case validly consecrated.[44]

Gabriel Glickman has found evidence of the purchase of Dodd's book by many Anglican clergy, and some approval by non-Catholic readers of its anti-Jesuit and anti-papal tone.[45] Yet Dodd's massive work made surprisingly little critical stir. To some extent this was because of its format. The work of Burnet and Strype had made it mandatory that any large-scale reformation history must have its load of documentary 'vouchers'. Where Burnet had relegated these to documentary appendices, however, and arranged them in the sequence in which they were cited in the text, Dodd's documents are distributed in a bewilderingly complex system throughout the three volumes, making continuous narrative development impossible. The book was chronically awkwardly arranged, its material broken down into endless subdivisions – records of clergy, gentry, parliament, bishops, cardinals and so on – which, together with the lack of adequate indices, made and make it a nightmare to use.

Dodd's book faced in two directions: inwards, addressing hoary internal conflicts within the Catholic community, outwards to the England of the late 1730s in which the monopoly of the Church of England was evidently under considerable pressure, and in which whig scepticism about the whole idea of a confessional state seemed propitious to attempts to question the national myth about the reformation. In the end, his book mattered more as a round in the boxing match being slogged out within the Catholic community than as a contribution to a shift in reformation historiography more generally. The book's short print run and provincial publication, and possibly the anti-Catholic scare which followed the '45 Rebellion, deprived it of much of a readership: by the 1790s it was considered a scarce book.

Dodd's was in any case by no means the only major Catholic exercise in reformation scholarship of the early 1740s: as his book was going through the press at Wolverhampton, Richard Challoner's *Memoirs of Missionary Priests* was being printed in London.[46] Challoner's book has a fair claim to be the only Catholic work of the period on the reformation which still retains some historical value. It set out modestly enough to present a part edition, part paraphrase of the best contemporary sources for the lives of the Elizabethan and Stuart martyrs: despite the inevitable limitations of such an enterprise, it remains a reliable, readable and moving source book, as much a classic in its own way as Foxe, and considerably less bitter in tone. But Challoner had no aspirations to offer an account of the reformation as a whole, there is no grand narrative and the reverential tone of his two volumes ensured that their audience was almost exclusively Catholic, their use devotional.

The 20 years after the '45 were an ambiguous time for the Catholics of England. The last throw of Jacobitism had helped fix, for those minded to attend to it, the association of popery and tyranny, popery and wooden shoes: anti-Catholic preaching and writing would add the '45 to the catalogue of proofs of Roman perfidy. But these were also years of a gradual relaxation of anti-Catholic attitudes, of cautious consolidation and even expansion of the Catholic community in London and elsewhere, and, within limits, the acceptance of Catholicism as part of the pluralism of Hanoverian England. Among the educated, animosity gave way to supercilious condescension.

The publication of Thomas Phillips' *Life of Cardinal Pole* in 1764 was in many ways well calculated to exploit this changing ethos.[47] Pole was the great unknown figure in the English reformation: a member of the royal family, a distinguished humanist, a known reformer within the Tridentine Church of Rome, a moderate in an age of extremes, he was a potentially sympathetic figure, despite the fact that he had been Bloody Mary's Archbishop of Canterbury, and had addressed a dauntingly harsh letter to Cranmer while the latter awaited execution. If a Catholic reading of the reformation was to be offered, it could hardly be better done than by a sympathetic presentation of Pole's career, for this would allow the English story to be placed in a wider European context, would involve an exploration of the character of the Council of Trent and the Tridentine reforms, and would place under the microscope the most notorious episode in the received anti-Catholic account of the reformation, the reign of Mary Tudor.

Thomas Phillips himself was a man of means who had travelled widely in Europe, a Jesuit who had left the Society as a result of a quarrel about his chosen course of studies, and who, having obtained a sinecure canonry of Tongres from Charles Edward Stuart, had served as domestic chaplain to the Earl of Shrewsbury and the Actons of Aldenham. At the time of the publication of his book, he was chaplain to the Berkeleys of Spetchley Park.[48]

Phillips' enterprise was made possible by the publication between 1744 and 1757 of a five-volume edition of Pole's *Letters* and other writings edited and introduced by Cardinal Angelo Maria Quirini, a distinguished Benedictine Renaissance scholar and the Vatican librarian.[49] For Pole's biography Quirini had relied heavily on the contemporary life of Pole by his protégé Ludovico Beccatelli. As reviewers were to demonstrate, a great deal of Phillips' work consisted of unacknowledged translation and paraphrase of Quirini's editorial matter and Beccatelli's life, disguised as original research. Much of the rest of the book was composed in a similar way by looting secondary authors, themselves often read at second hand, and most of Phillips' use of Protestant reformation historians like Burnet or Collier, for example, was in fact lifted directly from Dodd.

Phillips' book was presented with all the rhetoric of philosophical history – Hume's *History of England* had been completed only three years before. Judged rightly, Phillips told his readers, Pole's conduct would reveal itself as 'one uniform system of the most exalted and at the same time the most amiable virtues, which can adorn a man of Letters, a Patriot, a Christian, and a Prelate'. To see this, Protestant readers would have to step outside their prejudices – those who find this difficult 'are desired to step two hundred years back into the manners, religion and policy of the persons they either approve or find fault with; and consider the circumstances out of which their respective characters rise, and which form themselves about them ... to satisfy a Reader either unwilling or incapable of judging of men and actions by an impartial and universal standard is not in the nature of this undertaking'.[50]

Phillips, it has to be said, didn't take his own advice: for all the play of polite learning and eighteenth-century objectivity, his account of the reformers and their motives is uniformly hostile and one-sided: the style is the style of enlightenment man, but the voice is the voice of Sander. His account of Anne Boleyn, therefore, cites Protestant authorities like Fuller, Burnet, Collier and Echard; in fact, however, it is essentially a paraphrase of the account of Anne in the *Rise and Growth of the Anglican Schism*, sharpened to heighten the salacious element in her personality, right down to the description of her death:

Then laying herself down on the scaffold, and preserving a decency she had been unmindful of on other more important occasions, she drew her garments below her feet, and received the stroke which finished a life of levity, error and lewdness.[51]

Phillips' book did present a detailed account of the Council of Trent which attempted to do justice to the moderate position of Pole and his fellow *Spirituali*, and his account of Mary's reign offered a corrective to all previous writing about it, with an extended discussion of the work of Pole's Legatine Synod of Westminster, the first to describe in detail the measures Pole had proposed for the reform of the English Church – though he did not have access to Pole's legatine register. The atrocities of Mary's reign are blamed on Bonner and Philip of Spain, and on the Queen's understandable but doting fondness for a husband 12 years her junior, a foreigner who was proud, remote, cruel, and melancholic; they are partially apologised for on the grounds of the provocations of a Protestantism which was politicised and seditious. Phillips' picture of Philip II is, above all, of a foreigner who could speak not a word of English.

Phillips' book aroused more general interest – and was more widely reviewed – than any other Catholic historical enterprise of the century. Its appearance and the trickle of replies over the next two years coincided with a minor scare about the growth of popery in England, orchestrated by anti-Catholic agitators like Thomas Hollis; William Payne, the Protestant carpenter, had just begun his prosecutions against Catholic clergy in London, and journals like the whig *Monthly Review* ran coverage of the literature provoked by the Pole biography alongside reviews of alarmist schemes for limiting the growth of popery. The book was treated not as history, but as an apologia for the 'nonsensical tenets of the Romish church'.[52] Phillips' glaring plagiarism, laid bare by the ablest of the Protestant respondents to his book, Timothy Neve, prevented his portrayal of Tridentine Catholicism from having the effect it perhaps deserved, as did the book's unreconstructed Catholic partisanship, as vehement and unphilosophical as anything Sander had ever written.[53]

Catholic reflection on the reformation in the later decades of the eighteenth century was conditioned by two factors: the struggle for political liberties and the revolutionary upheavals in France. Under these two pressures, deep rifts opened within the Catholic community; the leading Catholic gentry, organised in the London 'Catholic

Committee' which met at the Freemason's Tavern, embraced a whiggish 'Cisalpine' position which emphasised the rationality, moderation and Britishness of the English Catholics.[54] Their clerical apologists, most notably the historian Joseph Berington, presented the history of the Catholic community in England as the story of a native Church denied its proper hierarchical structure by Rome and the religious orders; to Rome and the Jesuits Berington attributed the failure of the Catholic community to integrate into British society. In 1793 Berington published an edition of the *Memoirs of Gregorio Panzani*,[55] the bungling papal agent to the court of Charles I in the 1630s. The base text of the *Memoirs* came from the papers of Charles Dodd, and the historical preface offered a résumé of the Elizabethan and Jacobean religious situation, in which Elizabeth appears as a rational and wise ruler who begins by tolerating the Catholics, but was driven by papal intransigence and Jesuit plotting into harsh measures. Had Rome granted the English Church its own bishops and repudiated the Jesuits all would have been well.

Berington's view of Rome and the Jesuits was borrowed from the secular clergy tradition which passed through the writings of Dodd, sharpened and rendered more extreme by the impact of an Enlightenment Catholicism closer to the Jansenism of Scipio Ricci and the Synod of Pistoia than to Muratori, and by the French Revolution. It owed very little indeed to new historical evidence or a genuinely new historical approach, and Berington's brief account of the reformation period is worthless, his view of the Elizabethan government's attitude to Catholicism hopelessly naive, determined by the political agenda of the 1790s rather than the historical real-ities of the later sixteenth century. Berington was in fact a decent medievalist by the standards of eighteenth-century England, and he produced both a spirited and learned defence of the character and conduct of St Thomas Becket, as well as an English edition of the letters of Abelard and Héloïse.[56] But his historical insight, such as it was, abandoned him when he came to consider the history of the reformation and counter-reformation, where he writes for all the world like the anti-Catholic journalists of the *Monthly Review*; hardly a page of Panzani is without an insinuation or a sneer against the tyrannical court of Rome or the wily Jesuits. It is perhaps an irony that at the very moment when recusant historiography most decisively renounced the Sander tradition, it should have produced its least convincing account of the causes and course of the English reformation.

Till fairly recently, if the average modern reader had ever heard of Berington's friend and younger contemporary John Lingard, it was likely to be as the author of a much loved if rather loose paraphrase of the hymn Ave Maris Stella, *Hail Queen of Heaven, the Ocean Star*. A prolific pamphleteer and controversialist, Lingard's greatest achievement, the ten-volume history of England published between 1819 and 1830,[57] moulders now on the shelves of second-hand bookshops; you can buy a handsome leather-backed set on the internet for a good deal less than the value of the binding. Yet in his day, Lingard was a celebrity, the best-known and most widely read English Catholic writer. For a century his history was eagerly bought and read, within and beyond the English Catholic community. It ran through five large and expensive editions in his lifetime, and went on being printed after his death. It set a new benchmark for historical accuracy and balance: for historians of the generation after him, like Thomas Babington Macaulay or James Anthony Froude, Lingard's was the game to beat. His history was quickly translated into French and Italian, abridged into a single volume for use as a textbook in schools, and the whole work was reissued by Hilaire Belloc before the First World War with a continuation taking the narrative up to the reign of George V: Belloc's edition remained in print into the late 1920s. More than a century as a standard text is not a bad innings for an enormous and, if the truth be told, rather drily written work of history.

Lingard's Victorian celebrity is rather ironic, because he was to his very fingertips a man of the eighteenth-century Enlightenment. Educated in pre-revolutionary France at Douai College, he was one of the founding staff when the college moved back to England and eventually settled on a windblown moor at Ushaw, near Durham, and it was there he chose to lay his bones. Lindgard's body was brought to the college in true Victorian style, by train, from Hornby in Lancashire, where he had spent most of his priestly life. But though he lived till 1851, Lingard was a man of the Regency, and a recusant, born into an eighteenth century in which by the laws of English it was still a felony to celebrate Mass, and Catholic churches were disguised to look like factory buildings or nonconformist meeting houses. To the day of his death Lingard took it for granted that the Church in England could only win acceptance if Catholics accommodated themselves to the style and mindset of the Protestant society around them. He disliked all elaborate display or ceremony in the liturgy, allowed no music in his chapel and campaigned to have the recitation of the Litany of Our Lady and devotions to the Sacred Heart banned from English Catholic worship. He dismissed medieval hymns like the sweetly devotional *Jesu Dulcis memoria* – Jesus the very thought of thee – as 'pitiful rhapsodies, a farrago of amorous expressions', and that notable lack of empathy for the spirit of the Middle Ages was one of his main limitations as a historian. He hated Gothic architecture, thought Pugin a crank and deplored the influx of converted Anglicans from the Oxford movement as a gaggle of pious oddities. He viewed even John Henry Newman's conversion with suspicion and something not far short of contempt. Unsurprisingly, he deplored the style and extravagance with which Cardinal Wiseman and Pope Pius IX had reintroduced the Catholic hierarchy into England in 1850, and, famously, he refused to wear the newly fashionable clerical collar, sticking to the traditional eighteenth-century white cravat, and declaring that he hoped 'they would let an old man alone as to his throat, and not suffocate him with a Roman collar'.[58]

In recent times very large claims have been made for Lingard as a historian. He has been called 'The English Ranke', equal in originality and authority to the great German pioneer of suppos-edly value-free empirical history, whose methods and approach, it has been claimed, Lingard anticipated by more than a generation.[59] The Welsh scholar Ernest Jones has even suggested that Lingard is the greatest of all English historians, a pioneer of source criticism who, in the early nineteenth century, invented and deployed histor-ical techniques whose sophistication and thoroughness would not be equalled again till the late twentieth century, and Jones' claims have been accepted by historians as different and as distinguished as Norman Davies and the late Patrick Collinson.[60]

And certainly Lingard himself went out of his way to impress his neutrality and empiricism on his readers. So in the preface to the *History* he insisted that he had made it his strict rule 'to admit no statement merely upon trust, to weigh with care the value of the authorities on which I rely, and to watch with jealousy the secret workings of my own personal feelings and prepossessions'. Such vigilance, he claimed, was essential for any historian who aspires to truthfulness and impartiality: to do otherwise was 'to sacrifice the interests of truth to the interests of party, national, or religious, or political'.[61]

Lingard certainly believed what he said: but, as we shall see, his claims to impartiality can't quite be taken at face value, and to do so distorts both the nature, and the true achievement, of Lingard's historical work. For all his archival empiricism, he was no neutral historian. Rather, he wrote history as an apologist for the Catholic Church. Lingard lived in an age of struggle for Catholic Emancipation, and throughout his career he was a dedicated warrior for Catholic civil and religious rights, producing alongside his historical work a steady stream of pamphlets and polemical and apologetic journalism in the Catholic cause. In fact, everything Lingard wrote was designed to forward that cause: that is manifestly true of his first large-scale venture into historical writing, his first book, on the *Antiquities of the Anglo-Saxon Church* published in 1806.[62] A venerable Catholic historical tradition going back to Thomas Stapleton's Elizabethan translation of Bede's Ecclesiastical History saw Anglo-Saxon England as a resource for Catholic apologetic.[63] Lingard similarly deployed the history of the Anglo-Saxon Church to prove the antiquity and native Englishness of contemporary Catholic beliefs like the presence of Christ in the Eucharist, and Catholic practices like prayer for the dead. The same apologetic aim is less obviously present in his masterwork, the *History of England*, but it is central to its construction, and to overlook or play down this apologetic purpose and present Lingard as a pioneer of value-free history is to miss the most important fact about his life's work.

This is no new claim: much the same point was made 30 years ago by Dr Sheridan Gilley in a pioneering essay,[64] and Lingard's apologetic concerns have been exhaustively explored more recently by Dr Philip Cattermole.[65] But it is worth emphasising Lingard's essential continuity with the recusant historical enterprise by looking at one of the most characteristic and revealing aspect of Lingard's *History*, his handling of the English reformation under Henry VIII which, as we have seen, had been a battleground between Catholics and Protestants ever since the sixteenth century.

The basic Protestant reformation narrative had been inherited from Foxe's *Actes and Monuments*, and, like Sander's rival Catholic version, Foxe's work was dedicated to the creation of a myth. For Foxe, the story of the reformation is that of a great and providential liberation, the restoration of true Christianity and the deliverance of the English nation from the rule of the Roman antichrist. His book was written to reveal the hidden shape of history, an age-old cosmic struggle, between the Church of Christ on the one hand, consisting of Protestants and the medieval forerunners of Protestantism like the Lollards, and on the other, the Synagogue of Satan, led by the papal antichrist, perverting the truth and persecuting the saints from the time of Gregory the Great to Foxe's own day.

But though just as partisan and vitriolic as Sander's, Foxe's work made large historical claims. It was, according to the title page of the first edition, 'Faithfully gathered and collected according to the true copies and wrytings certificatory, as well of them that suffered: as also of the others that were the doers and workers therof.' And in his Latin introduction 'to the educated reader' Foxe contrasted the legends and fables of papistical martyrologies with his own book, which, he claimed, represented something entirely new in historical writing, since it had been 'drawn and woven together from the archives and registers of the bishops themselves, as well as the letters of the martyrs themselves'.[66]

Both Burnet and Strype wrote at the service of a national myth, in which England's reformation featured as the culmination of an age-old struggle between a free people and a tyrannical and superstitious Church. The break with Rome had liberated the nation for a providential future as the pioneer of political and religious freedom. Even historians who didn't share Burnet and Strype's religious commitments, like Hume, the atheistic philosopher whose *History of England* was the standard work by the end of the eighteenth century, followed Burnet and Strype in portraying Catholicism as a repressive and superstitious force, and the reformation accordingly as a great deliverance.

Lingard lived in an age when such anti-Catholic historical claims lay at the heart of British politics. The first 30 years of the nineteenth century saw a sustained struggle for nonconformist and Catholic civil rights, and Lingard set himself to break the hold of that traditional anti-Catholic narrative by writing a history that would challenge the selectivity of the sources on which it was based. He was not himself a great archival explorer: he worked from his small presbytery in the Lancashire village of Hornby, which he left seldom and with great reluctance. So Lingard relied heavily on printed sources, not so big a drawback as one might imagine. The Public Record Office did not yet exist, and the first volumes of the great Tudor historical projects like the *Calendar of the Letters and Papers of the Reign of Henry VIII* would not reach print till long after Lingard's death. But he lived in an age of blossoming interest in antiquities and historical sources, and the years in which he was writing saw the publication of a huge array of historical memoirs, letters and diaries: Evelyn's diary, first edition 1818, Pepys, 1825. Journals like *Archaeologia* regularly contained transcripts of historical source material. Lingard's Tudor volumes rely heavily on this kind of published source material, not least Foxe, Burnet and Strype.

But not exclusively. Lingard may not have been a pure empiricist, but he was the first historian to bring material from European and Catholic archives to bear on the traditional narrative, material which had never been used by English historians; he was an accomplished linguist, with an excellent nose for potentially important deposits of documents. He scrupulously followed up the archival hints found in often obscure published work drawn from all over Europe. So while he stayed at home in Hornby, a network of friends and agents went hunting on his behalf in the libraries and archives of Paris, Rome, Vienna, Valladolid and Simancas. All of them yielded documents setting English events in an unfamiliar and challenging European Catholic perspective: indeed, Lingard became nervous about drawing too much attention to material from the Vatican archives because he knew that its Roman provenance would be enough to discredit it in the eyes of many of his Protestant readers.

As we've already noted, very large claims have been made for Lingard's pioneering historical methods. And it is certainly true that he brought an entirely new level of thoroughness and balance to the writing of reformation history. He almost never made an unsupported claim, and was scrupulous in documenting every detail of his narrative. But for all that, he wrote to an agenda. As he told his friend and mentor John Kirk:

> Through the work I made it a rule to tell the truth, whether it be for or against us, to avoid all appearances of controversy, that I might not repel protestant readers, and yet furnish every proof in our favour in the notes: so if you compare my narrative to Hume's, for example, you will find that with the aid of the notes it is a complete refutation of him, without appearing to be so. This I think is preferable. In my account of the reformation I must say much to shock protestant prejudices: and my only chance of being generally read ... depends on my having the reputation of a temperate writer ... This however I can say: that I have not conceded a single proof in our favour ...[67]

This apologetic agenda explains some of the omissions as well as the inclusions in Lingard's account of the reformation. Many of his Catholic contemporaries, for example, felt he had said far too little in condemnation of the Dissolution of the Monasteries, and that his defence of the reputation of the Tudor monks was luke-warm and half-hearted. They were not far wrong: Lingard devoted in all just three paragraphs to the Dissolution, and his motives for this ludicrously cursory treatment were decidedly mixed. One of them was his reluctance to draw attention to monastic corruption. He had dutifully examined the records of the Henrician Visitation of the monasteries, whose hair-raising files were preserved in the Cotton manuscripts. Some of Lingard's most successful revisions came from bringing to bear a forensic scepticism to loaded source material of just this kind, and David Knowles' meticulous dissec-tion of the evidence in the twentieth century would show that the Henrician visitors' reports do indeed leave a lot to be desired as objective evidence for the state of the Tudor monasteries. But for once Lingard was inclined to take a source unfavourable to Catholics at face value, and he accepted the charges of superstition and financial and sexual corruption the files contained. Most Tudor monks, he thought, were 'a degenerate and time-serving class of men ... To have met the charge by denying it would have acted contrary to my conscience, since I believed it in many respects true, and contrary to sound policy because it might have provoked someone to lay before the public eye in a pamphlet or review that mass of whoredom and immorality contained in the [Cotton] Manuscripts.'[68]

Lingard's scrupulous conscience here, however, was not entirely a matter of historical objectivity. His involvement in some bitter contemporary disputes between the secular clergy and the religious orders undoubtedly coloured his views of monks in general, and inclined him to believe in Tudor monastic guilt; he despised religious orders of every kind, and considered that 'the discipline of . . . all the religious orders is the most absolute despotism, I never could admire it'. So the internal disputes of early nineteenth-century Catholicism help account for what is otherwise one of the most puzzling deficiencies in Lingard's treatment of the Henrician reforms.

Lingard's credentials as an archival historian are in any case not quite straightforward. He had himself worked through a good deal of the Tudor material in the Cotton library. But the searches for source material carried out on his behalf by agents and assistants in other archives and libraries were necessarily more hit and miss. They were rarely neutral trawls for everything which might happen to be in a particular archive. Instead, they were often targeted hunts for specific kinds of evidence which he hoped would set the record straight, and advance the cause of Catholic Emancipation. He commissioned his friend Robert Gradwell, Rector of the English College in Rome, to search out all the English material he could locate in the Vatican archives, but his interest was more focused than that open-ended commission suggested. As he wrote to Gradwell, 'In a word you see what I want: whatsoever may make the Catholic cause appear respectable in the eyes of a British public. I have the reputation of impartiality – therefore I have it more in my power to do so . . .' and Gradwell noted in his diary that Lingard 'wants proofs of Anne Boleyn's criminal conversation with Henry, and that Rome inculcated loyalty to English Catholics'.[69]

Still, these methods did turn up archival treasure in abundance – the despatches of the Imperial and French ambassadors to the courts of Henry, Mary, Elizabeth, throwing a flood of light on court intrigue and the motivation of the major actors: in the Vatican Gradwell copied a bundle of 17 love letters from Henry to Anne

Boleyn, enabling Lingard to blow a hole through the accepted and highly sanitised Protestant chronology of their relationship, to demonstrate that it had started before Henry had expressed any doubts about the validity of his marriage to Queen Catherine, and Lingard was able to show that Anne had indeed been pregnant before her wedding.[70]

Lingard was a massively thorough and cautious worker, and he rarely ventured an inch beyond what the sources warranted: his dry Augustan style, speculative caution and sardonic intelligence gave his historical judgements weight, and they have in fact worn better than those of almost any other nineteenth-century English historian. But many of his key contentions, soberly presented as the outcome of scrupulous research, and backed by multiple citations from the archives, in fact represented reworkings of polemical claims which had first been set out by Tudor Catholic polemicists. His overall interpretation of Henry's reign, as some critics noticed, owed a great deal to the writings of Cardinal Pole. So there was a familiar feel to Lingard's forensic and meticulously documented demolition of the characters of Anne Boleyn and of Archbishop Thomas Cranmer.

The extent to which, despite all his undoubted archival pioneering, Lingard worked within the Catholic historiographical tradition explored in this chapter can be gauged from his treatment of Archbishop Cranmer. Tudor Protestant propagandists like Foxe had been ambivalent about Cranmer. His involvement in the reigns of Henry and Edward in the trial, torture and execution of Protestant dissidents like Joan Boucher, and his own multiple recantations under Mary, made him a somewhat unsatisfactory martyr for the Protestant cause, though his heroic final gesture in holding his hand in the flames of his pyre did much to rescue his reputation. But by the time Burnet came to write in the late 1670s Cranmer had become an admired Protestant icon, and Burnet made generous allowances for the archbishop's lapses from grace. For Catholics, matters were of course otherwise. Cranmer was seen by them as the unscrupulous heresiarch who had given Henry spurious justification for two divorces – his own from Queen Catherine of Aragon, and England's from the Holy See. In Cranmer's own lifetime Catholic hostility had fastened on what they saw as the barefaced perjury with which

Cranmer had begun his archepiscopate. Before consecration, bishops and archbishops had to take an oath of loyalty to the Pope: Cranmer, who would soon be denouncing the Pope as antichrist, baulked at this oath, but Henry, who wanted no possible doubts about the validity of his new archbishop's credentials, insisted it must be taken. So, before the consecration, Cranmer quieted his conscience by swearing an affidavit before lawyers in the chapter house at Westminster, claiming that in taking the consecration oath he was not in fact committing himself to obey the Pope. In Mary's reign Cardinal Pole would bitterly reproach Cranmer, now awaiting trial and condemnation, for this perjured oath, which Pole believed had poisoned all Cranmer's actions as archbishop, and had been the first step on his road to damnation. The charge of perjury was hard to refute, though J. A. Froude would dismiss the incident as unimportant – 'It is idle trifling to build up, as so many writers have attempted to do, a charge of insincerity upon an action which was forced upon him', a claim which, however, sounds decidedly hollow, given that some of Cranmer's Catholic contemporaries would heroically endure an excruciating death rather than take a false oath.[71] As Cranmer's highly sympathetic modern biographer Diarmaid MacCulloch has observed, with considerable understatement, this 'morally dubious manoeuvre'... 'can reflect no credit on him at all'.[72] So, naturally, Cranmer's perjured oath was duly absorbed into the standard Catholic reformation polemics: as Sander wrote, by this act Cranmer 'took possession of the archbishopric like a thief'. Protestant historians did the best they could in extenuation, by claiming, falsely as it happens, that during the consecration ceremony Cranmer had publicly repeated the provisos he had sworn to in private, 'by which', Burnet wrote, 'if he did not wholly save his integrity, yet it was plain he intended no cheat, but to act fairly and above board'.[73] But this cut no ice with Catholics, for whom Cranmer's perjury provided the clue to his entire character: as Thomas Ward wrote in his 1710 verse riposte to Burnet's *History, England's reformation*,

Cranmer, who was steel within
And Brass against all checks of sin
Taught all of them how they might be
Just like himself, from conscience free.[74]

Unsurprisingly, therefore, Lingard reiterated this traditional Catholic condemnation of Cranmer's hypocrisy. 'By what casuistry could the archbishop elect . . . reconcile it with his conscience to swear canonical obedience to the pope', Lingard asked, 'when he was already resolved to act in opposition to papal authority?' In a carefully understated footnote he marshalled the surviving evidence to prove that Cranmer had made no public declaration at his consecration about the sense in which he took the oath: 'it was evidently his object to clothe it with all the canonical forms, but at the same time to conceal its purport from the public'.[75]

Lingard's dissection of Cranmer's character was relentless, and took him into territory unknown to earlier Catholic polemicists. When Anne Boleyn was arrested and accused of adultery and incest in May 1536, the entire Protestant cause which she had patronised and protected seemed under threat. At this juncture, Cranmer, whose patroness Anne had been, wrote Henry a famous letter expressing his amazement at the accusations against the Queen, but pleading with the King not to cast off the Gospel in casting off his wife. The letter, first published by Burnet, has always divided commentators, but Cranmer's advocates have put a benign face on it: Burnet thought the letter did Cranmer great credit, for it had 'all the softness that so tender a point required, in which he justified her as far as was consistent with prudence and charity'.[76] Diarmaid MacCulloch, slightly tetchily, compares those who see Cranmer's letter as 'a craven piece of toadying' to journalists 'braying' 'in complex situations for churchmen to give a moral lead with strong, simple answers', and he characterised the letter as 'a model of pastoral wisdom and courage'.[77]

This does not seem to me a compelling reading of a crucial document, and Lingard's less friendly interpretation is surely nearer the mark, for the rhetorical drive of Cranmer's letter seems very much at odds with its overt sentiments. Throughout the letter Cranmer carefully expresses his esteem for and indebtedness to Anne in the past tense: 'I never had better opinion in woman than I had in her', and while expressing the pious hope that she may be able to establish her innocence, he went on to say that 'if she be proved culpable, there is not one that loveth God and his gospel that will favour her, but must hate her above all other'. And the letter has a devastating postscript, in which Cranmer announces that, having now heard the evidence against Anne, he was deeply saddened that such faults could indeed be proved against her, thereby turning the letter into an acceptance of her guilt and 'that she hath deserved never to be reconciled to your grace's favour'. With the best will in the world, it is hard to avoid the conclusion that the purpose of Cranmer's letter was not to help Anne, but to extricate the evangelical cause from her ruin, while outwardly preserving the decencies he could hardly avoid, since both he and Henry knew that he owed his position to her patronage. That at any rate was how Lingard understood the letter, which becomes for him yet another proof of Cranmer's duplicity. As he wrote, it 'certainly does credit to the ingenuity of the archbishop in the dangerous position in which he thought himself placed: but I am at a loss to discover in it any trace of that high courage and chivalrous justification of the queen's honour which have drawn forth the praises of Burnet and his copiers'.[78]

Some of Lingard's most trenchant judgements, therefore, even when backed by reference to the documentation, echoed attitudes and claims deeply embedded in an older Catholic historiography. But where other Catholic historians deployed such claims and the evidence which supported them as knuckledusters for hand-to-hand sectarian street fighting, Lingard presented his gleanings from the archives with the sober precision of a pharmacist measuring out the ingredients of a laxative. His consummate and unemphatic judiciousness represented an entirely new and powerful kind of persuasion. The five editions which his vast and expensive *History* ran through in his lifetime was testimony to a readership well beyond the Catholic community.

Lingard's publisher perfectly well understood the value of the work as apologetic. An advertisement aimed in 1840 at potential Catholic purchasers of the *History* spelled the matter out:

Dr Lingard has done his account of the Reformation with exquisite tact. The superficial reader may think him cold when narrating the sufferings of Catholics during the long continuance of the penal laws. The acute thinker will rise from the perusal of Dr Lingard's pages with a much stronger abhorrence of those hateful penal laws, of that wasting series of persecutions, than if the author had coloured his narrative with even the most indignant and burning eloquence ... Few would ever suspect him of being a Catholic.[79]

Lingard's success in shaking the traditional Protestant account was deeply alarming to many, not least because in the mid-1820s the main contentions of his work were given far wider popular currency by the radical campaigner William Cobbett. Cobbett stripped Lingard's views of their judiciousness and balance, wrapped them in a torrent of invective and hurled them like bricks through the windows of the Church of England. His popular *History of the Protestant Reformation*, based on Lingard, was an all-out attack on the Anglican establishment as an elitist plot against the liberties of the common people of England.[80] J. A. Froude's great history of Tudor England was in many ways a riposte to Lingard and his imitators, and the ineffable Charles Kingsley, welcoming Froude's first volumes on Henry VIII five years after Lingard's death, articulated a widely shared unease about the influence of this Catholic challenge to the traditional grand narrative of the reformation.

Lingard is known to have been a learned man, and to have examined many manuscripts which few else had taken the trouble to look at; so his word is to be taken, no one thinking it worth while to ask whether he has either honestly read or honestly quoted the documents. It suited the sentimental and lazy liberality of the last generation to make a show of fairness by letting the Popish historian tell his side of the story, and to sneer at the illiberal old notion that gentlemen of his class were given to be rather careless about historic truth when they had a purpose to serve thereby; and Lingard is now actually recommended as a standard authority for the young by educated Protestants, who seem utterly unable to see that, whether the man be honest or not, his whole view of the course of British events since Becket first quarrelled with his king must be antipodal to their own; and that his account of all which has passed for three hundred years since the fall of Wolsey is most likely to be (and, indeed, may be proved to be) one huge libel on the whole nation, and the destiny which God has marked out for it.[81]

Kingsley was of course here being grossly unjust to Lingard: he had an irrational but unshakable conviction that every Catholic priest must be a liar and Kingsley was to apply that conviction gratuitously and directly to John Henry Newman in the course of another review of Froude's later volumes in 1863, thereby provoking the writing of Newman's *Apologia pro vita sua*. That prejudice blinded Kingsley to the scrupulous accuracy and the unrivalled mastery of his sources which Lingard brought to the writing and revision of English History. But if Kingsley was wrong about Lingard's historical reliability, he was not mistaken about the aim of Lingard's writing, or the secret of his success in establishing himself as a standard authority even for many Protestants. It was perfectly true that Lingard's view of the whole course of British events since Becket first quarrelled with his King was in Kingsley's phrase 'antipodal' to that of the entire Protestant historiographical tradition on which Victorian national identity had been based: from his perspective, Lingard's sceptical Catholic deconstruction of the received account of the English past really did represent a menace, 'one huge libel on the whole nation, and the destiny which God had marked out for her'.

Lingard's negative take on the leaders of the Tudor reformation would be eagerly taken up by the Tractarians. It was one of the contributory factors in Newman and Froude's developing contempt for Cranmer, and thereby contributed significantly to the rift between the Oxford movement and the older High Churchmanship. It is an irony that Lingard, who never took the Tractarian converts seriously, should have played so significant a role in their unsettling ambivalence towards the Church of England's reformation inheritance. But Lingard and Newman are linked in other ways, too. Lingard's *History* probably contributed more than any other single book to the rehabilitation of Catholicism as an intellectual force in early Victorian England. Newman's *Apologia* was the book which persuaded an even larger late Victorian reading public that a Catholic priest might also be a civilised and sympathetic Englishman. So it seems entirely fitting that the *Apologia* should have been triggered by a casual aside in a review of Froude's *History of Tudor England*, a book written at least in part to contest John Lingard's traditional Catholic take on England's reformation.

Notes

1   Elizabeth Evenden and Thomas S. Freeman, *Religion and the Book in Early Modern England, the making of John Foxe's 'Book of Martyrs'* (Cambridge, 2011); John N. King, *Foxe's Book of Martyrs and Early Modern Print Culture* (Cambridge, 2006); Thomas S. Freeman, 'Fate, Faction, and Fiction in Foxe's Book of Martyrs', *Historical Journal*, 43 (2000), pp. 601–23.

2   Eamon Duffy, *The Eoin MacNeill Lecture 2012: The Reformation and the Grand Narrative* (Irish Manuscripts Commission, Dublin, 2013).

3   Nicholas Harpsfield, *Dialogi sex contra summi pontificatus: monasticae vitae, sanctorum, sacrarum imaginum oppugnatores, et pseudomartyres/ab Alano Copo Londinensi editi auctiores nonnullis in locis & castigatiores . . . [etc.].* (Antuerpiae: ex officina Christophori Plantini, 1573); Harpsfield also contributed powerfully to recusant historiography of the reformation in two major works which circulated but remained unpublished till the nineteenth and twentieth centuries: Nicholas Pocock, (ed.) *A Treatise on the Pretended Divorce between Henry VIII and Catherine of Aragon* (Camden Society, new series, vol. 21, London, 1878), and *The Life and Death of Sir Thomas More* (ed.) Elsie Vaughan Hitchcock, Early English Text Society, original series, vol. 186 (London, 1932).

4   For some useful overviews of conflicting perspectives on the history of the reformation, from all of which I have benefitted, W. B. Patterson, 'The Recusant View of the English Past', in Derek Baker (ed.), *The Materials, Sources, and Methods of Ecclesiastical History* (Oxford, 1975), pp 249–62; Thomas Betteridge, *Tudor Histories of the English Reformation, 1530–83* (Aldershot, 1999) and Felicity Heal, 'Appropriating History: Catholic and Protestant Polemics and the National Past', *Huntington Library Quarterly*, 68.1–2 (2005), pp. 109–32.

5   Robert Persons, *De Persecutione Anglicana Epistola. Qua explicantur afflictiones, aerumna, & calamitates gravissimaem cruciatus etiam & tormenta & acerbissima martyria, quae Catholici nunc Angli, ob fidem patiuntur . . .* (Romae: Ferrarius, 1582).

6   Anthony Petti, 'Richard Verstegan and Catholic martyrologies', *Recusant History* vol. 5 (1959), pp. 64–90: Paul Arblaster, *Antwerp and the World: Richard Verstegan and the International Culture of Catholic Reformation* (Leuven, 2004); Frank Lestringant, *Le Théâtre des cruautés des hérétiques de notre temps de Richard Verstegan. En annexe, le Martyre des trente-neuf allant au Brésil de Louis Richeome. (Collection Magellane)* (Paris, 2005); Christopher Highley, 'Richard Verstegan's Book of Martyrs' in Christopher Highley and John N. King (eds), *John Foxe and His World* (Aldershot, 2002), pp. 183–97.

7   For the complex history and influence of Sander's book, Christopher Highley, '"A Pestilent and Seditious Book": Nicholas Sander's Schismatis Anglicani and Catholic Histories of the Reformation', *Huntington Library Quarterly*, 68 (2005), pp. 151–71.

8   Quotations are taken from the admittedly somewhat problematic Victorian translation, Nicholas Sander, *De Origine ac Progressu Schismatis Anglicani* (1585), trans. D. Lewis (London, 1877).

9   Gilbert Burnet, *The History of the Reformation of the Church of England*, vol. 1 (Oxford, 1829), p vi.

10   *Reginaldi Poli Cardinalis Britanni ad Henricum Octavem Britanniaeregem libri IV* (Rome, Antonio Blado [1536] 1538: English translation by Joseph G. Dwyer, *Pole's Defence of the Unity of the Church* (Westminster, Md., 1965).

11   *Pole's Defence*, p. 193.

12   Eamon Duffy, *Fires of Faith: Catholic England under Mary Tudor* (New Haven and London, 2009), pp. 34–44.

13   Ibid., pp. 45–8, 178–86; Carolyn Colbert, '"It is perilous stryvinge with princes": Henry VIII in works by Pole, Roper and Harpsfield' in Thomas Betteridge and Thomas S. Freeman (eds), *Henry VIII and History* (Farnham, 2012), pp. 65–85, and Victor Houliston, 'Fallen Prince and pretender of the Faith: Henry VIII as seen by Sander and Parsons', in ibid., pp. 119–34. On recusant downplaying of More's Erasmianism, J. K. McConica, 'The Recusant Reputation of Thomas More' in R. S. Sylvester and G. P. Marc'hadour (eds), *Essential Articles for the Study of Thomas More* (Hamden, 1977), pp. 138–49.

14   The immediate ascendancy of Sander's narrative is reflected in its adoption as the core round which Robert Persons constructed his monumental but never completed history of the English

reformation, *Certamen Ecclesiae Anglicanae*, commissioned by Pope Clement VIII, and intended as a continuation of Harpsfield's (at that time unpublished) *Historia Anglicana ecclesiastica a primis gentis svsceptae fidei incvnabvlis ad nostra fere tempora dedvcta, et in qvindecim centvrias distribvta/avctore Nicolao Harpsfeldio Archidiacono Cantvariensi. Adiecta breui narratione de diuortio Henrici VIII. regis ab vxore Catherina, & ab Ecclesia Catholica Romana discessione/scripta ab Edmvndo Campiano* (Douai, 1622); Jos. Simons (ed.) *Robert Persons S.J., Certamen Ecclesiae Anglicanae* (Assen 1965) introduction *passim* and p. 43: Houliston, 'Fallen Prince', pp. 128–32.

15   Sander, *De Origine*, p. 25.

16   For John Foxe's contrasting account of Anne, Thomas S. Freeman, 'Research, Rumour and Propaganda: Anne Boleyn in Foxe's "Book of Martyrs"', *Historical Journal*, 38 (1995), pp. 797–819.

17   'Notes as to the consecration of Archbishop Matthew Parker', by the Rev. Henry Barker MA. From Arthur Lowndes, *Vindication of Anglican Orders* (New York, 1911), reproduced in Project Canterbury, http://anglicanhistory.org/orders/orders1.html, accessed 21 June 2016.

'On the 12th of May, 1614, George Abbot, Archbishop of Canterbury, in the presence of these famous Bishops. John (King) of London, William (James) of Durham, Lancelot (Andrews) of Ely, James (Montague) of Bath and Wells, Richard (Neyle) of Lincoln and John (Buckeridge) of Rochester, produced Parker's Register and showed it to four Roman Catholics namely, Mr. Collington whom some people at that time called the Archpriest, Mr. Laithwaits, and Mr. Faircloth, Jesuits, and Mr. Leake, a Secular Priest, desiring them to carefully examine the same. "They" as Bishop Godwin remarks in his book De Prœsulibus, "looked at the Book, handled it, turned it over, perused it, as much as they pleased, but the Consecration of Parker especially they read, and turned over again and again, and having accurately and carefully considered the book, the letter, the matter and all other things contained in it, they at length bear testimony to the truth and validity of it; confessing that it seemed to them to be a book beyond all exception": these details are derived from the account of the 1614 inspection by Francis Godwin, *De praesulibus Angliae commentarius, omnium episcoporum necnon et cardinalium ejusdem gentis nomina, tempora, seriem, atque actiones maxime memorabiles ab ultima antiquitate repetita complexus. Ad fidem monumentorum in archivis regiis, Lamethanis, &c. &c/recognovit, plurimis in locis (adjectis annotationibus) ad veritatem reduxit, et perpetua demum serie ad praesens usque saeculum continuavit Gul. Richardson, S.T.P., Coll. Emman. Cant. Magister, et Eccles. Lincoln. Canonicus* (Cambridge, 1743), p. 219.

18   The lives by William Roper and Nicholas Harpsfield have been conveniently edited by E. E. Reynolds, *Lives of Sir Thomas More* (London, 1963).

19   Thomas Stapleton, *The Life and Illustrious Martyrdom of Sir Thomas More*, trans. Philip E. Hallett (London, 1928).

20   Thomas Bailey, *The Life and Death of that Renowned John Fisher Bishop of Rochester* (London, 1655).

21   Anthony Milton, *Laudian and Royalist Polemic in Seventeenth-Century England: The Career and Writings of Peter Heylyn* (Manchester, 2012); John Drabble, 'Thomas Fuller, Peter Heylyn and the English Reformation', *Renaissance and Reformation/Renaissance Et Réforme* New Series/Nouvelle Série 3.2 (1979), pp. 168–88.

22   Starkie, Andrew, 'Contested Histories of the English Church: Gilbert Burnet and Jeremy Collier', *Huntington Library Quarterly*, 68 (2005), pp. 335–51; Tony Claydon, 'Latitudinarianism and Apocalyptic History in the Worldview of Gilbert Burnet, 1643–1715', *Historical Journal*, 51 (2008), pp. 577–97.

23   S. L. Greenslade, 'The authority of the tradition of the early church in early Anglican thought' in G. Gassmann and V. Vajta (eds), *Tradition in Lutherismus und Anglicanismus* (Gutersloh, 1972), pp. 9–33; D. C. Douglas, *English Scholars 1660–1730* (London, 1951); Norman Sykes, *From Sheldon to Secker* (Cambridge, 1959); Jean-Louis Quantin, *The Church of England and Christian Antiquity* (Oxford, 2009).

24   Andrew Starkie, 'Henry VIII in History: Gilbert Burnet's History of the Reformation, 1679' in Betteridge and Freeman, *Henry VII and History*, pp. 151–63.

25   *ODNB* memoir by G. H. Martin and Anita McConnell.

26   James Cargill Thompson, 'John Strype as a Source for the Study of Sixteenth Century Church History' in *Studies in the Reformation, Luther to Hooker*, ed. C.W. Dugmore (London, 1980), pp. 192–201.

27   Burnet, *The History of the Reformation of the Church of England,* vol. III, part II (Oxford, 1829), quotation at p. xlix.

28   A representative example of late Restoration Catholic historical critique of the Church of England is George Anselm Touchet, *Historical Collections out of Several Grave Protestant Authors,* 1674: a copy of the 1686 reissue was in the library of John Dryden; see Thomas J. Clancy, *English Catholic Books 1641–1700* (Aldershot, 1996), nos 970 and 971.

29   Brief biography by Geoffrey Scott in *ODNB*: quotations from Ward's *England's Reformation* are from the two-volume edition of 1747: *England's Reformation (From the Time of K. Henry VIII to the End of Oates's Plot): A Poem in Four Cantos* (London, 1747).

30   *England's Reformation,* vol. 1, pp. 1–2.

31   Ibid., vol. 1, 'The Publisher to the Reader', unpaginated preface.

32   Ibid., vol. 1, pp. 17–18.

33   Ibid., pp. 94–5.

34   Ibid., pp. 200–216.

35   Ibid., vol. 2, pp. 65–73.

36   *The History of the Reformation of the Church of England,* vol. III, part II, pp. iv–v.

37   Jeremy Collier, *An Ecclesiastical history of Great Britain, chiefly of England: from the first planting of Christianity to the end of the reign of King Charles the Second. With a brief account of the affairs of religion in Ireland. Collected from the best ancient historians, councils, and records. In two volumes* (London, 1708–1714), vol. 2. p. 671.

38   Charles Dodd, *The Church History of England from the Year 1500 to the Year 1688, Chiefly with regard to Catholicks* ('Brussels', 1737).

39   *ODNB* memoir by Thompson Cooper and Alexander Du Toit.

40   *The History of the English College at Doway, from its first foundation in 1568, to the present time . . . . By R.C.* chaplain (London, 1713).

41   *The Secret Policy of the English Society of Jesus, Discover'd in a series of attempts against the clergy. In eight parts and twenty-four letters. Directed to their Provincial* (London, 1715, reissued 1717).

42   Dodd, *Church History of England,* vol. 1, p. iii.

43   Ibid., p. vii.

44   Dodd, *Church History of England,* vol. 2, pp. 269–90.

45   Gabriel Glickman, 'Gothic History and Catholic Enlightenment in the works of Charles Dodd (1672–1743', *Historical Journal,* 54 (2011), pp. 347–69.

46   Richard Challoner, *Memoirs of Missionary Priests, as well secular as regular; and of other Catholics, of both sexes, that have suffered death in England,* Anon. 2 vols (London, 1741–2). The best edition is that edited by John Hungerford Pollen (London, 1924).

47   Thomas Phillips, *The History of the life of Reginald Pole,* 2 vols (Oxford, 1764).

48   *ODNB* memoir by Thompson Cooper and Adam I. P. Smith.

49   Angelo Maria Quirini (ed.), *Epistolae Reginaldi Poli Cardinalis et aliorum ad ipsum,* 5 vols (Brescia, 1744–58).

50   *The history of the life of Reginald Pole,* vol. 1. pp. v–vi.

51   Ibid., vol. 1, pp 139–42.

52   *Monthly Review,* 31 (1764), pp. 131–42; 32 (1765), pp. 139–46.

53   For the critical response to Phillips, Timothy Neve, *Animadversions upon Mr. Phillips's History of the life of Cardinal Pole* (Oxford, 1766); Benjamin Pye, *The life of Cardinal Reginald Pole: written originally in Italian, by Lodovico Beccatelli, . . . and now first translated into English. With notes critical and historical* (London, 1766); Glocester Ridley, *A review of Mr. Phillips's History of the life of Reginald Pole* (London, 1766); Richard Tillard (London, 1765).

54   On Cisalpinism, see E. Duffy, 'Dr Douglass and Mr Berington: an eighteenth-century retraction', *Downside Review,* 88 (1970), pp. 246–69, and the three linked essays 'Ecclesiastical Democracy Detected', in *Recusant History,* 10 (1970), pp. 193-209 and pp. 309-31; vol. 13 (1974), pp. 123-48; Joseph Chinnici, *The English Catholic Enlightenment: John Lingard and the Cisalpine Movement, 1780–1850* (Shepherdstown, 1980); John Vidmar, *English Catholic Historians and the English Reformation, 1585–1954* (Sussex, 2005), chapter 2.

55   Joseph Berington, *The Memoirs of Gregorio Panzani: giving an account of his agency in England, in the years 1634, 1635, 1636* (Birmingham, 1793).

56   Joseph Berington, *The History of the reign of Henry II . . . In which the character of Thomas a Becket is vindicated* (Birmingham, 1790), 2 vols; *The history of the lives of Abeillard and Heloisa . . . with their genuine Letters* (Birmingham, 1788).

57   I have used the sixth revised and expanded edition, *The History of England from the First Invasion by the Romans to the Accession of William and Mary in 1688* (London, 1855).

58   The classic biography, highlighting all these traits, is Martin Haile and Edwin Bonney's delightful, *The Life and Letters of John Lingard* (London, 1911); this should now be read alongside the richly researched life by Peter Phillips, *John Lingard, Priest and Historian* (Leominster, 2008).

59   Donald Shea, *The English Ranke: John Lingard* (New York, 1969).

60   Ernest Jones, *John Lingard and the Pursuit of Historical Truth* (Brighton, 2001). Dr Jones set his account of Lingard in a broader historical argument in his remarkably powerful *The English Nation: the Great Myth* (Stroud, 1998), for the impact of which see Glenn Burgess, review of *The English Nation: the Great Myth* (review no. 88) http://www.history.ac.uk/reviews/review/88, accessed: 18 June 2016; Vidmar, *English Catholic Historians,* chapter 3.

61   Lingard, *History,* vol. 1, p. 6.

62   John Lingard, *The Antiquities of the Anglo-Saxon Church,* 2 vols (Newcastle, 1806).

63   *The History of the Church of Englande. Compiled by Venerable Bede, Englishman. Translated out of Latin into English by Thomas Stapleton Student in Divinitie* (Antwerp, 1565).

64   Sheridan Gilley, 'John Lingard and the Catholic Revival' in *Studies in Church History,* 14 (1977), pp. 313–27.

65   Philip H. Cattermole, *John Lingard: The Historian as Apologist* (Kibworth Beauchamp, 2013).

66   *The Unabridged Acts and Monuments Online* (HRI Online Publications, Sheffield, 2011). Available from: http//www.johnfoxe.org [Accessed: 20.06.2016, 1563 edn, pp 9–11.

67   Phillips, *Lingard,* p. 162.

68   Ibid., p. 217.

69   Haile and Bonney, *Lingard,* pp. 162–4; Phillips, *Lingard,* pp. 163, 212–14, 218. Cattermole, *Historian as Apologist,* p. 101; Cattermole marshals overwhelming evidence of Lingards apologetic selectivity in both the search for and the deployment of archival material, cf. *Historian as Apologist,* pp. 136–94.

70   The Boleyn letters were in fact available in print in the *Harleian Miscellany,* where Lingard had read them, but he suspected that material disgraceful to Anne had been suppressed by the editor, so he asked Gradwell to examine the holograph letters 'and if you find any expressions which seem to denote any improper liberties to have passed between them, to notice such passages for me'; Phillips, *Lingard,* p. 268 n. 38, Cattermole, *Historian as Apologist,* p. 199.

71   James Anthony Froude, *The History of England from the Fall of Wolsey to the Defeat of the Spanish Armada,* vol. 1 (London, 1879), p. 438, n. 1.

72   Diarmaid MacCulloch, *Thomas Cranmer: A Life* (New Haven and London, 1996), pp. 88–9.

73   Burnet, *History of the Reformation,* vol. 1, p. 261.

74   Ward, *England's Reformation,* vol. 1, p. 43.

75   Lingard, *History,* vol. 5, pp. 3–4.

76   The letter survives in the Cotton Manuscripts, Printed in J. E. Cox, *Miscellaneous Writings and Letters of Thomas Cranmer* (Cambridge, 1846), pp. 323–4; MacCulloch, *Cranmer,* p. 157.

77   MacCulloch, *Cranmer,* p. 157.

78   Lingard, *History,* vol. 5, p. 35, n. 3.

79   Rosemary Mitchell, *Picturing the Past: English History in Text and Image 1830–1870* (Oxford, 2000), p. 183.

80   *The History of the Protestant Reformation in England and Ireland,* 2 vols (London, 1829). Cobbett's book was endlessly reissued by Catholic publishers, and re-edited in the 1890s by Cardinal Gasquet.

81   Charles Kingsley, *Sir Walter Raleigh and his time* (Boston, Mass., 1859), p. 428.

PART THREE

The Godly and the Conversion of England

II

The Reformed Pastor in English Puritanism

In a series of brilliant and seminal publications extending over almost 30 years, culminating in his Birkbeck lectures *Peace in the Post-Reformation*,[1] John Bossy explored the relationship between Christian sacraments and ministry, and the making and healing of community. Bossy suggested that till the emergence of early modernity the Church understood its structures and rituals as primarily designed to create and sustain charity, and to defuse enmity. In this understanding, the priest was essentially a reconciler and healer, his sacramental ministrations designed to strengthen and sacralise natural bonds of kin and neighbourhood, and to infuse them with the supernatural grace of charity, which was itself understood as the life of heaven and of God himself. Baptism, penance and Eucharist were thus primarily acts of reconciliation and bonding, in which the restoration of peace to a chronically divided human society was the chief spiritual benefit: the heart of medieval experience of the Eucharist was therefore the kiss of peace. In such an understanding, teaching and preaching might and did have a place, but that place was subordinate to the minister's ritual and social functions as a maker and healer of community.

Bossy believed that somewhere round the beginning of the sixteenth century a shift which had been long preparing manifested itself, in which churchmen became increasingly uneasy at the interlocking of natural and supernatural bonds. Ecclesiastical reformers strove to drive a wedge between the sacred rites of the Church, and the structures of profane society. Baptism, long seen as a rite of passage into the web of kinship and neighbourhood, was projected as essentially and exclusively spiritual in character, no longer viewed by the hierarchy as the creation of ritual friendship, but, rather, a washing from original sin. Attempts were made to purge the institution of God-parentage, for example, to separate Christian sponsorship and proxy promise-making from the understanding of the role of the Godfather as social protector and patron – in much the sense we associate with Marlon Brando in the *Godfather* films.[2]

As understanding of the sacraments and the society that celebrated sacraments shifted, so, too, did understanding of the pastoral office. Bossy discerned among both Catholics as well as Protestants the emergence of a new type of priest, the 'new clerks', teaching and preaching an energetic form of Christianity in which charity was understood not as a social *state*, but in terms of *acts* of charity, a code of conduct. His chosen model for these new clerks was the seventeenth-century puritan Richard Baxter,[3] but he discerned them everywhere, not least among the Jesuits and in the influential figure of Carlo Borromeo, Christian activists questioning the profane solidarities of traditional society, for whom holiness was not sacramental solidarity, but moral separation: these new clergy were thus agents of separation, not of *communitas*.

Bossy's hypothesis can be criticised in a great many of its details, but it is enormously illuminating, and he was clearly on to something important. He pointed to the emergence of reformed concern for discipline as one of the principal symptoms of this new understanding of Christianity, and, in this understanding, discipline was designed not to unite but to separate the sheep from the goats. Hence it caused a lot of trouble, put people off and did more to divide parishes than to unite them.

In all this, Bossy had in mind such reformed self-presentations as George Gifford's *Countrie Divinitie* (1582).[4] Gifford was an Essex puritan cleric (Presbyterian by conviction), who composed the dialogue *Countrie Divinitie* in order to expound a reformed vision of salvation and to satirise the conventional conformist christianity of the archtypical English countryman or villager, Atheos. In a well-known and much anthologised exchange between Atheos and his puritan interlocutor, Zelotes, a 'curious and precise fellow', Gifford sets out the contrast between Christianity precisely as social solidarity and Christianity as moral separation in the starkest terms. Zelotes asks Atheos if they have a good minister in their parish, and is told that they have 'the best priest in the country'. Asked if their minister 'doth teach them to know the will of God and reprove naughtiness among the people', Atheos replies,

> Yea that he doth, for if there be any that do not agree, he will seek for to make them friends: for he will get them to play a game or two at bowls or cards, and to drink together at the alehouse. I think it is a godly way, to make charity: he is none of these busy controllers ...

Outraged, Zelotes responds,

> I do not mislike true friendship, which is in the Lord, knit in true godliness, but I mislike this vice, which overfloweth everywhere, that drunkards meet together and sit quaffing, and the minister that should reprove them, to be one of the chief ...

Against Atheos's lamentations for a bygone age of 'true love' when 'our forefathers lived in friendship and made merrie together in good neighbourhood', Zelotes replies that true love is that which 'admonishes and reproves naughtie vice'. Atheos retorts by condemning the puritan clergy as bringers of division and conflict:

> If they be so good and godly, how cometh it to pass then there is so much debate among them? For I know towns myself, which are even divided one part against another, since they had a preacher, which were not so before. This they gain, that whereas before they loved together, now there is dissension sown among them.

Zelotes replies scornfully,

> I pray you tell me, can ye put fire and water together but they will rumble? Will ye have light and darkness to agree as companions together? ... would ye have the godly and the wicked for to be at one?[5]

The contrast between a preaching ministry, and an older model of minister as peacemaker which underlay this exchange was a recurrent one in puritan rhetoric: as William Perkins wrote in his treatise *Of the Calling of the Ministrie*, 'They are greatly deceived, who thinke a Minister to discharge sufficientlie his dutie, though he preach not, if hee keepe good hospitalitie, and make peace amongst his neighbours ... for if a Minister preach not he hath no conscience, nor can have any comfort, for that is the principal dutie of a Minister ...'[6]

And preaching was envisaged as in essence likely to divide, for it was the instrument by which God called his own out of the corrupt mass of the damned. Preachers in England addressed a 'mixt people', and so, as Richard Bernard wrote in his treatise on ministry, *The Faithful Shepherd* (1607), the preacher must be aware of the two-edged nature of his preaching, taking care to 'preach mercy to whom mercy belongeth, and ... denounce judgement freely against the rest'.[7]

Thus Zelotes' question, 'Would ye have the godly and the wicked for to be at one?' resonated through much Protestant pastoral practice, and has conditioned perceptions of Protestant ministry in much recent historical writing. Puritan clergy with Zelotes' mindset and convictions saw the community of the godly not as coterminous with the 'mixt people' of the parish, but as a remnant within it. To whom therefore did the godly cleric minister? To all within the geographical area of his parish, or to the elect? Whose were the sacraments? Everyone who counted themselves a Christian, or those whose lives demonstrated the work of grace within them?

The impact of those questions on English puritan pastoral practice would take three generations to unfold, and would become most visible during the Cromwellian period, when episcopacy was abolished and the unity of the English Church splintered: pastoral experiment had a freer hand.[8] By and large, historians of puritanism had interpreted that unfolding as a retreat and a defeat, as puritan preoccupation with discipline manifested itself in the exclusion of the ungodly majority from full participation. Keith Wrightson, in a representative study, argued that the fencing of the communion tables and the exercise of discipline by puritan ministers, designed to sift the mixed people of the state Church, was inevitably fissiparous. We are familiar with the idea that puritans formed a church within a church, encouraged by their clergy to become 'gadding folk' travelling to sermons outside their own parishes, shopping around for

the ministrations of godly clergy in preference to their local incumbent, forming social alliances with other godly folk at regional
exercises and combination sermons. The result was the formation of
inner circles of the devout in many parishes, and the smuggling of
what were in practice gathered churches into the parochial system.
Predictably, what ensued in the civil war and its aftermath was 'the
disintegration of English puritanism into a multiplicity of denominations and sects' and the 'alienation from what remained of the
national church of those common people who found themselves
both the object of the cultural aggression of the godly and at the
same time excluded from the communion of the faithful'. Wrightson
illustrated his argument powerfully from the diary of Ralph Josselin,
an Essex puritan whose main pastoral energies were directed to an
inner group of less than 40 parishioners whom he called 'our society', in contrast to the 'sleepy hearers' who formed the majority, and
to whom he did not administer the sacrament. In the parishes of
England at the Restoration the result would be the emergence of
a large body of parishioners outwardly conforming but effectively
unchurched.[9]

There is in such a summary, of course, an element of distortion
and caricature. In fact, most puritan ministers struggled to reconcile
their duty to the 'mixt congregation' of the parish on the one hand,
and the natural affinity which they believed themselves to have with
the inner circle of the truly elect on the other. In the first place,
the divided preaching of law to the unregenerate and gospel to
the elect was by no means straightforward, for the preaching of the
law was an instrument by which God might awaken his elect from
their sins to conversion: the minister could afford to write off none
but the manifestly obdurate. Puritans worked with an Augustinian
ecclesiology, which not merely tolerated but expected the presence of the ungodly and unregenerate, cockle among the good
wheat, till the great division of judgement day. And perhaps more
to the point, non-separating puritans, like the rest of the reformed
ministry throughout Europe, recognised themselves to be working
within the constraints of a national, not a gathered Church: their
pastoral practice had to accommodate the unregenerate. We can
see both the determination to work within an established Church
and the tensions this created in the ministry of the most famous

of Elizabethan puritan ministers, Richard Greenham, vicar of Dry Drayton from 1570 till 1591. A significant theologian in his own right, and a notable and passionate preacher, who was obliged to change his sweat-drenched shirt after every sermon, Greenham was also a famous 'doctor of souls', consulted widely by fellow clergy and devout laity from all over the country about cases of conscience and matters of salvation. In an arrangement which Tom Webster has recently demonstrated was to become a widespread and distinctive feature of puritan ministerial training, Greenham turned his vicarage into a domestic seminary, to which a stream of earnest young graduates from Cambridge came to be instructed in practical theology and the care of souls.[10]

Greenham, famously, was reputed to have left Dry Drayton after 20 years in deep discouragement at the failure of the puritan message to penetrate the hard hearts of his parish: he is reported by Thomas Fuller to have said to his successor in the parish: 'Mr Warfield, God Bless you and send you more fruit of your labours than I have had: for I perceive no good wrought by [my] ministry on any but one family.' Samuel Clarke, the martyrologist, observed that Greenham left Dry Drayton because of 'the untractableness and unteachableness of that people among whom he had taken such exceeding great pains'.[11] This gloomy assessment of the ministry of the most revered puritan parish cleric of the Elizabethan age has recently been challenged by Eric Carlson, who has marshalled evidence for a more positive picture of the religious transformation of Dry Drayton under Greenham's preaching. But the evidence is mixed: soon after his arrival, for example, Greenham's parishioners began to have their children christened using biblical names – Peter, Appia, Daniel, Nathaniel, Samuel, Josiah, Sarah, Deborrah, Jehosabeth, Hannaniah, Gemimah, Solomon, Manasses, Moses, Joshua, Lot, Bathsheba. The use of names of this sort has been claimed by Nicholas Tyacke to be a reliable indicator of the internalisation of puritanism in a parish.[12] It is notable, however, that this practice ceased abruptly with Greenham's departure, when the parish reverted to the popular and conventional names of the region – William, Henry, John, Elizabeth, Alice, Margaret. Whatever change Greenham succeeded in making in the religious sensibilities of Dry Drayton was evidently not very deep-rooted.[13]

However that may be, Greenham's ministry was characterised by a conscious moderation which held the polarising tendency of predestinarian theology in check, in the interests of a parochial ministry which embraced the unregenerate or half-hearted as well as the godly. Certainly he was aware of the need to maintain parish solidarities. In language strikingly reminiscent of the rhetoric of Atheos's description of his ideal country parson, Samuel Clarke records that Greenham was remembered in Dry Drayton 'as a great friend to, and promoter of Peace and Concord amongst his neighbours and acquaintance, insomuch that is any had come to him who were at variance, he would either have made them friends himself, or if he could not prevail, he would have made use of other friends to reconcile them together, thereby to prevent their going to Law'.[14]

Greenham had been a fellow of Pembroke during the uproars in the university created by the radical puritan leader Thomas Cartwright's lectures on the Acts of the Apostles. Emphatically puritan himself, refusing the sign of the cross and the surplice, Greenham was nevertheless resolutely opposed to controversy about ceremonies or Church order, refused the terminology of 'the purest churches' as applied to Geneva. But his pastoral moderation went deeper: he was prepared to find evangelical meanings for popular observances like the churching of women and the wearing of white robes or veils during churching, he bent over backward to accommodate parishioners who in accordance with traditional custom refused to be present at their own children's baptisms and he never preached against even the ceremonies he himself could not use.

There is no mistaking the puritan character of Greenham's ministry at Dry Drayton: he introduced such familiar puritan institutions as weekday preaching, regular fasts and home visits for religious conference with his parishioners. He had a high and even imperious view of the minister's authority, so that 'he could not abide to bee crossed in his admonitions because it argued a proud and prefaract spirit, not that hee respected so much his private person, as that it was a thing against God's glory and truth, and would have men swift to hear admonitions, slow to cross'. He could give that conviction stark, even brutal, expression: at the funeral of the wife of a recalcitrant parishioner he told the bereaved man 'I feared God would bury something from you, because I saw you often bury mine instructions made unto you'.[15]

Greenham had been known to argue that the English Church's lack of Calvinist discipline was a blessing in disguise, because lacking discipline, the practice of godliness was a clear sign of sincerity, whereas 'many may seem godly in discipline which do it for fear not for love', and 'discipline would hide many hypocrites which are now discovered, and cover many christian true hearts, which now are knowen, for they that are godly now are godly of conscience, being a discipline to themselves'.[16] Yet he clearly instituted in the parish a system of voluntary discipline. There was a core of parishioners whom he recognised as the real godly: with these 'whome hee tendered most in the lord, and who had given him most credit by submitting themselves wholly to his ministry', he had a specially intense relationship. The pastoral implications of the submission to his ministry were sketched out in his account of what he expected of those whom he admitted to communion.

> Hee would take these promises of them, whom first hee admitted to the sacrament, and that in the sight of God and presence of some faithful witnesses, if it might bee first that beecaus the princuiples of religion and doctrine of beginnings were the word of god, or at least most consonant with the word and not the word of man, they would grow up in further confirming of them, by further knowledge of the word. Secondly they promised to depart from their former corrupt conversation, and to labour more for holiness of life. Thirdly that they would make conscience to keep the sabbath wholy, and throughout in godly exercises to the lord, and as far as their callings did permit that they would come to bee enstructed, both by publick preaching and by private conference, in the week daies, fourthly that if they did falter hereafter into any sin ... they would suffer themselves either publickly or privately to bee admonished of it, according to the censure and the quality of the fault, fifthly they promised that if they profited not in knowledge, they would be willingly suspended from the sacrament hereafter, until they had gotten more forwardeness in knowledge again.[17]

The Book of Common Prayer required communicants to give notice to the minister before presenting themselves at the table, and the procedure outlined here might be considered an elaboration of the Prayer Book provision. It quite clearly went beyond anything explicitly envisioned or authorised by the Prayer Book, however, and was plainly also an attempt to supply the lack of a formal reformed discipline within the Elizabethan Church. The agreements of the communicants to make a strict Sabbatarianism and attendance for private conference marks of their obedience, and their acceptance of Greenham's right to admonish them and if necessary withhold communion represents a covenant which must have marked some parishioners out as having 'submitted wholly to his ministry'. But it is quite clear that not all of Greenham's parishioners were willing either to accept the full programme of instruction, oversight and scrutiny outlined above, or to abstain from the table, and he clearly operated a two-tier system: Greenham is reported as having said that 'this was his manner in dealing with them that came to the communion, if they were but indifferently instructed therunto, hee by exhortation charged them to beware what they did, and hee said hee would not wish them to come, but if they came hee would not refuse them utterly, if they lay in noe sin'.[18]

It was a saying of Greenham that 'Care in superiours and fear in inferiours cause a godly government', and the efforts of individual ministers like Greenham were rarely a matter of unaided persuasion.[19] We know from the work of Tom Webster that godly clerical associations and networks of varying degrees of formality provided a broader framework in Elizabethan and Jacobean England for the implementation of discipline than any single parish could offer, and helped create a godly ethos which lent weight and authority to the endeavours of individual clergy.[20] But it was above all the alliance between godly ministers and godly magistrates that the reformed vision of Christian discipline could approach realisation in an English context. Samuel Clarke's account of the ministry of Samuel Fairclough at Barnardiston and Kedington in west Suffolk in the reign of Charles I demonstrates what might be achieved with Greenham's methods and priorities where they had the backing of powerful secular forces.[21] Early Stuart Kedington was an ungodly place before Fairclough's arrival, with the godly a distinct and belea-guered minority: – 'The town, when he first came to it, was very ignorant and prophane . . . there was not one family in twenty who did then call upon the name of the Lord or had the worship of God set up in it.'

However, 'there was one great advantage which that Town and corner had above most other places, and that was this, That the Magistracy and Ministry joined both together, and concurred in all things for the promoting of true piety and Godliness'.[22]

The town's principle landlord and patron of the living was Sir Nathaniel Barnardiston, himself an ardent puritan. He threw his full weight behind Fairclough's ministry, personally attending catechism sessions as well as sermons, and ensuring that all his family and tenants attended also. He persuaded the towns' other landlords and employers to do likewise, and when questions were asked which the young people or servants could not answer, Barnardiston or the other masters and heads of families answered on behalf of their dependants, 'which course being taken, it was incredible to consider how greatly knowledge was advanced thereby in that town'.

Instruction via preaching and catechising was one prong of reformed ministry, the other, and potentially divisive one, was the exercise of discipline. As Greenham had done at Dry Drayton, Fairclough introduced a form of baptismal covenant as a requirement for reception of communion. At Kedington, however, this arrange-ment was given special weight by the involvement of the parish grandees. Patron and minister, Clarke tells us, wished 'to hinder the intruding or approaching of the visibly prophane unto the Table of the Lord'. To prevent this, every intending communicant was required by Fairclough to publicly 'own his Baptismal Covenant for once, before his admission to the Lord's Supper'. Thereafter 'they should submit unto admonition, in case of visible and apparent breach of that Covenant' by a known sin. Barnardiston led the way, making a formal profession of faith before the assembled parish and undertaking to perform what his godparents had promised for him in baptism. 'He was then followed by all the rest who were about to receive.' This solidarity in submission to their minister's regime 'by all the serious and sober persons of that Town' was the key to the implementation at Kedington of a highly successful 'reformation of manners', so that 'Former prophaness was forced now to hide its head: drunkeness, swearing, cursing, bastardy, and the like, were scarce known'. Clarke paints a picture of the golden age of blessing which ensued, in which people from the surrounding county jostled to move to Kedington because 'there went a secret blessing along with the gospel . . . as to temporals as well as Spirituals. It was most visible that many of the Farmers did mightily thrive and grow rich, and the landlords revenue thereby did also increase and was augmented.'[23]

The modus vivendi which ministers like Fairclough evolved within the established Church, backed by the local men of substance and making a dramatic impact on the social and religious mores of their communities, must have looked like the future in early Caroline Suffolk. Informal alliances between magistrate or landlord or mayor on the one hand, and minister on the other, underlay the success of puritanism in transforming both urban and rural communities in seventeenth-century England, from Pat Collinson's Kent or Suffolk to David Underdown's Dorchester.[24] In fact, such alliances were to prove remarkably fragile, and the hawkishness of the Laudian episcopate was to outlaw many of the expedients by which puritan ministers accommodated themselves to ministering to the 'mixt people' of the English parish. It was out of this experience of frustration rather than any inbuilt tendency within puritan theology or practice, that alternative ecclesiologies, involving the formal repudiation of the Anglican settlement, would evolve. The late 1630s and 1640s therefore would see the emergence in England of radicalised versions of puritan churchmanship and a rallying both to Presbyterianism and to independency which made the breaking up of the pre-civil war synthesis and the emergence of separating nonconformity almost inevitable. In the final section of this chapter I want to turn to attempts in the Cromwellian Church to reconstruct a working ecclesiology which could transcend these polarising energies, and which would enable puritan ministers to minister not to gathered churches or to an exclusive denominational constituency, but to the whole parish. And in particular, I want to examine the activities of Richard Baxter and his circle.

The fracturing of the institutional unity of English Protestantism which was a feature of the 1650s was at one level the consequence of the abolition of episcopal oversight and the failure of Presbyterianism to establish itself as a working alternative. Puritans had never had any confidence in the Church courts as a means of exercising the discipline they believed the Gospel demanded. Now, as the devotional and doctrinal ethos of the English Church lurched strongly in a reformed direction, many ministers ceased to administer the communion to their parishes. Stephen Marshall, rector of Finchingfield and friend of the Barnardiston family and of Samuel Fairclough, became convinced in the early 1640s of the divine obligation of exercising discipline and fencing the table: dissatisfied 'in the parochial way as now we stand', he eventually refused communion to more than half of his parish, and dealt with the ensuing uproar by ceasing to administer communion at all for seven years, before abandoning parochial ministry altogether for a London lectureship. Others took a more drastic line, 'the way of separation ... and Gatherd Churches ... according to their several opinions, because the Parishes were so bad, that they thought them uncapable of discipline'.[25]

It is important to register that, whatever the motivation of his more radical separating colleagues, for men like Marshall the imperative to institute discipline or refuse communion was no mere pharisaic desire to preserve the purity of the Church at all costs, but a fundamentally pastoral response to what they saw as the desperate plight of their neighbours. Henry Oasland, one of Baxter's neighbours as curate of the Worcestershire living of Bewdley and 'the most lively, fervent and Moving Preacher in all the County', wrote of his frustration at the lack of discipline in his parish as he encounters parishioners whose lifestyle he believed was leading them to hell:

Sir, this state is not to be abided in, either I must do more, or I must be gone, the sight of their faces terrifies my conscience, which I have not done my best for. I cannot go along the street for grief to see and meet the ignorant and the unreformed ... here I must live in sin and not do half the work I am persuaded I could do if government [he means discipline] were erected for building, strengthening preventing sin keeping souls from wandering, acquainting more with knowledge.[26]

Baxter's reaction to the ecclesial confusions of the 1650s and these anguished ministerial laments for the absence of discipline was an emphatic emphasis on the parish community, and an insistence on the responsibility of the minister for all his people, 'poor ignorant carnal sinners' as well as the godly. A large section of his most enduring work, *The Saint's Everlasting Rest*, first published in 1650, was given over to a series of exhortations addressed to both the godly laity and the godly ministry, urging them to accept responsibility for the everlasting salvation of their neighbours. To the ministers in particular he urged

> Do not do as the lazy Separitists, that gather a few of the best together, and take them only for their charge, leaving the rest to sink or swim . . . O let it be not so with you! . . . If any walk scandalously and disorderly, deal with them for their recovery . . . if they prove obstinate after all, then avoid them and cast them off: but do not so cruelly as to unchurch them by hundreds and by thousands, and separate from them as so many Pagans, and that before any such means that been used for their recovery . . . I confess it is easier to shut out the ignorant than to bestow our pains night and day in teaching them; but wo to such slothful, unfaithful servants![27]

Baxter was acutely conscious of the central dilemma of the godly tradition in attempting to reconcile the divisive nature of Discipline with the unitive logic of parochial ministry: he spelled it out memorably early in 1655 in a published letter on the ministry in London addressed to the Lord Mayor of London, Christopher Packe.

> Do you not perceive what a strait your Teachers are in! The Lord Jesus requireth them to exercise his discipline faithfully and impartially. The work is, as to teach the ignorant and convince the unbelieving and gainsaying so to admonish the disorderly and scandalous. And to reject and cast out of the Communion of the Church the obstinate and impenitent and to set by the Leprous,

that they infect not the rest, and to separate thus the pretious from vile, by Christ's Discipline, that dividing separations and soul destroying transgressions may be prevented or cured.[28]

Like many others in his circle, Baxter recognised the force of the separatists' demands for discipline and the fencing of the tables. It was, he believed, an ordinance of Christ, 'greatly conducing to the honour of the church, which is not a common prophane society, nor a Sty of Swine, but must be cleaner than the Societies of Infidels and heathens'. Besides, he recognised the pragmatic value of exercising some form of discipline as a minimal basis for persuading those inclined to separation to join with the parish community. The trouble was, Baxter thought, that a rigorous implementation of discipline as conventionally conceived created more problems than it solved. If ministers obey Christ's imperative and enforce discipline

what a tumult, what clangours and discontents will be ready to rise up against them with hatred and scorn! If all the apparently obstinate and impenitent were cast out, what a stir would they make! And if Christ be not obeyed, what a stir will conscience make?[29]

Baxter resolved these dilemmas in his own parish of Kidderminster by the development there of a voluntary system of disicipline which drew on Elizabethan and Stuart puritan practice, and which is discernibly informed by the spirit of Richard Greenham. The parish itself was immense, 'a market town with twenty villages', 'near 20 miles about'. It contained 800 households, and an adult population of about 1,800. At Baxter's arrival it was an unregenerate place, 'there was about one Family in a street that worshipped God and called upon his name': by the time he left at his ejection in 1662, 'there was not past one family in the side of a street that did not do so', and 'on the Lord's Days there was no disorder to be seen in the streets, but you might hear an hundred Families singing psalms and repeating sermons'.[30] This is a Protestant literary trope, and one could produce a dozen or more examples of the transformation of the unregenerate and drunken town into a psalm-singing paradise from compendia of puritan lives like Samuel Clarke's *Martyrologie* or his *The Lives of*

Sundry Eminent Persons in this later Age. In the case of Kidderminster, however, there does seem to have been a spectacular transformation, testified to by the five galleries which the parish were obliged to build in the church for his hearers. But preaching was by no means the main part of his ministry. With the support of the local justices of the peace and leading citizens, Baxter established a voluntary system of household catechesis, scrutiny and discipline. Every Monday and Tuesday, Baxter saw a succession of different families, 14 in a week, each brought in turn to his house by the parish clerk, not only to recite and explain the catechism with them, but for 'personal Conference with every one about the state of their own souls' – the more zealous came again to evening prayer meetings where psalms were sung and sermons were repeated. The systematic catechesis of every household in the parish was remarkably successful, and Baxter claimed that only a handful of families refused to attend, in some cases because of their extreme poverty. The catechetical sessions were in turn used as the basis for a scrutiny to establish worthiness for attendance at communion, and here he was less successful – about six hundred communicants submitted to this further form of discipline, and the rest simply absented themselves from communion. Motives for abstention varied, and included some Prayer Book loyalists who had objections to the form in which he administered the sacrament, but Baxter seems to have managed to avoid alienating the non-communicants; as he later recorded, 'Those many that kept away, yet took it patiently, and did not revile us, as doing them wrong.' He was less strict about baptism than about communion, and baptised the children of any parishioner who displayed an elementary knowledge of the Christian faith and was not living in some notorious sin.[31]

Baxter's practice here was very close to that we have seen in use in Fairclough's Kedington 20 years earlier, but though he was very conscious of systematising and continuing earlier puritan practice, he knew also that his ministry was notably more successful. Looking back on these years, Baxter marvelled that 'God should thus abundantly encourage me, when the Reverend instructors of my youth, did labour Fifty years together in one place, and could scarecely say that they had converted one or two of their parishes!'[32] The success was more than just the flourishing of his own parish: in 1653 he was instrumental in establishing the Worcestershire Association, uniting about a third of the clergy of all opinions working in and around the county, who supported each other in the exercise of the sort of informal discipline Baxter had instituted at Kidderminster. Baxter drew up for the Association a Form of Agreement which was published, and proved hugely influential in triggering the establishment of similar county associations throughout the country. In 1656 Baxter published *Gildas Sylvianus or the Reformed Pastor*, an eloquent and fiery exposition of his pastoral ideals emphasising the primacy of catechising and personal conference as the central tool of parochial ministry: his postbag filled with letters from ministers eager to emulate his success in Kidderminster.[33]

The essence of Baxter's method lay in his conviction that the most unpromising individuals and households might be brought to a genuine and saving faith, and that pastoral gentleness and persistence, not severity, was the way to elicit this faith. 'If you will take all the Parish for your church', he told John Bryan, vicar of Holy Cross, Shrewsbury, 'you must exercise the rest of Christ's disicpline and not only keepe the unworthy from the sacrament: nay you must not suffer them to keepe away themselves. You must proceed with all the gross neglecters of such ordinances, and scandalous sinners, till you have either recovered them to repentance, or rejected them.'[34] But he thought outright rejection was a drastic and last resort. Conventional puritan discipline, he thought, was too trigger-happy. The 'multitude of the scandalous in almost all places is so great, and the effects of excommunicating so dreadful, that it would tend to the damning of multitudes of souls . . . contrary to the design of the Gospel . . . we have our power to edification and not to destruction'. To cut off the ungodly makes ministers 'the cruellest enemies of the souls of our poor people . . . for as soon as ever we have rejected them, and cast them under publique shame, they hate us to the heart . . .' Patience, private conference and gentle instruction designed to encourage parishioners to accept the responsibilities of church membership were the remedy: he told Thomas Wadsworth, curate of Newington Butts, 'O the abundant Prudence, the love, the meekness, the compassionate earnestness, the impartiality, but above all, the self-denyall, unwearied diligence and patience this is necessary to the faithful practice of Church government.'[35] 'It was my greatest care and contrivance . . . that we might neither make a meer

Mock-shew of Disicpline, nor with the Independents, unchurch the Parish church ... we told the people that we went not about to gather a new church, but taking the parish for the church, unless they were unwilling to own their own membership, we resolved to exercise that discipline with all.'[36]

Baxter's pastoral practice was based on a notably more positive assessment of the spiritual state of his parishioners than was common in puritan complaint literature. In 1658 he published an extended analysis of the spiritual state of his parishioners which acknow-ledged the presence among them of 'infidelity, heathen ignorance and wicked obstinacy', but characterised the majority far more positively, even the large number of non-communicants 'that are tractable and of willing minds, that ... seem to be ignorant of the very essentials of Christianity' but who 'when I have condescend-ingly better searcht and helped them, appeared to be certainly weak in the faith, but true Christians nevertheless'.[37]

Many of Baxter's admirers and imitators recognised and were uneasy about the openness of the anthropology which underlay his ministry, and they worried that Baxter should perhaps be sterner in excluding the ungodly, and in witholding what Giles Firmin called the 'seals of the covenant' from the ungodly.[38] Thomas Gouldstone, curate at Finchley, after reading *The Reformed Pastor* lamented his 'prophane, ignorant selfwilled ... desperately wicked' parishioners, and felt that Baxter's method 'was calculated aright for the merid-ian of Kedderminster not of Finchly. I buckle under the burden.'[39] Peter Ince, rector of Donhead St Mary in Wiltshire, wrote to Baxter that 'You say ... that there would not be many found notoriously ungodly amongst our people; but truly sir the greater part of my poore people that will have their children baptised hate instruction and are as ignorant of Christianity I meane of the plainest princi-ples ... as if they had never heard of them. I did not think rationall creatures subject to so grosse and affected ignorance; and unlesse I will baptise them in all haste they run away to some idle drunken fellows and thinke all well, and truly deare Sir it is not my case alone ...'[40]

Baxter's pastoral experiment in Kidderminster, and its imitation by members of the Association Movement, and by early readers of *The Reformed Pastor*, represents an attempt to renew the pastoral methods of an older puritanism in the fraught and tumultuous context of the 1650s. His successive accounts of his own pastoral practice, and the account of the nature and responsibilities of ministry advanced in *The Reformed Pastor* and a number of satellite publications, like his *Confirmation and Restauration the necessary means of Reformation* of 1658, represent the first elaborated puritan theology of pastoral as distinct from preaching ministry in English, an account that self-consciously drew on the writings and practice of 'our old English affectionate divines', but which also emphasised the novelty and inclusiveness of what Baxter and his associates had achieved. His methods were, of course, not universally successful elsewhere, but in any case, they were destined to be set aside, with the restoration of the monarchy and the episcopal order of the Church of England. With the return of the bishops and Church courts came a rewriting of the earlier history of the Church of England. The old nonconformity, that tradition which had sought an accommodation between reformed theology and pastoral practice on the one hand, and episcopal polity on the other, came to an end, and began to be written out of the history of the Church of England. The puritans who had been among the most effective, and respected, pastors of the church, now came to be viewed, both by their enemies and their friends, as the forefathers of dissent, an alien implant which had at last been cast out – or liberated – from the Church of England, and the search for discipline, though not entirely abandoned, became now the mark of a suspect minority. Baxter recognised what had happened, and was bitter. Despite the political disasters of the Interregnum, it had been an age of marvels, in which the puritan dream of a godly commonwealth had at last been within sight of pastoral realisation:

> God did so wonderfully bless the labours of his unanimous faithful ministers, that had it not been for the faction of the prelatists on one side that drew men off, and the factions of the Giddy and turbulent sectaries on the other (who pull'd down government, cried down the Ministers, and broke all in confusion . . .) had it not been for these Impediments, England had been like in a quarter of an age to have become a land of saints, and a pattern of Holiness to all the World, and the unmatchable Paradise of the earth. Never were such fair opportunities to sanctify a nation, lost

and trodden under foot, as have been in this land of late! Woe be to them that were the causes of it.[41]

Notes

1   John Bossy, *Christianity in the West 1400–1700* (Oxford 1985); idem, *Peace in the Post-Reformation* (Cambridge, 1998).
2   John Bossy, 'Blood and Baptism: Kinship, Community and Christianity in Western Europe from the Fourteenth to the Seventeenth centuries', *Studies in Church History*, 19 (1973), pp. 129–43.
3   Bossy, *Christianity in the West*, pp. 149–51.
4   George Gifford, *A Briefe discourse of certeine points of religion, which is among the common sort of Christians, which may be termed the Countrie Divinitie* (London, 1612).
5   Ibid., pp. 1–9.
6   William Perkins, *Of the Calling of the Ministrie: two Treatises, describing the Duties and Dignities of that Calling* (London, 1605), p. 24.
7   Richard Bernard, *The Faithful Shepherd* (London, 1607), preface, unpaginated.
8   Claire Cross, 'The Church in England 1646–1660' in G. E. Aylmer (ed.), *The Interregnum* (London, 1972), pp. 99–120; J. Collins, 'The church settlement of Oliver Cromwell', *History*, 87 (2002), pp. 18–40; Anne Hughes, 'The national church in interregnum England' in Christopher Durstan and Judith Maltby (eds), *Religion in Revolutionary England* (Manchester, 2006), pp. 95–103; Christopher Durstan, 'Policing the Cromwellian Church' in P. Little (ed.), *The Cromwellian Protectorate* (Woodbridge, 2007), pp. 188–205; John Morrill, 'The Puritan Revolution' in John Coffey and Paul Lim (eds), *The Cambridge Companion to Puritanism* (Cambridge, 2008), pp. 67–88.
9   Keith Wrightson, *English Society 1580–1680* (London, 1982), pp. 206–20.
10 For Greenham, Kenneth L. Parker and Eric J. Carlson, *Practical Divinity: The Works and Life of the Revd. Richard Greenham* (Aldershot, 1998) (hereafter *Practical Divinity*); Eric J. Carlson, 'Practical Divinity: Richard Greenham's ministry in Elizabethan England' in E. J. Carlson (ed.), *Religion and the English People 1500–1640: New Voices, New Perspectives* (Kirksville, 1998); Tom Webster, *Godly Clergy in Early Stuart England* (Cambridge, 1997).
11 *Practical Divinity*, p. 23.
12 'Popular Puritan Mentality in Late Elizabethan England' in N. Tyacke, *Aspects of English Protestantism c. 1530–1700* (Manchester, 2001), pp. 90–110; Patrick Collinson 'What's in a name? Dudley Fenner and the Peculiarities of Puritan Nomenclature' in Ken Fincham and Peter Lake (eds), *Religious Politics in Post-Reformation England: Essays in Honour of Nicholas Tyacke* (Woodbridge, 2006), pp. 113–27.
13 *Practical Divinity*, p. 75; and for the general context of such problems, Peter Lake, 'The Godly and their Enemies in the 1630s' in Christopher Durstan and Jacqueline Eales (eds), *The Culture of English Puritanism*, 1560–1700 (Basingstoke, 1996), pp. 145–83; Christopher Haigh, *The Plain Man's Pathways to heaven* (Oxford, 2007), pp. 122–41, 'The Godly and the Rest'.
14 *Practical Divinity*, p. 83.
15 Ibid., pp. 174, 184.
16 Ibid., p. 139.
17 Ibid., pp. 76–7.
18 Ibid., p. 191.
19 Ibid., p. 245.
20 Webster, *Godly Clergy*, chapter 4 *passim*.
21 Samuel Clarke, *The Lives of Sundry Eminent Persons in this later Age* (London, 1683), pp. 165 ff.; and see my treatment of these issues in Chapter 13 below. For a discussion of the context and purposes of Clarke's *Lives*, Peter Lake, 'Reading Clarke's Lives in political and polemical context'

in Kevin Sharpe and Steven N. Zwicker (eds), *Writing Lives: Biography and Textuality, Identity and Representation in Early Modern England* (Oxford, 2008), pp. 293–319.

22 Clarke, *Lives*, p. 166.

23 Ibid., pp. 169–70.

24 Patrick Collinson, 'Cranbrook and the Fletchers: popular and unpopular religion in the Kentish Weald' in his *Godly People* (London, 1983), pp. 399–428; David Underdown, *Fire from Heaven: Life in an English Town in the Seventeenth Century* (New Haven and London, 1994).

25 N. H. Keeble and Geoffrey F. Nuttall, *Calendar of the Correspondence of Richard Baxter* (Oxford, 1991), pp. 149–50.

26 Ibid., pp. 125–7.

27 Richard Baxter, *The Saints Everlasting Rest* (11th edn) (London, 1677), pp. 543–4 (part III, chapter 14, section viii).

28 Richard Baxter, *A Sermon of Judgement* (London 1655), sigs A2–A10v.

29 Ibid., A7v–A9.

30 Richard Baxter, *Confirmation and Restauration the necessary means of Reformation and Reconciliation* (London, 1658), pp. 157–65.

31 Matthew Sylvester (ed.), *Reliquiae Baxterianae* (London, 1696), pp. 83–5, 91.

32 Ibid., p. 85.

33 Richard Baxter, *Gildas Salvianus; the First Part: i.e. The Reformed Pastor* (Kidderminster, 1656). By far the fullest and best discussion of the sources, aims and distinctive emphases of *The Reformed Pastor* is William Black's *Reformation Pastors: Richard Baxter and the Ideal of the Reformed Pastor* (Waynsboro: Ga., 2004).

34 Keeble and Nuttall, *Correspondence of Richard Baxter*, pp. 230–31.

35 Ibid., p. 238.

36 Sylvester, *Reliquiae Baxterianae*, p. 91.

37 Baxter, *Confirmation and Restauration*, pp. 157–65: see also Chapter 12 below.

38 Correspondence of Richard Baxter, pp. 207–8.

39 Ibid., pp. 296–7.

40 Ibid., pp. 165–6.

41 Sylvester, *Reliquiae Baxterianae*, p. 91.

12

The Godly and the Multitude

On 14 July 1667 Samuel Pepys went picknicking on the Downs at Ashtead, Surrey, 'where a flock of sheep was'. He encountered there

> the most pleasant and innocent sight that I ever saw in my life . . . .
> a shepherd and his little boy reading, far from any houses or sight
> of people, the Bible to him. The shepherd did content himself
> mightily in my liking his boy's reading and did bless God for him,
> the most like one of the old Patriarchs that ever I saw in my life,
> and it brought those thoughts of the old age of the world in my
> mind for two or three days after.[1]

Pepys' delight in this vision of the Golden Age clearly has about it a good deal of Cockney nostalgia for the innocent country life. It also displays more than a little surprise at the very notion of a shepherd boy reading, and reading the Bible at that. In fact, literate shepherds may not have been all that rare in Stuart England,[2] but many recent historians of the period would probably share Pepys' sense of anomaly, at least at the boy's choice of reading matter. For it is well on the way to being an axiom that the poor in early modern England were hostile, or resistant, or at best indifferent to Protestant Christianity.

Protestantism, runs the axiom, being a religion of the book, was the preserve of the literate. It flourished among townsmen and prospering 'rural elites'. It was an instrument of social control, a form of moral, ideological and economic discipline. The world of minister and godly book, of Sabbath observance, sermon-gadding and repetition, sobriety, chastity, respectability and thrift, stood over against the world of the ale-house and the cunning-man, of ballad and broad-side, maypoles and dancing and Sunday sports, tabling and dicing, bowling and cards, cakes and ale and getting wenches with child. This was the world of disorder and social inversion, in which magic and survivals of the old religion provided a supernatural vehicle for the repudiation of law and order and social discipline, which the middling and better sorts sought to impose on the 'rabble that cannot read'. In different ways, and with differing degrees of direct-ness or qualification, the works of Christopher Hill, Keith Thomas, Peter Clark, Christopher Haigh and Keith Wrightson have contrib-uted to this general picture.[3]

There is much in this which is incontrovertible, and much more that could only be tested by extensive study of the localities. It does seem worthwhile, however, raising a number of question marks against the assumptions which appear to underlie such thinking about the godly and the multitude, and especially the poor.[4] Granted that puritanism seems to have been most successful among the middling and better sorts, to what extent can that be attributed to some inbuilt (or developed) puritan sourness and hostility towards the poor? Did seventeenth-century puritans increasingly see the common people as an 'earthly-minded multitude', imprisoned ines-capably in 'the darkness of their natural ignorance and the dung of their own corruption'? After the collapse of the puritan pastoral experiments of the 1650s, did puritanism follow the logic of its own predestinarian vision of society and 'simply accept' the 'incorrigible profanity of the multitude', as Keith Wrightson and David Levine argued in their influential study of Terling?[5] We can agree that the godly saw the demands of the Gospel as cutting across the lifestyle of the majority of their contemporaries. Can we therefore conclude that they were hostile to 'popular culture', and, if so, was that culture perceived by them as the culture especially of the poor? Finally, can any case at all be made for popular commitment to orthodox Protestant or puritan versions of Christianity, and can any conclu-sions be drawn about the character of any such popular Christianity? How unusual was Pepys' pious shepherd? How far can we penetrate his religious world, and if we do penetrate it, how likely are we to find his inner landscape peopled by characters from *Religion and the Decline of Magic* or *The World Turned Upside Down*?

Were the godly hostile to the poor? At the very outset we bark our shins on a problem of definition. Who *were* the poor? In his famous essay on 'William Perkins and the Poor' Christopher Hill focused on 'rogues, beggars and vagabonds', over against whom he set the bourgeoisie, the real beneficiaries of the puritan gospel.[6] In subsequent discussions of the relationship between puritanism and the poor the category was widened to include most of the potential occupants of the ale-house bench, in fact 'the mass of the parishioners'.[7] So our question must be not simply were the puritans hostile to beggars, but were they hostile to the mass of the parishioners?

It would be easy to construct a case arguing that they were. One cannot read very much of Richard Baxter, for example, without encountering equations of the 'Vulgar rabble all about us' with 'a malignant unhappy sort of people'.[8] Perkins' *Foundation of Christian Religion* opens with a notorious address to 'ignorant people':

Poore people, your manner is to soothe up yourselves, as though you were in a most happy estate: but if the matter come to a just triall, it will fall out far otherwise; For yee leade your lives in great ignorance ... Now where ignorance raigneth, there raigns sinne; and Where sinne raignes, there the divel rules; and where he rules, men are in a damnable case.[9]

The works of writers like Robert Bolton, George Gifford and Arthur Dent are crammed with denunciations of the immoral majority as 'swine', 'sottish scurrill wretches', who 'willfully wallow in the mud and filth of vanishing pleasures', allegations that 'the Popish dung doth sticke still between [their] teeth', or that the poor 'speake foolishly, and ignorantly in all that [they] say'.[10]

The violence and hostility of these expressions is inescapable: it was clearly based in part on the experience of social conflict between advocates of godliness and their opponents in Tudor and Stuart England. If Keith Wrightson, Pat Collinson and others have given us vivid and persuasive accounts of godliness triumphant, puritanism as the ideological platform of the socially dominant, it is important to remember that the experience of other godly people was different, that men like Richard Baxter's father found themselves on beleaguered islands of piety in a turbulent sea of profanity. The other, and closely related, source of this hostility was the doctrine of the small number of the elect. The majority of preachers in the period, puritan or not, believed that most people were bound for hell. The puritan tended to give particular imaginative vitality to that notion, and to flesh it out in terms of his own community. As Arthur Dent wrote:

> If we come to reason, we may rather wonder that any shall be saved, then so fewe shall be saved ... First let there be taken away from amongst us, all Papists, Atheists, and hereticks, Secondly let there be shoaled out all vicious and notorious evil livers: as swearers, drunkards, whoremongers, worldlings, deceivers, coseners, proud men, rioters, gamesters, and all the prophane multitude. Thirdly, let there be refused and sorted out, all hypocrites, carnall protestants, vaine professors, back-sliders, decliners and cold Christians. Let all these I say be separated and then tell me how many sound, sincere, faithfull, and zealous worshippers of God will be found amongst us? I suppose we should not need the art of Arithmetick to number them: for I thinke they would be very few in every Village, Towne and Citie. I doubt they would walk very thinly in the streets, so as a man might easily tel them as they goe.[11]

That perspective on the fate – and therefore the nature – of the 'prophane multitude', goes a long way towards explaining the tone of the writers we have been considering. But it would be misleading to leave the matter there, for puritan writers also placed strong emphasis on the duty of compassion and love for the multitude, especially the poor. To select their harsher utterances is therefore to distort their attitudes. Indeed, those harsh utterances themselves need to be placed in a context of *mission*, and therefore, however difficult this is for twenty-first-century sensibility to grasp, of compassion.

The theme of love for and compassion towards the common people among English Protestant writers is a neglected one. It is sometimes assumed, for example, that Protestant ideologues were prepared to look favourably only on a minority of the lower orders, the 'deserving poor', in contrast to a more traditional pre-reformation view that charity to the poor was meritorious in itself, whatever the character of the recipients.[12] This emphasis on Protestant limitation of charity — and therefore of regard — to the deserving poor, has certainly been overdone. John Rogers, in his much-read treatise *Of Love*, first published in 1629, made the usual distinctions between the deserving and undeserving poor, and the need for informed and discriminating charity where resources were limited,[13] but his impassioned insistence on the primacy of love and compassion in dealing with the poor in fact subverts any such distinctions. For Rogers, our attitude to the poor must reflect that of God towards us. We must give 'with compassion', out of 'a pitifull heart and feeling of others miseries', for 'Thus did the Lord to us, when we had plunged our selves into irrecoverable misery, he tooke pity on us.'[14] And since giving must proceed from love and a sense of our own sinfulness, it must go along with compassionate contact with the poor. We should 'goe and see the miseries of our Poor brethren, their ruinous and cold houses, poore fire ... empty cupboards, thin clothing ... If our heart be not made of an Adamant, this will move us.'[15] To the objection that the poor 'be so ill-tongued one may give them never so much, and they will not give one a good word' Rogers replied that 'though some be ill-tongued, yet all are not so: they that be, yet give them, and overcome them'. To the claim that 'They be so bad and so wicked, as its pitie to give them' he replied, 'We give it not to their badnesse, but to their povertie: and may be our goodnesse to them with good counsell may make them better.'[16]

Rogers' attitude can be amply paralleled elsewhere. John Hart, in a work first published in the 1650s, insisted that 'when you give to the poor, you give to Christ', and while accepting the principle that those who can work but will not should not be relieved, went on to qualify this:

> Yet to conclude it unlawful to give to any that beg, I dare not, Christ healed the blind Beggar ... and did not reprove him, for then begging. Besides, God hath given out a Rule, Luke 6.30 *Give to every one that asketh of thee;* which command would be void and useless, if I might not give to beggars.[17]

Richard Baxter himself argued in the *Christian Directory* that though in almsgiving '*caeteris paribus* a good man must be preferred before a bad', yet since more spiritual good can often be done by giving to the bad (for thereby one may influence them), 'oft-time a bad man, is to be preferred'.[18] Spiritual good, indeed, is the key to understanding the literature of complaint from which the current negative assessment of puritan thought about the 'rabble that cannot read' is drawn. For this literature of diatribe was *missionary* in intent. Even Perkins' savage onslaught on the self-regard of the poor forms the preface to a work designed to help 'ignorant people, that they may be fit to heare Sermons with profit, and to receive the Lord's supper with comfort'. [19] If one had to identify the one central preoccupation of godly ministers in Stuart England, it would be the urgent necessity of saving the multitude. As Francis Inman wrote in 1622, in the preface to *Light unto the unlearned*:

> There be many poore servants and laborers; many that are of trades and mannuall sciences; many aged persons of weak and decaied memories. Of these, some never learned so much as to reade, some very little and most of them have or will have small leisure to learne long discourses: the world, or other vanities, taking up their thoughts and cares. Yet all these have immortall soules, to remaine after a few daies in eternal ioye or in endless paines. Of these care must be had . . .[20]

Baxter was still hammering away at this theme in 1674, with a passionate plea to the rich, under pain of damnation, to have pity on the poor, 'so full of cares how to pay their rents and debts, that they have no heart to think of the greater business of their soules', unable even to 'spare their children from work while they learn to read'. [21]

This fervent concern for the spiritual welfare of the poor and uneducated produced one of the most remarkable and neglected aspects of Protestant pastoral activity in this period, the catechising movement. Professor Ian Green has identified more than a thousand surviving Protestant catechisms produced in England by 1740, some of them reaching 50 or 60 editions, and has pointed to the 'professional zeal and . . . desire to teach the simple and unlearned' which lay behind them.[22] Since for the puritan an essential dimension of religious instruction was the task of *awakening* the sinner to his need for grace and conversion,[23] this flood of catechetical material forms the essential background for understanding the denunciatory literature we are considering. It was the same fervent concern to teach and therefore to reach the unlettered and poor which produced the urgency and the vitriolic tone of much puritan comment on the poor. It would, of course, be naive to attempt to exclude all social and religious animus from the complaint literature, but its object was not to write off the multitude, but to shake them out of their religious complacency, and at the same time to alert the better-off to the scale of the evangelistic task. John Rogers, in justification of such harsh preaching and writing, argued that it was done 'to humble them and prepare them for God'. It had to be ferocious, since 'the people be like the Smiths dogge, who can lie under the hammers noyse, and the sparks flying, and yet fast asleepe'.[24] 'We are bid, *cry aloud*', wrote Richard Baxter, 'and tell them of their sin and danger, and yet we cannot get them to regard and feel, we cannot get them to awake, nor heare us like men that have the use of reason, and love themselves ... Sirs, This, this is the case of multitudes of our neighbours, and what would you have a Minister do in such a case? ... Would you have us let them quietly go to hell, for fear of displeasing them or others, or seeming to be unmannerly or uncivil with them?'[25]

One cannot discuss puritan attitudes to the people, without considering the attitudes of the godly to popular culture. To do so is to involve oneself in a much larger debate about the nature of religious reform in the early modern period as a whole. Historians of religion, both European and English-speaking, have suggested that reformation and counter-reformation alike should be seen as involving a conflict between 'high' and 'low' culture, in its religious form between Lent and Carnival, the world of orthodoxy, literacy and moral and social discipline, over against the world of magic and superstition, good fellowship and disorder.[26] Both Catholicism and puritanism in early modern England have been handled in this way.[27] I do not wish to engage here in this wider debate, though it seems to me that it begs many questions, not least in assuming that the mass of the people were irreligious in any other sense than that attributed to them by men whose standards were both high and narrow.[28] What I should like to suggest is that it is not self-evident that puritan polemic against the profane culture they saw around them was a polemic against 'popular culture' in the straightforward sense of the culture of the lower orders. This is clearly the implication of the equation of that culture with the world of the ale-house. It is not, I think, borne out uniformly by the sources.

Certainly, puritan critics of society did presuppose a radical contradiction between a godly and a worldly lifestyle. There is, wrote Rogers, 'a naturall enmitie between the *seed of the Woman* and the *seed of the Serpent*, which all are, till they be regenerate'.[29] Their separateness was never more evident than in the use they made of leisure. 'Nay my friend', declares George Gifford's minister, Zelotes, 'I do not allow that recreation which prophane men call so, which is no recreation, but a torment to a Godly mind.'[30] The servants of God, said Robert Bolton, were 'men of singularitie' who must differ from the corruptions of the times, 'familiaritie with graceless companions, the worldlings language, prophane sports; all wicked wayes of thriving, rising, and growing great in the world'.[31]

But as that last phrase suggests, the 'prophane sports' of 'gracclesse companions' were not necessarily the pastimes of the poor. When William Hinde condemned the 'vaine and profane exercise' of 'May-games, and Summer greenes ... Footraces and horseraces, matches on their Bowling greenes' and such 'sorry and sillie vanities', he was attacking the gentry, who were the source of these abuses, and only secondarily 'the inferiour rank also'. Similarly, George Gifford saw the ale-bench culture of drinking, swearing, railing, 'cards or tables or bowls' as the characteristic vices of the leisured, notably the clergy. Richard Baxter singled out these vices – 'cards, Dice, or dancing, hunting, bowling, cocking, stage-plays and such like' as sins not *of* the poor, but *against* the poor, for they wasted the resources of the well-to-do, which should be spent on relieving poor neighbours. It was, he thought, from the gentry that servants and children learned, 'and took the same course'.[32]

Indeed, a closer look at the 'prophane' in the complaint literature highlights the difficulties in equating them in any simple way with 'the rabble that cannot read'. In Dent's *Plaine Man's Path-Way* the plain man of the title, Asunetus, an illiterate, is ultimately converted. The hardened caviller who remains obdurate and damned, on the other hand, can read, and has an extensive library of 'merry books', which suggests that he has some spare cash to throw around. This point was not lost on Baxter, and when in the 1670s he composed *The Poor Man's Family Book*, a work designed to replace Dent's classic, his caviller is a rich man, Sir Elymas Dives, 'a Malignant contradicter, . . . accounted a man of wit, and learning'. The ignorant countryman in the book, Saul, is throughout shown as tractable and fundamentally decent, and ultimately, like Asunetus, he is converted.[33] When Gifford's ignorant countryman, Atheos, dismisses the godly ministry as 'busie controllers', he assures Zelotes that 'there are more of my mind'. 'Some poore men perhaps?' inquires Zelotes, but is told, 'Nay, the best in the parish'.[34] In Richard Rogers' *Seaven Treatises* the 'rude and common sort of people . . . as ignorant for the most part, as they are rude and barbarous' turn out to number prominently among their sins that of giving their *servant* 'liberties to do what they will',[35] thereby alerting us to the problem of interpreting language which might at first sight seem to translate directly across into socio-economic equivalents.[36]

Patrick Collinson has in fact suggested that if we are to identify profane activity and counter-culture with any specific social group, the *young* seem better candidates than the poor. One could certainly find support for this in the sources we are considering. 'How farre doe they runne on heapes', complains Zelotes, 'both men and women, unto feasts may-games, dauncing, playes, bearebaitings and other such vanities.' 'Youth will be doing', answers Atheos, 'ye must not blame them, they have time enough to be holy hereafter.' At any rate, the work of Martin Ingram on Wiltshire, and of James Sharpe on the Essex village of Kelvedon Easterford, suggests that the pattern discovered by Keith Wrightson at Terling, where godliness *was* the badge of a prosperous 'village elite', and profanity and godlessness that of the multitude of poor, cannot yet be safely generalised.[37]

I have been arguing that puritan attitudes to the 'prophane multitude' were both more complex and more positive than is often allowed, and were informed by a missionary and compassionate spirit which found expression in the movement to catechise the ignorant. What of the attitude of the multitude towards the Protestantism preached by the godly; were the multitude themselves irreligious?

In a compelling and sensitive brief account of Stuart religion, Keith Wrightson argued that on the whole they were.[38] He paid full due to the pastoral dedication of ministers like Baxter, and their determined efforts to reach the 'poore ignorant people' in the 1650s by catechising and private conference. But, he argued, 'it was a forlorn hope'. The exercise of discipline and the 'fencing' of the communion tables by many ministers led to the formation of inner circles of the devout in many parishes, forming effectively gathered churches within the parish system.[39] What ensued was 'the disintegration of English puritanism into a multiplicity of denominations and sects' and the 'alienation from what remained of the national church of those common people who found themselves both the object of the cultural aggression of the godly and at the same time excluded from the communion of the faithful'. He instanced the Essex parish of Earls Colne, where the vicar, Ralph Josselin, distinguished three groups: 'our society' of the committedly godly, numbering in the end only 34 communicants; the majority of 'my sleepy hearers'; and those that 'seldom hear', by implication 'the ruder sort' – i.e. the zealous, the indifferent and the absent. When the pressure of enforced godliness was removed at the Restoration the populace showed their true colours in a 'spontaneous wave of conspicuous ungodliness', and the years that followed confirmed that henceforth for most of the poor, baptisms, weddings, and burials would comprise 'the limits of their dealings with formal religion'.[40]

Persuasive as this account is, I suspect that it takes the analysis of the Stuart religious scene offered by men like Josselin too much at face value. Many of those dismissed by Josselin as 'sleepy hearers' may well have been sincerely religious parishioners who would not or could not accept Josselin's ministrations on his harsh terms. It seems likely that historians have drastically underestimated the amount of real grass-roots loyalty to Prayer Book Anglicanism in the mid-seventeenth century.[41] There were many who sincerely accepted the traditional forms of English Protestantism, above all the Prayer Book, and for that reason rejected the pattern of godliness offered by men like Josselin. There were, too, many 'honest protestants' who found the rigidities of puritanism excessive. When Antilegon told Philagathus in Dent's fable that his condemnation of ballads and merry books was 'more precise than wise' and that 'there be wiser men then you, which do both read, allow and take pleasure in those bookes', he was speaking, certainly, for the profane, but also for many who took a more humane view of what it was to be a Christian than the precise would allow. George Herbert's country parson was 'a Lover of old Customes, if they be good, and harmlesse; and the rather, because Countrey people are much addicted to them, so that to favour them therein is to win their hearts, and to oppose them therein is to deject them.'[42] Josselin's type of religion was not the only one possible, and if his church was empty, it may tell us more about the limitations of his ministry than the irreligion of his flock.

And indeed, something of this is demonstrable from a fascinating account of his parish at Kidderminster published by Richard Baxter in 1658, and which suggests that Josselin's glum threefold division of his parishioners was too crude. For Baxter found not three types of parishioner, but *twelve*! We may exclude from consideration his two last categories, 'one or two honest ignorant Professors, that are turned Anabaptists', and 'some Papists', and turn our attention to the other ten categories.

There were in Baxter's large parish ('near 20 miles about') some 'three or four thousand souls' in 800 households, of whom 1,800 'or more ... were at age to be Communicants'. Of these, about 500 'or perhaps somewhat more' were rated to be 'serious Professors of religion ... such as the vulgar call precise'. This group corresponds to Josselin's 'our society'. It was supplemented by the second category, about a hundred, 'of competent knowledge and exterior performance, and lives so blameless, that we can gather from them no certain Proofe, or violent presumption that they are ... not sincere'. This 600 formed the inner core of the parish, consenting to 'live under ... my pastoral charge'. The third group were 'some that are tractable and of willing minds, that ... *seem* to be ignorant of the very Essentials of Christianity', but who 'when I have condescendingly better searcht them and helped them', appeared merely 'weak in the Faith' but nevertheless true Christians. A fourth category were those 'of competent understanding, and of lives so blameless, that we durst not reject them', but who 'disown our administrations' out of loyalty to traditional Anglicanism. Of this sort, Baxter notes, 'there are many that truly fear God'. A fifth category were the 'secret Heathens', unbelievers who privately mocked religion but who for the sake of respectability 'will hear, and urge us to baptize their children, and openly make the most Orthodox Confessions'. The sixth category were 'many ... that have tollerable knowledge', but live in 'some notorious scandalous sins' such as drunkenness, ribaldry, whoredom, or neglect of the Sabbath. This group would 'sometimes [rise] up in tumults against the Officers that endeavour to punish a drunkard, or Sabbath breaker'.

The seventh group were 'of more tractable dispositions, but really know not what a Christian is; that heare us from day to day, yea ... learn the words of the Catechism ... confess that we must mend our lives and serve God', but are ignorant of even the most basic Christian doctrines, and have a Pelagian reliance on good works. One of them, 'of about fourscore years of age (now dead)' thought 'Christ was the Sunne that shineth in the Firmament; and the Holy Ghost was the Moone'. Many of this category joined 'heathenish ignorance and wicked obstinacy together' and would accept no teaching, though even they were sufficiently religiously minded to want 'their own will and way about the Sacrament, and all Church affairs'. The ninth category were those 'of tollerable knowledge, and no Drunkards or Whoremongers', but who yet 'live in idle or tipling company, or spend their lives in vanity', and who therefore detest 'Strict Professors, and ... our Churches and Administrations'. In order to arm themselves against Baxter's sacramental discipline, this group read 'all the books that are written for the admitting all to the Lord's table that they can light of'. Finally, there were antinomians, who 'give themselves to security and ungodliness', because, convinced that all is predestined by God, 'they cannot do nothing of themselves'. Some of these, Baxter thought, were Hobbesian infidels, but the majority were misunderstanders of the 'Doctrine of Predestination and Grace', 'as if they had been hired to disgrace it'. [43]

Baxter's analysis of his parishioners has been given at length here because its very thoroughness forces us to broaden our conception of the spectrum of religious opinion and commitment in Stuart England. Baxter, of course, agrees with his puritan colleagues that *real* religion is that which exists among 'such as the vulgar call precise', but he recognises in those who were *not* precise a subtler range of distinctions than either Josselin, or indeed most modern commentators, have been able, or prepared, to do; the 'many' God-fearing Anglican loyalists, the inarticulate but tractable and willing devout, the believers who live in sin, the unruly and riotous, who nevertheless value access to the sacraments. Even the 'Heathenish ignorant' are subdivided into those of 'tractable disposition' and the 'wicked obstinate'. This is an altogether more three-dimensional picture than any two-culture polarity. Moreover, it is clear that Baxter's categories cross social barriers, since he tells us elsewhere that many of the poor were godly, that 'some of the Poor men did competently understand the Body of Divinity' and could resolve disputed points, while 'Abundance of them were able to pray very *laudably* with their Families'. At Dudley, where he regularly preached at this time, 'the poor Nailers and other Labourers would not only crowd the Church as full as ever I saw any in London, but also hang upon the Windows, and the Leads without'.[44]

It would be preposterous to try to claim that Kidderminster was somehow typical of English parishes; Baxter himself thought it exceptional – 'as honest a Town as any I know in England'.[45] But it was certainly not unique,[46] and in any case what I am pointing to is not the level of pastoral success achieved there, but the range of recognisably religious positions he discerned among those Josselin might have simply written off. There *were* blasphemers, infidels, men and women who were as ignorant as 'the veryest Heathen in America', but the majority of those Baxter describes had some discernible contact with and affiliation to orthodox Christianity, if only that of informed lip service. As he was later to claim, even 'those Families which were the worst, being Inns and Alehouses, usually some persons in each House did seem to be Religious'.[47] Hardly any households refused private catechising, and few went without 'some tears, or seemingly serious promises for a Godly life'. Despite the drunks, the infidels and the mockers, the notion of an 'alternative society' does not seem helpful here.[48]

We have moved from the discussion of the attitudes of the godly towards the multitude, to the attitude of the multitude towards godliness.

It is time therefore to return to Pepys' shepherd, and the last of my set of question marks. Was there such a thing as popular Christianity: can we find a genuinely plebeian religious context into which to fit the Bible-loving shepherd? It's a huge question, and I doubt whether in the nature of the case it can ever be answered convincingly.[49] But if we are unlikely ever to be able to say with confidence what place orthodox Christian belief had in the hearts of the multitude, it should be possible to establish whether or not it had a place in their culture, at least their literary culture. For the 'multitude', including many of the poor, *did* read, or hear books read to them. The sale of almanacs alone in the 1660s, when Pepys encountered his shepherd, averaged 400,000 copies annually, enough for one in three families.[50] Printed ballads were almost as ubiquitous, so that as early as 1595 Nicholas Bownd was bemoaning their presence in the 'shops of Artificers, and cottages of poor husbandmen'. Even those who could not read 'have many new Ballads set up in their houses' so that literate neighbours could coach them as opportunity arose.[51] The chap-books hawked around the villages by pedlars were equally disturbing to reformers, and equally plentiful. Antilegon had 'many pleasant and merry books' to cure melancholy – 'the Court of Venus, the Pallace of Pleasure, Bevis of Southampton, Ellen of Rummin: The Merry Jest of the Friar and the Boy: The pleasant story of Clem of the Clough, Adam Bell, and William of Cloudesley. The odde Tale of William, Richard, and Humfrey, The pretie conceit of Iohn Splinters last will, and Testament', all of them, he assures Asunetus, 'excellent and singular bookes against hart-qualmes and . . . dumpishness'.[52]

In the early reformation, religious propagandists had harnessed the forms of popular culture, such as the ballad, to spread the Protestant Gospel, just as evangelists like Bernard Gilpin had welcomed Christmas and other seasonal festivities as good contexts for preaching. By the early Stuart period they had largely ceased to do so, perhaps because, as Bound claimed, 'many of the common Singing men are so ungodly, that it were better for them to have their mouths stopped, then once to open them to polute such holy and sacred songs'.[53] Certainly the godly clergy conducted a running battle with the chap-books, 'divised by the divel; seene, and allowed by the Pope: Printed in hel: bound up by Hobgoblin: and first published and dispersed, in *Rome, Italy* and *Spaine* . . . that thereby men might be kept from the reading of the Scriptures'.[54] Nevertheless, they found their way into godly households. Richard Baxter, following in the footsteps of his 'precise' father, was rebuking his playmates for profanity while still a child in petticoats, yet he was 'extremely bewitched with a love of Romances, Fables and old Tales'.[55] He later came to detest them as 'the Devils Psalms and Liturgy', 'the very poyson of youth, the prevention of grace, the fuel of wantoness and lust'. The frequency with which he urges his godly readers to shun them, however, suggests that such admonitions were very necessary.[56]

But if chapmen brought merry tales into the homes of the godly, they also carried godly books to the multitude. The 'poor pedlar' from whom Baxter no doubt bought some examples of his beloved

'Romances and idle tales' also brought to the door 'some good books', and one of them, a version of Richard Sibbes' *The Bruised Reed*, 'opened the *Love of God* to me, and gave me a livlier apprehension of the mystery of Redemption, and how much I was beholden to Jesus Christ'.[57] Margaret Spufford's analysis of the trade lists of chap-book publishers in the Restoration period reveals that as many as a third of the 278 advertised titles were religious.[58] The hostility of puritan moralists to the chap-books might suggest that the pedlars carried merry and godly books for different customers, but although this was no doubt sometimes true, it cannot have been universally so, as Baxter's testimony shows, and as the evidence of the chap-books themselves confirms. The publisher Jonah Deacon thought he could sell *The Adventures of Robin Hood, Bevis, The Seven Champions of Christendom* and *A Groat's-worth of Wit for a Penny* to the godly purchasers of *The Young Man's Last Legacy . . . with his last Dying Prayer*.[59] John Back regularly advertised a mixture of merry and godly titles at the back of his godly books.[60] It has to be said that this practice was not extended to the trade lists at the back of the profane chap-books, which advertised only more profane books, so that the traffic did not flow evenly in both directions. Nevertheless, if their readership was not coterminous, it clearly overlapped.

Discovering just who did read these godly chap-books is probably impossible. It is *conceivable* that they were all bought up by respectable householders like Baxter's father and that few of the 'multitude' read them. This seems improbable, however, since, as we shall see, the style and subject matter of many of them presuppose a humble readership, and a number state explicitly that they are written for 'the many' that '(it may be) cannot have choice larger pieces', or address 'my country auditors', or urge 'Christian friends of what degree soever' to read over 'or *tend to hear*' the reading of the book. And the mere fact that the godlies represent so large a proportion of the total market, and that many of them seem to have run through scores of editions, suggests that these little tuppenny or threepenny books were aimed at, and achieved, the widest possible readership.[61]

In the nature of things these flimsy little books have mostly disappeared down privies, into fires, or into pie dishes as lining. In the 1670s and 1680s, however, Samuel Pepys collected them, and although, predictably, he was keener on merry books than on godlies,

46 'Penny-Godlinesses' are preserved among his books at Magdalene College. They represent about a third of the total number of godlies available at that time. A comparison of the collection with 70 other titles advertised by the publishers from whom Pepys bought chap-books suggests that the 46 are a reasonably representative sample. It seems fair to assume, therefore, that these little books can tell us a good deal about popular religion, since they encapsulate the religion for which poor men in late Stuart England were prepared to part with money. If you can tell what people like by what they buy, then this is what a lot of people liked. If there was a popular religious culture, we can reasonably look for it here.[62]

The first thing to register about the godlies is their conventional character. In a popular religious literature aimed at a readership supposedly more interested in the magical, the sensational and the bizarre than in piety, one might expect to find a substantial element of the supernatural, the gruesome and the extraordinary. There is some of all this, but remarkably little. Only one of the chap-books qualifies on all counts, the story of a wife-murderer who has his neck burst open by a devil on the orders of an angel clad in grass green, who reassures the neighbours, and then disappears in 'a melodious harmony of delicious music'.[63] There are two other 'judgements' of a slightly less spectacular sort, a liar whose tongue swells up, and a bible stealer whose hands and legs rot off.[64] These, however, can be readily paralleled in better class religious literature, not only in Bunyan but in Beard's *Theatre of God's Judgements*, while the account of the bible thief's gangrene is a reasonably accurate boiling down of a much more elaborate work aimed at a genteel audience.[65] Supernatural elements of a sort surface in two other chap-books, a catechism and a book of comfort for persecuted nonconformists, both of which are preceded by accounts of 'trances' experienced by the authors just before their deaths, in which they see the fate of those in heaven and hell – 'Swearer and lyars, . . . hanged up by the Tongue . . . proud and wicked persons tormented with melted lead'. These 'trances' were clearly an attraction, as they are advertised on the title pages.[66]

The broad character of the religion of the readers of the chap-books can be drawn in rather more firmly, however, from the much larger group of sententious and catechetical chap-books, most of the former in rhyme. Six of the chap-books were devoted to instruction in faith, morality, or prayer, of which five had the title 'School of' Piety, Holiness, Godliness, etc.[67] To these can be added *Golden Drops of Christian Comfort*, a charming rhymed life of Christ emphasising his miracles and the patient love displayed in the passion. With its woodcuts of the Adoration of the Magi and Crucifixion, it was explicitly aimed at the Christmas and Easter seasonal trade.[68]

The catechisms offer brief summaries of the essentials of the faith, commandments, Lord's Prayer, graces and morning and night prayers, and rhymed psalm verses for devotional use. One of them includes encouraging sentences from the Fathers, and emphasises faith in Christ and worthy participation in the sacraments. Most include a scripture quiz, some of which read more like the *Guinness Book of Records* than a work of piety, asking the child who was the oldest, the most patient, the most hard-hearted, the wisest, or the strongest man. Their aim was clearly to get the youngster searching through his or her bible, and references were provided.[69] The catechism from which these examples are taken, indeed, is a curious mixture of religious and conventional wisdom: alongside instruction in 'the wholesome and sound Doctrine of fearing God' are guides to good manners for children. 'When thou blowest thy Nose make not thy Nose sound like a Trumpet and after look not within thy Handkerchief . . .'[70] This catechism, in fact, is closely modelled on the biblical wisdom literature found in Ecclesiastes and Proverbs, from which it lifts phrases and echoes, and a number of the chap-books correspond even more closely to that model, by using verse form and purporting to be the last uttered wisdom of parent to child. The religious content of these sententious godlies is heavily moralistic, even Pelagian, emphasising the virtues of loyalty to family, good neighbourliness, charity to the poor, with little or no reference to Christ or faith.

> Be mild and gentle in thy speech
> both unto Man and child
> Refuse not good and lawful gain
> with words be not beguil'd:
> Forget not any good turn done
> and help thy neighbours need
> Commit no ill in any case
> the hungry see thou feed.

This is instantly recognisable to anyone familiar with the polemic against the Pelagian religion of good works and common decency attributed to 'the plaine countrie plowmen, taylours and such-like' in the works of Dent, Giffard and others.[71] The catechisms by and large escape Pelagianism, since most of them have relatively extended discussions of the person and work of Christ and the need for faith in him. But these sententious books, based on models traceable to the fourteenth and fifteenth centuries, do not, and are clearly worlds removed from the requirements of evangelical puritanism. Here, certainly, is that 'popular' religion condemned by Zelotes, Theologus and their kind.[72]

It is completely swamped in importance and bulk, however, by the flood of godlies recognisably puritan in character calling for repentance and conversion, denouncing judgement on the sins of individual and nation, and dealing with the doctrine of assurance. The brevity of life, the terrors of death, the pains of hell feature in more than half the godlies, and the image of death with scythe or arrow is prominent among the surprisingly few woodcuts in the chap-books. Margaret Spufford, in her pioneering study of the Pepys collection, was prompted by the predominance of death and judgement in the godlies to describe the religion represented in them as gloomy and negative, filled with fear of rejection by an awful Judge, liable to produce the sort of terror that tormented John Bunyan for years – this 'constant threatening must have encouraged anxiety'.[73] This would fit well the notion of puritan hostility to the multitude – a religion of threat and rejection for an unregenerate people. However, one needs in fact to distinguish a number of different categories within this 'Judgement' material, and when this is done its overall impact can be read rather differently.

There were, certainly, a group of half a dozen or so godlies which laid great emphasis on personal sin and imminent judgement, with little in the way of compensating comfort or hope. The titles of some of these speak for themselves – *The Dreadful Character of a Drunkard, God's Hatred against Sin and Wickedness, Christ in the Clouds, Coming to Judgement.* Even this. group, however, explicitly sets out to awaken their readers to repentance – 'O I beseech you to make a speedy turn to the Lord; seek, seek for the fountain that ever springeth, and bathe your souls in the precious blood of Christ.'[74]

A second group of 'judgemental' chap-books lays even more stress on the imminence of the last day, but these tracts are concerned rather with the sins of society than of the individual. Their targets are breaches of justice, charity, neighbourliness. Their tone is ferocious – 'The wrath of God's fury hangs over you his scourging Rod, which will torment you. Hell lies under you, ready to swallow you up . . . the flames of Hell for evermore.' But the sins being denounced, pride, luxury, covetousness, malice, 'pinching and grinding the poor for gain', are 'our national sins'. They have brought down on England plague and famine and fire, scourges intended to turn the nation back to justice and mercy: 'Relieve thy poor brethren that are in want, so shall they bless thee . . . God shall Bless thee . . . and thou shalt be eternally blest hereafter in Heaven.'[75] With their polemic against usury, luxury, refusal of alms, these godlies are not likely to have produced personal anxiety among the multitude, who might well have welcomed the sweeping indictment they offered of 'churchmen that have been . . . Woolves . . . Judges . . . with bribes, Courtiers that have Flown upon the wings of Pride . . . Lawyers that have eaten up their clients . . . Citizens [who] . . . to buy lands [have] made away their souls, Farmers, Graziers and Countrymen who have grinded the faces of the poor . . . common beggars . . . whose mouths have been filled with cursings and with blasphemy'.[76]

The natural affinity of this group seems not so much with the grim denunciation of personal sin, as with another chap-book, the marvellous *The Charitable Christian. Or a Word of Comfort from the God of Comfort, to such as are truly Poor*, with its insistence that God had chosen the 'poor of the world, to be rich in Faith, and heirs of the Kingdom, which he hath promised to those that love him . . .' and its identification of unmercifulness to the poor as the principle sign of reprobation.[77] The appeal of such works to a humble readership needs little comment: several of the godlies in this group were continuously in print throughout the Restoration period.[78]

Two groups of 'awakening' chap-books remain to be discussed, a group of 'Alarms' to the unconverted[79] and a group offering assurance, consolation and comfort.[80] They are closely related, and must be dealt with together. The tone of the first group, which includes a skilfully shortened version of Baxter's famous 'alarm' *Now or Never*, is set by Andrew Jones' *Death Triumphant*. The title, and its illustration of a menacing skeleton, might lead a casual reader to assume that this was a conventional *memento mori*, and it does indeed begin like that, with its description of death as the 'worm's caterer', and its rhetorical 'Where is Alexander? Where is Pilate? Where is Julius Caesar?'[81] In fact, however, the thrust of this and all the other chap-books in this group is the urgent need to turn from sin and lay hold on Christ: 'Daily and hourly think upon the love of Christ, never enough to be thought upon, the gracious and admired work of thy Redemption, by the Blood of that immaculate and unspotted Lamb Christ Jesus.'[82] As the author of *Christ's Voice to England* insisted, 'there is a marvelous willingness in God and Christ to save and receive sinners'.[83] Judgement is ever-present in these works, but it is a judgement turned aside by trust in Christ: 'Let Christ be in your hand, and the promise in your eye, and no doubt, though thou has been a rebel and a Traytour, yet Jesus Christ . . . will shew mercy to thee, and receive thee.'[84]

Crucial to these books is a firmly evangelical rejection of reliance on works, an insistence on the need for a lively faith. This classical Protestant emphasis had produced in England an equally classical quest for assurance.[85] Our final group of godlies sought to provide that. Their dominant characteristic is an insistence on the free grace of God in Christ, the objectivity of man's salvation in the cross, and above all the love of God for sinners revealed in the life and death of Jesus. So, although *A Christian indeed, or Heaven's Assurance* insists, in classical puritan form, on the perils of mistaking 'counterfeit grace' for the true regeneration that comes from sincere conversion – 'you must be converted or condemned' – it goes on to place the assurance of that conversion not in subjective feeling, but in the overwhelming goodness of God in Christ:

Do but think what Love hath done for you, and think, if you can, what it means to do for you. This is the Love that yearned upon you . . . that took you up when you were robbed and wounded . . . This is the love, the expensive love that bought you from the power of darkness, from the eternal burnings . . . do you not remember how you were hungry, and it fed you, naked and it clothed you, strangers and it took you in . . . Oh . . . remember in what case he found you, and yet nothing could annihilate his heart, or divert the purpose of his love from you.

The focus of this confidence is the crucified Jesus:

> Ah sinners ... look upon your crucified Lord ... ah how those Holy hands, those unerring feet do run a stream to purge us! Alas, how that innocent Back doth bleed with cruel scourgings to save ours ... Lord, how do we make a shift to forget such a love as this ...[86]

The urgency of these pieces is unmistakable – 'Delay not then one moment longer; But up, and away! Put on, for a State of Grace! Lay out for Salvation and Glory! O never be content to be Christless.'[87] Urgency, however, is not the same as grimness, and these little tracts offer a rich and essentially positive message of trust in God, and the quest for holiness: 'Here ... is a good saying; let the Lord do what he will, and let us do what we should.'[88] The provenance of that message is unmistakable. It is the voice of what Baxter liked to call 'our old English affectionate Divinity', the central puritan tradition. Baxter himself had found it in a chap-book by Sibbes, and it had 'opened the *Love of God* to me, and gave me a livelier apprehension of the mystery of Redemption, and how much I was beholden to Christ'.[89] That aim remained central to the chap-books I have been discussing. Among them, indeed, was a skilfully shortened version of Thomas Hooker's classic *Poor Doubting Christian Drawn to Christ*, showing the continuity of the chap-books' objectives across the watershed of civil war. [90]

The mention of 'objectives' begs a question, however, for it implies direction. How are we to explain the presence of this dominant group of 'affectionate' puritan writings in a market which included the barely Christian sententious material we examined earlier? Is the contradictory range of material anything more than the outcome of speculative and eclectic publishing by the chap-book proprietors?

Ian Green has expressed strong scepticism about the puritan provenance of these 'Godly' chap-books. He has pointed to the sometimes drastic shortening of the original source material, the absence of signs of direct authorial involvement such as dedicatory epistles, addresses to the reader and the like, and the fact that at least four of the puritan authors to whom chap-books in the Pepys collection were attributed were recently deceased at the time of publication. He has therefore argued persuasively that the penny godlies represent a purely opportunistic commercial venture by the publishers.[91] And certainly some of the material was pirated. Baxter himself tells us that his bestselling *Call to the Unconverted* sold 20,000 copies in one year 'besides many thousands by stollen Impressions, which poor Men stole for Lucre sake'.[92] It is quite certain that a number of the godlies were simply 'stollen for Lucre's sake'; John Bunyan can hardly have had a hand in the appallingly inept version of his *Pilgrim's Progress*.[93] The chap-book account of the penitent murderer Thomas Savage published by Thackeray and Passinger, actually subverts the purpose of the original from which it was cribbed, turning a powerful demonstration of the power of grace to awaken even the worst sinner to assurance in Christ, into a conventional moral exemplar in which all Christological content is emptied away.[94]

Nevertheless, if it is indeed true that these little books were issued primarily with an eye to a potential market, it is equally true that there is a very marked coherence about the type of author and theology most commonly identifiable among the godlies. They are, overwhelmingly, works by ejected nonconformist ministers. In addition to Baxter, responsible for two of the godlies, I have identified nine ejected ministers whose work was drawn on for the godlies either contained in Pepys' collection or advertised there; I am confident that this list could be extended. And many of these men can be shown to have had a special concern with the evangelisation and instruction of the poor, particularly through books.[95]

Henry Stubbs, for example, 'a plain, moving, fervent preacher', devoted his ministry largely to catechising and instructing young people, and gave a tenth of his income to the provision of teaching for poor children, 'and buying them books'.[96] Thomas Wadsworth, as commonwealth incumbent of Newington Butts, had developed a pattern of ministry to the poor based on catechising and personal conference. Once a week he would 'bespeak a house in the Street at the end of an Alley, and thither he would send for the poor people out of the alleys, and spend much time in instructing them'. He followed this up by getting the poor themselves to gather to hear one of their number read awakening books. It may not be entirely coincidental that Newington Butts was a centre for the distribution of chap-books.[97] This preoccupation of the nonconformist clergy with the distribution of 'fit books' to the poor may well have been a deliberate supplement to, or substitute for, the preaching vocation they were now forbidden to exercise, as it certainly was in the case of Thomas Gouge, who founded a trust, with Baxter's help, to distribute awakening and catechetical books to the poor in Wales.[98]

The godlies were only occasionally catechetical, but many of them, as we have seen, were 'awakening', and the choice of authors as sources for the godlies can hardly be coincidental. The editing of Hooker's *Poor Doubting Christian* and of Baxter's *Now or Never* is sensitive and accurate, with none of the crass clumsiness of the chap-book *Pilgrim's Progress* or *Thomas Savage*, and one is tempted to see an informed and expert hand at work here. But in any case many of the awakening chap-books were purpose-written, and aimed at the poor. The author of *A Knock at the Door of Christless Ones* explained that he wrote so that 'many may have Benefit: And such as (it may be) cannot have choice larger pieces. I have written short designedly, that every one that will, may have them [and] make compannions of them'.[99] It is difficult to escape the conclusion that the mission to evangelise and instruct the poor which we noted in the pre-revolutionary cate-chising movement, and in the ministry of men like Baxter, Stubbs and Wadsworth in the 1650s, was being consciously, and in terms of readership, successfully continued and extended through the penny godlies, even if those responsible did so to make a profit.

The penny godlies were certainly popular literature; they were as likely to be read by the pious Surrey shepherd as by Pepys himself, with his background in the 'precise' Magdalene of the 1650s. If any religious writings of the seventeenth century have a claim to encapsulate 'popular religion', these little books do. They reveal a broad spectrum of religious types; they include striking examples of the quasi-Pelagian religion of decency and good neighbourliness condemned by puritan commentators and they contain sensational and supernatural elements. But more striking than these is their attractive emphasis on social justice, charity, and the dignity of God's poor, the prominent presence of orthodox Christian teaching, and above all the gospel of penitence, forgiveness and grace which was the centre and the best of English puritanism. The core of Pepys' collection is recognisably the religion preached by Baxter and his associates. Some of these books were avowedly written by preach-ers seeking every means to reach the hearts of the poor. If others were simply pirated by hard-headed businessmen with an eye to the market, that in itself is eloquent testimony to the acceptability of the message they contained. In that sense, too, they were popular literature. The set of questions with which this chapter opened can be summed up in one. Did the godly succeed in penetrating the culture of the people in seventeenth-century England? On the evidence of the chap-books, it looks as if they did.

Notes

1   *The Diary of Samuel Pepys*, eds Robert Latham and W. Matthews (London, 1995), vol. 8, pp. 338–9.

2   Margaret Spufford, 'First Steps in Literacy: the Reading and Writing Experience of the humblest seventeenth-century Autobiographers', *Social History*, 4 (1979), pp. 416–17, and *Small Books and Pleasant Histories: Popular Fiction and its Readership in Seventeenth-century England* (London, 1981), pp. 27–32. Pepys' shepherd, however, had once been a domestic servant, and this may have some bearing on his reading ability.

3   Christopher Hill, *The World Turned Upside Down* (London, 1972), and 'William Perkins and the Poor', *Puritanism and Revolution* (1958) (I have used the paperback edition, Panther Books, 1968), and 'The many-headed monster', *Change and Continuity in Seventeenth-century England* (1974); Keith Thomas, *Religion and the Decline of Magic* (London, 1971); Peter Clark, *English Provincial Society from the Reformation to the Revolution* (Harvest Press, 1977), and 'The Alehouse and the Alternative Society', D. Pennington and K. Thomas, *Puritans and Revolutionaries* (Oxford, 1978); Christopher Haigh, *Reformation and Resistance in Tudor Lancashire* (Cambridge, 1975), and 'Puritan Evangelism in Elizabethan England', *English Historical Review* (1978); Keith Wrightson and David Levine, *Poverty and Piety in an English Village. Terling 1525–1700* (New York, San Francisco, London, 1979); and K. Wrightson, *English Society 1580–1680* (London, 1982).

4   For an example of the runaway tendency of the view I have described here, see the bizarre account of eighteenth-century English religion offered in R. W. Malcolmson, *Life and Labour in England 1700–1780* (London, 1981), pp. 83–93; Malcolmson insists that 'the evidence currently available on popular religion is so insubstantial . . . that there is precious little to say'. However, he immediately launches into an account of popular religion which argues that religion had 'anything but a commanding presence in many English parishes' since 'few clergymen, it seems, devoted much time to pastoral labours'. He feels 'justified in omitting Methodism' from his account because there were 'only' 25,000 Methodists by 1770 (!!); instead of discussing religion, therefore, he spends eight pages discussing *magic*.

5   Wrightson and Levine, *Poverty and Piety*, pp. 12–13; cf. Wrightson, *English Society*, pp. 206–20, where the argument, though much more carefully nuanced, is essentially the same.

6   Hill, 'Perkins and the Poor', pp. 214, 223, 225.

7   E.g. William Hunt, *The Puritan Moment: The Coming of Revolution in an English County* (Harvard, 1983), pp. 130–55.

8   Matthew Sylvester (ed.), *Reliquiae Baxterianae*, part I (London, 1696), pp. 2–3, 31–2.

9   William Perkins, *The Foundations of Christian Religion gathered into six principles* (London, 1627), sigs A2–A4.

10   Robert Bolton, *Some General Directions for a comfortable walking with God*, 2nd edn (London, 1626), pp. 116–17; George Gifford, *A Briefe discourse of certaine points of religion, which is among the common sort of Christians, which may be termed the Countrey Divinitie* (London, 1612), p. 39; Arthur Dent, *The Plaine Man's Path-Way to Heaven* (London, 1601), pp. 30–31.

11   Dent, *Plaine Man's Path-Way*, pp. 285–7.

12   For warnings against this view, see Brian Tierney, 'The Decretists and the "Deserving Poor"', *Comparative Studies in Society and History*, 1 (1958–9), pp. 360–76; Richard Smith, 'Some Issues concerning Families and their Property in Rural England 1200–1800' in Richard Smith (ed.), *Land, Kinship and Life-Cycle* (Cambridge, 1984), especially pp. 78–85.

13   John Rogers, *A Treatise of Love*, 3rd edn (London, 1637), pp. 215–18.

14   Rogers, *Of Love*, pp. 220–21; cf. John Downame, *The Plea of the Poore, Or a Treatise of Beneficence* (London, 1616): 'Let us remember that Christ hath done the like for us; and we . . . doe it againe to our Saviour Christ.'

15   Rogers, *Of Love*; for similar views, Richard Baxter, *The Poor Man's Family Book* (London, 1674), pp. 100–102; Downame, *Plea of the Poore*, pp. 54–60.

16   Rogers, *Of Love*, p. 231; Downame, *Plea of the Poore*, pp. 240–44, for identical sentiments.

17   John Hart DD, *The Charitable Christian*, Pepys Library, Magdalene College, 'Penny Godlinesses', pp. 571–73 (this edn 1682).

18   Richard Baxter, *A Christian Directory* (London, 1673), book IV, p. 191; cf. Rogers, *Of Love*, pp. 141–2: 'Yea, they that be never so ignorant, profane, ungodly, whether rich or poore, we must wish well unto them, and seek their good . . . Our love towards them may be a meanes to winne them to God.'

19   Perkins, *The Foundation of Christian Religion*, title page.

20   Quoted in Pat Collinson, *The Religion of Protestants* (Oxford, 1982), p. 233.

21   Baxter, *Poor Man's Family Book*, pp. 101–2.

22   Quotation from an unpublished paper on 'The emergence of the English Catechism under Elizabeth and the early Stuarts'. I am grateful to Professor Green for permission to quote his paper: statistics from his *The Christian's ABC: Catechisms and Catechizing in England c 1530–1740* (Oxford, 1996), p. 51.

23   George Herbert, *A Priest to the Temple, or, The Countrey Parson* (1652), in *The Works of George Herbert*, ed. F.W. Hutchinson (Oxford, 1967), p. 257; William Crashaw, *Milke for babes, or a north-countrie catechism* (London, 1618), sig A2v (I am indebted to Dr Green for this reference); Richard Baxter, *Gildas Salvianus or The Reformed Pastor* (London, 1656), pp. 356–7, and see also ibid., p. 81.

24   John Rogers, *The Doctrine of Faith*, 6th edn (1634), pp. 97–9.

25   *Mr Thomas Wadsworth's last Warning to Secure Sinners . . . To which is prefixed an Epistle of Mr Richard Baxter* (London, 1677), sig C3v–4r.

26   For example, Robert Muchembled, *Culture populaire et culture des élites dans la France moderne* (Paris, 1978); Peter Burke, *Popular Culture in Early Modern Europe* (London, 1978). especially Chapter 8; and the discussion by Robert Muchembled and Jean Wirth in *Religion and Society in Early Modern Europe 1500–1800*, ed. Kasper von Greyerz (London, 1984), pp. 56–78.

27   For Catholicism, see Christopher Haigh, 'The Continuity of Catholicism in the English Reformation', *Past and Present*, no. 93 (1981) and 'From monopoly to minority', *TRHS*, 31 (1981). For puritanism, most of the writers cited in n. 3. But see also the important and judicious discussion by Professor Collinson in *The Religion of Protestants*, pp. 189–241.

28   Margaret Spufford, 'Can we count the Godly?', *Journal of Ecclesiastical History* (July 1985), pp. 428–38; John Bossy, *Christianity in the West 1400–1700* (Oxford, 1985), especially his remarks on p. viii.

29   Rogers, *Of Love*, pp. 31, 35

30   Gifford, *Countrie Divinitie*, p. 4.

31   Bolton, *Comfortable walking*, pp. 2–3.

32   William Hinde, A *Faithfull Remonstrance of the Holy Life and Happy Death of John Bruen* (London, 1641), pp. 104, 192; Gifford. *Countrie Divinitie*, pp. 4–5; Baxter, *A Treatise of Self-Denyall* (London, 1660), pp. 129–30; *Poor Man's Family Book* pp. 98, 145; see also Nicholas Bownd, *Sabbathum Veteris et Novi* (London, 1606), pp. 253–83, where gaming and profane activities are clearly associated with the *propertied*; I am indebted to Dr Ken Parker for a helpful discussion of the social scope of Sabbatarian complaint literature, on which see his *The English Sabbath: A Study of Doctrine and Discipline from the Reformation to the Civil War* (Cambridge, 2002).

33   Dent, *Plaine Mans Path-Way*, pp. 30, 408. Baxter, *Poor Man's Family Book*, pp. 89 ff.

34   Gifford, *Countrie Divinitie*, pp. 2–3.

35 Richard Rogers, *Seaven Treatises. Containing Such Directions as is gathered out of the Holy Scriptures*, 4th edn (London, 1627), p. 161.

36 Some of the pitfalls here can be seen in the passage from Robert Bolton's *Two Sermons preached at Northampton* (1635 edn, pp. 84–5), used by Keith Wrightson in both *Poverty and Piety* (p. 13) and *English Society* (p. 205). Bolton is discussing a range of people hostile to godliness and puritanism. The first group he singles out are 'naturall Puritans' or 'true Iusticiaries', that is, men and women 'with a great opinion of their own integrity', who accept the general notion of sin but do not apply specific sins to themselves. These people, of whom 'you shall finde many . . . especially among the common and ignorant people', were well described, Bolton thinks, by Dent in his *Plaine Man's Path-Way*. He claims that they are also described in the Book of Proverbs, and cites chapter 30, verse 12. This is the first verse of a unit of three, which runs 'There is a generation which arc pure in their own eyes, and yet is not washed from their filthiness. There is a generation, O how lofty are their eyes! and their eyelids are lifted up. There is a generation, whose teeth are as swords, and their jaw teeth as knives to devour the poor from off the earth, and the needy from among men.' Dent and Bolton are therefore not describing parishioners *in globo* (Bolton goes on to discuss *other* categories such as the 'civill honest' or merely respectable, the superstitious, the pharisaically self-righteous, 'the giddy separatist' as well as the truly godly), but a particular group found *among* the common people. The passage from Proverbs seems to rule out any simple identification with the mass of the poor; the ignorance intended by Bolton is ignorance of true religion, not simple illiteracy – that is, it is a type of ignorance which can as readily be found in a literate as an illiterate man. Yet in *Poverty and Piety* and even more in *English Society* this group is equated with 'the common people', the clergy's 'stubborn flocks'.

37 Collinson, *Religion of Protestants*, pp. 139–40, 224–30; cf. Gifford, *Country Divinitie*; Lewis Bayly, *The Practice of Piety* (London, 1629), pp. 448–50; Sylvester, *Reliquiae Baxterianae*, part III, p. 190, para 72; Martin Ingram, 'Religion, Communities and Moral Discipline in Late Sixteenth and Early Seventeenth Century England' in von Greyerz, *Religion and Society*, pp. 177–93; J. A. Sharpe, 'Crime and Delinquency in an Essex Parish 1600–1648', *Crime in England 1550–1800*, ed. J. S. Cockburn (London, 1977), pp. 90–109. See also the testimony of Richard Condor, the Cambridge puritan, converted as a young man from profane life by his horror at hearing the *Book of Sports* read in his parish church; he makes the point that Sabbath-breaking by games was the activity 'in our parish and many others', of 'the young men' – Spufford, *Contrasting Communities*, pp. 231–2. And see the comments at pp. 8–9 of Jeremy Goring's 1983 Dr Williams' Libran' Lecture, *Godly Exercises Or the Devils Dance? Puritanism and Popular Culture in Pre-Civil War England* (Dr Williams' Trust, 1983).

38 Wrightson, *English Society 1580–1680*, pp. 206–21.

39 Claire Cross, 'The Church in England 1648–1660' in *The Interregnum*, ed. G. E. Aylmer (London, 1972), p. 112; G. F. Nuttall, 'Congregational Commonwealth Incumbents', *Transactions of the Congregational Historical Society*, 14, pp. 155–67; *Poverty and Piety*, pp. 161–4.

40 Wrightson, *English Society*, p. 220.

41 John Morrill, 'The Church in England 1642–9', pp. 89–114, in *Reactions to the English Civil War*, ed. J. Morrill (London, 1982).

42 Dent, *Plaine Man's Path-Way*, pp. 409–10; Herbert, *Priest to the Temple*, pp. 283–4.

43 Richard Baxter, *Confirmation and Restauration the Necessary means of Reformation and Reconciliation* (London, 1658), pp. 157–65; Geoffrey F. Nuttall, *Richard Baxter* (London, 1965), pp. 46–7.

44 Sylvester, *Reliquiae Baxterianae*, part I, p. 85.

45 Nuttall, *Richard Baxter*, p. 47.

46 Cf. the account of Nottingham in Geoffrey Nuttall et al., *The Beginning of Nonconformity* (London, 1964), pp. 15–22; and of Dursley (Glos.) in Edmund Calamy, *An Account of the Ministers . . . Ejected or Silenced*, 2nd edn (London, 1713), vol. 2, pp. 319–27.

47 Sylvester, *Reliquiae Baxterianae*, part I, p. 85.

48 Baxter, *Confirmation*, p. 160.

49 Spufford, 'Can we count the godly?', *passim*.

50 Bernard Capp, *Astrology and the Popular Press: English Almanacks 1500–1800* (London, 1979), p. 23.

51 Bownd, *Sabbathum Veterum*, pp. 224–6.

52 Dent, *Plaine Man's Path-Way*, p. 408.

53 Bownd, *Sabbathum Veterum*, p. 424; he has the psalms in mind here, but the point holds.

54 Dent, *Plaine Man's Path-Way*, p. 409.

55 Sylvester, *Reliquiae Baxterianae*, part I, pp. 2–3; Nuttall, *Richard Baxter*, p. 5.

56 Baxter, *Treatise of Self-Denyall*, pp. 115, 126, 127; cf. e.g. *Christian Directory*, part I, chapter 2, p. 61, chapter 5, p. 292, part II, chapter 10, p. 548, chapter 12, p. 552, chapter 31, pp. 580–81; *Reliquiae*, part I, p. 2. And in general, Spufford, *Small Books*, pp. 45–82.

57 *Reliquiae*, part I, pp. 3–4.

58 Spufford, *Small Books*, table 2, p. 134. I have adjusted Professor Spufford's figures upwards, to give 94 rather than 79 'Godlies', since some of the 'Double books' on Thackeray's list were religious; if one counts the broadside carol 'Christus Natus Est', there were 52 religious items on Thackeray's trade list, printed in part, *Small Books*, pp. 262–7, and complete in Leslie Shephard, *John Pitts, Ballad Printer of Seven Dials* (London, 1969), pp. 20–21. I am deeply indebted to Margaret Spufford for this particular reference and for general clarification about religious chap-books though, as will be seen, I take a different view of them.

59 Pepys Library, Magdalene College, *Penny Godlinesses* (hereafter P.G.), no. 15, Deacon's List, p. 309. I am indebted to the Master and Fellows of Magdalene College for permission to quote from these pamphlets.

60 E.g. P.G. no. 24, pp. 508–9, P.G. no. 37, pp. 809–10. This practice was not, of course, confined to chap-book publishers; H. Brome, the publisher of Samuel Hardy's *A guide to Heaven: or Good Counsel How to close savingly with Christ* (1664), thought that his customers might buy *The Jovial Crew* or *The Love-Sick Conceit* as well as *Almost a Christian* or *Blood for Blood*. Hardy's work, though not a chap-book, is tiny enough to have been carried in a pedlar's pack, and was intended for 'a plaine people . . . in a familiar vulgar style'. The publisher had some titles on his list – *Crumbs of Comfort* and *The History of the Bible* – which appeared elsewhere as chap-books (Trinity College Library, Cambridge, D. 38.59).

61 Spufford, *Small Books*, chapters 3 and 5 on readership and distribution.

62 I have omitted any consideration of the religion of the *Almanacs* here, for which see Capp, *Astrology and the Popular Press*, chapter 5. For a discussion of the balance of Pepys' collection of chap-books in general, Spufford, *Small Books*, chapter 6. No category of chap-book represented in the trade lists is absent from Pepys' collection, with one exception. Thackeray's list for 1689 (see above, n. 58) includes a version of an Elizabethan classic, Philip Stubbes' life of his wife, *A Christall Glasse for Christian women . . . the godly life and christian death of mistress Katherine Stubbes* (1592). Pepys did not have this. So far as I can see, this is the only biographical 'godly' current in the later seventeenth century. Since nothing survives of many of the advertised 'godly' chap-books but their title, it is difficult to assess the overall balance of Pepys' collection. Fortunately chap-book titles tend to be fairly self-explanatory – *Tormenting Topeth, Sinners Sobs, Posie of Prayers* – and they suggest that Pepys' collection does indeed reflect what was available, rather than any personal idiosyncrasies.

63 *Murthers Reward: Being a true and exact Account of a most cruel and most barbarous Murther*, P.G. no. 45. The chap-book authenticates itself with names 'the chiefest that live in the Parish', – one 'esquire', one 'gent', five yeomen and five husbandmen.

64 *An Allarum from Heaven: or, a Warning to Rash Wishers* (1683), P.G. no. 46; *A warning to Wicked Livers, or. A faithful and true Account of the Life and Death of John Duncalf, whose Hands and Legs rotted off in Staffordshire*, P.G. no. 6.

65 Simon Ford, *A Discourse Concerning God's Judgements* (London, 1678). Both Ford and Illingworth, his co-author, were clients of the Foley family, and friends of Edward Reynolds and Richard Baxter.

66 *The School of Godliness: Or, Divine Lesson by Way of Question and answer . . . by that faithful minister of the Gospel, lately deceased. Mr. Jo. Williams.* P.G. no. 16 (trance on p. 313); *The Dying Minister's last sermon . . . with the last sayings of the faithful Divine. Mr Brooke.* P.G. no. 11 (trance on p. 200).

67 P.G. no. 43, *The School of Piety, Or, The Devout Christian's Duty*; P.G. no. 23, *The School of Holiness; or, The Penitent Souls Dayly Practice. Containing Godly Prayers for several Occasions: With Heavenly Meditations, and Graces before and after Meat. Together with a short Catechism for the better instruction in the Christian Religion. Also the Holy Sayings of several of the ancient Fathers of the Primitive Church, Very*

Profitable for all people, and useful for Families (1686); P.G. no. 20, *A School of Divine Meditation, relating to the Frailty of Man . . . Also, Some DIVINE CAUTIONS, how they may avoid that great Mistake of taking Moral Parts for Spiritual Duties. Whereunto is added. Certain Prayers and Graces . . . By that Reverend Divine Mr R.B.*; P.G. no. 16, *The School of Godliness: Or, Divine Lessons by way of Question and Answer . . . by that faithful minister lately deceased, Mr Jo. Williams, who after he had laine several days in a trance did write this his catechism . . . With the minister's speech when he came out of his trance. With Rules of Civility and Carriage becoming Children;* P.G. no. 9, *The New School of Education for the Behaviour of Children: and their Instruction in the Protestant Religion Practiced by Q. Elizabeth of Blessed Memory.* The sixth of these instructional works was P.G. no. 28, *The Poor Man's Help to Devotion; or his Family Prayer-Book For there Divided Times of Trouble,* attributed to Baxter.

68 *The Golden Drops of Christian Comfort, or, a safe Sanctuary for all True Penitent Sinners. Set for the Benefit of Youth, in order to their understanding of many Wonderful Things, which God in his Infinite Mercy has been pleased to perform for the Race of Mankind, by S.M.,* P.G. no. 25. Cf. Spufford, *Small Books,* pp. 206–7.

69 P.G. no. 23, pp. 465, 479, 480, 484–5; no. 16, pp. 318–24; no. 43, pp. 931–2, 935.

70 P.G. no, 16, pp. 315–16.

71 *The Mother's Blessing: Being Several Godly Admonitions . . . upon her Death-bed* (1685), P.G. no. 31, p. 658. See also P.G. no. 34, *Dying Man's last sermon* (prose); P.G. no. 7, *The Dying Christian's Pious Exhortation;* P.G. no. 15, *The Young Man's Last Legacy.*

72 For the medieval models of these sententious godlies, see *The Good Wife taught her Daughter,* ed. T. F. Mustanoja, *Annales Academiae Scientiarum Fennicae* (Helsinki, 1948), and *Peter Idley's Instructions to his Son,* ed. Charlotte D'Evelyn (Boston and Oxford, 1935). I am grateful to Dr Ian Doyle of the University Library, Durham, for alerting me to these medieval prototypes.

73 Gifford, *Countrie Divinitie,* pp. 10–11, 52. See *Small Books,* pp. 198–213.

74 P.G. nos 1, 26, 29, 35, 36, 39; the quotation is from no. 29, *A Serious Call to Obstinate Sinners, or a Sounding Trumpet to the Unconverted,* by William Knowles (1684), p. 609.

75 P.G. no. 5, *The Black Book of Conscience or God's High Court of Justice in the Soul . . . Very Seasonable for these Times . . .* , by Andrew Jones. P.G. no. 14, *An Almanack But for one Day, Or the Son of Man Reckoning with Man upon High Account Day;* P.G. no. 17 *The Great Assizes: or General Day of Judgement* (1681), by William Knowles, pp. 348–55: P.G. no. 21, *Heaven's Messengers, Denouncing Judgement Against this Sinful Nation: But Proclaiming Mercy to the Truly Pentient therein,* pp. 436–8.

76 P.G. no. 14. pp. 288–9.

77 *The Charitable Christian. Or, A Word of Comfort from the God of Comfort, to such as are truly Poor. And a word of Christian counsel and Advice to such as are Worldly Rich . . .* (1682), P.G. no. 27. The author is the mysterious 'John Hart D.D.' who also wrote as Andrew Jones (possibly his first publisher was John Andrews) and William Jones. Cf. John Summerville, *Popular Religion in Restoration England* (Gainesville, 1977), pp. 45–6.

78 *The Black book of Conscience* was in its forty-second edition by the time Pepys bought it; *The Charitable Christian* first appeared in the 1650s, was in its eighth edition by 1662, and was acquired by Pepys in an edition of 1682. *The Great Assizes* has a number of recorded editions for the 1660s, and was still in print in the 1680s.

79 P.G. no. 8, *The Door of Salvation Opened; or A Voice from Heaven to Unregenerate Sinners*; P.G. no. 12, *The Day of Grace, or Christ's Tears over Jerusalem* by Nathan Vincent; P.G. no. 19, *Death Triumphant; or, The most Reverend, Mighty, Puissant and irresistable Champion and Conqueror General of the whole world, Death, Described . . . by Andrew Jones*; P.G. no. 29, *A Serious Call to Obstinate Sinners, or a Sounding Trumpet to the Unconverted,* by William Knowles; P.G. no. 32, *Christ's Voice to England, Calling for Repentance*; P.G. no. 42, *Now or Never,* by Richard Baxter; P.G no. 44, *An Almanack for two Days, Viz the Day of Death, and the Day of Judgement.*

80 P.G. no. 2, *Saints Blessed for Ever, or God's People never Forsaken* by Roger Hough; P.G. no. 13, *The Christian's Triumph over Temptation, Tribulation and Persecution, or, a Sanctuary for the afflicted*; P.G. no. 22, *A Christian Indeed, or Heaven's Assurance*; P.G. no. 24, *The Danger of Dispair, Arising from a Guilty Conscience*; P.G. no. 30, *The Poor Doubling Christian Drawn to Christ* (by Thomas Hooker); P.G. no. 38 *A Knock at the Door of Christless Ones*; P.G. no. 40, *The Christian Temptation and Tryals, as a Sweet Cordial of Comfort for true Believers,* by Ralph Vennings.

81 P.G. no. 19, pp. 388, 392.

82 Ibid., p. 404.

83 P.G. no. 32, p. 677; cf. p. 691.

84 P.G. no. 8, p. 162.

85 For which see R. T. Kendall, *Calvin and the English Calvinists* (Oxford, 1979).

86 P.G. no. 22, pp. 453, 455–7.

87 P.G. no. 38, p. 828.

88 P.G. no. 30, *The Poor Doubting Christian Drawn unto Christ*. I have collated it with the fifth edition of Hooker's work of the same title (1638). The quotation is from p. 120 of the 1638 edition, and p. 635 of the P.G.

89 Sylvester, *Reliquiae Baxterianae*, part I, pp. 3–4.

90 P.G. no. 30; Pepys' copy is the 'ninth impression' dated, 1683. It is stated to be by 'EC – this is Elizabeth Clark, a chap-book publisher of the 1660s.

91 Ian Green, *Print and Protestantism in Early Modern England* (Oxford, 2000), pp. 472–9.

92 Sylvester, *Reliquiae Baxterianae*, part I, p. 115.

93 P.G. no. 41, *The Pilgrim's Progress to the Other World: or a Dialogue Between Two Pilgrims on their way to Paradise . . . by way of Visionary Representation. By J.B. an unworthy labourer in Christ's Vineyard* (London, 1684). Its quality can be judged from its opening: 'As I wandered through a wild and spacious forest, which was stowed with all manner of Rationals, Animals and Vegetives, I came to a mossy bank, and there laying my head upon the root of a blasted oak I fell asleep, and a dream soon seized my fancy; when I dreamed and low I saw a man in poor cloathing standing at a distance . . .'

94 P.G. no. 37, *The Wicked Life and Penitent Death of Thomas Savage*, n.d.; the original from which this is derived is *A Murderer Punished, and Pardoned. Or a True Relation of the Wicked Life, and Shameful-Happy death of Thomas Savage* . . . (London, 1668). Wing attributes this to Richard Alleine; Edward Calamy, *A Continuation of the Account* (London, 1727), vol. 2, p. 963, says it is by James Janeway, and this seems more plausible, since Alleine appears to have no connection with Savage, whereas Janeway is named in the pamphlet as one of the five ministers who visited Savage in Newgate, and is the only one whose words are not reported in the account, suggesting that he was indeed its author.

95 (i) Ejected ministers who were the authors of Godlies in the Pepys collection: Thomas Brooks (P.G. no. 11, *The Dying Ministers Last Sermon*); James Janeway (the author of the original from which P.G. no. 37; see note 95); George Swinnock (P.G no. 8, *The Door of Salvation Opened*); Ralph Venning (P.G. no. 40, *The Christian's Temptation and Trial*) Nathaniel Vincent (P.G. no. 12, *The Day of Grace*); Thomas Wadsworth (P.G. no. 36, *Christ in the Clouds*).
(ii) Ejected ministers who wrote godlies advertised in the trade lists in P.G.: T. Calvert, *The Wise Merchant or the Peerless Pearl*; Henry Stubbs, *A Voice from Heaven . . . with his last prayer* (Stubbs is also the true author of the 'will' published in P.G. no. 11, and there wrongly attributed to Brooks – see Calamy, ed. S. Palmer, *The Nonconformists Memorial*, 2nd edn (London, 1802), II, 240 ff.); Thomas Vincent, *God's Terrible Voice*. To these could be added Joseph Alleine, whose *Call to the Unconverted* is recommended in the anonymous P.G. no. 38, *A Knock at the Door*, which itself reads like a work by a nonconformist.

96 See the account of Stubbs in Calamy, *An Account of the Ministers . . . Ejected or Silenced*, 2nd edn (London, 1713), vol. 2 pp. 318–20. Stubbs learned his methods from Joseph Woodward, of Dursley, under whom he served for a time. Woodward passed this preoccupation with the catechising and conversion of the poor to his son Josiah, who was to become a pillar of and the principal apologist for the religious and reformation societies of William's and Anne's reigns, and an ardent supporter of SPCK. See his very revealing account of his father printed in Calamy, op. cit., pp. 324–7.

97 Richard Baxter's address 'To the Reader' prefixed to Thomas Wadsworth's *Last Warning to Secure Sinners* (London, 1677), sigs b2v–b3v. I am indebted to Margaret Spufford for the point about Newington Butts and the chap-book trade.

98 On Gouge's Trust and Baxter's involvement, and on the type of books circulated, see G. F. Nuttall, *Beginnings of Nonconformity*, pp. 26–32.

99 P.G. no. 38, p. 810.

13

The Long Reformation:
Catholicism, Protestantism and the Multitude

It is now more than 40 years since the first appearance of Jean Delumeau's *Catholicism between Luther and Voltaire*, in which he argued that despite their apparent mutual contradictions, 'the two Reformations – Luther's and Rome's – constituted . . . two complementary aspects of one and the same process of Christianization'.[1] The Christian Middle Ages, according to Delumeau, was a legend, at least 'as far as the (essentially rural) masses are concerned'. Christianity, he thought, had penetrated medieval society only superficially, and the whole of Europe in the sixteenth and seventeenth centuries was, therefore, '*pays de mission*', just as surely as the newly discovered pagan Indies, East and West.

Some scepticism is in order about Delumeau's central contention, and was in fact expressed by John Bossy in his introduction to the English translation. Something profound, and profoundly new, did indeed happen to European Christianity in the early modern period, but it seems maddeningly wrong-headed to describe that something as the achievement, after an apparently ineffective millennium of Christian activity in Europe, of 'Christianisation'. Elsewhere, indeed, Bossy has suggested that it may not always be very satisfactory even to describe the transformation by the term 'reformation', for to do so is to go along too easily with the notion that 'a bad form of Christianity was being replaced by a good one'.[2]

However that may be, in this chapter I want to focus on an insular aspect of the broader renewal or recasting of Christianity in the early modern period which Delumeau made much of, and which lent powerful support to his thesis. I want to consider the English dimension of the move all over Europe to devise new evangelistic methods, missionary strategies to reach populations widely thought of by zealous clergy as not merely unchurched, but actually unchristened. While such an assumption fitted particularly well with the Protestant conviction that the Reformation had rediscovered a gospel suppressed by centuries of popish error, it was not in any sense peculiar to Protestants, and indeed in many ways counter-reformation Catholicism embraced it with far greater energy and inventiveness than did the Protestant reformers. Catholic missionary strategists sometimes talked of the populations of rural Europe and of the great cities as pagans, and equated non-Christian 'heathenism' and the superstitious beliefs and practices of the European peasantry and urban poor. When the seventeenth-century missionary St Francesco de Geronimo asked his Jesuit superiors to send him to Japan and martyrdom, he was told instead to become 'the Apostle of the Indies of this city and kingdom of Naples'.[3]

Catholic Europe was, of course, no stranger to the idea of large-scale conversion or mission. The century before the Reformation had been marked by the activities of hugely popular urban evangelists such as Vincent Ferrar or Bernardino of Sienna.[4] But this was hit-and-run work by travelling friars: Vincent Ferrer averaged an annual 300 lengthy sermons in the restless travelling of his last 20 years, sermons often devoted to apocalyptic warnings about the imminent end of the world. Sixteenth- and seventeenth-century Europe came to feel that something with a longer-term perspective and a more gradualist and consistent pastoral strategy behind it was required, a pastoral strategy moreover which reached not merely the urban audiences which had gathered to hear St Bernardino or St Vincent, but which would touch and transform the much larger body of the rural poor, served as they often were by clergy as saturated in ignorance, cow dung and domestic cares as the people themselves. Trent took it as axiomatic that the solution to this pastoral dilemma lay in the rejuvenation of the parochial system, yet the engine eventually devised to breach the darkness of the parishes was not routine parochial ministry, but the revivalist machinery of the parish mission.

A sixteenth-century invention in which Spanish Jesuits played a key role, the parish missions of the counter-reformation, came into their own in the seventeenth and eighteenth centuries, and received their decisive shape in the activities of Vincent de Paul's Lazarists or Priests of the Mission, and Alphonsus de Ligouri's Redemptorists.[5] Preached by organised teams of specially trained religious, the missions were carefully adapted to the rhythms of peasant life. In its classical, and simplest, form, devised by St Vincent, it consisted of sermons preached at dawn for the benefit of those who had to be early in the fields, and which were designed to be awakening in more senses than one, catechising of children and young people in the afternoons, and the 'great catechism', systematic but also awakening instruction of all the parish, each evening. Mission preaching was concerned with practical reform, as well as the salvation of the soul, and targeted the objectionable features of popular culture – dancing, drinking, gambling, bad language, profanation of Sunday and holidays: there were ritual burnings of novels and ballads, smutty drawings and prints. Most missionary theorists – and the period saw a blossoming of missionary textbooks from John Eudes' *Catechism of mission* to Alphonsus de Ligouri's *Exercises of the missions* – emphasised the desirability of saturation bombing of a region. Missionaries stayed for anything up to eight weeks in an area, congregations were systematically bussed or, rather, processed in from the surrounding villages and the wider region, to ensure that the mission target area did not become a vulnerable island of the godly in a sea of sin and infidelity. Eyewitness accounts of the missions of St John Eudes record crowds of 12,000 or 15,000 covering the hillsides to hear him preach in the open air, and of confessors besieged by troops of penitents who had queued for a week or more to confess their sins. For the object of all missions was to bring the people to a state of penitence and to get them to make a general confession, intended to be the beginning of a much more regular penitential regime.[6] Ideally missions were arranged in four-, six- or eight-year cycles, with the aim of creating what was in effect a revivalist culture, periodic awakening consolidated by an intensified sacramental and devotional life between revivals. The lost souls of the country people of Europe were to be saved by conversion, confession and catechism.

Since Tridentine Catholicism was committed above all to the renewal of Christian life through the agency of the parish, there is a deep irony in the fact that the most effective and most characteristic counter-reformation machinery for that renewal should have been in essence non-parochial, the itinerant preaching of revival by specialist bands of vowed religious. Yet it was a brilliant and enduringly successful improvisation, which retained the integrity of the pastoral unit of the parish, while providing a disciplined machinery for injecting into the parishes the element of revivalist fervour and personal appropriation of religion which was central to counter-reformation spirituality.

But for Protestant Europe such a solution was not an option. The abolition of the religious life in effect reduced all ministry, at least in theory, to parochial ministry, and although within reformed church polity there was a recognition of diversity of function within the ministry, the essential localisation of such ministry within the parish everywhere in Protestant Europe set the agenda for all attempts at reform. Reform of the Christian life meant reform of the parish ministry, its conversion into a preaching ministry, and the Christian ordering of the lives of the people by parochial discipline. It has become something close to an historical orthodoxy that in this endeavour English Protestantism by and large failed, that the Reformation, unpopular to start with, never won the allegiance of the majority of the nation, and that the godly were at last forced to accept 'the incorrigible profanity of the multitude'.[7] Even Patrick Collinson, the subtlest and most sympathetic of modern historians of Puritanism, has reluctantly conceded that 'the pastoral ministry in post-reformation England was a long-term failure, the religious plurality and secularity of modern Britain its ultimate consequence and legacy'.[8]

I would be the last one to contest the unpopularity of the early reformation in England, or to minimise the difficulties of its first promoters in establishing it as a working religious system, but it does seem to me that Protestantism in late Elizabethan and Jacobean England must be judged, by any rational standards, a runaway success. I am struck by the extent to which, within two generations, England's Catholic past was obliterated, and how deeply impregnated seventeenth- and eighteenth-century English culture was by Protestant values. The criteria for success in the Reformation set by some historians seem to me as unreal as those set by Delumeau for the success of medieval Christianity. Certainly clerical activists in eighteenth-century England were complaining of the heathenism and ignorance of the people in much the same terms as sixteenth-century reformers, and the leaders of the Evangelical Revival spoke of the state of religion in England in terms uncannily similar to those used by the first reformers about medieval Catholicism.[9] But much the same complaints had been voiced by clerical activists in the tenth, thirteenth and fifteenth centuries, part of the perennial rhetoric of reform, and we should not try to deduce too much from them about what was happening on the ground. The achievement of a Christian society is, or was, an ongoing project which those charged with its attainment have never believed to be complete. The rhetoric of reform is not so much a measure of the failure of that project, but of the vitality of their commitment to it. My concern in this chapter, however, is not to attempt to adjudicate the success or failure of the Protestant project in England, the long reformation,[10] but to trace the history of just one of the preoccupations and problems it shared with the counter-reformation, the role of the parish ministry in the conversion of England.

In the first stages of Protestant evangelism in England the problem was acute. However much it might be feared, as Thomas Bilney told Cuthbert Tunstall, that 'Christ hath not been purely preached now a long time', short of a wholesale replacement of the existing non-preaching and popish ministry there was little that could be done.[11] Itinerant Protestant preaching was a vital factor in establishing islands of Protestant conviction, but without a base in the parishes could hardly sustain the communities thereby brought into being. And itineracy itself had no guarantee of a hearing. Hugh Latimer, a leading episcopal patron of itinerant preaching, told in a sermon before Edward VI how he himself on the eve of a holy day which fell during one of his episcopal journeys had sent word ahead to the next town that he would preach in the morning, for 'methought it was a holiday's work', only to find when he arrived the church locked and the congregation absent. At last one of the parish came to him and said 'Sir, this is a busy day with us, we cannot hear you; it is Robin Hood's day. The parish are gone abroad to gather for Robin Hood: I pray you let them not.'[12]

Latimer's courtly hearers dissolved in laughter that his 'rochet . . . was fain to give way to Robin Hood's men', but for him it was no laughing matter. A rampant semi-pagan popular culture which set the word of God at naught was the result of an unpreaching prelacy, the missionary failure of a Church which was content to have the people 'continue in their ignorance still'. The attempt to construct a Protestant missionary ministry in just such circumstances can be seen in the remarkable career of Bernard Gilpin, Elizabethan rector of Houghton-le-Spring in the diocese of Durham. Gilpin, an Erasmian humanist somewhat to the left, but very much in the mould, of his great-uncle and patron Cuthbert Tunstall, whom he served somewhat gingerly as archdeacon in Mary's reign, was an almost equally uneasy conformist in 1559, but then, as pastor with responsibility for some of the wildest border country in Northumberland, threw himself increasingly enthusiastically into a pioneering Protestant ministry until his death in 1584.[13]

Gilpin was much troubled by the 'desolation of the Church, and the ignorance of the common sort' which sprang from the abuse of lay impropriations. The parishes of the North East were full of 'poor base priests', only able to read the services, so that in many places 'the word of God was never heard of to be preached among them' and many congregations 'even dispersed and destitute of pastors'.[14] Gilpin therefore undertook an annual tour of itinerant evangelistic preaching in the most isolated and 'uncivil' parts of the region, Tynedale and Redesdale. He chose the Christmas season for this work, to take advantage of the great concourse of people in the churches then, thereby encountering head-on and even harnessing, the festal culture which had defeated Latimer's attempt at itineracy, and which was to feature so consistently as the great enemy of godliness in every account of Protestant ministry before George Herbert.[15]

In a region so sparely served with Protestant clergy, itineracy was an obvious expedient, and in the late 1570s Bishop Barnes drew up a circuit for every licensed preacher in the diocese, although few were willing to venture into the wilds as Gilpin did.[16] Yet Gilpin knew that these were stopgap solutions, and he tackled the need for settled preachers of God's word in two ways, coaxing able young clergy into the poorly endowed livings of the region, and cooperating with a godly London merchant who had purchased the dissolved estates of a local hospital to found and endow Kepier Grammar School at

Houghton. It was a foundation marked out by a distinctive emphasis on the godly formation of the pupils, explicitly intended to produce a stream of preachers for the region, 'the maintenance of Christ's holy gospel'. He also maintained a series of scholars at university, for the same purpose.[17]

Stopgap or not, however, Gilpin's missionary preaching had numerous parallels in the Elizabethan and Jacobean Church. The Elizabethan authorities appointed itinerating preachers not only for the Borders, Wales and Lancashire, but for other 'dark corners of the land'.[18] Collinson has shown that the preaching of occasionally itinerating ministers, often accompanied in their journeyings by clusters of godly groupies, 'gadding people', remained a feature of English Protestant life up to the civil war. Such preaching was a central element in the forming of a devout Protestant culture – it was too widespread and in many places too dominant to be called a subculture – which took in weekday lectures in other parishes, fast days, exercises and combination lectures, all extra-parochial dimensions of a ministry which nevertheless saw itself essentially in parochial terms. By such means the unity of the godly was fostered 'as if they had all been of one household'.[19]

In our context it is worth emphasising, however, that it was also a missionary device, part of the project to convert England, and such ministry, easily categorised as a process of consolidating and servicing a puritan consensus, was rarely described or conceived by those who practised it in isolation from the language of awakening, conversion.[20] Samuel Clarke's ministry in the Wirral in the 1620s, although based in Shotwick, was in effect an itinerant circuit, funded 'by a voluntary contribution' of 'divers godly and understanding Christians' scattered up and down the peninsula. The region was *pays de mission* with a vengeance, 'scarce a constant preacher besides my self' and reminiscent to that extent of Gilpin's Northumberland. The pattern of Clarke's ministry there, the 'public ordinances' of regular preaching and monthly sacraments, supplemented by 'days of conference' in the wealthier houses of the region, marked by searching catechising of young Christians, was well adapted to a region where the godly were few, and surrounded by the 'ethnical pastimes and sinful assemblies' of the ungodly: it was a ministry of the godly to the godly.[21]

Yet it was not addressed simply to the godly. Clarke commented that 'In this place I found the first seal of my ministry, by being an instrument of the conversion of many souls to God' and it was by the conversion of many, particularly among the young, that he reckoned the success of his subsequent ministry.[22] Conversions were indeed the distinctive 'seal' of a reformed ministry. The Cheshire preacher William Hinde, complaining that the majority of the people round about him were 'Popish and prophane', 'strangers from the commonwealth of Israel', with the 'mists of Samaria . . . yet in their eyes, and the calves of Bethel . . . yet in their hearts', nevertheless thanked God that 'he hath given me a seale of my ministry in the parish amongst them, and in the country round about them', by the converts he had 'gathered together into the fold and flocke of Christ Jesus'.[23] Hinde was a veteran of the wars between popery and Protestantism which were endemic in the North West, and Pat Collinson rightly emphasised the particular resonance and appropriateness of the language of conversion in a region in which a committed Protestant career might well begin with an act of renunciation of Catholicism.[24] Nevertheless, the language of conversion and new birth was by no means confined to the North West, and in the seventeenth century in particular is an ubiquitous feature of Protestant discourse.

For the rhetoric of conversion and of mission did not lapse as England became a more securely reformed nation. Even in the popish fastnesses of the North West by 1625 a zealous Protestant such as John Bruen could contrast the mid-Elizabethan period, when he had first begun 'to professe religion', being almost the only man in the shire 'acquainted with the power and practice of it . . . like a pelicane in the wilderness', with the happy present, in which 'the borders of the Church are much enlarged, the numbers of beleevers wonderfully increased, and blessed be God, every quarter, and corner of the countrey is now filled with the sweet savour of the Gospel'.[25] This was a conventional perception: late Elizabethan and Jacobean Protestants, however zealous in outreach to the perishing mass of the people, believed themselves to live in 'happy days . . . in this our peaceable land'.[26] Yet for all the growing company of preachers, they believed that the work of the gospel remained still to do, and even in this peaceable land, tens of thousands were on the way to perdition. 'If we come to reason', Arthur Dent wrote in a passage I have already quoted in chapter 12,

> we may wonder that any shall be saved, than so few shall be saved . . . First let there be taken away from amongst us all Papists, atheists, and heretics. Secondly let there be shoaled out all vicious and notorious evil livers: as swearets, drunkards, whoremongers, worldlings, deceivers, coseners, proud men, rioters, gamesters, and all the prophane multitude. Thirdly let there be refused and sorted out all hypocrites, carnal Protestants, vain professors, back-sliders, decliners and cold Christians. Let all these I say be separated and then tell me how many sound, sincere, faithful and zealous worshippers of God will be found amongst us? I suppose we should not need the art of arithmetic to number them: for I thinke they would be very few in every village, town and city. I doubt they would walk very thinly in the streets, so as a man might easily tell them as they go. [27]

There were two contrary energies operating in such a vision of society. One lived by and imaginatively fed on the notion of the necessary smallness of the number of the elect, and there was in such a theological vision an undertow towards separatism. Another, quite different, energy saw in the heedlessness of the multitudes not a sign of God's unsearchable decrees and their own condemnation, but a summons to vigorous activity, the task of awakening the people who 'be like the smith's dog, who can lie under the hammer's noise, and the sparks flying, and yet fast asleep'.[28] For men of this mind, the Protestant conformity that Christopher Haigh has christened 'parish Anglicanism' simply would not do: they were determined to sort out and transform the tepid religion of carnal Protestants and cold Christians into something more fiery and consuming.

> Hath God nothing to do with his mercy (think you) and Christ's blood, but to cast it away on those that can scarce think they need it, or will scarce thank him for it? No, God's mercies goe not a begging yet . . . Now we his ministers, his almoners to distribute his comforts . . . dare not lavish them out, and promise them to such lazy indifferents as these: but if wee see any ready to faint for

want, saying, give me drink or else I die, then we reach the cup of consolation to him, and bid him drink of it; neither dare we give it to any other. [29]

Conversion, therefore, meant not merely bringing the heathen to knowledge of the gospel, but bringing the tepid to the boil by awakening preaching, creating a godly people out of a nation of conformists. Converts were often the already decently conforming members of godly households, stirred to a personal appropriation of a religion which until then had been in some sense second hand. Richard Baxter, the son of a puritan father, recalled how even as a child hearing sermons and reading good books had made him 'love and honour godliness in the general' but that, until he was 15, he had 'never felt any other change by them on my heart'. A tattered and bowdlerised copy of a counter-reformation awakening treatise by the Jesuit Robert Persons changed all that, for by it 'it pleased God to awaken my soul, and show me the folly of sinning, and the misery of the wicked, and the unexpressible weight of things eternal, and the necessity of resolving on a holy life'. What he had known in theory before 'came now in another manner, with light, and sense and seriousness to my heart'.[30]

The reproduction of that movement on a universal scale, to bring the commonplaces of Christian catechesis 'with light and sense and seriousness' to the hearts of the people at large, was one of the fundamental drives of English Protestant ministry, and in England, as in the practice of counter-reformation missions, it led to the linking of catechism and conversion. Hinde's remarks about converts as the 'seal' of ministry come not from a book of sermons, as one might expect, but from the preface to a catechism prepared originally for use with the people of his own parish, and the linkage of catechesis and conversion is entirely conventional.

Ian Green has alerted us to the centrality of catechesis in Protestant ministry before the civil war. The sheer volume of works produced to help in this ministry is mind-boggling – Professor Green's finding list of catechetical works published in the century after the first appearance of the Prayer Book Catechism in 1549, many of which ran to 30, 40 or 50 editions, runs to 150 printed pages. Speculating as to why so many catechisms should have been produced in addition to the short form in the Prayer Book and the longer official work by Alexander Nowell, Green rules out in all except a handful of cases theological disquiet about the content of the Prayer Book Catechism. He suggests, rather, that practical considerations were decisive: what was wanted was a medium-length text, fuller than the Prayer Book form but not so long as Nowell, and one which would ensure that learners would interpret Christian fundamentals 'in a fully Protestant way'.[31]

This is perfectly right, but only so long as we don't confine 'in a fully Protestant way' to a matter of doctrinal understanding. The missing concept here is conversion. As a summary of the essentials of the faith as they had been defined at least since the Fourth Lateran Council – Creed, Commandments, Lord's Prayer – the Prayer Book Catechism was admirable: as an instrument of conversion, however, it was virtually useless. This was not a matter of its silence about such arcane matters as double predestination. The problem was that the Prayer Book form might have been written at any time since 1215, and it said nothing whatever about the distinctive Protestant *ordo salutis*, nothing about the Fall or Original Sin, it never discussed the nature of salvation, except in terms of duties towards God and neighbour, and it never once used the word faith. For a catechesis designed not merely to instruct in basics, but to arouse to faith, such a form simply would not do. So, William Hinde's catechism follows roughly the same layout as the Prayer Book form, but replaces the opening section of the Prayer Book version, which deals with the child's acceptance of the promises made by its godparents, with a section entitled 'Man's misery by Adam. His recovery by Christ', emphasising our need of a new birth, a share in the covenant of God, and the grace 'so to profess and maintain the Christian faith, that (we) may feel the power, and show forth the fruit of it'.[32] In the same way, William Perkins warned the ignorant people to whom his catechism was addressed not merely that they must rightly understand the Creed, Lord's Prayer and Commandments, as opposed to merely parroting them, but that they must also 'apply them inwardly to your hearts and consciences, and outwardly to your lives and conversation. This is the very point in which we fail.'[33]

The recognition of the role of catechesis in conversion modified Protestant emphasis on the uniqueness and centrality of the sermon.

Whereas in sermons, declared George Herbert, 'there is a kind of state, in catechising there is an humbleness very suitable to Christian regeneration'.[34] This was no High Church eccentricity. That ardent Protestant William Crashaw declared in 1618 that 'I find that cate-chising is the life of preaching, and such a meanes of knowledge as without it all preaching is to little purpose'.[35] There might be very much more to catechism than mere instruction. Catechising might lay bare the heart: as Herbert remarked, 'at sermons and prayers men may sleep or wander; but when one is asked a question, he must discover what he is'.[36]

When in the late 1620s Samuel Fairclough launched what was to become a model Protestant ministry in that cathedral of west Suffolk Protestantism, Kedington, he found a people emphatically in need of conversion, and the whole town, in words which by now will have a familiar ring to them, 'very ignorant and prophane, being generally aliens and strangers from the commonwealth of Israel'. Fairclough set himself to 'pull and snatch ... sinners, as brands out of the fire, by any ways or means he could think of'. Conversion dominated his thinking and pastoral strategy, and 'he left in his diary the names of some hundreds recorded there, who had all expressly owned him to be their spiritual father, and the proper means of their first conversion'. In this work preaching, which he did four times a week, played a central part, as anyone will know who has seen the great pulpit erected for Fairclough by his friend and patron, Sir Nathaniel Barnardiston, looming still in a church nowadays adorned with the Stations of the Cross and other Romish abominations. But preaching was only one element in his campaign to 'awaken the consciences of obstinate sinners; and then to make known to them the way of salvation'. His great aim, Samuel Clarke tells us, 'was to instruct the ignorant, which he found a very hard work to do'. He was assisted by Barnardiston, who persuaded the substantial men of the town to join him in ensuring the attendance of their whole households and dependants at catechising, 'both young and old, both governors and governed, one and other', and themselves partici-pating in the questions and answers, *pour encourager les autres*. As the second prong of this process, catechising was linked to admission to the Lord's Supper, Barnardiston and all the rest of the communicants agreeing that they would 'first publicly own ... [their] baptismal covenant for once . . . and that afterwards, they should submit unto admonition, in case of the visible and apparent breach of that covenant'. Barnardiston therefore made a public declaration of 'his faith in God through our Lord Jesus, and did undertake (through the assistance of the Holy Spirit) to perform whatever his sureties had promised in baptism upon his account'.[37]

Fairclough's activities at Kedington, at least as presented by Clarke, were a spectacularly successful example of a not uncommon type of godly ministry, a characteristically Reformed or Calvinist style in which a form of parochial discipline centred on rigorous catechising became the principal instrument not merely of instruction but of awakening, conversion and Christian formation and reformation. Sixteenth-century Protestant writing about the nature of ministry focused almost exclusively on the role of the preacher, but, in practice, in England as elsewhere in the reformed world, and in contrast to Lutheran Europe, a more complex, nuanced and resourceful understanding of ministry prevailed.[38]

The activities of Fairclough in Laudian Kedington testify to the centrality of evangelistic concerns in the pre-civil war Church of England, but those concerns became acute in the Cromwellian period. A heightened sense of expectation as the collapse of Laudianism and the establishment of Presbyterianism seemed to place within grasp the achievement of a godly and converted nation submitting to discipline, gave way to growing dismay at the non-arrival of a new godly order, and at the disorganisation and vulnerability of the Cromwellian Church to its enemies in the sects, and to its own internal disagreements. Yet these were years in which many yearned, worked for and expected the conversion of England. Almost any page at random of Samuel Clarke's admittedly hagiographic collections will yield examples, but the career of John Machin, a Staffordshire minister active in the 1650s, will serve. Himself converted from a youth of 'vanity and sin' at Cambridge in the 1640s, Machin became a dedicated evangelist, beginning with his own family, and then embracing a converting ministry based at Astbury. A tireless preacher in his own place, he set himself 'to promote and drive on the work of conversion whereever he came', his letters and prayers punctuated by fervent exclamations of longing, '*O that all Staffordshire and Cheshire might be saved!*' His spare

days 'he laid out to the utmost example of the Gospel, by forecast-
ing for heavenly work in the moorlands and other dark corners
in Staffordshire, where the Gospel in the power of it had scarce
ever come before'. He endowed a monthly lecture to be preached
in towns 'of great concourse' in the region – Newcastle, Leek,
Uttoxeter, Lichfield, Tamworth, Walsall, Wolverhampton, Pentbridge,
Stafford, Eccleshall, Stone and Mikleston. To reach the rural population, he organised groups of fellow ministers 'to meet him in those
parts, and to preach at several places near to each other, sometimes
three or four days together', an activity which had ample precedent
in puritan pastoral practice, but which also carries resonances of the
contemporary activities of Eudist and Lazarist counter-reformation
rural missions.[39]

Machin was a relatively obscure figure. Joseph Alleine of Taunton
was altogether more notable, and in the Restoration period was
to publish one of the best-known and most influential missionary
tracts of the century, his *Alarm to the unconverted*. His ministry in
Cromwellian Somerset, like Machin's in Staffordshire, demonstrates
an overriding concern with conversion. It was also characterised
by one of the most distinctive features of mid-century pastoral and
evangelistic strategy, namely household instruction and scrutiny.
Settling at Taunton, he established a model ministry there, preaching
not only to his own large congregation, but going frequently 'into
other parishes about the country, amongst poor ignorant people that
lived in dark corners, having none to take care of their souls'. He
organised many of the local clergy to do likewise, and with them
established combination lectures in several places. He shared in the
almost universal missionary preoccupation with the propagation of
the gospel in Wales.[40] Alleine laid enormous emphasis on the practice of catechising, and in particular on the characteristic reformed
pastoral practice of house-to-house visitation, in which he spent five
afternoons every week, to scrutinise the knowledge and the morals
of every parishioner. Far more was involved in such visitation than
the testing of knowledge of Christian fundamentals, for Alleine used
it as an explicitly evangelistic device, 'labouring to make them sensible of the evil and danger of sin, of the corruption and depravation
of our natures, the misery of an unconverted state, provoking them
to look after the true remedy proposed in the gospel, to turn from

all their sins unto God, to close with Christ upon his own terms, to follow after holiness, to watch over their hearts and lives, to mortify their lusts, to redeem their time, and to prepare for eternity'.[41]

Closely similar ministries, manifesting the same pastoral techniques and the same preoccupation with conversion, are a characteristic of the clergy who, after the great ejection of 1662, would form the Presbyterian party. Joseph Woodward of Dursley, a schoolmaster as well as a minister, brought his educational concerns to bear in an attack on illiteracy among the poor of his parish: his assistant, Henry Stubbs, was said to have spent a tenth of his income on teaching the poor to read and providing them with books. Woodward, 'in desire of reformation', christened his eldest son Josiah, although 'when he saw little hopes of it' he christened the next child Hezekiah.[42] Fairclough at Kedington had organised schooling for poor children, and he regularly distributed bibles, catechisms and good books, including bibles 'of a larger print' for the aged poor with decayed eyesight, and for the same purpose, gave away 'an incredible number of spectacles'.[43] Thomas Gouge, minister of the 'great and populous' parish of St Sepulchre's in London from 1638, devoted himself to a mission to the poor, pioneering work-relief schemes for the able-bodied, and catechising every morning throughout the year, to classes 'especially of the poorer sort', whose presence at classes he encouraged by random distributions of doles on a different day each week.[44]

Thomas Wadsworth, incumbent of the slum parish of Newington Butts, set about evangelising the tenements and alleys there. As we saw in Chapter 12, once a week he would 'bespeak a house in the street at the end of an Alley, and thither would he send for the poor people out of the alleys, and spend much time in instructing them, and praying with them'. These meetings were followed up by lay assistants, who gathered the poor families in subsequent weeks to answer catechism questions, to hear sermons repeated, or to have awakening tracts read to them. Wadsworth, whose pastoral strategy was deliberately modelled on that of Richard Baxter at Kidderminster, favoured Baxter's *Call to the Unconverted* and his *Making light of Christ* for the latter purpose. Wadsworth also hired a young graduate to come three days a week to teach the poor of the parish to read, and distributed tracts, catechisms and free copies of the New Testament. [45]

The pastoral and missionary ideals of these men and others like them were given decisive expression in the 1650s by Richard Baxter, whose own Kidderminster ministry became a model for others, and whose key role in the Association' Movement helped shape the most important single pastoral and ecclesial development of the mid-century. The Association Movement was at one level a response to crisis and breakdown, an attempt to provide a basis for unity within a voluntary structure for the parishes of the Cromwellian Church of England, by federating single ministers who agreed on the implementation of parochial discipline, along loosely 'Presbyterian' lines. It was consciously a ministerial response to a sense that the godly magistrate could no longer be relied on to protect and promote true religion. But it can also plausibly be thought of as the culmination of a century of puritan pastoral practice. The movement aimed to give spiritual reality to the geographical entity of the parish in ways which would not have struck Greenham or Bolton, Hinde or Fairclough as unfamiliar, by persuading the laity to accept catechising, scrutiny and discipline, and to associate themselves formally with the parish and the ministry of their pastor in an adult church covenant, based on acceptance of the Apostle's Creed and a commitment to the pursuit of holiness.[46]

Out of Baxter's experience came a classic textbook of puritan pastoral practice, *Gildas Salvianus, or the reformed pastor*, a landmark in English Protestant reflection on the nature of mission, conversion, reformation. In it he specifically and deliberately subordinated preaching to the practice of personal supervision, instruction and scrutiny of the flock. It was, he declared, 'but the least part of a minister's work, which is done in the pulpit', and like his contemporaries in counter-reformation France and Italy, he placed the main emphasis in conversion on catechising. He had found by experience, he claimed, 'that an ignorant sot that hath been an unprofitable hearer so long, hath got more knowledge and remorse of conscience in half an hours close discourse, than ... from 10 years publike preaching'.[47]

So much many a minister had said before him, but for Baxter the perception that the conversion of the nation must come less from preaching than from a systematic development of household instruction and scrutiny, a pastoral revolution, changed the familiar landmarks by which Protestant expectations were orientated. Ministers and private men had too long been prone to

> talk and write, and pray, and sigh, and long for reformation, and would little have believed that man that should have presumed to tell them that for all this their very hearts were against reformation, and that they that were praying for it, and fasting for it, and wading through blood for it would never accept it, but would themselves be rejecters and destroyers of it. Yet so it is ... they thought of a reformation to be given by God, but not of a reformation to be wrought on and by themselves. They considered the blessing, but never thought of the means of accomplishing it. As if ... the Holy Ghost should again descend miraculously; or every sermon should convert its thousands; or that the law of a parliament, and the sword of a magistrate would have converted or constrained all, and have done the deed. Little did they think of a reformation that must be wrought by their own diligence and unwearied labours, by earnest preaching, catechising, personal instructions, and taking heed to all the flock.[48]

For Baxter and his circle, the parish was indeed mission territory, containing many who 'really know not what a Christian is', men that 'know not almost any more than the veriest heathen in America'. Their conversion was a task to be tackled systematically, and through the later 1650s he issued a series of works designed to further different dimensions of that work. These included not only the *Reformed pastor* and its 1658 pendant, *Confirmation and restauration, the necessary means of reformation*, with its fascinating account of Baxter's own parish of Kidderminster, but also a series of awakening works directly aimed at conversion.[49] The famous *Call to the Unconverted* (1658), which he was later to claim sold over 20,000 copies in a single year, was aimed at impenitent sinners 'not yet so much as purposing to turn'. His *Directions and persuasions to a sound conversion*, published in the same year, by contrast was aimed at those that are already 'about the work', that they 'miscarry not in the birth'.[50]

In this perspective, conversion was a 'work', the new life a matter of what one of Baxter's associates called 'laborious holiness', and 'active and busy religiousness'.[51] It was also a social vision of conversion, in which the renewal of the individual meant the cleansing of society, reformation of manners. Henry Oasland, curate of Bewdley in Worcestershire, and an ardent evangelist who 'went up and down preaching from place to place', yet considered preaching 'the least part' of his work. He groaned for the conversion of his unregenerate flock and neighbours:

> the sight of their faces, terrifies my conscience . . . I cannot go along the street without grief to see and meet the ignorant and unreformed. Oh the wound, the words and time of sinners spoken and spent in alehouses have given me every time I go by the door! How many times have I stept in amongst them, to reason the case with them, though I might loose my life or limbs!'[52]

So the conversion of England was for them a process which might, and must, make use of every available means, from the laborious fostering of devotion by good books or the encouragement of private meetings for edification of the godly, especially the godly young, to the enforcement by the magistrates of laws against vice and drunkenness, profanity, scorn of godliness and Sabbath-breaking.[53] What these men were after was not merely the conversion of individuals, but the transformation of a community, and accounts of their work are peppered with idealised pictures of such transformations. Fairclough at Kedington made

> a very effectual reformation in that town. Former prophaneness was forced now to hide its head; drunkenness, swearing, cursing, bastardy, and the like, as they were not practiced, so they were scarce known; divers persons having lived many years in that parish . . . never heard an oath sworn, or ever saw one person drunk, as they have professed.

Even in godly Suffolk,

> it was expected . . . that every inhabitant of Kedington should be distinguished from others, not only by the more savouriness of their discourse, but also by the universal strictness and piety of their lives and conversations.[54]

393

Alcester, where Samuel Clarke laboured, 'which before was called Drunken Alcester, was now exemplary, and eminent for religion, all over the country'.[55] At his coming to Dursley, Joseph Woodward's son recalled, it was

> a place at the time very dissolute insomuch that it had the name of drunken Dursley, but if he found it so it was very much altered by his labours ... and became one of the most wealthy and best trading towns in the neighbourhood. Some of them having told me that they cleared a thousand pounds a year by the trade of clothing, in the time of his residence there. His presence in the streets ... made the sober to rejoice, and the guilty to hide themselves in corners ... and every one's zeal seemed inflamed by the flame he beheld in his neighbour; so that I have heard that there was the most composed and affected congregation that could anywhere be seen. [56]

When Baxter came to Kidderminster first, he recalled,

> there was about one family in a street that worshipped God and called on his name, and when I came away there were some Streets where there was not past one family in the side of a street that did not so ... And those families that were the worst, being inns and alehouses, usually some persons in each house did seem to be religious. [57]

Baxter believed that the Commonwealth years had brought the dream of the conversion of England closer than it had ever been. As we saw in chapter 11, he marvelled that he himself should have achieved so much, 'when the reverend instructors of my youth did labour fifty years together in one place, and could scarcely say that they had converted one or two of their parishes!' The godly had always had an uneasy relationship with the parish community, passionately committed to the notion of a preaching minister in every parish, yet gathering the godly from outside it, gadding abroad to sermons, forging loyalties at exercises, fasts and combination sermons, which transcended it, and always haunted by a theology which refused to equate the elect with membership of the visible church.

The activities of Baxter and his associates in the 1650s represented the reformed tradition's best shot in England at coming to terms with the parish, of establishing a stable relationship and a substantial overlap between the visible and the invisible churches. We need not, indeed we should not, take them at their own estimation. Baxter's success in persuading the majority of households in his parish to accept discipline and submit to his pastoral regime was as unusual in mid-Stuart England as the five galleries he had to construct to hold the hearers who flocked to his sermons, and probably led him to exaggerate the effectiveness of the pastoral revolution which he saw around him in the 1650s. The problems of operating a voluntary discipline of this sort within the parochial system, involving as it did the exclusion of substantial numbers of the parish from communion, were more evident elsewhere than they were at Kidderminster, where most of those excluded 'yet took it patiently, and did not revile us as doing them wrong'.[58] Nevertheless, Baxter came to believe that the pastoral experiments and successes which culminated in the 1650s established beyond all doubt the centrality of the parish in the work of conversion, and that 'it is a better work to reform the parishes, than to gather churches out of them'.[59]

But any such success was destined to be short-lived. With the exodus of almost 2,000 ministers in 1662, many of them the most committed practitioners of the Baxterian parochial model, the Restoration put an end to short-term hopes for the conversion of England through the parishes. It did not, however, eclipse the ideal, even within the Church of England. Many moderates who shared Baxter's hopes and methods conformed in 1662, and the children of many who could not do so carried their fathers' ideals into the establishment. Joseph Woodward rejected the Restoration settlement, but his sons Josiah and Hezekiah, named for reformation, conformed and pursued clerical careers, and, as we shall see, the cause of reform, within the national church. But in the 1660s and 1670s the missionary impulse we have been discussing was more evident within the ranks of nonconformity, as Alleine, Wadsworth, Baxter himself and a host of others pursued evangelistic careers outside the law. In some cases at least, their methods could be as histrionic as any of their counter-reformation opposite numbers, and not such as were likely to win approval in a Church increasingly suspicious of the enthusiasm that had overthrown Church and state. Henry Oasland would press on his Nonconformist congregation the need to accept Christ and then demand that anyone present who made light of the offer and 'reused Christ' should leave the building: he would then sit down and a long wait ensued, which ended only when Oasland 'perceiving that they all stayed . . . rose up as one in an extasy of joy, and said "Now I hope every one of you is espoused to Jesus Christ"'.[60]

Exclusion from parochial ministry forced on them other expedients, some of them, such as the gathering of congregations, profoundly distasteful to them, others hallowed by long practice among the godly, such as wide-scale itineracy.[61] They also developed further existing Protestant sensitivity to the role of print.[62] Baxter and his associates poured out a stream of material designed to convert, from Baxter's own tract *Now or Never* in 1662, to Alleine's *Alarm to unconverted sinners* in 1672, and a life of Alleine, by his wife and others, in the same year. Baxter did much to maintain this stream of publications, providing prefaces to a number of them, such as the *Alarm* and Alleine's biography, and later to a posthumous edition of awakening sermons of Thomas Wadsworth, and to Samuel Clarke's *Lives of sundry eminent persons* of 1683. Clarke's collection gathered together a set of biographies of figures like Machin, Alleine, Wadsworth, and of older, prototype figures such as Fairclough, and it can be read as a manifesto for the evangelistic enterprise choked off by the Restoration settlement, a gallery of portraits designed to illustrate the pastoral tragedy of 1662.[63]

For English Protestantism, then, 1662 marked a parting of the ways as momentous as any event since the break with Rome. Not unnaturally, there has been a tendency for historians to be mesmerised by it into editing the 'godly' dimension out of Restoration church life, to see the ideals and practice of the pre-Restoration puritan tradition as having been decisively excluded from the national church in 1662 and having thereafter flowed into separating nonconformity. This is particularly true in the area of soteriology: we are accustomed to think of the Restoration as the period of 'the rise of moralism', the replacement of an earlier evangelical emphasis on faith and grace by a laborious and somewhat gloomy works religion, represented in devotional classics such as Allestree's *The whole duty of man*. It is a picture which leading Restoration churchmen themselves encouraged. Simon Patrick denounced the rhetoric of puritan conversion as a cloak for antinomianism:

> It is called a casting of ourselves upon Christ, a relying on his merits, a shrouding our selves under the robes of his righteousness; and though sometimes it is called a going to him for salvation, yet there is this mystery in the business, that you may go, and yet not go, you may go, and yet stand still . . . or if you take one little step, and be at pains to come to him, the work is done, and you need not follow him.

He urged the devout reader to 'put your hands to pull down that idol of faith, which hath been set up with so much devotion, and religiously worshipped so long among us: that dead image of faith which so many have adored, trusted in, and perished (by)'.[64] John Eachard spelt this out:

> I do most heartily wish that such as have spent their time in read-ing of books and sermons about experiences, getting of Christ, and the like, would change them all away for *The whole duty of man*, that abounds with very pious and intelligible rules of godly living, and useful knowledge tending to salvation.[65]

As will be plain from what has been said about the puritan ideal of a 'laborious holiness', however, and from Baxter's denunciation of those who 'thought of a reformation to be given by God, but not of a reformation to be wrought on and by themselves', there was an element of shadow-boxing about all this. Insofar as these insinuations of an antinomian emphasis on faith were aimed at the mainstream of nonconformity, they were wide of the mark. *The whole duty of man* was promoted by Restoration bishops, and distrib-uted by the basketful to Restoration parishioners, but it was also one of the 'helps' specifically recommended to the godly by Baxter and other puritan activists.[66] A shared godly culture persisted into the Restoration, with no impermeable walls between conforming and nonconforming participants in it. In the margin of page 108 of the Trinity College, Cambridge, copy of Baxter's *Treatise of self-denyall*, published in 1660 and containing a resounding puritan attack on play-books and romances, Sabbath-breaking, sports and profanity, someone has written, 'July 6th 1662 Francis Limly was convinced of his sins by the hearing of this place read at Christ Church on a sabbath day morning.'[67]

The awakening literature which poured from the presses of Restoration England, in the production of which ejected ministers played a major role, sustained a culture within which conversion and missionary concerns remained central. In the process, some of the missionary forms associated with the end of the century, and generally interpreted as a response to the new problems created for the Church of England by the calamities of the late Stuart period, emerged from the roots we have been discussing. In the early 1670s Thomas Gouge, ejected minister of St Sepulchre's in London, read the life of Joseph Alleine, and was fired with zeal by the account of Alleine's involvement in the propagation of the gospel in Wales. Gouge devoted the remaining years of his life to an extraordinary peripatetic mission to Wales, which focused on the provision of schools for the poor, and the translation of good books into Welsh for them to read. Gouge established a trust to print Welsh Bibles, and he distributed puritan favourites such as Lewis Bailey's *The practice of piety*. But he also distributed Welsh editions of the Book of Common Prayer, the Church Catechism and commentaries on it, and *The whole duty of man*. His work, which was carried out in cooperation with Nonconformist activists, nevertheless also had the somewhat uneasy blessing of the Welsh episcopate, and forms a striking link between the evangelistic ferment of the 1650s and the later work of the SPCK.[68]

But if there was still a shared culture of the godly, it was one which had been profoundly fractured by the ejections of 1662, above all along the uneasy and fragile junction between that culture's parochial and its charismatic elements. The Restoration Church of England continued to seek fervour and conversion from its members, but its profound distrust of the traditional godly language by which that fervour had been elicited and expressed left it prone to a duty-bound formalism. Restoration piety can seem stifling, scrupulous, churchy.

The godly Anglican now was encouraged to express a deeper dedication and a changed heart by a closer attention to the duties of a churchman, more frequent attendance at the sacraments, a devouter celebration of the Church's year. Such a calendrical piety, however deeply felt, was bound to alienate those of the godly who had suffered exclusion because of their objections to Prayer Book observance. Penitential, joyless and duty-bound, it could seem not much better calculated to attract the multitudes of 'parish Anglicans', for whom the Prayer Book and its feasts were valued, not so much as the framework for a profound and scrupulous conversion of life, but rather as the scaffolding for social decency, and markers in the natural cycle of rites of passage and the hallowing of time. Conversion of life and parish conformity, successfully joined in counter-reformation Europe, were decisively divorced in England in 1662.

It is in the light of this growing rift in the godly tradition that we need to consider the extraordinary flurry of pious and evangelistic activity in the last decades of the seventeenth and the early decades of the eighteenth century, of which the SPCK was to become the epitome. Modern discussion of the religious societies, the societies for the reformation of manners, of the SPCK, and the charity school movement has usually placed these various movements for reform against the polarising of Church politics in the era of the Glorious Revolution. The religious societies have been seen as self-consciously and exclusively Anglican devotional groups dedicated to consolidating a Church-based piety, while the societies for the reformation of manners, in which many Dissenters were involved, have been seen, by contrast, as a mark of Low Church abandonment of distinctive claims of Anglican hegemony in society. Where High Churchmen sought a cure for society's moral corruption in the revival of the discipline of the Church and its courts, Low Churchmen settled for the enforcement of public morality by the secular arm. [69]

The religious societies, with their scrupulous and self-consciously exclusive Anglicanism, seem on the face of it the least likely candidates for inclusion in a pedigree which stretches back through Richard Baxter to the English puritan tradition. Origins have been sought for them in the *collegia pietatis* of German Pietism, or in the sodalities and confraternities of the French counter-reformation, as mediated through the life of De Renty, a favourite book with many Protestants in Restoration England.[70] Yet our best and earliest contemporary account of their origins, by Josiah Woodward, leaves little doubt that it is primarily in the tradition we have been discussing that they should be placed. Woodward describes how the awakening sermons of two London preachers in the late 1670s, William Smythies, curate of St Giles Cripplegate, and Anthony Horneck, preacher at the Savoy Chapel, had converted groups of young men. Josiah Woodward interviewed one of them,

> who with floods of tears lamented that he had not till then had any affecting apprehensions of the glorious majesty and perfections of Almighty God, nor of his infinite love to men in his son Jesus Christ. And that he had not before felt any just convictions of the immense evil of every offence against God ... But now he saw, and groan'd under all this, in very sharp and pungent convictions. And withal, perceiving the universal corruption of human nature, and the deplorable crookedness and deceit of man's heart, and with what a world of temptations we are encompass'd ... when he considered all this, his soul was even poured out within him, and he was in danger of being overwhelmed with excessive sorrow.[71]

The gathering of young men of this mentality to take advice from their spiritual guides, to pray and to perform works of charity was in conformity with the well-established practice of the godly, for such weekday meetings 'about soul affairs' were a normal part of puritan pastoral practice. The activities of these Anglican societies also conformed to well-tried formulae, like the society in the parish of St Martin-in-the-Fields in 1681 which met for prayer, Bible-reading and sermon repetition, or the society begun by the minister at Old Romney in Kent about 1690, to revive 'the divine ordinance of singing psalms', to increase 'spiritual fervency' among the young, and to encourage attendance on the 'public ordinances of God'.[72]

But there were significant differences, and a decisive narrowing of appeal about the societies. In the fraught climate of Charles II's reign it was inevitable that the piety of the societies should be self-consciously loyal to the Church. Meetings about soul affairs in the godly tradition had always been vulnerable to charges of conventicling, and it was inevitable that the societies should deliberately distance themselves from any association with separatism. Moreover, the revival of sacramental piety which is a feature of Restoration devotion meant that the meetings of the societies were initially largely concerned with preparation for reception of communion. Fervour at the sacrament was a characteristic of the puritan tradition, too, and such preparation meetings had been a feature of puritan devotion, but in Restoration England reception of the sacrament was a political as well as a devotional act, a barrier between the godly rather than the bond of their fellowship. The societies might have a devotional root in the tradition, but the circumstances of the time made them a stumbling stone to the principal heirs of that tradition, excluded as they were (or as others thought they should be) from the sacramental sealing of the unity of the godly.

The movement for the reformation of manners was closely connected to a providentialist reading of the Revolution of 1688. The God who had shown his special favour to the nation by delivering them from the tyranny of popery would now demand a corresponding response, the cleansing of the nation from sins which cried out to heaven for judgement. As Josiah Woodward declared,

A public sinner does not only sin against his own soul, but against the community of which he is a member . . . Our overlooking of any gross sin is a taking the guilt of it into our own bosom; yea, 'tis a spreading and diffusing of the curses due unto it upon the face of the whole city and nation in which we dwell. [73]

To invoke the magistrate against public vice, therefore, was not a secular but a religious act, the search for a godly nation through the conversion or at any rate the containment and punishing of the vicious, in the time-honoured alliance between minister and magistrate. As Woodward further declared,

thou shalt appeal to the minister, and to the magistrate; not against the man, but against the sin. Thou shalt tell it to the Church, and thou shalt inform the bench (the seat of justice) of it, that all fit spiritual censures and temporal chastisements may be applied to him in time, that his soul perish not to all eternity. [74]

Josiah Woodward, as already remarked, had been 'named for reformation' by his puritan father, and it is hardly surprising to find him deploying the familiar rhetoric of godly reformation. His own career was devoted to a strenuous campaign of education and catechesis in his own parish of Maidstone, and also, through pamphleteering and preaching, against Sabbath-breaking, profanity and vice in every form, in works with titles such as *A kind caution to profane swearers.* In him the godly agenda of the 1650s and before can be seen still alive and active. But he was by no means alone. Another key figure in the movement for reformation of manners was the remarkable and eccentric Gloucestershire lawyer Edward Stephens, who founded the first Reformation Society and became a tireless publicist for the movement.[75] His later liturgical preoccupations, his advocacy of the 1549 Prayer Book and foundation of a Protestant convent, and his desire for reunion with the Churches of Greece and Rome, make Stephens seem an unlikely heir of the puritans. Yet he too had direct links backward to the Baxter circle, for he was the son-in-law of Sir Matthew Hale, and there is no mistaking the provenance of the reforming rhetoric he pressed into service in the aftermath of the Glorious Revolution.

In a series of pamphlets in aid of religious and moral reform beginning in 1689 Stephens advanced a providentialist reading of the history of England under the Stuart monarchy which would not have disgraced the fast sermons of the Long Parliament. He denounced the moves by which the godly had been squeezed out of the national church – the discouraging and oppression of true piety 'by reproachful names of Puritans and precisions', particularly by 'that impious and abominable project of the Book of Sports', and 'the cursed dividing of the church and nation, by that mischievous Act of Uniformity', by which 'many good and useful men' were excluded from service in the Church.[76] For Stephens, enforcement of laws against vice was not a secular usurpation of the Church's rights, but a prelude to their recovery. He denounced the first reformers, and the Church of England ever since, for failure to introduce a proper Christian discipline of excommunication. Cranmer's commination service deplored the absence of such a discipline, but this lament, renewed in the liturgy of every Ash Wednesday, was rank hypocrisy, for the Church had systematically 'opposed and suppressed those who have desired it, and instead thereof retained only a popish relict and abuse of it'.[77] The need for reformation of manners on a voluntary basis sprang from the failure of the Church and the Crown to fulfil their covenanted obligations to a God who had manifested his saving providence to the nation again and again.

Support for the movement for reformation of manners was at first widespread among devout members of the Church of England, including many and perhaps most members of the religious societies, but its wider appeal was doomed by the very fact that it presented itself as a response to a godly agenda patronised by the Crown, and by Queen Mary in particular.[78] William's victory at the battle of Aughrim on 11 July 1691, for example, was attributed by the *Athenian Mercury* to the adoption in a proclamation the day before of the cause of reformation of manners by the Middlesex justices of the peace, and by September 1691 Edward Stephens was denouncing opponents of reformation of manners as Jacobites.[79] For the many churchmen with queasy consciences about the deposition of James II this was a problematic pedigree, and reformation of manners became a party issue, with a consequent division of the godly, if only for prudential reasons. Most members of religious societies withdrew overt support as party tensions heightened, and it was probably in the wake of their departure that Dissenters were first recruited, to take their places.

It has been generally recognised that the movement did command a good deal of high-placed Church support, notably that of Archbishop Tillotson and, to begin with at least, Archbishop Sharp of York, and of a good many other Revolution bishops – Gilbert Burnet, Edward Fowler, Richard Kidder, Simon Patrick, Humphrey Humphreys, Nicholas Stratford, John Hough. These men are often described as 'Latitudinarians', and Mark Goldie has characterised support for reformation of manners, along with comprehension and Latitudinarianism, as forming a nexus, distinct from 'High-Church preoccupations'.[80] What the word 'Latitudinarian' is in danger of concealing here is the 'godly' origins of some of the key figures in these Revolution disputes. Tillotson himself had succeeded Fairclough as vicar of Kedington, and he retained a good deal of sympathy for the religious programme of those driven into nonconformity. He was the funeral eulogist of Thomas Gouge, and an admirer of the practical holiness preached by nonconforming clergy. Similarly, Kidder, the biographer of Anthony Horneck, had himself been ejected for nonconformity in 1662. Fowler was the friend, patron and employer of William Smythies whose awakening preaching had begun the religious societies, and he was to lend Stephens his city church for daily communion services later in the reign. Many of the clergy who supported the reformation societies did so because, like the Archdeacon of Durham, Robert Booth, who had 25 people in a single day clapped in the stocks for Sabbath-breaking, they saw in the societies a revival of the aspiration for a godly nation which had lain at the heart of Protestant mission to England for a century and a half.[81] The programme of the movement for reformation of manners, with its attacks on Sabbath-breaking, profanity, public drunkenness and prostitution, has many similarities, even down to the institution of professional informers, with the programme of legislation against profaneness and for reformation which Richard Baxter was advocating in the late 1650s.[82] The links were not lost on opponents, and Henry Sacheverell denounced the movement for reformation of manners as a 'mongrel institution' designed to 'insinuate an insufficiency in the Church's discipline', to 'betray its power into the hands of a lay-eldership and fanaticism'.[83]

The religious societies and the reformation societies sprang, therefore, from the same cluster of godly preoccupations with ways and means of conversion and reformation. Their separation represents the fracture, under the pressure of late Stuart politics, of a single vision of a Reformed England, and a single programme for its achievement in the parishes. Low as well as High Churchmen came to have reservations about the reformation movement in the 1690s and early 1700s, precisely because they did not wish to see the unity of that reforming vision divided into different agencies. Tillotson's successor, Archbishop Thomas Tenison, veteran of a distinguished slum ministry at St Martin-in-the-Fields which had the approval and support of Richard Baxter, thought that bishops should not support the societies for reformation of manners, but instead proposed 'the doing of something ourselves, it being, I thought, most absurd for the college of bishops to be led in such a manner'.[84] He wrote in April 1699 to the other bishops deploring the 'sensible growth of vice and profaneness in the nation', and urging the clergy to combat it by meeting together in local groups 'to consult and advise', by enlisting the support of magistrates and the laity 'of the greatest esteem and authority in their parishes', by suppressing vice and encouraging virtue, and above all by diligent catechising to 'lay the foundations of piety and morality'.[85] His letter, decidedly reminiscent of the expedients of the clergy of the Association Movement of the 1650s, came within a month of the founding of a reform agency which was to dominate much of the eighteenth-century Church of England's practical work, the SPCK.

The SPCK was the brainchild of Thomas Bray, an unpleasant but phenomenally active clerical educator, dedicated to the propagation of orthodox Protestantism in England and the colonies. He envisaged his Society for Promoting Christian Knowledge as a Church of England response to the Roman Catholic *Congregatio de Propaganda Fide*, but it was also designed to combat Dissenters and Quakers in the interests of the 'pure and primitive Christianity which we profess'.[86] Originally intended as a clerical initiative, and, despite firm support for the Hanoverian succession, retaining the support of a broad-based clerical constituency, it quickly became an essentially lay agency, promoting Anglican reform in all its manifestations – charity schools, catechising and the distribution of edifying literature, defence of Church principles, encouragement of more frequent attendance at the sacrament, patronage of the religious societies. It was also a vigorous patron of the reformation societies, however, publishing epitomes of the legislation against vice, issuing advice to constables and magistrates, and using its network of book distributors to disseminate blank warrants for use in the war against the ungodly. It embodied, then, most aspects of the awakened piety which had characterised the godly tradition we have been considering, and represented not merely the response of churchmen to the crisis of the 1690s, but the continuation of a long-term preoccupation with the conversion of the nation. Yet once again, the political environment in which it was born, and the concern of its directors to secure the widest possible base within the Church of England, turned it into an instrument against the Dissenters, and therefore a stumbling stone for many of the inheritors of that same godly tradition.

The ambivalences within the pedigree of the SPCK were recognised by contemporaries, and reflected in the early response to its work. The coincidence of the founding of the SPCK and the appearance of the archbishop's invitation to the clergy to associate for the promotion of reformation, led many to identify the SPCK as an official episcopal instrument of reform. A group of 13 Berkshire clergy told the secretary of the SPCK in 1700 that they had established a clerical association,

> out of a true zeal ... for the salvation of the souls of our poor brethren, and out of a just concern for the true interest of that truly primitive and apostolical church whereof we are members; as also in obedience to our most reverend metropolitan's circular letter, and ... in compliance with the reasonable request of the society.

But the clergy of Kent, perhaps alert to the overtones of the word 'association', took a different view, judging the SPCK to be 'a reviving of presbyterian classes ... an usurpation of the rights of convocation and an inlet to division and separation'.[87] The reception of the society in Wales, that long-standing focus of missionary zeal, illustrates these ambivalences. The society's objectives were easily recognised as part of a long tradition of godly reformation. One Welsh supporter listed the remedies for the 'corruptions of the age': 'discipline must be restored, catechizing seriously applied to and the magistrate be vigorous and resolv'd in punishing vice'. This was an agenda in which Richard Baxter would warmly have collaborated.

But although many clergy welcomed the help of an external agency in tackling the 'reigning diseases' of 'ignorance and unconcernedness' among the vulgar, and the SPCK was to play a crucial role in the stabilising of Welsh Anglicanism in the eighteenth century, in the last years of the Stuart monarchy its pan-parochial, extra-diocesan character was a cause of suspicion. It was reported that there, too, 'some cavil at the word association', and there were fears that the activities of the society might erode the Church's distinctive jurisdiction.[88]

John Spurr has criticised the Restoration religious societies for having undermined the integrity of the parish. The voluntary piety of the societies, he suggests, was ultimately elitist because it needed a clerical and liturgical apparatus which 'was simply not available outside London', and the societies, designed, as Woodward said, as mutual support for the godly, 'to maintain their integrity in the midst of a crooked and perverse generation', were in fact a retreat on sectarianism, an abandonment of the claims of the Church of England to be the church of the whole nation. This led some Anglicans, he believes, to recognise that they had no monopoly on holiness, and that among the Nonconformists there were many who might have been 'instruments of reforming the parochial churches by example, admonition and assisting the exercise of discipline'. Such admissions were 'straws in the wind blowing from the eighteenth century', precursors of a world 'where the zealous of different denominations might have more in common with each other than with the lukewarm of their own communion'.[89]

But historical winds don't blow backwards, and the limitations Spurr ascribes to the Restoration and Revolution religious societies were precisely the limitations of the godly tradition in general. The religious societies were not the forerunners of modern-day religious voluntarism. They were, rather, part of the wreckage of the English reformation's attempt to bring together and hold together the routinisation of religion in the parish, and the personal conversion and zeal which were the essential marks of the godly. It is not clear that so difficult a bonding could ever have been perfectly achieved. The counter-reformation may be judged to have made a better stab at it, but with the help of three inestimable advantages. The first of these was the presence of the religious orders, and in particular of orders like the Jesuits, Lazarists and Redemptorists, operating alongside the parish ministry and supplementing it with the specialised professionalism of the missions. The second was, within those missions, a hospitality to ritual and drama – the use of dramatic penitential gestures, the wearing of hoods, torchlight processions, the dramatic display of life-sized crucifixes, the use of *tableaux vivants* and costume to represent sacred truths, the encouragement of emotional and emotive devotional practices, all of which enabled Catholic missions simultaneously to attack the profane dimensions of popular culture, yet to put up some plausible rival attractions, and to become itself an aspect of popular culture – in David Gentilcore's words, meeting popular culture half way.[90]

The third, and arguably the decisive advantage, was the harnessing of the centuries-old obligation of confession into the service of a newer and more demanding style of Christian commitment. The confessional was the ultimate weapon of the counter-reformation, the perfect forum for the meeting and integration of routinisation and the zeal of conversion, and Protestantism had nothing to rival it. Yet up until the Restoration, the godly tradition in England did at least present a coherent front to the society it sought to convert and subdue, its vision of a godly nation pursued simultaneously through the pulpit, the catechism class, the house visit, the prayer meeting and the magistrate's bench. Cromwellian Kedington or Dursley, Alcester or Kidderminster would not have been to modern taste, with constables and ministers combing the pubs during service time, the sound of psalm-singing in every street no compensation for the powerful dryness of those long, hot Sunday afternoons. But they were at least a serious attempt to embody the central dream of the English reformation. The dream persisted, and was still a powerful one in the eighteenth century: it is one of the foundation stones of the Evangelical Revival. But after 1662 it was never viable as a possibility for the whole nation, and the ejection of the majority of the clergy most committed to that dream, and best equipped to pursue it, signed its death warrant. The Church of England entered the eighteenth century with all the elements of that Protestant dream of a Christian nation intact – parochial conformity, suppression of public vice, the cultivation of serious personal religion. But they were beads without a string, forces whose individual impact was fatally weakened by their lack of a common focus. The transformation of England into a godly nation remained a concern in the Hanoverian Church. As a realistic project, however, it died in 1662.

Notes

1   J. Delumeau, *Le Catholicisme entre Luther et Voltaire* (Paris, 1971), English translation, with an introduction by John Bossy, *Catholicism between Luther and Voltaire* (London, 1977): quotation from the Foreword (unpaginated).
2   J. Bossy, *Christianity in the West 1400–1700* (Oxford, 1985) p. 91.
3   D. Gentilcore '"Adapt yourselves to the people's capabilities": missionary strategies, methods and impact in the kingdom of Naples, 1600–1800' (hereafter 'Missionary strategies'), *Journal of Ecclesiastical History*, 45 (1994), p. 272.
4   M. Aston, *The Fifteenth Century: The Prospect of Europe* (London, 1968), p. 167; I. Origo, *The World of San Bernardino* (London, 1963); F. Oakley, *The Western Church in the Later Middle Ages* (Cornell, 1979), pp. 261–70; L. Chatellier, *La religion des pauvres* (Paris, 1993), pp. 17–21.

5   Delumeau, *Catholicism between Luther and Voltaire*, pp. 189–94; Chatellier, *Religion des pauvres*, pp. 51–121 and *passim*; J. W. O'Malley, *The first Jesuits* (Harvard, 1993), pp. 126–7; F. M. Jones, *Alphonsus de Liguori* (Dublin, 1992), pp. 246–61; Gentilcore, 'Missionary strategies', pp. 269–96.

6   H. Joly, *Life of St John Eudes* (London, 1932), pp. 59–62: the witness here was Baron Gaston de Renty.

7   K. Wrightson and D. Levine, *Poverty and Piety in an English Village: Terling 1525–1700* (New York, San Francisco and London, 1979), pp. 12–13; the classic exposition of this view is that of Christopher Haigh, 'Puritan evangelism in the reign of Elizabeth I', *English Historical Review*, 92 (1977), pp. 30–58.

8   P. Collinson, 'Shepherds, sheepdogs, and hirelings: the pastoral ministry in post-Reformation England' in *The Ministry, Clerical and Lay*, W. J. Sheils and D. Wood (eds) (Studies in Church History, vol. 26, 1989), p. 220.

9   J. Gregory, 'The eighteenth-century Reformation: the pastoral task of Anglican clergy after 1689' in *The Church of England c.1689–1833*, J. Walsh, C. Haydon & S. Taylor (eds) (Cambridge, 1993), pp. 67–85.

10   But for a tentative stab at something like this, see Chapter 12 above.

11   J. Foxe, *The acts and monuments*, S. R. Cattley and G. Townsend (eds) (London, 1837), vol. 4, p. 636.

12   G. E. Corrie (ed.), *Sermons by Hugh Latimer* (Parker Society, Cambridge, 1844), p. 208.

13   The essential source is George Carleton, *The life of Bernard Gilpin* (London, 1629): there is a helpful modern assessment by D. Marcombe, 'Bernard Gilpin: anatomy of an Elizabethan legend', *Northern History*, 16 (1980), pp. 20–39, which, however, oversimplifies Gilpin's religious positions in the reigns of Edward and Mary.

14   Carleton, *Gilpin*, p. 19

15   Carleton, *Gilpin*, pp. 27–8: Gilpin's preaching was characterised by a particular emphasis on the reconciliation of feuding factions in the Marches, a preoccupation which also characterised Lazarist and Eudist preaching in upland France and Italy. Joly, *St John Eudes*, pp. 61, 64; P. Coste, *The Life and Labours of Saint Vincent de Paul* (London, 1935), vol. 3, pp. 45, 50–51.

16   J. Raine (ed.), *Ecclesiastical Proceedings of Bishop Barnes* (Surtees Society 22, 1850), pp. 81–91: Marcombe, 'Gilpin', p. 32.

17   Carleton, *Gilpin*, p. 21: Marcombe, 'Gilpin', pp. 31–4; W. Gilpin, *The life of Bernard Gilpin* (London, 1753), p. 223: M. James, *Family, Lineage and Civil Society* (Oxford, 1974), pp. 63, 97, 99.

18   C. Hill, 'Puritans and the "dark corners of the land"', in *Continuity and Change in Seventeenth-Century England* (London, 1974). p. 5.

19   P. Collinson, *The Religion of Protestants* (Oxford, 1982), pp. 257–64; S. Clarke, *The lives of sundry eminent persons in this later age* (London, 1683), p. 4.

20   Collinson, *Religion of Protestants*, pp. 242–4.

21   The phrasing comes from a 1592 order of the Northern High Commission: R. W. Hoyle, 'Advancing the Reformation in the North: orders from the York High Commission, 1583 and 1592', *Northern History*, 28 (1992), p. 225.

22   Clarke, *Lives of eminent persons*, p. 5.

23   W. Hinde, *A path to pietie, leading to the way, the truth and the life, Christ Jesus. Drawn upon the ground, and according to the Rule of Faith* (London, 1626), Epistle Dedicatorie.

24   P. Collinson, '"A magazine of religious patterns": an Erasmian topic transposed in English Protestantism', in *Renaissance and Renewal in Christian History*, D. Baker (ed.) (Studies in Church History, 14 (1977), pp. 240–42.

25   W. Hinde, *A faithfull remonstrance of the holy life and happy death of John Bruen of Bruen Stapleford, in the County of Chester, Esquire* (London, 1641), pp. 216–17.

26   W. Harrison, *The difference of hearers* (London, 1614), p. 93.

27   Dent, *Plaine Man's Path-Way* (London, 1601), pp. 285–7.

28   J. Rogers, *The doctrine of faith* (London, 1634). pp. 97–9.

29   Ibid., pp. 185–6.

30   M. Sylvester (ed.), *Reliquiae Baxterianae* (London, 1696), p. 3: for the treatise in question, B. S. Gregory, '"The true and zealous service of God": Robert Persons, Edmund Bunny, and The First Booke of the Christian Exercise', *Journal of Ecclesiastical History* 45 (1994), pp. 238–68.

31   I. Green, '"For children in yeeres and children in understanding": the emergence of the English catechism under Elizabeth and the early Stuarts', *Journal of Ecclesiastical History* 37 (1986), pp.

397–425. *The Christian's ABC: Catechisms and Catechizing in England c. 1530–1740* (Oxford, 1996), pp. 580–751 for the finding list of the catechisms.

32   Hinde, *Path to pietie*, pp. 1–3.

33   W. Perkins, *The foundation of Christian religion gathered into six principles* (London, 1627), Epistle 'to all ignorant people that desire to be instructed', sig A4.

34   F. E. Hutchinson (ed.), *The Works of George Herbert* (Oxford, 1967), p. 255.

35   Green, 'Emergence', p. 417.

36   Hutchinson, *Works of George Herbert*, p. 257.

37   Clarke, *Lives of eminent persons*, pp. 165–82. For a salutary caution about treating Clarke's *Lives* as neutral historical sources, Peter Lake, 'Reading Clarke's Lives in political and polemical context' in Kevin Sharpe and Steven N. Zwicker (eds), *Writing Lives: Biography and Textuality, Identity and Representation in Early Modern England* (Oxford, 2008), pp. 293–319: and see Patrick Collinson, '"A Magazine of Religious Patterns": an Erasmian Topic Transposed in English Protestantism' in *Godly People* (London, 1983) pp. 499–526, and see chapter 11 above.

38   For a more tentative although not contradictory discussion of the nature and development of ministry in England than is here implied, see P. Collinson, 'Shepherds, sheepdogs and hirelings: the pastoral ministry in post-Reformation England' in *The Ministry, Clerical and Lay*, W. J. Sheils and D. Wood (eds) (*Studies in Church History*, vol. 26, 1989), pp. 185–220; see also, in the same collection, I. Green '"Reformed pastors" and *Bons Curés*: the changing role of the parish clergy in Early Modern Europe', pp. 249–86.

39   Clarke, *Lives of eminent persons*, pp. 83–92; E. Calamy, *Nonconformists' memorial*, S. Palmer (ed.) (2nd edn, London, 1802–3), vol. 1, pp. 343–4.

40   For which see Hill, 'Puritans and the "dark corners of the land"', *passim*, and A. M. Johnson, 'Wales during the Commonwealth and Protectorate' in D. Pennington and K. Thomas (eds), *Puritans and revolutionaries* (Oxford, 1978), pp. 233–56.

41   Clarke, *Lives of eminent persons*, pp. 140–44; Calamy, *Nonconformists' memorial*, vol. 3, pp. 208–11.

42   Calamy, *Nonconformists' memorial*, vol. 2, pp. 234–44.

43   Clarke, *Lives of eminent persons*, p. 180.

44   Ibid., pp. 203 ff.

45   This account of Wadsworth's ministry is based on Richard Baxter's prefatory 'to the reader', prefixed to Wadsworth's posthumous *Last warning to secure sinners, being his two last sermons* (London, 1677); see also Calamy, *Nonconformists' memorial*, vol. 1, pp. 138–42; for Wadsworth's pastoral indebtedness to Eaxter, N. H. Keeble and G. F. Nuttall (eds), *Calendar of the correspondence of Richard Baxter*, vol. 1 (Oxford, 1991) pp. 200–201, 203–4.

46   *Christian concord: or the agreement of the associated pastors and churches of Worcestershire. With Rich. Baxter's explication and defence of it* (London, 1653).

47   N. H. Keeble, *Richard Baxter, Puritan man of letters* (Oxford, 1982), pp. 81–2; K. Wrightson, *English Society 1580–1680* (London, 1982), p. 216.

48   W. Orme (ed.), *The practical works of the Revd. Richard Baxter*, vol. 14 (London, 1830), (Gildas Salvianus), pp. 266–7.

49   Chapter 12 above: Orme, *Practical Works of Richard Baxter*, vol. 14, pp. 401–594.

50   For Baxter's discussion of the place of these publications in his overall evangelistic scheme, Keeble, *Puritan man of letters*, pp. 74–6.

51   *Baxter correspondence*, vol. 1, p. 88.

52   Ibid., pp. 112, 126.

53   Ibid., pp. 145–8, 222–6.

54   Clarke, *Lives of eminent persons*, p. 169.

55   Ibid., pp. 6–7.

56   Calamy, *Nonconformists' memorial*, vol. 2, p. 258.

57   Sylvester, *Reliquiae Baxterianae*, Part 1, pp. 84–5.

58   For lesser success with the same methods elsewhere, see, for example, the rueful and envious comments of T. Wadsworth: *Baxter correspondence*, vol. 1, p. 204; see also I. Green's remarks on the 'rose-tinted glass colouring Baxter's view of the wider success of the movement by 1659' in *The*

Christian's ABC, pp. 222–7, esp. p. 226. For a discussion of similar moves in Warwickshire, and their limitations, see Anne Hughes, *Godly Reformation and its Opponents in Warwickshire, 1640–1662* (Dugdale Society Occasional Papers, 35, 1993).

59 Sylvester, *Reliquiae Baxterianae*, p. 85.

60 Calamy, *Nonconformists' memorial*, vol. 3, p. 386.

61 M. R. Watts, *The Dissenters*, vol. 1 (Oxford, 1978), pp. 221–62.

62 *Baxter correspondence*, vol. 1, p. 160.

63 For a complete list of works to which Baxter provided prefaces, see Keeble, *Puritan man of letters*, pp. 170–72.

64 Simon Patrick, *The parable of a pilgrim: written to a friend* (London, 1679), pp. 138–43.

65 J. Eachard, *Some observations upon the answer to an enquiry* (London, 1671), p. 140; cited in J. Spurr, *The Restoration Church of England 1646–1689* (New Haven and London, 1991), p. 283.

66 Keeble, *Puritan man of letters*, p. 38.

67 Trinity College Cambridge, Wren Library, shelfmark K 4 13.

68 Clarke, *Lives of eminent persons*, pp. 203–5; Calamy, *Nonconformists' memorial*, vol. 1, pp. 184–8; Watts, *The Dissenters*, vol. 1, p. 281.

69 G. V. Portus, *Caritas Anglicana* (London, 1912); D. W. R. Bahlman, *The Moral Revolution of 1688* (New Haven, 1957); E. Duffy, '"Primitive Christianity reviv'd": religious renewal in Augustan England', in *Renaissance and Renewal in Christian History*, D. Baker (ed.) (Studies in Church History, vol. 14, 1977), pp. 287–300; F. W. B. Bullock, *Voluntary Religious Societies 1520–1799* (St Leonards-on-Sea, 1963); T. Isaacs 'The Anglican hierarchy and the reformation of manners, 1688–1738', *Journal of Ecclesiastical History* 33 (1982), pp. 391–411; A. G. Craig, *The movement for the reformation of manners 1688–1715* (PhD thesis, Edinburgh University, 1980); J. Spurr, 'The church, the societies and the moral revolution of 1688', in J. Walsh, C. Haydon and S. Taylor (eds), *The Church of England c. 1689–1833* (Cambridge, 1993), pp. 127–42.

70 E. Duffy, 'Wesley and the counter-reformation' in J. Garnett and C. Matthew (eds), *Revival and Religion since 1700: Essays for John Walsh* (London, 1993), pp. 2–5; see also Baxter's letter 'to the reader' prefacing James Janeway, *Invisible realities demonstrated in the holy life and triumphant death of Mr John Janeway* (London, 1690).

71 J. Woodward, *An account of the rise and progress of religious societies in the city of London*, D. E. Jenkins (ed.) (Liverpool, n.d.), pp. 32–3; Spurr, 'The church, the societies and the moral revolution of 1688', pp. 135–42, is the only account known to me which does justice to the 'godly' pedigree of the societies.

72 Spurr, 'The church, the societies', p. 133; Woodward, *Account*, pp. 45–6.

73 Woodward, *The duty of compassion to the souls of others, by endeavouring their reformation* (London, 1698), pp. 14, 29.

74 Woodward, *Duty of compassion*, p. 27.

75 A study of Stephens is badly needed: see Craig, 'Reformation of manners', pp. 13 ff.: Portus, *Caritas Anglicana*, pp. 37–9.

76 E. Stephens, *The true English government, and misgovernment of the four last Kings . . . Briefly noted in two little tracts* (London, 1689), 'To the King' pp. 4–5, 'A caveat against flattery', pp. 8, 24–5.

77 Ibid., p. 23: many of the same points are made in his *The beginning and progress of a needful and hopeful reformation in England* (London, 1691), and *A seasonable and necessary admonition to the gentlemen of the first society for the reformation of manners* (London n.d. but c. 1700).

78 M. Goldie, 'John Locke, Jonas Proast and religious toleration 1688–1692' in Walsh, Haydon and Taylor (eds), *The church of England c. 1689–1833*, p. 164.

79 Craig, 'Reformation of manners', pp. 29–30, 42.

80 Walsh, Haydon and Taylor (eds), *The church of England c. 1689–1833*, p. 167.

81 Craig, 'Reformation of manners', p. 230; Portus, *Caritas Anglicana*, pp. 124–5.

82 *Baxter correspondence*, vol. 1, pp. 222–6.

83 H. Sacheverell, *The character of a low churchman* (London, 1702), pp. 11–12.

84 Tennison to Archbishop Sharp, 7 April 1699, quoted in Craig, 'Reformation of manners', p. 268.

85 E. Cardwell, *Documentary annals of the reformed Church of England* (Oxford, 1839), vol. 2, pp. 347–52.

86   On the founding of the SPCK, see E. Duffy, 'The SPCK and Europe', in *Pietismus und Neuzeit*, vol. 7 (1981), pp. 28–42, and C. Rose 'The origins of the SPCK 1699–1716', in Walsh, Haydon and Taylor (eds), *The church of England c. 1689–1833*, pp. 172–90; on the international protestant context, E. Duffy, 'Correspondence fraternelle': the SPCK, the SPG, and the churches of Switzerland in the war of the Spanish succession', in *Reform and Reformation: England and the Continent c. 1500–1750*, D. Baker (ed.) (Oxford, 1979), pp. 251–80. Much of the devotional ethos, and a survey of the various types of activity promoted by members of the SPCK, is provided in the 'Representation of the several ways and methods of doing good' included in a book by one of the leading lay supporters of the society: R. Nelson, *An address to persons of quality and estate* (London, 1715), pp. 100–116.

87   Duffy, 'The SPCK and Europe', p. 31.

88   M. Clement (ed.), *Correspondence and minutes of the SPCK relating to Wales, 1699–1740* (Cardiff, 1952), pp. 7–9 and *passim*.

89   Spurr, 'The church, the societies', pp. 141–2.

90   Gentilcore, 'Missionary strategies', p. 274.

14

George Fox and the Reform of the Reformation

The other chapters in this section of the book have been concerned with attempts by puritan clergy and their lay supporters to reform the national church. The subject of this chapter, George Fox, saw it as one of his prime responsibilities to tear down the institutional church altogether, and made a point of harassing precisely those 'painful and godly' ministers who are the subject of Chapters 11, 12 and 13. In 1657 Richard Baxter could declare that the Quakers

> deny and revile the Church and Ministers of Christ, and yet cannot tell us of any Church or Ministry which is indeed the right, and to be preferred before those that they do despise ... They take the same course against the Church and Cause of God as the malicious enemies in all ages have done; even to oppose the best and painfullest Ministers.[1]

Baxter is a biased witness, for he had early become a particular target for Quaker hostilities. They barracked him in his pulpit and disrupted his services with shouts. But a multitude of other ministers in the 1650s also experienced Quaker hostility to the existing Churches, and Fox himself placed rejection of the visible Church of his day high on the list of special commissions he had received from God.

> And I was to bring people off from all the world's religions, which are vain, that they might know the pure religion; might visit the fatherless, the widows, and the strangers, and keep themselves from the spots of the world ... And I was to bring them off from all the world's fellowships, and prayings, and singings, which stood

in forms without power; that their fellowship might be in the Holy Ghost, and in the Eternal Spirit of God ... And I was to bring people off from Jewish ceremonies, and from heathenish fables, and from men's inventions and worldly doctrines, by which they blew the people about this way and the other, from sect to sect; and from all their beggarly rudiments, with their schools and colleges for making ministers of Christ, – who are indeed ministers of their own making, but not of Christ's; and from all their images, and crosses, and sprinkling of infants, with all their holy-days (so called), and all their vain traditions, which they had instituted since the Apostles' days, against all of which the Lord's power was set: in the dread and authority of which power I was moved to declare against them all.[2]

For Quakerism was the most militantly separatist of all the separatist movements of the seventeenth century. In its repudiation of vestments, of liturgy, of a professional ministry, of the parish churches, of the authority of the very scripture itself, it could and did seem to be an essentially negative and destructive movement. It never achieved large numbers, and even a sympathetic assessment of it must come to terms with the fact that in Fox's movement we are dealing with the final refinement of that strand of the Reformation which had long seemed to threaten the dissolution of the visible Church, in any sense that would be understood by the majority of Protestants, their rulers or their pastors.

To understand why, we need to consider the background from which Fox emerged. He attained manhood in an England in which the notion of the Church had already been deeply and radically challenged by events in the immediate past. The 1630s had seen the rise to dominance in England of Archbishop Laud and his associates, and the imposition of forms of Anglican observance which seemed to many to represent a betrayal of the Protestant past. Ritual, church order, the observance of patterns of piety, Laud and his supporters saw as means of encapsulating the beauty of holiness, but for many Englishmen and women they represented a wallowing in the filth of popery.[3] The Revolution of 1641 overturned all that. Episcopacy was howled down as tyrannical priestcraft, and a torrent of long-pent religious grievances burst out. Sectarian activity erupted from the dark alleys of Southwark into the broad light of day, and religious conservatives watched with horror as the attack on episcopacy slid into what seemed a general rejection of religious order and discipline.

Contemporary fears of religious anarchy were, in fact, greatly exaggerated: the sects were never as numerous as their opponents feared, and elements of the Anglicanism of the nation at large survived in a remarkable number of parishes. Meanwhile, England became in 1646 officially a Presbyterian country. This meant the substitution of one clerically dominated Church system for another: as John Milton pointed out in his poem 'On the new forcers of conscience in the Long Parliament', 'New Presbyter was but old Priest writ large'. The new Church never caught on, and in some places the result was a period of deep-seated religious uncertainty and of a bewildering variety of religious options.[4] Distracted conservatives, like the Presbyterian Thomas Edwards in his eloquently titled *Gangraena*, reported the universal spread of heresy and schism. England, he wrote, 'is become in many places already a chaos, a Babel, another Amsterdam . . . and in the high way to Munster'.[5] The Laudian regime had alienated from the broad bounds of the established Church many who under easier rule had managed to contain themselves within it: further left, sectarianism flourished.

But only for a while. Episcopacy had collapsed on a wave of millennial expectation, and the men and women of the sects hoped to see the reign of King Jesus inaugurated in their day, or, at the least, to find within the intense life of the gathered churches a new dimension of godliness which would prepare hearts and minds for the imminent coming of the Saviour. But millennial hopes did not always survive the non-arrival of the Parousia. Those who sought in the claustrophobic discipline of the sects the power of Godliness found themselves still sinners, and the world still set in its old ways. All over England there emerged a new phenomenon, the twice disillusioned – men and women who had abandoned the national worship for the more intense and committed life of the sects, only to find that the freedom from formalism, and the power of holiness they sought, was not to be found there either.

These dispossessed souls were known collectively as Seekers. They were not a coherent movement, but, rather, a scattering of individuals and small groups united only in their search for a deeper worship, and a rejection of existing forms: 'spiritual orphans', 'going from one form of religion to another, wandering up and down among dry hills and mountains'. Often they joined together, eschewing ordinances – their custom when they met together 'neither To preach nor pray vocally butt to Read the Scriptures & Discourse of Religion, Expecting a farther Manifestation', often sitting in silence rather than engaging in formal prayer.[6] They were men and women who believed that there had been a general apostasy, and they awaited a sign.

And it is as a Seeker that we first encounter Fox. He was the product of a puritan household in Leicestershire, his father a weaver, 'an honest man, and there was a Seed of God in him. The neighbours called him "Righteous Christer"'.[7] His mother was also an upright woman, 'of the family of the Lagos and of the stock of the martyrs'. Fox seems never to have been much troubled by a sense of sinfulness: 'I had a gravity and stayedness of mind and spirit not usual in children', and he claimed to have known 'pureness and righteousness' from the age of 11.

But in the immediate wake of the downfall of Laud, Fox, a youth of 19, found himself increasingly at odds with the religion of his friends and relations. He experienced an overwhelming sense of the hollowness of conventional religion. The trigger seems to have been an incident at Atherstone fair in Warwickshire, when a pious cousin, ostensibly a 'professor' or earnest Christian, with another friend invited Fox to share a jug of beer with them, and he, being thirsty, went with them, 'for I loved any who had a sense of good, or that sought after the Lord.' But before long, his companions

> began to drink healths, and called for more drink, agreeing together that he that would not drink should pay all. I was grieved that any who made profession of religion should offer to do so ... Wherefore I rose up, and, putting my hand in my pocket, took out a groat, and laid it down upon the table before them, saying, 'If it be so, I'll leave you.'

The incident had a disproportionate effect on him. He

> returned home; but did not go to bed that night, nor could I sleep, but sometimes walked up and down, and sometimes prayed

and cried to the Lord, who said unto me: 'Thou seest how young people go together into vanity, and old people into the earth; thou must forsake all, young and old, keep out of all, and be as a stranger unto all.'[8]

He began a restless pilgrimage the length and breadth of the Midlands and south, seeking religious comfort and assurance from clergy and the lay godly, but finding none. One minister advised him to cure his melancholy by smoking tobacco and singing psalms, 'but Tobacco was a thing I did not love, and psalms I was not in an estate to sing: I could not sing'.[9] A characteristic story has him consulting a Doctor Craddock in the Parliamentary garrison town of Coventry in 1646. Fox earnestly enquired of Craddock

> the ground of temptation and despair and how trouble came to be wrought in man ... Now, as we were walking together in his garden, the alley being narrow, I chanced, in turning, to set my foot on the side of a bed, at which the man was in a rage, as if his house had been on fire. Thus all our discourse was lost, and I went away in sorrow, worse than I was when I came. I thought them miserable comforters, and saw they were all as nothing to me, for they could not reach my condition.[10]

Fox in those years was often, by his own account, under great temptations to despair at his own religious powerlessness, at times doubting even the existence of God.

> I fasted much, walked abroad in solitary places many days, and often took my Bible, and sat in hollow trees and lonesome places till night came on ... for I was a man of sorrows in the time of the first workings of the Lord in me.[11]

His journeyings in the 1640s trace an odyssey through the religious eccentricities of revolutionary England, in which he encountered a host of oddities, vividly evoked in his *Journal*. There were the people that 'relied much on dreams', who were later to become Friends, and the group 'that held that *women have no souls ... no more than a goose ...* But I reproved them and told them that was not right for

Mary said "My soul doth magnify the Lord".' Then there was the woman in Lancashire who fasted for 22 days, and whom he travelled north specially to see, only to perceive that 'she was under a temptation'.[12]

At the root of Fox's distress was a perennial religious problem, which was felt with special vividness in those years – that of the deadness or opaqueness of religious practice, the bankruptcy of the existing means of grace. For Fox, as for many other seekers, this focused itself on Calvinist teaching about sin in the regenerate man. The person justified by faith was saved, but their righteousness was imputed, not intrinsic. Though a saint, they would go on being a sinner. Arthur Dent, in *The Plaine Man's Path-Way to Heaven*, the most popular work of religious instruction of the early seventeenth century, explained the standard Calvinist teaching clearly.

> For some of Gods deare children, in whom no doubt the inward worke is truly and soundly wrought: yet are so troubled and encombred, with a crabbed and crooked nature, and so clogged with some master sinne, as some with anger, some with pride, some with covetousnesse, some with lusts, some one way, and some another: all which breaking out in them, doo so blemish them & their profession, that they cannot so shine forth unto men, as otherwise no doubt they would: and this is their wounde, their griefe, and their heart smart, and that which causeth them many a teare, and many a prayer: and yet can they not get the full victorie over them, but still they are left in them, as their pricke in the flesh to humble them.[13]

For Fox and his like this seemed a flat denial of the power of grace, a proof that conventional Protestantism was an impotent and mortal confidence trick, which deluded people into resting in their own wickedness. The ministry were 'roaring up for sin' when they should have been proclaiming the power and life of God to make men and women holy. What was needed was some living and vital force which would transform a man within and without. That was the Spirit of Christ, the power of God. All else, even the scriptures themselves, was the letter that killeth. Fox came to believe that faith in

Christ, however fervent, as a force *outside* oneself, was useless. Christ must live in the soul, as a principle of renewal and enlightenment. Salvation history was not a series of events *out there*, in the past, but was enacted within the heart of every human being. The Fall, the giving of the Law, the wandering in the wilderness, the death and resurrection of Jesus, all had indeed happened in the external world. But if they were to mean anything for us, they must happen within every individual's spirit.

So Fox's illumination, when it came, followed the theological leading of the Gospel of St John, with its emphasis on Christ as the light of the world, rather than the epistles of St Paul, with their intense awareness of the dominion of sin in the human will. Christ was the light of God in every one, renewing and transforming the heart. To become a Christian was in some sense to become Christ, and to experience a return to Paradise.

> Now was I come up in spirit, through the flaming sword, into the paradise of God. All things were new, and all the creation gave another smell unto me than before, beyond what words can utter. I knew nothing but pureness, innocency, and righteousness, being renewed up into the image of God by Christ Jesus; so that I was come up to the state of Adam, which he was in before he fell. The creation was open to me; and it was showed me, how all things had their names given them, according to their nature and virtue. I was at a stand in my mind, whether I should practise physic for the good of mankind, seeing the nature and virtues of the creatures were so opened to me by the Lord. But I was immediately taken up in spirit, to see into another or more steadfast state than Adam's in innocency, even into a state in Christ Jesus, that should never fall.[14]

It was in this new-found power that Fox's true mission began. The divine light of Christ, he was convinced, was given to all men and women. Fox felt himself commanded to call everyone to submit themselves to that Christ within them. His language here was characteristically dualistic. In everyone there were two powers – the seed of God and the seed of the devil, the light and the dark: everyone must choose to serve one or the other.

'Convincement' or conversion involved the submission of the mind and heart and will to the power of the light, allowing it to overcome and destroy all that was dark within. The process might take years, as it had in Fox, and it was traumatic and painful. It was an internalised Armageddon, in which the soul became the battle-ground of Good and Evil. This apocalyptic language, the imagery of a cosmic struggle between the forces of light and dark, the king-dom of Christ and the kingdom of the Devil, was a commonplace of the time, and was central to much both of the mainstream and of extremist religious thought. Apocalyptic expectation informed the Fifth Monarchy Men who sought by political means to attain the millennium, but also the writings of moderates like Richard Baxter.[15]

What is distinctive about Fox's message is that his eschatology is internalised apocalypse written in the heart of man. One of Fox's first converts was Francis Howgill, a Westmorland tailor and farmer who had been a strict puritan since the age of 12. Becoming oppressed by his own sinfulness, he found the conventional teaching on the subject useless, and became terrified of receiving commu-nion unworthily. Ministers tried to console him by bidding him believe that Christ had died for him and taken away his sins, but that the experience of guilt might remain 'while he lived'. This seemed to Howgill 'a miserable salvation', for 'the witness in my conscience told me I was a servant of sin while I committed it'.[16]

Howgill abandoned parish worship and became first an Independent, then a Baptist, ultimately a Seeker. In the summer of 1653 Fox came among the Seekers of Westmorland, proclaim-ing the Christ within. 'And immediately', wrote Howgill, 'as soon as I heard him declare the light of Christ in man was the way to Christ, I believed the eternal word of truth, and that of God in my conscience sealed it, with many hundred more.'[17] The experience was traumatic, a horrifying revelation of his spiritual bankruptcy. 'The dreadful power of the Lord fell upon me: plague, pestilence, and famine, and earthquake, and fear and terror, for the sights that I saw with my eyes; and that which I heard with my ears, sorrow and pain. And in the morning I wished it had been evening, and in the evening I wished it had been morning and I had no rest, but trouble on every side . . .'

For some this experience could unhinge: for Howgill, as for many more, it brought at last a sense of wholeness.

> ... and as I bore the indignation of the Lord, somthing rejoyced, the Serpents head began to be bruised, and the Witnesses which were slain, were raised ... [another eight sentences of biblical woes and apocalyptic judgements listed here] and as I did give up all to the Judgement, the captive came forth out of prison and rejoyced, and my heart was filled with joy, and I came to see whom I had pierced, and my heart was broken, and the blood of the Prophets I saw slaine, and a great lamentation; and then I saw the Crosse of Christ, and stood in it, and the enmity slaine upon it, and the new man was made, and so peace came to be made, and so eternall life was brought in through death and judgement, and then the perfect gift I received which was given from God, and the holy Law of God was revealed unto me, and was written in my heart, and his feare and his word which did kill now makes alive; and so it pleased the Father to reveal his son in me through death, and so I came to witnesse cleansing by his blood which is eternall, Glory unto him for ever, and am a Minister of that word of eternall life which endures for ever, Glory un|to his name for ever, and have rest and peace in doing the will of God, and am entred into the true rest, and lie down in the fold with the lambs of God, where the Sons rejoyce together, and the Saints keep holy-day, Glory unto him for ever.[18]

Howgill's convincement – the overwhelming sense of the splendour and the terror of the light within, exposing and burning away all that is sinful, and then the welling up of a new power, the life of Christ, is the archetypal early Quaker experience. In the 1650s his experience was repeated over and over again among the 'shattered Baptists' and Seekers of the north Midlands and the North West, above all in the 'Quaker Galilee' of the Lake District. Fox's coming meant life to many. '... the Kingdom of Heaven did gather us, and catch us all as in a Net', recalled Howgill 20 years on, 'and his Heavenly Power at one time drew many Hundreds to Land, that we came to know a place to stand in, and what to wait in; and the Lord appeared daily to us, to our Astonishment, Amazement, and great Admiration, insomuch that we often said one unto another, with great joy of Heart, What, is the Kingdom of God come to be with men? And will he take up his Tabernacle among the Sons of Men, as He did of old?'[19]

By 1654 Fox was sending out missionaries for the Kingdom, two by two, supported by funds raised by Margaret Fell of Swarthmoor, whose home now became the Quaker headquarters. Already the existence of the new 'society of Friends of the Truth' was alarming the orthodox. Well it might do so, for Fox's message was as uncompromising as his temperament. His proclamation of the inner light was anything but a pietist retreat into mysticism. The conflict of light and dark within the soul was one with that conflict in the universe at large. Those possessed of the power of Christ were called to proclaim the day of the Lord, to express the characteristic Quaker sense of overwhelming indignation at the signs of sin everywhere in the society about them, sins above all against the poor and helpless.

I was sorely exercised in going to their courts to cry for justice, in speaking and writing to judges and justices to do justly; in warning such as kept public houses for entertainment that they should not let people have more drink than would do them good; in testifying against wakes, feasts, May-games, sports, plays, and shows, which trained up people to vanity and looseness, and led them from the fear of God . . .

In fairs, also, and in markets, I was made to declare against their deceitful merchandise, cheating, and cozening; warning all to deal justly, to speak the truth, to let their yea be yea, and their nay be nay, and to do unto others as they would have others do unto them; forewarning them of the great and terrible day of the Lord, which would come upon them all.

As I travelled through markets, fairs, and diverse places, I saw death and darkness in all people where the power of the Lord God had not shaken them. And as I was passing on in Leicestershire I came to Twycross, where there were excise-men and I was moved of the Lord to go to them, and warn them to take heed of oppressing the poor; and people were much affected with it.[20]

These protests could take spectacular form, expressed in prophetic symbolism. William Simpson 'was moved to go naked and barefoot to markets, courts, towns and cities, priests houses and great houses, and tell them so should they all be stripped naked as he was stripped naked . . . And much sufferings did this poor man go through and whippings with horse-whips and coach-whips, stonings and imprisonment . . . But the Mayor of Cambridge did nobly to him, he put his gown about him and took him into his house.'[21]

Behind all this lay the conviction that the light laid bare all human pretence and hypocrisy, exposed all corruption and sin. Those who stood in the light were the judges of the world, and must call others to stand in the light, and be judged themselves. In the light, all were equal, there was no master and no servant. Fox even denied the subjection of women (since it was a consequence of the Fall). Quakers refused to doff their hats to anyone, or to use the polite 'you' form instead of 'thee' and 'thou' to their social 'superiors'. In an age which put enormous weight on due subordination such gestures brought on them savage persecution, as social revolutionaries. Fox would let no awe of persons obscure the fact that before God all men were equal. When in 1664 he appeared at the Lancaster Assizes before Sir Thomas Twysden for refusal to swear the oath of allegiance, the Judge, who in fact was known for speaking fiercely against dissent but treating dissenters themselves leniently, demanded, 'Sirrah, will you take the oath?' Fox was having none of this. 'I am none of thy sirrahs, I am no sirrah, I am a Christian. Art thou a judge and sits there and gives names to prisoners? It does not become either thy grey hairs or thy office.' Rather feebly, Twysden, protested, 'I am a Christian too', to which Fox replied unrelentingly, 'Then do Christian works.'[22] Here, as in all his trials, one cannot escape the feeling that it is Fox's captors who are in the dock.

For Fox, nothing could be mere ceremony, nothing second-hand. Even the scriptures could not be used as shelter. Margaret Fell's conversion began when Fox turned up at a religious meeting at Swarthmoor in which biblical texts were being bandied about. Fox cut through the verbiage. 'You will say, Christ saith this, and the apostles say this, but what canst thou say?'[23] The same impatience with mere forms made him dismiss a minister as 'a mere notionist', who was not a possessor of that which he spoke, and it made him tell the worshippers in York Minster that they dwelt among words.[24] For Fox, the scriptures themselves had no intrinsic *authority*. He loved and revered them because they proceeded from the same Spirit which lighted the hearts of believers, but the scriptures themselves could become a substitute for the experience of the Light.

That emphasis led historians like Christopher Hill to minimise the difference between the early Quakers and the antinomian Ranters who allegedly used the notion of an indwelling Christ to sweep away moral as well as religious constraints.[25] But this is a grave mistake. The early Quaker vision was one of harmony between all the expressions of the spirit of Christ, not the replacement of one by another. The Ranter spirit is evident in the story the Presbyterian heresiographer Clement Walker told of the Cromwellian soldier who interrupted worship in the parish church of Walton-on-Thames in the spring of 1649, soon after the execution of the King. Having announced the divine abolition of the Sabbath, of tithes, of ministers and of magistrates, the soldier pulled a bible from his pocket and declared, 'Here is a Booke ye have in great veneration, consisting of two parts, the Old and the New Testament; I must tell you, it is abolished: It containeth beggarly rudiments, milk for Babes: But now Christ is in Glory amongst us and imparts a fuller measure of his Spirit to his Saints than this can afford, and therefore I am commanded to burne it before your faces; so taking the Candle out of his Lanthorne, he set fire of the leaves.'[26]

In 1649, Fox had encountered such views in gaol. 'But when I came into the gaol where the prisoners were a great power of darkness struck at me, and I sat still, having my spirit gathered into the love of God. They began to rant and vapour and blaspheme ... They said they were God ... Then seeing they said they were God, I asked them, if they knew whether it would rain tomorrow. They said they could not tell. I told them God could tell.'[27]

Yet to many of his contemporaries, Fox's identification of his inner Light with the Spirit of Christ seemed itself the wildest blasphemy, and it is not hard to see why. Here is part of Fox's examination before the magistrates at Carlisle:

They asked me if I were the son of God.
I said 'Yes'.
They asked me if I had seen God's face.
I said 'Yes'.[28]

Fox, of course, believed that all who stood in the light could claim to be Christ. 'He that hath the same spirit that raised up Jesus Christ is equal with God . . . As Jesus Christ which is the mystery, hath passed before, so the same spirit takes upon it the same seed and is the same where it is made manifest.'[29] The claim reveals a radical weakness in Quaker Christology, and it could have startling expression. Fox's converts at Swarthmoor could write to him like this:

> O our life, we hope to see thee again that our joy may be full; for in thy presence is fullness of joy, and where thou dwells is pleasure for evermore. O thou fountain of eternal life, our souls thirsts after thee, for in thee alone is our life and peace, and without thee have we no peace: for our souls is much refreshed by seeing theem and our life is preserved by thee, O thou father of eternal felicity.[30]

Down that same road James Naylor, arguably almost as important a figure as Fox himself in early Quakerism, would travel to the end. In 1656 Naylor rode into Bristol, while his female disciples, one of whom believed herself to have been raised from the dead by him, cast their cloaks before his horse's hooves while they sang 'Holy Holy Holy'. The incident brought a savage conservative reaction and persecution of the Quakers. Parliament ordered Naylor himself to be whipped, branded and to have his tongue bored through with a red hot spike.[31] But Naylor was expressing in an extreme form the sense of immediacy of the divine life which all early Quakers felt. In Fox, this showed itself most startlingly in his miracles. He worked, or believed himself to have worked, many. Here is a typical example.

> And as I came out of Cumberland one time I went to Hawkshead, and lighted at a Friend's house, and there was young Margaret Fell with me and William Caton; and it being a very cold season we lighted, and the lass made us a fire, her master and dame being gone to the market. And there was a boy lying in the cradle which they rocked, about eleven years old, and he was grown almost double; and I cast my eye upon the boy, and seeing he was dirty I bid the lass wash his face and his hands, and get him up and bring him unto me. So she brought him to me and I bid her take him

and wash him again, for she had not washed him clean, then I was moved of the Lord God to lay my hands upon him and speak to him, and so bid the lass take him again and put on his clothes, and after we passed away.

And some time, after I called at the house, and I met his mother, but did not light. 'Oh stay,' says she, 'and have a meeting at our house; for all the country is convinced by the great miracle that was done by thee upon my son; for we had carried him to Wells and the Bath, and all doctors had given him over, for his grandfather and father feared he would have died and their name have gone out, having but that son: but presently, after you was gone (says she), we came home and found our son playing in the streets' . . . And this was about three years after, that she told me of it, and he was grown to be a straight, full youth then; and so the Lord have the praise.[32]

Fox's motive here had been pure compassion, but such actions frightened and angered his contemporaries. Many thought him bewitched, rumours spread that he hung ribbons on people's arms 'which made them follow me'. They feared his eyes: the 'rude scholars' at Cambridge tried to pull his companions from their horses, but drew back from Fox. 'I kept on my horse-back and rid through them in the Lord's power. Oh said they, he shines, he glisters.'[33]

He was not always so fortunate. At Ulverstone the mob, egged on by justices and ministers and constables, dragged him through the mire to the common outside the town and beat him senseless with stakes and clubs and stones.

There I lay a pretty space, and when I recovered myself again, and saw myself lying on a watery common, and all the people standing about me, I lay a little still, and the power of the Lord sprang through me, and the eternal refreshings refreshed me, that I stood up again in the eternal power of God, and stretched out my arms amongst them all, and said again with a loud voice, 'Strike again; here is my arms, my head, and my cheeks.' And there was a mason, a rude fellow, a professor called; he gave me a blow with all his might just atop of my hand as it was stretched out, with his walking rule-staff; and my hand and arm was so numbed and bruised that I could not draw it in to me again but it stood out as it was. Then the people cried out, 'He hath spoiled his hand for ever having any use of it more.' The skin was struck off my hand and a little blood came, and I looked at it in the love of God, and I was in the love of God to them all that had persecuted me. And after a while the Lord's power sprang through me again, and through my hand and arm, that in a minute I recovered my hand and arm and strength in the face and sight of them all and it was as well as it was before, and I never had another blow afterward.[34]

Almost every element in the Quaker programme can be paralleled in the sectarian background from which it emerged – refusal of hat-honour among the Levellers, silent worship among the Seekers, refusal of pagan names for the days and months among the Baptists. What is distinctive about Fox is the coherence and power he brought to a movement which without him must inevitably have run off into mere protest and fanaticism. It was, of course, Fox who was to create the structure and order within the Quaker movement itself which helped it to survive the savage persecution it endured during the Restoration. That is another story, and one in which Fox features in the paradoxical role of one seeking to restrain religious enthusiasm and fanaticism, and attacked by dissident Quakers as a persecutor – Bishop Fox, they called him, and those he excluded, Fox's martyrs.

In any case, the society that emerged into the eighteenth century was scarcely recognisable as the charismatic movement of protest and prophecy of Fox's heyday. But Fox's real contribution to the project of reformation was to create and hold in the light of day one of the most compelling embodiments of Johannine Christianity ever achieved; to eschew creeds and forms, and yet to give shape to an unmistakably authentic embodiment of New Testament Christianity, pointing beyond sacrament and structure to the realities they hint at. In the process, he gave classic expression to the perennial prophetic protest against the forces of formalism and insincerity within the churches. His was emphatically a message centred in Christ, not the mere belief in conscience and liberty which Quakerism would later be in danger of becoming. 'I like not that word "liberty of conscience"', Fox is reported to have said: 'there is no liberty out of the light.'[35]

Fox's Christianity possessed something of the same charismatic blend of literalness and freedom as that of Francis of Assisi, but was more devastatingly sharpened against the opacities of official Christianity. Yet it did not evaporate into fanaticism or mere protest. His followers were in no doubt that his power sprang from his own closeness to God. William Penn, as unlike Fox as chalk is to cheese, could write 'The most awful, Living, Reverent frame I ever Felt or Beheld, I must say, was His in Prayer. And truly it was a Testimony he knew and lived nearer to the Lord than other Men.'[36]

He could be a hard man. His *Journal* is full of accounts of the judgements that had befallen those who resisted the Light or harassed Friends, like John Line, a persecuting constable 'who grievously rotted away alive, and so did his wife also'.[37] But in the end it is his essential humanity that lay behind his power to challenge and illuminate. The soldier who came to his rescue from the mob at Ulverstone had it right. 'Sir', said he, 'I am your servant, I am ashamed that you should be thus abused, for you are a man.'[38]

The Quaker movement distilled out of the chaos of the Revolution and the tawdry material of half-baked mysticism a form of mystical and ethical identification with Christ which turned men and women not inwards but outwards, to their fellows, to the poor and oppressed, even to their enemies, and to the rich, on whom also they had compassion. In the midst of an acrimonious debate with an old clerical enemy, 'Priest Stephens', Fox said, as he reached out and took his opponent's hand – 'Nathaniel, give me thy hand': and then 'I told him I would not quench the last measure of God in any, much less put out his starlight.'[39]

It was entirely characteristic of him. The Quaker movement was his movement: his journal stands, arguably the most remarkable religious document of the English seventeenth century, a permanent witness against form without life. It is the warmth of a living man that informs it, and that won, and held, the hearts of his Friends. That warmth, and the power it wrought, is nowhere clearer than in the story of the healing of John Banks, with which I end. The narrator is Banks himself.

About this time a pain struck into my shoulder, which gradually fell down into my arm and hand, so that the use thereof I was wholly deprived of; and not only so, but my pain greatly increased both day and night: and for three months I could neither put my clothes on nor off myself, and my arm and hand began to wither, so that I did seek to some physicians for cure, but no cure could I get by any of them: until at last, as I was asleep upon my bed, in the nighttime, I saw in a vision, that I was with dear George Fox; and I thought I said to him, 'George, my faith is such, that if you see the way to lay your hand upon my shoulder, my arm and hand shall be whole throughout.'

Which remained with me after I awaked, two days and nights, (that the thing was a true vision), and that I must go to G. F. until at last, through much exercise of mind, as a near and great trial of my faith, I was made willing to go to him; he being then at Swarthmore, in Lancashire, where there was a meeting of Friends, being on the first day of the week. And some time after the meeting, I called him aside into the hall, and gave him a relation of my dream, showing him my arm and hand; and in a little time, we walking together silent, he turned about and looked upon me, lifting up his hand, and laid it upon my shoulder, saying, 'The Lord strengthen thee, both within and without.' And so we parted, and I went to Thomas Lower's, of Marsh Grange, that night; and when I was sate down to supper in his house, immediately, before I was aware, my hand was lifted up to do its office, which it could not do for long before. This struck me with great admiration, and my heart was broke into tenderness before the Lord; and the next day I went home, with my hand and arm restored to its former use and strength without any pain. The next time that G. F. and I met, he readily said, 'John, thou mended, thou mended'; I answered, 'Yes, very well in a little time.' 'Well,' said he, 'give God the glory.'[40]

Notes

1   Richard Baxter, *One Sheet against the Quakers* (London, 1657), pp. 1, 6.
2   The journal was first edited for publication by Thomas Ellwood in 1694, and Ellwood's tidied and sanitised version was the basis for all editions till Norman Penney (ed.), *The Journal of George Fox* (Cambridge, 1911), 2 vols, a transcription of Fox's dictations, edited *verbatim et literatim*, from the so-called 'Spence manuscript', and so the closest we can get to Fox's own voice. But its adherence to Fox's erratic spelling, and the many inserted documents, makes it extremely challenging for the general reader. For quotations from Fox's *Journal* I have therefore used the standard modern

edition by J. L. Nickalls (ed.), *The Journal of George Fox: A Revised Edition, with an Introduction by Geoffrey F. Nuttall* (London, 1975) (hereafter *Journal*), p. 35; for the problems in establishing a 'standard' text of the *Journal*, see T. Edmond Harvey's introduction to Penney's edition, vol. 1, pp. ix–xli, and Thomas N. Corns, 'No Man's Copy: The Critical Problem of Fox's Journal' in Thomas N. Corns and David Lowenstein (eds), *The Emergence of Quaker Writing: Dissenting Literature in Seventeenth-Century England* (Portland, Oreg., 1995), pp. 99–112. There is also another scholarly edition closely based on the Spence manuscript by Nigel Smith (ed.) *George Fox, the Journal* (Harmondsworth, 1998).

3   Nicholas Tyacke, *Anti-Calvinists: the Rise of English Arminianism c 1590–1640* (Oxford, 1987); Julian Davies, *The Caroline Captivity of the Church: Charles I and the Remoulding of Anglicanism* (Oxford, 1992); Sylvia Watts, 'The Impact of Laudianism on the Parish: The Evidence of Staffordshire and North Shropshire', *Midland History*, 33 (2008), pp. 21–42; Andrew Foster, 'Church Policies of the 1630s' in Richard Cust and Ann Hughes (eds), *Conflict in Early Stuart England* (London, 1989), pp. 193–223.

4   Useful brief overview in John Morrill, 'The Puritan Revolution' in John Coffey and Paul Lim (eds), *The Cambridge Companion to Puritanism* (Cambridge, 2008), pp. 67–88. Still the profoundest guide to the theology and spirit of the separatists is G. F. Nuttall, *Visible Saints 1640–1660* (Oxford, 1967).

5   For a detailed study of Edwards' classic expression of conservative horror at the eruption of religious radicalism, Ann Hughes, *Gangraena and the Struggle for the English Revolution* (Oxford, 2004).

6   Norman Penney (ed.), *The First Publishers of Truth* (London, 1907), p. 18.

7   *Journal*, p. 1.

8   Ibid., p. 3.

9   Ibid., pp. 5–6.

10   Ibid., p. 6.

11   Ibid., p. 9.

12   Ibid., pp. 8–9, 18.

13   Arthur Dent, *The Plaine Man's Path-Way to Heaven. Wherein every man may clearly see, whether he shall be saved or damned. Set forth Dialogue wise, for the better understanding of the simple* (London, 1601), pp. 22–3.

14   *Journal*, p. 27.

15   William M. Lamont, *Richard Baxter and the Millennium* (London, 1979).

16   Details in Howgill's autobiographical tract, *The Inheritance of Jacob discovered, after his return out of Egypt* (1655–6), printed in Hugh Barbour and Arthur O. Roberts (eds), *Early Quaker Writings 1650–1700* (Grand Rapids, Mich., 1973), pp. 167–79, quotations at pp. 171, 172.

17   Barbour and Roberts, *Early Quaker Writings*, p. 173.

18   Ibid., p 174: in this extract I have collated the modernised version in *Early Quaker Writings* against Howgill's original, and have restored his spelling.

19   The quotation is from Howgill's 'Testimony', prefixed to *The memorable works of a son of thunder and consolation namely that true prophet and faithful servant of God and sufferer for the testimony of Jesus, Edward Burroughs, who dyed a prisoner for the word of God in the city of London, the fourteenth of the twelfth moneth, 1662* (London, 1672) unpaginated.

20   *Journal*, pp. 37, 49.

21   Ibid., pp. 407–8.

22   Ibid., p. 468.

23   William C. Braithwaite, *The Beginnings of Quakerism* (London, 1923), p. 101.

24   *Journal*, p. 78.

25   Christopher Hill, *The World Turned Upside Down* (Harmondsworth, 1975), pp. 184–258: see also the useful collection of essays edited by J. F. McGregor and B. Reay, *Radical Religion in the English Revolution* (Oxford, 1984); Andrew Bradstock, *Radical Religion in Cromwell's England* (London, 2011), pp. 75–116; for debate about the existence of the Ranters, J. C. Davis, *Fear, Myth and History: The Ranters and the Historians* (Cambridge, 1986), and Gerald Aylmer, 'Did the Ranters Exist?', *Past & Present*, 117 (Nov. 1987), pp. 208–19.

26 Clement Walker, *Anarchia Anglicana, or, the History of Independency. The Second Part . . . by Theodorus Verax* (London, 1649), pp. 152–3.

27 *Journal*, p. 47.

28 *Journal*, p. 159.

29 *The Works of George Fox* (Philadelphia, 1831), p. 592.

30 Braithwaite, *Beginnings*, p. 105.

31 Ibid., pp. 241–78.

32 *Journal*, pp. 171–2.

33 Ibid., pp. 218–19.

34 Ibid., pp. 127–8.

35 H. Larry Ingle, *First Among Friends: George Fox and the Creation of Quakerism* (Oxford, 1996), p. 260 (quoting William Penn).

36 William Penn, *A Briefe Account of the Rise and progress of the People called Quakers*, in *A Collection of the Works of William Penn* (London, 1726,) vol. 1, p. 883.

37 *Journal*, p. 442.

38 Ibid., p. 128.

39 Ibid., p. 184.

40 Henry Joel Cadbury (ed.), *George Fox's Book of Miracles* (Cambridge, 1948), pp. 136–7.

Acknowledgements

Chapter 1 incorporates material from my introduction to the Folio Society's edition of *Praise of Folly*.

An earlier version of Chapter 2 appeared in George M. Logan (ed.), *The Cambridge Companion to Thomas More* (Cambridge, 2011), pp. 191–215.

An earlier version of Chapter 3 appeared in Peter Clarke and Charlotte Methuen (eds), *The Church and Literature, Studies in Church History*, 48 (Woodbridge, 2012), pp. 133–54.

Chapter 4 is a revised and expanded version of an essay which first appeared in Eamon Duffy and David Loades (eds), *The Church of Mary Tudor* (Abingdon, 2006), pp. 176–200.

Chapter 5 is a revised and expanded version of an essay which first appeared in *Recusant History*, 22 (1995), pp. 265–290, on which my memoir of Allen in the Oxford Dictionary of National Biography was based.

Chapter 7 is simultaneously published in James E. Kelly and Susan Royal (eds), *Early Modern English Catholicism: Identity, Memory and Counter-Reformation* (Leiden, 2016).

Chapter 8 is a revised and expanded version of an essay which first appeared in the *Journal of Ecclesiastical History*, 34 (1983), pp. 214–30.

Chapter 9 is a revised and expanded version of an essay which first appeared in the *Journal of Ecclesiastical History*, 28 (1977), pp. 291–317.

Chapter 10 incorporates material from my inaugural Ushaw College lecture on John Lingard, delivered in 2013.

Chapter 11 is a revised version of an essay which first appeared in Theo Clemens and Wim Janse (eds), *The Pastor Bonus: Papers Read at the British-Dutch Colloquium at Utrecht 18–21 September 2002* (Leiden and Boston, 2004), pp. 216–34.

Chapter 12 is a revised and expanded version of an essay which first appeared in N. Tyacke (ed.), *England's Long Reformation* (London, 1997), pp. 33–70.

Chapter 13 is a revised and expanded version of an essay which first appeared in *The Seventeenth Century*, vol. 1 (1986), pp. 31–55.

Chapter 14 is a revised version of an essay which first appeared in *Epworth Review*, 12 (1985), pp. 85–95.

Index